Lecture Notes in Computer Science

Lecture Notes in Artificial Intelligence 16780

Founding Editor

Jörg Siekmann

Series Editors

The series Lecture Notes in Computer Science (LNCS), including its subseries Lecture Notes in Artificial Intelligence (LNAI) and Lecture Notes in Bioinformatics (LNBI), has established itself as a medium for the publication of new developments in computer science and information technology research, teaching, and education.

LNCS enjoys close cooperation with the computer science R & D community, the series counts many renowned academics among its volume editors and paper authors, and collaborates with prestigious societies. Its mission is to serve this international community by providing an invaluable service, mainly focused on the publication of conference and workshop proceedings and postproceedings. LNCS commenced publication in 1973.

Lukas Malburg · Kerstin Bach
Editors

Case-Based Reasoning Research and Development

34th International Conference, ICCBR 2026
Bremen, Germany, August 13–16, 2026
Proceedings

Springer

Editors
Lukas Malburg
Trier University and German Research Center for Artificial Intelligence
Trier, Germany

Kerstin Bach
Norwegian University of Science and Technology
Trondheim, Norway

ISSN 0302-9743 ISSN 1611-3349 (electronic)
Lecture Notes in Artificial Intelligence
ISBN 978-3-032-33864-8 ISBN 978-3-032-33865-5 (eBook)
https://doi.org/10.1007/978-3-032-33865-5

LNCS Sublibrary: SL7 – Artificial Intelligence

This Springer imprint is published by the registered company Springer Nature Switzerland AG
The registered company address is: Gewerbestrasse 11, 6330 Cham, Switzerland

Preface

This volume contains the papers presented at the 34th International Conference on Case-Based Reasoning (ICCBR 2026), held August 13–16, 2026, at the University of Bremen, Germany. ICCBR is the premier annual meeting of the Case-Based Reasoning (CBR) research community. ICCBR 2026 brought the CBR community to Bremen in co-location with ECAI/IJCAI 2026. The conference program reflected both the continuing foundations of CBR and its current connections to wider developments in artificial intelligence. Prominent themes included CBR with large language models, retrieval-augmented generation, explainable AI, uncertainty-aware CBR, neuro-symbolic methods, adaptation, retrieval, similarity, temporal and process-oriented CBR, responsible AI, and applied CBR systems.

ICCBR 2026 received 221 submissions in total. Of these, 85 papers proceeded to full review following an initial screening by the Program Chairs. The review process was single-blind. Each paper received at least two reviews, with a third and/or a meta-review provided by the Advisory Committee (AC) where needed. The program includes 21 papers selected for oral presentation and 15 for poster presentation, for an overall acceptance rate of 17%. These contributions were selected and organized under the guidance of the Program Chairs, with support from the Program Committee, additional reviewers, and the AC.

The scientific program featured two keynote talks: "XAI is in Trouble, but is CBR?" by Rosina O. Weber, and "In any case, or maybe not? Towards uncertainty-aware CBR" by Eyke Hüllermeier. The program also included the Doctoral Consortium, a poster session, community events, and the Workshop on Memory-Based Reasoning for Responsible GenAI, providing opportunities for discussion across the main conference and its co-located activities.

We gratefully acknowledge the support of all those whose contributions made ICCBR 2026 possible. We thank the authors for submitting their work, the reviewers and Program Committee for their careful evaluations and constructive feedback, and the ICCBR Advisory Committee for its guidance. We are grateful to the organizing team, the local organizers at the University of Bremen, and the Local Chair, Felix Putze, for hosting the conference in Bremen. We also thank the keynote speakers for their contributions to the program and Springer for its continued support in publishing the proceedings.

We also thank our funders and sponsors for their generous support: Deutsche Forschungsgemeinschaft (DFG, German Research Foundation, 583776511).

Springer Nature, Empolis Information Management GmbH, Denkbares GmbH, Trier University, German Research Center for Artificial Intelligence GmbH (DFKI), Norwegian University of Science and Technology (NTNU), Norwegian Research Center for

AI Innovation (NorwAI), and the Norwegian Open AI Lab. Special thanks go to the Artificial Intelligence Journal for their continued support of the Doctoral Consortium.

August 2026

Kerstin Bach
Lukas Malburg

Competing Interests The authors have no competing interests to declare that are relevant to the content of this manuscript.

Organization

Program Chairs

Kerstin Bach	Norwegian University of Science and Technology, Norway
Lukas Malburg	Trier University/German Research Center for Artificial Intelligence (DFKI), Germany

Local Chair

Felix Putze	University of Bremen, Germany

Workshop Chair

Marta Caro-Martínez	Universidad Complutense de Madrid, Spain

Publicity Co-chairs

Lasal Jayawardena	Robert Gordon University, UK
Brian Schack	Air Force Research Laboratory, USA

Doctoral Consortium Chairs

Mirjam Minor	Goethe University Frankfurt, Germany
Jean Lieber	Université de Lorraine, CNRS, Inria, LORIA, France

Poster Chair

Kyle Martin	Robert Gordon University, UK

Advisory Committee

Ralph Bergmann	Trier University/German Research Center for Artificial Intelligence (DFKI), Germany
Isabelle Bichindaritz	State University of New York Oswego, USA
David Leake	Indiana University Bloomington, USA
Mirjam Minor	Goethe University Frankfurt, Germany
Juan A. Recio Garcia	Universidad Complutense de Madrid, Spain
Nirmalie Wiratunga	Robert Gordon University, UK

Program Committee

Betül Bayrak	Norwegian University of Science and Technology, Norway
Shahina Begum	Mälardalen University, Sweden
Marta Caro-Martínez	Universidad Complutense de Madrid, Spain
Jörg Cassens	University of Hildesheim, Germany
Sutanu Chakraborti	Indian Institute of Technology Madras, India
Sarah-Jane Delany	Technological University Dublin, Ireland
Eoin Delaney	Trinity College Dublin, Ireland
Belén Díaz-Agudo	Universidad Complutense de Madrid, Spain
Viktor Eisenstadt	TIB - Leibniz Information Centre for Science and Technology, Germany
Jonah Fernandez	University of Girona, Spain
Michael Floyd	Knexus Research, USA
Béatrice Fuchs	iaelyon, Université Jean Moulin Lyon 3, LIRIS, France
Thomas Gabel	Frankfurt University of Applied Sciences, Germany
Devi Ganesan	Capgemini, New Zealand
Ashok Goel	Georgia Institute of Technology, USA
Mehmet H. Goker	Aionics, USA
Lisa Grewenig	German Research Center for Artificial Intelligence (DFKI), Germany
Mir Riyanul Islam	KTH Royal Institute of Technology, Sweden
Mark Keane	University College Dublin, Ireland
Joseph Kendall-Morwick	Washburn University, USA
Mirko Lenz	German Research Center for Artificial Intelligence (DFKI), Germany
Beatriz Lopez	University of Girona, Spain

Jean Lieber	Université de Lorraine, CNRS, Inria, LORIA, France
Kyle Martin	Robert Gordon University, UK
Stefania Montani	Università del Piemonte Orientale "A. Avogadro", Italy
David Ménager	Parallax Advanced Research, USA
Hector Muñoz Avila	Lehigh University, USA
Pierre-Alexandre Murena	Hamburg Technical University, Germany
Emmanuel Nauer	Université de Lorraine, CNRS, Inria, LORIA, France
Ikechukwu Nkisi-Orji	Robert Gordon University, UK
Enric Plaza	IIIA-CSIC, Spain
Luigi Portinale	Università del Piemonte Orientale "A. Avogadro", Italy
Brian Schack	Air Force Research Laboratory, USA
Barry Smyth	University College Dublin, Ireland
Manuel Striani	Università del Piemonte Orientale "A. Avogadro", Italy
Antonio A. Sánchez-Ruiz	Universidad Complutense de Madrid, Spain
Rosina Weber	Drexel University, USA
Wolfgang Wilke	Trier University, Germany
David Wilson	University of North Carolina at Charlotte, USA
Xiaomeng Ye	Berry College, USA
Christian Zeyen	German Research Center for Artificial Intelligence (DFKI), Germany

Additional Reviewers

Opy Das	Norwegian University of Science and Technology, Norway
Jonah Fernandez	University of Girona, Spain
Prateek Goel	Drexel University, USA
Odd Erik Gundersen	Norwegian University of Science and Technology, Norway
Lasal Jayawardena	Robert Gordon University, UK
Folke Jernbert	Norwegian University of Science and Technology, Norway
Anders Kofod-Petersen	Norwegian University of Science and Technology, Norway
Craig Pirie	Robert Gordon University, UK
Christopher Rauch	Drexel University, USA

Alexander Schultheis	Trier University/German Research Center for Artificial Intelligence (DFKI), Germany
Tolga Tel	Goethe University Frankfurt, Germany
Kokulan Thanabalan	Trier University/German Research Center for Artificial Intelligence (DFKI), Germany
Ximing Wen	Drexel University, USA
Kaitlynne Wilkerson	Indiana University Bloomington, USA
Zachary Wilkerson	Indiana University Bloomington, USA

Invited Talk Abstracts

XAI Is in Trouble, But is CBR?

Rosina O. Weber

Drexel University, USA

Abstract. This keynote examines why Explainable AI (XAI), despite its popularity, has not yet delivered sufficiently mature solutions for AI explainability. It discusses problems of scope, definitions, motivation, and evaluation, and uses this analysis as a starting point for reflecting on CBR. Although CBR is not commonly described as being in trouble, it remains a valuable yet non-mainstream AI field. The talk asks whether CBR faces an identity problem between symbolic and subsymbolic AI and considers how recent work on AI alignment, additive feature attribution benchmarks, and large language models points to strategic opportunities for the CBR community.

In Any Case, or Maybe Not? Towards Uncertainty-Aware CBR

Eyke Hüllermeier

Ludwig-Maximilians-Universität München, Germany

Abstract. This keynote addresses the representation and handling of uncertainty in Case-Based Reasoning. It connects CBR with two active lines of research in machine learning: the distinction between aleatoric and epistemic uncertainty, and conformal prediction as a methodology for producing set-valued predictions with formal coverage guarantees. The talk discusses how these uncertainty frameworks can contribute to a formal foundation for uncertainty-aware CBR and highlights the specific challenges that arise when bringing them into the CBR setting.

Contents

Foundations, Retrieval, and the State of CBR

The Changing Shape of Case-Based Reasoning

A Topic-Level Analysis and Call-to-Action for Modern CBR

Barry Smyth(✉)

School of Computer Science, University College Dublin, Dublin, Ireland
barry.smyth@ucd.ie

Abstract. We present a large-scale, topic-level analysis of case-based reasoning (CBR) research. Our results suggest that CBR functions as a translational framework, importing ideas from core AI subfields while exporting CBR principles into applied domains. We find that CBR maintains a stable core, but exhibits weaker publication and author growth than the wider research ecosystem. Research on nearest-neighbour methods is expanding rapidly, but despite its strong conceptual connection to CBR, this growth has not translated into renewal for CBR itself. We conclude by outlining opportunities for CBR in light of the resurgence of data-driven, retrieval-centric AI.

Keywords: case-based reasoning · topic analysis · scientometrics

1 Introduction

Case-based reasoning (CBR) emerged in the 1980s as a memory-based reasoning paradigm within artificial intelligence [1,19–21,28]. It demonstrated the value of episodic memory, retrieval, and reasoning from experience as an alternative to the prevailing rule-based, knowledge-engineering approaches [33]. Since then, CBR principles have diffused widely across machine learning, AI, and many application domains [3,5–7,9,11,13,16,25,32,39,41]. This diffusion raises important questions for the CBR community: Is the field expanding or consolidating? How cohesive is its core, and how does it relate to adjacent research areas?

Prior scientometric work on CBR identified a striking asymmetry: a compact core coexisting with a larger periphery [34]. That work analysed CBR in aggregate. Here we conduct a thematic analysis spanning four decades to identify areas of growth and decline while exploring the conditions for renewal; see also [35]. Our findings reveal CBR as a translational framework, importing advances from core AI subfields while exporting CBR principles into applied domains. CBR retains strong citation influence and areas of growth, yet its overall momentum is weaker and less coordinated than the broader research ecosystem.

We also observe a divergence between CBR and related nearest-neighbour (kNN) research [12]. The latter shows strong growth in output, impact, and

L. Malburg and K. Bach (Eds.): ICCBR 2026, LNAI 16780, pp. 3–18, 2027.
https://doi.org/10.1007/978-3-032-33865-5_1

participation, reflecting expanding opportunities in retrieval-centric, data-driven AI. However, despite the close historical and conceptual connection between CBR and kNN, this growth has not translated into renewal for CBR itself.

This paper makes three contributions. First, we present a large-scale topic-level scientometric analysis of CBR. Second, we introduce a multidimensional momentum framework, using publication, citation, and author dynamics to analyse the structural evolution of CBR topics. Third, we identify emerging growth patterns and structural divergences, particularly between CBR and kNN, to highlight opportunities for future CBR expansion and renewal.

2 Datasets, Communities, and Metrics

This study uses Semantic Scholar (SS), which provides publication and citation data for more than 230 million papers across many fields [18]. Data were collected in December 2025 using the Semantic Scholar Datasets API.

2.1 The CBR Universe

Following [34], we construct a *CBR universe* of 2,784,208 papers by 4,490,008 unique authors from the following SS subsets:

- V_p: 1,576 *venue* papers from IC/EC/EW/UK-CBR and their workshops.
- S_p: 26,381 papers returned by a query-based SS search for CBR papers[1]
- C_p: 27,920 CBR papers, where $C_p = V_p \cup S_p$.
- L_p: 494,944 *linked* papers that cite, or are cited by, papers in C_p.
- A_p: 2,419,625 *related* papers by authors in C_p.

The CBR universe is $U_p = C_p \cup L_p \cup A_p$. Author sets ($C_a, L_a, A_a$) are defined similarly with $U_a = C_a \cup L_a \cup A_a$; see Fig. 1(a) & (b). Relative to [34], the number of CBR papers and authors has increased by 3× and 5×, respectively.

2.2 Inside and Outside Communities

Smyth [34] found two largely distinct communities: (i) an *inside* community publishing in the core CBR venues (IC/EC/EW/UK-CBR), and (ii) an *outside* community not publishing in these venues. A CBR paper is an *inside paper* if at least one author is a venue author; an author is an *inside author* if they have authored an inside paper (Eqs. 1–2). This author-lineage definition captures community membership even when CBR work appears outside core venues.

$$I_p = \{\, p \in C_p \mid \exists u \in \text{Authors}(p) \wedge u \in V_a \,\}. \tag{1}$$

[1] CBR papers were identified using *strong* (e.g. 'case-based reasoning', 'derivational analogy'), *moderate* (e.g. 'case base', 'nearest-neighbour'), and *weak* (e.g. 'CBR', 'knowledge container') terms and a suitable scoring system to prioritise high precision and recall.

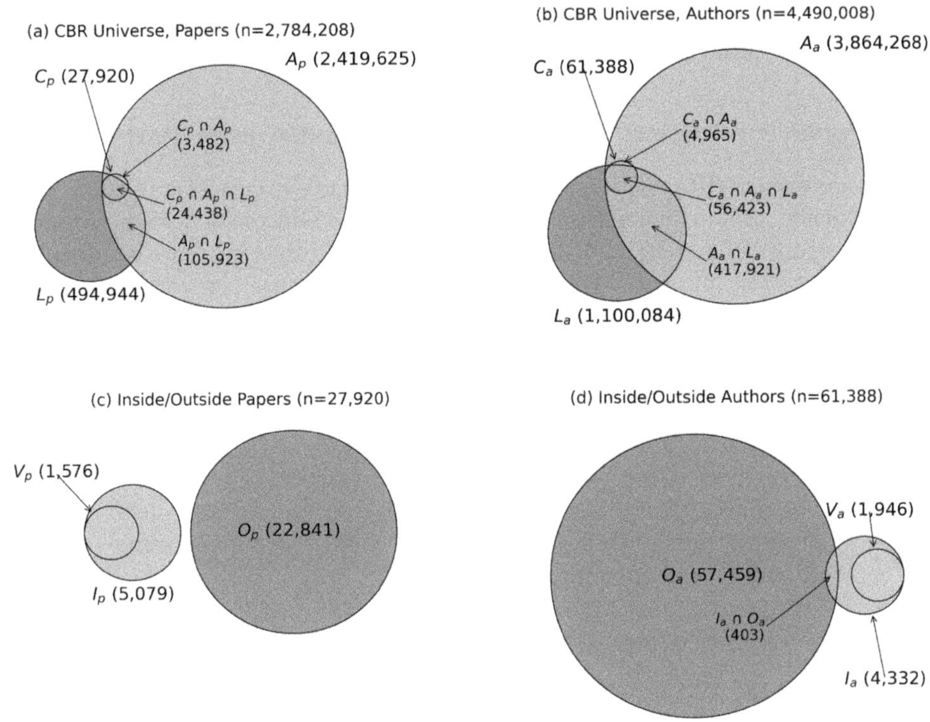

Fig. 1. The structure of the CBR universe and the inside/outside communities.

$$I_a = \{u \in C_a \mid \exists p \in I_p \wedge u \in \text{Authors}(p)\} \tag{2}$$

Outside papers and authors are defined as:

$$O_p = C_p \setminus I_p \tag{3}$$

$$O_a = \{u \in C_a \mid \exists p \in O_p \wedge u \in \text{Authors}(p)\} \tag{4}$$

Figure 1(c) & (d) summarise these. As in [34], the outside community remains the larger—$> 4x$ papers and $> 13x$ authors—and recent growth has been driven mainly by it; inside papers increased by >40%, whereas outside papers grew by 500%. Author growth is similarly uneven, 150% for I_a but 600% for O_a; cf. [34].

2.3 CBR vs kNN: The Pure CBR Dataset

It is useful to view C_p as being made up of K_p, papers matching nearest-neighbour (kNN) terms but without CBR-specific matches, and C'_p, papers matching CBR terms and (optionally) kNN terms; $C_p = C'_p \cup K_p$ with $C'_p \cap K_p = \varnothing$. Overall, 25% of C'_p are inside papers while <1% of the 7,932-paper kNN-only subset K_p are inside papers. This does not imply kNN methods are absent from the inside community; rather, when present they are framed within CBR.

2.4 Paper Production, Citation Influence, and Author Participation

We characterise CBR research along three dimensions: production output, citation influence, and author participation. Production and participation are measured as counts of papers and unique authors aggregated by year, community, or topic. Citation influence requires normalisation because citation counts vary across fields and publication age. We therefore adopt a windowed variant of field-weighted citation impact (FWCI) [30].

$$c_W(p) = \sum_{t=y_p}^{y_p+W-1} c(p,t), \tag{5}$$

Let $c(p,t)$ denote citations received by paper p in year t, with y_p its publication year. For a window of W years (here $W = 3$), Eq. 5 counts citations received within the first W years after publication.

$$\mu_W(f,y) = \text{mean}\left\{c_W(p') : \text{FoS}(p') = f,\ \text{Year}(p') = y\right\}. \tag{6}$$

$$\text{FWCI}_W(p) = \frac{c_W(p)}{\mu_W(\text{FoS}(p), \text{Year}(p))}. \tag{7}$$

Each SS paper is associated with one or more *fields of study* (FoS); we use the first-listed field as the primary FoS. For each primary FoS, f, and publication year y, the expected citation count is given by Eq. 6. The windowed FWCI of p (Eq. 7) compares p to papers in the same field and year: values > 1 indicate above-expected impact, while values < 1 indicate below-expected performance.

3 The Role of CBR in the Universe of Research

CBR research does not exist in isolation. In this section, we consider the role it plays within the universe of related research, U_p. First, we identify distinct research themes (topics) within U_p and examine how they relate to CBR research (C_p). Second, we quantify the extent to which *core* CBR research acts as a net importer or exporter of ideas relative to adjacent research areas. We do this by treating citations as directional knowledge transfers: if p cites q, then p is importing ideas from q or, equivalently, q is exporting ideas to p.

3.1 Topic Discovery and Model Selection

Topics in U_p are discovered using an unsupervised, density-based clustering pipeline designed to operate at scale and to accommodate highly skewed topic sizes. Focusing on English-only papers, each paper is embedded using the pretrained sentence-transformer model `all-MiniLM-L6-v2`, producing a dense semantic representation from titles and abstracts [42]. These embeddings are projected into a lower-dimensional space using UMAP [24] to preserve local neighbourhood structure while enabling efficient clustering. Topic discovery is performed using HDBSCAN [10], allowing both large, well-established research areas and smaller, more specialised or emerging topics to be identified.

A key hyperparameter is *minimum cluster size* (MCS): it controls the smallest number of documents required for a group to be a cluster. Based on a sweep over candidate values ($20 \leq MCS \leq 1000$) for U_p, we select $MCS = 300$ as the knee point in the relationship between cluster size and count. Topic labels are generated by extracting representative keyphrases (unigrams and bigrams) from each cluster, ranked by within-topic frequency and penalised for corpus-wide commonality, to ensure labels are semantically informative and discriminative.

3.2 Topics in the Universe

This process identifies 154 topics within U_p, spanning 16 primary fields of study. Topic sizes range from $3,684$ (*classical* • *quantum computing*) to $47,871$ (learning • student) papers, with a mean size of $13,120.61 \pm 7,247.14$ papers. The most common field of study is Computer Science (69 topics, 903,900 papers), followed by Medicine (31 topics, 405,575 papers), Engineering (24 topics, 305,287 papers), and Environmental Science (9 topics, 92,881 papers).

Most (55%) topics are from outside Computer Science and 27% of C_p papers appear in these non-CS topics. Only one topic (*laser* • *sensor*) contains no papers from C_p. The mean C_p overlap with U_p topics is 131.88 ± 625.61 and the largest overlap contains $7,733$ C_p papers (*case-based* • *knowledge*), which we revisit below. Most topics contain dozens of C_p papers; 42 topics contain > 100 C_p papers, and several contain substantially more. This pattern reflects the broad diffusion of CBR ideas across the wider research universe.

Due to limited space, it is not feasible to show all identified topics. Instead, Table 1 presents three illustrative top-10 lists: (a) the ten largest topics overall; (b) the ten topics with the greatest overlap with C_p; and (c) the ten largest non–Computer Science topics. For each topic, we report the primary field of study, the median publication year, the total number of papers, the C_p, I_p, and O_p overlap counts, and the total number of citations to papers in the topic. Once again, it is worth noting that four of the top five topics in (a) are outside Computer Science. This further demonstrates the degree to which CBR has diffused throughout a diverse collection of fields.

As above, the largest CBR-concentrated topic is *case-based* • *knowledge* – the top topic in Table 1(b) – with 10,883 papers, 7,733 (71%) of which belong to C_p. This is by far the greatest concentration of CBR papers within any single topic. Importantly, this topic emerges from an entirely bottom-up discovery process, rather than from our carefully curated C_p definition. We therefore interpret it as the empirically grounded structural core of the CBR field and denote it T_{CBR}.

Viewed in this light, T_{CBR} is a semantically coherent and internally dense cluster representing canonical CBR research. The C_p papers in surrounding top-

Table 1. Sample topics with labels, abbreviated fields of study, median publication years, overall topic sizes, the number of C_p, I_p, and O_p papers, and total citation count. For variety, three tables are presented: (a) top-10 by overall topic size; (b) top-10 by overlap with C_p; (c) top-10 by size for non–CS topics.

(a) Top 10 overall	FoS	Year	Overall	C_p	I_p	O_p	Cites
learning • student	Education	2012	47,871	302	42	260	3,270,654
patient • cell	Medicine	2016	46,445	27	1	26	3,437,310
learning • classific	Comp Sci	2014	34,904	719	69	650	4,273,911
design • product	Eng	2009	30,883	312	36	276	920,522
power • energy	Eng	2016	29,909	86	12	74	950,880
word • text	Comp Sci	2017	28,666	151	59	92	3,318,412
patient • risk	Medicine	2015	28,478	24	0	24	2,136,190
requirement • code	Comp Sci	2010	27,885	281	86	195	1,264,639
eeg • brain	Comp Sci	2017	24,334	298	6	292	1,446,114
decision • criteria	Comp Sci	2011	24,147	154	27	127	1,443,892
(b) Top 10 CBR	FoS	Year	Overall	C_p	I_p	O_p	Cites
case-based • knowl	Comp Sci	2007	10,883	7,733	2,524	5,209	396,415
ML • prediction	Medicine	2020	18,271	563	15	548	887,138
medical • health	Medicine	2014	22,676	409	108	301	903,914
fault • maintenance	Eng	2014	24,031	360	35	325	859,366
robot • reinforc.	Comp Sci	2015	22,187	318	153	165	1,482,926
legal • law	Law	2013	6,880	307	58	249	247,264
recommend • user	Comp Sci	2016	15,705	287	142	145	822,483
cancer • detection	Medicine	2016	15,135	276	7	269	600,621
topic • document	Comp Sci	2013	9,215	250	23	227	491,390
intrusion • network	Comp Sci	2018	15,261	240	16	224	714,534
(c) Top 10 non-CS	FoS	Year	Overall	C_p	I_p	O_p	Cites
heart rate • detection	Medicine	2016	17,474	196	14	182	699,493
building • cost	Eng	2013	17,187	150	10	140	659,802
financial • credit	Econ	2013	14,782	138	17	121	1,404,774
segment • image	Medicine	2019	17,720	135	8	127	1,011,907
clinical • learning	Medicine	2014	19,867	132	4	128	2,054,113
forest • sensing	Env Sci	2015	18,178	124	2	122	1,295,181
evac. • response	Eng	2014	7,450	113	7	106	226,465
gait • emg	Eng	2016	16,968	104	0	104	809,783
spectral • quality	Ag/Food	2015	9,385	102	1	101	361,579
transport • predict.	Eng	2014	15,104	94	5	89	503,804

ics ($C_p \setminus T_{\text{CBR}}$) align more closely with their host topics, rather than T_{CBR}, but they remain CBR in nature. These papers operate as boundary contributions, linking T_{CBR} to adjacent computational and applied areas. Together, this structure reveals the split personality of CBR: a clear structural core, T_{CBR}, alongside extensive diffusion across diverse and often high-impact research domains.

3.3 CBR Knowledge Transfer Between Topics

To analyse idea transfer at the topic level, we aggregate citations into a directed topic graph. If a paper in topic T_i cites a paper in T_j, we treat this as a citation from T_i to T_j. We interpret this as T_i *importing* from T_j (or T_j *exporting* to T_i). In this section, we analyse these flows between each topic T_i and the T_{CBR} core because we are primarily concerned with the export of CBR ideas from T_{CBR} to other topics, and the import of non-CBR ideas into T_{CBR} from other topics.

The *CBR export share* for T_i is the fraction of citations to T_{CBR} coming from papers in T_i (Eq. 8). Because citations from T_i to T_{CBR} are instances in which T_i draws on CBR ideas, the numerator counts exports from T_{CBR} to T_i, while the denominator normalises by total exports from T_{CBR} to all topics. High values imply CBR exports disproportionately to T_i relative to other topics.

$$\text{ExportShare}(T_i) = \frac{\sum_{p \in T_i} \#\{\, q \in T_{\text{CBR}} \mid p \to q \,\}}{\sum_{r} \#\{\, q \in T_{\text{CBR}} \mid r \to q \,\}}. \tag{8}$$

Analogously, the *CBR import share* of T_i is the fraction of all citations made by T_{CBR} that go to papers in T_i (Eq. 9). High values indicate that the CBR core relies strongly on ideas coming *from* T_i relative to other topics.

$$\text{ImportShare}(T_i) = \frac{\sum_{q \in T_{\text{CBR}}} \#\{\, p \in T_i \mid q \to p \,\}}{\sum_{q \in T_{\text{CBR}}} \#\{\, r \mid q \to r \,\}}. \tag{9}$$

Figure 2 plots each topic (excluding T_{CBR} for clarity) according to its CBR import (x-axis) and export (y-axis) share, with marker size indicating the number of C_p papers in the topic. To improve readability, most topics are greyed out but a selection of topics from Table 1 are highlighted and colour-coded based on their primary FoS; the numbers in brackets after the topic label indicate the overall topic size and the number of C_p papers, respectively.

Most topics lie close to the diagonal, indicating a broadly reciprocal exchange of ideas between CBR and neighbouring areas. CBR is neither purely an exporter nor importer of ideas. Systematic asymmetries nevertheless exist. For example, most of the topics above the diagonal (e.g. *medical • health, requirement • code, design • product*) are application oriented, often in non-Computer Science fields, and their position above the diagonal indicates that T_{CBR} exports more ideas to these topics than it imports from them. In contrast, foundational methodological topics (e.g. *learning • classification, topic • document, word • text*) lie below the diagonal, indicating that T_{CBR} imports more from these foundational topics than it exports to them. These patterns suggest that CBR often functions as a translational framework, importing advances from core AI subfields while exporting CBR principles into applied domains.

The overlap between CBR and the universe topics, and the citation flows to and from the CBR core, suggest a field that is structurally concentrated yet intellectually porous. CBR maintains a coherent methodological core (T_{CBR}) while remaining deeply embedded in, and responsive to, broader developments in artificial intelligence. At the same time, its principles continue to inform important

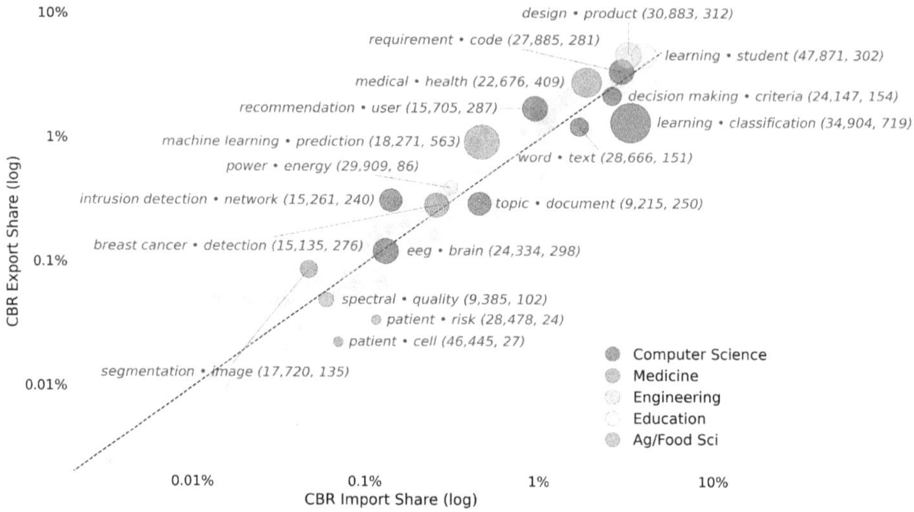

Fig. 2. Topics by CBR import/export share. Each marker is a topic in U_p. Marker sizes reflect the number of C_p papers in a topic, and highlighted topics are colour-coded by FoS and show the overall topic size and number of C_p papers.

application domains, including medicine, engineering, and even materials science and agricultural and food sciences. This dual character—stable at the centre but dynamically engaged at the periphery—has important implications for how the field evolves and sustains influence over time.

4 The Evolution of CBR

We return now to the curated CBR corpus (C_p) and its variants (C'_p, I_p, O_p, K_p) to understand how CBR itself is evolving and how this compares to the evolution of the wider universe. For each CBR variant we construct a topic system using the same approach as Sect. 3. We denote these systems by C'_T, I_T, O_T, and K_T. Our objectives are twofold: (i) to characterise the thematic composition of CBR and its variants and (ii) to assess whether the field exhibits expansion, contraction, or structural realignment—and what this implies about the health of CBR research today. Note, a detailed description of topics is not feasible in the space available, but we will accompany descriptions of specific topics with references to highly cited papers to serve as exemplars for the topic.

4.1 Identifying CBR Topics

To characterise the internal structure of CBR research, we apply the same embedding and density-based clustering framework, using the titles and abstracts of English papers, as described in Sect. 3. This ensures methodological consistency. Because C'_p is substantially smaller than U_p, and because our goal is to capture specialised and emerging research themes, we adopt a smaller minimum cluster size ($MCS = 50$). This allows niche subtopics to emerge while retaining robustness against noise. The resulting topic system, C'_T, contains 83 topics ranging in size from 64 papers (*retrieval • manufacturing*, e.g. [15,38]) to 729 papers (*case-based • knowledge*, e.g. [1,28,37]), with a mean topic size of 222.28 ± 145.12 papers.

Let T_p be the set of papers in topic T. Then, the *inside bias* of T is the normalised share of its papers that belong to the inside subset, I_p; see Eq. 10. If $\text{inside\_bias}(T) \geq \frac{1}{2}$, then T is *inside-leaning*, otherwise it is *outside-leaning*.

$$\text{inside\_bias}(T) = \frac{|T_p \cap I_p|/|I_p|}{|T_p \cap I_p|/|I_p| + |T_p \cap O_p|/|O_p|}. \tag{10}$$

We apply the same topic discovery procedure to K_p (with $MCS = 40$) to produce K_T ($|K_T| = 62$). Altogether, we analyse five topic systems derived from five paper datasets: U_T from U_p, C'_T from C'_p, and K_T from K_p, plus the inside- and outside-leaning subsets I_T and O_T defined within C'_T.

4.2 Topic Momentum

To characterise each topic T over a time interval $\Delta = [y_{\min}, y_{\max}]$, let

$$T_\Delta = \{p \in T_p \mid \text{Year}(p) \in \Delta\}$$

denote the set of papers in topic T published during Δ. We define three basic topic dimensions to capture publication output ($P_\Delta(T)$), citation impact ($C_\Delta(T)$), and author participation ($A_\Delta(T)$), as shown in Eqs. 11–13.

$$P_\Delta(T) = |T_\Delta|. \tag{11}$$

$$C_\Delta(T) = \sum_{p \in T_\Delta} \text{FWCI}_W(p). \tag{12}$$

$$A_\Delta(T) = \left| \bigcup_{p \in T_\Delta} \text{Authors}(p) \right|. \tag{13}$$

Next, *topic momentum*, $M_X(T)$, is defined as the relative change in a topic's performance over two consecutive, equal-duration intervals, Δ_{recent} and Δ_{prior}:

$$M_X(T) = \frac{X_{\Delta_{\text{recent}}}(T)}{X_{\Delta_{\text{prior}}}(T)}, \qquad X \in \{P, C, A\}. \tag{14}$$

Since FWCI_W uses a three-year window, the recent period must allow for a full three years' worth of citation accrual. As our dataset ends in 2025, the most recent admissible intervals are $\Delta_{\text{recent}} = [2020, 2022]$ and $\Delta_{\text{prior}} = [2017, 2019]$.

Figure 3 shows the 83 C'_T topics projected onto the publication–citation plane. The origin ($M_P = M_C = 1$) denotes structural equilibrium; distance from

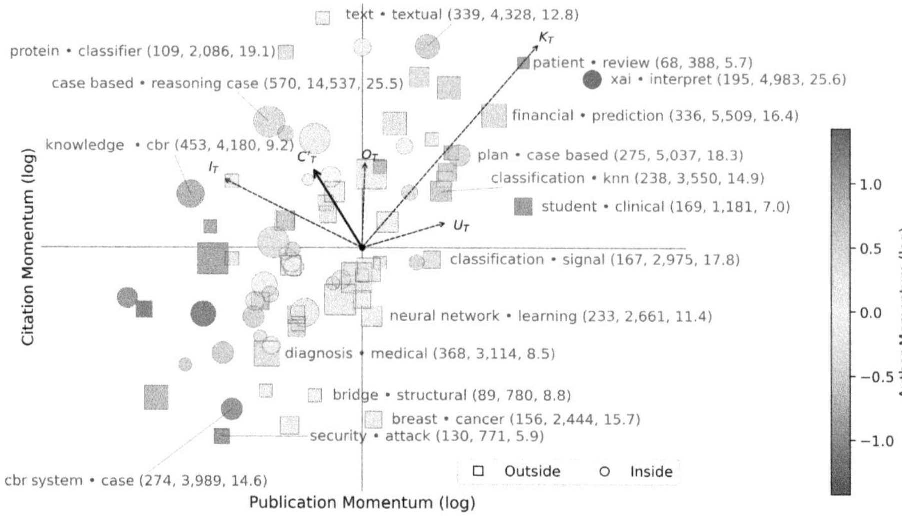

Fig. 3. Pure CBR (C'_p) topics in log-momentum space. Marker colour encodes $\log M_A$, size reflects topic size, and shape indicates inside or outside-leaning. The text in brackets shows topic size, citation count, and citations per paper for highlighted topics.

it indicates momentum intensity, and quadrant position, direction of change. The log transformation places growth and contraction on a symmetric additive scale. Marker colour encodes $\log M_A$, marker size reflects topic size, and shape distinguishes inside- from outside-leaning topics. Each topic is also classified as per Eq. 15:

$$\text{state}(T) = \begin{cases} \text{growing}, & \text{if } M_P(T) > 1 \wedge M_C(T) > 1 \wedge M_A(T) > 1, \\ \text{declining}, & \text{if } M_P(T) < 1 \wedge M_C(T) < 1 \wedge M_A(T) < 1, \\ \text{mixed}, & \text{otherwise.} \end{cases} \quad (15)$$

Mostly, the upper-right quadrant has growing topics, while lower-left topics are declining. For example, *XAI • interpretable* is an inside-leaning topic with strong publication, citation and author momentum; it includes high-impact papers such as [17,29]. The outside-leaning *financial • prediction* (e.g. [4,22]) topic is also growing in all three dimensions. In contrast, the inside-leaning *CBR system • case* (e.g. [8,27]) and outside-leaning *security • attack* (e.g. [2]) topics are declining in publications, citations and authors. In both of these quadrants there are a minority of topics with contrary author momentum; e.g. *bridge • structural* [26] is declining in publications and citations but has some positive author momentum as indicated by its fill colour.

Other quadrants are asymmetric. Upper-left topics have positive citation but declining publication momentum and, usually, declining author momentum, consistent with mature domains sustained by accumulated citation capital. Lower-right topics show publication growth but citation decline. Some have growing author counts (e.g. *classification • signal* [40]), which may suggest recent expansion if lagging citation impact has yet to materialise; they might transition into the upper-right, growth quadrant in time. Other lower-right topics have declining author momentum (e.g. *neural network • learning* [31], *breast • cancer* [14]), which may suggest they are destined to transition into the lower-left quadrant, representing overall decline.

4.3 Comparing Topic Systems

To compare topic systems, we treat each topic as a mass-weighted vector in three-dimensional log-momentum space, see Eq. 16. Each topic is assigned a mass weight proportional to the square root of its recent publication count (Eq. 17) so larger topics exert greater influence, without allowing a small number of dominant topics to overwhelm aggregate behaviour. The aggregate per-mass drift vector is defined as shown in Eq. 18. Its components correspond to net per-mass forces for publications, citations, and authors in log-momentum space. The magnitude $|\bar{\mathbf{V}}|$ captures overall structural intensity.

$$\mathbf{v}_T = \big(\log M_P(T), \log M_C(T), \log M_A(T)\big) \tag{16}$$

$$w_T = \sqrt{P_{\Delta_{\text{recent}}}(T)}. \tag{17}$$

$$\bar{\mathbf{V}} = \frac{\sum_T w_T \mathbf{v}_T}{\sum_T w_T} \tag{18}$$

$$coherence = \frac{\|\sum_T w_T \mathbf{v}_T\|}{\sum_T w_T \|\mathbf{v}_T\|} \tag{19}$$

We define coherence in Eq. 19. The denominator is the total weighted magnitude of topic-level change, while the numerator is the magnitude of their aggregate (net) drift. Coherence therefore captures the degree of directional alignment among topics: if all topics move in the same direction in log-momentum space, coherence tends to 1; if topic movements diverge, coherence approaches 0.

In Fig. 3, the labelled drift arrows show the projection of $\bar{\mathbf{V}}$ onto the publication–citation plane for C'_T, U_T, I_T, O_T, and K_T. Although U_T and K_T topics are not shown, their drift vectors are included to allow for direct visual comparison. The drift arrow for C'_T indicates modest overall citation growth accompanied by publication contraction, which is driven mostly by inside-leaning topics, since O_T's publication momentum is marginally positive. The U_T arrow shows balanced positive publication and citation momentum for the wider universe, whereas K_T (kNN-only topics) displays even stronger and more coherent expansion.

Figure 4(a–f) summarises this structural composition and these dynamical forces across the topic systems. Panel (a) shows that the CBR-derived systems

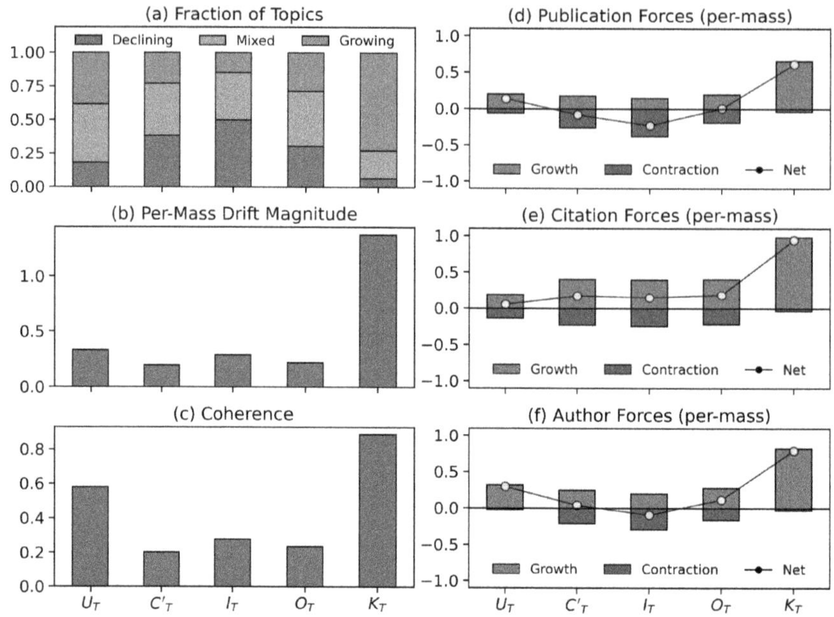

Fig. 4. The structural composition and dynamical forces across topic systems.

(C'_T, I_T, and O_T) are more contraction-heavy than U_T and K_T. I_T exhibits the largest share of declining topics and the smallest share of growing topics among the CBR systems, whereas K_T is dominated by growth with few declining topics. In (b), per-mass drift magnitude is much higher for K_T, indicating stronger aggregate structural movement; the CBR systems cluster just below U_T. Coherence (c) further differentiates the systems: K_T displays very high alignment of topic-level dynamics, while C'_T, I_T, and O_T exhibit far less coordination. Publication forces (d) lead to negative net publication momentum for CBR systems, but K_T exhibits strong positive publication force with minimal contraction. Citation forces (e) are net positive, confirming sustained influence even where publication expansion is limited, but again are strongest for K_T; C'_T, I_T, and O_T have stronger citation momentum than U_T. Author forces (f) show negative author momentum for I_T and weak momentum for C'_T and O_T, while U_T and especially K_T show strong positive author growth with little opposing contraction.

These results show that CBR publication and author momentum are modest at best, with low coherence, especially in inside-leaning topics. There is growth but it is concentrated and lacks the strong coherence evident in kNN growth.

5 Discussion

These results portray CBR as influential but constrained. Its core remains coherent and citation-active, but growth is fragmented and less aligned than related research areas. At the same time, related retrieval-centric areas, especially kNN research, are expanding. This combination suggests not a crisis of relevance, but a gap between intellectual influence and field-level renewal. What explains this gap and what strategic responses follow from it?

5.1 The kNN Paradox and Retrieval-Centric AI

Perhaps the most striking result is the contrast between CBR and closely related nearest-neighbour methods. Why doesn't kNN growth benefit CBR? One explanation is terminological drift: contemporary kNN research is embedded in data-driven, retrieval-centric AI (retrieval-augmented generation, embedding-based search, metric learning, etc.) and it appears to have lost its connection to CBR. A second explanation is conceptual decoupling: kNN is treated as a computational primitive rather than an integral part of a broader reasoning paradigm grounded in adaptation, explanation, and structured experiential memory. In either case, the opportunity for reintegration is clear and should be pursued.

5.2 Actionable Priorities

The evidence doesn't indicate crisis, but it does suggest an important inflexion point for the field. Given this, we propose the following priorities to strengthen alignment and renewal within the CBR community:

(i) Reintegrate kNN within the CBR narrative. Position modern kNN advances (e.g. embedding retrieval, vector databases, and hybrid symbolic–neural similarity learning) as contemporary instantiations of CBR principles. Framing CBR as the conceptual foundation of retrieval-centric AI could redirect adjacent growth toward field-level renewal.

(ii) Engage directly with retrieval-centric AI. Retrieval-augmented generation, memory-augmented neural networks, approximate nearest-neighbour algorithms (e.g. [23]), and prompt retrieval/reuse are closely aligned with case retrieval. Workshops, shared benchmarks, and joint challenges will strengthen intellectual bridges and increase structural integration.

(iii) Shift from applications to infrastructure. Invest in reusable assets: benchmark libraries, open-source retrieval, adaptation, explanation frameworks, evaluation standards, interoperable case-memory architectures, etc. Infrastructure lowers entry barriers and broadens participation.

(iv) Broaden author renewal. Encourage early-career engagement through doctoral consortia, cross-disciplinary supervision, and curricular integration of CBR concepts within mainstream AI. Actively welcome kNN into CBR venues; there has been no explicit mention of nearest-neighbour methods in the ICCBR call-for-papers for more than fifteen years!

(v) Strengthen theoretical uniqueness. Formalise CBR's unique reasoning strengths (adaptation, learning, explanation) to distinguish CBR from retrieval-only paradigms, and highlight the value CBR can bring.

CBR remains influential but it is becoming structurally narrower than adjacent fields. Meanwhile, kNN—CBR's methodological core—is expanding rapidly.

If CBR can reconnect its identity to data-driven, retrieval-centric AI, it may convert influence into expansion and selective consolidation into broader renewal.

6 Conclusion

We have presented a large-scale, topic-level analysis of the CBR research landscape, integrating publication, citation, and author dynamics to enable direct comparison across multiple topic systems. CBR may be at an inflexion point: citation momentum remains positive, selected themes continue to grow, yet overall momentum and coherence lag behind those of the wider research ecosystem.

This should not be read as decline, but as divergence. Closely related nearest-neighbour research is enjoying coordinated growth fueled by advances in data-driven, retrieval-centric AI. Despite kNN's historical, conceptual, and methodological connection with CBR, this growth has not translated into renewed expansion for CBR. Reasserting the conceptual and methodological link between CBR, kNN, and modern retrieval-centric AI represents a clear strategic opportunity to address this. At stake is not simply incremental growth for CBR, but the field's capacity to convert influence into substantial renewal.

Beyond CBR, this study demonstrates the value of multidimensional scientometric analysis for diagnosing structural dynamics in research fields. Our momentum framework provides a systematic basis for constructing relevant datasets, identifying coherent topic structures, and analysing patterns of concentration, diffusion, and renewal. A similar approach may prove useful for understanding the evolution of specialised domains within and beyond AI.

Acknowledgements. This research is supported by the Insight Research Ireland Centre for Data Analytics (12RC2289P2), with thanks to Prof. Padraig Cunningham for feedback during preparation.

Generative AI and Data Availability Statement. The author used AI for grammar and spell checking. The author reviewed and edited the content and takes full responsibility for the publication's content. Data supporting this research are available at [36].

References

1. Aamodt, A., Plaza, E.: Case-based reasoning: Foundational issues, methodological variations, and system approaches. AI Commun. **7**(1), 39–59 (1994)
2. Abutair, H.Y., Belghith, A.: Using case-based reasoning for phishing detection. Procedia Comput. Sci. **109**, 281–288 (2017). 8th International Conference on Ambient Systems, Networks and Technologies
3. Aha, D.W.: The omnipresence of case-based reasoning in science and application. Knowl.-Based Syst. **11**(5–6), 261–273 (1998)
4. Ahn, H., Jae Kim, K.: Bankruptcy prediction modeling with hybrid case-based reasoning and genetic algorithms approach. Appl. Soft Comput. **9**(2), 599–607 (2009)

5. Allen, B.P.: Case-based reasoning: business applications. Commun. ACM **37**(3), 40–43 (1994)
6. Bannour, W., Maalel, A., Ben Ghezala, H.H.: Emergency management case-based reasoning systems: A survey of recent developments. J. Exp. Theoret. Artif. Intell. **35**(1), 35–58 (2023)
7. Bichindaritz, I., Marling, C.: Case-based reasoning in the health sciences: What's next? Artif. Intell. Med. **36**(2), 127–135 (2006)
8. Bonzano, A., Cunningham, P., Smyth, B.: Using introspective learning to improve retrieval in cbr: A case study in air traffic control. In: Leake, D.B., Plaza, E. (eds.) Case-Based Reason. Res. Dev., pp. 291–302. Springer, Berlin Heidelberg, Berlin, Heidelberg (1997)
9. Bridge, D., Göker, M.H., McGinty, L., Smyth, B.: Case-based recommender systems. Knowl. Eng. Rev. **20**(3), 315–320 (2005)
10. Campello, R.J.G.B., Moulavi, D., Zimek, A., Sander, J.: Hierarchical density estimates for data clustering, visualization, and outlier detection. ACM Trans. Knowl. Discov. Data **10**(1), 1–51 (2015). https://doi.org/10.1145/2733381
11. Cui, D., Guo, J., Liu, P., Zhang, X., Liu, W.: Case-based causal reasoning for elite sport training. In: International Conference on Case-Based Reasoning, pp. 378–391. Springer, Cham (2025)
12. Cunningham, P., Delany, S.J.: k-Nearest neighbour classifiers–a tutorial. ACM Comput. Surv. **54**(6), 1–25 (2021)
13. Delaney, E.: Case-based explanations for black-box time series and image models with applications in smart agriculture. ICCBR DC **1613**, 0073 (2022)
14. Elter, M., Schulz-Wendtland, R., Wittenberg, T.: The prediction of breast cancer biopsy outcomes using two CAD approaches that both emphasize an intelligible decision process. Med. Phys. **34**(11), 4164–4172 (2007)
15. Hashemi, H., Shaharoun, A.M., Sudin, I.: A case-based reasoning approach for design of machining fixture. Int. J. Adv. Manuf. Technol. **74**(1–4), 113–124 (2014)
16. Keane, M.T., Smyth, B.: Good Counterfactuals and Where to Find Them: A Case-Based Technique for Generating Counterfactuals for Explainable AI (XAI). In: Watson, I., Weber, R. (eds.) ICCBR 2020. LNCS (LNAI), vol. 12311, pp. 163–178. Springer, Cham (2020). https://doi.org/10.1007/978-3-030-58342-2_11
17. Kenny, E.M., Keane, M.T.: Twin-systems to explain artificial neural networks using case-based reasoning. In: Proceedings of the Twenty-Eighth International Joint Conference on Artificial Intelligence, IJCAI-19, pp. 2708–2715 (2019)
18. Kinney, R., et al.: The semantic scholar open data platform. arXiv preprint arXiv:2301.10140 (2023)
19. Kolodner, J.: Case-based reasoning. Morgan Kaufmann (2014)
20. Kolodner, J.L.: Towards an understanding of the role of experience in the evolution from novice to expert. Int. J. Man Mach. Stud. **19**(5), 497–518 (1983)
21. Kolodner, J.L.: Retrieving events from a case memory: A parallel implementation. In: Proceedings of the DARPA Workshop on Case-Based Reasoning, pp. 233–249. Morgan Kaufmann, San Mateo, CA (1988)
22. Li, H., Sun, J.: Gaussian case-based reasoning for business failure prediction with empirical data in China. Inf. Sci. **179**(1), 89–108 (2009)
23. Li, W., Zhang, Y., Sun, Y., Wang, W., Zhang, W., Lin, X.: Approximate nearest neighbor search on high dimensional data — experiments, analyses, and improvement (v1.0). arXiv preprint arXiv:1610.02455 (2016)
24. McInnes, L., Healy, J., Melville, J.: UMAP: Uniform manifold approximation and projection for dimension reduction. arXiv preprint arXiv:1802.03426 (2018)

25. Montani, S., Jain, L.C., et al.: Successful case-based reasoning applications, vol. 305. Springer, Cham (2010)
26. Morcous, G., Rivard, H., Hanna, A.M.: Modeling bridge deterioration using case-based reasoning. J. Infrastruct. Syst. **8**(3), 86–95 (2002)
27. Ottersen, S.G., Bach, K.: Automatic adjusting global similarity measures in learning CBR systems. In: Recio-Garcia, J.A., Orozco-del Castillo, M.G., Bridge, D. (eds.) Case-Based Reasoning Research and Development, pp. 17–32. Springer Nature Switzerland, Cham (2024)
28. Riesbeck, C.K., Schank, R.C.: Inside Case-Based Reasoning. Lawrence Erlbaum Associates, Hillsdale, NJ (1989)
29. Rudin, C., Chen, C., Chen, Z., Huang, H., Semenova, L., Zhong, C.: Interpretable machine learning: Fundamental principles and 10 grand challenges. CoRR abs/2103.11251 (2021)
30. Scelles, N., Teixeira da Silva, J.A.: Making the impact of publications within a field comparable by improving the field-weighted citation impact (FWCI): the case of sport management. Scientometrics **130**(3), 1571–1586 (2025)
31. Shin, C.K., Yun, U.T., Kim, H.K., Park, S.C.: A hybrid approach of neural network and memory-based learning to data mining. IEEE Trans. Neural Netw. **11**(3), 637–646 (2000)
32. Shokouhi, S.V., Skalle, P., Aamodt, A.: An overview of case-based reasoning applications in drilling engineering. Artif. Intell. Rev. **41**(3), 317–329 (2014)
33. Slade, S.: Case-based reasoning: A research paradigm. AI Mag. **12**(1), 42–55 (1991)
34. Smyth, B.: A Tale of Two Communities: An Analysis of Three Decades of Case-Based Reasoning Research. In: Bach, K., Marling, C. (eds.) ICCBR 2019. LNCS (LNAI), vol. 11680, pp. 343–357. Springer, Cham (2019). https://doi.org/10.1007/978-3-030-29249-2_23
35. Smyth, B.: People who liked this also liked. ACM Trans. Recommender Syst. **4**(2), 1–41 (2025)
36. Smyth, B.: The changing shape of case-based reasoning. FigShare (2026). https://doi.org/10.6084/m9.figshare.32314362.v1
37. Stanfill, C., Waltz, D.: Toward memory-based reasoning. Commun. ACM **29**(12), 1213–1228 (1986)
38. Wang, H., Rong, Y.K.: Case-based reasoning method for computer aided welding fixture design. Comput. Aided Des. **40**(12), 1121–1132 (2008)
39. Wiratunga, N., et al.: CBR-RAG: case-based reasoning for retrieval augmented generation in LLMs for legal question answering. In: International Conference on Case-Based Reasoning, pp. 445–460. Springer, Cham (2024)
40. Yazdani, A., Ebrahimi, T., Hoffmann, U.: Classification of EEG signals using Dempster–Shafer theory and a k-nearest neighbor classifier. In: 2009 4th International IEEE/EMBS Conference on Neural Engineering, pp. 327–330 (2009)
41. Yeh, I.C., Hsu, T.K.: Building real estate valuation models with comparative approach through case-based reasoning. Appl. Soft Comput. **65**, 260–271 (2018)
42. Yin, C., Zhang, Z.: A study of sentence similarity based on the all-minilm-l6-v2 model with "same semantics, different structure" after fine-tuning. In: 2024 2nd International Conference on Image, Algorithms and Artificial Intelligence (ICIAAI 2024), pp. 677–684. Atlantis Press (2024)

Exploring Embedding Spaces for Case-Based Reasoning: Geometry, Coherence, and Human Alignment

Antonio A. Sánchez-Ruiz(✉)

Department of Software Engineering and Artificial Intelligence, Instituto de Tecnologías del Conocimiento Universidad Complutense de Madrid, Madrid, Spain
antsanch@ucm.es

Abstract. Similarity plays a central role in case-based reasoning systems. When cases contain unstructured data, neural networks are commonly used to learn embeddings and measure similarity as distance in the resulting embedding space. However, it remains unclear to what extent these distances capture the similarity perceived by a human expert.

In this work, we compare six neural embedding architectures (autoencoders, VAEs, classifiers, triplet networks, and hybrid models) trained on the MNIST dataset, and evaluate the resulting spaces along three complementary axes: class structure, geometry, and round-trip coherence. We further assess the alignment between embedding distances and human similarity judgements collected via a triplet-based annotation study.

Our results show that discriminative models produce spaces with tighter inter-class separation but poorer alignment with expert-perceived intra-class similarity. The Prototypical Variational Autoencoder (Proto-VAE), which combines generative regularisation with explicit class prototypes, achieves the best overall expert alignment (85.0% triplet accuracy), suggesting that prototype-based structure is a promising direction for human-aligned similarity in CBR.

Keywords: Case-based Reasoning · Similarity · Embedding Spaces · Deep Learning · Expert Alignment

1 Introduction

Similarity is a fundamental concept in artificial intelligence, and in case-based reasoning (CBR) in particular. In CBR, similarity between cases is the mechanism that enables the retrieval of relevant cases for a new problem and the reuse of their solutions, adapted to the new context [14]. In classical CBR systems, cases are represented symbolically (typically as attribute-value tuples) and similarity is defined through explicit functions that combine local attribute similarities weighted by their relative importance. This approach is both interpretable and controllable, but requires considerable knowledge engineering effort.

L. Malburg and K. Bach (Eds.): ICCBR 2026, LNAI 16780, pp. 19–34, 2027.
https://doi.org/10.1007/978-3-032-33865-5_2

When cases contain unstructured data (images, text, audio, video), the classical approach is no longer viable, and neural networks are instead used to automatically extract task-relevant features represented as numerical vectors, or *embeddings*. This vector representation is not easily interpretable, so similarity between cases is measured as the distance between the embeddings produced by the network. This approach has proven effective for retrieval tasks, but raises questions that are rarely addressed systematically: what properties does the resulting embedding space have, and to what extent do distances in that space capture the similarity between cases as perceived by a human expert?

These questions matter because different training objectives (reconstruction, classification, metric learning) can produce embedding spaces with very different geometries. A space well suited for classification may be inadequate for capturing intra-class similarity, which is particularly important for the reuse phase of the CBR cycle. Furthermore, similarity is not only a retrieval mechanism but also the foundation for explainability in CBR: retrieved cases justify the system's decisions, so similarity that is misaligned with expert intuition undermines trust in the system. Systematic introspection of the embedding space is therefore a prerequisite for explainable CBR over unstructured data.

In this work, we address these questions empirically by comparing six embedding architectures trained on the MNIST dataset [11]. While MNIST is relatively simple as a classification benchmark, the variation in handwriting style (digits of the same class differ in stroke width, slant, and writing style) makes intra-class similarity a genuinely interesting problem. This work therefore focuses on image embeddings as a controlled first step; extending the analysis to other case representations (attribute-value tuples, graphs, tabular data) is left as future work (Sect. 8). The research questions guiding this work are:

RQ1. What geometric properties characterise the resulting embedding spaces?
RQ2. How coherent and navigable are these embedding spaces?
RQ3. Do embedding distances align with expert-perceived similarity?

The main contributions of this paper are: (a) a systematic evaluation framework for embedding spaces covering three complementary axes: class structure, geometry, and round-trip coherence; (b) an empirical comparison of six commonly used neural embedding architectures; and (c) an expert alignment study based on triplet judgements.[1]

The rest of the paper is organised as follows. Section 2 reviews related work. Sections 3 and 4 describe the dataset and the neural architectures compared. Sections 5 and 6 present the results of the embedding space analysis and the expert alignment study, respectively. Section 7 discusses the findings and their implications, and Sect. 8 presents the conclusions and future work.

2 Related Work

Computing similarity between cases is one of the most studied topics in CBR research. When cases have complex structure, similarity must account for the

[1] Code and annotations: https://github.com/antsanchucm/iccbr2026.

Fig. 1. Examples of MNIST handwritten digit images.

relationships between case components [2], which has led to a wide range of approaches based on logic, graphs, and neural networks. For logic-based representations, measures grounded in formal language semantics have been proposed, such as subsumption [7] and edit distance in formula space [15]. For graph-based representations, measures based on subgraph isomorphism, maximal common subgraphs, and graph edit distance have been explored [1].

The use of embeddings in CBR has been explored in several recent works. Leake et al. [9] compared three feature extraction approaches for an image classification task, showing the advantage of post-dense layer embeddings in example-sparse domains. Leake et al. [10] extended this analysis to the impact of network architecture on extracted feature quality, assessed through retrieval accuracy. Wilkerson et al. [18] showed that transfer learning improves feature quality in low-data domains compared to training from scratch. These works assess embedding quality through downstream system performance (retrieval or classification accuracy); our work complements this line by evaluating the intrinsic properties of the embedding space (class structure, geometry, and coherence) and their alignment with expert judgements.

The alignment between computational similarity measures and human perception has also received attention in CBR. Díaz-Agudo et al. [5] studied similarity perception between artworks through user evaluations and proposed a methodology for learning similarity weights that reflect individual perception. Dapica and Peinado [4] used expert judgements to validate similarity measures in a CBR system for flight simulation, finding notable inter-annotator variability. More recently, Lenz et al. [12] showed that large language models can assess similarity in CBR, and that pairwise preferences align better with human perception than absolute scores, with best results obtained by letting the LLM decide how to combine local similarity measures. However, these results apply to symbolic domains; it remains unclear whether they generalise to unstructured data and neural embedding spaces, which is the focus of our work.

3 Dataset

The MNIST dataset [11] contains 60 000 training and 10 000 test 28×28 greyscale images of handwritten digits across 10 classes (see Fig. 1).

The choice of this dataset is motivated by several reasons: its manageable size allows multiple models to be trained quickly for embedding space analysis; the generated images can be interpreted without domain-specific expertise; and, most importantly, it presents non-trivial intra-class variation (instances of the

Table 1. Neural architectures compared and their training objectives.

Model	Superv.	Loss function	Parameters	Decoder
Autoencoder	No	$\mathcal{L} = \|x - \hat{x}\|^2$		Yes
VAE	No	$\mathcal{L} = \|x - \hat{x}\|^2 + \beta\, D_{\mathrm{KL}}$	β=10^{-3}	Yes
Classifier	Yes	$\mathcal{L} = \mathcal{H}(y, \hat{y})$		No
TripletNet	Yes	$\mathcal{L} = \max(0,\, d_+ - d_- + m)$	m=0.5	No
ClassifierAE	Yes	$\mathcal{L} = \|x - \hat{x}\|^2 + \alpha\, \mathcal{H}(y, \hat{y})$	α=1	Yes
ProtoVAE	Yes	$\mathcal{L} = \|x - \hat{x}\|^2 + \beta\, D_{\mathrm{KL}} + \gamma\, \|\mu - p_y\|^2$	β=10^{-3}, γ=0.1	Yes

same digit differ in stroke width, slant, and writing style), which makes intra-class similarity a genuinely challenging problem.

4 Embedding Architectures

We compare six commonly used neural architectures for image embedding, organised into three groups based on the type of information they use and their training objective: (a) generative models without class supervision (Autoencoder, VAE); (b) discriminative models with class supervision but no decoder (Classifier, TripletNet); and (c) hybrid models with class supervision and a decoder (ClassifierAE, ProtoVAE). Table 1 summarises the six architectures.

All models share the same encoder block: two convolutional blocks (16 and 32 filters, 3 × 3 kernels, each followed by max-pooling), producing a flattened representation of 1568 units, followed by a fully connected layer that projects to a 32-dimensional embedding space. Models with a decoder use a nearly symmetric architecture for reconstruction: a fully connected layer projecting back to 1568 units, reshaped into a 7 × 7 × 32 feature map, followed by three transposed convolutional layers that reconstruct the 28 × 28 output image. All models were trained for 10 epochs with a batch size of 128. The training objective of each model is described below.

The **Autoencoder** [6] learns to reconstruct its input after compressing it through a bottleneck, which forces the network to learn a latent representation that captures the essential visual structure. This model has no access to class labels, so its loss is based solely on pixel-level reconstruction.

$$\mathcal{L} = \|x - \hat{x}\|^2$$

The **Variational Autoencoder** (VAE) [8] extends the autoencoder by learning a probabilistic distribution over the latent space. Rather than encoding each input as a fixed point, the encoder outputs a mean μ and standard deviation σ parametrising a Gaussian distribution from which the embedding z is sampled. The loss combines reconstruction with a KL divergence term that regularises the latent space towards a standard Gaussian $\mathcal{N}(0, I)$, encouraging a smoother and more uniformly populated embedding space.

$$\mathcal{L} = \|x - \hat{x}\|^2 + \beta\,\mathrm{KL}(\mathcal{N}(\mu, \sigma^2) \,\|\, \mathcal{N}(0, I))$$

The **Classifier** is the most common discriminative architecture: an encoder followed by a softmax layer that predicts the digit class. The loss is the cross-entropy between the predicted probability distribution and the ground-truth label. Embeddings are extracted from the pre-softmax layer, which organises images according to their class.

$$\mathcal{L} = \mathcal{H}(y, \hat{y}) = -\sum_{c} y_c \log(\hat{y}_c)$$

The **TripletNet** [16] uses metric learning to separate classes in the embedding space without an explicit classification layer. It is trained on triplets (a, p, n), where a is an anchor, p is a positive example (same class as a), and n is a negative example (different class). The loss enforces a margin m between the anchor-to-negative and anchor-to-positive distances.

$$\mathcal{L} = \max(0,\ d(a, p) - d(a, n) + m)$$

Finally, we include two hybrid models that combine reconstruction and classification objectives. The **ClassifierAE** uses a shared encoder with two output heads: a decoder for reconstruction and a softmax head for classification. The loss is a weighted combination of both tasks, controlled by hyperparameter α.

$$\mathcal{L} = \|x - \hat{x}\|^2 + \alpha\,\mathcal{H}(y, \hat{y})$$

The **ProtoVAE** [17] extends the VAE with a set of k learnable prototype vectors, one per class, representing prototypical instances in the latent space. In addition to reconstruction and KL regularisation, the loss includes a term that encourages each embedding μ to remain close to the prototype of its class p_y. This allows the prototypes to impose prior structure on the latent space; in this work we use randomly initialised learnable prototypes, without explicit inter-class structure.

$$\mathcal{L} = \|x - \hat{x}\|^2 + \beta\,\mathrm{KL}(\mathcal{N}(\mu, \sigma^2) \,\|\, \mathcal{N}(0, I)) + \gamma\,\|\mu - p_y\|^2$$

5 Embedding Space Analysis

Once the six models are trained on the training set, we evaluate their embedding spaces using the test set. For each model, we compute the embedding coordinates for all test images and apply a battery of objective metrics, using Euclidean distance throughout, characterising class structure, embedding space geometry, and round-trip coherence.

5.1 Class Structure

This set of metrics evaluates the extent to which the embedding space organises images according to the digit they represent. Good class structure means that images of the same digit form compact clusters well separated from the others, which is relevant for CBR retrieval as it facilitates finding neighbours of the same class or semantic category. To characterise this property we use three complementary metrics: the accuracy of a leave-one-out k-NN classifier (k=1), the silhouette coefficient, and the mean intra-class to inter-class distance ratio. Results are shown in Table 2.

Table 2. Class structure metrics. I/E: mean intra-class to inter-class distance ratio.

Model	kNN↑	Silhouette↑	I/E↓
Autoencoder	0.967	0.098	0.925
VAE	0.967	0.092	0.998
Classifier	0.987	0.414	0.355
TripletNet	0.983	**0.431**	**0.354**
ClassifierAE	**0.989**	0.348	0.423
ProtoVAE	0.933	0.213	0.543

Table 3. Embedding space geometry. P.R.: participation ratio; I.D.: intrinsic dimensionality (PCA at 90% variance); D.C.: distance concentration (coefficient of variation).

Model	P.R.↑	I.D.↑	D.C.↑	Hubness↓
Autoencoder	0.382	**17**	0.203	0.842
VAE	**0.453**	14	0.183	0.795
Classifier	0.174	6	**0.284**	0.795
TripletNet	0.210	8	0.252	1.111
ClassifierAE	0.213	9	0.263	0.852
ProtoVAE	0.192	6	0.269	**0.426**

All models achieve high k-NN accuracy since MNIST is a relatively easy benchmark, but clear differences emerge between discriminative models (98.3%–98.9%) and generative ones (93.3%–96.7%). The highest value is obtained by ClassifierAE, suggesting that the decoder helps preserve visually discriminative information. The lowest is obtained by ProtoVAE, possibly because the learnt prototypes are not sufficiently separated and class boundaries are not sharp.

The silhouette coefficient reveals that purely discriminative models produce more compact and well-separated clusters, whereas unsupervised generative models do not form well-defined clusters even though they remain separable by k-NN. ProtoVAE occupies an intermediate position, indicating that prototype anchoring improves cluster cohesion compared to the plain VAE.

The mean intra/inter-class distance ratio confirms these findings. In particular, the VAE obtains a value close to 1, indicating that the mean intra-class distance is nearly equal to the mean inter-class distance. As before, purely discriminative models achieve the greatest separation, with hybrid models in between.

5.2 Embedding Space Geometry

This set of metrics characterises the geometry of the embedding space independently of class labels, i.e., how embeddings are distributed and what properties that distribution has. These properties affect the quality of the similarity ranking of retrieved cases. Results are shown in Table 3.

The participation ratio measures isotropy: how variance is distributed across dimensions of the embedding space. It is defined as

$$\mathrm{PR} = \frac{(\sum_i \lambda_i)^2}{D \sum_i \lambda_i^2},$$

where λ_i are the eigenvalues of the embedding covariance matrix and D=32 is the embedding dimension. Values close to 1 indicate that all dimensions contribute equally to the total variance, while low values indicate that the space is dominated by a few dimensions. Complementarily, intrinsic dimensionality is the smallest number of PCA components needed to explain 90% of the variance. Both metrics reveal that discriminative models collapse to a low-dimensional subspace, while generative models distribute variance more uniformly. This is expected, as reconstruction requires preserving intra-class variation, whereas classification can be solved with a small number of class-invariant dimensions. Notably, hybrid models do not gain effective dimensions despite combining both objectives, suggesting that classification loss dominates.

Distance concentration, measured as the coefficient of variation of pairwise distances, quantifies how much distances vary between points in the embedding space [3]. Higher values are preferable for CBR because they indicate that some neighbours are clearly closer than others, making the similarity ranking more informative and discriminative. Discriminative models tend to cluster embeddings of the same class into compact regions, which increases the relative variance of distances.

Hubness [13] measures the skewness of the k-NN occurrence distribution: how often each point appears as a neighbour of others. High values indicate the presence of "hubs" (points that dominate retrieval results regardless of the query), which can distort similarity-based retrieval. ProtoVAE achieves the lowest hubness, suggesting that prototype anchoring distributes embeddings more evenly.

Table 4. Relative round-trip error (RTE) on real (10 000 test embeddings), interpolated (6 000 points: 2 000 random pairs $\times\ \alpha \in \{0.25, 0.5, 0.75\}$), and sampled (2 000 points from the empirical Gaussian) latent points.

Model	RTE real↓	RTE interp.↓	RTE sampl.↓
Autoencoder	**0.071**	**0.135**	**0.254**
VAE	0.212	0.211	0.368
ClassifierAE	0.118	0.191	0.426
ProtoVAE	0.191	0.189	0.266

5.3 Round-Trip Coherence

For models with a decoder, we can evaluate round-trip coherence: how faithfully the latent space supports encode–decode cycles. We define the relative round-trip error (RTE) as the distance between a latent point z and its reconstruction obtained by decoding and re-encoding, normalised by the mean pairwise embedding distance to make it comparable across models with different scales:

$$\mathrm{RTE}(z) = \frac{\|z - f_{\mathrm{enc}}(f_{\mathrm{dec}}(z))\|_2}{\bar{d}},$$

where $\bar{d}$ is the mean Euclidean distance between pairs of test embeddings.

We measure RTE on three types of latent points: (a) real points (embeddings of test images); (b) interpolated points (linear combinations of pairs of real embeddings); and (c) randomly sampled points drawn from a Gaussian fitted to the test embeddings. This allows us to evaluate not only coherence on observed data, but also the navigability of the latent space in regions not seen during training.

Round-trip coherence matters for the reuse phase of the CBR cycle, where case adaptation may involve interpolating in the latent space; a uniform RTE indicates that the encode–adapt–decode cycle is reliable beyond the training support. Results for the four models with a decoder are shown in Table 4.

The Autoencoder achieves the lowest error overall, particularly for real points, but error grows substantially for interpolated and sampled points. In contrast, VAE and ProtoVAE show higher errors on real points but little increase for interpolated ones. Overall, ProtoVAE shows the smallest gap across the three conditions, indicating a more coherent and navigable latent space at the cost of lower reconstruction precision.

Figures 2 and 3 provide complementary qualitative evidence. The interpolation figure shows smooth, semantically coherent transitions between class centroids 5 and 6 for VAE and ProtoVAE, while the Autoencoder transitions more abruptly—a consequence of its unregularised latent space, which does not impose smoothness on regions between training points. The sampled reconstructions reveal a different aspect: the Autoencoder generates sharp images near the training support but produces artefactual outputs for out-of-distribution points, consistent with its large gap between RTE real (0.071) and RTE sampled (0.254).

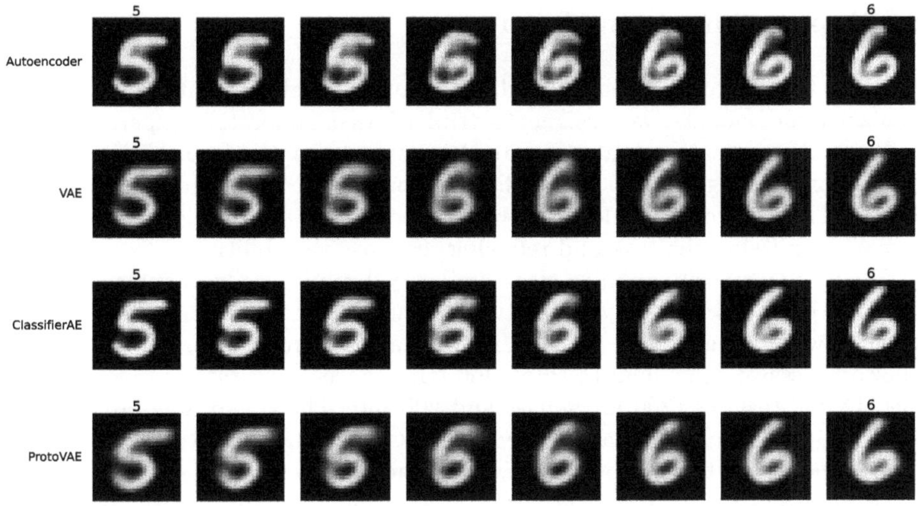

Fig. 2. Digits decoded from linearly interpolated points between class centroids 5 and 6 in the latent space, for the four models with a decoder (one row per model).

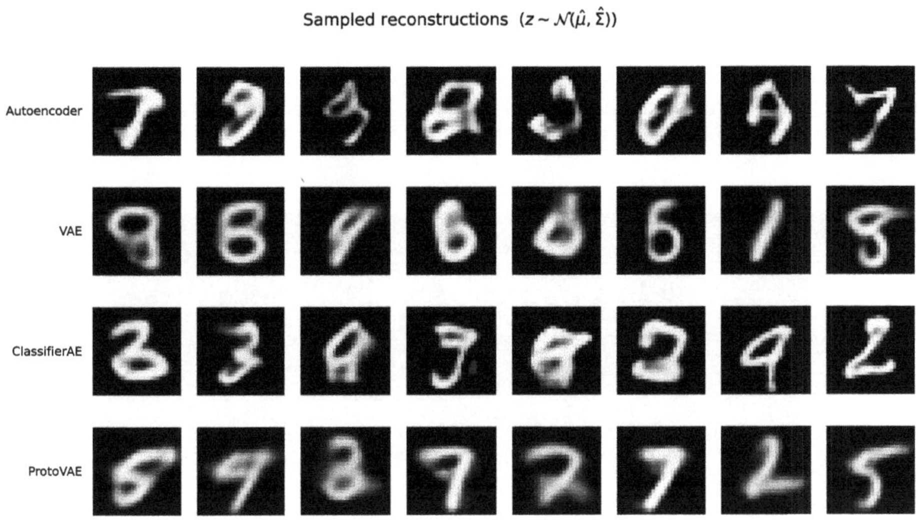

Fig. 3. Digits decoded from points sampled from the empirical Gaussian $\mathcal{N}(\hat{\mu}, \hat{\Sigma})$ fitted to the test embeddings of each model (one row per model).

VAE and ProtoVAE remain plausible and diverse under sampling, and ClassifierAE samples are visually homogeneous, reflecting its more clustered embedding geometry.

6 Expert Alignment Study

To assess the extent to which embedding distances are aligned with human expert similarity judgements, we designed a triplet-based annotation experiment. We built a web application that presents the annotator with an anchor image and two options, asking them to select which option is more similar to the anchor (see Fig. 4). This forced-choice format avoids the need to assign absolute similarity scores, simplifying the task and reducing response variability.

We focus primarily on intra-class similarity, but also evaluate inter-class similarity in triplets where only one option belongs to the same class as the anchor. Triplets with images from three different classes were not considered as they caused excessive confusion. In total, 400 triplets were generated randomly from the MNIST test set (200 intra-class and 200 inter-class) and annotated by the expert. Option order was randomised and the annotator was required to always choose one of the two options, even under uncertainty.

Table 5 reports the *triplet accuracy* of each model, defined as the fraction of triplets in which the option chosen by the expert matches the option closest to the anchor in the embedding space. Results are shown globally and broken down by triplet type.

As expected, the annotator always selected the option from the same class as the anchor in inter-class triplets, confirming that class membership is a dominant factor in similarity perception. All models achieve high accuracy on this type of triplet, but discriminative models clearly outperform generative ones, with Classifier and TripletNet leading at 99.0%.

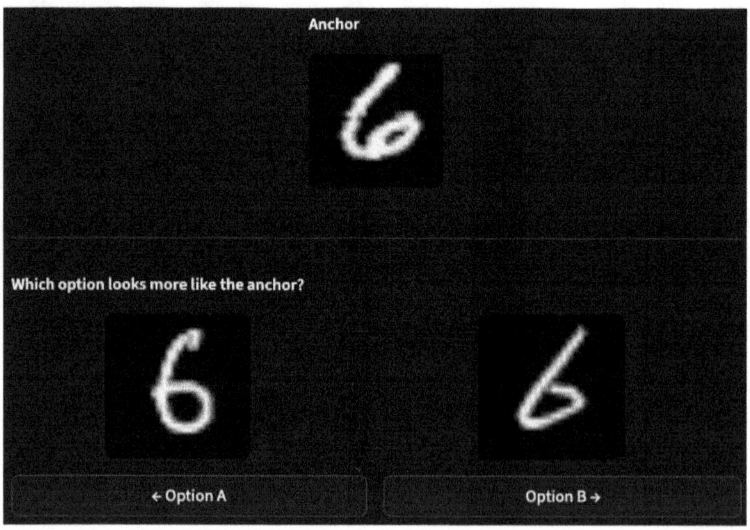

Fig. 4. Triplet annotation interface. The anchor image is shown at the top centre; the two options are displayed at the bottom with their respective selection buttons.

Table 5. Expert alignment for all six models. Global, intra-class, and inter-class triplet accuracy over 400 triplets (50% intra, 50% inter).

Model	Global	Intra-class	Inter-class
Autoencoder	0.775	0.725	0.825
VAE	0.780	0.745	0.815
Classifier	0.823	0.655	**0.990**
TripletNet	0.825	0.660	**0.990**
ClassifierAE	0.820	0.670	0.970
ProtoVAE	**0.850**	**0.765**	0.935

Intra-class accuracy is substantially lower across all models, reflecting the greater difficulty of this task. Other explanations may also contribute—for instance, inherent ambiguity in human judgements at fine stylistic differences—and disentangling them would require a multi-annotator study with repeated trials. Here the pattern reverses: generative models outperform discriminative ones, with ProtoVAE achieving the best result (76.5%). Although discriminative models are highly effective at detecting that two digits belong to different classes, their ability to correctly rank similarity within the same class is much more limited. ProtoVAE is the only model that combines competitive intra-class accuracy (76.5%) with high inter-class accuracy (93.5%), yielding the best overall result.

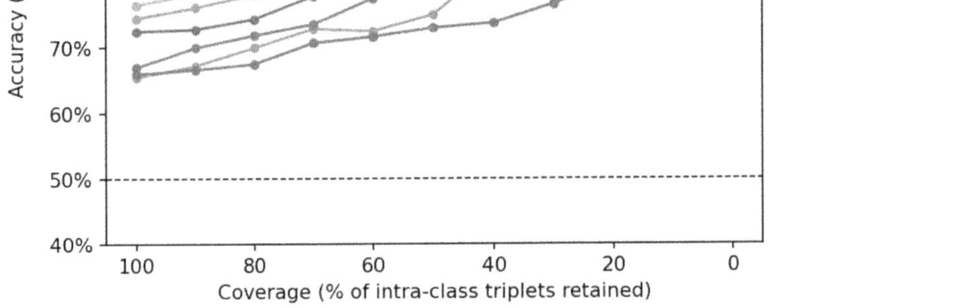

Fig. 5. Coverage–accuracy curve for intra-class triplets: accuracy as triplets are filtered by decreasing relative margin.

Beyond mean accuracy, we examine whether the embedding distance itself can serve as a confidence signal for prediction quality. For each intra-class triplet, we define the relative margin as:

$$m = \frac{|d_{\text{farther}} - d_{\text{closer}}|}{d_{\text{farther}} + d_{\text{closer}}}$$

where d_{closer} and d_{farther} are the distances from the anchor to the closer and farther option, respectively. A high margin indicates a confident prediction; a low margin indicates ambiguity.

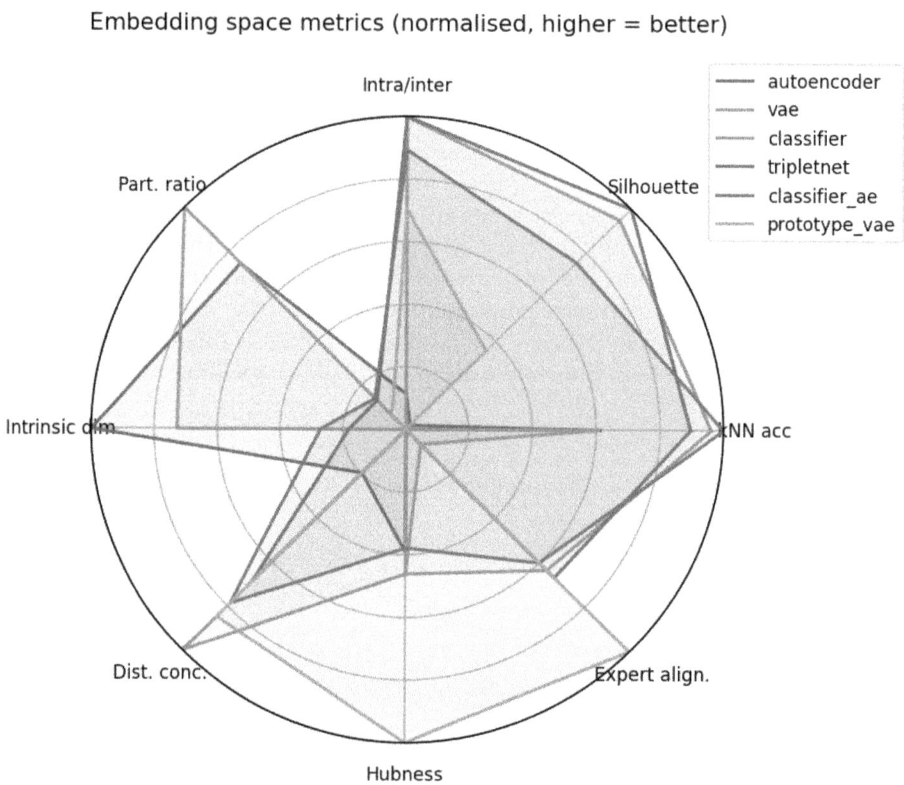

Fig. 6. Radar chart of normalised embedding space metrics for all six models (higher is better on all axes). Each metric is min-max normalised across models; metrics where lower values are better (I/E ratio and hubness) are inverted before normalisation.

Figure 5 shows the intra-class accuracy for each model as a function of coverage (triplets filtered by increasing margin threshold). ProtoVAE achieves the highest intra-class accuracy at full coverage (76.5%). As coverage decreases, all models improve consistently, confirming that the relative margin is a useful confidence signal regardless of the model. Generative models remain consistently better than discriminative ones throughout the curve, reinforcing that their embedding spaces better reflect expert-perceived intra-class similarity.

7 Discussion

The results presented in the previous sections allow several conclusions to be drawn that go beyond a purely numerical comparison of models. Figure 6 provides a visual summary of all metrics, showing how each model performs across the full evaluation profile.

First, the choice of training objective profoundly shapes the structure of the embedding space, and different objectives produce spaces with very different properties. Models trained with classification loss collapse to a low-dimensional subspace (6–9 out of 32 available dimensions) with compact and well-separated class clusters. Generative models, having no access to class labels, distribute variance more uniformly and use more effective dimensions. This difference is reflected consistently in both the geometric metrics (participation ratio, intrinsic dimensionality) and the alignment with expert judgements on intra-class triplets.

A notable finding is the convergence between Classifier and TripletNet: despite their conceptually different loss functions (cross-entropy vs. triplet loss), they produce spaces with very similar metrics. This suggests that separating 10 classes in MNIST has a low-dimensional solution that both objectives discover independently of their optimisation path.

More effective dimensions do not translate into better expert alignment: the VAE and Autoencoder use more dimensions than ProtoVAE, yet their similarity rankings are less aligned with expert judgements. What matters is the type of information preserved, not its amount—generative models encode pixel-level variation, whereas the expert perceives similarity more globally.

Regarding round-trip coherence, the Autoencoder is the most precise model for real embeddings (RTE 0.071), but its error grows substantially for points outside the training support (0.254 sampled). ProtoVAE is not the most precise in any individual condition, but it is the most consistent: its error varies little across conditions (0.191 real, 0.189 interpolated, 0.266 sampled), indicating a better-covered latent space where interpolating between points yields predictable results.

ProtoVAE achieves the best overall expert alignment (85.0%) and the lowest hubness, making it a promising option that may have been underexplored in the CBR context. Its ability to organise the latent space around class prototypes promotes alignment with expert-perceived similarity, albeit at the cost of lower k-NN accuracy (93.3%). This suggests that prototype anchoring introduces some ambiguity at class boundaries, which may be a disadvantage for classification tasks but an advantage for intra-class similarity-based retrieval.

The choice of architecture will ultimately depend on the primary goal of the system: retrieving cases of the same class (intra-class similarity) or discriminating between classes (inter-class similarity). For the former, generative models and ProtoVAE in particular appear more suitable; for the latter, discriminative models such as Classifier or TripletNet are clearly superior. In any case, none of the models studied achieves strong alignment with expert-perceived intra-class similarity, even on a dataset as simple as MNIST, highlighting the difficulty of learning embedding spaces that reflect human similarity perception. Such alignment is a fundamental requirement for case-based explanations to be comprehensible and trustworthy.

Limitations. This study has several limitations worth acknowledging. First, MNIST is a controlled benchmark whose intra-class variation is stylistic (stroke width, slant, writing style) rather than semantic. In real domains such as medical images or engineering data, intra-class variation may carry functional meaning and results could differ. Second, triplet annotations were produced by a single annotator, so inter-annotator reliability is unknown. Third, the architectures evaluated are deliberately simple, enabling a controlled comparison of training objectives but leaving out larger and more recent designs such as vision transformers and pre-trained foundation encoders (e.g., DINO, CLIP), whose embedding spaces may exhibit different properties. Finally, the 400 annotated triplets identify general trends but are insufficient for a per-class-pair analysis.

8 Conclusions and Future Work

In this work, we compared six neural embedding architectures on the MNIST dataset along three complementary axes: class structure, embedding space geometry, and round-trip coherence. We also conducted an expert alignment study based on triplet annotation. The three research questions posed in the introduction can now be answered as follows.

RQ1 (geometry): The training objective profoundly shapes the geometry of the embedding space. Discriminative models produce compact, anisotropic spaces with few effective dimensions and strong inter-class separation. Generative models distribute variance more uniformly and use more effective dimensions.

RQ2 (coherence): The Autoencoder is the most precise model for real embeddings, but its error grows substantially outside the training support. ProtoVAE shows the most consistent behaviour across conditions, making it better suited to support latent-space interpolation for case adaptation.

RQ3 (alignment): ProtoVAE achieves the best overall expert alignment, particularly on intra-class triplets. Discriminative models are near-perfect on inter-class triplets but weak on intra-class ones. No model exceeds 77% intra-class accuracy, underscoring the difficulty of learning embedding spaces that reflect the similarity perceived by a human expert within the same class, even on a controlled dataset such as MNIST.

A promising direction for future work is the incorporation of expert knowledge during model training to improve alignment between the learned embedding space and human similarity perception. Active learning approaches could be used to select the most informative triplets, collect expert feedback, and use those annotations to guide embedding learning.

Equally important is evaluation in real domains with semantically meaningful intra-class variation, such as medical images or engineering data, where expert-perceived similarity may have direct consequences for the quality of adapted solutions.

Although this study focuses on image embeddings, the framework applies to any vectorised case representation, including attribute-value tuples, graphs, and tabular data via modern embedding techniques (e.g., text or graph encoders). Assessing whether the geometric and coherence properties observed here transfer to these representations is an open question of direct interest to the CBR community.

Further secondary directions include extending the alignment study to multiple annotators to measure inter-annotator reliability, and exploring more expressive architectures such as ProtoVAE with multiple prototypes per class or transformer-based encoders.

Acknowledgments. This work has been partially funded by the Ministry of Science, Innovation and Universities (PID2021-123368OB-I00) and the Complutense University of Madrid (Group 921330).

Declaration on Generative AI. During the preparation of this work, the author used GenAI tools in order to: paraphrase and reword, improve writing style, and grammar and spelling check. After using these tools, the author reviewed and edited the content as needed and takes full responsibility for the publication's content.

References

1. Bergmann, R., Gil, Y.: Similarity assessment and efficient retrieval of semantic workflows. Inf. Syst. **40**, 115–127 (2014). https://doi.org/10.1016/J.IS.2012.07.005
2. Bergmann, R., Kolodner, J.L., Plaza, E.: Representation in case-based reasoning. Knowl. Eng. Rev. **20**(3), 209–213 (2005). https://doi.org/10.1017/S0269888906000555
3. Beyer, K., Goldstein, J., Ramakrishnan, R., Shaft, U.: When Is "Nearest Neighbor" Meaningful? In: Beeri, C., Buneman, P. (eds.) ICDT 1999. LNCS, vol. 1540, pp. 217–235. Springer, Heidelberg (1999). https://doi.org/10.1007/3-540-49257-7_15
4. Dapica, R., Peinado, F.: Evaluation of Similarity Measures for Flight Simulator Training Scenarios. In: Sánchez-Ruiz, A.A., Floyd, M.W. (eds.) ICCBR 2021. LNCS (LNAI), vol. 12877, pp. 17–31. Springer, Cham (2021). https://doi.org/10.1007/978-3-030-86957-1_2
5. Díaz-Agudo, B., Jimenez-Diaz, G., Jorro-Aragoneses, J.L.: User Evaluation to Measure the Perception of Similarity Measures in Artworks. In: Sánchez-Ruiz, A.A., Floyd, M.W. (eds.) ICCBR 2021. LNCS (LNAI), vol. 12877, pp. 48–63. Springer, Cham (2021). https://doi.org/10.1007/978-3-030-86957-1_4
6. Hinton, G.E., Salakhutdinov, R.R.: Reducing the dimensionality of data with neural networks. Science **313**(5786), 504–507 (2006). https://doi.org/10.1126/science.1127647
7. Hutchinson, A.: Metrics on terms and clauses. In: van Someren, M., Widmer, G. (eds.) ECML 1997. LNCS, vol. 1224, pp. 138–145. Springer, Heidelberg (1997). https://doi.org/10.1007/3-540-62858-4_78

8. Kingma, D.P., Welling, M.: Auto-encoding variational bayes. In: Bengio, Y., LeCun, Y. (eds.) 2nd International Conference on Learning Representations, ICLR 2014, Banff, AB, Canada, April 14-16, 2014, Conference Track Proceedings (2014). http://arxiv.org/abs/1312.6114
9. Leake, D., Wilkerson, Z., Crandall, D.: Extracting case indices from convolutional neural networks: A comparative study. In: Keane, M.T., Wiratunga, N. (eds.) Case-Based Reasoning Research and Development - 30th International Conference, ICCBR 2022, Nancy, France, September 12-15, 2022, Proceedings, pp. 81–95. Lecture Notes in Computer Science, Springer, Cham (2022). https://doi.org/10.1007/978-3-031-14923-8_6
10. Leake, D., Wilkerson, Z., Vats, V., Acharya, K., Crandall, D.J.: Examining the impact of network architecture on extracted feature quality for CBR. In: Massie, S., Chakraborti, S. (eds.) Case-Based Reasoning Research and Development - 31st International Conference, ICCBR 2023, Aberdeen, UK, July 17-20, 2023, Proceedings. pp. 3–18. Lecture Notes in Computer Science. Springer, Cham (2023). https://doi.org/10.1007/978-3-031-40177-0_1
11. LeCun, Y., Cortes, C., Burges, C.: Mnist handwritten digit database. ATT Labs Inc. **2** (2010). http://yann.lecun.com
12. Lenz, M., Hoffmann, M., Bergmann, R.: Llsim: Large language models for similarity assessment in case-based reasoning. In: Bichindaritz, I., López, B. (eds.) Case-Based Reasoning Research and Development - 33rd International Conference, ICCBR 2025, Biarritz, France, June 30–July 3, 2025, Proceedings, pp. 126–141. Lecture Notes in Computer Science, Springer, Cham (2025). https://doi.org/10.1007/978-3-031-96559-3_9
13. Radovanovic, M., Nanopoulos, A., Ivanovic, M.: Hubs in space: Popular nearest neighbors in high-dimensional data. J. Mach. Learn. Res. **11**, 2487–2531 (2010). https://doi.org/10.5555/1756006.1953015
14. Richter, M.M., Weber, R.O.: Case-Based Reasoning: A Textbook, 1st edn. Springer Publishing Company, Incorporated (2016)
15. Sánchez-Ruiz, A.A., Ontañón, S., González-Calero, P.A., Plaza, E.: Measuring similarity of individuals in description logics over the refinement space of conjunctive queries. J. Intell. Inf. Syst. **47**(3), 447–467 (2016). https://doi.org/10.1007/S10844-015-0374-3
16. Schroff, F., Kalenichenko, D., Philbin, J.: Facenet: A unified embedding for face recognition and clustering. In: IEEE Conference on Computer Vision and Pattern Recognition, CVPR 2015, Boston, MA, USA, June 7-12, 2015, pp. 815–823. IEEE Computer Society (2015). https://doi.org/10.1109/CVPR.2015.7298682
17. Snell, J., Swersky, K., Zemel, R.S.: Prototypical networks for few-shot learning. In: Guyon, I., et al. (eds.) Advances in Neural Information Processing Systems 30: Annual Conference on Neural Information Processing Systems 2017, December 4-9, 2017, Long Beach, CA, USA. pp. 4077–4087 (2017). https://proceedings.neurips.cc/paper/2017/hash/cb8da6767461f2812ae4290eac7cbc42-Abstract.html
18. Wilkerson, Z., Leake, D., Vats, V., Crandall, D.: Extracting indexing features for CBR from deep neural networks: A transfer learning approach. In: Recio-García, J.A., Orozco-del-Castillo, M.G., Bridge, D. (eds.) Case-Based Reasoning Research and Development - 32nd International Conference, ICCBR 2024, Merida, Mexico, July 1-4, 2024, Proceedings. pp. 143–158. Lecture Notes in Computer Science. Springer, Cham (2024). https://doi.org/10.1007/978-3-031-63646-2_10

An Adaptation-Guided and Efficient Case Retrieval Approach Based on a Dichotomy of the Case Space

Jules Sipp and Jean Lieber(✉)

LORIA, Université de Lorraine, CNRS, Inria, Nancy F-54000, France
{jules.sipp,jean.lieber}@loria.fr

Abstract. This paper presents an approach to retrieval that is adaptation-guided in the strong sense: the adaptation effort to solve the target problem thanks to the retrieved case is minimal. It uses the principle of dichotomy: the search space is cut in half at each iteration, which involves a complexity in a logarithm of the size of the case base. Then, it is applied to the framework of the general adaptation system Olaaaf, and the approach is evaluated in this framework.

Keywords: case-based reasoning · case retrieval · adaptation-guided retrieval

1 Introduction

The process model of case-based reasoning (CBR) considers in sequence the retrieval and adaptation steps (see e.g. [13]) also known as *retrieve* and *reuse* steps in the 4 Rs model of [1]. Now, this process model should not hide the deep connection between retrieval and adaptation: the retrieved case is the one that is used by adaptation.[1] Some early studies on CBR have highlighted this connection, such as the work on *adaptation-guided retrieval* (AGR [16]) which states that, at least, the retrieved case has to be adaptable.

A more constrained vision of AGR could state that the retrieved case is the one that involves the "best adaptation". Following this view supposes to rank two adaptation processes: in this article, it is assumed that such a ranking is done thanks to a cost that measures the "adaptation effort". A lower cost corresponds to a more plausible adaptation effort. In this paper, a retrieval process is said to be adaptation-guided (in the strong sense) if the retrieved case is not only adaptable to solve the target problem but is also the one that minimizes the adaptation effort.

A naive adaptation-guided retrieval consists in applying the adaptation on every case of the case base and selecting the one that minimizes the adaptation effort. The complexity of this naive retrieval approach is linear in the size of the case base. The objective of this paper is to propose a retrieval algorithm that is based on dichotomy search that is logarithmic in this size.

[1] This includes the situations of "retrieval only" CBR systems. For such systems, either adaptation by copy is deemed sufficient (the solution of the retrieved case is a solution proposed to the target problem) or the adaptation is left to the system user.

L. Malburg and K. Bach (Eds.): ICCBR 2026, LNAI 16780, pp. 35–50, 2027.
https://doi.org/10.1007/978-3-032-33865-5_3

After some preliminaries including the presentation of a running example in the cooking domain (Sect. 2), a presentation of CBR is made, introducing some notations and making some assumptions (Sect. 3). Then the general approach of case retrieval based on dichotomy of the case space is presented in Sect. 4. This general approach is presented independently of the case representation formalism. Then, this general approach is instantiated for the representation formalism of Olaaaf, which is an adaptation engine presented in [9]. This instantiation has given birth to a retrieval engine called Olrrrf, that is presented with details in Sect. 5 and evaluated in Sect. 6.[2] For the purpose of reproducibility and usability, the Olrrrf retrieval engine is available online[3], together with the Olaaaf adaptation engine. Section 7 concludes the paper and presents some research directions.

Some additional technical details, such as proofs, can be found in [15].

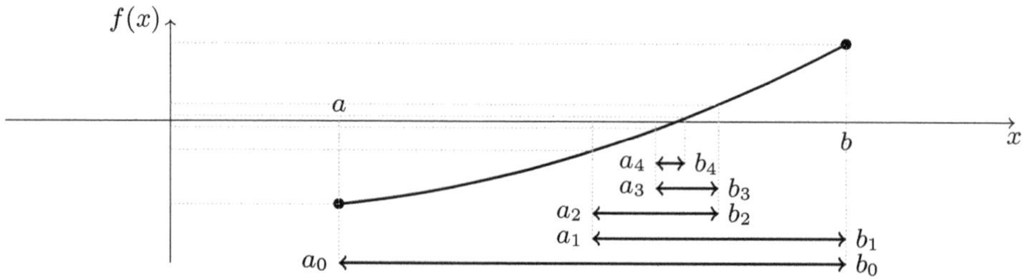

Fig. 1. Illustration of the dichotomy search of a root of $f(x) = 0$.

2 Preliminaries and Introduction of the Running Example

This section recalls some mathematical notions and notations used in the paper.

Basic Notations. Given two sets A and B, $A \cap B$ denotes the intersection of the two sets and $A \setminus B$, their difference ($a \in A \setminus B$ iff $a \in A$ and $a \notin B$).

The set of integers is denoted by $\mathbb{Z}$. The set of rational numbers is denoted by $\mathbb{Q}$. For $a, b \in \mathbb{Z}$ with $a \leq b$, $[\![a, b]\!]$ denotes the integers k such that $a \leq k$ and $k \leq b$. The set of real numbers is denoted by $\mathbb{R}$. The set of nonnegative real numbers and positive real numbers are denoted, respectively, by $\mathbb{R}_+$ and $\mathbb{R}_+^*$. For $a, b \in \mathbb{R}$ such that $a \leq b$, $[a, b]$ denotes the set of $x \in \mathbb{R}$ such that $a \leq x$ and $x \leq b$. For $x \in \mathbb{R}$, the ceil of x is $\lceil x \rceil = \min\{a \in \mathbb{Z} \mid x \leq a\}$.

[2] The name Olrrrf has been chosen as a solution of the following analogical equation (with unknown x): "adaptation is to retrieval as Olaaaf is to x".

[3] Code available at https://github.com/OlaaafEngine/Olrrrf/.

The Dichotomy Search for a Root of a Function. (also known as the bisection method) is a classical mathematical method to find a root of some equations and has been an inspiration for the retrieval approach proposed in this paper. It is recalled briefly below and illustrated in Fig. 1. Let $a, b \in \mathbb{R}$ such that $a < b$ and f be a continuous function from $[a, b]$ to $\mathbb{R}$ such that $f(a)f(b) < 0$. According to the intermediate value theorem, there is at least one root $r \in [a, b]$ of the equation $f(x) = 0$. The dichotomy search aims to give an approximate value of such a root, with an error below a given $\varepsilon > 0$. Starting with the interval $[a_k, b_k] = [a, b]$ and $k = 0$, at each iteration $[a_k, b_k]$ is updated as follows, with $m = (a_k + b_k)/2$: $[a_{k+1}, b_{k+1}] = \begin{cases} [m, b_k] & \text{if } f(m) < 0 \\ [a_k, m] & \text{else} \end{cases}$. The process ends when $b_k - a_k \leq 2\varepsilon$ and the value $(a_k + b_k)/2$ approximates the root with an error $e \leq \varepsilon$. It can be proven that the number of iterations is $\lceil \log_2((b - a)/(2\varepsilon)) \rceil$.

Pseudo-Distance Functions. Let $\mathcal{U}$ be a set. A *pseudo-distance function* on $\mathcal{U}$ is a mapping $\mathtt{dist} : \mathcal{U} \times \mathcal{U} \to \mathbb{R}_+$ such that:

$$\text{for } u, v \in \mathcal{U}, \qquad \mathtt{dist}(u, v) = 0 \quad \text{iff} \quad u = v \tag{1}$$

The *symmetric* of a pseudo-distance dist is a pseudo-distance tsid defined by $\mathtt{tsid}(u, v) = \mathtt{dist}(u, v)$ for each $u, v \in \mathcal{U}$.

Given dist, a pseudo-distance on $\mathcal{U}$, A and B, two nonempty subsets of $\mathcal{U}$, and $u \in \mathcal{U}$, the classical notations $\mathtt{dist}(A, u)$, $\mathtt{dist}(u, B)$ and $\mathtt{dist}(A, B)$ are used:

$$\mathtt{dist}(A, u) = \inf\{\mathtt{dist}(a, u) \mid a \in A\} \qquad \mathtt{dist}(u, B) = \inf\{\mathtt{dist}(u, b) \mid b \in B\}$$
$$\mathtt{dist}(A, B) = \inf\{\mathtt{dist}(a, b) \mid a \in A \text{ and } b \in B\}$$

Given a nonempty subset A of $\mathcal{U}$ and $r \in \mathbb{R}_+$, the *dilation* of A by r according to the pseudo-distance dist on $\mathcal{U}$ is the set $\mathtt{Dil}_{\mathtt{dist}}(A, r)$ defined by

$$\mathtt{Dil}_{\mathtt{dist}}(A, r) = \{u \in \mathcal{U} \mid \mathtt{dist}(A, u) \leq r\}$$

The *closed ball* of radius $r \in \mathbb{R}_+$ and center $c \in \mathcal{U}$ for a pseudo-distance dist on $\mathcal{U}$ is denoted by $B_{\mathtt{dist}}(c, r)$ and defined by

$$B_{\mathtt{dist}}(c, r) = \{u \in \mathcal{U} \mid \mathtt{dist}(c, u) \leq r\}$$

It can also be equivalently defined by $B_{\mathtt{dist}}(c, r) = \mathtt{Dil}_{\mathtt{dist}}(\{c\}, r)$.

A *distance function* on $\mathcal{U}$ is a pseudo-distance function on $\mathcal{U}$ that satisfies the following properties:

$$\text{for each } u, v \in \mathcal{U}, \qquad \mathtt{dist}(u, v) = \mathtt{dist}(v, u)$$
$$\text{for each } u, v, w \in \mathcal{U}, \qquad \mathtt{dist}(u, w) \leq \mathtt{dist}(u, v) + \mathtt{dist}(v, w)$$

It can be noted that the symmetric tsid of a distance function dist is itself: $\mathtt{tsid} = \mathtt{dist}$.

3 CBR: Notions, Notations, Assumptions and Introduction of the Running Example

This section introduces case-based reasoning in a rather general setting, with some notations and assumptions, together with the introduction of an example in the cooking domain, in which the cases represent recipes.

Cases. There are at least two ways to consider cases: one of them represents them as problem-solution pairs but, in this article, it has appeared simpler to consider the more general representation of specific problem-solving episodes. In the running example, a case represents a (specific) recipe. For instance, given an apple pie recipe, it corresponds to a single case but answers several problems, such as "Give me a recipe of a dessert with apples." or "Give me a pie recipe with fruits."

In a given domain, let Ω be a set —called the *case space*— in which every element x is a specific problem-solving experience. Let $\mathcal{L}$ be a representation language of some subsets of Ω, using in particular the binary connective $\wedge$: if $\alpha, \beta \in \mathcal{L}$ then $\alpha \wedge \beta \in \mathcal{L}$. A *formula* is an element of $\mathcal{L}$. The semantics of this language is given by a mapping $\mathcal{M} : \mathcal{L} \to 2^{\Omega}$, that is, for $\alpha \in \mathcal{L}$, $\mathcal{M}(\alpha)$ is a subset of the case space. The semantics of $\wedge$ is given by $\mathcal{M}(\alpha \wedge \beta) = \mathcal{M}(\alpha) \cap \mathcal{M}(\beta)$. The entailment relation $\models$ is defined by $\alpha \models \beta$ if $\mathcal{M}(\alpha) \subseteq \mathcal{M}(\beta)$, which gives birth to the logic $(\mathcal{L}, \models)$. An $\alpha \in \mathcal{L}$ is *satisfiable* if $\mathcal{M}(\alpha) \neq \emptyset$.

A *case* $\mathtt{c}$ is a representation of a specific problem-solving experience: $\mathtt{c} \in \mathcal{L}$ and $\mathcal{M}(\mathtt{c})$ is a singleton of Ω. In the cooking domain, a case $\mathtt{c}$ is the formal representation of a recipe $x : \mathcal{M}(\mathtt{c}) = \{x\}$. There are two kinds of cases: "correct cases" and "incorrect cases", though the knowledge for distinguishing correct from incorrect cases is usually not completely available to the CBR system. In the cooking domain, $\mathtt{c}$ is correct if $\mathcal{M}(\mathtt{c}) = \{x\}$ and x is a "good recipe": this distinction is supposed to exist but is difficult, if not impossible, to formalize with certainty.

However, there is a finite and nonempty set CB of cases that are known to be correct. They are called the *source cases* and CB is the *case base*. For a $\mathtt{c}^s \in \mathtt{CB}$, the only element of $\mathcal{M}(\mathtt{c}^s)$ is denoted by $\mathcal{I}^s$. The case base of the running example is $\mathtt{CB} = \{\mathtt{c}^s\}_{s \in [\![1,4]\!]}$ with

$$\mathtt{c}^1 = \text{a banana milkshake with cow milk recipe} \tag{2}$$

$$\mathtt{c}^2 = \text{a kiwi milkshake with almond milk recipe} \tag{3}$$

$$\mathtt{c}^3 = \text{a strawberry milkshake with cow milk recipe} \tag{4}$$

$$\mathtt{c}^4 = \text{a banana and strawberry milkshake with cow milk recipe} \tag{5}$$

Domain Knowledge. The domain knowledge of the CBR system is a formula DK that gives *necessary* conditions for a case $\mathtt{c}$ to be correct: if $\mathtt{c}$ is correct, then $\mathtt{DK} \wedge \mathtt{c}$ must be satisfiable. In the running example, DK is the conjunction of the formulas expressing this:

DK1. Bananas, kiwis and strawberries are the only 3 types of fruits available.

DK2. Almond milk and cow milk are the only 2 types of milks available.
DK3. The mixture of cow milk and kiwis give a bitter taste and, therefore, their association should be avoided (in dessert recipes).

Every source case $\mathtt{c}^s$ is supposed to be correct, so $\mathtt{DK} \wedge \mathtt{c}^s$ is satisfiable.

$(\mathcal{L}, \models)$ as a query language on CB. Let $\mathtt{q} \in \mathcal{L}$. Such a formula can be interpreted as a query on CB: the execution of this query returns the set $\{\mathtt{c}^s \in \mathtt{CB} \mid \mathtt{c}^s \models \mathtt{q}\}$. This corresponds to querying in database systems, which is a highly optimized process and is assumed, in this paper, to be efficient.

The Target Query. is a formula $\mathtt{q}^{\mathtt{tgt}}$ such that $\mathtt{DK} \wedge \mathtt{q}^{\mathtt{tgt}}$ is satisfiable. Let $\mathtt{c}^s \in \mathtt{CB}$ be such that $\mathtt{c}^s \models \mathtt{q}^{\mathtt{tgt}}$ (which is equivalent to $\mathtt{c}^s \wedge \mathtt{q}^{\mathtt{tgt}}$ is satisfiable, since $\mathcal{M}(\mathtt{c}^s)$ is a singleton). If such a source case exists, then it answers the target query, without any need for adaptation. For example, if

$$\mathtt{q}^{\mathtt{tgt}} = \text{Give me a milkshake recipe with bananas.}$$

then $\mathtt{c}^s \models \mathtt{q}^{\mathtt{tgt}}$ for $s = 1$ and $s = 4$. By contrast, the following target query does not have an exact match in the case base (i.e. $\mathtt{c}^s \not\models \mathtt{q}^{\mathtt{tgt}}$ for every $\mathtt{c}^s \in \mathtt{CB}$):

$$\mathtt{q}^{\mathtt{tgt}} = \text{Give me a strawberry milkshake with almond milk recipe.} \tag{6}$$

Assumptions About Adaptation. The contribution of this article is about an adaptation-guided retrieval approach, hence the necessity of introducing some definitions and assumptions about adaptation.

First, in this work, it is assumed that case reuse is done thanks to a single adaptation procedure (though the approach could be extended to multiple adaptation). Therefore, adaptation is a function that takes as inputs:

- A source case $\mathtt{c}^s$ (that is, the output of the retrieval procedure);
- The target query $\mathtt{q}^{\mathtt{tgt}}$;
- The CBR system knowledge containers, in particular DK.

and returns either a case $\mathtt{c}^{\mathtt{tgt}}$ that answers the query ($\mathtt{c}^{\mathtt{tgt}} \models \mathtt{q}^{\mathtt{tgt}}$) or the value `failure`.

Given a source case $\mathtt{c}^s$ and a target problem $\mathtt{x}^{\mathtt{tgt}}$, it is assumed that the adaptation process gives, as a byproduct, a nonnegative value measuring the so-called "adaptation effort", denoted by $\mathtt{effort}(\mathtt{c}^s, \mathtt{q}^{\mathtt{tgt}})$. The assumption is that the adaptation process makes the least adaptation effort and that the lower this adaptation effort is, the more likely $\mathtt{c}^{\mathtt{tgt}}$ is a correct case. For $\mathcal{I} \in \Omega$ and $B \subseteq \Omega$, $\mathtt{effort}(\mathcal{I}, B)$ is assumed to be defined, that satisfies the fact that, if $\mathcal{M}(\mathtt{c}^s) = \{\mathcal{I}\}$ and $\mathcal{M}(\mathtt{q}^{\mathtt{tgt}}) = B$, then $\mathtt{effort}(\mathcal{I}, \mathtt{q}^{\mathtt{tgt}}) = \mathtt{effort}(\mathtt{c}^s, \mathtt{q}^{\mathtt{tgt}})$.

Several assumptions about the `effort` mapping can be made. The first one is:

$$\mathcal{I} \in B \quad \text{iff} \quad \mathtt{effort}(\mathcal{I}, B) = 0 \tag{7}$$

This entails that if $\mathtt{c}^s \models \mathtt{q}^{\mathtt{tgt}}$ then no adaptation effort is needed: $\mathtt{c}^s$ already answers $\mathtt{q}^{\mathtt{tgt}}$ and there is no risk involved by considering that $\mathtt{c}^s$ solves $\mathtt{q}^{\mathtt{tgt}}$.

The second one is (for $\mathcal{I} \in \Omega$, $B_1 \subseteq \Omega$ and $B_2 \subseteq \Omega$):

$$\mathtt{effort}(\mathcal{I}, B_1 \cup B_2) = \min(\mathtt{effort}(\mathcal{I}, B_1), \mathtt{effort}(\mathcal{I}, B_2)) \tag{8}$$

An example may be helpful to understand (8). Let us consider the following target queries:

$$\mathtt{q}^{\mathtt{tgt}} = \text{Give me an apple pie recipe with almonds or walnuts.}$$
$$\mathtt{q}_1^{\mathtt{tgt}} = \text{Give me an apple pie recipe with almonds.}$$
$$\mathtt{q}_2^{\mathtt{tgt}} = \text{Give me an apple pie recipe with walnuts.}$$

Let $B = \mathcal{M}(\mathtt{q}^{\mathtt{tgt}})$, $B_1 = \mathcal{M}(\mathtt{q}_1^{\mathtt{tgt}})$ and $B_2 = \mathcal{M}(\mathtt{q}_2^{\mathtt{tgt}})$. It comes that $B = B_1 \cup B_2$: every result of the query $\mathtt{q}^{\mathtt{tgt}}$ is a result of $\mathtt{q}_1^{\mathtt{tgt}}$ and/or of $\mathtt{q}_2^{\mathtt{tgt}}$. If the adaptation of $\mathtt{c}^s$ to answer $\mathtt{q}_1^{\mathtt{tgt}}$ (resp. $\mathtt{q}_2^{\mathtt{tgt}}$) gives the result $\mathtt{c}_1^{\mathtt{tgt}}$ (resp. $\mathtt{c}_2^{\mathtt{tgt}}$) with an adaptation effort ae_1 (resp. ae_2), then the adaptation of $\mathtt{c}^s$ to answer $\mathtt{q}^{\mathtt{tgt}}$ can return $\mathtt{c}_1^{\mathtt{tgt}}$ or $\mathtt{c}_2^{\mathtt{tgt}}$, choosing the one that minimizes the adaptation effort, hence an adaptation effort of $\min(ae_1, ae_2)$, which is in agreement with equation (8).

A direct consequence of (8) is that, for $\mathcal{I} \in \Omega$ and $B_1, \ldots, B_p$, p subsets of Ω, $\mathtt{effort}(\mathcal{I}, B_1 \cup \ldots \cup B_p) = \min\{\mathtt{effort}(\mathcal{I}, B_k) \mid k \in [\![1, p]\!]\}$. Generalizing this to potentially infinite unions gives the following assumptions:

$$\mathtt{effort}(\mathcal{I}, B) = \inf\{\mathtt{effort}(\mathcal{I}, \{\mathcal{J}\}) \mid \mathcal{J} \in B\} \tag{9}$$

Now, let $\mathtt{dist}$ defined for $\mathcal{I}, \mathcal{J} \in \Omega$ by $\mathtt{dist}(\mathcal{I}, \mathcal{J}) = \mathtt{effort}(\mathcal{I}, \{\mathcal{J}\})$. According to (7), $\mathtt{dist}(\mathcal{I}, \mathcal{J}) = 0$ iff $\mathcal{I} = \mathcal{J}$. Therefore, $\mathtt{dist}$ is a pseudo-distance on Ω. Moreover, according to (9), $\mathtt{effort}(\mathtt{c}^s, \mathtt{q}^{\mathtt{tgt}}) = \mathtt{dist}(\mathcal{M}(\mathtt{c}^s), \mathcal{M}(\mathtt{q}^{\mathtt{tgt}}))$.

Another notion can be introduced about adaptation. The higher the adaptation effort is, the less plausible of correctness is the produced case $\mathtt{c}^{\mathtt{tgt}}$. Then, an approach consists in defining a threshold value `MaxAdEff` such that if $\mathtt{effort}(\mathtt{c}^s, \mathtt{q}^{\mathtt{tgt}}) > \mathtt{MaxAdEff}$ then the adaptation must return `failure`. If, in contrast, no such threshold is given, this is modeled by $\mathtt{MaxAdEff} = \infty$.

Adaptation-Guided Retrieval. Since this work focuses on simple case adaptation, retrieval aims at selecting a simple $\mathtt{c}^s \in \mathtt{CB}$ to be adapted. The best selection choice is the one that will provide the best adaptation, hence the least adaptation effort. *Adaptation-guided retrieval* is defined as retrieval making such an optimal choice. Therefore, it comes that, with the above assumptions on adaptation, a retrieval procedure is adaptation-guided (in the strong sense) iff, for every case base CB and every target query $\mathtt{q}^{\mathtt{tgt}}$, the retrieved case $\mathtt{c}^s$ is such that it minimizes $\mathtt{dist}(\mathcal{M}(\mathtt{c}^s), \mathcal{M}(\mathtt{q}^{\mathtt{tgt}}))$, for $\mathtt{c}^s \in \mathtt{CB}$.

Now, let n be a positive integer characterizing the complexity of the case space Ω. In particular, if an interpretation is defined with a set of attributes with simple types (e.g. `float`), then n is the number of these attributes. The complexity of a retrieval algorithm usually depends on n and $|\mathtt{CB}|$.

4 Case Retrieval Based on Dichotomy of the Case Space

For a source case $\mathtt{c}^s$, it is recalled that $\mathcal{M}(\mathtt{c}^s) = \{\mathcal{I}^s\}$. For a target query $\mathtt{q}^{\mathtt{tgt}}$, let $\mathtt{Q}^{\mathtt{tgt}} = \mathcal{M}(\mathtt{DK} \wedge \mathtt{q}^{\mathtt{tgt}})$. So, according to the assumptions given in the previous section, retrieval aims to select an $\mathcal{I}^s$ such that $\mathtt{dist}(\mathcal{I}^s, \mathtt{Q}^{\mathtt{tgt}})$ is minimal. Figure 2(a) presents an illustration of $\mathtt{c}^s$'s and of $\mathtt{q}^{\mathtt{tgt}}$ in the Euclidean plane. Section 4.1 presents a naive algorithm for adaptation-guided retrieval, Sect. 4.2, a less naive algorithm, and Sect. 4.3, the approach proposed in this article.

4.1 A Naive Algorithm: Balls Growing Around Source Cases

Figure 2(b) illustrates the approach presented here, which is based on the equality:

$$\mathtt{dist}(\mathcal{I}^s, \mathtt{Q}^{\mathtt{tgt}}) = \inf\{r \in \mathbb{R}_+ \mid B_{\mathtt{dist}}(\mathcal{I}^s, r) \cap \mathtt{Q}^{\mathtt{tgt}} \neq \emptyset\} \tag{10}$$

Therefore, retrieval can be computed as follows, for some $\varepsilon > 0$ assumed to be small:

- $r \leftarrow 0$
- **While** for every $\mathtt{c}^s \in \mathtt{CB}$, $B_{\mathtt{dist}}(\mathcal{I}^s, r) \cap \mathtt{Q}^{\mathtt{tgt}} = \emptyset$ **do**
  - $r \leftarrow r + \varepsilon$
- **End While**
- **Return** a $\mathtt{c}^s \in \mathtt{CB}$ such that $B_{\mathtt{dist}}(\mathcal{I}^s, r) \cap \mathtt{Q}^{\mathtt{tgt}} \neq \emptyset$.[4]

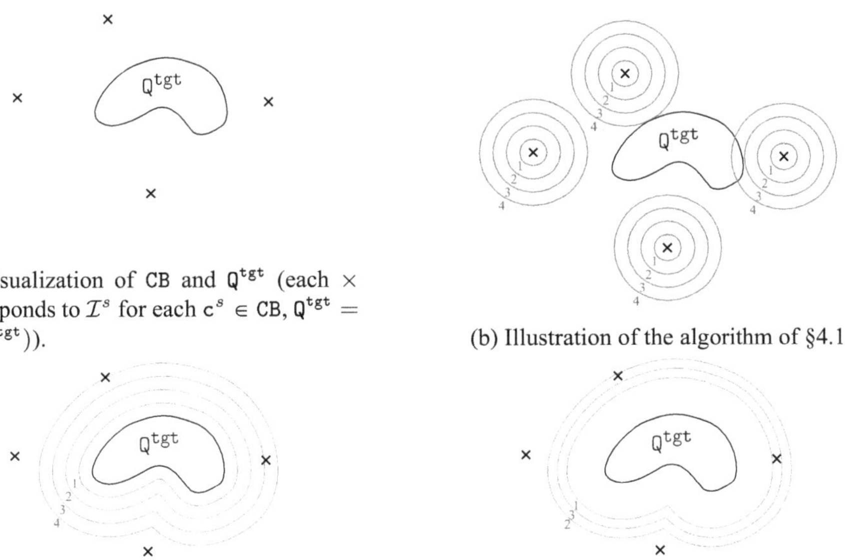

(a) Visualization of CB and $\mathtt{Q}^{\mathtt{tgt}}$ (each × corresponds to $\mathcal{I}^s$ for each $\mathtt{c}^s \in \mathtt{CB}$, $\mathtt{Q}^{\mathtt{tgt}} = \mathcal{M}(\mathtt{q}^{\mathtt{tgt}})$).

(b) Illustration of the algorithm of §4.1.

(c) Illustration of the algorithm of §4.2.

(d) Illustration of the algorithm of §4.3.

Fig. 2. Three retrieval approaches. The number on every dilation represents the step in which it is computed.

Let $\texttt{dist}^* = \min\{\texttt{dist}(\mathcal{I}^s, \texttt{Q}^{\texttt{tgt}}) \mid \mathsf{c}^s \in \mathsf{CB}\}$. The number of iterations of the while loop is $\lceil \texttt{dist}^*/\varepsilon \rceil$. The test of this loop is also complex (though difficult to estimate without assumptions): it considers each source case (hence a factor $|\mathsf{CB}|$) and the test $B_{\texttt{dist}}(\mathcal{I}^s, r) \cap \texttt{Q}^{\texttt{tgt}} = \emptyset$, which amounts to a satisfiability test in $(\mathcal{L}, \models)$, which may be costly (this depends in particular on the chosen formalism).

4.2 A Less Naive Algorithm: Dilating the Target Problem

Figure 2(c) illustrates the approach presented here, which is based on the following equality:

$$\texttt{dist}(\mathcal{I}^s, \texttt{Q}^{\texttt{tgt}}) = \inf\{r \in \mathbb{R}_+ \mid \mathcal{I}^s \in \texttt{Dil}_{\texttt{tsid}}(\texttt{Q}^{\texttt{tgt}}, r)\} \qquad (11)$$

where $\texttt{tsid}$ is the symmetric of the pseudo-distance $\texttt{dist}$. Therefore, retrieval can be computed as follows, for some $\varepsilon > 0$ assumed to be small:

- $r \leftarrow 0$
- **While** for every $\mathsf{c}^s \in \mathsf{CB}, \mathcal{I}^s \notin \texttt{Dil}_{\texttt{tsid}}(\texttt{Q}^{\texttt{tgt}}, r)$ **do**
  - $r \leftarrow r + \varepsilon$
- **End While**
- **Return** a $\mathsf{c}^s \in \mathsf{CB}$ such that $\mathcal{I}^s \in \texttt{Dil}_{\texttt{tsid}}(\texttt{Q}^{\texttt{tgt}}, r)$.

This algorithm has the same number $\lceil \texttt{dist}^*/\varepsilon \rceil$ of iterations of the while loop as the algorithm of the previous section. The advantage of this algorithm is that the test $\mathcal{I}^s \notin \texttt{Dil}_{\texttt{tsid}}(\texttt{Q}^{\texttt{tgt}}, r)$ amounts to an exact querying, with a query q such that $\mathcal{M}(\mathsf{q}) = \texttt{Dil}_{\texttt{tsid}}(\texttt{Q}^{\texttt{tgt}}, r)$ (once this query has been computed).

4.3 An Exact Retrieval Based on Dichotomy of the Search Space

The proposed approach for exact retrieval is based on the idea of dichotomy. The idea is to consider an interval $[a, b]$ $(0 \leq a \leq b)$ such that $\texttt{dist}^* \in [a, b]$ at each time, and such that the length $b - a$ of this interval is divided by 2 at each iteration, until $b - a \leq \varepsilon$.

The initial value of a is set to 0. For setting the initial value of b, a first idea is to consider a random source case c^s and to compute $d^s = \texttt{dist}(\mathsf{c}^s, \texttt{Q}^{\texttt{tgt}})$. Therefore, setting b to d^s ensures that $\texttt{dist}^* \in [a, b]$. Another idea is to use $\texttt{MaxAdEff}$: if $\texttt{dist}^*$ is greater than this threshold, the adaptation following any retrieval (exact or not) would fail. Therefore, the choice for the initial value of b is $b = \min(d^s, \texttt{MaxAdEff})$. So, the proposed retrieval process is:

- Initialize a and b (as detailed above).
- **While** $b - a > \varepsilon$ **do**
  - $m \leftarrow (a + b)/2$
  - **If** for every $\mathsf{c}^s \in \mathsf{CB}, \mathcal{I}^s \notin \texttt{Dil}_{\texttt{tsid}}(\texttt{Q}^{\texttt{tgt}}, m)$
    - **then** $b \leftarrow m$
    - **else** $a \leftarrow m$

[4] If there are several of them, then the closest to $\texttt{Q}^{\texttt{tgt}}$ must be chosen. The smaller ε is, the less frequently this situation occurs, so the extra-computation of this choice is not considered in this paper, neither for this algorithm, nor for the next ones.

End If

▶ **End While**

▶ **Return** a $\mathtt{c}^s \in \mathtt{CB}$ such that $\mathcal{I}^s \in \mathtt{Dil}_{\mathtt{tsid}}(\mathtt{Q}^{\mathtt{tgt}}, m)$

This algorithm requires $O(-\log_2 \varepsilon)$ iterations, which is much less (for small values of ε) than the number of iterations $\lceil \mathtt{dist}^*/\varepsilon \rceil$ of the previous algorithm, with a close computing time of one iteration.

5 Olrrrf: Application of Retrieval Based on Dichotomy to an Adaptation-Guided Retrieval System

5.1 Olaaaf Formalism

The formalism of Olaaaf uses variables of different types: real numbers, integers, Booleans, and enumerated types. To simplify the explanations, only real variables are used in the following. Moreover, only the connectives $\wedge$ and $\vee$ are considered there (the negation raises technical difficulties that can be overcome, at the cost of tedious explanations). With these restrictions, the formulas of Olaaaf are:

- Linear constraints, i.e. expressions of the form $a_1x_1 + \ldots + a_nx_n \leq b$ where $a_1, \ldots, a_n, b \in \mathbb{Q}$ and $x_1, \ldots, \mathtt{x}_n$ are n variables.
- Of one of the forms $\alpha \wedge \beta$ and $\alpha \vee \beta$ where α and β are Olaaaf formulas.

Other expressions can be used as abbreviations. For example $a_1x_1 + \ldots + a_nx_n = b$ is an abbreviation for $(a_1x_1 + \ldots + a_nx_n \leq b) \wedge (-a_1)x_1 + \ldots + (-a_n)x_n \leq -b$.

The semantics of this formalism is defined as follows. An interpretation $\mathcal{I}$ is a mapping from $\mathcal{V}$, the set of variables, to $\mathbb{R}$. Ω is the set of the interpretations. The function $\mathcal{M}$ is defined recursively as follows. For a constraint $\alpha = (a_1x_1 + \ldots + a_nx_n \leq b)$, $\mathcal{M}(\alpha)$ is the set of $\mathcal{I} \in \Omega$ such that $a_1\mathcal{I}(x_1) + \ldots + a_n\mathcal{I}(x_n) \leq b$. For two formulas α and β, $\mathcal{M}(\alpha \wedge \beta) = \mathcal{M}(\alpha) \cap \mathcal{M}(\beta)$ and $\mathcal{M}(\alpha \vee \beta) = \mathcal{M}(\alpha) \cup \mathcal{M}(\beta)$.

For example, the domain knowledge presented in Sect. 3 is represented by:

$$\begin{aligned}
\mathtt{DK} = \mathtt{DK}_1 \wedge \mathtt{DK}_2 \wedge \mathtt{DK}_3 \text{ with } \mathtt{DK}_1 &= (\mathit{banana}_{\mathrm{g}} + \mathit{kiwi}_{\mathrm{g}} + \mathit{strawberry}_{\mathrm{g}} = \mathit{fruit}_{\mathrm{g}})\\
\mathtt{DK}_2 &= (\mathit{cowMilk}_{\mathrm{g}} + \mathit{almondMilk}_{\mathrm{g}} = \mathit{milk}_{\mathrm{g}})\\
\mathtt{DK}_3 &= (\mathit{cowMilk}_{\mathrm{g}} = 0) \vee (\mathit{kiwi}_{\mathrm{g}} = 0)
\end{aligned}$$

Moreover, the dilation as defined in Sect. 2 can be defined on a formula by:

$$\mathtt{Dil}_{\mathtt{dist}}(\alpha, r) = \mathtt{Dil}_{\mathtt{dist}}(\mathcal{M}(\alpha), r)$$

where the chosen $\mathtt{dist}$ is a weighted Manhattan distance:

$$\mathtt{dist}_w(\mathcal{J}, \mathcal{I}) = \sum_{x \in \mathcal{V}} w_x \cdot |\mathcal{I}(x) - \mathcal{J}(x)| \tag{12}$$

$$\text{with} \left| \begin{array}{l} w_{\mathit{banana}_{\mathrm{g}}} = w_{\mathit{kiwi}_{\mathrm{g}}} = w_{\mathit{strawberry}_{\mathrm{g}}} = 1 \\ w_{\mathit{cowMilk}_{\mathrm{g}}} = w_{\mathit{almondMilk}_{\mathrm{g}}} = 1 \\ w_{\mathit{fruit}_{\mathrm{g}}} = w_{\mathit{milk}_{\mathrm{g}}} = 10 \end{array} \right. \quad |l \tag{13}$$

5.2 Computation of the Dilation

In this section, different ways of computing the dilation of a given formula α, depending on its form, are explored.

General and DNF Form. Any formula α can be put under disjunctive normal form (DNF): $\alpha \equiv \alpha_{DNF}$ with $\alpha_{DNF} = \bigvee_i \bigwedge_j c_{ij}$, with c_{ij} a linear constraint. Therefore, since the dilation on sets is union-distributive [12], it can be shown that $\mathtt{Dil}(\alpha, r) \equiv \bigvee_{i=1}^{p} \mathtt{Dil}\left(\mathcal{M}\left(\bigwedge_{j=1}^{q_i} c_{ij}\right), r\right)$.

The computation of the dilation in the general situation can therefore be done by computing the dilation of every conjunction of linear constraints in its DNF form.

Conjunctive Form. When α is a conjunction of linear constraints, computing its dilation $\mathtt{Dil}(\alpha, r)$ can be done in three steps:

1. The formula α describes a convex region in space using constraints (that represent halfspaces). Computing the dilation requires finding all vertices of this region (vertex representation). This conversion has been shown to be, in the worst case, exponential in regards to the *dimension* [4], i.e. the number of variables $|\mathcal{V}|$.
2. The dilation can be viewed as a geometric expansion of the region. With the vertex representation, this expansion can be computed in polynomial time [18].
3. Finally, the dilated region—in vertex form—is converted back into a set of inequalities using a convex hull algorithm, in exponential time according to the dimension [3].

Since our goal is to dilate a formula in high dimensions, these first and last steps, and therefore the dilation when α is in conjunctive form, are computationally intractable.

Simplified Forms. If α is a fully-constrained formula, $\mathcal{M}(\alpha)$ is a singleton $\{\mathcal{J}\}$. In this specific form, it follows that $\mathcal{M}(\mathtt{Dil}(\alpha, r)) = B_r(\mathcal{J})$.

Computing the dilation of α is therefore equivalent to computing a closed ball for a weighted L1 distance function, which is itself characterized by 2^n linear constraints of the form $\sum_{i=1}^{n} \mathtt{sgn}_i w_i(x_i - \mathcal{J}_i) \leq r$, with $\mathtt{sgn}_i \in \{-1, 1\}$ for every $i \in [\![1, n]\!]$.

Another, more common, specific form is when α is partially constrained —that is, fully-constrained on a set $\mathcal{V}_c$ of n_c variables, yet free on $n - n_c = n_f$ other variables. Under this assumption, the dilation of α has to be done only on $\mathcal{V}_c$, therefore reducing the number of dimensions that the algorithm needs to work on and consequentially its runtime.

5.3 An Approach Based on Overapproximation

The dilation of a formula in Olaaaf has been shown to be computationally expensive. This has motivated the design of a variation of this algorithm based on an overapproximation of the dilation which can be computed in linear time complexity, in regards to the dimensionality. Each step of its structure is detailed in Sects. 5.4 to 5.6:

1. Since the case base CB is a set of fully-constrained cases, it is indexed using a point-indexed data structure allowing the execution of range queries (Sect. 5.4).
2. For a given target query $\mathtt{q}^{\mathtt{tgt}}$, a dichotomic search is applied (as explained in Sect. 4) with an overapproximation instead of the dilation. Under the Olaaaf formalism, an example target query for our running example is:

$$\mathtt{q}^{\mathtt{tgt}} = (\mathit{strawberry}_{\mathrm{g}} = 150.) \wedge (\mathit{almondMilk}_{\mathrm{g}} = 250.) \quad (14)$$

   More importantly, our retrieval requires to take the domain knowledge into account. Thus, the query is $\mathtt{DK} \wedge \mathtt{q}^{\mathtt{tgt}}$. This step, covered in Sect. 5.5, yields a set of *p candidate cases* $(\mathtt{c}^i)_{i \in [\![1,p]\!]}$ for the execution of $\mathtt{DK} \wedge \mathtt{q}^{\mathtt{tgt}}$ that should, in theory, be such that $\mathtt{effort}(\mathtt{c}^i, \mathtt{DK} \wedge \mathtt{q}^{\mathtt{tgt}}) \leq d$ with d the dilation value.
3. This hypothesis is verified by computing the adaptation effort $\mathtt{effort}(\mathtt{c}^i, \mathtt{DK} \wedge \mathtt{q}^{\mathtt{tgt}})$ for every candidate case.
   (a) If at least one i for which $\mathtt{effort}(\mathtt{c}^i, \mathtt{DK} \wedge \mathtt{q}^{\mathtt{tgt}}) \leq d$ is found, the source case $\mathtt{c}^s$ is such that $\mathtt{effort}(\mathtt{c}^s, \mathtt{DK} \wedge \mathtt{q}^{\mathtt{tgt}}) = \min_{i \in [\![1,p]\!]} (\mathtt{effort}(\mathtt{c}^i, \mathtt{DK} \wedge \mathtt{q}^{\mathtt{tgt}}))$.
   (b) Else, a *backtracking* step, explained in Sect. 5.6, is applied, going back one step through the dichotomic search and exhaustively computing the adaptation effort of every encountered case, looping back to step 3.

In the worst case, our overapproximation of the dilation is too loose and it is required to compute the adaptation effort for every case of CB, akin to a naive adaptation-guided retrieval. The average time complexity of this approach is discussed in Sect. 6.

5.4 Indexing of the Case Base

In Olaaaf, the case-base $\mathtt{CB} = \{\mathtt{c}^s\}_{s \in [\![1,4]\!]}$ of the running example is formalized by:

$$\mathtt{c}^1 = (\mathit{banana}_{\mathrm{g}} = 120.) \wedge (\mathit{fruit}_{\mathrm{g}} = 120.) \wedge (\mathit{cowMilk}_{\mathrm{g}} = 250.) \wedge (\mathit{milk}_{\mathrm{g}} = 250.) \wedge \cdots \quad (15)$$

$$\mathtt{c}^2 = (\mathit{kiwi}_{\mathrm{g}} = 100.) \wedge (\mathit{fruit}_{\mathrm{g}} = 100.) \wedge (\mathit{almondMilk}_{\mathrm{g}} = 250.) \wedge (\mathit{milk}_{\mathrm{g}} = 250.) \wedge \cdots \quad (16)$$

$$\mathtt{c}^3 = (\mathit{strawberry}_{\mathrm{g}} = 150.) \wedge (\mathit{fruit}_{\mathrm{g}} = 150.) \wedge (\mathit{cowMilk}_{\mathrm{g}} = 250.) \wedge (\mathit{milk}_{\mathrm{g}} = 250.) \wedge \cdots \quad (17)$$

$$\mathtt{c}^4 = (\mathit{banana}_{\mathrm{g}} = 120.) \wedge (\mathit{strawberry}_{\mathrm{g}} = 75.) \wedge (\mathit{fruit}_{\mathrm{g}} = 195.) \wedge (\mathit{cowMilk}_{\mathrm{g}} = 250.) \wedge (\mathit{milk}_{\mathrm{g}} = 250.) \wedge \cdots \quad (18)$$

The "$\cdots$" corresponds to the conjunction of $(x = 0)$ for the variables x not occurring before in the formula.

As previously stated, the case base CB is a set of fully-constrained cases on which queries are executed. In other words:

1. For every $c^s \in \texttt{CB}$, each variable is specified in c^s (i.e. for every x, there exists a value v such that $c^s \models (x = v)$);
2. Every formula α can be seen as a query on CB and the execution of the query can be done efficiently to retrieve the set of $c^s \in \texttt{CB}$ such that $c^s \models \alpha$.

Data structures fitting both these prerequisites are numerous. Therefore, Olrrrf was built as a modular system for which any case base satisfying both conditions can be used. In particular, this paper discusses a version of Olrrrf using a k-d tree-indexed case base. k-d trees can be seen as generalizations of binary search trees extended to index data in k dimensions [5]. The remainder of this paper uses n to denote the dimensionality of our search space. For the sake of historical and conventional norms regarding k-d trees, this section uses k instead. This data structure is therefore capable of storing high-dimensional cases, hence satisfies our first condition on CB. It is, however, only able to perform range queries under the assumption that they are axis-aligned, and therefore requires a small modification to fully satisfy our second condition.

Executing a Range Query for k-d Trees for a Generic Formula. Let α be any formula. A range query of the case base CB is performed to find all cases c^s such that $c^s \models \alpha$. To achieve this, its *Axis Aligned Bounding Box* (AABB) is computed, an over-approximation of α consisting of $2k$ constraints of the forms:

$$x_j \geq \ell_j \quad \text{and} \quad x_j \leq u_j \quad \text{for } j \in [\![1, k]\!],$$

where x_j denotes the variable corresponding to the j-th dimension of the search space, and $[\ell_j, u_j]$ is the projection along the x_j axis of the convex hull of $\mathcal{M}(\alpha)$, that is:

$$\text{with } S = \{v \in \mathbb{R} \mid \alpha \wedge (x_j = v) \text{ is satisfiable}\}, \quad \ell_j = \min S \text{ and } u_j = \max S$$

$[\ell_j, u_j]$ can be computed by solving the linear optimization problems "minimize x_j for $x \in \mathcal{M}(\alpha)$" and "maximize x_j for $x \in \mathcal{M}(\alpha)$".

The resulting AABB is thus the tightest axis-aligned hyper-rectangle enclosing the set of solutions of α that can be executed as a query to CB. Using simple substitutions of the candidate results of the AABB query in each constraint of α, it is then easy to determine all cases c^s such that $c^s \models \alpha$, therefore, executing a range query on a k-d tree indexed case base for a generic formula.

Time Complexity. Indexing a k-d tree can be computed in $O(|\texttt{CB}| \log |\texttt{CB}|)$ [6,8]. Performing an axis-aligned range query can be done in $O(|\texttt{CB}|^{1-\frac{1}{k}} + m)$, with m the number of cases returned from the query [5]. Since computing an AABB takes $2k$ linear optimizations, each polynomial in terms of dimensionality in the worst case. It is known that, in the average case, this task is well optimized and can be reasonably computed [2]. This query can therefore be executed in a reasonable time and, in addition, can be done lazily by pausing its execution whenever a single candidate case is found.

5.5 Overapproximation of the Dilation by Translation of Constraints

As shown in Sect. 5.2, computing the dilation of a given formula α to a radius r is, in the general case, intractable. An *overapproximation* of the dilation is therefore defined, named $\texttt{Dil}^+(\alpha, r)$ and is defined as shown in Proposition 1.

Proposition 1. *Let* $\alpha = \bigwedge_{i=1}^{m} (a_{i1}x_1 + \cdots + a_{in}x_n \le b_i)$ *for* $a_{ij}, b_i \in \mathbb{R}$. *Let* $\lambda \in \mathbb{R}^m$ *and* $M \in \mathbb{R}^m$ *such that, for* $i \in [\![1, m]\!]$, $M_i = \max_{j=1}^{n} \frac{|a_{ij}|}{w_j}$ *and* $\lambda_i = M_i \cdot r$.

Now, let $\texttt{Dil}^+(\alpha, r) = \bigwedge_{i=1}^{m} (a_{i1}x_1 + \cdots + a_{in}x_n \le b_i + \lambda_i)$. *Intuitively,* $\texttt{Dil}^+(\alpha, r)$ *is the translation of* α *by* λ_i *along the axis* x_j, *for each* $j \in [\![1, n]\!]$. $\texttt{Dil}^+(\alpha, r)$ *is an overapproximation of* $\texttt{Dil}_{d^1}(\alpha, r)$: $\mathcal{M}(\texttt{Dil}_{d^1}(\alpha, r)) \subseteq \mathcal{M}(\texttt{Dil}^+(\alpha, r))$ *and* λ *is the smallest value that satisfies this inclusion.* $\texttt{Dil}^+(\alpha, r)$ *is therefore the smallest overapproximation of the dilation of* α *by a weighted* L^1 *distance to r, defined by translation of its constraints.*

Thanks to this proposition, the overapproximation of the dilation can be computed in linear time in regards to the number of constraints m of α by pre-computing the M_i. Each M_i can be computed in $O(n)$ time, where n is the dimension of the space (or in $O(n_i)$ time if only the n_i non-zero coefficients of constraint i are considered).

Therefore, the Olrrrf algorithm uses this overapproximation to query the case base at each dichotomy step: if a case is in the overapproximation of the dilation, its distance is computed using a linear optimization on the distance.

5.6 Adaptation-Guided Retrieval with Backtracking

The computation of the overapproximation defined in the previous section has a low time complexity compared to a general dilation and is a strong candidate for a dichotomy search, as defined in Sect. 4. However, it can yield false positives compared to the exact dilation. Therefore, a two-phase dichotomy was chosen: a coarse search phase relying only on the overapproximation, and a fine search phase verifying the exact distance of each candidate case. This part of the algorithm is quite technical and is described in details in [15].

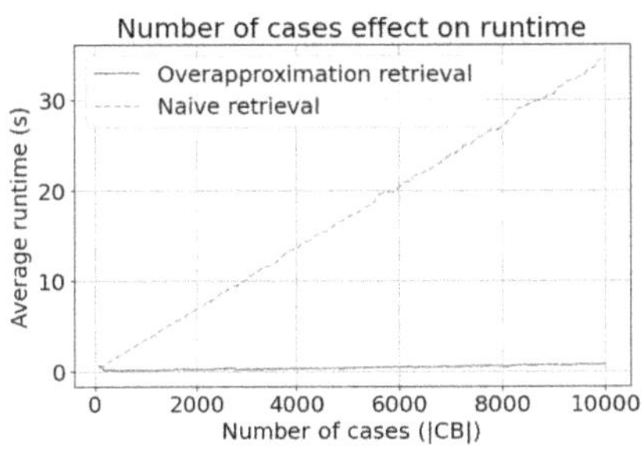

(a) Evolution of runtime depending on the number of cases in CB.

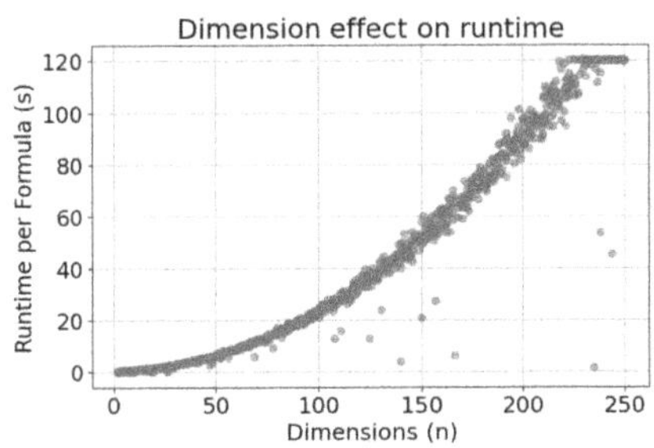

(b) Evolution of runtime depending on the dimension n.

Fig. 3. Evolution of runtime depending on the number of cases in CB (a) and on the dimension n (b).

6 Evaluation

The runtime of Olrrrf was evaluated as a function of the number of cases in $\mathtt{CB}$, and the dimension n. This was experimented with a laptop with an Intel Core Ultra 7 255H and 32 GB of RAM. More details are given in [15].

To estimate the effect of the number of cases $|\mathtt{CB}|$ of Olrrrf, visible in Fig. 3a, a benchmark from 100 to 10 000 cases was run, querying on 10 randomly generated formulas in dimension 10. A benchmark on a naive algorithm was also run, with Olrrrf executions being capped at 2 times the naive time to avoid very long runs on already impractical values of $|\mathtt{CB}|$. As it can be seen in Fig. 3a, these timeouts were only reached when $|\mathtt{CB}|$ was small, where the naive algorithm is particularly fast and therefore yields a low timeout threshold.[5]

To study the effect of the dimension n of Olrrrf, visible in Fig. 3b, a benchmark from 2 to 250 dimensions was run, querying on 5 randomly generated formulas in dimension n. A timeout at 120 seconds was used. Figure 3b suggests that the runtime of Olrrrf as a function of the dimension n is in $O(2^{\frac{n}{50}})$, with all 5 executions for $n = 250$ reaching the 120 seconds timeout.[6]

7 Conclusion

This paper has proposed a general approach to case retrieval based on the combination of dilation of the target query and exact matching in the case base. This idea of retrieval based on modifications of the target query is not new (though it seems to be quite rare in the CBR literature). Indeed, in a 1993 paper, a memory-based reasoning system proposed an approach to retrieval based on the transformation of SQL queries [14]. A similar approach has been applied in a knowledge graph representation setting, using transformations of SPARQL queries and applied, in particular, to the case-based cooking system Taaable [7]. A difference with these related studies is that, in this paper, the retrieval is adaptation-guided in the strong sense and enables one to minimize a distance measuring an adaptation effort.

From a computational viewpoint, the dichotomy of the search space provides a retrieval process whose complexity is logarithmic in the size of the case base. Now, for the application of this algorithm to the setting of the Olaaaf system, it has appeared that, in worst case situations, the dilation can be intractable, in particular for a target query involving numerous variables. This has motivated a two-step approach using first an overapproximation of the retrieval that returns quickly a few candidate source cases followed by a potential selection among these candidates (if there are more than one candidate). This is not unlike the MAC/FAC approach to retrieval [10], with the difference that the closest case is necessarily returned by the proposed approach, nor unlike Footprint-based retrieval [17], in which the first step consists of searching a compact

[5] Pipeline available at: https://github.com/OlaaafEngine/Olrrrf/blob/main/evaluation/cb_size.ipynb.

[6] Pipeline available at: https://github.com/OlaaafEngine/Olrrrf/blob/main/evaluation/dimension_size.ipynb.

precomputed footprint set rather than an overapproximation of a target problem dilation.

Now, Olrrrf and Olaaaf form a case-based inference engine with exact retrieval, in a formalism with a high expressivity power: in this paper, only real variables are considered whereas this engine uses also integers, Booleans and values of enumerated types.

A future work is the implementation of the retrieval approach in other representation frameworks. In [11], an exact retrieval algorithm has been designed in a formalism of cases and domain knowledge based on propositional logic (which is a fragment of the Olaaaf formalism), that is based on similar principles. The strength of this work is that it integrates by design adaptation rules, represented in a so-called variation logic, so the case returned by an exact retrieval process is the one using a well-informed adaptation process, using, when available, adaptation rules. The combination of both approaches is planned first by a study of a variation logic for Olaaaf, enabling a well-founded representation of adaptation rules for both adaptation and adaptation-guided retrieval.

Acknowledgments. The authors wish to thank the anonymous reviewers for their relevant remarks. For instance, they have both noticed that the adjective "exact" for an adaptation-guided retrieval in the strong sense was misguided. This adjective has been removed in this final version and replaced with "adaptation-guided". They also would like to thank professor Manuel Rebuschi for his relevant advices.

Declaration on Generative AI. During the preparation of this work, the authors used ChatGPT, Perplexity and Writefull in order to: Paraphrase and reword, improve writing style, and grammar and spelling check. After using these tools/services, the authors reviewed and edited the content as needed and take full responsibility for the publication's content.

References

1. Aamodt, A., Plaza, E.: Case-based reasoning: foundational issues, methodological variations, and system approaches. AI Commun. **7**(1), 39–59 (1994)
2. Achterberg, T., Wunderling, R.: Mixed integer programming: analyzing 12 years of progress. In: Facets of Combinatorial Optimization: Festschrift for Martin Grötschel. Springer Berlin Heidelberg (2013). https://api.semanticscholar.org/CorpusID:59830161
3. Avis, D., Fukuda, K.: A pivoting algorithm for convex hulls and vertex enumeration of arrangements and polyhedra. In: Proceedings of the Seventh Annual Symposium on Computational Geometry, pp. 98–104 (1991)
4. Avis, D., Fukuda, K.: Reverse search for enumeration. Discrete Appl. Math. **65**(1), 21–46 (1996). https://doi.org/10.1016/0166-218X(95)00026-N, https://www.sciencedirect.com/science/article/pii/0166218X9500026N, first International Colloquium on Graphs and Optimization
5. Bentley, J.L.: Multidimensional binary search trees used for associative searching. Commun. ACM **18**, 509–517 (1975). https://api.semanticscholar.org/CorpusID:13091446
6. Brown, R.A.: Building a Balanced K-D Tree in O(KN log N) Time. ArXiv **abs/1410.5420** (2014). https://api.semanticscholar.org/CorpusID:16995974

7. Bruneau, O., Gaillard, E., Lasolle, N., Lieber, J., Nauer, E., Reynaud, J.: A SPARQL query transformation rule language - application to retrieval and adaptation in case-based reasoning. In: ICCBR 2017 - Case-Based Reasoning Research and Development, 25th International Conference on Case-Based Reasoning. Trondheim, Norway (2017). https://inria.hal.science/hal-01661651
8. Cormen, T.H., Leiserson, C.E., Rivest, R.L., Stein, C.: Introduction to algorithms. Chapitre 9. 4th Edition. MIT Press (2022)
9. Diebold, E., et al.: Olaaaf: a general adaptation prototype. In: International Conference on Case-Based Reasoning (2024). https://api.semanticscholar.org/CorpusID:271098746
10. Forbus, K.D., Gentner, D., Law, K.: MAC/FAC: a model of similarity-based retrieval. Cogn. Sci. **19**(2), 141–205 (1995)
11. François, N., Lieber, J.: A knowledge representation approach for reasoning with adaptation rules. In: Bichindaritz, I., Lopez, B. (eds.) Case-Based Reasoning Research and Development33rd International Conference, ICCBR 2025, Biarritz, France, June 30–July 3, 2025, Proceedings. vol. 15662, pp. 204–219. I. Bichindaritz and B. Lopez, Springer, Biarritz, France (2025). https://hal.science/hal-05408527
12. Heijmans, H.J.: Mathematical morphology: an algebraic approach (1987)
13. Riesbeck, C.K., Schank, R.C.: Inside Case-Based Reasoning. Lawrence Erlbaum Associates Inc, Hillsdale, New Jersey (1989)
14. Shimazu, H., Kitano, H., Shibata, A.: Retrieving cases from relational data-bases: another stride towards corporate-wide case-based systems. In: Proceedings of the 13th International Joint Conference on Artificial Intelligence (IJCAI'93), Chambéry, pp. 909–914 (1993)
15. Sipp, J., Lieber, J.: An exact and efficient case retrieval approach based on a dichotomy of the case space (extended version). Research report, available at https://inria.hal.science/hal-05557272 (2026)
16. Smyth, B., Keane, M.T.: Using adaptation knowledge to retrieve and adapt design cases. Knowl.-Based Syst. **9**(2), 127–135 (1996)
17. Smyth, B., McKenna, E.: Footprint-based retrieval. In: Althoff, K.D., Bergmann, R., Branting, L. (eds.) Case-Based Reasoning Research and Development, pp. 343–357. Springer, Berlin Heidelberg, Berlin, Heidelberg (1999)
18. Weibel, C., Fukuda, K.: Computing faces up to K dimensions of a Minkowski sum of polytopes. In: Canadian Conference on Computational Geometry (2005). https://api.semanticscholar.org/CorpusID:9454671

Failure-Aware Matching-Based Adaptation for Generalisable Reuse

Ikechukwu Nkisi-Orji(✉), Pedram Salimi, and Nirmalie Wiratunga

School of Computing, Engineering and Technology, Robert Gordon University, Aberdeen, UK

{i.nkisi-orji,p.salimi1,n.wiratunga}@rgu.ac.uk

Abstract. Case-based reasoning (CBR) is appealing for structured decision tasks because of its interpretability, data efficiency, and support for memory-based reuse. However, reliable adaptation remains difficult when solutions are structured and must be recombined from multiple cases. Even highly similar cases can yield incomplete or incorrect solutions and many existing reuse methods remain tied to domain-specific representations. We propose CARM, a generalisable framework for failure-aware solution reuse that represents problems as sets of needs and solutions as graphs of reusable components. The framework formulates adaptation as affinity-driven matching between query needs and candidate components, introduces cardinality-aware optimisation to control solution size, and uses failure-aware acceptance to decide whether to accept a constructed solution or expand the retrieval neighbourhood. We evaluate CARM on two structurally different domains, MultiWOZ task-oriented dialogue and O*NET occupation data, comparing against nearest-neighbour reuse, matching-based reuse variants, and LLM baselines. Results show that cardinality-aware matching with conditional-probability affinity improves component selection across domains, demonstrating the value of general, representation-independent reuse mechanisms for structured CBR adaptation.

Keywords: Adaptation · Matching-based reuse · Failure detection · Solution graphs · Generalisable reuse

1 Introduction

Case-based reasoning (CBR) reuses prior solutions for new problems, but adaptation remains difficult when solutions are structured and multi-component. Direct reuse of highly similar cases may produce incomplete or incorrect solutions, especially when solutions must be recombined from several neighbours. Existing matching-based approaches support such recombination [20], but are often tied to specific domains or representations.

This paper proposes a generalisable framework for failure-aware solution reuse. We represent each case using a problem description, a set of needs, and a

L. Malburg and K. Bach (Eds.): ICCBR 2026, LNAI 16780, pp. 51–66, 2027.
https://doi.org/10.1007/978-3-032-33865-5_4

structured solution expressed as a graph of reusable components. This abstraction decouples the reuse mechanism from domain-specific representations while supporting different kinds of solution structure. Our approach extends matching-based reuse in four ways. First, it represents solutions as solution graphs, allowing sets, sequences, and more complex structures to be handled within a single framework. Second, it replaces similarity-based matching with a more flexible affinity formulation for modelling compatibility between problem needs and solution components. Third, it introduces a cardinality-aware optimisation mechanism to control the number of selected components, together with optional ordering where required by the solution structure. Fourth, it incorporates post-hoc failure detection mechanisms grounded in CBR principles to estimate the reliability of constructed solutions from neighbourhood consistency, alignment quality, and novelty signals.

We use generalisability to mean that the same case abstraction, affinity-based matching, cardinality objective, and failure-aware stopping mechanism are applied across datasets without dataset-specific adaptation rules. The contributions of this paper are as follows:

1. We propose a domain agnostic case and solution representation based on solution graphs, unifying sets, sequences, and other structured solutions within a single framework.
2. We extend matching-based reuse with an affinity-driven formulation that decouples adaptation from domain-specific similarity measures.
3. We introduce a cardinality-aware optimisation mechanism, with optional ordering, to better control the structure of constructed solutions.
4. We incorporate CBR-inspired failure detection mechanisms that use neighbourhood evidence to assess solution quality and support acceptance decisions during reuse.

2 Related Work

Adaptation remains a major challenge in CBR systems, particularly for complex and structured solution spaces [13,24]. Two of the well known adaptation approaches are weighted majority voting and case difference heuristics (CDH) [23]. Weighted majority voting aggregates the solutions of the k-nearest neighbours, typically selecting the value of k through validation procedures such as leave-one-out testing [12,22]. In contrast, CDH-based methods learn adaptation rules from pairs of cases by modelling the relationship between differences in problem descriptions and differences in solutions [4,8,10,16,25]. Although traditionally applied to simple structure classification and regression tasks, modern advancements such as deep learning CDH (DL-CDH) use deep neural networks to extract features from non-symbolic data (e.g., images) and predict solution differences without requiring manually engineered domain features [26]. Other work has sought more general adaptation models for numerical, parametric, and substitutional settings, including differential adaptation, Grey Relational Analysis-based weighting, and analogical substitution frameworks [3,7,15].

These approaches broaden adaptation beyond simple classification but remain less suited to constructing multi-component structured solutions.

However, many real-world applications require the reuse of complex, structured solutions that cannot be adequately represented or adapted as single entities. Early work in CBR recognised the importance of compositional reuse, where solutions are constructed by combining elements from multiple cases rather than reusing a single retrieved solution [2,9,24]. In the domain of Process-Oriented CBR (POCBR), compositional reuse has been advanced through workflow streams, which decompose procedural cases into reusable sub-fragments to incrementally compensate for deficiencies in a retrieved solution [17,18]. Malburg et al. [13] also proposed encoding complex structural modifications as rules within the Drools rule engine, providing a more intuitive and maintainable format for domain experts than proprietary graph-fragment formats. Furthermore, the integration of Large Language Models (LLMs) offers a new frontier for domain-agnostic adaptation, where the LLM implements transformational, compositional, or generative operations through its inherent reasoning and generation functions [6].

Recently, Nkisi-Orji et al. [20] proposed a matching-based reuse framework for structured case solutions, specifically for adaptation of explanation strategies. Their method aligns query elements with candidate solution elements from neighbouring cases using similarity-driven preferences derived from Sentence-BERT embeddings and constructs composite solutions through stable matching. Our work builds on this line by broadening the representation, replacing similarity with affinity-based matching, and incorporating cardinality-aware selection and detector-based acceptance.

3 Proposed Method

Figure 1 provides an overview of our method, CARM (*Cardinality-Aware Reuse Matching*). Given a query case, we retrieve a ranked neighbourhood and progressively expand a reusable solution component pool. At each expansion step, we construct a candidate solution through matching-based reuse and build a solution graph. We then apply an acceptance policy (match-based or detector-based) to decide whether to stop expansion. The following subsections formalise each stage.

3.1 Problem Formulation

We represent a case as a tuple $c = (x, L, S)$ where x is the problem description, $L = \{l_1, \ldots, l_m\}$ is a set of needs relevant to x, and $S = (V, E)$ is the case solution. The set of needs L can be obtained through a function $L = \phi(x)$ which extracts structured elements from the problem description. In structured domains (e.g. tabular problem description), ϕ may be the identity function. We represent solutions as graphs $S = (V, E)$, where $V = \{s_1, \ldots, s_n\}$ is a set of solution components and E encodes relations between them. This formulation

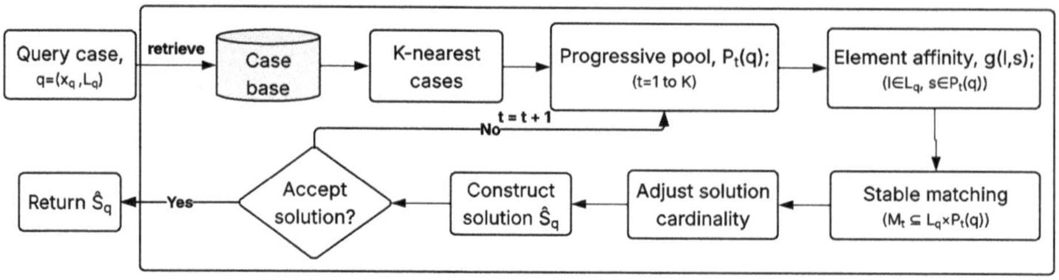

Fig. 1. CARM overview: failure-driven neighbourhood expansion with reuse with stable matching and solution cardinality optimisation, candidate graph construction, and threshold-based acceptance.

generalises both unordered solutions ($E = \emptyset$) and ordered sequences. Given a query case $q = (x_q, L_q)$, the goal is to construct a solution $\hat{S}_q$ by reusing the solutions of retrieved cases.

3.2 Matching-Based Reuse

We first retrieve the top-K most similar cases from the case base using a similarity function $\text{sim}(x_q, x_i)$ which produces an ordered set of neighbours $c_1, \ldots, c_K$. Rather than relying on a single retrieved case, we construct a candidate pool $P_t(q)$ of reusable solution components by aggregating components from multiple neighbours:

$$P_t(q) = \bigcup_{j=1}^{t} V(j), \quad t = 1, \ldots, K.$$

This pool defines the space of components that can be reused for the query. By increasing t, the pool grows to include more diverse components which enables flexible recombination while preserving locality to the query.

We adopt the matching framework introduced in [20], which includes the Gale–Shapley-based (GSA) and non-deferred acceptance (NDA) variants. These methods construct a matching $M_t \subseteq L_q \times P_t(q)$ based on element-wise preference rankings. In the original formulation, preferences are derived from a pairwise similarity function that captures inner compatibility between elements to produce a similarity matrix used to guide the matching process.

In this work, we generalise this formulation by replacing the similarity function with a more flexible *affinity function*, $g(l, s)$, which quantifies the compatibility between needs $l \in L_q$ and candidate solution components $s \in P_t(q)$. This formulation captures the strength of association between elements and may be instantiated using semantic similarity, statistical dependence, learned compatibility scores, or other domain-specific measures. The resulting affinity matrix $A \in \mathbb{R}^{m \times n}$, defined over $L_q \times P_t(q)$ with entries $a_{ij} = g(l_i, s_j)$, subsumes traditional similarity matrices while enabling broader modelling choices. The induced preference rankings are then used to compute the matching M_t.

We retain the deferred acceptance (Gale–Shapley) algorithm as the core matching mechanism as it guarantees convergence to a stable matching. As detailed in [20], the algorithm iteratively refines pairings based on mutual preferences until no blocking pairs exist. Our contribution lies in redefining the construction of preference rankings through the proposed affinity formulation.

3.3 Cardinality-Aware Reuse

As case solutions have variable component cardinality, a key design question is how many components should be included in the constructed solution for a query. In the GSA approach [20], a limitation is that the number of predicted solution components is determined by the number of query needs. Since stable matching links query needs to candidate solution components in a one-to-one manner, the number of components selected cannot exceed the number of needs in the query. This introduces a structural bias where the size of the constructed solution is constrained by the query representation rather than by the complexity of the solution suggested by the retrieved neighbourhood.

In CARM, we address this limitation by decoupling solution cardinality from the number of query needs. The stable matching step in Sect. 3.2 identifies an initial core set of solution components which is treated as a seed rather than the final output. After matching, additional neighbourhood signals are used to adjust the number of retained components upward or downward.

First, the remaining solution components in the candidate pool (i.e. those not selected by matching) are ranked using a combination of query relevance and neighbourhood support. For each component $s \in P_t(q)$ at step t, the ranking score is

$$\text{rank\_score}^{(t)}(s) = w_a f_{\text{aff}}^{(t)}(s) + w_s f_{\text{sup}}^{(t)}(s),$$

with

$$f_{\text{aff}}^{(t)}(s) = \max_{l_i \in L_q} g(l_i, s),$$

$$f_{\text{sup}}^{(t)}(s) = \frac{\sum_{i=1}^{t} \rho_i \, \mathbf{1}[s \in V(i)]}{\max_{s' \in P_t(q)} \sum_{i=1}^{t} \rho_i \, \mathbf{1}[s' \in V(i)]}.$$

Here, $f_{\text{aff}}^{(t)}(s)$ is the maximum affinity between component s and any query need l_i, and $f_{\text{sup}}^{(t)}(s)$ is the normalised neighbourhood support of s, computed from weighted neighbour occurrence (ρ_i: retrieval score of the case containing s). w_a and w_s control the contribution of relevance and support respectively. This is a standard linear signal-fusion form used in ranking and information retrieval [14].

Next, the final solution component list is constructed in two stages: matched core components are ordered by descending matched affinity, and the remaining non-core components are appended in descending rank_score order. Cardinality selection then adjusts the retained set upward by extending into the appended components, or downward by truncating the ordered list while preserving core-priority ordering. For each query, a cardinality-selection objective $J(k)$ is used to decide how many components k to keep in the final solution. Specifically, it optimises

$$J_t(k) = Q_t(k) - \lambda\, C_t(k), \qquad k \in \{k^{(t)}_{\min}, \ldots, k^{(t)}_{\max}\}$$

where

$$Q_t(k) = \frac{1}{k} \sum_{s \in \text{prefix}_k(\Pi_t)} \text{rank\_score}^{(t)}(s)$$

is the average score of the first k components, Π_t is the ordered candidate list, and

$$C_t(k) = \left(\frac{k - \mu_t}{\Delta_t}\right)^2; \mu_t = \frac{\sum_{i=1}^{t} \rho_i \,|V_i|}{\sum_{i=1}^{t} \rho_i}, \qquad \Delta_t = \max\!\left(k^{(t)}_{\max} - k^{(t)}_{\min}, 1\right)$$

penalises deviation from the typical solution length in the retrieved neighbourhood, with μ_t the similarity-weighted average neighbour solution length and Δ_t a normalisation constant based on the candidate size range. The parameter λ controls the strength of this cardinality regularisation: smaller values allow more flexible expansion or contraction of the solution, while larger values favour solutions whose size is closer to that of the local neighbourhood. In this way, the method allows the final solution size to reflect both the query-specific matches and the broader structure of similar cases in the neighbourhood. This formulation follows standard regularisation principles in statistical learning, where objective functions are augmented with penalty terms to control structural properties of the solution [1,5]. The quadratic form of $C_t(k)$ corresponds to an L2 penalty, which is commonly used due to its smoothness and strong penalisation of large deviations. From a probabilistic perspective, this is analogous to a maximum a posteriori estimation with a Gaussian prior over solution size centred at μ [19]. In the context of CBR, neighbouring cases provide empirical evidence for solution construction, justifying the use of neighbourhood-derived statistics to guide the selection of solution structure.

3.4 Solution Graph Construction

Given selected components $\hat{V}_q$, we define a solution structure $\hat{S}_q = (\hat{V}_q, \hat{E}_q)$. In domains where solution component order matters (e.g. robot action planning), we model $\hat{E}_q$ as directed sequence edges. In domains where order is less central (e.g. ingredient lists), the framework can be used with an unordered output ($\hat{E}_q = \emptyset$). To infer ordering, we use retrieved neighbours that contain each component. For each $s \in \hat{V}_q$, we compute its retrieval-score-weighted average position across those neighbours, and then sort components by this score to obtain an ordered list $\hat{V}_q = (s_1, \ldots, s_n)$. We then construct sequence edges between consecutive components:

$$\hat{E}_q = \{(s_i, s_{i+1}) \mid i = 1, \ldots, n-1\}.$$

This yields an ordering consistent with local neighbourhood patterns (a sequence graph).

3.5 Failure-Driven Expansion, Solution Acceptance and Failure Detectors

A central challenge in reuse is determining the number of neighbours to use. A very small neighbourhood may under-cover required solution components, whereas a large neighbourhood may reduce precision by introducing noisy or conflicting components. Following [20], we adopt a failure-driven expansion strategy that starts from the most similar retrieved case and incrementally enlarges the candidate reuse pool until the constructed solution is deemed sufficiently reliable. We propose *match-based* and *detector-based* acceptance as alternative stopping policies over the expansion loop. At each step t, the retrieved neighbourhood is expanded, a candidate pool $P_t(q)$ is formed, and a candidate solution $\hat{S}_q^{(t)}$ is constructed by reuse.

Under match-based acceptance, we accept the first step that exceeds a threshold τ_{match}. This is evaluated on the post-selection component set (i.e. after cardinality adjustment). Let $\hat{V}_t$ be the selected components at step t. We use

$$\text{score}_{\text{match}}(\hat{S}_q^{(t)}) = \frac{1}{|\hat{V}_t|} \sum_{s \in \hat{V}_t} \max_{l \in L_q} g(l, s),$$

and accept $\hat{S}_q^{(t)}$ when $\text{score}_{\text{match}}(\hat{S}_q^{(t)}) \geq \tau_{\text{match}}$. This score evaluates the constructed solution by taking, for each selected component, its highest affinity to any query need, and then averaging these values over all selected components.

Under detector-based acceptance, we score the constructed candidate solution with a failure detector and accept when the detector score exceeds its detector-specific threshold τ_{det}. Here, a *detector* is a scoring function that estimates the reliability of the constructed candidate solution under the current neighbourhood context. We consider four domain-agnostic detectors grounded in CBR principles:

1. *Neighbourhood Consistency Detector (NCD)*: Measures average set overlap (Jaccard similarity) between predicted components and each retrieved neighbour's components.

$$\text{NCD}(\hat{S}_q^{(t)}) = \frac{1}{t} \sum_{i=1}^{t} \text{Jacc}\Big(\hat{V}_t, V(i)\Big).$$

2. *Weighted Neighbourhood Consistency Detector (WNCD)*: A retrieval-weighted version of NCD, which gives higher influence to more similar neighbours.

$$\text{WNCD}(\hat{S}_q^{(t)}) = \frac{\sum_{i=1}^{t} \rho_i \, \text{Jacc}\Big(\hat{V}_t, V(i)\Big)}{\sum_{i=1}^{t} \rho_i},$$

ρ_i is the non-negative retrieval weight for neighbour i (derived from retrieval score).

3. *Embedding Novelty Detector (END)*: Fits an anomaly model on case base solution embeddings and scores how "in-distribution" the predicted solution is. Let z_t be the embedding of $\hat{V}_t$, and $f_{\mathrm{IF}}(z_t)$ the Isolation-Forest [11] decision score; we map it to $(0, 1)$ through

$$\mathrm{END}(\hat{S}_q^{(t)}) = \sigma(f_{\mathrm{IF}}(z_t)) = \frac{1}{1 + e^{-f_{\mathrm{IF}}(z_t)}}.$$

4. *Neighbourhood Transformation Alignment Detector (NTAD)*: Learns a local linear mapping from problem-space similarity to solution-space similarity within the retrieved neighbourhood, then scores residual alignment error for the query prediction. If $\bar{e}_t$ is the retrieval-weighted mean residual, the detector score is

$$\mathrm{NTAD}(\hat{S}_q^{(t)}) = \exp(-\gamma \bar{e}_t),$$

$\gamma > 0$ controls the sharpness of NTAD's error-to-confidence mapping.

Higher detector scores indicate higher confidence that the current candidate solution is reliable. Under detector-based acceptance, we accept the first step t such that

$$\mathrm{score}_{\mathrm{det}}(\hat{S}_q^{(t)}) \geq \tau_{\mathrm{det}},$$

where $\mathrm{score}_{\mathrm{det}}$ is one of the detector scores above. We set detector acceptance thresholds using a calibration step on the case base. For calibration, each detector score is tested against candidate cutoff values, and we choose the cutoff that best separates reliable from unreliable solutions. This gives an acceptance threshold per detector, which is then used during neighbourhood expansion.

With either match-based or detector-based method, if acceptance is not reached, expansion proceeds to $t+1$. If no step is accepted, then the best-scoring solution across explored steps is retained.

4 Evaluation

We evaluate the proposed case adaptation framework under a common retrieval-and-reuse pipeline.

4.1 Dataset

Our experiments use the MultiWOZ 2.2[1] task-oriented dialogue and O*NET[2] occupation datasets. For MultiWOZ, cases are derived from over 10,000 annotated dialogue turns in the original dataset. O*NET consists of 438 structured task-to-skill data, where each record links an occupational description and task profile with associated skill elements.

---

[1] https://github.com/budzianowski/multiwoz/tree/master/data/MultiWOZ_2.2.

[2] https://www.onetcenter.org/database.html.

4.2 Case Construction and Preprocessing

Following the proposed dataset structure, both datasets are converted into cases of the form (`problem, needs, solution`). All text is normalised by lowercasing and collapsing whitespace to minimise variability. For MultiWOZ, each system turn is treated as one case (example in Fig. 2). The problem representation consists of the dialogue service, the immediately preceding user utterance, and when available, the dialogue state encoded as slot-value pairs. The needs field decomposes this context into matching units, including a service token and the user utterance. The solution field is extracted from the annotated dialogue acts for the corresponding system turn, preserving action order. This results in a structured representation in which the problem captures dialogue context and the solution captures the response action sequence. The solution can be considered as a target response plan (what to inform/request/select, in order) which a response generator can use to respond to the user (i.e. system's response).

Raw data	**Constructed case**
`dialogue_id=PMUL3484.json`	`case_id=train:PMUL3484.json:turn3`
`turn_index=3`	`problem={service-booking | user=...}`
`previous_utterance=` *I would like to book a reservation...*	`needs=[service-booking, user=...]`
`raw_dialog_act=`	`solution=[`
`Booking-Inform: none`	`booking:inform(none),`
`Booking-Request:`	`booking:request(bookday),`
`bookday=?`	`booking:request(bookpeople),`
`bookpeople=?`	`booking:request(bookstay)`
`bookstay=?`	`]`

Fig. 2. Example of case construction from MultiWOZ dataset content.

The O*NET experiment dataset is constructed from multiple O*NET files, including occupation metadata, skill ratings, and task statements. Tasks and skills are filtered using O*NET Data Values (standardised 1–5 scales of importance or frequency), thereby retaining only descriptors with values greater than 4 to focus on highly salient occupation skills and core tasks. For each occupation, the remaining tasks and skills are aggregated into sets: the case problem consists of the occupation title and description, the tasks form the need, and the case solution corresponds to the skills for the occupation.

4.3 Experiment Setup

For each query, we retrieve the top-$K = 5$ nearest cases from the case base using Sentence-BERT [21] over the problem representation, and construct a solution graph from the retrieved cases. We compare the proposed CARM method against BM, NDA, and GSA from [20]. BM reuses the solution of the single closest neighbour. GSA applies Gale-Shapley stable matching, while NDA is the corresponding non-deferred variant. CARM differs from GSA in that it treats the number of retained solution components as an explicit optimisation problem rather than accepting the cardinality induced by stable matching.

For NDA, GSA, and CARM, we evaluate three affinity functions for matching query needs to candidate solution components: `embed_cos`, which uses Sentence-BERT embeddings with cosine similarity; `condprob`, which uses a smoothed estimate of $P(\text{solution component} \mid \text{need})$ from case-base co-occurrence; and `pmi`, which uses smoothed normalised pointwise mutual information computed from the same co-occurrence statistics. We also include three LLM baselines: zero-shot (LLM-Zero), few-shot (LLM-FewShot), and retrieval-augmented generation (LLM-RAG). All LLM methods use `llama3.1:8b` with deterministic decoding ($T = 0$) and predict component IDs from a provided candidate inventory rather than generating free-form labels, to ensure that outputs are comparable with the fixed gold component vocabulary used for Node-F1 and Edge-F1 evaluation.

We evaluate component selection using *Node-F1*, computed over predicted and gold component sets, and ordering using *Edge-F1*, computed over predicted and gold edges. For match-based acceptance, the threshold τ_{match} is selected separately for each affinity method using internal 5-fold cross-validation on the case base to maximise Node-F1. For detector-based acceptance, we evaluate a one-dimensional grid of score-quantile thresholds and choose τ_{det} to maximise failure-detection Node-F1. For rank_score (Sect. 3.3), we set $w_a = 0.8$ and $w_s = 0.2$ based on a coarse grid search.

Code and datasets used in the experiments (including LLM prompts, data splits and raw results) are publicly available on GitHub[3].

4.4 Results

Experiment results are shown in Table 1 and Table 2 for MultiWOZ and O*NET, respectively. Node-F1 evaluates what components are selected, while Edge-F1 evaluates how those components are sequenced. Results are averaged over five random seed runs (each seed samples new data for the case base and test data). For each seed, we sample a 200-case base and a disjoint 50-case test set from each dataset.

For brevity, we report results for three variants (unique combinations of affinity and solution acceptance methods i.e. Affinity/Accept. in result tables) of NDA, GSA and CARM: V1 (`embed_cos`/α) embedding similarity as affinity method with match-based acceptance; V2 (`condprob`/α) conditional probability as affinity with match-based acceptance; and V3 (`condprob/NTAD`) conditional probability with detector-based acceptance using NTAD for success/fail detection. V1 aligns with previous work that explored NDA and GSA [20], while V2 and V3 were generally the best-performing combinations for these techniques.

[3] https://github.com/ike01/cbr-fda.

Table 1. Node-F1 and Edge-F1 using MultiWOZ dataset. For NDA, GSA, and CARM, three variants (V1, V2, V3) based on affinity and solution acceptance methods are reported

Method	Affinity/Accept.	Node-F1	Edge-F1	Cases used
BM	–	0.321 ± 0.021	**0.110 ± 0.018**	1.000 ± 0.000
LLM-Zero	–	0.214 ± 0.015	0.011 ± 0.009	0.000 ± 0.000
LLM-FewShot	–	0.077 ± 0.010	0.010 ± 0.011	3.000 ± 0.000
LLM-RAG	–	0.349 ± 0.022	0.078 ± 0.025	3.000 ± 0.000
NDA (V1)	embed_cos/α	0.315 ± 0.018	0.068 ± 0.029	1.436 ± 0.289
NDA (V2)	condprob/α	0.319 ± 0.019	0.063 ± 0.030	2.072 ± 0.233
NDA (V3)	condprob/NTAD	0.314 ± 0.020	0.065 ± 0.030	3.136 ± 0.137
GSA (V1)	embed_cos/α	0.315 ± 0.018	0.068 ± 0.029	1.436 ± 0.289
GSA (V2)	condprob/α	0.319 ± 0.019	0.063 ± 0.030	2.072 ± 0.233
GSA (V3)	condprob/NTAD	0.314 ± 0.020	0.065 ± 0.030	3.136 ± 0.137
CARM (V1)	embed_cos/α	0.320 ± 0.027	0.087 ± 0.046	1.800 ± 1.071
CARM (V2)	condprob/α	**0.384 ± 0.020**	0.071 ± 0.036	2.684 ± 0.181
CARM (V3)	condprob/NTAD	0.363 ± 0.019	0.069 ± 0.030	3.340 ± 0.107

On MultiWOZ (Table 1), CARM outperformed GSA equivalents, indicating that cardinality-aware construction benefits. CARM (V2) achieves the highest Node-F1 (0.384) and improves substantially over GSA (V2) (0.319). Among all methods, BM remains strongest on Edge-F1 (0.11), while LLM-RAG is competitive on Node-F1 (0.349). CARM reused the most cases for constructing solutions (Cases used 3.34).

On O*NET (Table 2), BM and CARM (V2) have the best Node-F1 scores. On the surface, BM exhibits surprisingly strong performance. However, because we retained only highly ranked skills in each solution, the variability of the solution sets may have been reduced. As a result, an occupation that is similar in title and description may have a relatively high probability of containing the same solution components (skills). Once again, CARM clearly outperforms GSA/NDA equivalents. Across both datasets, the same directional trend is observed for stable-matching family methods: V2/V3 are consistently stronger than V1, supporting the role of affinity/acceptance design in reuse quality. NDA and GSA exhibited identical performance on MultiWOZ and very similar performance overall, which indicates that deferred acceptance in the stable-matching step provided no measurable advantage under our experimental conditions.

Overall, these results support the proposed framework, particularly regarding the selection of appropriate components for reuse. However, how candidate solutions should be structured requires further investigation. The consistent gains of CARM (V2 and V3) indicate that cardinality-aware optimisation is a promising direction for problems with multi-component solutions.

Table 2. Node-F1 and Edge-F1 using O*NET dataset. For NDA, GSA, and CARM, three variants (V1, V2, V3) based on affinity and solution acceptance methods are reported

Method	Affinity/Accept.	Node-F1	Edge-F1	Cases used
BM	–	**0.622 ± 0.026**	**0.314 ± 0.027**	1.000 ± 0.000
LLM-Zero	–	0.291 ± 0.018	0.025 ± 0.004	0.000 ± 0.000
LLM-FewShot	–	0.352 ± 0.020	0.077 ± 0.011	3.000 ± 0.000
LLM-RAG	–	0.599 ± 0.028	0.102 ± 0.023	3.000 ± 0.000
NDA (V1)	embed_cos/α	0.503 ± 0.033	0.231 ± 0.025	1.420 ± 0.102
NDA (V2)	condprob/α	0.590 ± 0.030	0.276 ± 0.034	2.040 ± 0.196
NDA (V3)	condprob/NTAD	0.603 ± 0.027	0.293 ± 0.015	3.120 ± 0.105
GSA (V1)	embed_cos/α	0.512 ± 0.035	0.235 ± 0.039	1.420 ± 0.130
GSA (V2)	condprob/α	0.591 ± 0.030	0.278 ± 0.035	2.040 ± 0.198
GSA (V3)	condprob/NTAD	0.603 ± 0.027	0.295 ± 0.019	3.120 ± 0.105
CARM (V1)	embed_cos/α	0.524 ± 0.031	0.252 ± 0.011	1.760 ± 0.115
CARM (V2)	condprob/α	**0.622 ± 0.025**	0.311 ± 0.031	2.640 ± 0.092
CARM (V3)	condprob/NTAD	0.620 ± 0.024	0.305 ± 0.029	3.320 ± 0.009

5 Discussion

Structure of Solutions: Edge-F1 is consistently low, but this result should be interpreted with care. In our evaluation, Edge-F1 measures overlap in adjacent directed transitions derived from the ordered solution sequence, rather than a richer notion of solution structure. For O*NET (Table 2), the ordering of skills appears to carry limited semantic meaning and is often highly regular across solutions. As a result, structural differences between methods are less informative, and BM is advantaged because, whenever it retrieves the correct components, it is also likely to reproduce the corresponding local ordering.

In MultiWOZ (Table 1), ordering is more consequential because task-oriented dialogue requires actions such as requesting missing slots, confirming constraints, and presenting results in a coherent sequence. At the same time, not all local permutations are equally important: for example, requests for `bookday` and `bookpeople` in a hotel-booking dialogue may occur in either order without materially affecting solution quality. This may partly explain why Edge-F1 remains low even when node-level performance is reasonable. Overall, the results suggest that selecting the correct components is currently easier than reconstructing their ordered transitions, and that stronger methods for representing flexible or partially ordered solution structure remain an important direction for future work.

Impact of Case-Base Size: To better understand the effect of case-base scarcity and abundance on performance, we repeated the evaluation using two additional case-base sizes for BM, which served as a strong baseline in our setting, and for the V2 and V3 variants of the GSA family, which performed strongly in the earlier experiments. For both datasets, we considered a small case base of 50 cases with 50 test cases and a medium case base with 200 cases and 50 test cases. We also considered a larger case base of 500 cases for MultiWOZ and 388 cases for O*NET, each again with 50 test cases; the latter corresponds to the largest feasible training set in O*NET, which contains 438 instances in total. We report Node-F1 averaged over five runs with different random seeds in Table 3.

Table 3. Comparison of reuse methods and selected variants on different case-base sizes. The best result for each case-base size category per dataset is in **bold**

Case-base size	Method with variant	MultiWOZ Node-F1	O*Net Node-F1
Small	BM	0.306 ± 0.015	0.510 ± 0.026
	GSA (V2)	0.292 ± 0.033	0.505 ± 0.014
	GSA (V3)	0.293 ± 0.025	**0.524 ± 0.025**
	CARM (V2)	**0.324 ± 0.037**	0.510 ± 0.026
	CARM (V3)	**0.324 ± 0.038**	0.521 ± 0.017
Medium	BM	0.321 ± 0.021	**0.622 ± 0.026**
	GSA (V2)	0.319 ± 0.019	0.591 ± 0.030
	GSA (V3)	0.314 ± 0.020	0.603 ± 0.027
	CARM (V2)	**0.384 ± 0.020**	**0.622 ± 0.025**
	CARM (V3)	0.363 ± 0.019	0.620 ± 0.024
Large	BM	0.328 ± 0.050	**0.572 ± 0.035**
	GSA (V2)	0.331 ± 0.043	0.533 ± 0.030
	GSA (V3)	0.338 ± 0.040	0.565 ± 0.033
	CARM (V2)	0.345 ± 0.049	0.571 ± 0.036
	CARM (V3)	**0.367 ± 0.043**	0.555 ± 0.034

On MultiWOZ, the CARM variants continued the trend observed in Table 1, remaining the strongest-performing methods across case-base sizes. On O*NET, although the differences are small, the effect of case-base scarcity is more visible for BM. With a case base of 50, GSA (V3) performs best, CARM (V2) matches BM, and CARM (V3) outperforms BM. At a case-base size of 200, BM is the joint best with CARM (V2) as also reported in Table 1. When the case base is increased to 388, BM becomes slightly stronger than CARM (V2). This pattern is intuitive: as the case base becomes denser, the likelihood of retrieving a highly suitable reuse instance increases, reducing the benefit of considering additional neighbourhood cases.

Affinity and Acceptance Methods: Table 4 analyses CARM on MultiWOZ across all affinity methods (`embed_cos`, `pmi`, and `condprob`) and solution-acceptance strategies, including match-based acceptance (α) and detector-based acceptance (NCD, WNCD, END, and NTAD). The best result is achieved by `condprob` with α, corresponding to CARM (V2), with a Node-F1 of 0.385. The second-best result is obtained by `condprob` with NTAD, corresponding to CARM (V3).

Table 4. Node-F1 of CARM on MultiWOZ for solution acceptance methods using different element affinity methods

Affinity Method	Match-based acceptance (α)	Detector-based acceptance			
		NCD	WNCD	END	NTAD
embed_cos	0.320 ± 0.051	0.325 ± 0.034	0.325 ± 0.034	0.325 ± 0.034	0.315 ± 0.015
pmi	0.320 ± 0.044	0.325 ± 0.034	0.325 ± 0.034	0.330 ± 0.036	0.330 ± 0.046
condprob	**0.385 ± 0.046**	0.326 ± 0.034	0.326 ± 0.034	0.330 ± 0.036	0.364 ± 0.035

NCD and WNCD show nearly identical performance across affinity types, suggesting that the additional weighting signal used in neighbourhood-consistency estimation had little effect in this setting. By contrast, NTAD is substantially more sensitive to affinity choice, achieving its best score with `condprob` (i.e. CARM (V3)) and the overall worst score with `embed_cos`. This pattern suggests that affinity modelling becomes more important when acceptance decisions depend on structurally informed detector signals rather than a fixed matching threshold.

6 Conclusion

This paper presented a general framework for case-based adaptation that unifies heterogeneous solution structures through solution graphs, supports domain-agnostic reuse through affinity-driven matching, and improves solution construction through cardinality-aware optimisation. Across the experiments, CARM with conditional-probability affinity and match-based acceptance achieved the strongest overall performance. More broadly, the results show that the proposed framework is effective at selecting suitable components for reuse, while also highlighting that reconstructing solution structure, particularly ordered transitions, remains more challenging. The experiments also revealed that the interaction between affinity modelling and acceptance strategy is important. In particular, conditional-probability affinity was consistently strong, and its advantage was most pronounced in settings where acceptance depended on richer neighbourhood-structure signals. At the same time, simple retrieval-based baselines remained competitive, especially in settings where solution ordering carries limited semantic meaning or where the case base is sufficiently dense.

Future work will focus on three directions. First, retrieval should be strengthened, as the current system relies on SBERT-based retrieval with uniform weighting, and stronger retrieval may further improve reuse quality. Second, solution structure requires deeper investigation, especially with respect to ordering, flexible or partially ordered solutions, and domains in which action order is more strictly constrained, such as robot action planning. Third, the interaction between affinity functions and acceptance methods should be studied more systematically in order to better understand when richer structural signals provide the greatest benefit.

Acknowledgment. The authors acknowledge Robert Gordon University for providing research facilities and support for this work.

Declaration on Generative AI. During the preparation of this work, the author(s) used Generative AI tool (ChatGPT) to paraphrase and reword parts of the manuscript. After using this tool/service, the author(s) reviewed and edited the content as needed and take(s) full responsibility for the publication's content.

References

1. Bishop, C.M., Nasrabadi, N.M.: Pattern Recognition and Machine Learning, vol. 4. Springer (2006)
2. Cunningham, P., Smyth, B.: Case-based reasoning in scheduling: reusing solution components. Int. J. Prod. Res. **35**(11), 2947–2962 (1997)
3. Fuchs, B., Lieber, J., Mille, A., Napoli, A.: Differential adaptation: an operational approach to adaptation for solving numerical problems with CBR. Knowl.-Based Syst. **68**, 103–114 (2014)
4. Hanney, K., Keane, M.T.: Learning adaptation rules from a case-base. In: Smith, I., Faltings, B. (eds.) EWCBR 1996. LNCS, vol. 1168, pp. 179–192. Springer, Heidelberg (1996). https://doi.org/10.1007/BFb0020610
5. Hastie, T., Tibshirani, R., Friedman, J.: The elements of statistical learning (2009)
6. Hatalis, K., Christou, D., Kondapalli, V.: Review of case-based reasoning for LLM agents: theoretical foundations, architectural components, and cognitive integration. arXiv preprint arXiv:2504.06943 (2025)
7. Hu, J., Qi, J., Peng, Y.: New CBR adaptation method combining with problem-solution relational analysis for mechanical design. Comput. Ind. **66**, 41–51 (2015)
8. Jalali, V., Leake, D., Forouzandehmehr, N.: Learning and applying case adaptation rules for classification: an ensemble approach. In: IJCAI, pp. 4874–4878 (2017)
9. Leake, D.B.: Case-Based Reasoning: Experiences, Lessons and Future Directions. MIT Press (1996)
10. Liao, C.K., Liu, A., Chao, Y.S.: A machine learning approach to case adaptation. In: IEEE First International Conference on Artificial Intelligence and Knowledge Engineering (AIKE), pp. 106–109. IEEE (2018)
11. Liu, F.T., Ting, K.M., Zhou, Z.H.: Isolation forest. In: Eighth IEEE International Conference on Data Mining, pp. 413–422. IEEE (2008)
12. Lowe, D.G.: Similarity metric learning for a variable-kernel classifier. Neural Comput. **7**(1), 72–85 (1995)
13. Malburg, L., Hotz, M., Bergmann, R.: Improving complex adaptations in process-oriented case-based reasoning by applying rule-based adaptation. In: International Conference on Case-Based Reasoning, pp. 50–66. Springer (2024)

14. Manning, C.D.: Introduction to Information Retrieval. Syngress Publishing (2008)
15. Manzoni, S., Sartori, F., Vizzari, G.: Substitutional adaptation in case-based reasoning: a general framework applied to p-truck curing. Appl. Artif. Intell. **21**(4–5), 427–442 (2007)
16. McSherry, D.: An adaptation heuristic for case-based estimation. In: Smyth, B., Cunningham, P. (eds.) EWCBR 1998. LNCS, vol. 1488, pp. 184–195. Springer, Heidelberg (1998). https://doi.org/10.1007/BFb0056332
17. Müller, G., Bergmann, R.: Generalization of workflows in process-oriented case-based reasoning. In: FLAIRS, pp. 391–396 (2015)
18. Munoz-Avila, H., Cox, M.T.: Case-based plan adaptation: an analysis and review. IEEE Intell. Syst. **23**(4), 75–81 (2008)
19. Murphy, K.P.: Machine Learning: A Probabilistic Perspective. MIT Press (2012)
20. Nkisi-Orji, I., Palihawadana, C., Wiratunga, N., Wijekoon, A., Corsar, D.: Failure-driven transformational case reuse of explanation strategies in cloodcbr. In: International Conference on Case-Based Reasoning, pp. 279–293. Springer (2023)
21. Reimers, N., Gurevych, I.: Sentence-bert: sentence embeddings using siamese bert-networks. arXiv preprint arXiv:1908.10084 (2019)
22. Wettschereck, D., Aha, D.W.: Weighting features. In: Veloso, M., Aamodt, A. (eds.) ICCBR 1995. LNCS, vol. 1010, pp. 347–358. Springer, Heidelberg (1995). https://doi.org/10.1007/3-540-60598-3_31
23. Wilke, W., Vollrath, I., Althoff, K.D., Bergmann, R.: A framework for learning adaptation knowledge based on knowledge light approaches. In: Proceedings of the Fifth German Workshop on Case-Based Reasoning, pp. 235–242 (1997)
24. Yan, A., Cheng, Z.: A review of the development and future challenges of case-based reasoning. Appl. Sci. **14**(16), 7130 (2024)
25. Ye, X., Leake, D., Jalali, V., Crandall, D.J.: Learning adaptations for case-based classification: a neural network approach. In: Sánchez-Ruiz, A.A., Floyd, M.W. (eds.) ICCBR 2021. LNCS (LNAI), vol. 12877, pp. 279–293. Springer, Cham (2021). https://doi.org/10.1007/978-3-030-86957-1_19
26. Ye, X., Zhao, Z., Leake, D., Wang, X., Crandall, D.: Applying the case difference heuristic to learn adaptations from deep network features. arXiv preprint arXiv:2107.07095 (2021)

Case-Based Adaptation and Retrieval-Augmented Self-reflection for Multi-label Classification

Lasal Jayawardena[1(✉)], Nirmalie Wiratunga[1], Ikechukwu Nkisi-Orji[1], and Darren Nicol[2]

[1] The Robert Gordon University, Aberdeen, UK
{l.jayawardena,n.wiratunga,i.o.nkisi-orji}@rgu.ac.uk
[2] William Nicol (Aberdeen) Limited, Aberdeen, UK
darren.nicol@williamnicol.co.uk

Abstract. Large language models (LLMs) can perform multi-label classification, but they do not provide calibrated label-wise scores, and token probabilities are a poor confidence proxy. This makes label set identification difficult because a fixed threshold cannot be assumed. We therefore use prompt-based numerical and Likert scoring to derive per-label signals for thresholding. Fine-tuning LLMs at scale is not cost-efficient in industrial settings, making post-hoc thresholding techniques essential, but these cannot be directly applied without calibrated scores. To address this, we propose two complementary case-based reasoning (CBR) mechanisms built on Rapt (Retrieval-Augmented Post-hoc Thresholding). First, **Reflective Prompting** feeds aggregated neighbourhood knowledge back to the LLM as external evidence, derived from the model's own performance on similar past cases rather than from individual neighbours as in few-shot prompting. This neighbourhood context informs an iterative generate-refine prompting cycle, allowing the LLM to revise its label scores across multiple passes. Second, **Score Adaptation** adjusts prompt-elicited LLM scores using ground-truth residuals from retrieved neighbours, requiring no additional LLM calls. Experiments on the WM Nicol industrial multi-label document classification dataset show that score adaptation substantially improves zero-shot LLM classification. The strongest Rapt configuration, combining adaptation with iterative Self-Reflection, achieves 0.803 Micro-F1 and 0.737 Macro-F1, exceeding few-shot baselines at lower token cost.

Keywords: Multi-Label Classification · Large Language Models · Retrieval Augmented Generation · Thresholding · Self-Reflection

1 Introduction

Multi-label document classification, assigning multiple relevant labels to a single document, is a critical component of intelligent document processing (IDP) pipelines [2]. In such systems, classification is a key routing step: its output

L. Malburg and K. Bach (Eds.): ICCBR 2026, LNAI 16780, pp. 67–82, 2027.
https://doi.org/10.1007/978-3-032-33865-5_5

determines which downstream extraction tasks are executed, making errors at this stage costly. A false negative prevents the relevant extraction task from running; a false positive triggers an inappropriate prompt, producing irrelevant fields and increasing verification effort.

The core technical challenge lies not in learning good label rankings, since modern classifiers already produce informative per-label scores, but in converting those scores into a final label set by deciding which labels to include in the prediction. Per-class optimal thresholds can range from below 0.1 to above 0.7, yet in practice the most common default is a fixed global threshold of $\tau = 0.5$. This mismatch is especially acute in industrial settings where label cardinality varies across instances and label co-occurrence patterns differ across regions of the instance space [7]. This challenge is compounded by label imbalance, a common characteristic in industrial settings, where standard thresholds tend to favour over-represented classes, making classifier confidence unreliable for rare or ambiguous document types.

Large language models (LLMs) have emerged as versatile alternatives for text classification, offering zero-shot capability without task-specific training. In multi-label settings, however, direct binary label assignment can be too coarse for reliable set prediction. We therefore elicit graded per-label scores, which preserve more decision information for constructing the final label set. However, these scores still require thresholding to determine the final label set. Recent work shows that LLMs exhibit fundamentally different multi-label behaviour from supervised task-specific classifiers, with token distributions becoming more concentrated on a single label as model scale increases [17].

Applying existing thresholding methods to LLMs is not straightforward. Traditional supervised classifiers, metric learners, fine-tuned transformers, produce embeddings and calibrated logit scores as a natural byproduct of their architecture. For LLMs, however, extracting hidden states is impractical: most models are accessed through APIs where internal representations are not exposed, and even for open-source models, extracting and calibrating hidden-layer embeddings requires custom infrastructure not available in standard deployment settings. Furthermore, fine-tuning LLMs is expensive: it demands significant GPU resources, instruction-formatted training data, and risks catastrophic forgetting, making it impractical for domain-specific industrial tasks with limited labelled data. A prompt-driven approach is therefore the most practical alternative: we elicit per-label confidence scores via structured prompts (percentage, verbal, or numerical rating scales) that the LLM produces as text output, avoiding hidden-state extraction and fine-tuning entirely.

RAPT (Retrieval-Augmented Post-hoc Thresholding) was introduced in our earlier work as a case-based reasoning (CBR) wrapper for metric-learning and transformer-based classifiers [12]. For each query document, RAPT retrieves similar prior classification instances from a case base, applies a local adaptation rule that corrects the query's scores using neighbourhood residuals, and produces the final label set via dynamic thresholding. Because RAPT operates post-hoc on predicted scores without requiring any separately trained component, it is a natural candidate for bridging the calibration gap identified above. In this work, we investigate whether these case-based adaptation principles transfer to LLM-based multi-label classification. Accordingly we make the following contributions.

1. An extension of RAPT's neighbourhood-based score adaptation from supervised classifiers to prompt-elicited LLM confidence scores, calibrating LLM outputs without additional model calls or fine-tuning.
2. Self-Reflection Prompting, a retrieval-augmented generate-refine mechanism that feeds aggregated case-based evidence back to the LLM, enabling iterative score revision grounded in external neighbourhood feedback rather than internal self-critique.
3. Evaluation on a representative industrial document processing dataset from a real-world information extraction pipeline, across two LLMs, four scoring scales, and multiple thresholding and prompting regimes, including label-anonymised settings.

2 Related Work

Converting real-valued scores to label sets is a fundamental step in multi-label classification [24]. A global threshold ($\tau = 0.5$) is the simplest approach but ignores per-class score distributions; label-specific strategies such as SCut [27] and gap-based cutoffs such as MCut [15] improve upon this default but all such strategies remain static at test time [7]. Instance-adaptive methods learn to estimate per-instance cutoffs [23], but typically require additional training or model modification. RAPT provides instance-adaptive thresholds through case-based retrieval without additional training [12]. Key to RAPT is the construction of an adaptation case base from the training data, with each case pairing predicted label scores with the corresponding ground truth label set. In this work, we study how to construct such an adaptation case base for LLMs, pairing elicited per-label scores with ground truth label sets to form reusable adaptation knowledge.

LLMs can perform multi-label classification through prompting, either via binary yes/no judgements per label or by eliciting confidence scores on verbal or numerical scales [5]. However, recent work reveals that autoregressive LLMs exhibit fundamentally different multi-label behaviour from fine-tuned classifiers: token distributions show lower entropy and higher single-label confidence at each generation step, with models tending to suppress all but one label [17]. This makes mapping scores to label selection decisions particularly challenging for LLMs. Deriving calibrated confidence scores from generative LLMs remains an open problem: the generative architecture inherently lacks direct class-level probabilities, and approaches such as token-level marginalisation [22] or post-hoc calibration of elicited scores [19] have been proposed, though none address instance-adaptive thresholding for multi-label classification.

A growing body of work addresses the miscalibration of LLM confidence estimates. Surveys [8] identify systematic overconfidence in LLM probability estimates, with RLHF training producing particularly spiky token distributions [16].

Calibration pipelines combining logit-based scores with post-hoc methods have been explored for single-label settings [11], and QA-calibration methods provide formal guarantees for elicited confidence scores [19]. However, these methods focus on single-label classification or question answering; the multi-label setting, where per-instance label cardinality varies and labels are not mutually exclusive, introduces additional challenges that existing calibration methods do not address.

Self-Refine [18] showed that LLMs can iteratively improve their outputs through feedback and revision, with gains reported across tasks such as code generation, reasoning, and text generation. However, a recent survey of self-correction methods [13] found that such improvements are much less reliable when feedback is generated internally. Without external feedback, LLMs may exhibit self-bias and can even degrade their original outputs. This has motivated approaches such as CRITIC [9], which incorporate external tool-interactive feedback to support verification and refinement. Together, these findings suggest that effective iterative refinement depends not merely on repeated revision, but on the availability of informative external feedback signals. In this work, such feedback is provided by neighbourhood knowledge retrieved from the adaptation case base, which guides iterative refinement of the LLM's per-label scores.

The kNN-LM [14] demonstrated that interpolating a language model with a kNN model over a data store improves perplexity without additional training, a principle conceptually related to our approach, though applied to language modelling rather than classification calibration. Emerging work has begun to explore CBR–LLM synergies from complementary angles. CBR-RAG (Case-Based Reasoning Retrieval-Augmented Generation), which draws on CBR's vocabulary, case base, and similarity knowledge containers to retrieve relevant cases for use as LLM context [26]. One line of work addresses the knowledge acquisition bottleneck by prompting LLMs to generate vocabulary and case base content for CBR systems [4], but does not use CBR to improve LLM outputs. Another complementary direction uses LLMs to perform similarity assessment and adaptation over retrieved cases for medical triage [25]. Although access to a nearest-neighbour case improved classification accuracy, LLM-based retrieval matched external k-NN selection only 20–28% of the time, and the model hallucinated case attributes that required manual filtering. A recent research manifesto [3] consolidates these findings, identifying prompt-based adaptation accuracy, output validation, and the absence of robust external retrieval mechanisms as key open challenges for hybrid CBR–LLM systems. Our Self-Reflection Prompting extends this line of work: instead of retrieving documents for knowledge grounding, we retrieve adaptation cases to provide calibration evidence that the LLM uses to revise its own confidence scores, thus making use of CBR's retrieve, reuse and adapt stages.

3 Methodology

We present four methodological contributions: (1) LLM scoring methods for multi-label classification; (2) a case base constructed from the training set, where each instance stores the LLM generated label scores together with the ground truth multi-label assignment for external feedback; (3) Self-Reflection Prompting for iterative score revision with external case-based feedback; and (4) RAPT score adaptation and thresholding of the final LLM generated solution. Figure 1 summarises the main stages of the framework: case embedding for retrieval, the iterative generate-refine prompting phase, and subsequent solution adaptation for final multi-label prediction. A key component of the methodology is the construction of a case base from the validation dataset. This accumulated case knowledge is then exploited within the iterative generate-refine cycle to enable prompt-based self-reflection.

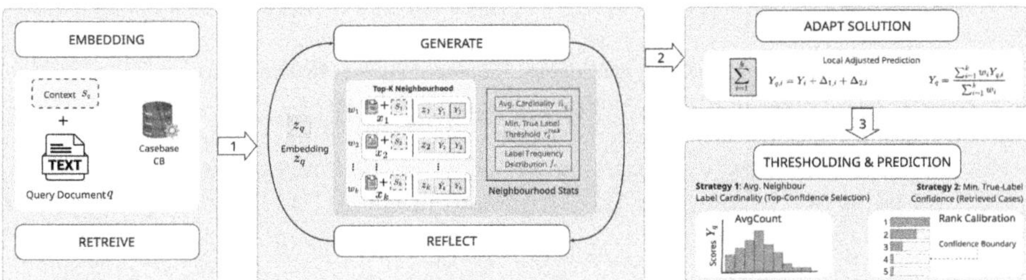

Fig. 1. Case-based Self-Reflection pipeline. A query document is embedded and its top-K neighbours are retrieved from the case base. Two paths, Self-Reflection Prompting (iterative LLM score revision using neighbourhood statistics as external feedback) and Score Adaptation (Δ_1/Δ_2 correction using ground-truth residuals), feed into RAPT thresholding (AvgCount or RankCal) to produce the final multi-label output.

3.1 LLM Multi-label Scoring

Given a document d and a set of candidate labels $\mathcal{L} = \{l_1, \ldots, l_C\}$, where $C = |\mathcal{L}|$, the LLM is prompted to produce a score vector $\mathbf{s} \in [0, 1]^C$. Figure 2 illustrates the prompt structure and score mapping for each scale. We evaluate four scoring scales:

We consider four prompt based scoring schemes for obtaining per label confidence scores from the LLM. In the *five point verbal scale*, the model assigns one of five verbal categories, *Definitely Not*, *Probably Not*, *Possibly*, *Probably*, and *Definitely*, which are mapped to scores in $\{0, 0.25, 0.5, 0.75, 1\}$. In the *ten point numerical scale*, labels are rated on a 1 to 10 scale and linearly normalised to $[0, 1]$. In the *percentage scale*, the model outputs a confidence percentage between 0 and 100, again normalised to $[0, 1]$. In the *binary scale*, the model makes a direct yes or no decision for each label, producing scores in $\{0, 1\}$.

3.2 Case Base Creation for Self-reflection Prompting

A case base $\mathcal{CB} = \{(e_i, \mathbf{s}_i, \mathbf{y}_i)\}_{i=1}^{N}$ is constructed from validation data, where e_i is the document embedding, $\mathbf{s}_i \in [0, 1]^C$ is the model's predicted score vector,

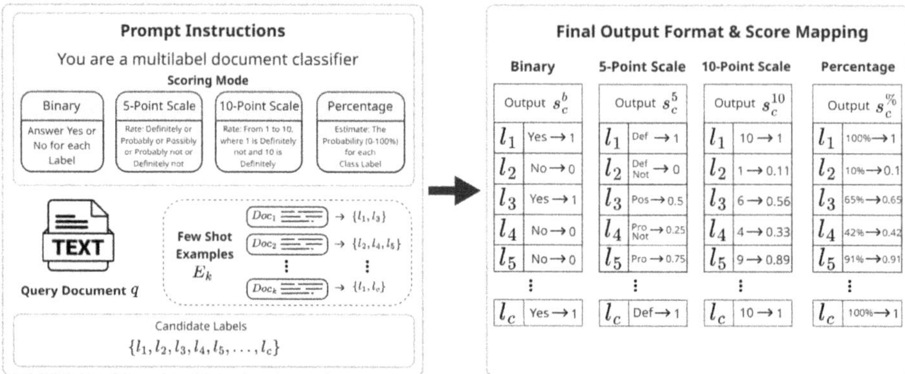

Fig. 2. LLM multi-label scoring prompts. A structured prompt comprising system instructions, a scoring mode, optional few-shot examples $\mathcal{E}_k$, the query document, and the candidate labels is processed by the LLM. Depending on the selected scoring mode, the LLM produces a per-label score using one of four output formats: Binary ($s_c^{(b)}$), Five-point ($s_c^{(5)}$), Ten-point ($s_c^{(10)}$), or Percentage ($s_c^{(\%)}$). These outputs are then mapped to the interval $[0, 1]$.

and $\mathbf{y}_i \in \{0,1\}^C$ is the ground-truth label vector. For LLM-based classifiers, the LLM's internal representations are inaccessible through standard APIs, so the embedding e_i is instead obtained from a separate pre-trained sentence encoder applied to the document text. This decouples the retrieval space from the scoring model, which is an intended design choice, to accommodate both locally run and hosted LLMs. The score vector $\mathbf{s}_i$ is the LLM's prompt-elicited output. For a query document q, we compute its embedding e_q and retrieve the top K nearest neighbours, denoted by $\mathcal{N}_K(q)$, from the case base using cosine similarity. Each retrieved neighbour $i \in \mathcal{N}_K(q)$ is associated with a similarity weight w_i, which is used to compute the neighbourhood summary statistics for reflection.

3.3 Neighbourhood Feedback for Generate-Refine Prompt Cycles

We implement self-reflection as a two-stage generate-reflect cycle to refine LLM-based multi-label predictions. For a query document q, the LLM first generates an initial score vector $s_q^{(1)}$. We then retrieve the top K neighbouring cases and summarise their label behaviour using neighbourhood statistics. These statistics serve as external case based evidence in the reflection step, enabling the LLM to revise its initial scores using signals derived from similar past cases.

Given the K nearest neighbours retrieved from the case base, we compute three neighbourhood aggregated statistics that serve as external feedback for reflection. The first is the expected label cardinality $\bar{n}_q$, defined as the similarity weighted average number of active labels across the retrieved neighbours. The second is the rank threshold τ_q^{rank}, defined as the similarity weighted estimate of the minimum true label score in the neighbourhood and used as a confidence boundary between likely relevant and irrelevant labels. The third is a label frequency distribution f_q, where each component $f_q[c] = \sum_{i \in \mathcal{N}_K(q)} \frac{w_i}{\sum_j w_j} y_{i,c}$ denotes the similarity weighted frequency of label, c, across the retrieved neighbours. Together, these statistics provide a compact summary of the local label structure around the query.

The Generate-Reflect cycle uses the neighbourhood statistics as fixed external feedback across all refinement iterations. In the first iteration, the Generate step conditions only on the query document q and produces an initial score proposal $\tilde{\mathbf{s}}_q^{(1)}$. From the second iteration onwards, it additionally conditions on the refined score vector from the previous pass, enabling progressive revision of the model's confidence estimates. At each pass, the resulting proposal $\tilde{\mathbf{s}}_q^{(p)}$ is then passed to the Reflect step, where the LLM receives the original document together with the neighbourhood summary $(\bar{n}_q, \tau_q^{\text{rank}}, f_q)$ and revises the scores in light of the local label structure of similar past cases. After P iterations, the procedure returns a final refined score vector $\mathbf{s}_q^{(P)}$, which is subsequently passed to the thresholding stage to obtain the predicted label set. The overall process is summarised in Algorithm 1.

Algorithm 1. Iterative Generate–Reflect Cycle with Neighbourhood Evidence

Require: Query document q, case base $\mathcal{CB}$, neighbourhood size K, number of iterations P

Ensure: Final refined score vector $\mathbf{s}_q^{(P)}$

```
Compute query embedding e_q
Retrieve the top K neighbours N_K(q) from CB
Compute neighbourhood statistics (n̄_q, τ_q^rank, f_q) from N_K(q)
for p = 1 to P do
  Generate
    if p = 1 then
        Obtain score proposal s̃_q^(p) ← LLM(q)
    else
        Obtain score proposal s̃_q^(p) ← LLM(q, s_q^(p-1))
    end if
  Reflect
    Revise using neighbourhood evidence:
        s_q^(p) ← LLM(q, s̃_q^(p), n̄_q, τ_q^rank, f_q)
end for
return s_q^(P)
```

3.4 RAPT: Score Adaptation and Thresholding

RAPT (Retrieval-Augmented Post-hoc Thresholding) is a model-agnostic CBR wrapper that can be applied post hoc to any classifier producing embeddings and per-label scores. It operates through three stages: case base construction, retrieval, and dynamic thresholding. The casebase creation and retrieval infrastructure is shared with Self-Reflection Prompting (Sect. 3.3). In this section, we focus on dynamic thresholding, which adapts generated scores to rank candidate labels and uses neighbourhood knowledge about typical label patterns in the local space to determine the final label set.

Score Adaptation (Δ_1/Δ_2). RAPT can *adapt the scores themselves* using the classical CBR adaptation step. For each neighbour i, we compute a predicted shift $\Delta_{1,i} = \mathbf{s}_q - \mathbf{s}_i$ (how the query's scores differ from the neighbour's predictions) and a residual correction $\Delta_{2,i} = \mathbf{y}_i - \mathbf{s}_i$ (how the neighbour's predictions deviated from its ground truth). The locally adjusted prediction for neighbour i is:

$$\mathbf{y}_{q,i} = \mathbf{y}_i + \Delta_{1,i} + \Delta_{2,i} = \mathbf{s}_q + 2(\mathbf{y}_i - \mathbf{s}_i)$$

The adapted score is the similarity-weighted average across all neighbours, clipped to $[0, 1]$:

$$\mathbf{s}_q^{\text{adapt}} = \text{clip}\left(\sum_{i \in \mathcal{N}_K(q)} \frac{w_i}{\sum_j w_j} \cdot \mathbf{y}_{q,i},\ 0,\ 1 \right) \tag{1}$$

The adapted scores $\mathbf{s}_q^{\text{adapt}}$ replace the raw scores $\mathbf{s}_q$ and are then passed through any thresholding method (static τ, AvgCount, or RankCal). This adaptation corrects systematic biases in the LLM's scores: if the model consistently over-predicts a label, the neighbourhood residuals ($\mathbf{y}_i - \mathbf{s}_i < 0$) pull the score downward, and vice versa. Crucially, adaptation requires no additional LLM calls, it operates entirely on cached scores and ground-truth labels from the case base.

Dynamic Thresholding: AvgCount. The AvgCount strategy estimates the expected label cardinality from the weighted average number of positive labels in the neighbourhood:

$$\bar{n}_q = \sum_{i \in \mathcal{N}_K(q)} \frac{w_i}{\sum_j w_j} \cdot |\mathbf{y}_i|$$

where $|\mathbf{y}_i| = \sum_{c=1}^{C} y_{i,c}$ is the label cardinality of neighbour i. The final prediction selects the top $\lceil \bar{n}_q \rceil$ labels ranked by score:

$$\hat{\mathbf{y}}_q = \mathbb{1}\left[\text{rank}(s_{q,c}) \leq \lceil \bar{n}_q \rceil\right] \tag{2}$$

Dynamic Thresholding: RankCal. The Rank Calibration strategy derives a confidence threshold from the minimum true-label score observed across retrieved neighbours. For each neighbour i with at least one positive label, define the minimum confidence among its ground-truth positive labels:

$$\tau_i = \min_{c: y_{i,c}=1} s_{i,c}$$

The dynamic threshold is the similarity-weighted average of these minimum confidences:

$$\tau_q^{\text{rank}} = \sum_{i \in \mathcal{N}_K(q)} \frac{w_i}{\sum_j w_j} \cdot \tau_i$$

The final prediction applies this threshold:

$$\hat{\mathbf{y}}_q = \mathbb{1}\left[s_{q,c} \geq \tau_q^{\text{rank}}\right] \tag{3}$$

4 Evaluation

We conduct a comprehensive evaluation across the following axes:

- **Scoring scales** (4): Binary yes/no, 5-point verbal, 10-point numerical, percentage (Sect. 3.1).
- **Thresholding methods** (8): Four base strategies (fixed $\tau = 0.50$, fixed $\tau = 0.60$, RAPT$_{\#}$/AvgCount Eq. 2, and RAPT$_{\geq}$/RankCal Eq. 3) are each evaluated with and without ADAPT+ score adaptation (Eq. 1), which applies Δ_1/Δ_2 neighbourhood residual correction to raw LLM scores before thresholding, yielding eight combinations in total.
- **Prompting regimes** (4): Zero-shot, few-shot ($k \in \{1, 3, 5\}$), single-pass Self-Reflection, and iterative Self-Reflection (up to 5 passes, with and without justification).
- **Label anonymisation**: All zero-shot, few-shot, Self-Reflection, and iterative experiments are repeated on an anonymised variant of the dataset where class labels are replaced with generic identifiers (`Label_1`, ..., `Label_11`), removing semantic information from label names while keeping document text unchanged.

Experiments are conducted on the **WM Nicol** dataset, a human-labelled representative subset of a real-world waste-management intelligent document processing (IDP) pipeline in which classification acts as the decision gate for downstream information extraction. In production, this pipeline processes hundreds of thousands of documents, where correct multi-label classification determines which extraction templates are applied to each document. The WM Nicol dataset comprises 11 document types and contains 1,134 training, 284 validation, and 355 test instances. Documents include cleanliness certificates, delivery notes, invoices, job tickets, purchase orders, SEPA notes, waste transfer notes, weighbridge tickets, and others. Label cardinality varies across documents, with some requiring 1–2 labels and others 3–5. Results are reported for two LLMs:

- **GPT-4o-mini** (`openai/gpt-4o-mini`): A compact, efficient model from OpenAI optimised for speed and cost [21].
- **GPT-OSS-20B** (`openai/gpt-oss-20b`): A 20-billion parameter open-source model, representing a smaller, locally-deployable alternative [20].

The CBR retrieval uses $k = 5$ nearest neighbours via a FAISS index built on top of text-embedding-3-small, a 1536-dimensional embedding model, from OpenAI[1]. In total, the evaluation comprises 832 experimental conditions: 208 unique combinations per model (25 zero-shot, 3 few-shot Binary baselines, and 180 iterative Self-Reflection configurations), evaluated on both original and anonymised labels across 2 models.

We report Micro-F1, Macro-F1, micro/macro precision and recall, and Hamming loss for every experimental condition. For brevity, the main tables include only Micro-F1, which reflects aggregate performance, and Macro-F1, which gives equal weight to each class; full results, including precision, recall, and Hamming loss, will be released separately. We emphasise Macro-F1 as the primary metric because it reveals whether a method handles rare document types, a critical requirement in industrial workflows where each document type triggers distinct downstream processing.

5 Results

We evaluate 832 experimental conditions and trace the progressive improvement as each methodological layer is added. Table 1 reports the single best configuration at each stage on the original dataset; the zero-shot and few-shot reference rows show Binary scoring only as a standard baseline, while all scoring scales were also evaluated for these regimes. Table 2 repeats this analysis on label-anonymised data.

The dominant finding in Table 1 is that the bottleneck in LLM multi-label performance is score calibration, not model capability. Score adaptation (Stage 3) produces the single largest incremental gain on both models (+7.1 pp Micro-F1 on GPT-4o-mini, +22.1 pp on GPT-OSS-20B), correcting systematic biases via neighbourhood residuals with zero additional LLM calls. Crucially, GPT-OSS-20B with adaptation (0.780) surpasses GPT-4o-mini without it (0.726), confirming that a mathematical correction on a weaker model outperforms a stronger model left uncalibrated. The final stage reveals two complementary optimisation paths: mathematical adaptation maximises Micro-F1 (peaking early at Pass 2), while iterative revision with justification improves Macro-F1 across multiple passes by targeting rare-class recall. Self-Reflection benefits GPT-4o-mini (+2.1 pp Macro-F1) but degrades GPT-OSS-20B (−1.5 pp Macro-F1), indicating a model capability threshold for LLM-driven revision. The best Micro-F1 and Macro-F1 configurations each surpass the strongest few-shot baseline ($k = 3$) by +5.7 pp and +4.2 pp respectively, without any in-context examples.

To test whether LLM classification fundamentally depends on semantic label names, and to simulate deployment with proprietary or arbitrary taxonomies where labels carry no inherent meaning, we repeat the evaluation on a label-anonymised variant of WM Nicol. Class names are replaced with generic identifiers (`Label_1`, ..., `Label_11`), removing all semantic information while keeping document text unchanged (Table 2).

[1] https://developers.openai.com/api/docs/models/text-embedding-3-small.

Table 1. Progressive improvement on WM Nicol (original labels). Each stage adds one methodological layer; the best configuration at that stage is reported. Best per model in **bold**.

Stage	Best Configuration	Mi-F1	Ma-F1
GPT-4o-mini			
1. Static threshold	Pct + $\tau = 0.50$	0.689	0.622
2. + Rapt threshold	5pt + Rapt$_{\#}$	0.726	0.658
3. + Score adaptation	Pct + Adapt+Rapt$_{\#}$	0.797	0.678
4. + Self-Reflection	SelfRef(Pct) + Adapt+Rapt$_{\#}$	0.799	0.699
5. + Iterative (best Mi)	**P2(plain) + Adapt+Rapt$_{\#}$**	**0.803**	0.702
5. + Iterative (best Ma)	P5(just.) + Rapt$_{\geq}$	0.775	**0.737**
Reference: Zero-shot	Binary	0.688	0.593
Reference: Few-shot	Binary $k = 3$	0.746	0.695
Reference: Few-shot	Binary $k = 5$	0.716	0.659
GPT-OSS-20B			
1. Static threshold	Pct + $\tau = 0.50$	0.511	0.435
2. + Rapt threshold	Pct + Rapt$_{\#}$	0.559	0.482
3. + Score adaptation	Pct + Adapt+Rapt$_{\#}$	0.780	0.600
4. + Self-Reflection	SelfRef(Pct) + Adapt+Rapt$_{\#}$	0.774	0.585
5. + Iterative	**P5(plain) + Adapt+Rapt$_{\#}$**	**0.789**	**0.671**
Reference: Zero-shot	Binary	0.591	0.499
Reference: Few-shot	Binary $k = 3$	0.507	0.430
Reference: Few-shot	Binary $k = 5$	0.518	0.426

The near-total collapse in Stage 1 is expected and confirms that LLM classification relies heavily on label semantics: the document text is identical, yet without meaningful class names the model cannot assign scores. Score adaptation (Stage 3) breaks this dependency: because neighbourhood residuals encode the ground-truth mapping between scores and labels, they substitute distributional knowledge for the semantic signal the LLM has lost, recovering to within 2–6% of original performance. Few-shot prompting also degrades severely (−20–30% Mi-F1 on GPT-4o-mini, −50–78% on GPT-OSS-20B), confirming that in-context examples cannot compensate for semantic loss and that their effectiveness is largely mediated through label names. With iterative refinement (Stage 5), the most robust configurations close to within 3–4% of original performance on both models. These findings have direct practical relevance: adaptation enables competitive classification on tasks where labels are proprietary codes or carry no inherent meaning, which is common in industry settings.

Table 2. Progressive improvement on label-anonymised WM Nicol. Class names replaced with generic identifiers (`Label_1` ... `Label_11`).

Stage	Best Configuration	Mi-F1	Ma-F1
GPT-4o-mini			
1. Static threshold	Pct + $\tau = 0.50$	0.059	0.047
2. + RAPT threshold	5pt + $\text{RAPT}_{\geq}$	0.133	0.130
3. + Score adaptation	10pt + $\text{ADAPT+RAPT}_{\#}$	0.750	0.487
4. + Self-Reflection	SelfRef(Pct) + $\text{ADAPT+RAPT}_{\#}$	0.746	0.463
5. + Iterative (best Mi)	**P4(plain) +** $\textbf{ADAPT+RAPT}_{\#}$	**0.775**	0.529
5. + Iterative (best Ma)	P4(just.) + $\text{ADAPT+RAPT}_{\geq}$	0.755	**0.588**
Reference: Zero-shot	Binary	0.125	0.102
Reference: Few-shot	Binary $k = 3$	0.600	0.508
Reference: Few-shot	Binary $k = 5$	0.503	0.413
GPT-OSS-20B			
1. Static threshold	Pct + $\tau = 0.50$	0.157	0.141
2. + RAPT threshold	5pt + $\text{RAPT}_{\#}$	0.186	0.116
3. + Score adaptation	5pt + $\text{ADAPT+RAPT}_{\#}$	0.761	0.503
4. + Self-Reflection	SelfRef(Pct) + $\text{ADAPT+RAPT}_{\#}$	0.755	0.505
5. + Iterative (best Mi)	**P3(just.) +** $\textbf{ADAPT+RAPT}_{\#}$	**0.763**	0.509
5. + Iterative (best Ma)	P3(just.) + $\text{ADAPT+RAPT}_{\geq}$	0.753	**0.579**
Reference: Zero-shot	Binary	0.012	0.022
Reference: Few-shot	Binary $k = 3$	0.111	0.183
Reference: Few-shot	Binary $k = 5$	0.260	0.208

6 Discussion

Prompt-elicited LLM scores exhibit systematic, document-dependent biases that vary by scoring scale: coarser scales discretise probabilities into a few levels, while continuous scales spread more evenly but with per-document offsets. Adaptation corrects these biases using the residual between the LLM's scores and ground truth on retrieved neighbours, which is why gains are largest where initial calibration is poorest and universally beneficial across all scales. Our approach preserves the LLM's document-level reasoning about label relevance; CBR provides post-hoc calibration infrastructure (score correction and instance-adaptive thresholding) rather than replacing the LLM's predictions. The LLM contributes semantic understanding of the document, while the case base contributes distributional knowledge about score-to-label mappings. Self-Reflection Prompting extends this by presenting neighbourhood statistics as external evidence for the LLM to reason about, instantiating CBR's revise step; its failure on weaker models suggests that effective revision requires sufficient instruction-following capability to integrate statistical evidence without over-correcting.

Table 3 profiles token usage and latency on GPT-4o-mini. The most striking observation is the cost–performance inversion between Self-Reflection and few-shot prompting. The best Micro-F1 configuration (SelfRef-P2, plain, + ADAPT+RAPT$_{\#}$: **0.803**) consumes only 1,624 tokens/doc, while the best few-shot baseline ($k = 3$, binary: 0.746) requires 4,556, 2.8× more tokens for 5.7 pp *lower* F1. Even the most expensive Self-Reflection variant (SelfRef-P5, justified: 4,844 tokens) uses 34% fewer tokens than few-shot $k = 5$ (7,199–7,379 tokens), which itself performs worse than $k = 3$. This gap is structural, not incidental: few-shot token budgets scale with $k \times C$ (number of examples × number of classes), so in real-world taxonomies with tens or hundreds of labels the cost grows rapidly. Self-Reflection avoids this scaling problem entirely because it feeds aggregated neighbourhood statistics, a fixed-size summary, rather than individual labelled examples.

Table 3. Inference profiling on WM Nicol (355 test documents, GPT-4o-mini). SelfRef-Pn denotes iterative Self-Reflection after n cumulative passes, with token usage and latency compounded across all passes; *plain* feeds only neighbourhood statistics, while *justified* additionally requests the LLM to provide reasoning for each score revision.

Methodology	Scoring	Tokens/doc	Latency (ms)	P95 (ms)	doc/s
Zero-shot	binary	588	412.3	678.5	2.43
Zero-shot	fivepoint	821	2098.7	2812.4	0.48
Zero-shot	tenpoint	792	2221.1	2911.7	0.45
Zero-shot	percentage	742	2173.6	2865.5	0.46
Few-shot ($k = 3$)	binary	4556	681.0	1081.1	1.47
Few-shot ($k = 3$)	fivepoint	4735	2122.3	2763.1	0.47
Few-shot ($k = 3$)	tenpoint	4701	2237.3	4561.5	0.45
Few-shot ($k = 3$)	percentage	4700	1988.0	2478.1	0.50
Few-shot ($k = 5$)	binary	7199	848.0	1916.6	1.18
Few-shot ($k = 5$)	fivepoint	7379	2947.5	6192.3	0.34
Few-shot ($k = 5$)	tenpoint	7341	2865.0	5002.8	0.35
Few-shot ($k = 5$)	percentage	7341	2261.5	3074.9	0.44
SelfRef-P2 (plain)	percentage	1624	2498.3	3247.8	0.40
SelfRef-P3 (plain)	percentage	2513	2651.7	3447.2	0.38
SelfRef-P4 (plain)	percentage	3402	2812.4	3656.1	0.36
SelfRef-P5 (plain)	percentage	4291	2968.9	3859.6	0.34
SelfRef-P2 (justified)	percentage	1764	3688.4	4794.9	0.27
SelfRef-P3 (justified)	percentage	2792	3892.1	5059.7	0.26
SelfRef-P4 (justified)	percentage	3819	4103.5	5334.6	0.24
SelfRef-P5 (justified)	percentage	4844	4298.7	5588.3	0.23

Score adaptation (Adapt+) represents the most cost-efficient improvement available: it lifts zero-shot percentage from 0.689 to **0.797** Micro-F1 with zero additional LLM calls and minimal overhead (<50 ms/doc for FAISS retrieval and thresholding combined), making it effectively negligible at inference time. Binary scoring is the fastest modality (∼412 ms/doc) but provides no continuous scores for downstream calibration; scored scales (percentage, tenpoint) are slower (∼2.1–2.2 s) but enable the full adaptation and thresholding pipeline that drives our best results.

The same score adaptation and thresholding mechanisms that improved metric learners and transformers in the original Rapt framework [12] now yield comparable gains on LLMs, establishing CBR as a model-agnostic calibration infrastructure for any upstream scorer producing confidence scores.

Two directions are particularly promising. First, high-stakes domains with extreme label spaces, such as legal document classification (EUR-LEX with ∼4,000 EUROVOC descriptors [6]) and medical coding (OHSUMED with medical codes [10]), would test whether adaptation scales to hundreds of classes and whether the few-shot cost argument ($k \times C$) becomes decisive. Second, in production systems where the case base grows as classified documents are verified by domain experts, investigating how adaptation quality improves with case base size, and whether active case selection can reduce the labelling budget, connects directly to core CBR research on case base maintenance [1].

7 Conclusion

We have shown that Rapt's case-based calibration principles transfer effectively from metric-learning classifiers to LLMs for multi-label classification, with score adaptation emerging as the single most impactful mechanism. By correcting prompt-elicited scores using neighbourhood ground-truth residuals, adaptation improves both tested models substantially, with zero additional LLM calls, minimal overhead, and no dependence on semantic label names, while Self-Reflection Prompting provides complementary gains on sufficiently capable models through iterative, evidence-grounded score revision. The best configurations surpass an equivalent few-shot baseline while consuming 64% fewer tokens per document, a cost advantage that grows with label set size since few-shot budgets scale with the number of classes. For industrial deployment, these properties are decisive: adaptation requires no fine-tuning, no retraining when models are updated, and no access to hidden states. It wraps any LLM that produces per-label scores, making it immediately deployable in existing classification pipelines. The robustness demonstrated under label anonymisation further confirms suitability for proprietary taxonomies where labels carry no inherent meaning, a common scenario in enterprise document processing. These results are demonstrated on a single industrial dataset with 11 classes and two LLM variants; generalisation to larger label spaces and diverse domains remains to be established.

Acknowledgements. The authors thank WM Nicol (Aberdeen) Pvt Ltd for providing the proprietary industrial dataset used in this study. We also gratefully acknowledge Robert Gordon University for providing the research facilities that supported this work.

Generative AI Statement. During the preparation of this manuscript, the authors used generative AI tools for assistance with writing refinements and formatting. All intellectual content, research design, methodology, experiments, data analysis, and interpretation were conducted solely by the authors, who reviewed and approved the final manuscript. The authors take full responsibility for the content of this publication.

References

1. Aamodt, A., Plaza, E.: Case-based reasoning: foundational issues, methodological variations, and system approaches. AI Commun. **7**(1), 39–59 (1994). https://doi.org/10.3233/AIC-1994-7104
2. Achachlouei, M.A., Patil, O., Joshi, T., et al.: Document Automation Architectures: Updated Survey in Light of Large Language Models (2023). https://doi.org/10.48550/arXiv.2308.09341
3. Bach, K., Bergmann, R., Brand, F., et al.: Case-Based Reasoning Meets Large Language Models: A Research Manifesto for Open Challenges and Research Directions (2025). https://hal.science/hal-05006761
4. Brand, F., Malburg, L., Bergmann, R.: Large language models as knowledge engineers. In: Workshop Proceedings of the 32nd International Conference on Case-Based Reasoning (ICCBR). CEUR Workshop Proceedings, vol. 3708, pp. 3–18. CEUR-WS.org (2024)
5. Chae, Y., Davidson, T.: Large language models for text classification: from zero-shot learning to instruction-tuning. Sociol. Methods Res. (2025). https://doi.org/10.1177/00491241251325243
6. Chalkidis, I., Fergadiotis, E., Malakasiotis, P., et al.: Large-scale multi-label text classification on EU legislation. In: Proceedings of the 57th Annual Meeting of the Association for Computational Linguistics, pp. 6314–6322. ACL, Florence, Italy (2019). https://doi.org/10.18653/v1/P19-1636
7. Dembczyński, K., Waegeman, W., Cheng, W., et al.: On label dependence and loss minimization in multi-label classification. Mach. Learn. **88**(1–2), 5–45 (2012). https://doi.org/10.1007/s10994-012-5285-8
8. Geng, J., Cai, F., Wang, Y.: A survey of confidence estimation and calibration in large language models. In: Proceedings of the 2024 Conference of the North American Chapter of the Association for Computational Linguistics (NAACL), pp. 6577–6595 (2024)
9. Gou, Z., Shao, Z., Gong, Y., et al.: CRITIC: large language models can self-correct with tool-interactive critiquing. In: Proceedings of the International Conference on Learning Representations (ICLR) (2024)
10. Hersh, W., Buckley, C., Leone, T.J., et al.: OHSUMED: an interactive retrieval evaluation and new large test collection for research. In: SIGIR 1994, pp. 192–201. Springer, London (1994)
11. Hovsepian, K., Liu, D., Murugesan, S.: Label with confidence: effective confidence calibration and ensembles in LLM-powered classification. In: Proceedings of the 1st Workshop on Generative AI for E-Commerce (GenAIECommerce), co-located with CIKM 2024 (2024)

12. Jayawardena, L., Wiratunga, N., Nkisi-Orji, I., Nicol, D.: RAPT: Retrieval-Augmented Post-hoc Thresholding for Multi-Label Classification (2026). https://doi.org/10.48550/arXiv.2605.16535
13. Kamoi, R., Zhang, Y., Zhang, N., et al.: When can LLMs actually correct their own mistakes? A critical survey of self-correction of LLMs. Trans. Assoc. Comput. Linguist. **12**, 1417–1440 (2024)
14. Khandelwal, U., Levy, O., Jurafsky, D.: Generalization through memorization: nearest neighbor language models. In: Proceedings of the International Conference on Learning Representations (ICLR) (2020)
15. Largeron, C., Moulin, C., Géry, M.: MCut: a thresholding strategy for multi-label classification. In: Hollmén, J., Klawonn, F., Tucker, A. (eds.) IDA 2012. LNCS, vol. 7619, pp. 172–183. Springer, Heidelberg (2012). https://doi.org/10.1007/978-3-642-34156-4_17
16. Leng, J., Dong, R., Zhang, Y., et al.: Taming overconfidence in LLMs: reward calibration in RLHF. In: Proceedings of the International Conference on Learning Representations (ICLR) (2025). https://doi.org/10.48550/arXiv.2410.09724
17. Ma, M., Chochlakis, G., Pandiyan, N.M., et al.: Large language models do multi-label classification differently. In: Proceedings of the 2025 Conference on Empirical Methods in Natural Language Processing, pp. 2472–2495. ACL, Suzhou, China (2025)
18. Madaan, A., Tandon, N., Gupta, P.: Self-refine: iterative refinement with self-feedback. In: Advances in Neural Information Processing Systems 36 (NeurIPS), pp. 46534–46594 (2023)
19. Manggala, P., Mastakouri, A., Kirschbaum, E., et al.: QA-calibration of language model confidence scores. In: Proceedings of the International Conference on Learning Representations (ICLR) (2025)
20. Agarwal, S., Ahmad, L., et al.: gpt-oss-120b & gpt-oss-20b Model Card (2025). https://doi.org/10.48550/arXiv.2508.10925
21. Hurst, A., Lerer, A., et al.: GPT-4o System Card (2024). https://doi.org/10.48550/arXiv.2410.21276
22. Praharaj, A., Kasundra, J.: Token-Level Marginalization for Multi-Label LLM Classifiers (2025). https://doi.org/10.48550/arXiv.2511.22312
23. Shamatrin, D.: Adaptive Thresholding for Multi-Label Classification via Global-Local Signal Fusion (2025). https://doi.org/10.48550/arXiv.2505.03118
24. Tsoumakas, G., Katakis, I.: Multi-label classification: an overview. Int. J. Data Warehous. Mining (IJDWM) **3**(3), 1–13 (2007). https://ideas.repec.org/a/igg/jdwm00/v3y2007i3p1-13.html
25. Wilkerson, K., Leake, D.: On implementing case-based reasoning with large language models. In: Proceedings of the 32nd International Conference on Case-Based Reasoning (ICCBR), vol. 14775, pp. 404–417. Springer (2024)
26. Wiratunga, N., Abeyratne, R., Jayawardena, L.: CBR-RAG: case-based reasoning for retrieval augmented generation in LLMs for legal question answering. In: Case-Based Reasoning Research and Development, vol. 14775, pp. 445–460. Springer, Cham (2024)
27. Yang, Y.: A study of thresholding strategies for text categorization. In: Proceedings of the 24th Annual Int. ACM SIGIR Conference on Research and Development in Information Retrieval, SIGIR 2001, pp. 137–145. ACM, New York, NY, USA (2001)

An Empirical Investigation of Bias and Unfairness in Case-Based Adaptation

Thomas Gabel[(✉)]

Faculty of Computer Science and Engineering, Frankfurt University of Applied Sciences, 60318 Frankfurt am Main, Germany
tgabel@fra-uas.de

Abstract. When constructing artificially intelligent systems, it may happen that bias and unfairness against a protected group, that do exist in the real world or in real-world data, are mapped into the digital world. If such systems are then used in practice for decisions that influence humans' life, the obvious question is: Do the algorithms just pass through, perhaps mitigate, or even exacerbate such undesirable characteristics? That question has recently been addressed for the retrieve and retain phase of Case-Based Reasoning (CBR) systems. The paper at hand aims at providing an answer to that question for the *reuse* step in CBR, viz for case-based adaptation in k-nearest neighbor classification tasks.

1 Introduction

The consideration of fairness and bias as well as ethical implications of machine learning algorithms and their application to sensitive domains has become a topic of active research in recent years. Accordingly, a plethora of fairness metrics has been developed and, correspondingly, a large number of (meta) analyses has been published [12,30]. Research in Case-Based Reasoning (CBR) has started to address fairness issues in previous years, too. Knowing that the CBR paradigm advocates that "Similar problems have similar solutions" [36], one might adapt that principle to a human-focused and fairness-related setting by requiring that "Similar individuals should be given similar decisions" [11]. Thus, unfairness may arise in a CBR system, if it underpredicts a desirable outcome for a specific group of people (e.g. a credit approval decision for a specific gender), or, likewise, overpredicts a non-desirable outcome for some group (e.g. crime recidivism prediction for people of some specific skin color or race).

Blanzeisky et al. [10] have shown that nearest neighbor retrieval, that usually resides at the core of a CBR system, is generally not bias-free. They target this issue by suggesting a multi-objective approach for learning a similarity metric that yields less biased retrieval results. In later work [9], the same authors have focused on the case data itself. The case base stores experience, and if that experience reflects biased decisions taken in real life, then predictions made on their basis might be easily biased, too. Thus, they propose a case-base maintenance approach that removes cases from the case base that cause unfair classifications.

L. Malburg and K. Bach (Eds.): ICCBR 2026, LNAI 16780, pp. 83–99, 2027.
https://doi.org/10.1007/978-3-032-33865-5_6

Based on Richter' knowledge container model [35], we observe that the similarity knowledge and the case data container have been subject to fairness-related studies, but the vocabulary and adaptation knowledge containers have, to the best of the author's knowledge, remained unexplored. The paper at hand attempts to fill a part of that gap by investigating how and to which extent case-based adaptation approaches can yield unfair decisions. More specifically, we restrict our focus to classification problems and utilize adaptation as a mean to combine the solutions (i.e. class labels) of a query's k nearest neighbors to one uniquely predicted class membership. Past reuse research has addressed both, the question of (a) how many nearest neighbors should be considered as well as (b) how specifically to amalgamate their predictions. Traditionally, the focus has been mostly on performance-related issues like classification accuracy or scores, but not on aspects of fairness. Our goal is, thus, to highlight aspects of fairness in the context of the reuse phase for case-based k-nearest neighbor (k-NN) classification. An analysis of more sophisticated reuse approaches such as structural or transformational case adaptation [24] is, however, beyond our scope.

Fairness and bias in machine learning have been a topic of active research for many years. We therefore devote Sect. 2 to a concise review of relevant related work and foundations on approaches to assess bias and fairness in machine learning. We discuss sources of unfairness, practically adopted approaches to quantify it, derive factors that reinforce it and, in so doing, bridge the gap to established k-nearest neighbor reuse methods in CBR. Section 3 presents the methodological approach and contributions required for our empirical investigations on the impact of case reuse on fairness. Section 4 outlines our experiments and the characteristics of the classical fairness-impaired data sets we utilized. Moreover, a comprehensive overview of our results is given, including detailed analyses on the influence of k on fairness subject to the characteristics of the case data as well as with respect to the specific reuse approach taken.

2 Foundations and Related Work

In this section, we introduce the necessary vocabulary, paying special attention to bridging the gap between terms used in the fairness literature and in the CBR community. Additionally, we interweave relevant related work.

2.1 Notation

We start by clarifying the notation used throughout the paper, aligning fairness-related and CBR-related concepts. As indicated, our focus is on classification tasks. Since a case c from the set of all cases $\mathcal{M} = (\mathbb{X}, Y)$ consists of a problem part x and a solution part y, i.e. $c = (x, y)$, the solution is an element of a set of class labels Y. We also denote the solution as the target variable. By contrast, the problem part x comprises the case's features, i.e. $x \in \mathbb{X} = (X_1 \times \cdots \times X_d)$. As usual, $sim : \mathbb{X} \times \mathbb{X} \rightarrow [0, 1]$ denotes a similarity measure to assess the similarity between two cases' problem parts or between a query and problem.

One or more of these features are considered to be *sensitive* ones, such as gender, race, handicaps or others, which must be treated carefully. Without loss of generality, we stick to the existence of exactly one such sensitive feature S in the remainder of this paper, i.e. $\exists s \in \{1, \ldots, d\}$ with $S = X_s$. Moreover, we say that individuals in the protected group, which are potentially subject to discriminatory treatment, have the sensitive feature value of 0 (i.e. $x_s = 0$ or, for short, $S = 0$) whereas the rest has $S = 1$.

In classification, there is usually a desired prediction – a class label that is generally considered better than other outcomes (e.g. a loan granted vs. not granted). Without loss of generality, we subsequently stick to two classes and denote the desired outcome by $y = 1$ and the non-desirable one by $y = 0$. We also differentiate between the solution y of a case and the predicted solution $\hat{y}(q) \in Y$ for a new query $q \in \mathbb{X}$. If the context is clear, we write $\hat{y}$ for brevity.

Finally, for a given case data set $\mathcal{D} \subset \mathcal{M}$ we will repeatedly refer to the commonly used pairwise disjoint decomposition into a training set (the case base) $\mathcal{C}$, a validation set $\mathcal{V}$, and a test set $\mathcal{T}$ with $\mathcal{D} = \mathcal{C} \cup \mathcal{V} \cup \mathcal{T}$.

2.2 Background on Bias and Fairness

A widely accepted distinction concerning potential causes for unfairness and bias is made by [26]. First, unfairness may arise from *prejudice* that is due to some statistical dependence between the sensitive feature S and the target variable Y *or* between S and non-sensitive features from $\mathbb{X}$. Then, the (in)direct use of S during decision-making yields a predictor that basically supports discrimination with respect to S. While there exist approaches towards removing prejudice [26], in a CBR context this may be addressed by the contents of the vocabulary knowledge container [35], which is beyond the focus of this paper.

Second, *negative legacy* is frequently highlighted as a source of unfairness. It refers to biased sampling or case labelling habits in the real world that made it into the data. For example, if prison inmates' early release decisions were affected by judges disadvantaging some minority group due to skin color, race, or other sensitive features, then the recorded case data distribution will be skewed. This type of bias is notably problematic in a CBR setting which fundamentally relies on storing and re-using past experience. Addressing that type of prejudice falls into the realm of CBR's retain phase [1] and has already been examined in [9].

The third source of prejudice is called *underestimation* and denotes a decision model that generalizes too much and is thus susceptible to making unfair classifications as it does not regard minorities sufficiently. One might expect that CBR is rather robust against that kind of bias, as it does not build a model in a supervised way that might underfit the data. However, underestimation can nonetheless emerge in a CBR system, as the similarity measure employed in the retrieve phase may select nearest neighbors in a biased way. Moreover, the way in which the neighbors' solutions are adapted and combined may give rise to unfairness as well. While the former, i.e. the learning of a similarity measure that is geared towards fairness, has been addressed in [10], fairness and underestimation issues during the reuse step are the topic of the paper at hand.

2.3 Quantifying Unfairness

There exists an abundance of fairness measures in the literature, for a concise review the reader is referred to [11] or [12]. A discrimination measure that is widely referred to in the judicial system (e.g. in US courts or in the UK Sex Discrimination Act), is the *disparate impact* [17], also denoted as slift [34] or impact ratio [44]. It represents the ratio of desired outcomes ($\hat{y} = 1$) for the protected group ($S = 0$) to the desired outcomes for the non-protected (majority) group on a given test data set $\mathcal{T} \subset \mathcal{M}$:

$$DI_S(\mathcal{T}) = \frac{P(\hat{y}(q) = 1 | (q, y) \in \mathcal{T}, q_s = 0)}{P(\hat{y}(q) = 1 | (q, y) \in \mathcal{T}, q_s = 1)}, \text{ or for short, } DI_S^{\mathcal{T}} = \frac{P(\hat{y} = 1\, S = 0)}{P(\hat{y} = 1\, S = 1)}. \quad (1)$$

In legal practice, it is commonly assumed that discriminatory behavior is present if $DI_S < \tau := \frac{4}{5}$, i.e. if the desired outcomes for the protected group are 20% or more below those of the general group. Interestingly, the DI measure may also be applied to the full training data set (or case base) and, thus, hint to the amount of discrimination in the given data. We will return to that point in Sect. 3.1.

When assessing the additional unfairness introduced by a machine learning-based system, [8] suggest the *underestimation score* which is a simplified, group-specific modification of the underestimation index from [26]. For a group $g \in S$, the underestimation score is defined for a train ($\mathcal{C}$) and test case set ($\mathcal{T}$) as

$$US_{S=g}(\mathcal{C}, \mathcal{T}) = \frac{P(\hat{y}(q) = 1 | (q, y) \in \mathcal{T}, q_s = g)}{P(y = 1 | (x, y) \in \mathcal{C}, q_s = g)}, \text{ short, } US_{S=g} = \frac{P(\hat{y} = 1\, S = g)}{P(y = 1\, S = g)} \quad (2)$$

and it tells whether the desired outcome (1) for a considered group g is actually lower ($US < 1$), equal, or higher ($US > 1$) than what one would expect from the training data. In particular, if $US_{S=0} \ll US_{S=1}$, one has to attest a severe amount of unfairness specifically against protected group $g = 0$.

Factors for Underestimation. In [8], the authors identify four factors that may contribute to the degree of underestimation a learning algorithm is subject to. Besides (1) noise (irreducible error), (2) imbalance among the target classes, and (3) under-represented groups – all of which refer to the given training data, i.e. the learner itself is not liable for them – they point to (4) the level of regularization an algorithm applies and confirm for various classic learning algorithms that regularization impacts underestimation and generally reduces the US value.

In line with that, Blanzeisky et al. have proposed two approaches to mitigate underestimation in CBR. They learn a less biased similarity metric using particle swarm optimization [10] where the solution found approaches Pareto optimality with respect to accuracy *and* underestimation. Furthermore, they eliminate cases from the case base [9] that enforce an underestimation of the desirable outcome for the protected group. Both approaches can be interpreted as regularizing the system – they regularize the similarity measure and prune the case base, accepting minor negative impacts on classification performance in exchange for fairness gains. Our intent is to complement these pieces of work by analyzing how bias, underestimation and, hence, unfairness can arise in CBR's reuse phase.

2.4 *k*-Nearest Neighbor Reuse Methods

The goal of the CBR cycle's [1] second phase (reuse) is to adapt, combine or merge a query's k nearest neighbors' solutions to a new suggested solution [36]. As we focus on classification, the new solution must be a class label from Y, reducing the reuse phase to some variant of voting among the k nearest neighbors.

2.4.1 *k*-NN-Based Classification Formally, given a case base $\mathcal{C} \subset \mathcal{M}$ of n cases, a query $q \in \mathcal{M}$, some similarity measure sim, and $k \geq 1$, a CBR system's retrieve step determines a sorted list $\mathcal{N}_k$ of k cases from $\mathcal{C}$ that are most similar to q. Thus, $\mathcal{N}_k = [c_1, \ldots, c_k]$ is sorted by similarity of its entries to q, i.e. $sim(q, c_i) \geq sim(q, c_j) \forall i < j$. As a shortcut, we refer to these similarities by s_i subsequently ($s_i := sim(q, c_i) \forall c_i \in \mathcal{N}_k$). Moreover, we refer to the cases' solutions by y_i, i.e. if $c_i = (a, b)$, then $y_i := b \in Y$.

The question how to combine the nearest neighbors' solutions (i.e. the actual reuse) has been studied for decades, starting with the introduction of the k-NN rule by [18]. The general k-NN rule determines the suggested solution $\hat{y}$ as:

$$\hat{y}(q) = \arg\max_{l \in Y} \sum_{i=1}^{k} w_i \delta(y_i, l) \ \ (=: \hat{y} \text{ for short}), \tag{3}$$

where the Kronecker δ gives one, if its two arguments are equal, and zero otherwise. Here, the crucial question becomes how to define the weights w_i and how to set k in relation to n. For example, the mentioned early k-NN rule implements a simple majority voting due to using constant weights ($1/k$), but much work has focused on deriving and analyzing more elaborated variants (cf. Sect. 2.4.2).

2.4.2 Interpretation of *k*-NN as a Regularizer It is well-known that the number k of nearest neighbors used in case-based classification can be interpreted as a regularization mechanism. The bias of the 1-nearest neighbor classifier is often low at a high variance, as it reuses only the class label of the query's most similar case [23]. For larger k, the reused class label depends on the k most similar neighbors and can thus, e.g., mitigate noise by exerting more bias while reducing variance. Cover and Hart [13] have shown that asymptotically the error of the 1-nearest neighbor classifier is never more than twice the Bayes-optimal error. Moreover, it has been shown that the original, simple majority vote is optimal for $n \to \infty$, if $k \to \infty$ and $\frac{k}{n} \to 0$ [14].

Practical applications typically favor finite k values and non-uniform weighting. Since the best k is dictated by the model's bias and variance characteristics, this technical choice directly affects the classifier's fairness. Consequently, optimizing for accuracy can unintentionally bias the results when sensitive features are involved. While fairness has received little attention in conjunction with k-nearest neighbor voting, there exist k-NN classification methods specifically tailored for imbalanced data sets which aim at re-weighting neighbors accordingly [4, 15, 42]. Likewise, there are approaches that determine a good value of k

on the fly [3,20,38] or that take the distribution of feature values into account when weighting cases [29,33]. Moreover, there are reuse approaches that advocate the mingling of cases to form centroids per class, so-called local mean non-parametric classifiers, and make the classification decision using those adapted cases (original work in [31] with many follow-up approaches).

Since a full coverage of all existing approaches is not feasible, we have devised a selection of rather simple, though established approaches from the literature that we compare with one another, subsequently (cf. Sect. 3.2). Our selection is by far not exhaustive, which is why the interested reader is referred to [19] and [2] for comprehensive overviews of many further k-NN reuse methods.

3 Methods

There exists a rich body of methods for fairness analyses as well as for k-NN-based case reuse. We complement this by some selective enhancements.

3.1 Fairness as a Result of Balanced Under and Overestimation

The established underestimation score also covers overestimation situations for values of $US_{S=g}$ larger than one. This hints to a critical point when using the underestimation score as a measure for comparing the fairness of different systems in case that some system *over*estimates the desirable outcome. One group, for example, the protected one, may feature the desired outcome far less in the data, i.e. $P(y = 1|S = 0) \ll P(y = 1|S = 1)$ with $P(y = 1|S = 0)$ near zero. As a consequence, for some overestimating classifier the numerical value $US_{S=0}$ may take rather large values $\gg 1$ due to the small denominator in Eq. 2 which are hard to compare with scores < 1 for genuine underestimation. Thus, comparing US values is fine, as long as the focus is exclusively on underestimation, but underestimation scores larger than one should be treated with care.

A learning system that has been trained on some data set $\mathcal{C} \subsetneq \mathcal{D}$ may – if it exerts some bias – generally affect not just a single group of instances unfair (e.g. the sensitive group), but probably all groups. For example, a trained classifier may grant credit approvals to 20% of the female applicants (from test set $\mathcal{T} \subsetneq \mathcal{D}$), while 30% of the females within $\mathcal{C}$ obtained the credit. Clearly, this is unfair. We might also observe that the group of male applications contained in $\mathcal{C}$ received the credit in 40% of the cases and, hence, conclude that the training data is subject to negative legacy. What is even worse, however, is when, at the same time the classifier grants credits to 50% of the male applicants from $\mathcal{T}$ at application time. Therefore, we suggest to consider underestimation for the sensitive group jointly with under-/overestimation for the other (e.g. majority) group, and vice versa. This point has been indicated by other authors in the fairness literature, coining differing terms for it [7,28], and is reflected in the original definition of disparate impact (cf. Eq. 1).

As pointed out in Sect. 2.3, we propose to utilize the disparate impact measure to assess the unbalancedness within the given case base $\mathcal{C}$. We therefore define

$$DI_S(\mathcal{C}) = \frac{P(y=1|(x,y) \in \mathcal{C}, x_s = 0)}{P(y=1|(x,y) \in \mathcal{C}, x_s = 1)} \text{ or, for short, } DI_S^{\mathcal{C}} = \frac{P(y=1\, S=0)}{P(y=1\, S=1)} \tag{4}$$

as the baseline disparate impact that quantifies the level of unequal treatment among the sensitive ($S = 0$) and remaining ($S = 1$) group as it is given by the case data $\mathcal{C}$. Putting into relation the actually observed disparate impact $DI_S^{\mathcal{T}}$ on test cases (Eq. 1) and the baseline disparate impact (Eq. 4), we propose the *relative disparate impact*

$$RDI(\mathcal{C}, \mathcal{T}) = \frac{DI_S(\mathcal{T})}{DI_S(\mathcal{C})} \ (=: RDI \text{ for short}), \tag{5}$$

as a measure to quantify the additional amount of unfairness introduced by a learned prediction system. With some basic algebraic manipulations we see that

$$RDI = \frac{DI_S^{\mathcal{T}}}{DI_S^{\mathcal{C}}} = \frac{P(\hat{y}=1\, S=0)}{P(y=1\, S=0)} \cdot \frac{P(y=1\, S=1)}{P(\hat{y}=1\, S=1)} = \frac{US_{S=0}(\mathcal{C},\mathcal{T})}{US_{S=1}(\mathcal{C},\mathcal{T})} \underset{\text{short}}{=} \frac{US_{S=0}}{US_{S=1}}.$$

In alignment with the original definition of the DI and its frequent use in different areas (cf. Sect. 2.3), we propose to ascribe a relative disparate impact to some classifier, if $RDI \notin [\tau, \frac{1}{\tau}]$ with the commonly used value $\tau = \frac{4}{5}$, i.e. if it underestimates or overestimates one or the other group by more than 20%.

3.2 Utilized k-Nearest Neighbor Classification Rules

As argued in Sect. 2.4.1, deciding for a class label in a case-based way using the suggestions of a query's k nearest neighbors represents a (possibly weighted) voting problem (cf. Eq. 3). A large body of k-NN rules has been proposed, which can be broadly categorized into four groups:

a) The *simple majority vote* (cf. Sect. 2.4) is made by the original k-NN rule [18] using a constant weight w_i (e.g. $w_i = 1$ or $1/k$).
b) *Similarity-weighted approaches* apply some function f to the numeric similarity s_i between query and the ith neighbor from $\mathcal{N}_k$, i.e. $w_i = f(s_i)$ (where $s_i = sim(q, \mathcal{N}_k[i])$).
c) *Rank-weighted approaches* apply some function g to the rank i of c_i within the list of q's nearest neighbors, i.e. $w_i = g(i)$.
d) Specialized variants: These may include, but are not limited to
   - *combinations* of b) and c) that apply some function h to both, the similarity s_i and rank i of some neighbors c_i from $\mathcal{N}_k$: $w_i = h(s_i, i)$, or
   - *class-based normalizations* that additionally adjust the weight w_i of each neighbor c_i from $\mathcal{N}_k$ w.r.t. the frequency of its class y_i within $\mathcal{N}_k$.

Since an exhaustive coverage of such rules in infeasible, we have selected a few representatives for each such category that we include in our investigations (see Table 1). Notably, rule R_7 has been highlighted for offering good performance across many domains [21]. Moreover, the selection also includes two rules that we propose (R_{12} and R_{13}). Although the underlying ideas are not fundamentally new, their specific formulation appears to be novel within the existing literature.

Table 1. k-NN rules considered in the remainder of this paper. Note that each rule that features a fraction also covers the special case of a zero denominator by letting $w_i = 1$. If the rules allow for parameter adjustments, we work with fixed settings throughout this paper: $\alpha = \beta = 1$. For R_{12} and R_{13} see the text for full explanations.

Cat.	No.	$w_i =$	Description	Origin
a)	R_1	$const$	simple majority vote	[18]
b)	R_2	s_i	similarity-based vote	[16]
	R_3	$s_i - s_k$	similarity-based vote relative to base similarity	
	R_4	$\frac{s_i - s_k}{s_1 - s_k}$	normalized similarity-based vote	[16]
	R_5	s_i^2	squared similarity-based vote	[40]
	R_6	$e^{\alpha s_i^\beta}$	exponential similarity-based vote	[41]
	R_7	$\frac{s_i - s_k}{s_1 - s_k} \cdot \frac{s_k + s_1}{s_k + s_1 - s_i}$	dual-normalized similarity-based vote	[21]
c)	R_8	$k - i + 1$	rank-based vote	[16]
	R_9	$\frac{1}{i}$	inverse rank-based vote	[22]
	R_{10}	$w_{i+1} + w_{i+2}$	Fibonacci-based vote	[32]
d)	R_{11}	$\frac{s_i - s_k}{s_1 - s_k} \cdot \frac{1}{i}$	multiplicative combination of R_4 and R_9	[22]
	R_{12}	cf. Eq. 7	class representatives-based similarity vote	Sect. 3.3.1
	R_{13}	cf. Eq. 8	sim-based vote normalized by class frequency	Sect. 3.3.2

3.3 *k*-NN Rules Under Imbalanced Data

For imbalanced data sets where one class $y \in Y$ dominates the data a voting among a large number k of neighbors becomes (for increasing k) more and more biased since the majority class will dominate the result. Similarity-weighted voting rules, for instance, represent a first approach to mitigate that problem. The issue becomes even more prevalent, however, if we know that there is some protected group $g \in S$ that is presumed to having been treated unfair in practice and, therefore, is represented in the data in a biased way. The underlying idea of both of the following rules is to take into account the distribution of case solutions in the vicinity of the query.

3.3.1 Class Representatives-Based Similarity Vote The idea is to split the list of nearest neighbors $\mathcal{N}_k$ into sublists with respect to the classes of the cases contained. Voulgaris and Magoulas have pursued a similar approach, with the difference of forming multiple lists upfront [39]. Thus, for each possible solution $y \in Y$ we obtain $\mathcal{N}_k^y = [c_j \in \mathcal{N}_k | c_j = y]$, a sorted list with at most k entries. If there exists an $y \in Y$ with $\mathcal{N}_k^y = \emptyset$, then the vote is unambiguous for the other solution (in case of two classes). If there are multiple $y \in Y$ with $|\mathcal{N}_k^y| > 0$, then we denote by κ the number of cases belonging to the class with the least number of instances within $\mathcal{N}_k$, i.e. $\kappa = \min_{y \in Y} |\mathcal{N}_k^y|$. We then use the class y as the suggested solution whose κ top entries in $\mathcal{N}_k^y$ have the highest average similarity to q:

$$\hat{y}(q) = \arg\max_{y \in Y} \frac{1}{\kappa} \sum_{i=1}^{\kappa} sim(q, \mathcal{N}_k^y[i]) \tag{6}$$

As a side node, this definition of $\hat{y}$ can easily be integrated into the weight-based framework from above (cf. Eq. 3) by letting

$$w_i = \begin{cases} s_i & \text{if } |\{c_j \in \mathcal{N}_k | j \leq i, y_i = y_j\}| \leq \kappa \\ 0 & \text{else.} \end{cases} \tag{7}$$

Thus, the weights are query-specific and derived during retrieval with minimal computational effort, which is in contrast to related approaches like [15].

3.3.2 Normalized Class Similarity Support The previous weighting scheme focussed equally on the same number of (top) representatives from each class. We next utilize the entire retrieval result $\mathcal{N}_k$, normalizing each case's weight by the frequency of its class in $\mathcal{N}_k$. If all cases in $\mathcal{N}_k$ belong to the same class, again, the vote is unambiguous, otherwise:

$$w_i = \frac{s_i}{|\mathcal{N}_k^{y_i}|} \tag{8}$$

As a matter of fact, this yields vote results that are identical to those that would arise if we would assign to $\hat{y}$ the class whose cases within $\mathcal{N}_k$ have on average the highest similarity to q. A similar idea has been used by [43] in conjunction with a feature weighting approach. An appealing characteristic of this approach is that the influence of the majority class is constrained. Of course, some noisy data point c_η with y_η might take the lead for small k, but for larger k – where we expect to find further non-noisy neighbors within $\mathcal{N}_k$ that have class y_η as well – the averaging of similarities will filter out the noise.

3.4 Optimization of *k* with Respect to Fairness

We follow a straightforward procedure to analyze the optimizability of k for the goal of fair case reuse. As mentioned, the given case data $\mathcal{D}$ is randomly split into three disjoint sets: $\mathcal{C}$ forms the actual case base, while a smaller part is used as a separate test query set $\mathcal{T}$ on which final classifier performance is measured and reported. Moreover, there is a validation set $\mathcal{V}$ that we use to search (brute force) for the value of $k^\star$ that maximizes some optimization criterion $\mathcal{L}$ over $\mathcal{V}$, i.e. $k^\star = \arg\max_{k\in\{1,\dots,n\}} \mathcal{L}(\mathcal{V})$. We compare the simple F_1 score [37] on $\mathcal{V}$

$$\mathcal{L}_1 = F_1(\mathcal{V}) = \frac{2TP}{2TP+FP+FN} = \frac{2P(\hat{y}=1, y=1|(q,y)\in\mathcal{V})}{P(\hat{y}(q)=1|(q,y)\in\mathcal{V}) + P(y=1|(q,y)\in\mathcal{V})} \tag{9}$$

with a multi-objective criterion that additionally takes into account a fair treatment of groups using the relative disparate impact:

$$\mathcal{L}_2 = F_1(\mathcal{V}) \cdot \begin{cases} RDI(\mathcal{C},\mathcal{V}) & \text{if } RDI(\mathcal{C},\mathcal{V}) \leq 1 \\ \frac{1}{RDI(\mathcal{C},\mathcal{V})} & \text{else} \end{cases} \tag{10}$$

Using $\mathcal{L}_2$ we are thus interested in the value of k that brings about both, good performance (measured with F_1) on the validation set as well as a relative disparate impact as near to one as possible.

Table 2. Data sets used for our analyses: The last column provides a reference to the source where U indicates the UCI Machine Learning Repository [27] and K stands for a Kaggle dataset [25].

Dataset Name (and Area)	#Features and #Cases	Sensitive Feature	Protected group (and Share of)	Desired Outcome (and Share of)	Src
Adult (finance)	14/30162	gender	female (32.4%)	earns >50k/yr (24.9%)	U
Bank (marketing)	16/45211	marital	single (28.3%)	sale made (11.7%)	K
Credit (finance)	20/1000	gender	female (31.0%)	creditworthy (70.0%)	U
Credit Card (fin.)	15/653	gender	female (31.1%)	card approved (45.3%)	U
Heart (health)	13/270	age	midage (51.1%)	ill (44.4%)	U
Liver (health)	10/579	gender	female (24.2%)	ill (71.5%)	K
Recidivism$_1$ (law)	7/7214	race	black (51.2%)	no recidivism (54.9%)	[5]
Recidivism$_2$ (law)	47/16198	race	black (56.1%)	no recidivism (42.2%)	K
Titanic	6/887	gender	male (64.6%)	survived (45.3%)	K

4 Experiments

We performed an extensive empirical evaluation using standard datasets to examine the interplay of classifier performance and classifier fairness subject to the algorithmic parameters of CBR's reuse phase, viz the choice of the reuse method and its nearest neighbor weighting as well as the dependency on k.

4.1 Experimental Approach, Datasets and Performance Measures

In all our experiments, we use a large fraction (80%) of the given data $\mathcal{D}$ as case base $\mathcal{C}$ and employ the remainder (10%) as a validation set $\mathcal{V}$ to analyze the domain of possible k values as well as an independent test set $\mathcal{T}$ (10%). All experiments were repeated 100 times (for the smaller data sets) or 10 times (for the much larger ones) to form average values.

We selected a number of datasets frequently used in fairness research. Instances with missing or unknown feature values were omitted. Table 2 summarizes their core characteristics. The retrieve phase utilizes a knowledge-poor default similarity measure modelled according to the local-global principle [6].

4.2 Bias as a Function of k: Visualizing Underestimation

We start by focusing on the classic Adult domain where the task is to predict whether a human earns more than 50k$ per year. With a disparate impact of $DI_S(\mathcal{C}) = 0.362$ this domain is known to be heavily biased against females and has, thus, been frequently used in fairness studies.

The left part of Fig. 1 shows what happens, if we perform k-NN classification for increasing k (log-scaled abscissa denoting k/n) using the simple majority voting rule (R_1). The thick-plotted data series show – separately for the sensitive group (gray, $S = 0$) and the remaining group (black, $S = 1$) – that the true negative rates converge to one, while the true positive rates converges to zero since the k-NN classifier becomes more likely to assign more queries to the majority class (which is not earning $50k\$/yr$) for increasing k. Thus, for $k/n > 0.35$ the classifier is the trivial one always returning the non-desired, i.e. negative class.

The thin series in the same chart show how k-NN achieves this, setting the number of false/true positives of the k-NN classifier in relation to the number of false/true positives of the 1-NN classifier. Obviously, *both* the number of false (dashed) positives and true (solid) positives drops much faster for the sensitive group ($S = 0$) compared to the decline for the non-sensitive group ($S = 1$). Of course, this heavily impacts the underestimation scores $US_{S=0}$ and $US_{S=1}$ and, accordingly, the relative disparate impact as can be seen in the right part of Fig. 1. The widely used threshold for disparate impact ($\tau = 0.8$) is undercut for $k/n \geq 0.00035$. Additionally, that chart plots (y_2 axis) some performance measures for the obtained k-NN classifier. All of those (accuracy, balanced accuracy, F_1 and P_4 score [37]) take nearly the same shape with maxima in the interval $k/n \in [10^{-2}, 10^{-1}]$ where k-NN's RDI is critical between 0.6 and 0.75.

4.3 k as a Driver for Disparate Impact and Underestimation

We next extend our scope by focusing on multiple domains with fairness issues (Table 2). The bottom-left chart of Fig. 2 conveys an overview of the domains' core characteristics. It plots the share of desired outcomes against the share of the protected group within the case data, using data point bubble sizes to indicate the amount of data-inherent bias as expressed by the disparate impact

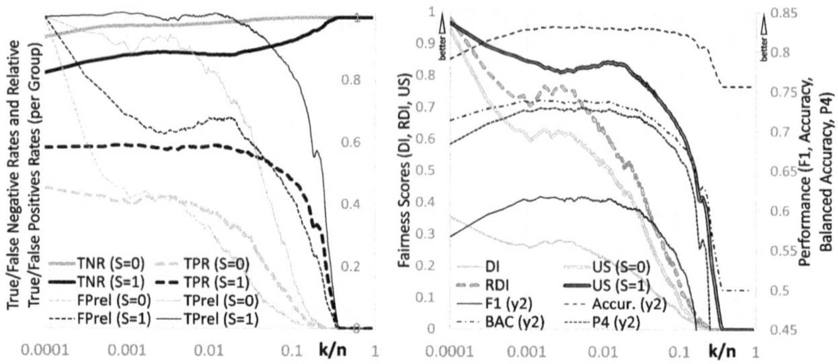

Fig. 1. Left: k-NN classification using the simple majority vote for increasing values of k/n. Separately for the protected group ($S = 1$) and the rest, the chart visualizes the development of true negative and true positive rates as well as the shrinking share of positive classifications, i.e. of desired outcomes. Right: For the same data, this chart plots the underestimation scores for both groups, the relative disparate impact as well as four different performance measures (y_2) of the resulting case-based classifier.

measure $DI_S(\mathcal{C})$ (Eq. 4). While each of the domains considered is subject to fairness problems ($DI < 1$), in some of them the protected group takes actually the role of a majority (y value larger than 0.5), and in some of them the desired outcome happens to occur in more than half of the cases (x value larger than 0.5).

The impact of the latter can be seen in the three bottom right charts of Fig. 2. With $k/n \to 1$, the majority class (here, the desired outcome) outnumbers the non-desired outcome resulting in strong overestimation (black curve with US scores larger than one). We also see that domains with roughly balanced shares of the protected group and of the desired outcome (near 0.5/0.5, e.g. Heart oder Recidivism) are only mildly influenced by additional disparate impact due to the k-NN classifier (RDI values mostly within $[\frac{4}{5}, \frac{5}{4}]$ except for extreme k/n values) which is in line with notes by [8] on imbalance among the target class as a source for underestimation. Finally, we identify domains which either come with a low $DI_S(\mathcal{C})$ (small bubbles) value upfront or with a strong imbalance between protected and non-protected group and an imbalance in the class label distribution. For those domains (Bank, Heart, Titanic) both, the underestimation score as well as the disparate impact decline rapidly for growing k values.

4.4 Experiments on the Bias of Case Reuse Methods

Returning to the Adult domain, we examine the impact of the employed reuse methods on underestimation, disparate impact, and the actual performance of the resulting classifier when altering k. Figure 3 contrasts representatives from each of the categories listed in Table 1. Purely sim-based voting methods (R_2 and R_{12}) produce a rather fast decline of the US and (R)DI scores, approaching zero for $k/n > 0.2$, while there are negligible differences in classifier peak performance

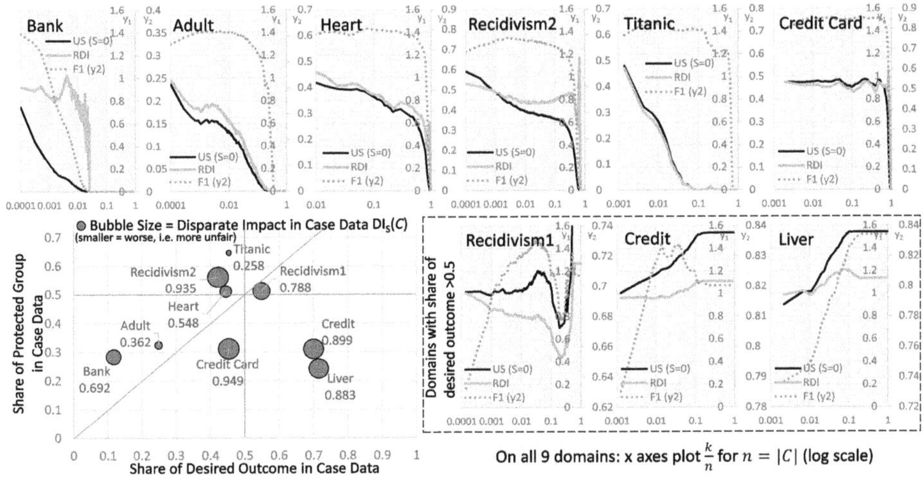

Fig. 2. The bottom-left chart gives an overview of the fairness-related characteristics of the domains considered. The remaining charts visualize for each of the domains the level of underestimation of the protected group subject to k/n as well as the resulting relative disparate impact of the k-NN classifier. F_1 scores are given as a reference to indicate the range of k values that would be practically relevant.

at $k/n \approx 10^{-2}$. For the two reuse methods where rank information is included in the vote (R_9, R_{11}) all fairness-related curves are less steep, approaching values larger zero for $k/n \to 1$. Although this might suggest an improvement in terms of handling biased data, the best value of k, which a practitioner would select using some validation set, yields nearly identical fairness (RDI ~ 0.7) and performance ($F_1 \sim 0.62$) characteristics as the previously discussed sim-based rules.

In contrast to those, rule R_{13} (right in Fig. 3) strongly overestimates the desired outcome for both groups. Since this kind of overestimation is even more pronounced for the protected group, the RDI grows to values larger than one, thus "repairing" some of the disparate treatment among groups in the given case data. While this comes generally at the cost of an impaired F_1 score for smaller values of k, the best value of k found ($k/n = 0.335$) also produces the best F_1 score among *all* k-NN rules from Table 1 with no underestimation and a relative disparate impact within the desirable interval ($1.187 \in [\frac{4}{5}, \frac{5}{4}]$).

Search for Fair Values of k In another large-scale series of experiments we iterated over all 9 domains and 13 rules and compared the quality of a k-NN classifier and its fairness properties for 7 specific settings of k. Besides the 1-NN classifier (for which all rules behave identically), we set k to increasing shares of the case base size ($n = |\mathcal{C}|$), viz $\frac{k}{n} \in \{0.001, 0.005, 0.01, 0.05, 0.1, 0.5\}$. Moreover, we used the values $k^\star$ resulting from the optimization procedure described in Sect. 3.4 for a separate validation set $\mathcal{V}$ with optimization criteria $\mathcal{L}_1$ and $\mathcal{L}_2$.

Part a) of Fig. 4 plots F_1 and RDI on the test cases $\mathcal{T}$ and shows (except for a few outliers) how "clusters" for the different levels of k arise. It is remarkable

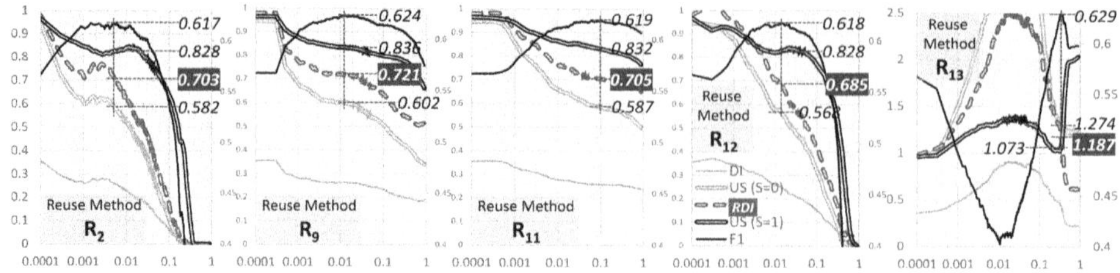

Fig. 3. Adult domain: k is varied from 1 to n. We contrast 5 out of the listed (cf. Table 1) k-NN voting methods w.r.t. their influence on the (R)DI and underestimation for the (non-)protected group (primary y-axis). Additionally, the F_1 score of the resulting classifier on independent test data is shown on the secondary ordinate, including markers for the F_1 maximum value and belonging fairness assessments. Used reuse methods from left to right: similarity-based vote, inverse rank-based, multiplicative combination, class representatives-based sim vote, and sim-based vote normalized by class frequency. Mind the differently scaled y_1 axis for the latter one.

how the $\mathcal{L}_1$-optimized (i.e. geared towards optimal F_1 score) classifiers "gather" in the bottom-right part of the zoomed-in sub-chart. Likewise, the rules whose k values have been optimized w.r.t. fairness (via $\mathcal{L}_2$ and the incorporation of RDI) appear to be shifted to the top-left compared to their $\mathcal{L}_1$ counterparts. Stated differently, on average a loss of ~ 0.015 in terms of the classifiers' F_1 scores (from ~ 0.695 to ~ 0.68) is compromised for an RDI increase of about 0.12 (from ~ 0.82 to ~ 0.94, roughly using the centers of the ellipses in Fig. 4 as indicator). This shows empirically that case adaptation in CBR's reuse phase can be designed towards reduced bias and unfairness against protected groups.

Rule Ranking. We finish our study with a brief comparison across our selection of k-NN rules. The bar chart in part b) of Fig. 4 reports aggregate performance of all rules over all domains. Within each specific setting of k (e.g. $k/n = 0.05$) we *ranked* all 13 rules by both, their achieved F_1 score and RDI value, respectively, and awarded each rule $13 - r$ points, if it achieved rank r, forming averages over all settings of k considered previously. Apparently, R_{13} performs best in terms of fairness by keeping the RDI close to one, whereas R_7 is best-in-class with respect to maximizing F_1 (which is in line with [21]). Be aware that these numbers are averages over a wide range of k values including those that might be practically irrelevant – which is why the bars are merely meant as a general indication as to what extent each rule trades fairness for classification performance.

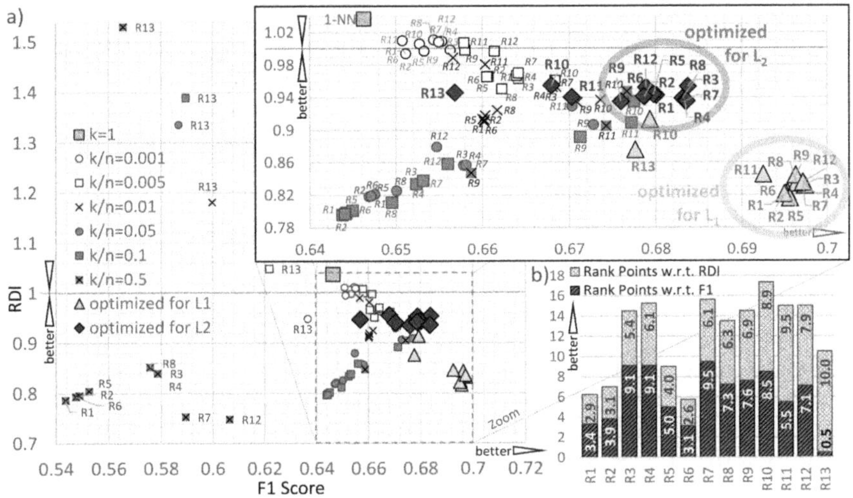

Fig. 4. a) Trade-off between performance (F_1 on x) and fairness (RDI on y), averaged over all domains. The zoomed-in subgraph clarifies specific combinations of reuse method and k setting. b) Attempt to discern the 13 used reuse methods by their average rank (as achieved for different k values) regarding both, performance and fairness.

5 Conclusion

We have focused on the algorithmic bias of the reuse step in CBR. For the special case of k-nearest neighbor classification we have systematically analyzed how the specific value of k in conjunction with the employed voting rule exerts bias by treating members of a protected group disparately. In a comprehensive empirical study with established fairness research datasets we found that fairness can be improved at a moderate cost in classification performance by selecting a tailored value of k in combination with favoring appropriate k-NN rules over others.

Declaration of GenAI Use. Writing this manuscript, the author used Lumo and ChatGPT for disambiguating word meanings and LaTeX assistance. He reviewed and edited the content as needed to take full responsibility for the paper.

References

1. Aamodt, A., Plaza, E.: Case-based reasoning: foundational issues, methodological variations, and system approaches. AI Commun. **7**(1), 39–59 (1994)
2. Abdalla, H., Amer, A.: Enhancing data classification using locally informed weighted kNN algorithm. Expert Syst. Appl. **276** (2025)
3. Acikkar, M., Tokgöz, S.: Improving multi-class classification: scaled extensions of harmonic mean-based adaptive k-nearest neighbors. Appl. Intell. **55** (2025)
4. Ando, S.: Classifying imbalanced data in distance-based feature space. Knowl. Inf. Syst. **46**(3), 707–730 (2016)

5. Angwin, J., Larson, J., Mattu, S., Kirchner, L.: Machine Bias (2016)
6. Bergmann, R., Richter, M., Schmitt, S., Stahl, A., Vollrath, I.: Utility-oriented matching: a new research direction for CBR. In: GWCBR (2001)
7. Berk, R., Heidari, H., Jabbari, S., Kearns, M.: Fairness in criminal justice risk assessments: the state of the art. Soc. Methods Res. **50**, 3–44 (2017)
8. Blanzeisky, W., Cunningham, P.: Algorithmic factors influencing bias in machine learning. In: Machine Learning and Principles and Practice of Knowledge Discovery in Databases (ECML PKDD 2021), pp. 559–574. Springer (2021)
9. Blanzeisky, W., Cunningham, P.: Addressing underestimation bias in CBR through case-base maintenance. In: 31st International Conference on Case-Based Reasoning (ICCBR 2023), Aberdeen, Scotland, pp. 233–243. Springer (2023)
10. Blanzeisky, W., Smyth, B., Cunningham, P.: Algorithmic bias and fairness in case-based reasoning. In: Proceedings of the 30th International Conference on Case-Based Reasoning (ICCBR 2022), Nancy, France, pp. 48–62. Springer (2022)
11. Castelnovo, A., Crupi, R., Greco, G., Regoli, D., Penco, I.: A clarification of the nuances in the fairness metrics landscape. Nat. Sci. Rep. **12**, 4209 (2022)
12. Caton, S., Haas, C.: Fairness in ML: a survey. ACM Comput. Surv. **56**(7) (2024)
13. Cover, T., Hart, P.: Nearest neighbor pattern classification. IEEE Trans. Inf. Theory **13**, 21–27 (1967)
14. Devroye, L., Gyorfi, L., Lugosi, G.: A Probabilistic Theory of Pattern Recognition. Springer (1996)
15. Dubey, H., Pudi, V.: Class based weighted k-nearest neighbor over imbalance dataset. In: 17th Pacific-Asia Conference on Advances in Knowledge Discovery and Data Mining (PAKDD), Goald Coast, Australia, pp. 305–316. Springer (2013)
16. Dudani, S.: The distance-weighted k-nearest neighbor rule. IEEE Trans. Syst. Man Cybern. SMC **6**, 325–327 (1976)
17. Feldman, M., Friedler, S., Moeller, J., Scheidegger, C.: Certifying and removing disparate impact. In: 21th ACM SIGKDD International Conference on Knowledge Discovery and Data Mining, Sydney, Australia, pp. 259–268. ACM Press (2015)
18. Fix, E., Hodges, J.: Discriminatory Analysis. Nonparametric Discrimination: Consistency Properties. Technical Report 4, USAF School of Aviation Medicine, USA (1951)
19. Geler, Z., Kurbalija, V., Radovanovic, M., Ivanovic, M.: Comparison of different weighting schemes for the kNN classifier. Knowl. Inf. Syst. **48**, 331–378 (2016)
20. Ghosh, A.: On optimum choice of k in nearest neighbor classification. Comput. Stat. Data Anal. **50**(11), 3113–3123 (2006)
21. Gou, J., Du, L., Zhang, Y., Xiong, T.: A new distance-weighted k-nearest neighbor classifier. J. Inf. Comput. Sci. **9**, 1429–1436 (2012)
22. Gou, J., Xiong, T., Kuang, Y.: A novel weighted voting for K-nearest neighbor rule. J. Comput. **6**(5), 833–840 (2011)
23. Hastie, T., Tibshirani, R., Friedman, J.: The Elements of Statistical Learning. Data Mining, Inference, and Prediction. Springer (2013)
24. Hotz, M., Malburg, L., Bergmann, R.: Advanced search techniques for determining optimal sequences of adaptation rules in process-oriented CBR. In: 33rd International Conference on CBR (ICCBR 2025), Biarritz, France, pp. 236–251 (2025)
25. Kaggle Inc.: Data Science Community and Competitions Repository (2026). https://www.kaggle.com. Accessed Mar 2026
26. Kamishima, T., Akaho, S., Asoh, H., Sakuma, J.: Fairness-aware classifier with prejudice remover regularizer. In: Machine Learning and Knowledge Discovery in Databases (ECML PKDD 2012), Bristol, UK, pp. 35–50. Springer (2012)

27. Kelly, M., Longjohn, R.: The UCI ML Repository. https://archive.ics.uci.edu
28. Kusner, M., Loftus, J., Russell, C., Silva, R.: Counterfactual fairness. In: Proceedings NeurIPS, pp. 4066–4076. NIPS Foundation, Long Beach, USA (2017)
29. Liu, W., Chawla, S.: Class confidence weighted kNN algorithms for imbalanced data sets. In: Huang, J.Z., Cao, L., Srivastava, J. (eds.) PAKDD 2011. LNCS (LNAI), vol. 6635, pp. 345–356. Springer, Heidelberg (2011). https://doi.org/10.1007/978-3-642-20847-8_29
30. Mehrabi, N., Morstatter, F., Saxena, N., Lerman, K., Galstyan, A.: A survey on bias and fairness in machine learning. ACM Comput. Surv. **54**(6), 1–35 (2021)
31. Mitani, Y., Hamamoto, Y.: A local mean-based nonparametric classifier. Pattern Recogn. Lett. **27**(10), 1151–1159 (2006)
32. Pao, T.-L., Chen, Y.-T., Yeh, J.-H., Cheng, Y.-M., Lin, Y.-Y.: A comparative study of different weighting schemes on KNN-based emotion recognition in mandarin speech. In: Huang, D.-S., Heutte, L., Loog, M. (eds.) ICIC 2007. LNCS, vol. 4681, pp. 997–1005. Springer, Heidelberg (2007). https://doi.org/10.1007/978-3-540-74171-8_101
33. Patel, H., Thakur, G.: A hybrid weighted nearest neighbor approach to mine imbalanced data. In: International Conference on Data Mining (DMIN 2016), pp. 106–110 (2016)
34. Pedreschi, D., Ruggieri, S., Turini, F.: Measuring discrimination in socially-sensitive decision records. In: 9th SIAM International Conference on Data Mining (SDM), pp. 581–592. Society for Industrial and Applied Mathematics, Sparks, USA (2009)
35. Richter, M.: Knowledge Containers. Readings in CBR. Morgan Kaufmann (2003)
36. Richter, M., Weber, R.: Case-Based Reasoning. A Textbook. Springer (2013)
37. Sitarz, M.: Extending F1 Metric, Probabilistic Approach. arXiv:2210.11997 (2022)
38. Song, Y., Huang, J., Zhou, D., Zha, H., Giles, C.: IKNN: informative k-nearest neighbor pattern classification. In: ECML PKDD, pp. 248–264. Springer (2007)
39. Voulgaris, Z., Magoulas, G.: Extensions of the k nearest neighbour methods for classification problems, pp. 23–28. ACTA Press (2008)
40. Wu, X., et al.: Top 10 algorithms in data mining. Knowl. Inf. Syst. **14**, 1–37 (2008)
41. Zavrel, J.: An empirical re-examination of weighted voting for k-NN. In: 7th Belgian-Dutch Conference on Machine Learning (BeNeLearn-97), pp. 139–145 (1997)
42. Zhang, X., Li, Y.: A positive-biased nearest neighbour algorithm for imbalanced classification. In: 17th Pacific-Asia Conference on Advances in Knowledge Discovery and Data Mining (PAKDD), Goald Coast, Australia, pp. 293–304. Springer (2013)
43. Zhou, Z., Pan, G., Wang, X.: Classification based on attribute positive correlation and average similarity. Res. J. Appl. Sci. Eng. Technol. **5**(4), 1420–1423 (2013)
44. Zliobaite, I.: Measuring discrimination in algorithmic decision making. Data Min. Knowl. Disc. **31** (2017)

Hierarchical Contrastive Learning with Explanation-Aware Training for Case-Based APT Recognition

Wenjie Liu[1,2], Zhen Xu[1(✉)], Yan Zhang[1], Qian Tan[1], and Huading Su[1,2]

[1] Institute of Information Engineering, Chinese Academy of Sciences, Beijing, China
{liuwenjie,xuzhen,zhangyan,tanqian,suhuading}@iie.ac.cn
[2] School of Cyber Security, University of Chinese Academy of Sciences, Beijing, China

Abstract. Advanced Persistent Threat (APT) attacks are characterized by their stealthy, multi-stage nature, posing significant challenges for traditional detection. While Case-Based Reasoning (CBR) offers a promising paradigm for APT recognition by leveraging historical incidents, its efficacy is often hindered by the difficulty of learning discriminative and explainable case representations from complex, large-scale provenance graphs. In this paper, we propose a novel representation learning framework for case-based APT recognition via explanation-aware hierarchical contrastive learning. We model each APT instance as a case consisting of a directed heterogeneous provenance graph. To bridge the gap between raw system logs and high-level attack semantics, we develop a heterogeneous graph encoder trained with hierarchical supervised contrastive learning, which captures multi-granularity attack patterns (sub-technique, technique, and tactic) from the MITRE ATT&CK framework. Furthermore, we introduce an explanation-aware triplet constraint that forces the encoder to focus on critical malicious sub-structures during training, ensuring that the learned embeddings are inherently grounded in task-relevant evidence. During the retrieval phase, similar cases are identified through a class-wise case retrieval mechanism, providing both multi-level labels and a supporting case as a natural explanation. Experimental results on real-world APT datasets demonstrate that our method significantly outperforms baseline models in multi-granularity recognition and provides more robust, interpretable case retrieval, highlighting the synergy between deep representation learning and the CBR cycle in security analysis.

Keywords: Case-Based Reasoning · APT Recognition · Provenance Graphs · Hierarchical Contrastive Learning · Explainable Graph Neural Networks

1 Introduction

Advanced Persistent Threat (APT) attacks represent one of the most challenging threats in modern cybersecurity. Unlike traditional attacks that focus on

L. Malburg and K. Bach (Eds.): ICCBR 2026, LNAI 16780, pp. 100–115, 2027.
https://doi.org/10.1007/978-3-032-33865-5_7

short-term exploitation, APT campaigns are typically stealthy, multi-stage, and long-lasting. Attackers gradually progress through multiple phases such as reconnaissance, privilege escalation, lateral movement, and data exfiltration [2]. These activities often span long periods of time and generate complex system interaction traces [24], making APT detection particularly difficult.

In security operations, detection decisions must not only be accurate but also actionable for analysts. Beyond predicting attack labels, analysts need to understand the reasoning behind alerts, such as which prior attack behaviors they resemble and what evidence supports the decision. However, most existing APT detection approaches focus primarily on node-level anomaly detection [5,19,20], often without providing case-level reasoning support. Although deep learning models have achieved strong performance in these tasks, they typically produce representations that are not directly interpretable or comparable in a way that aligns with analysts' investigative workflows. Moreover, these methods generally rely on sufficient labeled data for each attack category, while real-world APT datasets are often limited and imbalanced across different tactics and techniques [11].

Case-Based Reasoning (CBR) offers a natural paradigm for explainable decision making in such scenarios. Instead of making isolated predictions, CBR solves new problems by retrieving and reusing similar historical cases [1]. When applied to APT detection, a CBR system can justify its decision by presenting historical attack cases that resemble the current observation. This similarity-based reasoning aligns well with the investigative workflow of security analysts, who frequently analyze new incidents by comparing them with previously observed attacks. Motivated by this property, we model each APT attack instance as a case and perform detection through similarity-based retrieval from a case base. In this work, we focus on learning high-quality case representations that enable both accurate detection and explainable case retrieval.

Despite these advantages, applying CBR to APT detection raises two key challenges. **Challenge 1: Case representation with hierarchical attack semantics.** APT knowledge is inherently hierarchical, consisting of tactics, techniques, and sub-techniques. Effective case retrieval therefore requires representations that preserve such multi-level semantic relationships so that attacks sharing similar tactics or techniques can be organized appropriately in the embedding space. **Challenge 2: Explainable similarity reasoning.** While CBR retrieves similar historical cases, analysts often need to understand the behavioral evidence that explains why two attack cases are considered similar. However, most existing approaches treat explanation as a post-hoc analysis step rather than integrating explainability objectives into the representation learning process.

To address these challenges, we propose a novel case-based reasoning framework for APT detection. In our approach, each APT provenance graph is modeled as a case, and a graph neural network is used to learn its embedding representation. To address **Challenge 1**, we introduce a hierarchical supervised contrastive learning strategy that incorporates multiple levels of attack labels, including sub-technique, technique, and tactic categories, enabling the learned case embeddings to preserve multi-granularity attack semantics. To address **Challenge 2**, we design an intrinsic explanation-aware contrastive constraint. This constraint incorporates discriminative subgraphs into the contrastive training loop, encouraging the model to ground its representations in critical malicious interactions rather than spurious correlations. During inference, the system performs class-wise case retrieval and provides historical supporting cases as evidence to justify the detection decisions.

We evaluate the framework on real-world APT datasets and compare it against multiple baselines. Results show superior accuracy across all attack granularities, and ablation studies confirm the importance of the hierarchical strategy and explanation-aware constraint for learning robust case representations.

The main contributions of this paper are summarized as follows:

- We propose a novel case-based reasoning framework for APT detection that models each APT provenance graph as a case and performs similarity-based reasoning over a case base.
- We introduce a hierarchical supervised contrastive learning strategy to capture multi-level attack semantics, ensuring that case embeddings preserve the structured relationships between tactics, techniques, and sub-techniques.
- We design an intrinsic explanation-aware constraint that incorporates discriminative subgraphs into the contrastive training loop, encouraging the model to ground its reasoning in critical malicious interactions.
- We develop a class-wise case retrieval mechanism and conduct extensive experiments on real-world datasets to demonstrate that our approach achieves superior recognition accuracy while providing supporting cases.

The remainder of this paper is organized as follows. Section 2 reviews related work on APT detection and recognition, case-based reasoning for cybersecurity, and graph representation. Section 3 presents the proposed CBR framework for APT recognition. Section 4 describes the experimental setup and evaluation results. Finally, Sect. 5 concludes the paper and discusses future research directions.

2 Related Work

2.1 APT Detection and Recognition

Provenance graph analysis is the standard approach for APT detection due to its ability to capture causal relationships [25]. Early methods primarily focus on binary anomaly detection at the node or graph level [5,19,20]. However, these approaches provide limited tactical insights for security analysts. To address this, rule-based systems like HOLMES [12] and the deep learning-based TREC [11] attempt to recognize specific attack techniques. Despite their progress, these methods typically treat attack categories as independent labels, ignoring the three-level hierarchy (tactics, techniques, and sub-techniques) defined by the MITRE ATT&CK framework. This motivates our hierarchical representation learning approach for more precise case indexing.

2.2 Case-Based Reasoning for Cybersecurity

CBR offers an interpretable paradigm by justifying decisions through similar historical incidents [1]. Recent advances include multi-agent systems for distributed detection [14] and diffusion models for ransomware feature refinement [18]. A notable inspiration is MicroCBR [10], which utilizes spatio-temporal knowledge graphs for troubleshooting. However, its reliance on exact graph matching is computationally prohibitive for large-scale APT provenance graphs. While Siamese GNNs have proven effective for similarity learning in process-oriented CBR [6], their application to complex, hierarchical APT cases remains underexplored. Our work bridges this gap by integrating GNNs into a CBR framework to handle large-scale, graph-structured cases efficiently.

2.3 Graph Representation and Contrastive Learning

Heterogeneous GNNs, such as HAN [21] and HGT [7], have become standard for modeling complex system dependencies. To improve representation quality, supervised contrastive learning (SupCon) [8] has been adapted for malware [4] and intrusion detection [22]. Nevertheless, existing contrastive methods fail to exploit the hierarchical relationships inherent in attack taxonomies. Furthermore, while XAI techniques like gradient-based importance [23] and exemplar-based explanations [3] provide foundations for transparency, they are rarely integrated into the training process. We address these limitations by introducing an explanation-aware hierarchical contrastive constraint that grounds case embeddings in critical attack sub-structures.

3 Methodology

In this section, we present a case-based reasoning (CBR) framework for APT recognition with hierarchical label prediction. We first define the structure of a case and construct the case base from provenance graphs. We then introduce a heterogeneous graph-based case representation learning module, which integrates hierarchical supervised contrastive learning with an explanation-aware constraint to emphasize discriminative substructures. Finally, we describe the case retrieval mechanism based on learned embeddings. The overall framework of the proposed method is illustrated in Fig. 1.

3.1 Case Definition and Representation

Following the data collection procedure described in [11], each APT attack instance is modeled as a *case* $\mathcal{C} = (G, y_{\text{sub}}, y_{\text{tec}}, y_{\text{tac}})$, where G is a directed heterogeneous provenance graph, and $y_{\text{sub}}, y_{\text{tec}}, y_{\text{tac}}$ denote the sub-technique, technique, and tactic labels respectively (according to the MITRE ATT&CK framework).

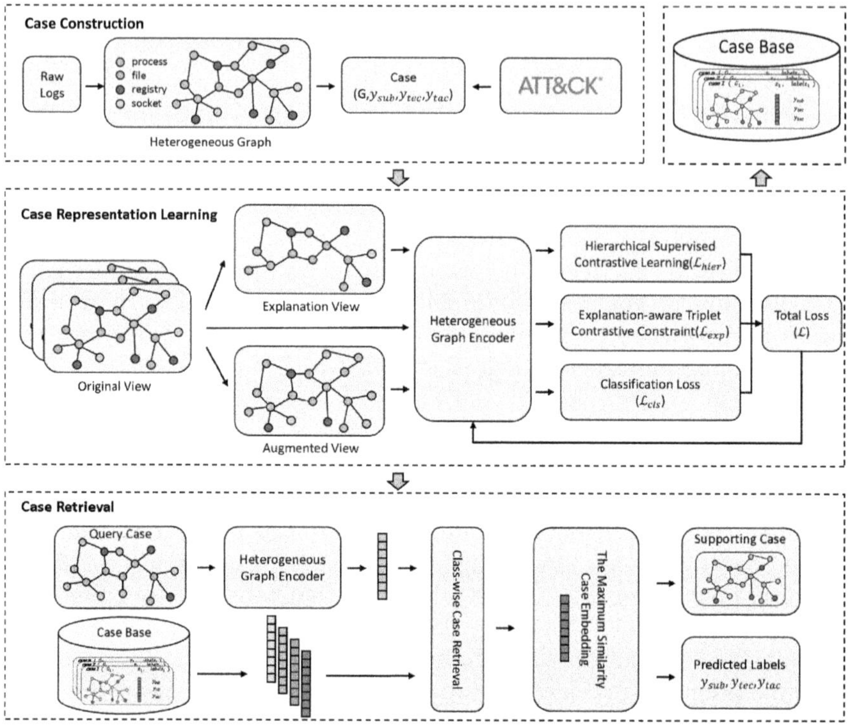

Fig. 1. Overall Framework of the Proposed CBR-based APT Recognition Method.

Graph Structure. The provenance graph $G = (\mathcal{V}, \mathcal{E})$ is constructed from kernel-level audit logs. The nodes represent system entities and are categorized into four types: *process* ($\mathcal{V}_p$), *file* ($\mathcal{V}_f$), *registry* ($\mathcal{V}_r$), and *socket* ($\mathcal{V}_s$). Edges represent system events, and each edge is a triple (u, v, op), where u is the subject, v is the object, and op denotes the operation (e.g., read, write, execute). Following [11], we consider 21 distinct edge types based on the combination of source/target node types and the operation. Table 1 summarizes these types.

Node Feature Initialization. For each node $v_i \in \mathcal{V}$, we compute a 42-dimensional initial feature vector $\mathbf{e}_i^{(0)}$ that captures its local interaction pattern. Specifically, we count the number of incoming edges of each of the 21 types (placed in the first 21 dimensions) and the number of outgoing edges of each type (placed in the last 21 dimensions). This results in:

$$\mathbf{e}_i^{(0)} = [a_1, \ldots, a_{21}, a_{22}, \ldots, a_{42}], \tag{1}$$

where a_k $(1 \leq k \leq 21)$ is the count of incoming edges of type k, and a_{k+21} is the count of outgoing edges of type k. Such statistics reflect the behavioral roles of nodes and have been shown effective for APT detection [11].

Table 1. The types of nodes and edges

Node Type Pairs	Edge Types
process - process	launch
process - file	create, read, write, close, delete, enum
process - registry	open, query, enumerate, modify, close, delete
process - socket	send, receive, retransmit, copy, connect, disconnect, accept, reconnect

Case Base Construction. All historical cases are stored in the case base $\mathcal{B} = \{\mathcal{C}_1, \ldots, \mathcal{C}_N\}$. To support efficient retrieval, we adopt a two-tier storage: the raw graph G is kept for explanation generation, while the embedding vector $\mathbf{z} = \text{Enc}(G)$ (computed by the trained encoder) can be optionally stored for fast similarity search. The incremental addition of new cases and periodic model updating are left as future work.

3.2 Case Representation Learning

To enable effective retrieval, each raw case must be mapped to a low-dimensional embedding vector that preserves hierarchical semantics and is sensitive to critical substructures. We achieve this by training a heterogeneous graph encoder with carefully designed contrastive objectives.

Encoder Architecture. We design a lightweight heterogeneous graph encoder, denoted $\text{Enc}(\cdot)$, inspired by the Heterogeneous Graph Transformer [7], but simplified for small-data scenarios. The encoder consists of L layers of relation-aware message passing, followed by a node-type aware attention pooling to produce a graph-level embedding.

Type-Specific Projection. For each node type $t \in \{\text{process}, \text{file}, \text{registry}, \text{socket}\}$, a learnable linear layer projects the initial feature vector into a hidden space of dimension d_h:

$$\mathbf{h}_v^{(0)} = \mathbf{W}_t \, \mathbf{e}_v^{(0)}, \tag{2}$$

where $\mathbf{W}_t \in \mathbb{R}^{d_h \times 42}$.

Relation-Aware Message Passing. At each layer l $(1 \leq l \leq L)$, for every directed edge (u, v) of relation r (where r encodes the source node type, target node type, and operation), we compute a message from u to v as:

$$\mathbf{m}_{u \to v}^{(l)} = \mathbf{W}_r^{(l)} \, \mathbf{h}_u^{(l)}, \tag{3}$$

with $\mathbf{W}_r^{(l)} \in \mathbb{R}^{d_h \times d_h}$. The messages from all neighbors of v are aggregated, and a residual connection followed by layer normalization is applied:

$$\mathbf{h}_v^{(l+1)} = \text{LayerNorm}\left(\mathbf{h}_v^{(l)} + \sum_{u \in \mathcal{N}(v)} \mathbf{m}_{u \to v}^{(l)}\right). \tag{4}$$

After L layers, we obtain the final node embeddings $\mathbf{h}_v^{(L)}$ for all $v \in \mathcal{V}$.

Graph-Level Pooling. To produce a fixed-size case embedding, we employ a node-type aware attention mechanism. For each node type t, we compute attention scores for nodes of that type:

$$\alpha_v = \frac{\exp\left(\mathbf{q}_t^\top \tanh(\mathbf{W}_t^{\text{att}} \mathbf{h}_v^{(L)})\right)}{\sum_{u \in \mathcal{V}_t} \exp\left(\mathbf{q}_t^\top \tanh(\mathbf{W}_t^{\text{att}} \mathbf{h}_u^{(L)})\right)}, \tag{5}$$

where $\mathbf{q}_t$ and $\mathbf{W}_t^{\text{att}}$ are learnable parameters. The type-specific representation is then the weighted sum:

$$\mathbf{z}_t = \sum_{v \in \mathcal{V}_t} \alpha_v \mathbf{h}_v^{(L)}. \tag{6}$$

Finally, all type vectors are concatenated and passed through a linear layer to obtain the graph-level embedding:

$$\mathbf{z} = \mathbf{W}_{\text{out}} \left[\mathbf{z}_{\text{proc}} \| \mathbf{z}_{\text{file}} \| \mathbf{z}_{\text{reg}} \| \mathbf{z}_{\text{sock}}\right], \tag{7}$$

where $\|$ denotes concatenation and $\mathbf{W}_{\text{out}} \in \mathbb{R}^{d \times 4d_h}$. The encoder is trained end-to-end with the objectives described below. Unlike TREC [11] and HAN [21] which rely on manually predefined meta-paths to capture semantic relations, our encoder adopts a relation-aware message passing mechanism that implicitly learns multi-hop dependencies through stacked layers. This design avoids the need for labor-intensive and potentially incomplete meta-path selection, and is more flexible in capturing the diverse and evolving patterns of APT attacks directly from the graph structure.

Hierarchical Supervised Contrastive Learning. The embedding space must reflect the hierarchical relationships among sub-techniques, techniques, and tactics. To achieve this, we apply supervised contrastive learning [8] separately for each granularity. For a mini-batch of B cases with embeddings $\{\mathbf{z}_i\}_{i=1}^B$ and corresponding labels $y_i^{\text{sub}}, y_i^{\text{tec}}, y_i^{\text{tac}}$, we define three contrastive losses.

Loss for Sub-technique. For sub-technique, the set of positives for sample i is $\mathcal{P}_{\text{sub}}(i) = \{j \neq i \mid y_j^{\text{sub}} = y_i^{\text{sub}}\}$. The loss is:

$$\mathcal{L}_{\text{sub}} = \sum_{i=1}^{B} \frac{-1}{|\mathcal{P}_{\text{sub}}(i)|} \sum_{p \in \mathcal{P}_{\text{sub}}(i)} \log \frac{\exp(\mathbf{z}_i \cdot \mathbf{z}_p / \tau_{\text{sub}})}{\sum_{j \neq i} \exp(\mathbf{z}_i \cdot \mathbf{z}_j / \tau_{\text{sub}})}, \tag{8}$$

where τ_{sub} is a temperature parameter. Similarly, $\mathcal{L}_{\text{tec}}$ and $\mathcal{L}_{\text{tac}}$ are defined using technique and tactic labels with temperatures τ_{tec} and τ_{tac}, respectively. And we set $\tau_{\text{sub}} < \tau_{\text{tec}} < \tau_{\text{tac}}$ to reflect the class granularity: finer-grained classes (sub-technique) require a lower temperature to enforce tighter clustering, whereas coarser-grained classes (tactic) benefit from a higher temperature to allow more structural diversity within the same tactic.

The total hierarchical contrastive loss is:

$$\mathcal{L}_{\text{hier}} = \alpha_{\text{sub}}\mathcal{L}_{\text{sub}} + \alpha_{\text{tec}}\mathcal{L}_{\text{tec}} + \alpha_{\text{tac}}\mathcal{L}_{\text{tac}}. \tag{9}$$

Explanation-Aware Triplet Contrastive Constraint. To make the learned representations amenable to explanation, we encourage the encoder to focus on the discriminative substructures within each case. For each case G in the batch, we construct two additional views:

- **Explanation subgraph** G_{exp}: extracted by retaining only the nodes with highest importance scores (detailed in Sect. 3.3). This subgraph is intended to capture the core malicious operations of the attack.
- **Augmented graph** G_{aug}: obtained by applying mild augmentations to G, such as randomly masking a fraction of node features or dropping a fraction of edges. Augmentations simulate variations in the attack and improve robustness.

Using the shared encoder, we obtain three embeddings: $\mathbf{z} = \text{Enc}(G)$, $\mathbf{z}_{\text{exp}} = \text{Enc}(G_{\text{exp}})$, and $\mathbf{z}_{\text{aug}} = \text{Enc}(G_{\text{aug}})$. We then enforce semantic consistency among them via a triplet InfoNCE loss:

$$\mathcal{L}_{\text{exp}} = \frac{1}{3}\Big(\text{InfoNCE}(\mathbf{z}, \mathbf{z}_{\text{exp}}) + \text{InfoNCE}(\mathbf{z}, \mathbf{z}_{\text{aug}}) + \text{InfoNCE}(\mathbf{z}_{\text{exp}}, \mathbf{z}_{\text{aug}})\Big), \tag{10}$$

where $\text{InfoNCE}(\mathbf{a}, \mathbf{b})$ treats $\mathbf{b}$ as the positive sample for $\mathbf{a}$ and all other samples in the batch as negatives. This loss encourages the explanation subgraph to retain the core discriminative information of the original graph and improves robustness to variations.

Overall Training Objective. In addition to the contrastive losses, we add a lightweight auxiliary classification loss to stabilize training. A three-layer MLP classifier is attached to the embedding $\mathbf{z}$ to predict the tactic and technique labels (tactic is coarser and easier, sub-technique is finer). The classification loss is:

$$\mathcal{L}_{\text{cls}} = \text{CE}(\hat{y}_{\text{tac}}, y_{\text{tac}}) + \text{CE}(\hat{y}_{\text{tec}}, y_{\text{tec}}) + \text{CE}(\hat{y}_{\text{sub}}, y_{\text{sub}}), \tag{11}$$

where CE denotes cross-entropy. The final training objective combines all components:

$$\mathcal{L} = \lambda_{\text{hier}}\mathcal{L}_{\text{hier}} + \lambda_{\text{exp}}\mathcal{L}_{\text{exp}} + \lambda_{\text{cls}}\mathcal{L}_{\text{cls}}, \tag{12}$$

with balancing hyperparameters $\lambda_{\text{hier}}, \lambda_{\text{exp}}, \lambda_{\text{cls}}$. After training, the encoder $\text{Enc}(\cdot)$ is fixed and used to embed any case for retrieval and explanation.

3.3 Case Retrieval and Explanation

Class-Wise Case Retrieval Given a query case q with embedding $\mathbf{z}_q = \text{Enc}(G_q)$, we retrieve the most relevant cases from the case base $\mathcal{B}$. To ensure both accuracy and explainability, we adopt a class-wise maximum similarity strategy to predict the sub-technique label:

$$\hat{y}_{\text{sub}} = \arg\max_{c} \left(\max_{\mathbf{z} \in \mathcal{B}_c} \cos(\mathbf{z}_q, \mathbf{z}) \right), \tag{13}$$

where $\mathcal{B}_c$ denotes the set of case embeddings belonging to sub-technique c, and $\cos(\cdot, \cdot)$ represents the cosine similarity. The corresponding technique and tactic labels are subsequently derived via the predefined mappings SUB2TEC and SUB2TAC.

The retrieved case achieving the maximum similarity within the predicted class is designated as the *supporting case*, which provides a direct, evidence-based explanation for the detection decision. This class-wise retrieval mechanism (conceptually a k-nearest neighbor scheme with $k = 1$) offers two distinct advantages: (i) it inherently yields an interpretable reference for security analysts, and (ii) it mitigates the influence of majority-class bias often found in standard k-NN voting, making it particularly robust for handling imbalanced APT data.

Explanation Subgraph Generation. To explain why the query q and its supporting case c are similar, we extract discriminative subgraphs using a gradient-based importance method. For a case G with embedding $\mathbf{z}$, the importance score of node v is computed as:

$$s_v = \left\| \frac{\partial \|\mathbf{z}\|_2}{\partial \mathbf{h}_v} \odot \mathbf{h}_v \right\|_1, \tag{14}$$

where $\mathbf{h}_v$ denotes the node embedding from the final encoder layer. This score reflects the contribution of node v to the overall graph representation. For each node type, we retain the top $n\%$ highest-scoring nodes to construct the explanation subgraph G_{exp}, where $n\%$ is hereafter referred to as the *keep_rate*.

Due to the large scale of provenance graphs (typically thousands of nodes per instance), directly visualizing G_{exp} is impractical. Instead, we treat the extracted subgraph as a structured explanation, which captures the most critical entities and interactions responsible for the similarity between cases. Importantly, the same importance mechanism is integrated into training, where G_{exp} serves as an explanation-aware view for contrastive learning. This establishes a closed loop between representation learning and explanation extraction, enabling the model to learn more discriminative and semantically grounded representations.

3.4 Case Revision and Retention

The proposed framework primarily focuses on the representation learning and retrieval stages of CBR, while formal revision and retention mechanisms are reserved for future exploration. In practical deployments, once a newly detected APT incident is verified, it can be incorporated into the case base as a new case to facilitate future reasoning.

However, continuous accumulation of cases may lead to case base swamping or performance degradation due to redundancy and concept drift. To address this, we envision an incremental learning and maintenance strategy leveraging our explanation-aware framework. Specifically, the explanation subgraphs can serve as a metric for case-base maintenance: cases with highly overlapping or low-quality explanation structures could be identified as redundant or noisy and subsequently pruned. Furthermore, we plan to investigate periodic fine-tuning of the graph encoder using these distilled subgraphs to ensure the model remains robust to evolving attack variants. This adaptive retention process will ensure a compact yet highly informative case base for long-term APT detection.

4 Experiments

In this section, we evaluate the effectiveness of the proposed framework for case-based APT analysis on provenance graph data. We first introduce the experimental setup, including the dataset, evaluation strategies, and implementation details. We then compare the proposed method with several baseline models. Finally, we conduct ablation studies and provide visualization examples to demonstrate the interpretability of the proposed approach.

4.1 Experimental Setup

Dataset. We evaluate our approach on the Kellect4APT dataset [15], a publicly available provenance graph dataset designed for APT tactic and technique recognition. The dataset is constructed based on the MITRE ATT&CK framework [16], which provides a hierarchical taxonomy of adversary tactics, techniques, and sub-techniques. To simulate APT behaviors, the Atomic Red Team [13] library is used to execute individual ATT&CK techniques, ensuring that each execution corresponds to a single technique instance. The dataset comprises 298 provenance graph samples, covering 9 tactics and 43 sub-techniques. Each sample is stored as a JSON file containing a sequence of system events, which we transform into a heterogeneous graph with four node types (process, file, registry, socket) and multiple edge types representing system operations. Table 2 summarizes the main statistics of the dataset. For evaluation, we adopt a stratified split with a ratio of 9:1 for training and testing. For sub-techniques with only one available sample, the sample is excluded from training and retained solely in the case base as a supporting case for retrieval.

Evaluation Strategies. Following the hierarchical structure of the MITRE ATT&CK framework, we evaluate our method performance at three levels: sub-technique, technique, and tactic. SubACC, TecACC, TacACC are used as evaluation metrics, which stand for accuracies of APT sub-technique recognition, APT technique recognition, and APT tactic recognition, respectively.

Table 2. Dataset statistics at different hierarchy levels.

Level	Classes	Min	Max	Avg
Sub-technique	43	1	20	6.93
Technique	25	1	53	11.92
Tactic	9	2	133	33.11

Implementation Details. The proposed framework is implemented using PyTorch and the Deep Graph Library (DGL). Graph neural network encoders are trained using the Adam optimizer. The embedding dimension is set to 128, following TREC [11]. For hierarchical contrastive learning, the temperature parameters are set to $\tau_{\text{sub}} = 0.07$, $\tau_{\text{tec}} = 0.2$, and $\tau_{\text{tac}} = 0.4$, following the intuition that finer-grained classes require tighter clustering. The loss weights are set to $\alpha_{\text{sub}} = 0.2$, $\alpha_{\text{tec}} = 0.3$, and $\alpha_{\text{tac}} = 0.5$. For the overall objective, we set $\lambda_{\text{hier}} = 0.3$, $\lambda_{\text{exp}} = 0.3$, and $\lambda_{\text{cls}} = 0.3$. For fair comparison, all models are evaluated using the same training and test sets, with the same case embedding dimension and number of training epochs. All experiments were repeated 10 times, and we report the average performance.

4.2 Comparison Experiments

In this section, we compare the proposed framework with several representative baseline models. The baselines are grouped into three categories according to their modeling strategies: homogeneous graph baselines, heterogeneous graph baselines, and contrastive learning baselines.

- **Homogeneous Graph Baselines.** These methods treat each provenance graph as a homogeneous graph and perform graph classification using standard graph neural networks. Although they have been widely used for graph representation learning, they do not explicitly model different node and edge types in provenance graphs. We evaluated two representative models in this category, including GAT [17] and GCN [9], each followed by graph pooling and a cross-entropy classification objective.
- **Heterogeneous Graph Baselines.** These methods explicitly model the heterogeneous structure of provenance graphs by considering different node and relation types. Such approaches are particularly suitable for system provenance data where entities such as processes, files, and network connections interact through different types of relations. We evaluated two representative heterogeneous graph neural networks: HAN [21] and HGT [7].
- **Contrastive Learning Baselines.** Recent studies have shown that contrastive learning can effectively improve representation quality by encouraging similar samples to have closer embeddings in the representation space. To compare with recent contrastive learning-based approaches for APT analysis, we include TREC [11] as a baseline method, which learns representations of

provenance subgraphs using a contrastive learning objective for APT tactic and technique recognition.

These baselines allow us to evaluate the proposed framework from multiple perspectives, including standard graph representation learning, heterogeneous graph modeling, and contrastive learning paradigms.

Table 3. Overall Performance on APT Analysis Tasks

Category	Method	SubACC	TecACC	TacACC
Homogeneous	GCN	0.217	0.267	0.433
	GAT	0.233	0.300	0.533
Heterogeneous	HAN	0.325	0.367	0.596
	HGT	0.389	0.445	0.567
Contrastive	TREC	0.433	0.600	0.767
	OURS	**0.633**	**0.733**	**0.867**

Results Analysis. Table 3 reports the classification performance of different methods at the sub-technique, technique, and tactic levels. From the results, we observe several important findings:

- Homogeneous graph models such as GCN and GAT, achieve reasonable performance but fail to fully capture the heterogeneous structure of provenance graphs. As a result, their performance is generally lower than models designed for heterogeneous graph learning.
- Heterogeneous graph neural networks such as HAN and HGT, achieve improved performance by explicitly modeling different node and relation types. This demonstrates the importance of leveraging heterogeneous structural information when analyzing provenance graphs.
- The contrastive learning-based baseline TREC further improves representation quality by incorporating a contrastive learning objective. However, compared with TREC, the proposed framework achieves superior performance by learning more discriminative graph representations that preserve hierarchical attack semantics. This improvement is attributed to two key components: the hierarchical contrastive learning strategy, which captures multi-granularity attack semantics, and the explanation-aware representation learning mechanism, which enhances the discriminative power of case embeddings.

Across all methods, performance consistently improves from sub-technique to tactic level, reflecting increasing semantic granularity. Overall, the proposed framework achieves the best performance across all classification levels, demonstrating its effectiveness in learning discriminative and interpretable representations for case-based APT analysis.

4.3 Ablation Experiments

To analyze the contributions of different components of the proposed framework, we conduct ablation experiments by removing key modules from the full model. Specifically, we evaluate the following variants:

- **w/o Explanation**: The explanation-aware training component is removed. Specifically, the model is trained without the explanation subgraph-based contrastive constraint, and only uses the original graph representations for learning.
- **w/o Hierarchical**: The hierarchical supervised contrastive learning objective is removed. Instead, all labels are treated independently without modeling the hierarchical relationships among sub-techniques, techniques, and tactics.
- **w/o Classification**: The auxiliary classification objective is removed. The model is trained solely with contrastive learning objectives, without additional supervision from label prediction.
- **Full Model**: The complete proposed framework, which integrates hierarchical supervised contrastive learning, explanation-aware subgraph-based contrastive constraints, and the auxiliary classification objective.

Results Analysis. Table 4 presents the ablation results evaluating the contribution of each component. Removing the explanation-aware component (**w/o Explanation**) leads to a consistent performance drop, indicating that the subgraph-based constraint helps focus on informative structures and reduces noise from irrelevant parts of the graph. The degradation in **w/o Hierarchical** highlights the importance of modeling the hierarchical relationships among sub-techniques, techniques, and tactics. Treating labels independently weakens the semantic structure of the embedding space and reduces accuracy. Similarly, **w/o Classification** shows that the auxiliary classification objective provides complementary supervision, improving alignment between embeddings and label semantics.

Overall, the full model achieves the best performance, demonstrating that the three components are complementary: explanation-aware learning enhances representation quality, hierarchical contrastive learning preserves multi-level semantics, and classification supervision improves discriminability.

Table 4. Ablation study of the proposed framework.

Variant	SubACC	TecACC	TacACC
w/o Explanation	0.433	0.600	0.744
w/o Hierarchical	0.504	0.596	0.773
w/o Classification	0.478	0.567	0.778
Full Model	**0.633**	**0.733**	**0.867**

We further study the effect of the *keep_ rate* n% used to construct explanation subgraphs. Specifically, we vary the *keep_ rate* from 0.1 to 0.7 and evaluate the performance at the sub-technique, technique, and tactic levels, as illustrated in Fig. 2. The results show that the best performance is consistently achieved when the *keep_ rate* is set to 0.3 across all three levels. When the *keep_ rate* is smaller (e.g., 0.1 or 0.2), the performance degrades, suggesting that overly aggressive pruning may remove important nodes and thus weaken the model's ability to capture critical attack patterns. On the other hand, increasing the *keep_ rate* beyond 0.3 (e.g., 0.4–0.7) also leads to inferior performance. This indicates that including more nodes introduces redundant or less relevant information, which may dilute the discriminative signals in the learned representations.

These results demonstrate that a moderate level of pruning achieves the best trade-off between information preservation and noise reduction. More importantly, they highlight the necessity of the explanation-aware constraint: provenance graphs typically contain substantial redundancy, and focusing on a compact yet informative subgraph is crucial for effective representation learning.

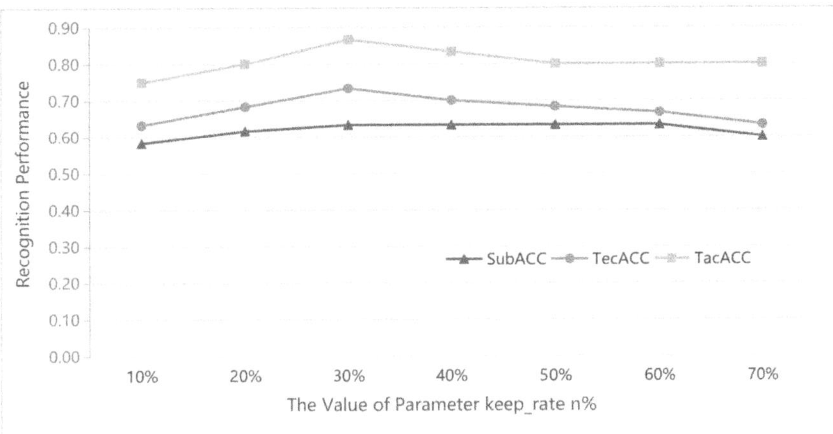

Fig. 2. The Tuning of Parameter *keep_ rate n%*.

5 Conclusion

In this paper, we present a CBR-based framework for APT recognition that leverages hierarchical contrastive learning and explanation-aware training to learn discriminative and semantically structured case representations. Experimental results demonstrate its effectiveness across multiple attack granularities. In future work, we plan to explore incremental case-base updating strategies and more advanced explanation mechanisms to further enhance the adaptability and interpretability of the framework.

Acknowledgments. This work was supported by the National Key Research and Development Program of China (No. 2023YFB3106302).

Declaration on Generative AI. During the preparation of this work, the authors used ChatGPT in order to improve language readability, grammar, and spelling. After using this tool/service, the authors reviewed and edited the content as needed and take full responsibility for the publication's content.

References

1. Aamodt, A., Plaza, E.: Case-based reasoning: foundational issues, methodological variations, and system approaches. AI Commun. **7**(1), 39–59 (1994)
2. Alshamrani, A., Myneni, S., Chowdhary, A., Huang, D.: A survey on advanced persistent threats: techniques, solutions, challenges, and research opportunities. IEEE Commun. Surv. Tutor. **21**(2), 1851–1877 (2019)
3. Armgaan, B., Jain, E., Pandey, H., Chandran, M., Ranu, S.: Gnnxemplar: exemplars to explanations-natural language rules for global GNN interpretability. arXiv preprint arXiv:2509.18376 (2025)
4. Barros, P.H., Chagas, E.T., Oliveira, L.B., Queiroz, F., Ramos, H.S.: Malware-smell: a zero-shot learning strategy for detecting zero-day vulnerabilities. Comput. Secur. **120**, 102785 (2022)
5. Han, X., Pasquier, T., Bates, A., Mickens, J., Seltzer, M.: Unicorn: runtime provenance-based detector for advanced persistent threats. arXiv preprint arXiv:2001.01525 (2020)
6. Hoffmann, M., Malburg, L., Klein, P., Bergmann, R.: Using siamese graph neural networks for similarity-based retrieval in process-oriented case-based reasoning. In: International Conference on Case-Based Reasoning, pp. 229–244. Springer (2020)
7. Hu, Z., Dong, Y., Wang, K., Sun, Y.: Heterogeneous graph transformer. In: Proceedings of the Web Conference 2020, pp. 2704–2710 (2020)
8. Khosla, P., et al.: Supervised contrastive learning. Adv. Neural. Inf. Process. Syst. **33**, 18661–18673 (2020)
9. Kipf, T.N., Welling, M.: Semi-supervised classification with graph convolutional networks. arXiv preprint arXiv:1609.02907 (2016)
10. Liu, F., et al.: Microcbr: case-based reasoning on spatio-temporal fault knowledge graph for microservices troubleshooting. In: International Conference on Case-Based Reasoning, pp. 224–239. Springer (2022)
11. Lv, M., et al.: TREC: APT tactic/technique recognition via few-shot provenance subgraph learning. In: Proceedings of the 2024 on ACM SIGSAC Conference on Computer and Communications Security, pp. 139–152 (2024)
12. Milajerdi, S.M., Gjomemo, R., Eshete, B., Sekar, R., Venkatakrishnan, V.: Holmes: real-time apt detection through correlation of suspicious information flows. In: 2019 IEEE Symposium on Security and Privacy (SP), pp. 1137–1152. IEEE (2019)
13. Red Canary: Atomic red team. GitHub repository (2025). https://github.com/redcanaryco/atomic-red-team. Accessed 16 Mar 2025
14. Schoenborn, J.M., Althoff, K.D.: A multi-agent case-based reasoning intrusion detection system prototype. In: International Conference on Case-Based Reasoning, pp. 359–374. Springer (2023)
15. The Kellect Team: Kellect4APT dataset (2025). https://www.kellect.org/#/kellect-4-aptdataset. Accessed 16 Mar 2025

16. The MITRE Corporation: ATT&CK matrix for enterprise (2025). https://attack.mitre.org/. Accessed 16 Mar 2025
17. Veličković, P., Cucurull, G., Casanova, A., Romero, A., Lio, P., Bengio, Y.: Graph attention networks. arXiv preprint arXiv:1710.10903 (2017)
18. Wang, H., Hardy, J., Kandah, F.: Case-based reasoning with diffusion model for ransomware detection. In: International Conference on Case-Based Reasoning, pp. 469–483. Springer (2025)
19. Wang, Q., et al.: You are what you do: hunting stealthy malware via data provenance analysis. In: NDSS (2020)
20. Wang, S., et al.: Threatrace: detecting and tracing host-based threats in node level through provenance graph learning. IEEE Trans. Inf. Forensics Secur. **17**, 3972–3987 (2022)
21. Wang, X., et al.: Heterogeneous graph attention network. In: The World Wide Web Conference, pp. 2022–2032 (2019)
22. Wu, C., Sun, J., Chen, J., Alazab, M., Liu, Y., Xiang, Y.: TCG-IDS: robust network intrusion detection via temporal contrastive graph learning. IEEE Trans. Inf. Forensics Secur. **20**, 1475–1486 (2025). https://doi.org/10.1109/TIFS.2025.3530702
23. Ying, Z., Bourgeois, D., You, J., Zitnik, M., Leskovec, J.: Gnnexplainer: generating explanations for graph neural networks. Adv. Neural. Inf. Process. Syst. **32** (2019)
24. Zhu, T., et al.: General, efficient, and real-time data compaction strategy for apt forensic analysis. IEEE Trans. Inf. Forensics Secur. **16**, 3312–3325 (2021)
25. Zipperle, M., Gottwalt, F., Chang, E., Dillon, T.: Provenance-based intrusion detection systems: a survey. ACM Comput. Surv. **55**(7), 1–36 (2022)

Explainable, Multimodal, and Responsible CBR

Combining Deep Learning and Large Language Models for Retrieval-Based Image Classification

Zachary Wilkerson(✉), David Leake, and David Crandall

Luddy School of Informatics, Computing, and Engineering, Indiana University, Bloomington, IN 47408, USA
zachwilk@iu.edu

Abstract. Image classification is challenging for traditional case-based methods because of the difficulty of crafting an image feature vocabulary. DL-CBR hybrid classification models address this issue by extracting features from a neural network trained for the image classification task and using those features for similarity assessment to guide retrieval. The hybrid classification approach benefits both from DL models' ability to extract relevant features from raw data and from the ability of CBR to support inertia-free case learning and to effectively use small data sets. The advent of large language models (LLMs) able to process images provides a new potential source for refining similarity assessment decisions in these hybrid models. To investigate the benefit of bringing LLMs to bear in the hybrid classification process, this paper presents two case studies combining a DL-CBR feature extractor/case retrieval model with an LLM that performs a second stage of similarity assessment to determine classification predictions. In experimental tests, this new hybrid model achieves higher classification accuracy than the baseline DL-CBR model while retaining the inertia-free learning, small-data effectiveness, and explanation benefits of the original approach, and is at least as accurate as (and more consistent than) the LLM applied alone. These results highlight the potential benefit of applying DL, CBR, and LLMs in concert for image classification, especially for small-data tasks.

1 Introduction

Accurate case-based classification depends on effective similarity assessment. For many domains, similarity assessment can be based on a comprehensive feature vocabulary developed through knowledge engineering based on human expertise and existing domain knowledge (e.g., [10,18,27]). However, this approach is costly and is not feasible for poorly understood domains or domains such as image classification, in which inputs do not readily align with human-understandable features. Much work has been done to address feature acquisition issues by incorporating (DL) approaches into the (CBR) data pipeline to extract features from raw data and facilitate similarity assessment during retrieval (e.g., [26,28,35]).

L. Malburg and K. Bach (Eds.): ICCBR 2026, LNAI 16780, pp. 119–134, 2027.
https://doi.org/10.1007/978-3-032-33865-5_8

In contrast to pure DL classifiers, such hybrid DL-CBR approaches provide interpretability through the ability to present the cases on which classification is based. In addition, because new cases can be added without retraining, they provide inertia-free learning. Our previous work has focused on improving the classification accuracy of DL-CBR hybrid approaches [19,20,33–35], investigating the effects of different neural architectures and algorithms and different DL-CBR interfaces (esp. on datasets containing limited training data, traditionally considered an area of strength for CBR). Experimental tests of these approaches have shown them to be successful, especially compared with analogous DL-only models in small-data case studies; they retained accuracy comparable to or exceeding that of pure DL models while enabling explanation by prior cases and being more robust to limited training data (e.g., [34,35]).

The DL-BR models that we have described generally build on training a network for the classification task (we describe an alternative training approach in [34]). Thus, model accuracy depends on the availability and characteristics of the training data, albeit less directly than a DL–only model, because of the use of cases as an additional data source. Our previous work illustrates the benefit of using pre-trained DL models [35].

Large language models (LLMs) today benefit from enormous training data sets that have been shown to provide broad-spectrum capabilities. Visual language models provide these capabilities for image data. We hypothesize that LLMs are capable of processing image data and/or extracted features in ways that complement the DL-only and DL-CBR models used in our previous work.

Being able to include information provided by LLMs in the classification process offers a number of potential benefits. First, LLMs exhibit significant potential in handling multimodal cases, and their input flexibility enables them to handle feature vocabularies consisting of diverse modalities or resulting from different levels of pre-processing, while exploiting broad knowledge acquired from training in diverse domains. By contrast, the DL-CBR approach of our previous work requires translating raw data or knowledge into numeric vectors for distance calculation during similarity assessment. Second, due to the flexibility of text-based prompting, LLMs possess significant leeway in how they make decisions. As applied to our work, LLMs could leverage general knowledge from their extensive initial training for similarity assessment (e.g., as in [15]), and potentially perform adaptation to build upon retrieval results, ideally leading to higher classification accuracy than a more rigid DL-CBR system.

This paper presents a two-stage retrieval model (which bears similarity to [11]), combining DL-CBR for feature extraction and retrieval with a LLM for final similarity assessment and decision-making. In this pipeline, our previous DL-CBR model performs feature extraction, with the features used by (KNN) to select an initial set of candidate cases similar to a query case. Then, the LLM selects the nearest neighbor from the field of cases and makes the overall model's classification decision based on the ground truth class of the selected case. Reflecting this data pipeline organization, we name this approach **D**eep learning for feature **E**xtraction and **L**arge language models for **CBR** (DEL-CBR).

This paper also presents two case studies highlighting the effectiveness of DEL-CBR. The case studies consider two datasets, the Animals with Attributes 2 (AwA2) dataset and Augmented Alzheimer MRI Dataset (AAMRI), two distinct domains for an image classification task. DEL-CBR exhibits classification accuracy values that are greater than baseline previous DL-CBR approaches and rival or exceed classification accuracy values for the analogous LLM models used alone, and the significance of these results is corroborated by Student's T-test results. Taken together, these results highlight DEL-CBR as a promising neurosymbolic approach that bridges DL, CBR and LLM approaches.

2 Related Work

Knowledge acquisition of case indices and features is a thoroughly-researched area of CBR. Foundational research in this area focuses on knowledge engineering to establish feature vocabularies (e.g., [10,18,27]) as well as symbolic learning methods to generate and refine indices (e.g., [5,6,8,12]. However, for tasks such as image classification, where limited or no symbolic knowledge may be available, a different approach is required.

2.1 Research Context on Combining DL and CBR

Multiple projects have explored combining symbolic methodologies (including CBR) with non-symbolic models such as neural networks. Many of these integration approaches focus on increased interpretability of the DL model. These include so-called "inherently interpretable networks," where neural models are constructed to leverage prototypical intermediate features within an image (e.g., a beak, wing, etc. that helps describe/classify an image of a bird and may be more readily understood by humans) to inform model decisions [7,23,25]. Other "twin system" models take a different approach, where DL and CBR models are applied in parallel; the CBR model ideally approximates the accurate, black-box decision of the DL model, and then an explanation may be extracted from the CBR model via retrieved case presentation. Still other applications modify the DL structure to conceptually imitate nearest-neighbor algorithms (i.e., in NN-KNN [38]) and leverage DL models within the CBR cycle to perform similarity assessment (e.g., [24]) or case adaptation (e.g., [21]).

Multiple projects have used DL models to extract similarity features for the CBR retrieval process (e.g., [1,26,28]). DL-based feature extraction has shown great success in novel class detection, where a DL model is uncertain about the class label of a given image (e.g., one on which it was not trained) [28]. To address this, features are extracted and passed to a CBR model, which performs implicit classification based on case clustering that can identify groups of cases belonging to novel classes. Additionally, DL models have been shown to successfully handle other multi-dimensional raw data, as in the human activity recognition domain [26]. In these experiments, DL models extract features from tri-axis sensors that lead to higher model performance than features developed using standard transformation techniques.

2.2 Our Previous Work Refining DL-CBR for Feature Extraction

Our previous work explores how DL model architecture [20,35], feature extraction location [19], (pre)training and evaluation techniques [35], and inclusion of existing knowledge-engineered features [33] impact classification accuracy.

Recently, our work has considered more complex integrations of DL and CBR models for improved model performance. For one, investigations into using Siamese network models leveraging triplet loss techniques to encourage the neural model to learn features that correlate with class-level similarity between examples have shown potential for improved classification accuracy in some domains [30]. For another, the Deep Ensemble Feature Extraction for Retrieval (DEFER) model uses ensembles of DL replica models for feature extraction in imitation of a random forest, where each replica specializes in extracting features associated with a subset of the classes in the given task [34]. In addition to this more specialized feature extraction, DEFER employs a discriminator model that funnels per-replica case retrieval based on its top-n predicted classes, as well as a weighted voting framework that weights the contributions of each replica's retrieved case based on its similarity score. DEFER is our most accurate DL-CBR architecture to date as evaluated on our benchmark datasets.

2.3 Neuro-Symbolic Approaches Leveraging LLMs

With the advent and continuing success of LLMs, it is appealing to consider how LLMs may be incorporated into neuro-symbolic systems for CBR [3]. Much work interfaces LLMs with knowledge-based approaches through retrieval-augmented generation, either by leveraging database information to augment their decision-making process or by incorporating knowledge graphs (e.g., [14]).

CBR principles have also been used to augment LLMs [22,36], and CBR-LLM integrations have been applied to LLM decision-making to discourage the LLM from hallucinating data [32]. In these experiments, LLMs are directed to ground their decisions in specific cases (i.e., prompting the LLM to perform CBR), and when they hallucinate, follow-up prompts refocus the LLM to retrieve real cases. LLMs have been used to develop explanations based on visual question answering [4]. This work shows how image-to-text algorithms can be paired with LLMs to retrieve relevant similar explanations for image classification decisions based on natural language similarity assessment.

3 Our Approach

We propose a model structure that combines our existing DL-CBR architecture with an LLM model into a single hybrid model (Fig. 1). Specifically, the DLCBR

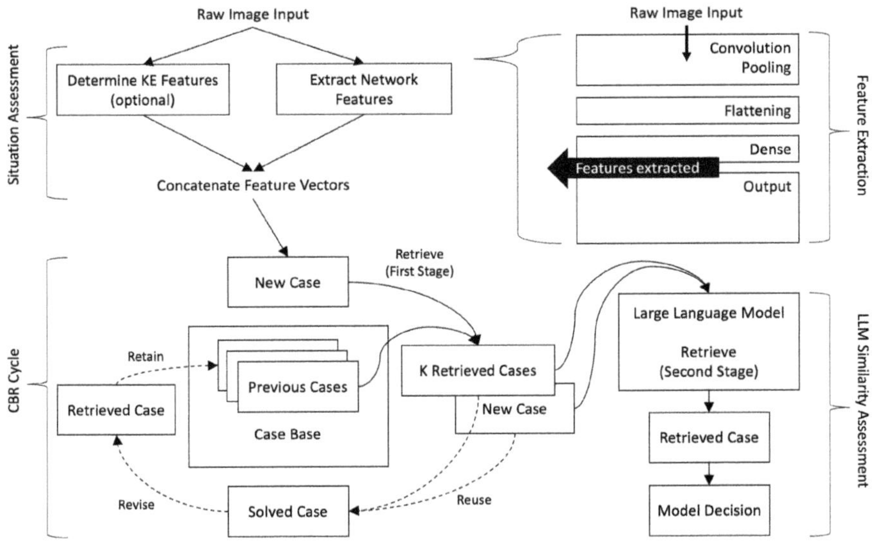

Fig. 1. Data flow through the DEL-CBR model, starting with feature extraction (top right), case creation, potentially involving knowledge-engineered (KE) features when applicable (top left), retrieving the field of k candidate cases (bottom left), and the LLM-driven model decision (bottom right).

system performs feature extraction and the first stage of a two-stage KNN process, where the most relevant k cases to the query in the case base are selected. These cases are passed to the LLM, which identifies the single nearest neighbor case, whose ground truth class becomes the model's classification decision.

There are multiple promising integrations of LLMs with DL-CBR systems, but many such hybridizations incur significant spatial or temporal overhead. For example, extracting features using the LLM may be inconsistent due to hallucinations and the generative nature of LLMs on the whole, and having the LLM perform pairwise similarity assessment may cause an excessive number of queries. Thus, performing KNN with the LLM is appealing, but providing the whole case base as context is costly and invites hallucination.

Our approach addresses the limitations of these potential integrations, minimizing temporal and spatial overhead by limiting the number of queries to the LLM (i.e., one per test case) as well as the context required for each query (i.e., by supplying a high-graded field of k candidate cases to the LLM for consideration). The model design also seeks to maintain the explainability benefits of case presentation that exist for other CBR and DL-CBR systems through performing case retrieval using the LLM. Our model architecture consists of the following sub-systems (Algorithm 1):

1: $DL \leftarrow$ pretrained neural model
2: $LLM \leftarrow$ large language model (no fine-tuning)
3: $cb \leftarrow$ input case base
4: $k \leftarrow$ number of neighbors to retrieve using KNN
5: $DL \leftarrow$ fine-tune(DL, train examples, train labels)
6: **for** (example, label) in training data **do**
7: $f \leftarrow$ feature vector extracted from DL(example)
8: add case(f, example, label) to cb
9: **end for**
10: **for** query, _ in testing data **do**
11: $f \leftarrow$ feature vector extracted from DL(query)
12: $q \leftarrow$ case(f, query, _)
13: $nn \leftarrow$ retrieve k-nearest neighbors(cb, q, k)
14: prediction $\leftarrow LLM(q, nn)$
15: **end for**

Algorithm 1: The DEL-CBR algorithm. DEL-CBR incorporates DL model training/fine-tuning (line 5), case base instantiation (lines 6-9), and two-stage KNN-based classification (lines 10-15). In the first stage, the DL-CBR model retrieves a field of k nearest neighbors (line 13), and the LLM selects the most relevant of these (line 14) to determine the prediction.

DL Feature Extraction. Feature extraction in DEL-CBR follows our previous work [35]. Namely, a DL model is trained to classify the images provided in the training set, and indexing features for each case (both during case base instantiation and for query cases during testing) are extracted by passing the corresponding image through the DL model and extracting the intermediate feature embeddings. Thus, each case consists of a raw image, its indexing feature vector extracted from the DL model, and its ground truth class.

Retrieval Stage 1. A critical design requirement for our system is that the LLM is not overwhelmed with input from a large case base (potentially increasing the probability of hallucination). We satisfy this constraint by dividing case retrieval into two steps. The first step is controlled by the DL-CBR model, which takes the query case as input and outputs a field of k candidate cases (i.e., performing true KNN rather than 1-NN as in our previous papers). These candidate cases are then passed to the LLM for secondary processing.

Retrieval Stage 2. Once the field of k candidate cases is determined, they are passed along with the query to the LLM, which selects the most relevant case to retrieve. Parameterizations for this selection mechanism are discussed in Sect. 4 (esp. LLM fine-tuning and how the LLM performs similarity assessment). Using the LLM in this secondary role assumes that its similarity measure is potentially distinct from that of the DL-CBR system. Once the retrieved case is identified, the system uses that case's ground truth class for its final decision.

4 Hypotheses and Evaluation

Broadly, the goals of this experiment center on improving the DL-CBR approach outlined in our previous work [34,35] by leveraging LLMs in our model pipeline. In that context, we investigate three primary hypotheses:

1. **DEL-CBR will exhibit higher classification accuracy than our existing DL-CBR model alone.** We expect that this will be evident for various training set sizes, because the LLM may bring additional implicit knowledge to the task because of its extensive initial training.
2. **DEL-CBR will achieve higher classification accuracy than the corresponding LLM classifier alone.** Similar to the benefits discussed in our previous work (e.g., [35]), we expect that the access to cases will provide additional performance benefits compared with the LLM used alone.
3. **Newer LLMs will perform better in DEL-CBR, and tuning the value of k for case retrieval will impact classification accuracy.** We expect that newer LLMs will be more capable (e.g., due to more effective pretraining), and that the LLM's classification accuracy will be significantly impacted by its access to cases, which is determined by the value of k.

4.1 Experimental Setup

Architecture. Our evaluation of these hypotheses is conducted using a DL-CBR architecture built on the DenseNet121 neural architecture [16], which was shown to be especially effective in our prior work [34,35]. Most experiments use Llama 4 Scout for the LLM system component, but some additional experiments also employ Gemini 2.5 Flash Lite as an easily accessible commercial model [13]. The DenseNet base model is pretrained on ImageNet [9], and the LLM architectures are taken as-is (i.e., no fine-tuning). Our system bases its decisions on case retrieval only; there is no adaptation component. Furthermore, retrieval during the first stage occurs using KNN based on a Manhattan distance metric operating on the extracted feature vectors. The LLM performs the second stage of retrieval based on raw image data for the cases passed from the first stage of retrieval and provided prompts. Our experimental code can be found online[1].

LLMs are prompted with a single instruction for retrieval: "In the provided list of images, the first is a query for a k-nearest neighbors problem, and the others are potential neighbors. Select the nth image that is the most similar to the first, and return the value of n. n cannot be 1, since that is the query. Provide no other information or formatting." In the control test where the LLM makes the classification decision directly, based only on the query example, the prompt is modified to "What is the class of this image? Possible classes are [comma-separated list of classes]. Provide no other information or formatting." Ideally, using the raw image data in the second stage encourages the LLM to analyze the candidate cases thoroughly (e.g., rather than performing a simple distance calculation, as the DL-CBR model would by itself).

[1] https://github.com/zwilk314/ICCBR2026_DELCBR.

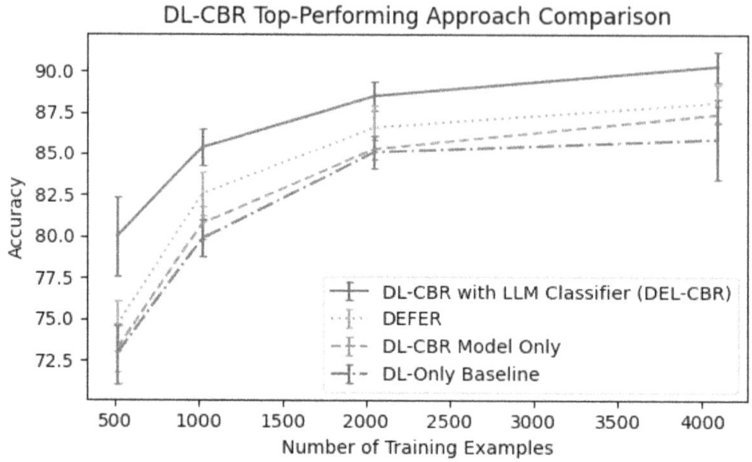

Fig. 2. Comparison between DEL-CBR, DEFER [34], our DL-CBR model used alone, and a DL-only baseline [35]. Classification accuracy values are reported as a function of training set size; error bars represent one standard deviation.

Datasets and Training. For the experiments described in this paper, we leverage two datasets for DL model fine-tuning and experimental evaluation. Most experiments are conducted using the images contained in the Animals with Attributes 2 (AwA2) dataset, which contains images of animals belonging to fifty different classes [37]. In addition, one set of experiments leverages the AAMRI dataset that consists of MRI brain scan images that belong to one of four classes pertaining to diagnosed severity of Alzheimer's disease [29].

For these experiments, the training set consists of 8, 16, 32, or 64 batches of 64 training examples each (in specific additional experiments, 128 batches are also used). Elements of the training set are selected randomly with a uniform distribution over the domain classes. The model weights are instantiated using pretrained values based on ImageNet [9], and the model is trained during fine-tuning until convergence using early stopping at two epochs (i.e., when the accuracy does not improve for two epochs, training stops).

Evaluation Approach. For evaluation, 16 batches of 64 images are selected independently in the same manner as the training data (instead of leave-one-out testing). Each image is passed through the DL model for feature extraction to create the query case. Then, DEL-CBR performs retrieval using the two-part KNN retrieval process described above to facilitate classification. Each evaluation experiment, from training/fine-tuning through evaluation, is repeated thirty times to produce reliable mean and standard deviation statistics (with the exception of the tests using Gemini 2.5 Flash Lite, which are repeated up to three times each due to resource constraints for the free-access model).

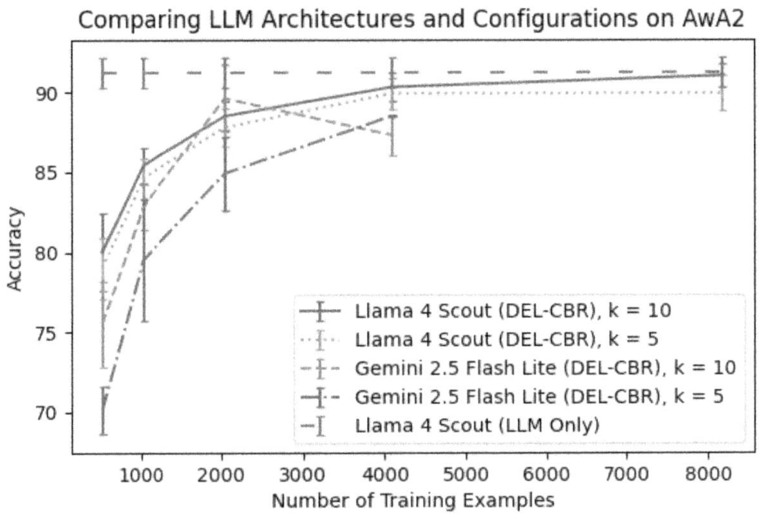

Fig. 3. Classification accuracy values as a function of training set size in the AwA2 case study. Experiments vary the LLM model and value of k used by DEL-CBR, comparing them to the corresponding LLM-only baseline (which has no additional training/fine-tuning). Error bars represent one standard deviation.

5 Results and Discussion

Our results are presented in Figs. 2, 3 and 4. From these data, we note several broad trends that align strongly with our hypotheses. First, DEL-CBR significantly outperforms both the DL-only baseline and each of our existing DL-CBR models, including DEFER [34]. This strongly supports our first hypothesis; while the data suggest a more nuanced conclusion for the second hypothesis, DEL-CBR appears capable of achieving at least as high classification accuracy as a LLM-only approach, and it can be significantly higher for some domains. Finally, it appears that the newer Llama 4 Scout model is more accurate in general than Gemini 2.5 Flash Lite, and that there appears to be a relative maximum for classification accuracy around $k = 5$ or $k = 10$, depending on the model. Tentatively, these results support our third hypothesis as well.

5.1 DEL-CBR Versus DL-CBR Baselines

One of the most dramatic results from these experiments is the relative performance increase for DEL-CBR relative to other DL-CBR approaches in the AwA2 case study. In particular, DEL-CBR achieves higher classification accuracy for all numbers of training examples investigated, often by a margin exceeding one standard deviation (thus, supporting our first hypothesis). The significance of these results is supported by Student's T-test values of $p \leq 1.158 * 10^{-8}$ across all comparisons comparing DEL-CBR and DEFER (our next-most performant

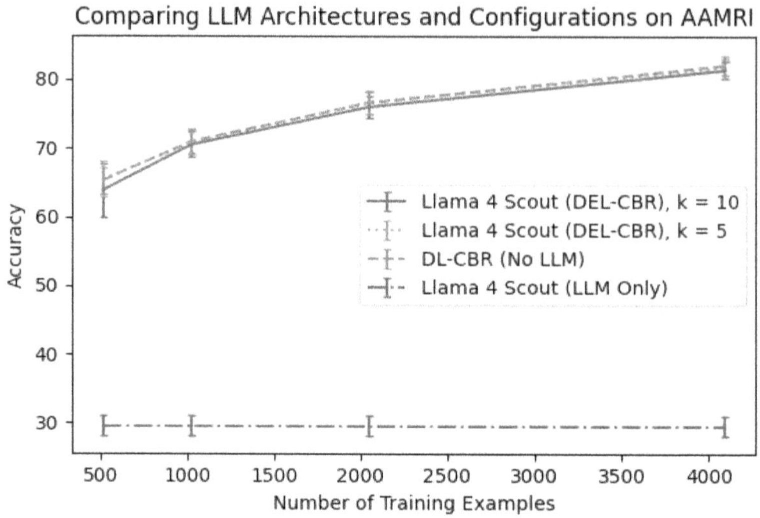

Fig. 4. Classification accuracy values as a function of training set size in the AAMRI case study. Experiments vary the value of k used by DEL-CBR and compare results to a standard DL-CBR model and to the corresponding LLM-only baseline (which has no additional training/fine-tuning). Error bars represent one standard deviation.

DL-CBR model), suggesting statistical significance with near-certain confidence. Interestingly, this margin does not carry over into the AAMRI case study at all; instead, DEL-CBR performs very similarly to a baseline DL-CBR model (which is more accurate than DEFER for this dataset), supported by Student's T-test values of $p \leq 8.87 * 10^{-1}$.

These accuracy results suggest that the utility offered by including an LLM in the DL-CBR process is domain-dependent. This claim is tempered by the fact that we do not fine-tune the LLM, and so generality may be significantly limited by the data to which the LLM has been exposed during its initial training (we explore this more deeply in Sect. 5.2). If this is the case, and/or if fine-tuning does not adequately mitigate any domain-related issues in LLM performance, combining the LLM with DL-CBR does appear to have a stabilizing effect (e.g., versus the performance of the LLM by itself).

5.2 DEL-CBR Versus the LLM Alone

The answer to our second hypothesis is much less clean-cut than the answer to our first, in that DEL-CBR's performance relative to the LLM baseline is more nuanced. Specifically, for the AwA2 dataset, and for the number of training examples explored in this paper, DEL-CBR achieves at most roughly the same classification accuracy as the LLM applied by itself. By contrast, on the AAMRI dataset, DEL-CBR significantly outperforms the LLM baseline, which achieves only slightly better than random-guess accuracy. These results suggest that an off-the-shelf LLM's performance is strongly domain-dependent. That is, for some domains like AwA2, LLMs appear to possess sufficient general domain familiarity to make accurate decisions without fine-tuning. By contrast, for more specialized domains like the MRI dataset, the LLM lacks sufficient prior knowledge/experience, leading to a significant decrease in accuracy.

The results also speak to interesting interplay between the DL-CBR system and the LLM. For one, there exists a threshold at which point the classification accuracy of DEL-CBR rivals that of the LLM by itself (i.e., for 128 training batches). Therefore, at this point, any additional explanatory power afforded by using KNN for retrieval-based classification is a bonus for DEL-CBR. Furthermore, it can be argued that DEL-CBR could outperform an LLM-only model if provided enough training data for the domain, though given the diminishing accuracy returns for larger numbers of training batches, it is likely that any such difference would be small. For another, the LLM's innate general knowledge, which is cultivated due to extensive initial training, understandably may be superior to a standard DL-CBR model that is fine-tuned on a relatively small dataset. However, a model like DEL-CBR holds the potential for additional benefit by optimizing trade-offs and additional parameters that are available when including the DL-CBR system in the decision-making process (e.g., see Sect. 5.4), with the caveat that if the DL-CBR system fails to select a candidate neighbor with the correct ground truth class in the first stage of KNN, then the LLM cannot select a correct case to retrieve without hallucinating.

Finally, these comparisons hold interesting implications for the primary motivations for this DL-CBR research. For one, our DL-CBRDL-CBR models consistently achieve higher classification accuracy for small-data case studies than DL-only models, supporting the claim that they need less training data to achieve reasonable classification accuracy. This claim could be seen as less powerful when also considering an LLM system, which even without fine-tuning has been initially trained on an extensive corpus of data. Similar reasoning underlies our motivations for not fine-tuning the LLM, which might require significantly more data to meaningfully bias the model without overfitting. Thus, the question becomes how best to quantify the impact of training data (and by extension, the definition of "limited training data") in a system containing two DL models–and especially whether model pretraining is exempt from this consideration.

5.3 Using Different LLMs in DEL-CBR

At first glance, it appears that Llama 4 Scout enables slightly higher classification accuracy on average than Gemini 2.5 Flash Lite. Additionally, Gemini 2.5 Flash Lite records higher standard deviation values than Llama 4 Scout. However, both models achieve roughly the same maximum classification accuracy (roughly 90%), albeit with differences in the parameterizations that lead to that maximum performance. Specifically, Gemini 2.5 Flash Lite achieves its maximum average classification accuracy when trained on 32 training batches and when $k = 5$. For Llama 4 Scout, it is 64 training batches (we do not consider the 128-batch experiment since one was not conducted for Gemini) and $k = 10$.

These results could be due to multiple potential influences. At the outset, it is possible that some of the mean and standard deviation values for the Gemini model are not completely representative of the true values due to fewer experimental iterations. Beyond that, it is also interesting to consider the mechanisms by which both LLM models receive image data via prompting. Specifically, both models recommend in their documentation to provide image data to the LLM by converting it to bytes and then combining the reformatted data with the query prompt. Perhaps this medium encourages the models to interpret image data in certain ways that may be distinct from other forms of data encoding (e.g., compared with vision-language models that can process the raw data directly) and could favor one model over the other. Finally, any differences in performance may simply be due to the fact that Llama 4 Scout is the newer model, potentially enabling access to more or more refined data, better internal algorithms, and/or superior initial training.

5.4 Importance of the Field of k Cases

Another way in which DEL-CBR may be compared against an LLM-only model (and against itself) is by considering the number of cases in the field supplied by the DL-CBR system. Specifically, it is evident (esp. in the experimental results for Gemini 2.5 Flash Lite) that at least at a certain point, the overall accuracy of DEL-CBR appears to decrease as the number of cases provided to the LLM increases. This makes intuitive sense since, given a greater amount of information to process at once, there is a greater opportunity for the LLM to hallucinate, over-generalize, or otherwise make a mistake. Importantly, though, it also supports the conclusion that LLMs require domain-specific fine-tuning and/or input from another system (e.g., the DL-CBR system) for effective KNN similarity assessment. Otherwise, it is likely that performance suffers

Different rules apply for smaller values of k, more in line with the performance of the discriminator in the DEFER model [34] and top-n accuracy in DL model evaluation. That is, having a large value of k increases the likelihood that a case with the correct ground truth class relative to the query is among the candidates (i.e., top-n accuracy intuitively increases as n increases). Thus, the value of k is an optimizable parameter. If k is too large, the LLM's classification accuracy is suboptimal, likely due to too many choices; if k is too small, then the LLM provides minimal additional utility to a DL-CBR retrieval that dominates the decision-making process.

5.5 Final Thoughts and Implications for Explainability

Taken together, these results illustrate DEL-CBR's significant accuracy improvement over other DL-CBR methods. Furthermore, they show the influence that number of training examples, value of k, and LLM model have on DEL-CBR's performance, especially with respect to an LLM used by itself. Overall, it appears that, while an LLM-only approach can achieve strong classification accuracy off-the-shelf for domains (e.g., AwA2) that are closely correlated with day-to-day experience, DEL-CBR can at least rival that performance when provided enough training data. For other domains (e.g., the AAMRI dataset) that are more specialized, DEL-CBR (or even a regular DL-CBR approach) excels.

Given this successful comparison, it is also important to assess how DEL-CBR's explanation capability compares with LLMs in general and with DLCBR models. In our previous works, we have asserted that DL-CBR models are likely more explainable than DL-only models, since they perform classification using DL-supported case retrieval rather than based only on forward propagation through the network model. This claim becomes more complex when introducing LLMs into the context. On one hand, it can be argued that LLMs are better able to explain their decisions than other DL models, since their natural language capability enables them to generate textual explanations that are understandable to humans and may be appealing to users. On the other, LLMs do not offer any additional structural transparency compared with other DL models, and LLM-generated explanations can be unreliable in some tasks (e.g., due to probability of hallucination). We believe that DEL-CBR is promising for explainability because of leveraging the natural language explanation capability of LLMs combined with grounded explanations by case presentation, as provided by CBR. Although recent research has shown that LLM hallucinations may affect cases, it has also demonstrated the possibility to detect and repair such hallucinations to support trustworthiness of the cases used [32].

6 Potential Opportunity for Case Adaptation

The previous sections present a retrieval-based classification method, without an explicit case adaptation step. In general, case adaptation for classification remains challenging, although both knowledge-based (e.g., [2]) and knowledge-light methods have been proposed (e.g., [17]), and case-difference-heuristic methods have been applied to learning to adapt numerical values associated with images (e.g., for age prediction from faces [39]). In the study reported in this paper, the task for the LLM is only to select a prior case. However, a natural next step would be to prompt the LLM not only to select, but to adapt the classification of the selected case as needed. LLM-based adaptation appears promising for non-image-based classification [31], but to our knowledge has not been tested for image data. If successful, it could enable moving beyond retrieval to a full CBR process for image classification.

7 Conclusions and Future Work

This paper presents DEL-CBR, an approach that combines DL, CBR, and LLM methods into a single hybrid model to increase classification accuracy on small-data domains, with the potential for greater explainability than the models individually. Increased accuracy is supported by case study experiments which highlight DEL-CBR's performance relative to existing DL-only and DL-CBR models, as well as relative to an LLM-only baseline. Additionally, the results continue to support DL-CBR hybridization as an effective approach for classification in small-data domains, and suggest that multi-stage KNN is an effective way to harness the decision-making power of LLMs, while reducing the risk of hallucination by providing only a selected subset of case information to the LLM (i.e., in the form of the field of k candidate cases).

Looking beyond these experiments, future research could include performing experiments using additional datasets, different LLM architectures, modified LLM prompting/incorporation into the data pipeline, and/or ensembles of LLMs for improved performance and consistency. Additionally, testing more values of k could provide insight into the optimal size of the field of candidate cases provided to the LLM, and further analysis of LLM-driven retrieval methods could help optimize LLM integration into the DL-CBR data pipeline. Prompting the LLM to perform adaptation would turn the pipeline into a full CBR process, potentially providing accuracy gains. Finally, it is appealing to evaluate the explainability of this model and other DL-CBR approaches quantitatively (e.g., through a human subjects study), against DL-only or LLM-only baselines.

Acknowledgments and Generative AI Statement. This work was funded by the US Department of Defense (Contract W52P1J2093009) and supported in part by Lilly Endowment, Inc., through its support for the Indiana University Pervasive Technology Institute. No generative AI was used in the preparation of this paper.

References

1. Amin, K., Kapetanakis, S., Althoff, K.-D., Dengel, A., Petridis, M.: Answering with Cases: A CBR Approach to Deep Learning. In: Cox, M.T., Funk, P., Begum, S. (eds.) ICCBR 2018. LNCS (LNAI), vol. 11156, pp. 15–27. Springer, Cham (2018). https://doi.org/10.1007/978-3-030-01081-2_2
2. Ashley, K.: Modeling Legal Argument: Reasoning with Cases and Hypotheticals. MIT Press, Cambridge (1990)
3. Bach, K., et al.: Case-Based Reasoning Meets Large Language Models: A Research Manifesto For Open Challenges and Research Directions (2025). https://hal.science/hal-05006761
4. Bastardo-Rojas, A., Caro-Martinez, M.: Visual question answering to generate case-based explanations for image classification. In: Case-Based Reasoning Research and Development, ICCBR 2025. Springer, CHam (2025)
5. Bhatta, S., Goel, A.: Model-based learning of structural indices to design cases. In: Proceedings of the IJCAI-93 Workshop on Reuse of Design, pp. A1–A13. IJCAI, Chambery, France (1993)
6. Bonzano, A., Cunningham, P., Smyth, B.: Using introspective learning to improve retrieval in CBR: A case study in air traffic control. In: Leake, D.B., Plaza, E. (eds.) ICCBR 1997. LNCS, vol. 1266, pp. 291–302. Springer, Heidelberg (1997). https://doi.org/10.1007/3-540-63233-6_500
7. Chen, C., Li, O., Tao, D., Barnett, A., Rudin, C., Su, J.K.: This looks like that: Deep learning for interpretable image recognition. In: Advances in Neural Information Processing Systems, vol. 32, pp. 8930–8941. Curran (2019)

8. Cox, M., Ram, A.: Introspective multistrategy learning: On the construction of learning strategies. Artif. Intell. **112**(1–2), 1–55 (1999)
9. Deng, J., Dong, W., Socher, R., Li, L.J., Li, K., Fei-Fei, L.: Imagenet: A large-scale hierarchical image database. In: 2009 IEEE Conference on Computer Vision and Pattern Recognition, pp. 248–255 (2009)
10. Domeshek, E.: Indexing stories as social advice. In: Proceedings of the Ninth National Conference on Artificial Intelligence, pp. 16–21. AAAI Press, Menlo Park, CA (1991)
11. Forbus, K.D., Gentner, D., Law, K.: MAC/FAC: A model of similarity-based retrieval. Cogn. Sci. **19**(2), 141–205 (1995)
12. Fox, S., Leake, D.: Introspective reasoning for index refinement in case-based reasoning. J. Exp. Theoret. Artif. Intell. **13**(1), 63–88 (2001)
13. Google: Gemini 2.5 flash-lite (2026). https://gemini.google.com
14. Han, H., et al.: Rag vs. graphRAG: A systematic evaluation and key insights. ArXiv abs/2502.11371 (2025). https://api.semanticscholar.org/CorpusID:276408622
15. Hoffmann, M., Bergmann, R.: Informed machine learning for improved similarity assessment in process-oriented case-based reasoning (2021). https://arxiv.org/abs/2106.15931
16. Huang, G., Liu, Z., van der Maaten, L., Weinberger, K.Q.: Densely connected convolutional networks (2016). https://arxiv.org/abs/1608.06993
17. Jalali, V., Leake, D., Forouzandehmehr, N.: Learning and applying adaptation rules for categorical features: an ensemble approach. AI Commun. **30**(3–4), 193–205 (2017)
18. Leake, D.: An indexing vocabulary for case-based explanation. In: Proceedings of the Ninth National Conference on Artificial Intelligence, pp. 10–15. AAAI Press, Menlo Park, CA (1991)
19. Leake, D., Wilkerson, Z., Crandall, D.: Extracting case indices from convolutional neural networks: A comparative study. In: Case-Based Reasoning Research and Development, ICCBR 2022 (2022)
20. Leake, D., Wilkerson, Z., Vats, V., Acharya, K., Crandall, D.: Examining the impact of network architecture on extracted feature quality for cbr. In: Case-Based Reasoning Research and Development, ICCBR 2023, Springer, Cham (2023). https://doi.org/10.1007/978-3-031-40177-0_1
21. Leake, D., Ye, X.: Harmonizing Case Retrieval and Adaptation with Alternating Optimization. In: Sánchez-Ruiz, A.A., Floyd, M.W. (eds.) ICCBR 2021. LNCS (LNAI), vol. 12877, pp. 125–139. Springer, Cham (2021). https://doi.org/10.1007/978-3-030-86957-1_9
22. Lenz, M., Hoffmann, M., Bergmann, R.: Llsim: Large language models for similarity assessment in case-based reasoning. In: Bichindaritz, I., López, B. (eds.) Case-Based Reasoning Research and Development, pp. 126–141. Springer, Cham (2025)
23. Li, O., Liu, H., Chen, C., Rudin, C.: Deep learning for case-based reasoning through prototypes: A neural network that explains its predictions. ArXiv abs/1710.04806 (2018)
24. Mathisen, B.M., Aamodt, A., Bach, K., Langseth, H.: Learning similarity measures from data. Progress Artif. Intell. (10 2019)
25. Moffett, J., et al.: Cosine similarity is almost all you need (for prototypical-part models), WACV Open Access (2026)
26. Sani, S., Wiratunga, N., Massie, S.: Learning deep features for knn-based human activity recognition. In: 25th International Conference on Case-Based Reasoning (ICCBR 2017) (2017)

27. Schank, R., et al.: Towards a general content theory of indices. In: Proceedings of the 1990 AAAI spring symposium on Case-Based Reasoning, AAAI Press, Menlo Park, CA (1990)
28. Turner, J.T., Floyd, M.W., Gupta, K., Oates, T.: NOD-CC: A Hybrid CBR-CNN Architecture for Novel Object Discovery. In: Bach, K., Marling, C. (eds.) ICCBR 2019. LNCS (LNAI), vol. 11680, pp. 373–387. Springer, Cham (2019). https://doi.org/10.1007/978-3-030-29249-2_25
29. Uraninjo: Augmented alzheimer MRI dataset (2015). https://www.kaggle.com/datasets/uraninjo/augmented-alzheimer-mri-dataset/data
30. Vats, V., Wilkerson, Z., Sato, H., Leake, D., Crandall, D.: Learning case features with proxy-guided deep neural networks. In: Case-Based Reasoning Research and Development, ICCBR 2025, Springer, Cham (2025)
31. Wilkerson, K., Leake, D.: On implementing case-based reasoning with large language models. In: Case-Based Reasoning Research and Development - 32nd International Conference Proceedings, vol. 14775, pp. 404–417. Springer, Cham (2024). https://doi.org/10.1007/978-3-031-63646-2_26
32. Wilkerson, K., Leake, D.: Case hallucinations and steps toward repair. In: Proceedings of the ICCBR 2025 Workshop on Case-Based Reasoning and Deep Learning. p. 54 (2025), Workshops Proceedings for the 2025 International Conference on Case-Based Reasoning (ICCBR 2025), CEUR Workshop Proceedings. https://ceur-ws.org/Vol-3993/
33. Wilkerson, Z., Leake, D., Crandall, D.: On combining knowledge-engineered and network-extracted features for retrieval. In: Case-Based Reasoning Research and Development, ICCBR 2021, pp. 248–262 (2021)
34. Wilkerson, Z., Leake, D., Crandall, D., Wilkerson, B.: Extracting features with deep learning for ensemble-driven case-based classification. In: Case-Based Reasoning Research and Development, ICCBR 2025. Springer, Cham (2025). https://doi.org/10.1007/978-3-031-96559-3_23
35. Wilkerson, Z., Leake, D., Vats, V., Crandall, D.: Extracting indexing features for CBR from deep neural networks: A transfer learning approach. In: Case-Based Reasoning Research and Development, ICCBR 2024, Springer, Cham (2024). https://doi.org/10.1007/978-3-031-63646-2_10
36. Wiratunga, N., et al.: CBR-RAG: Case-based reasoning for retrieval augmented generation in LLMs for legal question answering. In: Case-Based Reasoning Research and Development. ICCBR 2024, pp. 445–460. Springer, Cham (2024)
37. Xian, Y., Lampert, C.H., Schiele, B., Akata, Z.: Zero-shot learning - a comprehensive evaluation of the good, the bad and the ugly. In: IEEE Transactions on Pattern Analysis and Machine Intelligence (T-PAMI) (2018)
38. Ye, X., Leake, D., Wang, Y., Zhao, Z., Crandall, D.: Towards network implementation of CBR: Case study of a neural network K-NN algorithm. In: Case-Based Reasoning Research and Development - 32nd International Conference, ICCBR-24. LNCS, vol. 14775, pp. 354–370. Springer, Cham (2024). https://doi.org/10.1007/978-3-031-63646-2_23
39. Ye, X., Zhao, Z., Leake, D.B., Wang, X., Crandall, D.J.: Applying the case difference heuristic to learn adaptations from deep network features. ArXiv **abs/2107.07095** (2021). https://api.semanticscholar.org/CorpusID:235899183

SSNN-XCBR: A Siamese-Spiking Neural Network Architecture for Audio Case-Based Explanations

Pedro A. Martín-Peláez(✉) and Marta Caro-Martínez

Department of Software Engineering and Artificial Intelligence, Universidad Complutense de Madrid, Madrid, Spain
{pedrma07,martcaro}@ucm.es

Abstract. Explainable Artificial Intelligence has become one of the fastest-growing fields in Artificial Intelligence in recent years. Since AI models are now more complex, improving user trust has emerged as a critical challenge. In this context, Case-Based Reasoning has been successfully used to generate factual and counterfactual explanations. Despite significant advances in xAI, research on audio-related tasks remains limited. Generating explanations for audio data is essential, as such tasks are typically addressed using black-box neural networks due to the complex, unstructured, and difficult-to-interpret nature of audio signals. In this work, we propose a novel approach to generate factual and counterfactual explanations by integrating Siamese and Spiking Neural Networks within a CBR framework to better handle the nature of audio data. We compare our approach with state-of-the-art methods, obtaining promising results in terms of explanation quality.

Keywords: xAI · Case-based explanations · Audio-based explanations · Siamese Neural Networks · Spiking Neural Networks

1 Introduction

Nowadays, the complexity of Artificial Intelligence (AI) models has become extremely high. Although this complexity goes hand in hand with increased accuracy when solving problems and generating predictions, it also provokes lack of users' trust, especially in critical domains like medicine or security [4]. When this happens, users may abandon the use of AI tools and systems [4]. Explainable Artificial Intelligence (xAI) emerged as a field that employs specialized techniques to justify models' behaviour to users. This way, users can understand the reasons behind a prediction, which leads to increasing AI utility [15]. Research in xAI has focused on explaining problems when tabular data or images are involved. Other domains where audio data predominates lack the variety of explanation methods available for tabular and visual data [1]. Despite this, audio-based explanations are essential for accessibility or in-vehicle environments, for example. To date, most audio explanation techniques (also called

L. Malburg and K. Bach (Eds.): ICCBR 2026, LNAI 16780, pp. 135–151, 2027.
https://doi.org/10.1007/978-3-032-33865-5_9

explainers) for audio found in the literature are focused on adapting well-known explainers, such as LIME or Grad-CAM [1].

Instance-based explanations show examples to the user that are past cases similar to the current prediction obtained with an AI model [13]. They are often implemented using Case-Based Reasoning (CBR) to provide factual explanations (also called explanations-by-examples), if the prediction is the same as the past case, or counterfactual if the prediction is different to the past case [13]. Existing literature explores instance-based approaches that could be applied to audio, but in fact, they are not model-agnostic explainers designed for audio tasks, and in most of the cases, they have not been proved or evaluated in audio scenarios [1].

In this work, we introduce SSNN-XCBR, a novel model-agnostic case-based explanation approach that obtains explanation cases to offer both explanations-by-examples and counterfactuals for audio classification. This approach is domain-agnostic but designed to address the specific audio features inherent in audio-related tasks. Audio is a type of unstructured data, whose information and knowledge is distributed through frequencies and time series [25]. Due to the nature of the audio features, we have combined two different deep learning architectures, Siamese Neural Networks (SmNN) and Spiking Neural Networks (SpNN), to carry out the CBR retrieval process. Our explanation approach is local, post-hoc and model-agnostic, which is a novelty within the instance-based explanations for audio found in the literature [1].

On the one hand, SmNNs are a neural network-based architecture whose objective is to identify similarities between problems, for example in image matching. Moreover, SmNNs learn knowledge by comparing feature spaces, obtaining discriminative representations, which makes it suitable for audio tasks where capturing relevant features is particularly challenging [20]. On the other hand, SpNNs are a neural network-based architecture that is designed to transmit information through a specific path of neurons in the layers, instead of transmitting the information to all neurons in every layer, as occurs in Feed Forward Neural Networks [28]. Their most important characteristic is that this knowledge is sent in time sequences, in individual spikes over time, which makes audio processing more efficient [28]. A key strength of the SSNN-XCBR approach is that audio and semantic knowledge is used to obtain explanation cases, which can also be leveraged to enrich these explanations in the future. We have evaluated our approach, by comparing the *proximity* and the *diversity* of the explanation cases obtained with it and with audio-based similarity metrics found in the state-of-the-art. We have also evaluated the *efficiency* and the *robustness* of our model. The results show that we keep the *proximity* and *diversity* of the explanation cases when improving the *robustness* and *efficiency*.

The paper is organised as follows. In Sect. 2 we describe previous works about instance-based explanations for audio classification, as well as the use of SmNN and SpNN in xAI and audio related tasks. Section 3 depicts the method that we introduce in this work. The evaluation process and the results achieved are shown in Sect. 4. Finally, we provide some conclusions and future lines of work in Sect. 5.

2 Related Work

xAI techniques are widely focused on tabular and visual related tasks. For audio-related tasks, there is not as much research done, even though it remains a significant challenge since the AI models used to solve these tasks are black-boxes, such as deep learning models (CNN, RNN or transformers) [1]. In Akman and Schuller's review [1], we find that there are some generic explainers and specific explainers for audio-based tasks that adapt well-known explainers in the literature, such as LIME, SHAP, Integrated Gradients or Grad-CAM. These methods are local and model-specific and use spectrograms or waveforms as input representation. They also focus on explaining the task using feature attributions.

We also find instance-based explanations, called prototype-based. They are local and model-specific, and use spectrograms as input representation. In particular, we find three approaches [17,22,24] in the Akman and Schuller's review [1]. Olah et al. [22] introduces a generative AI-based approach that creates images that are explanations-by-examples. These images are created from noise, adding lines and textures, until real objects appear in the explanation image. In Pruthi et al.'s work [24], the TracIn explainer is introduced. It can be applied to explain any AI model that uses Stochastic Gradient Descent, and it is domain independent. TracIn analyses the network error when using a different training example in the learning process. Koh and Liang [17] propose using influence functions to detect which examples are the most important ones to obtain the prediction. The authors evaluate the approach to explain CNN and non-convexity and non-convergence models. These three approaches are not evaluated for audio-related tasks, and authors do not mention the possible application in this domain.

In the context of factual explanations, we find another relevant approach: SonicProtoPNet [11], a model-specific explainer for CNN used to solve audio classification. The approach uses a convolutional solution to find components across multiple explanation examples that are similar to components in the audio to explain. The method does not use the input data as a waveform, it needs to transform it into a Log-Mel Spectrogram. In the context of counterfactual explanations, we find the thesis [12]. This work feeds the dataset with semantic knowledge to find local and global counterfactuals for any type of classification for several types of data. The approach has been tested in several domains, including in audio classification for COVID-19 diagnosis. For this evaluation, the sounds of coughs and voices are transformed to MEL spectrograms and enriched through an ontology. Therefore, this method requires the audio in spectrogram format and semantic knowledge to find similarities between the cases.

Although there are some works in the CBR community that have explored the use of SmNN to detect similarities between cases [2,16], only a few have applied this approach to xAI. One of them is the work by Ye et al. [29], which introduces the method class-to-class siamese network (C2C-SN) for classification tasks, implemented for image classification. Instead of implementing a traditional case-based classification method, where similar cases to the query are obtained using a similarity metric, the C2C-SN method uses a siamese network to learn similarities and differences. The method can also provide supportive and contrastive cases as explanations together with the classification. Another relevant work is the proposed by Rocha Pinto [23], where an xAI method has been developed using an improved siamese network to provide prototypes to explain identity recognition through images.

Our work proposes a model- and domain-agnostic approach designed for audio classification specifically, using waveforms without any additional knowledge, which represents a novelty in the xAI for the audio field.

3 Audio Explanations Based on SSNN

In this work, we propose a case-based explanation approach that provides factual and counterfactual audio explanations using a combined architecture of Siamese Neural Networks and Spiking Neural Networks (SSNN). The approach designed in this work is a post-hoc, local and model-agnostic explainer for audio classification. Therefore, it is an approach that can explain any prediction obtained with any AI model. However, in contrast to other related works that we have described in the previous section, this approach proposes the following novelties: (1) the approach is designed considering the audio-specific features, (2) the audio waveform is the input for the explainer, and it is not transformed into a spectrogram, (3) it is totally model- and domain-agnostic, and (4) it does not require additional knowledge apart from the audio data.

Audio is a type of data that has particular features, which are different from other types of data, that should be treated in a suitable and specific fashion. Audio data is non-structured data that consists of a continuous signal, i.e. a vector of continuous values that represents the waveform space through time [30]. Therefore, audio data depends on: time, amplitude, and frequency [7]. Amplitude represents the sound intensity in a particular time: the higher the amplitude, the stronger the sound. Frequency represents the pitch in a specific time: a higher frequency means a higher pitch. On top of that, there are specific features for noise, voice, music, etc. [14]. Although there are existing model-agnostic explainers that could be used for audio data, they are not adapted to the particular features inherent to audio. Designing an explanation approach that leverages these particular features can improve the quality of the explanations provided.

Since audio is non-structured data, we opted for Siamese Neural Network (SmNN) to find the similarities between the cases. Using SmNN allows us to find similarities capturing shared complex relationships and patterns that other similarity metrics cannot discover [18,29]. SmNNs are a deep learning architecture that receives two inputs (two audio samples in our approach) that are going to be processed by two identical Neural Networks (ANN). This means both ANNs use the same weights for the data attributes. As a result, the ANNs return two embeddings that represent each of the audios. After that, a similarity metric is going to be used to compare the embeddings. The metric returns a similarity value that represents that similarity between the two audio samples [8]. In our approach, instead of using the most common ANNs, Spiking Neural Networks (SpNN) have been used within SmNN. The reason behind this choice is twofold: (1) to capture audio features through time, and (2) to provide greater interpretability than other types of ANN [28]. The main difference between SpNN and ANN is the mechanisms for broadcasting and propagating information through the cells within the network. SpNN neurons propagate signals in time events: when they receive a spike from other neurons, they adjust their own synaptic weights, adding the new knowledge. When this weight is greater than a threshold, after an accumulation of spikes, they will send their own spike to the following neurons, as a spike event in a particular time [28]. To carry out a classification, some neurons are related to different classes. The class associated with the neurons that spiked the most times will be the class predicted. For our case-based explanation approach, using SpNN provides us with time features to be captured within the SSNN architecture and can provide a method to read the activated neurons to enrich the explanation cases in the future.

Next, we describe the audio case-based approach process, including the case base formalisation, the retrieval process and the SSNN architecture. An overview of this process is shown in Fig. 1.

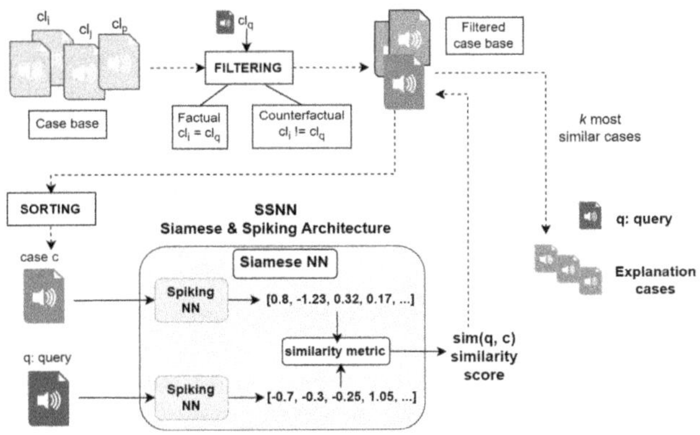

Fig. 1. Overview of the SSNN audio case-based explanation method. *cl* denotes class for the cases in the case base.

3.1 Case-Based Explanation Method

The proposed explanation method does not use knowledge or reasoning from the audio classification AI model. It does not require any other additional knowledge either. The explanation method takes as input the classified audio itself, represented as a waveform, along with the class predicted by the black-box AI model. Therefore, the case base C is structured as follows: $\forall c_i \in C,\ c_i = \langle D_i, S_i \rangle$, where every case $c_i \in C$ has a description D_i and a solution S_i. The description is formalised as $D_i = \{w_i, cl_i\}$, where w_i is the waveform that represents the audio for the case c_i, and cl_i is the class predicted for c_i by the black-box model. The solution $S_i = \{exc_i\}$ contains the set of explanation cases that explains the class cl_i for the case c_i. The set of explanation cases exc_i is defined as $exc_i = \{(e_j, f_j) \mid j = 1, \ldots, k\}$, where k is the number of explanation cases retrieved, e_j is the explanation case itself, and f_j represents the latent factors extracted from the SpNN for e_j. These latent factors represent knowledge about temporal features that are important to find similarities between the case c_i and the explanation e_j. These features will be used in future work to enrich the explanation cases.

Given a query q, we perform a MAC/FAC (many-are-called, few-are-chosen) retrieval process [10] to find the explanation cases. In the *filtering step* (MAC), we carry out a selection of cases from the case base depending on the type of explanation that we need to retrieve. If we need to retrieve a factual explanation, in the filtering step we are going to select only the cases that have the same class as the query. However, if we need to retrieve counterfactuals, the cases that we are going to select are the ones that do not share the class with the query.

$$c_{mac} = mac(cl_q, C, exp) = \begin{cases} \{c_i \in C \mid cl_q = cl_i\}, & \text{if } exp = \text{factual} \\ \{c_i \in C \mid cl_q \neq cl_i\}, & \text{if } exp = \text{counterfactual} \end{cases}$$

where cl_q is the query class, and $exp \in \{factual, counterfactual\}$ the type of explanation to create. Once we have the set of explanation cases c_{mac}, we perform the *sorting step* (FAC). In this step, we calculate the similarities between the query q and the cases in c_{mac}. However, after finding the similarity values, we apply an additional filter to extract counterfactual explanations in order to maximize the diversity of the explanation cases. Given the similarity values between q and the cases in c_{mac}, we select the most similar case for each class different to the query class cl_q. For instance, if we are working with the AudioMNIST dataset (see Sect. 4.1 for further details), the case base contains classes from 0 to 9. If the query q belongs to class $cl_q = 0$, this filtering & sorting step selects: the most similar case with class $cl_i = 1$, the most similar case with class $cl_i = 2$, and so on for all classes $cl_i \neq cl_q$. Therefore, we will have a case base of size equal to the number of classes different from cl_q. Finally, we select the top-k similar cases in this filtered case base.

Nevertheless, to obtain factual explanations, we select the k most similar cases within c_{mac} to the query q, without applying the previous filter. The formalisation of the sorting step, for both factual and counterfactual explanations, is the following:

$$c'_{mac} = mac'(q, C, exp, c_{mac}) = \begin{cases} c_{mac}, & \text{if } exp = \text{factual} \\ \{\hat{c}(cl_i) \mid cl_i \neq cl_q\}, & \text{if } exp = \text{counterfactual} \end{cases}$$

$$\text{where } \hat{c}(cl_i) = \underset{\substack{c_i \in c_{\text{mac}} \\ \text{class}(c_i) = cl_i}}{\arg\max} \ \text{sim}(q, c_i)$$

$$exc_q = fac(q, c'_{mac}, k) = \left\{(e_j, f_j) \mid e_j \in \arg\max^k_{e \subset c'_{mac}} \text{sim}(q, e)\right\}$$

$exc_q = \{(e_j, f_j) \mid j = 1, \ldots, k\}$ is the set of explanation cases that have the same class to the query (factual explanations) or different class to the query (counterfactual explanations). e_j is the audio case example, while f_j is the set of features that characterised the similarity between q and e_j. The similarity values computed between q and the cases $c_i \in c_{mac}$, and the features within f_j are obtained using the Siamese and Spiking Neural Network architecture proposed in this work. We describe this architecture below.

3.2 Siamese-Spiking Neural Network Architecture

To find similarities between the case q and the cases in C, we propose an SSNN: a Siamese-Spiking Neural Network architecture. While the SmNN is able to find similarities between two instances (audio in our approach), the SpNN discovers relevant features in non-structured and event-based data, such as audio. First, we define and implement a model based on SpNN to be used as a backbone for the SmNN architecture. This way, we can extract the important data features focusing not only on achieving high accuracy, but also on being explainable by design. To achieve this, we propose a 1-dimensional convolutional SpNN architecture that we have called *PopNetAudio*. This architecture is organised into two main modules (see an overview in Fig. 2):

- **Feature Extractor**. As we mentioned before, our approach does not need to transform the audio data into a spectrogram or another format, so the feature extractor module accepts raw audio as input. This module consists of a sequence of two 1D convolutional layers, each followed by *Leaky Integrate and Fire* (LIF) and *Batch Normalization* layers, with a *MaxPooling* layer positioned between the two convolutional blocks. The first convolutional layer, with a *kernel size* = 80 and *stride* = 4, is designed to capture low frequency variations from raw audio. Therefore, this layer captures general audio features. Later, to preserve the spiking characteristics, we use *Leaky Integrate and Fire (LIF)* layers to transform the data into spiking signals. This way, we are keeping event-based knowledge in a more interpretable fashion. Finally, we add some *Batch Normalisation* layers to stabilise the layer outputs. Later, a *MaxPooling* layer reduces temporal dimensions. Next, the second convolutional layer extracts again temporal patterns using a smaller kernel (*kernel size* = 3). This second convolutional layer is thus extracting more detailed features. Again, after the convolutional layer, we add LIF and *Batch Normalisation* layers. Finally, we include a *Linear* layer, It is crucial to note that, unlike standard Feed-forward Networks, the linear projection to the expert layer is applied independently at each discrete time step $t \in T$ during the SpNN simulation loop. Consequently, the temporal dimension is never flattened or lost; the backbone outputs a 3D tensor preserving the exact chronological sequence of spikes for each expert neuron.
- **Expert Layer and Population Encoding**. To design an explainable model by design, avoiding black box-related problems, we decided to add this second module using a *Population Encoding* approach. As shown in Fig. 2, the

module is divided into *cl* discrete sub-populations, where each *cl* represents one class. Each sub-population is formed by 25 neurons. The output is read as a "voting" process, where each expert or sub-population "votes" whether the given input belongs to its own class or not. The final output is determined by counting how many times each expert votes for its class. The most voted class is the class predicted. As a *loss function*, and to ensure each sub-population is the expert of only one class, we use a binary mask (expert masks) a binary mask suppresses the output of incorrect experts by setting their activations to zero and penalizing them. By comparing this with the higher activation of the correct expert, the model learns to route each class to its own dedicated neuron group, ensuring an explainable-by-design representation. For implementing our approach, the class prediction is not the important result of the training process, but the features that the module extracts, since we can obtain similarities between the audio cases.

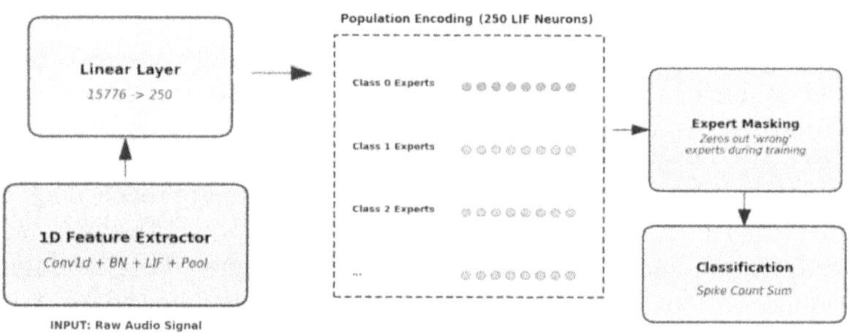

Fig. 2. Visual representation of the backbone architecture.

To find audio similarities between the query q and the cases in the case base C, we implement an SmNN architecture, using the previously described SpNN-based model as a backbone. Its main purpose is to map the spike trains into a 512-dimensional latent space, where semantic and audio features are preserved through a Euclidean space. The proposed SmNN architecture consists of the following modules and functions (see an overview in Fig. 3):

- **Temporal Filtering.** Since the backbone preserves the chronological spike sequence as a 3D tensor, we can extract fine-grained temporal dynamics. Inspired by how the Van Rossum metric works (see Sect. 4.3 for further details), we implement a 1D convolutional layer with *kernel size* = 25 and *padding* = 12. By using grouped convolutions, the network learns a temporal smoothing filter for each expert neuron, converting discrete binary events into continuous ones. This way, the network does not lose temporal knowledge during this process.
- **Temporal Aggregation.** To reduce dimensionality without losing the temporal structure of the raw audio, we use an *Adaptive Average Pooling* layer.

This layer divides the filtered signal into 16 discrete temporal bins (or phases), to capture the temporal evolution of the audio signal.
- **Non-linear Projection**. The aggregated features (the previous vector) are passed through a *Multi-Layer Perceptron* (MLP), comprising a hidden layer of 1024 nodes with *Batch Normalization*, *Leaky-ReLU activation* and *Dropout* to prevent overfitting. The final output projects the data into a 512-D embedding.
- **Loss Function**. The whole model uses a *Contrastive Loss*, forcing the model to minimise the distance between audios of the same class, and separating the audios from different classes.

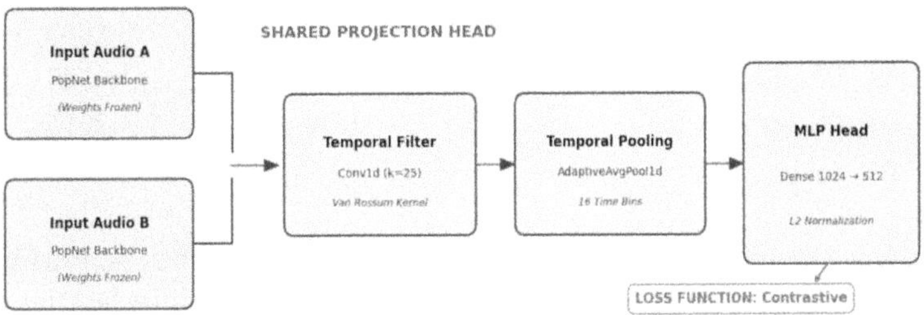

Fig. 3. Siamese architecture visual representation.

As a result, the SSNN returns a 512-D embedding for both the query q and the case c_i. We use Euclidean Distance to compare both embeddings and eventually find the similarity value $sim(q, c_i)$ that represents the similarity between both.

3.3 SSNN-XCBR: a Practical Application

To demonstrate the retrieval capabilities of the SSNN-XCBR method, this section presents a practical application focused on retrieving factual and counterfactual explanations for digit classification using the AudioMNIST dataset. The source audio files used, including the query, the factual examples, and the counterfactual examples, are available via our GitHub repository[1]. Moreover, several visualisations that illustrate the example are also available in the repository.

The query q (file 4_41_42.wav) with class $cl_q = 4$ is a recording where a male voice pronounces the digit "four" with a distinct emphasis on the fricative "f" and the open "o" vowel sound. By setting the neighbourhood parameter to $k = 3$, the SSNN-XCBR method retrieves the examples shown in Table 1 as factual and counterfactual cases. On the one hand, the most similar factual example (file 4_08_31.wav) features a male voice speaking the digit "four". It is identified as the closest instance, because it shares a nearly identical phonetic structure and vowel resonance with the query, particularly regarding the "r" colouring at

[1] https://github.com/PedroAMP22/SHOUX/tree/main/example.

the end of the utterance. On the other hand, the most similar counterfactual (file 1_48_20.wav) consists of a male voice speaking the digit "one". Despite belonging to a different class, it is retrieved due to its high acoustic similarity to the query. Its vocal profile, such as pitch, timbre, and the spectral envelope of the initial transition, mimics the temporal spiking patterns of the "four" sound.

Table 1. A practical example of the factual and counterfactual explanations obtained using the SSNN-XCBR method. EC denotes "Explanation Case", and ED denotes "Euclidean Distance" scores obtained between the query q and the explanation case.

Factual ECs			Counterfactual ECs		
EC File	EC Class	ED	EC File	EC Class	ED
4_08_31.wav	4	0.0152	1_48_20.wav	1	0.8672
4_08_22.wav	4	0.0252	5_16_1.wav	5	1.0726
4_02_28.wav	4	0.0275	2_18_15.wav	2	1.2515

In Fig. 4, we provide a visualisation for these explanations computing the Mel spectrogram heat-maps for both the $k = 1$ factual and counterfactual examples shown in Table 1.

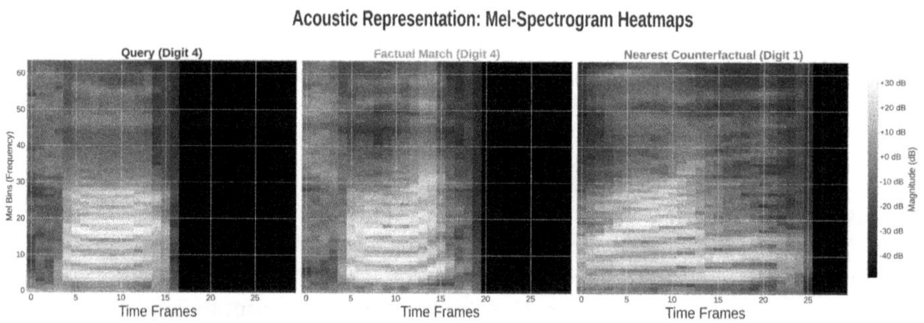

Fig. 4. Mel spectrogram heat-map of the query, top one factual and counterfactual.

4 Evaluation

The main goal of the evaluation carried out was to test the quality of the explanation cases provided by our SSNN-based methodology when generating factual and counterfactual explanations. We hypothesize that the explanation cases retrieved by the SSNN-XCBR will surpass those retrieved by the state of the art, since the SSNN architecture is designed to keep and use the event-based knowledge inherent to audio data. To perform the evaluation, we compare these explanation cases with the cases retrieved by several state-of-the-art similarity metrics in terms of four explanation case features: (1) *proximity* to the query (the instance to be explained), (2) explanation cases' *diversity*, (3) *robustness* of the similarity approach, and (4) method's *efficiency*. The complete code developed to perform this evaluation is available in our GitHub repository[2].

In this section, we detail the process performed, and the results obtained. First, we start by introducing the dataset that we have used (Sect. 4.1). Next, we define the evaluation metrics that we have used (Sect. 4.2). We then describe the experimental setup, including the baselines (Sect. 4.3). Finally, we show and discuss our results in Sect. 4.4.

4.1 Dataset

For the purpose of this evaluation, we worked with the AudioMNIST dataset [5]. It is a standard dataset for audio-related tasks being the audio version of the MNIST image dataset. AudioMNIST consists of 30,000 audio samples of spoken English digits, from 0 to 9. These samples were recorded by 60 distinct speakers, comprising men and women of different ages. We have the records for each speaker uttering every digit 50 times. The audio samples were recorded in a quiet room and later saved in 16-bits format.

To carry out the evaluation, we divided the dataset according to a Group-Based Splitting or Subject-Independent Splitting [19]. Taking into account this splitting, we divided the data set into three different subsets: training (which consists of 80% of speakers), validation (10% of speakers) and testing (10% of speakers). The training set contains 24,000 samples in total from 48 speakers; and the validation and test sets, 3,000 samples from 6 speakers, each. This way, the SpNN does not learn the particularities of individual speakers to classify the digits. Instead, it is forced to learn how each digit is spoken, as well as its acoustic characteristics and temporal patterns.

4.2 Evaluation Metrics

To compare our proposed method and the baseline methods, we employ different metrics. These metrics measure the *proximity* between the cases and the query, the *diversity* of the explanation cases, the *robustness* of the SSNN approach, adn the *efficiency* of the methods. To measure *proximity* and *diversity*, we use the *Root Mean Square Error* (RMSE) metric, which returns a score that represents the difference between the amplitudes of two cases at each time step. Before applying RMSE, we apply *Wav2Vec 2.0* [3], a self-supervised transformer-based model that extracts deep semantic embeddings to transform the audio samples into feature vectors. The evaluation metrics used in our evaluation are:

- ***Proximity***. Using RMSE, we calculate the distance between the query q and the k explanation cases. If $k > 1$, the proximity score value is the mean RMSE

[2] https://github.com/PedroAMP22/SHOUX.

values for all case compared with the query. The lower the proximity value, the better: similar cases to q can help users to identify the class.
- ***Diversity***. Using RMSE, we calculate the difference between all the k explanation cases exc_q. The higher the diversity value, the better: the target user can compare a wider variety of cases.
- ***Robustness***. This metric is inspired by the *Remove and Debias* (ROAD) metric [26], which indicates how important some regions in the audio are to understand a class. To evaluate *robustness*, we selectively remove the most significant audio segments following a *Most Relevant First* (MRF) approach. Later, using a similarity metric, we compare the original audio and the perturbed audio. The higher the robustness value, the better. Higher values indicate that the evaluated model is more sensitive to critical audio segments, as the distance between the original sample and the perturbed sample increases significantly when key explanatory regions are removed.
- ***Efficiency***. It is calculated as the average execution time per query, expressed in milliseconds (ms). The lower, the better.

4.3 Baselines and Experimental Setup

We evaluate our proposed method by comparing it against several state-of-the-art audio similarity metrics. These metrics serve as a baseline for retrieving factual and counterfactual explanation cases. These baselines are:

- **Mel-Frequency Cepstral Coefficients (MFCC)** [9]. A spectral representation that maps audio onto the Mel scale to mimic human perception.
- **Discrete Wavelet Transform (DWT)** [21]. DWT provides multi-resolution analysis, capturing both temporal and frequency transients.
- **Pearson Correlation Coefficient** [6]. A statistical metric used to measure the linear relationship between audio feature vectors.
- **Van Rossum Distance** [27]. This metric is used to measure similarity with high temporal precision. For our evaluation, the Van Rossum distance serves as the performance ceiling, since it uses the same backbone as our proposed model to extract features.

For both our method and our baselines, we generate $k \in \{1, 3, 5\}$ cases for factual and counterfactual explanations. To ensure a fair and rigorous comparison across different baselines, the retrieval of the factual and counterfactual cases is performed within the native feature space of each method. To do that, we use Euclidean distance for the SSNN and DWT embeddings, whereas Cosine distance is applied to the MFCC and Pearson. We perform the Group-Based Splitting described before, using the evaluation metrics *proximity*, *diversity*, and *efficiency* as explained in the previous section. *Diversity* is omitted when $k = 1$, since we do not have cases to compare. In particular, to calculate *robustness*, we randomly select 50 audio samples from the dataset. We remove 10%, 20%, 30%, 40%, and 50% of the audio samples, using an MRF approach. The results are presented in the following section.

4.4 Results

Table 2. Results for *efficiency*, *proximity*, and *diversity* when obtaining $k \in \{1, 3, 5\}$ explanation cases for factual and counterfactual explanations. In the columns: T/Q represents Time per query in ms, P, Proximity, D, Diversity, F, Factual, and CF, Counterfactual. The best results for each column are marked in bold.

		k = 1		k = 3				k = 5			
Method	T/Q (ms)	P-F	P-CF	P-F	P-CF	D-F	D-CF	P-F	P-CF	D-F	D-CF
SSNN-XCBR	2.10	0.14	**0.17**	0.14	**0.17**	3.95	5.13	0.14	0.18	3.96	**5.10**
V.R	1709.24	**0.13**	**0.17**	**0.13**	**0.17**	3.82	**5.14**	**0.13**	0.18	3.86	**5.10**
MFCC	2.72	**0.13**	**0.17**	**0.13**	**0.17**	3.73	5.05	**0.13**	**0.17**	3.75	5.03
DWT	**0.23**	**0.13**	0.18	**0.13**	0.18	3.82	5.10	**0.13**	0.18	3.85	5.02
Pearson	41.33	0.14	**0.17**	0.14	**0.17**	**4.08**	5.02	0.14	0.18	**4.10**	5.03

Finally, we present the experimental results of our proposed method, comparing its performance with the baseline metrics previously described. In Table 2, we show the results obtained for *proximity*, *diversity*, and *efficiency*. Regarding *proximity* and *diversity* metrics, the scores across the table are very similar. A key point to highlight is that there is almost no variation in the metrics across different k values. This might be a consequence of the simplicity of the dataset, as there is not much variation between recordings, neither background noise nor distinct voice features. All voices were recorded at a monotonic pitch. However, SSNN-XCBR achieves the highest counterfactual diversity (5.10 for $k = 5$), reaching the upper bound set by the Van Rossum method while outperforming MFCC (5.03). Therefore, SSNN-XCBR seems to be the best approach when retrieving counterfactual explanation cases. SSNN-XCBR also demonstrates notable efficiency. The proposed method records a mean latency of only 2.10 ms per query, surpassing MFCC by 0.62 ms and Pearson by nearly 40 ms. Across all other metrics, SSNN-XCBR maintains performance parity with the top-tier results, demonstrating an optimal trade-off between *proximity*, *diversity*, and *efficiency*. MFCC achieves slightly better results mainly because *Wav2Vec 2.0* is designed to work with continuous sound features, which aligns with the MFCC representation. SSNN, on the other hand, converts sounds into simple discrete spikes, removing less important details and keeping only the most important patterns. Because of this simplification, SSNN delivers performance comparable to the baselines, but this is not a weakness: this simplification helps SSNN be more robust, less sensitive to noise, and better at isolating semantic features.

Figure 5 shows that the SSNN-based approach outperforms the baselines in terms of explanation *robustness*. SSNN demonstrates particular robustness when 10% of the most important parts are removed, outperforming a score of 0.65, compared to Pearson's 0.2. We can conclude from these results that the performance gap between SSNN-XCBR and the baselines widens when the key explanatory regions of the audio are removed.

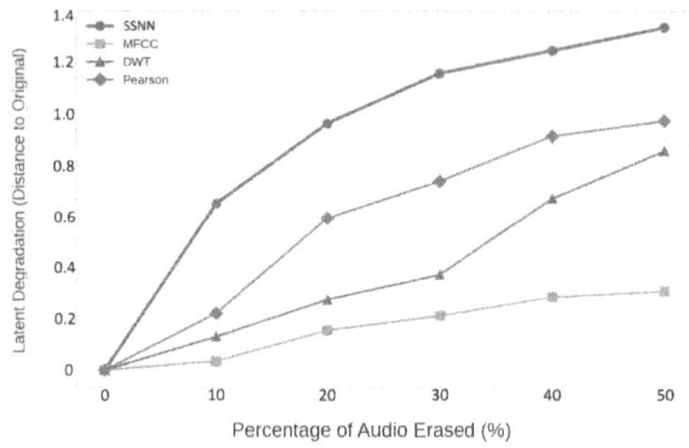

Fig. 5. Comparative results regarding *robustness*.

To visualise the *robustness* of the different approaches, we show the resulting latent spaces for each metric, illustrated in Fig. 6. The proposed SSNN-based method produces significantly more separated clusters compared to the baselines. This separation is the result of the model's ability to cluster instances based on the shared semantic features of the audio samples. Notably, the Van Rossum metric, unlike the other methods, it does not generate its own explicit feature vectors. Instead, it utilises the embeddings provided by the backbone and calculates the distance between them directly. In conclusion, our results demonstrate that the SSNN-XCBR organises the explanation cases in a more structurally coherent fashion. This capability of SSNN can be leveraged to enrich the explanation cases using shared semantic and audio features in the future.

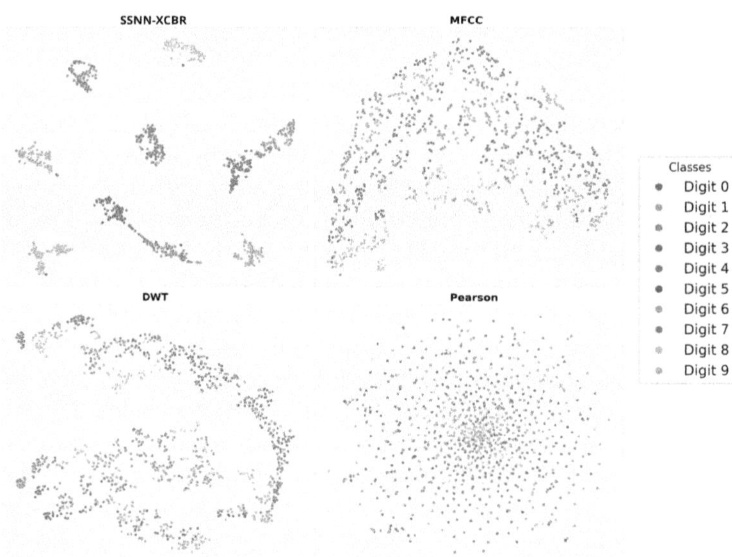

Fig. 6. Visual representation of latent spaces found by SSNN-XCBR and the baselines.

5 Conclusion and Future Work

In this work, we propose SSNN-XCBR, a CBR method to retrieve factual and counterfactual explanations for audio classification, using a Siamese-Spiking Neural Network architecture. It is a post-hoc and model-agnostic explainer whose novelty lies in its design: it has been developed to address the non-structured and time-based nature of the audio data during similarity computation between the query and the explanation cases. SSNN creates a robust latent space that enables the retrieval of near, diverse, and robust factual and counterfactual instances using semantic knowledge. The method was evaluated in an audio domain, confirming the quality of the instances retrieved. Leveraging the structured latent space, the semantic knowledge, and the acoustic features that we can obtain using SSNN-XCBR, in future work, we aim to enrich the explanation cases in a CBR adaptation step. We will explore the extraction of audio characteristics, such as frequency, spectral centroid or wave amplitudes, and the adaptation of SSNN-XCBR in different audio domains. Finally, we will investigate the integration of SSNN-XCBR to build a multimodal model where audio is involved.

Acknowledgments. This work is supported by the SHOU-X project (PR17/24-31890), funded by the Community of Madrid (CAM) through the UCM program supporting projects led by early-career PhD researchers (Line A, within the framework of VI PRICIT 2022–2025). This work is also supported by Grant PID2023-150566OB-I00 (AUDITIA-X) funded by MCIN/AEI/10.13039/501100011033 and the SI4/PJI/2024-00032 project funded by the Comunidad de Madrid through the UAM.

Declaration on Generative AI. During the preparation of this work, the authors used Gemini in order to only take advice on paraphrase and reword, improve writing style, and Grammar and spelling check. After using these tools, the authors adapted the content as needed according to the advice generated taking full responsibility for the publication's content.

References

1. Akman, A., Schuller, B.W.: Audio explainable artificial intelligence: a review. Intell. Comput. **3**, 0074 (2024)
2. Amin, K.: Cases without borders: automating knowledge acquisition approach using deep autoencoders and Siamese networks in case-based reasoning. In: IEEE 31st International Conference on Tools with Artificial Intelligence (ICTAI), pp. 133–140. IEEE (2019)
3. Baevski, A., Zhou, H., Mohamed, A., Auli, M.: wav2vec 2.0: a framework for self-supervised learning of speech representations. In: Proceedings of the 34th International Conference on Neural Information Processing Systems. NIPS '20, Curran Associates Inc, Red Hook, NY, USA (2020)
4. Barredo Arrieta, A., et al.: Explainable artificial intelligence (xAI): concepts, taxonomies, opportunities and challenges toward responsible ai. Inf. Fusion **58**, 82–115 (2020)

5. Becker, S., Vielhaben, J., Ackermann, M., Müller, K.R., Lapuschkin, S., Samek, W.: Audiomnist: exploring explainable artificial intelligence for audio analysis on a simple benchmark. J. Franklin Inst. **361**(1), 418–428 (2024)
6. Benesty, J., Chen, J., Huang, Y., Cohen, I.: Pearson Correlation Coefficient, pp. 1–4. Springer, Berlin, Heidelberg (2009)
7. Bhangale, K.B., Kothandaraman, M.: Survey of deep learning paradigms for speech processing. Wireless Pers. Commun. **125**(2), 1913–1949 (2022)
8. Chicco, D.: Siamese neural networks: an overview. Artifi. Neural Netw. 73–94 (2021)
9. Davis, S., Mermelstein, P.: Comparison of parametric representations for monosyllabic word recognition in continuously spoken sentences. IEEE Trans. Acoust. Speech Signal Process. **28**(4), 357–366 (1980)
10. De Mantaras, R.L., McSherry, D., Bridge, D., Leake, D., Smyth, B., Craw, S., et al.: Retrieval, reuse, revision and retention in case-based reasoning. Knowl. Eng. Rev. **20**(3), 215–240 (2005)
11. Fedele, A., Guidotti, R., Pedreschi, D.: This sounds like that: explainable audio classification via prototypical parts. In: International Conference on Discovery Science, pp. 348–363. Springer (2024)
12. Filandrianos, G.: Generation and evaluation of semantic counterfactual explanations. Thesis (2025)
13. Gao, Y., Gu, S., Jiang, J., Hong, S.R., Yu, D., Zhao, L.: Going beyond xAI: a systematic survey for explanation-guided learning. ACM Comput. Surv. **56**(7) (2024)
14. Gemmeke, J.F., et al.: Audio set: an ontology and human-labeled dataset for audio events. In: 2017 IEEE International Conference on Acoustics, Speech and Signal Processing (ICASSP), pp. 776–780 (2017)
15. Gunning, D., Aha, D.: Darpa's explainable artificial intelligence (XAI) program. AI Mag. **40**(2), 44–58 (2019)
16. Hoffmann, M., Malburg, L., Klein, P., Bergmann, R.: Using Siamese graph neural networks for similarity-based retrieval in process-oriented case-based reasoning. In: International Conference on Case-Based Reasoning, pp. 229–244. Springer (2020)
17. Koh, P.W., Liang, P.: Understanding black-box predictions via influence functions. In: International Conference on Machine Learning, pp. 1885–1894. PMLR (2017)
18. Leake, D., Wilkerson, Z., Ye, X., Crandall, D.J.: Enhancing case-based reasoning with neural networks. Compendium Neurosymbolic Artif. Intell. **369**, 387 (2023)
19. Lee, K.F., Hon, H.W.: Speaker-independent phone recognition using hidden Markov models. IEEE Trans. Acoust. Speech Sign. Process. **37**(11), 1641–1648 (1989)
20. Li, Y., Chen, C.P., Zhang, T.: A survey on Siamese network: methodologies, applications, and opportunities. IEEE Trans. Artifi. Intell. **3**(6), 994–1014 (2022)
21. Mallat, S.: A theory for multiresolution signal decomposition: the wavelet representation. IEEE Trans. Patt. Anal. Mach. Intell. **11**(7), 674–693 (1989)
22. Olah, C., Mordvintsev, A., Schubert, L.: Feature visualization. Distill **2**(11), e7 (2017)
23. Pinto, M.A.R.: Generalized Prototypical Parts Siamese Networks for Explainable Identity Recognition. Master's thesis, Universidade do Porto (Portugal) (2025)
24. Pruthi, G., Liu, F., Kale, S., Sundararajan, M.: Estimating training data influence by tracing gradient descent. Adv. Neural. Inf. Process. Syst. **33**, 19920–19930 (2020)
25. Purwins, H., Li, B., Virtanen, T., Schlüter, J., yiin Chang, S., Sainath, T.N.: Deep learning for audio signal processing. IEEE J. Selected Top. Sign. Process. **13**, 206–219 (2019)

26. Rong, Y., Leemann, T., Borisov, V., Kasneci, G., Kasneci, E.: A consistent and efficient evaluation strategy for attribution methods. arXiv preprint arXiv:2202.00449 (2022)
27. Rossum, M.C.W.v.: A novel spike distance. Neural Comput. **13**(4), 751–763 (2001)
28. Tavanaei, A., Ghodrati, M., Kheradpisheh, S.R., Masquelier, T., Maida, A.: Deep learning in spiking neural networks. Neural Netw. **111**, 47–63 (2019)
29. Ye, X., Leake, D., Huibregtse, W., Dalkilic, M.: Applying class-to-class Siamese networks to explain classifications with supportive and contrastive cases. In: International Conference on Case-based Reasoning, pp. 245–260. Springer (2020)
30. Zaman, K., Sah, M., Direkoglu, C., Unoki, M.: A survey of audio classification using deep learning. IEEE Access **11**, 106620–106649 (2023)

Case-Based Interpretability in Graph-Level Anomaly Detection via Contrast with Normal Prototypes

Qiuran Zhao, Kai Ming Ting(✉), and Xinpeng Li

State Key Laboratory for Novel Software Technology, School of Artificial Intelligence, Nanjing University, Nanjing 210023, China
{zhaoqr,lixp}@lamda.nju.edu.cn, tingkm@nju.edu.cn

Abstract. The task of graph-level anomaly detection (GLAD) aims to identify graphs that deviate significantly from the majority in a dataset. While existing deep learning methods achieve strong detection performance, they operate as black boxes that provide anomaly scores without human-interpretable explanations. Recent explainable GLAD methods either highlight suspicious substructures without referencing normal patterns, or rely on abstract latent vectors as prototypes that cannot be directly inspected by domain experts. We propose **Proto**type-based **G**raph-**L**evel **A**nomaly **D**etection (ProtoGLAD), an intrinsically interpretable framework that draws on core principles of case-based reasoning (CBR) to address these limitations. ProtoGLAD maintains a case base of normal prototype graphs discovered directly from the dataset using a density-adaptive point-set kernel. Given a graph, the framework retrieves its nearest normal prototype, which is a concrete, real graph instance, and determines anomalousness based on the similarity to its closest normal cluster. For each detected anomaly, ProtoGLAD generates a contrastive case-based explanation by explicitly comparing the anomalous graph with its nearest normal prototype at the node level, highlighting which substructures deviate from the normal reference and which align with it. This retrieve-and-contrast paradigm provides transparent, instance-grounded explanation that is lacking in existing GLAD methods. Extensive experiments demonstrate that ProtoGLAD achieves competitive detection performance while providing more human-interpretable case-based explanations compared to state-of-the-art methods.

Keywords: Graph-Level Anomaly Detection · Interpretability · Prototype-Based Explanation · Contrastive Explanation · Similarity-Based Retrieval

1 Introduction

Graphs are data structures widely used to represent complex relationships in various domains such as chemistry, traffic systems, and social networks. Recently,

L. Malburg and K. Bach (Eds.): ICCBR 2026, LNAI 16780, pp. 152–168, 2027.
https://doi.org/10.1007/978-3-032-33865-5_10

graph-level anomaly detection (GLAD) has emerged as a critical but challenging task in the graph data mining community [4,6,11,26,29–31]. The task of GLAD aims to identify graphs that deviate significantly from the majority of graphs in a dataset of graphs. Reliable GLAD methods support applications such as toxic compound detection, malicious network pattern discovery, and abnormal brain connectivity identification.

Despite their promising detection performance, most advanced methods for GLAD operate as black-box models. They detect anomalies based on anomaly scores derived from, for example, the reconstruction error of a graph autoencoder [6,12], the learning discrepancy from a knowledge distillation framework [13], the consistency score from cross-view mutual information maximization [11], the distance to a learned hypersphere center in one-class classification [16,30], or the decision boundary learned with pseudo-anomalous graphs [4]. The anomaly scores offered by these methods are self-referential, which means they measure how well a graph conforms to a compressed version of itself or to an augmented view of itself, rather than comparing it to normality. Consequently, it is unclear how the detected anomalies can be understood when the detectors cannot provide human-interpretable explanations or verify whether their detected anomalies are indeed rare and different from the majority of the graphs.

Recent studies [11,26,29] seek to provide explanations for detected anomalies. However, they have notable limitations: they either lack a comparative normal reference to verify why a detected anomaly is deviant, or they rely on learnable latent vectors as prototypes. Such latent prototypes may diverge from actual normal graphs, yielding unreliable baselines for both detection and explanation.

We contend that the limitations above stem from a common root cause: existing methods lack the reasoning paradigm of **learning from concrete cases**. In case-based reasoning (CBR) [1], a new problem is solved by retrieving similar past cases from a case base, comparing the new instance with the, and reusing the associated solutions or explanations. This paradigm is naturally suited to the GLAD task: if a case base of representative normal graphs can be constructed from the dataset, then a new graph can be assessed by retrieving its most similar normal case. If the new graph is dissimilar to all normal cases, it is identified as anomalous, and the contrast between the new graph and its nearest normal case directly provides a human-interpretable explanation for the detection result.

Therefore, we propose **Proto**type-based **G**raph-**L**evel **A**nomaly **D**etection (ProtoGLAD), an intrinsically interpretable framework that leverages case-based reasoning for GLAD. ProtoGLAD constructs a case base of normal prototype graphs and their associated normal clusters. Each prototype is a real graph from the dataset, serving as a representative normal case. Given an anomalous graph, ProtoGLAD retrieves its nearest normal prototype and determines anomalousness based on the similarity to its corresponding closest normal cluster. This design naturally aligns with the CBR cycle of *retrieve*, *reuse*, and *retain*: each detected anomaly can be directly contrasted with its nearest typical normal case, providing an inherent basis for ante-hoc interpretability.

The main contributions of this work are:

- Proposing ProtoGLAD, an interpretable GLAD framework based on the principle of case-based reasoning. ProtoGLAD constructs a case base of normal prototype graphs directly from the dataset and detects anomalies based on their similarity to the nearest normal prototype and its associated cluster.
- Developing a node-level, contrastive explanation mechanism that identifies the specific substructures, both in the detected anomalous graph and in its nearest normal prototype, that contribute to its anomalousness, providing a fine-grained, contrastive explanation.
- Conducting extensive experiments on multiple real-world and synthetic datasets, demonstrating that ProtoGLAD achieves competitive detection performance compared to state-of-the-art GLAD methods, while providing more human-interpretable, case-based explanations.

2 Related Work

In this section, we review existing works from three perspectives: graph-level anomaly detection methods, explainable GLAD methods, and case-based reasoning with prototype-based explanations.

2.1 Graph-Level Anomaly Detection

GLAD methods are used to identify anomalous graphs that exhibit significant deviations from the majority of graphs in a dataset. Existing GLAD methods can be broadly categorized into two types: **two-step** methods and **end-to-end** methods. **Two-step methods** first generate graph-level embeddings using graph kernels [23] or self-supervised learning [27], then apply a detector such as LOF [3] or Isolation Forest [10]. MUSE [6] also follows this pipeline but uses a GNN-based autoencoder to extract reconstruction error representations for a one-class classifier. **End-to-end methods** leverage GNNs [7] to jointly learn graph representations and detect anomalies in a unified framework. Among them, some approaches presume that the anomaly labels of the graphs are accessible during model training, and thus frame GLAD as a supervised classification problem [28,29]. However, their strong dependence on labeled anomalies renders their application difficult in a real-world scenarios where such annotations are few or, more often than not, nonexistent. Therefore, most approaches focus on unsupervised learning, under the assumption that only normal samples are used during the training phase. For example, some of them adopt GNN-based graph reconstruction [12], where anomalies are identified as graphs that are poorly reconstructed by the model, while some others like GLocalKD [13] and KDGAE [31] use a knowledge distillation framework where anomalies are detected as those having large knowledge discrepancies. In addition, OCGTL [16] combines one-class classification with graph transformation learning to learn a compact normal boundary, while AGDiff [4] leverages latent diffusion models to generate pseudo-anomalous graphs for enhancing the decision boundary.

2.2 Explainable GLAD

Explainable graph-level anomaly detection has attracted increasing attention, and several recent methods have attempted to provide explanations for their detected anomalies. SIGNET [11] identifies the specific substructures within a single graph that contribute to its anomaly score. It is done by extracting an important "bottleneck" subgraph using the information bottleneck (IB) principle. While it highlights the suspicious subgraph of the detected anomaly, it fails to provide a contrastive reference to a normal counterpart, making it difficult to verify why the highlighted subgraph is considered deviant.

GLADPro [26] aims to provide a general understanding of the model's behavior by learning global prototypes. It extends the IB principle to learn a set of prototypes that capture important subgraph patterns across the entire dataset. However, a key limitation is that these prototypes are modeled as learnable vectors in a latent space, rather than actual graphs directly discovered from the dataset, and high-dimensional latent vectors are difficult for humans to interpret.

More recently, X-GAD [29] aggregates common structural and attribute characteristics across anomalous graphs to construct anomaly prototypes. By contrasting graphs with these learned anomaly prototypes, X-GAD provides explanations that highlight recurring anomalous patterns shared among abnormal graphs. However, X-GAD relies on the availability of anomaly labels during training, which are often expensive or inaccessible. Furthermore, the presupposition of anomaly prototypes is a restrictive assumption, as anomalies do not necessarily exhibit consistent patterns.

2.3 Case-Based Reasoning and Prototype-Based Explanation

Case-based reasoning (CBR) [1] solves new problems by retrieving and adapting solutions from similar past cases stored in a case base. Prototype-based methods represent a specific CBR paradigm that constructs case bases from typical instances, for example, performing classification by comparing a query to learned class prototypes [18]. A core principle of CBR is that similar problems yield similar solutions, which has a natural connection to explainability: the system can present the retrieved cases as concrete evidence to justify its decisions [2]. Prototype-based explanations have been explored in various domains, especially in deep learning for image recognition [5,9], where predictions are explained by comparing an input to similar prototypical instances.

3 Preliminaries

3.1 Problem Definition

Let $M = \{\mathcal{G}_i\}_{i=1}^{n}$ be a set of n attributed graphs, where each graph $\mathcal{G}_i = (\mathcal{V}_i, \mathcal{E}_i)$ has a set of nodes $\mathcal{V}_i$ and a set of edges $\mathcal{E}_i$. Each node $v \in \mathcal{V}$ is associated with an attribute vector $\mathbf{x}_v \in \mathbb{R}^m$ with m attributes. We assume the majority of graphs in M are normal and can be grouped into k distinct normal clusters

$C = \{C_j\}_{j=1}^k$, where each cluster has a prototype P_i. The anomalous graphs are few and dissimilar from the majority of the graphs in M. This process requires a similarity measure $sim(\cdot,\cdot)$ that computes the similarity between a single graph and a set (or distribution) of graphs.

Definition 1 (Graph-Level Anomaly Detection). *Graph-level anomaly detection aims to identify anomalous graphs which have characteristics different from those of the* ***majority*** *of the graphs in the given set M of graphs, and to rank all the graphs on the basis of their anomaly scores such that the anomalous graphs are ranked higher than the normal ones.*

Definition 2 (Normal and Anomalous Graphs). *Given $M = \{\mathcal{G}_i\}_{i=1}^n$, a set of k normal clusters $C = \{C_j\}_{j=1}^k$ discovered from M, and a point-set similarity function $sim(\mathcal{G}, C_j)$ that measures the similarity between a graph $\mathcal{G}$ and the distribution of cluster C_j:*

- *A graph $\mathcal{G}^N$ is* ***normal*** *if it belongs to a cluster C_j and is close to that cluster's overall distribution.*
- *A graph $\mathcal{G}^A$ is* ***anomalous*** *if it does not belong to any cluster and is dissimilar to all normal clusters' distributions.*

and they have the following relationship:

$$\max_j \left(sim(\mathcal{G}^N, C_j)\right) \gg \max_j \left(sim(\mathcal{G}^A, C_j)\right)$$

3.2 Weisfeiler-Lehman Graph Kernels

Graph kernels are a class of methods for measuring the similarity between graphs. One of the most influential embedding techniques is the Weisfeiler-Lehman (WL) scheme [8,17], which captures the dependencies in a graph in the form of subtrees. There have been several extensions and variations of the WL scheme, for instance, a different version [22] of the WL scheme has been proposed to handle attributed graphs. In this approach, each graph is encoded as a histogram that reflects the distribution of node embeddings produced by the WL process.

Let $\mathcal{G} = (\mathcal{V}, \mathcal{E})$ be an attributed graph and $\mathcal{N}(v)$ be the set of nodes in the 1-hop neighborhood of node v, excluding v.

Definition 3. *A Weisfeiler-Lehman (WL) scheme [22] that embeds node v associated with $\mathcal{G}$, denoted as $\mathcal{G}(v)$, is defined as $\mathbf{x}_v^{(h)} = [\mathbf{x}_v^0, \mathbf{x}_v^1, \ldots, \mathbf{x}_v^h]$, where $\mathbf{x}_v^h$ represents the embedding of $\mathcal{G}(v)$ at iteration h:*

$$\mathbf{x}_v^h = \frac{1}{2}\left(\mathbf{x}_v^{(h-1)} + \frac{1}{|\mathcal{N}(v)|}\sum\nolimits_{u\in\mathcal{N}(v)} \mathbf{x}_u^{(h-1)}\right)$$

3.3 Isolation Kernel

Isolation kernel (IK) is a data-dependent kernel that derives directly from data without explicit learning, and it has no closed-form expression [21].

Let $D = \bigcup_{v \in \mathcal{V}_i, i \in [1,n]} \mathbf{x}_v$ be the set of all node vectors in the given dataset M of graphs. Here we use IK to map each node vector $\mathbf{x}_v \in \mathbb{R}^m$ into a vector $\varphi(\mathbf{x}_v \mid D) \in \{0,1\}^{t \times \psi}$ as is done in [25], where the use of IK has been shown to be the key to improving the discriminative power of the WL scheme.

Let $\mathbb{H}_\psi(D)$ denote the set of all partitionings H admissible from $\mathcal{D} \subset D$, where each point $\hat{\mathbf{x}}_v \in \mathcal{D}$ has equal probability of being selected from D and $|\mathcal{D}| = \psi$. Each $\theta[\hat{\mathbf{x}}_v] \in H$ isolates a point $\hat{\mathbf{x}}_v \in \mathcal{D}$.

Definition 4 ([15,21])**.** *The IK of $\mathbf{x}_1$ and $\mathbf{x}_2$ is defined to be the expectation taken over the distribution of partitionings $H \in \mathbb{H}_\psi(D)$ that both $\mathbf{x}_1$ and $\mathbf{x}_2$ fall into the same isolating partition $\theta[\hat{\mathbf{x}}_v] \in H$, where $\hat{\mathbf{x}}_v \in \mathcal{D} \subset D$, $\psi = |\mathcal{D}|$:*

$$\begin{aligned} \kappa_\psi(\mathbf{x}_1, \mathbf{x}_2 \mid D) &= \mathbb{E}_{\mathbb{H}_\psi(D)} \left[\mathbb{1}(\mathbf{x}_1, \mathbf{x}_2 \in \theta \mid \theta \in H) \right] \\ &\approx \frac{1}{t} \sum_{i=1}^{t} \mathbb{1}(\mathbf{x}_1, \mathbf{x}_2 \in \theta \mid \theta \in H_i) \\ &= \frac{1}{t} \sum_{i=1}^{t} \sum_{\theta \in H_i} \mathbb{1}(\mathbf{x}_1 \in \theta) \mathbb{1}(\mathbf{x}_2 \in \theta) \end{aligned} \tag{1}$$

where $\mathbb{1}(\cdot)$ is an indicator function; κ_ψ is constructed using a finite number of partitionings H_i, $i = 1, \dots, t$, where each H_i is created using randomly subsampled $\mathcal{D}_i \subset D$; and θ is a shorthand for $\theta[\hat{\mathbf{x}}_v]$.

Definition 5 (Feature Map of Isolation Kernel.[20]**).** *For node vector $\mathbf{x}_v \in \mathbb{R}^m$, the feature mapping $\varphi : \mathbb{R}^m \to \{0,1\}^{t \times \psi}$ of κ_ψ maps $\mathbf{x}_v$ into a vector that represents the partitions in all the partitionings $H_i \in \mathbb{H}_\psi(D)$, $i = 1, \dots, t$, where $\mathbf{x}_v$ falls into either one of the ψ hyperspheres or none in each partitioning H_i.*

Rewriting Eq. 1 using φ gives:

$$\kappa_\psi(\mathbf{x}_1, \mathbf{x}_2 \mid D) = \frac{1}{t} \langle \varphi(\mathbf{x}_1 \mid D), \varphi(\mathbf{x}_2 \mid D) \rangle$$

4 Proposed Framework: ProtoGLAD

ProtoGLAD performs graph-level anomaly detection through three steps: (1) **Case representation**: each graph is embedded into a fixed-dimensional vector; (2) **Case base construction and retrieval**: a density-adaptive point-set kernel discovers normal prototypes and clusters from the dataset, and a new graph is assessed by retrieving its nearest normal cluster; (3) **Case-based explanation**: for each detected anomaly, a contrastive explanation is generated by comparing it with its nearest normal prototype at the node level. An overview of ProtoGLAD and an illustration of its contrastive explanation is provided in Fig. 1.

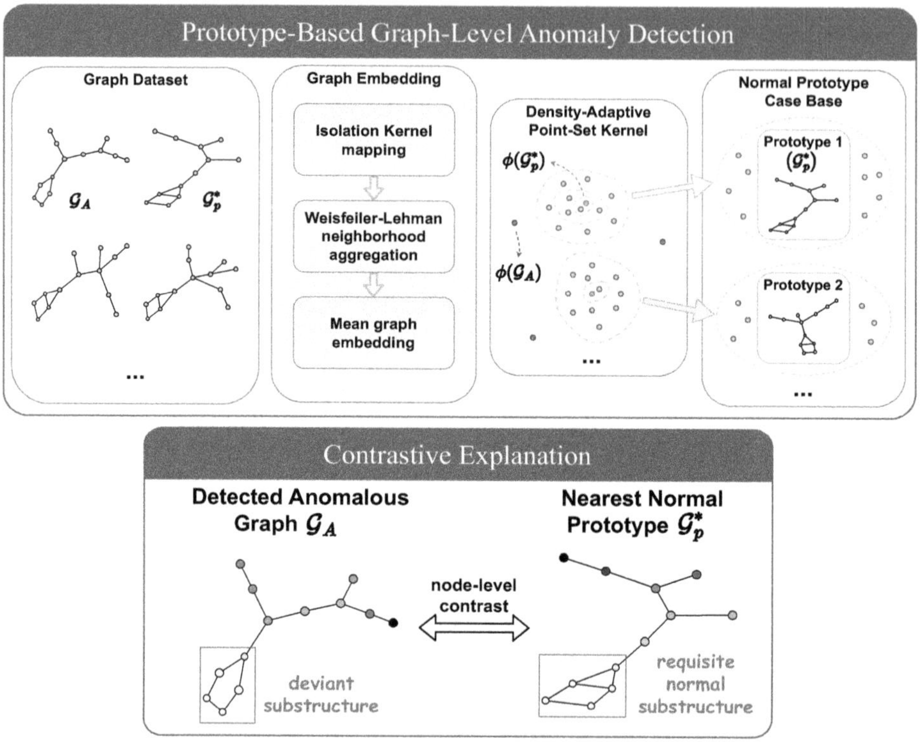

Fig. 1. An overview of ProtoGLAD and the contrastive explanation it generates.

4.1 Graph Embedding

The Weisfeiler-Lehman (WL) embedding used here is identical to what we introduced in Sect. 3.2. The only exception is that we use the IK mapped vector $\varphi(\mathbf{x}_v)$ rather than node vector $\mathbf{x}_v$ as the input representation of the WL scheme, which is the same as in [25].

Let $\varphi^0(\mathbf{x}_v) = \varphi(\mathbf{x}_v)$ be the IK mapped node vector $\mathbf{x}_v$ for a node v in a graph $\mathcal{G}$. The WL embedding at iteration $h > 0$ is recursively defined as:

$$\varphi^h(\mathbf{x}_v) = \frac{1}{2}(\varphi^{h-1}(\mathbf{x}_v) + \frac{1}{|\mathcal{N}(v)|}\sum_{u\in\mathcal{N}(v)} \varphi^{h-1}(\mathbf{x}_u)) \tag{2}$$

We see each graph $\mathcal{G} = (\mathcal{V}, \mathcal{E})$ as having a representative sample of WL-embedded node vectors $\varphi^h(\mathbf{x}_v)$ ($\forall v \in \mathcal{V}$) of an unknown distribution, where each node vector is represented using the IK-WL embedding. Then, a mean embedding can be used to represent each graph.

For a graph $\mathcal{G} = (\mathcal{V}, \mathcal{E})$, its embedding is given as the mean embeddings of all nodes in $\mathcal{G}$:

$$\phi(\mathcal{G}) = \frac{1}{|\mathcal{V}|}\sum_{v\in\mathcal{V}} \varphi^h(\mathbf{x}_v).$$

The similarity between any pair of two graphs is calculated by a dot product between the two mean embeddings or feature mean maps, *i.e.*,

$$sim(\mathcal{G}, \mathcal{G}') = \langle \phi(\mathcal{G}),\ \phi(\mathcal{G}') \rangle$$

4.2 Anomalous Graph Detection

Once graph-level embeddings are obtained for each graph in the dataset, the GLAD problem can be reformulated as a point anomaly detection task in the embedding space. Each graph $\mathcal{G}_i$ is represented by a fixed-dimensional vector $\phi(\mathcal{G}_i)$ to capture its structural and semantic properties.

The point-set kernel [19] between a point x and a set C of points is:

$$K(x, C) = \langle \varphi(x), \Phi(C) \rangle$$

and

$$\Phi(C) = \frac{1}{|C|} \sum\nolimits_{y \in C} \varphi(y)$$

where $\langle a, b \rangle$ denotes a dot product between two vectors a and b; Φ is the kernel mean map of K; and φ is the feature map of a point-to-point kernel κ, for which we use IK as it has a finite-dimensional feature map, and its similarity adapts to local density of the data distribution of a given dataset.

ProtoGLAD, as detailed in Algorithm 1, is an extension of the `psKC` algorithm [19] to deal with graph data. ProtoGLAD employs the point-set kernel K to discover clusters by first locating a high-density data point, which is treated as the prototype for that cluster. A cluster is then "grown" from this prototype by absorbing all points that are similar to the cluster, based on a growth rate ρ. The process repeats for subsequent clusters using the set Π of unassigned points. It continues until Π is empty or no remaining point has a similarity to an existing cluster greater than a threshold τ. The final anomaly score for any graph $\mathcal{G}_i$ is the negative of its point-set similarity to its nearest cluster. Graphs that are most dissimilar to all clusters are thus identified as anomalies.

4.3 Contrastive Case-Based Explanation

Upon obtaining the anomaly score for a detected anomalous graph $\mathcal{G}_A$, we identify its most similar normal prototype $\mathcal{G}_p^*$. Then, for $\mathcal{G}_A$, we assign each node $u \in \mathcal{V}_A$ a score measuring how well it aligns with $\mathcal{G}_p^*$. We define the node normality score as the inner-product similarity between the node embedding and the nearest normal prototype embedding:

$$c(u) = \langle \varphi^h(u), \phi(\mathcal{G}_p^*) \rangle.$$

Intuitively, a low $c(u)$ indicates that node u contributes little to the similarity between $\mathcal{G}_A$ and the normal prototype $\mathcal{G}_p^*$, thereby highlighting this node's contribution to the anomalousness of $\mathcal{G}_A$. Analogously, scores for nodes in $\mathcal{G}_p^*$

Algorithm 1. ProtoGLAD: Prototype-Based Graph-Level Anomaly Detection

Input: Graph dataset $M = \{\mathcal{G}_i = (\mathcal{V}_i, \mathcal{E}_i)\}_{i=1}^n$, similarity threshold τ, growth rate ϱ
Output: Anomaly scores $S = \{s_i\}_{i=1}^n$, normal prototype graphs $P = \{\mathcal{G}_p^j\}_{j=1}^k$

Obtain graph embedding $g_i = \phi(\mathcal{G}_i)$ for each graph $\mathcal{G}_i$ in M, $G_{all} = \{g_i\}_{i=1}^n$
$\Pi = G_{all}$, $k = 0$
while $|\Pi| > 1$ **do**
  $g_p = \arg\max_{g \in \Pi} K(g, \Pi)$
  $g_q = \arg\max_{g \in \Pi \setminus \{g_p\}} K(g, \{g_p\})$
  $\gamma = (1 - \varrho) \times K(g_q, \{g_p\})$
  if $\gamma \leq \tau$ **then**
    break
  end if
  $k = k + 1$
  $\mathcal{G}_p^k = g_p$, $C^k = \{g_p, g_q\}$
  while $\gamma > \tau$ **do**
    $C^k = \{g \in \Pi \mid K(g, C^k) > \gamma\}$
    $\gamma = (1 - \varrho)\gamma$
  end while
  $\Pi = \Pi \setminus C^k$
end while
for $i = 1$ to n **do**
  $s_i = -\max_{j=1,\ldots,k} K(g_i, C^j)$
end for
return $S = \{s_i\}_{i=1}^n$, $P = \{\mathcal{G}_p^j\}_{j=1}^k$

can also be computed w.r.t. $\mathcal{G}_A$. This identifies the lowest-scored nodes in $\mathcal{G}_p^*$ that are least similar to the nodes in $\mathcal{G}_A$, *i.e.*, the normal substructure that $\mathcal{G}_A$ lacks.

The pair of $\mathcal{G}_A$ and $\mathcal{G}_p^*$, along with their respective lowest-scored nodes, provides a comprehensive, contrastive explanation of the divergence between the anomalous graph $\mathcal{G}_A$ and its most similar normal prototype $\mathcal{G}_p^*$. Specifically, this contrastive view not only highlights the deviant substructure present within $\mathcal{G}_A$ that leads to its anomalousness, but also identifies the requisite normal substructure from $\mathcal{G}_p^*$ that $\mathcal{G}_A$ should have possessed. Notably, while the contrastive explanation produced by ProtoGLAD is similar to counterfactual explanations, it remains distinct: whereas counterfactuals focus on modifying the input to alter the model's output [24]—typically by generating synthetic instances—our approach retrieves concrete, normal prototypes directly from the case base.

5 Experiments

In this section, we evaluate ProtoGLAD by addressing three research questions:

- **RQ1.** How accurately does ProtoGLAD detect anomalous graphs?
- **RQ2.** Can ProtoGLAD provide a human-interpretable, high-quality explanation for each of its detected anomalies?

- **RQ3.** How do the key components of ProtoGLAD contribute to its overall anomaly detection effectiveness?

5.1 Experimental Setup

Datasets. We employ 10 publicly available real-world datasets from the TUDataset benchmark [14], covering bioinformatics (AIDS, BZR, COX2, DD, MUTAG, PROTEINS, NCI1, DHFR) and social networks (IMDB-BINARY, REDDIT-BINARY). Following standard GLAD evaluation protocols [13,30], the minority class in a binary dataset is treated as anomalous and the majority as normal.

In addition, we construct three synthetic datasets with ground-truth explanation annotations, following [11]. Each graph is composed of a base structure (tree, ladder, or wheel with 25–35 nodes) and one or more attached motifs that determine its label. For B-TYPE (motif type), normal graphs have a house motif and anomalies have a 5-cycle motif. For B-COUNT (motif count), normal graphs have 1–2 house motifs and anomalies have 3–4. For B-SIZE (motif size), normal graphs have a cycle with 3–5 nodes and anomalies have a cycle with 6–8 nodes. Each dataset contains 500 graphs with a 10% anomaly ratio. The ground-truth anomalous substructures are defined as the nodes and edges within the motifs. Quantitative evaluations are based on 5-fold cross-validation for all datasets.[1]

Baselines. Eight unsupervised GLAD methods are selected as baselines:

- **Two-step Methods**: *WL-iForest* [10,17] and *MUSE* [6].
- **End-to-End Deep Learning Methods**: Six state-of-the-art end-to-end GLAD methods based on deep learning are used: *GLADC* [12], *GLocalKD* [13], *OCGTL* [16], *SIGNET* [11], *GLADPro* [26], and *KDGAE* [31].

Among these baselines, only SIGNET and GLADPro are capable of providing explanations for their detection results.

5.2 Anomaly Detection Performance (RQ1)

We adopt the Area Under the ROC Curve (AUC) for quantitative performance evaluation as it is a robust metric for handling the severe class imbalance inherent in GLAD tasks [13,29,30]. Higher AUC indicates better performance.

As shown in Table 1, ProtoGLAD achieves the best average rank across all 13 datasets, ranking first on 9 datasets and second on 3. Two points stand out. First, ProtoGLAD consistently outperforms all baselines on molecular datasets (BZR, COX2, MUTAG, PROTEINS) with large margins, suggesting that the density-adaptive prototype discovery is effective when normal graphs form multiple distinct clusters. Second, on the two social network datasets (IMDB-B and REDDIT-B) that lack node attributes, ProtoGLAD ranks second, behind GLADC. This is expected, as the IK-WL embedding relies on node features, and its discriminative power is reduced when only structural information is available.

[1] Code is available at https://github.com/IsolationKernel/ProtoGLAD.

Table 1. Anomaly detection performance in terms of AUC (%). For each dataset, the best result is presented in **boldface**, and the second best result is underlined.

Dataset	WL-iForest	MUSE	GLADC	GLocalKD	SIGNET	OCGTL	GLADPro	KDGAE	ProtoGLAD
AIDS	61.4	**99.8**	96.7	96.9	97.6	97.5	52.6	83.3	98.7
BZR	52.8	68.0	61.1	68.1	77.9	61.8	60.6	55.3	**85.6**
COX2	51.2	67.3	57.7	60.2	64.5	57.9	63.7	55.2	**70.9**
DD	70.4	80.3	57.2	75.3	71.2	78.5	76.6	73.6	**81.1**
MUTAG	71.1	85.1	73.2	83.3	76.6	79.5	89.1	67.1	**89.8**
PROTEINS	62.1	72.3	75.8	76.1	73.3	70.7	73.6	58.2	**79.4**
NCI1	50.4	70.1	68.3	65.3	71.3	58.1	59.2	59.1	**72.1**
DHFR	51.7	62.5	60.4	61.8	**63.4**	51.0	60.9	52.4	62.4
IMDB-B	59.9	63.3	**65.4**	49.9	63.0	60.1	62.1	59.2	64.9
REDDIT-B	55.7	74.4	**82.1**	77.9	71.4	73.9	63.1	58.0	79.1
B-TYPE	78.1	72.6	53.0	75.9	78.6	74.7	69.9	54.8	**86.2**
B-COUNT	88.7	87.7	82.6	75.8	70.0	87.9	66.7	74.0	**91.2**
B-SIZE	76.2	60.0	64.3	74.9	65.7	79.6	69.5	63.6	**88.3**
Avg. Rank	7.00	3.77	5.46	4.54	4.23	5.23	5.69	7.69	**1.38**

5.3 Case-Based Explanations (RQ2)

We assess the interpretability of ProtoGLAD from two aspects: (1) whether the node score $c(u)$ correctly localizes anomaly-inducing substructures on synthetic data with available node- or edge-level ground truth, and (2) whether ProtoGLAD provides more informative explanations than the two explainable GLAD methods, SIGNET and GLADPro, on real-world data.

Synthetic Data Validation. Leveraging ground-truth annotations of anomalous motifs from synthetic datasets, we evaluate the explanations quantitatively via node-level AUC (N-AUC) and edge-level AUC (E-AUC), which measure the ability to rank nodes or edges belonging to the anomalous motifs lower than normal ones [11,26]. We compare ProtoGLAD with SIGNET and GLADPro, the only two baselines capable of providing explanations.

Table 2. Quantitative evaluation of explanations on synthetic datasets (AUC, %).

Method	B-TYPE		B-COUNT		B-SIZE	
	N-AUC	E-AUC	N-AUC	E-AUC	N-AUC	E-AUC
SIGNET	81.3	83.2	60.9	60.7	82.1	86.4
GLADPro	63.3	58.5	63.0	59.7	68.8	67.1
ProtoGLAD	**88.4**	**91.6**	**64.4**	**67.2**	**91.5**	**94.2**

The evaluation results are reported in Table 2. ProtoGLAD achieves the best N-AUC and E-AUC on all three datasets. The advantage is most pronounced on

B-TYPE and B-SIZE, where the anomaly is characterized by a structurally distinct motif—ProtoGLAD's contrastive comparison with a concrete normal prototype directly exposes the differing substructure. On B-COUNT, where normal and anomalous graphs share the same motif type and differ only in the number of occurrences, all methods find the task more challenging, but ProtoGLAD still achieves the best results. GLADPro's relatively low scores reflect the difficulty of interpreting abstract latent prototypes at the node level.

Table 3. Contrastive explanations produced by ProtoGLAD on the synthetic datasets. Each detected anomaly is shown alongside its retrieved normal prototype. Darker nodes indicate high similarity to the prototype; lighter nodes indicate anomaly-inducing substructures, which are highlighted by red bounding boxes.

Dataset	B-TYPE	B-COUNT	B-SIZE
Anomalous Graph	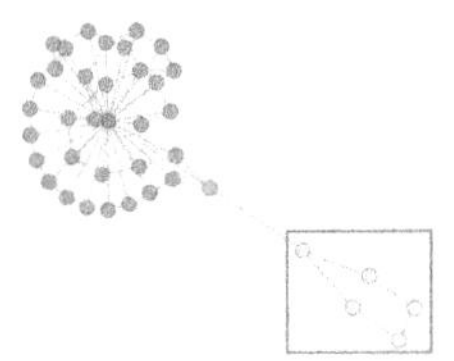	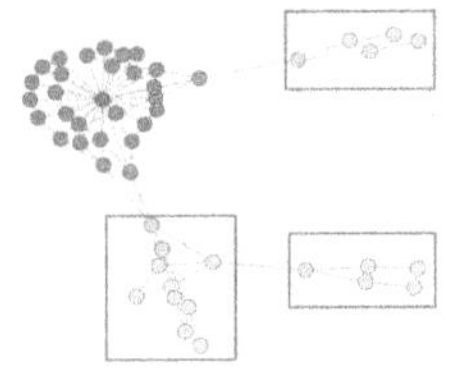	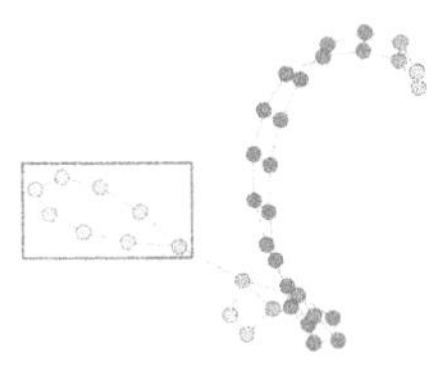
Normal Prototype	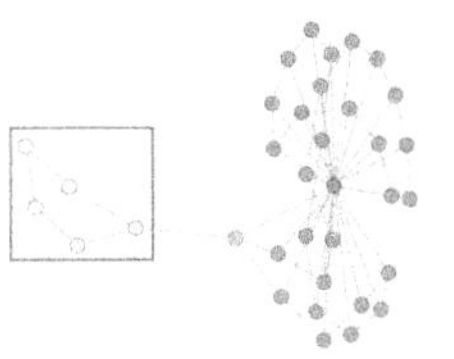	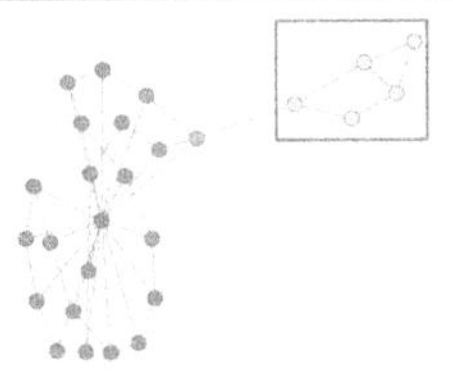	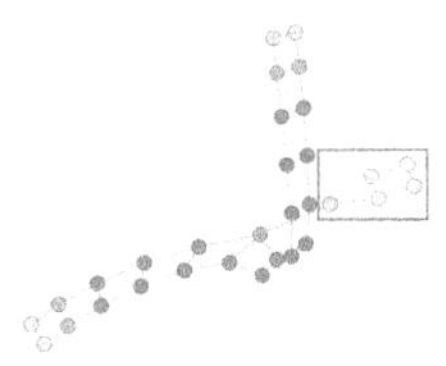

Table 3 visualizes ProtoGLAD's case-based explanations on the three synthetic datasets, where the ground-truth anomalous motif is known. Each detected anomaly is presented alongside its corresponding retrieved normal prototype. Node colors indicate the normality score $c(u)$: darker nodes are consistent with the prototype, while lighter nodes highlight the anomaly-inducing motifs. Across all three datasets, the lighter regions align well with the ground-truth motifs, confirming that ProtoGLAD's contrastive explanation mechanism correctly identifies the substructures responsible for anomalousness.

Real-world Data Validation. We provide a qualitative comparison of the explanations produced by ProtoGLAD, SIGNET, and GLADPro on the MUTAG dataset in Table 4. For each detected anomaly, the retrieved normal prototype provides a concrete reference for comparison, and the node colors reveal where the anomaly deviates from its nearest normal case.

- **SIGNET** highlights a "bottleneck subgraph" within each anomalous graph, but does not provide a normal reference, making it difficult to verify whether

Table 4. Comparison of explanations produced by SIGNET, GLADPro, and ProtoGLAD on MUTAG. For each method, we show the top-2 anomalous graphs detected, their normal prototype graphs, and additional normal reference graphs. For ProtoGLAD, prototypes are real graphs discovered from the dataset. For GLADPro, the closest graph to its latent prototype is shown. For SIGNET which does not identify prototypes, we use ProtoGLAD to provide the normal reference.

Method	Anomalous Graph	Normal Prototype	Additional Normal Reference Graphs
SIGNET	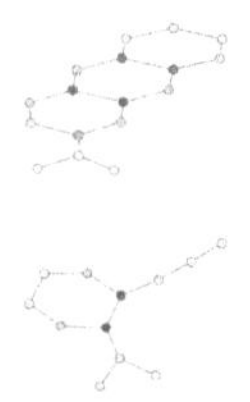	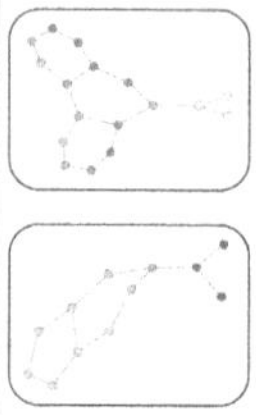	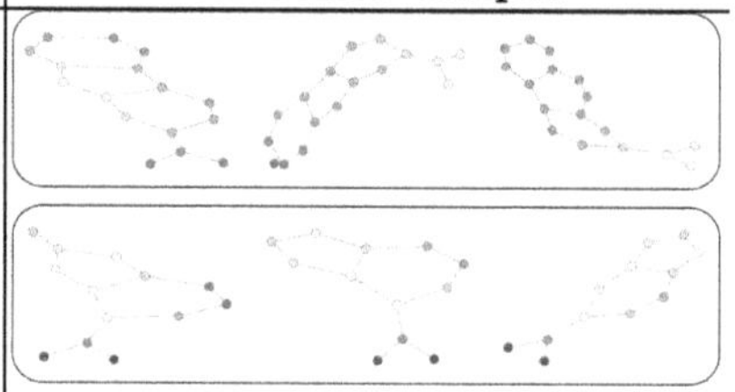
GLADPro	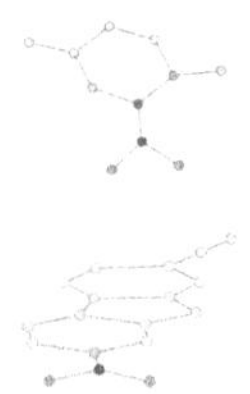		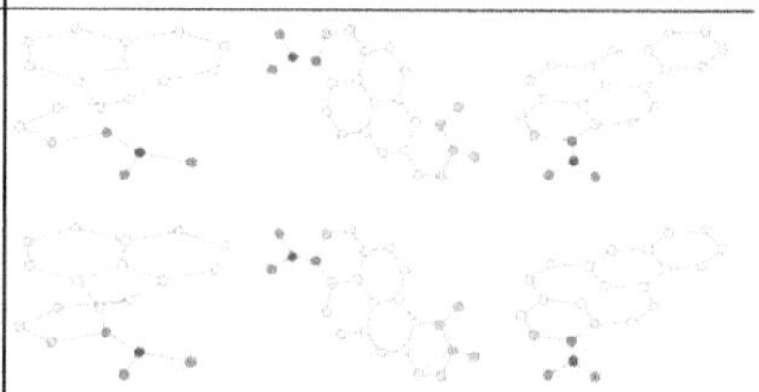
ProtoGLAD	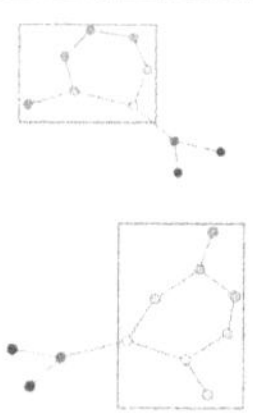	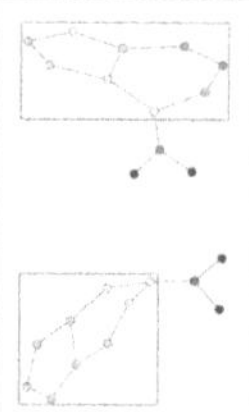	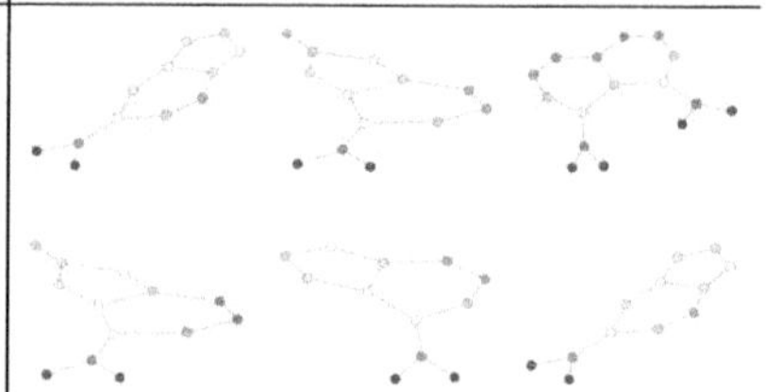

the detected anomaly truly deviates from the majority. Notably, its top-1 ranked anomaly (the first row in Table 4) is identified as normal by both GLADPro and ProtoGLAD. For visual comparison, we use ProtoGLAD to obtain the normal prototype and cluster examples for the anomalous graphs detected by SIGNET. As illustrated, the top-1 anomalous graph detected by SIGNET is visually similar to its nearest normal prototype as well as to other graphs within the corresponding normal cluster. This also highlights the risk of misinterpretation when no contrastive normal reference is available.

- **GLADPro** learns global prototypes. However, as its prototypes are abstract latent vectors, they can only be visualized indirectly by retrieving a set of top-k similar graphs from the dataset. While this provides a general sense of normal patterns, no explicit summary of normal graphs is available.
- **ProtoGLAD** provides a direct, contrastive explanation for each detected anomaly. Not only does ProtoGLAD highlight the anomalous substructure, but it also finds the specific real normal prototype to which the anomaly

Table 5. A comparison of identified prototypes on the MUTAG dataset.

Method	Identified Prototypes
GLADPro	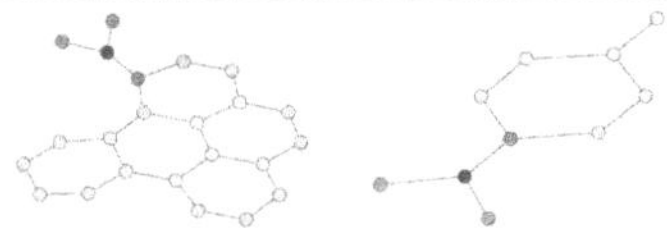
ProtoGLAD	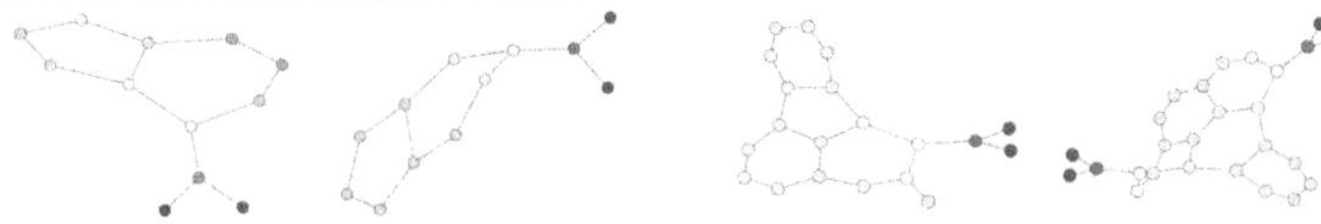

is most similar. Node colors describe the similarity to the prototype: darker nodes indicate consistency with normality (high similarity), while **lighter nodes highlight the anomalous deviations** (low similarity).

A notable observation from Table 4 is that GLADPro incorrectly flags a ground-truth normal graph as the second detected anomaly. We attribute this to the inherent instability of its prototype learning mechanism: since its prototypes are randomly initialized learnable vectors, these vectors may drift into sparse regions that do not correspond to any dense normal distribution. This is evidenced in Table 5, where the second prototype retrieved by GLADPro is structurally more similar to the first anomalous graph shown in Table 4 rather than a typical normal graph. In contrast, ProtoGLAD explicitly identifies four concrete prototypes. Not only does ProtoGLAD capture the dominant normal pattern identified by GLADPro, but it also manages to identify others that GLADPro fails to discover. This confirms that the data-dependent approach of ProtoGLAD ensures both the *validity* and the *coverage* of the normal reference set.

5.4 Ablation Study (RQ3)

To verify the contribution of each component in ProtoGLAD, we evaluate three variants: (1) **w/o IK**: replace IK with the original node features as input to the WL scheme; (2) **w/o WL**: remove WL neighborhood aggregation and use only the IK-mapped node vectors averaged as the graph embedding; (3) **w/o Prototypes**: replace the multi-prototype clustering with a single global center.

As shown in Table 6, the multi-prototype mechanism is the most critical component in ProtoGLAD, yielding an average AUC drop of 24.3% upon its removal. This confirms that normal graphs form multiple clusters that cannot be adequately represented by a single center. Removing WL aggregation leads to an average drop of 10.8%, indicating that neighborhood structural information is essential. Removing IK causes a moderate drop of 5.4%, validating that density-adaptive similarity improves the quality of graph embeddings and case retrieval.

Table 6. Performance of the variants of ProtoGLAD in terms of AUC (%). Δ denotes the average AUC drop relative to the full ProtoGLAD method.

Variant	AIDS	BZR	COX2	DD	MUTAG	PROT.	NCI1	DHFR	IMDB	REDDIT	B-TYPE	B-CNT	B-SIZE	Avg.Δ
w/o IK	95.9	67.8	55.9	78.8	86.7	77.2	67.4	60.6	62.1	72.3	85.2	83.7	85.5	−5.4
w/o WL	61.1	79.8	69.7	77.2	72.6	69.6	62.7	61.7	59.5	42.6	80.3	87.7	84.6	−10.8
w/o Proto.	98.7	55.8	46.3	20.3	12.2	32.3	31.7	59.0	51.1	76.8	80.9	87.1	81.5	−24.3
Full	**98.7**	**85.6**	**70.9**	81.1	**89.8**	**79.4**	72.1	**62.4**	**64.9**	79.1	**86.2**	**91.2**	**88.3**	—

6 Conclusions

We present ProtoGLAD, an interpretable framework that brings case-based reasoning to the task of graph-level anomaly detection. ProtoGLAD constructs a case base of normal prototype graphs directly from the dataset using a density-adaptive point-set kernel, assesses new graphs by retrieving their nearest normal cases, and explains each detected anomaly through a contrastive comparison with its retrieved prototype, identifying substructures leading to anomalousness.

Experiments on 10 real-world and 3 synthetic datasets demonstrate that ProtoGLAD achieves the best average rank among 8 baselines in detection performance, while providing quantitatively and qualitatively superior case-based, contrastive explanations compared to existing explainable GLAD methods.

Acknowledgments. Kai Ming Ting is supported by the National Natural Science Foundation of China (Grant No. 92470116). This project is also supported by Fundamental and Interdisciplinary Disciplines Breakthrough Plan of the Ministry of Education of China (No. JYB2025XDXM118).

Disclosure of Interests. The authors have no competing interests to declare that are relevant to the content of this article.

Declaration on Generative AI. During the preparation of this work, the authors used Claude in order to assist with paraphrasing, stylistic refinement, and grammatical check. After using this tool, the authors thoroughly reviewed and edited the content as needed and take full responsibility for the final work.

References

1. Aamodt, A., Plaza, E.: Case-based reasoning: foundational issues, methodological variations, and system approaches. AI Commun. (1994)
2. Bastardo-Rojas, Á., Caro-Martínez, M.: Visual question answering to generate case-based explanations for image classification. In: Proceedings of the International Conference on Case-Based Reasoning, pp. 37–51. Springer (2025)
3. Breunig, M.M., Kriegel, H.P., Ng, R.T., Sander, J.: LOF: identifying density-based local outliers. In: Proceedings of the ACM SIGMOD International Conference on Management of Data, pp. 93–104 (2000)
4. Cai, J., Zhang, Y., Liu, F., Ng, S.K.: Leveraging diffusion model as pseudo-anomalous graph generator for graph-level anomaly detection. In: Proceedings of the 42nd International Conference on Machine Learning (2025)

5. Chen, C., Li, O., Tao, D., Barnett, A., Rudin, C., Su, J.K.: This looks like that: deep learning for interpretable image recognition. Adv. Neural Inf. Process. Syst. (2019)
6. Kim, S., et al.: Rethinking reconstruction-based graph-level anomaly detection: limitations and a simple remedy. Adv. Neural. Inf. Process. Syst. **37**, 95931–95962 (2024)
7. Kipf, T.N., Welling, M.: Semi-supervised classification with graph convolutional networks. arXiv:1609.02907 arXiv preprint (2016)
8. Leman, A., Weisfeiler, B.: A reduction of a graph to a canonical form and an algebra arising during this reduction. Nauchno-Technicheskaya Informatsiya (1968)
9. Li, O., Liu, H., Chen, C., Rudin, C.: Deep learning for case-based reasoning through prototypes: a neural network that explains its predictions. In: Proceedings of the AAAI Conference on Artificial Intelligence (2018)
10. Liu, F.T., Ting, K.M., Zhou, Z.H.: Isolation forest. In: Proceedings of the 8th IEEE International Conference on Data Mining, pp. 413–422 (2008)
11. Liu, Y., Ding, K., Lu, Q., Li, F., Zhang, L.Y., Pan, S.: Towards self-interpretable graph-level anomaly detection. Adv. Neural. Inf. Process. Syst. **36**, 8975–8987 (2023)
12. Luo, X., et al.: Deep graph level anomaly detection with contrastive learning. Sci. Rep. **12**(1), 19867 (2022)
13. Ma, R., Pang, G., Chen, L., van den Hengel, A.: Deep graph-level anomaly detection by glocal knowledge distillation. In: Proceedings of the 15th ACM International Conference on Web Search and Data Mining, pp. 704–714 (2022)
14. Morris, C., Kriege, N.M., Bause, F., Kersting, K., Mutzel, P., Neumann, M.: TUDataset: a collection of benchmark datasets for learning with graphs. In: ICML 2020 Workshop on Graph Representation Learning and Beyond (2020)
15. Qin, X., Ting, K.M., Zhu, Y., Lee, V.C.: Nearest-neighbour-induced isolation similarity and its impact on density-based clustering. In: Proceedings of the AAAI Conference on Artificial Intelligence, vol. 33, pp. 4755–4762 (2019)
16. Qiu, C., Kloft, M., Mandt, S., Rudolph, M.: Raising the bar in graph-level anomaly detection. arXiv:2205.13845 arXiv preprint (2022)
17. Shervashidze, N., Schweitzer, P., Van Leeuwen, E.J., Mehlhorn, K., Borgwardt, K.M.: Weisfeiler-Lehman graph kernels. J. Mach. Learn. Res. **12**(9) (2011)
18. Snell, J., Swersky, K., Zemel, R.: Prototypical networks for few-shot learning. In: Advances in Neural Information Processing Systems (2017)
19. Ting, K.M., Wells, J.R., Zhu, Y.: Point-set kernel clustering. IEEE Trans. Knowl. Data Eng. (2023)
20. Ting, K.M., Xu, B.C., Washio, T., Zhou, Z.H.: Isolation distributional kernel: a new tool for kernel based anomaly detection. In: Proceedings of the 26th ACM SIGKDD International Conference on Knowledge Discovery & Data Mining (2020)
21. Ting, K.M., Zhu, Y., Zhou, Z.H.: Isolation kernel and its effect on SVM. In: Proceedings of the 24th ACM SIGKDD International Conference on Knowledge Discovery & Data Mining, pp. 2329–2337 (2018)
22. Togninalli, M., Ghisu, E., Llinares-López, F., Rieck, B., Borgwardt, K.: Wasserstein weisfeiler-lehman graph kernels. Adv. Neural. Inf. Process. Syst. **32** (2019)
23. Vishwanathan, S.V.N., Schraudolph, N.N., Kondor, R., Borgwardt, K.M.: Graph kernels. J. Mach. Learn. Res. **11**, 1201–1242 (2010)
24. Warren, G., Delaney, E., Guéret, C., Keane, M.T.: Explaining multiple instances counterfactually: User tests of group-counterfactuals for XAI. In: Proceedings of the International Conference on Case-Based Reasoning, pp. 206–222. Springer (2024)

25. Xu, B.C., Ting, K.M., Jiang, Y.: Isolation graph kernel. In: Proceedings of the AAAI Conference on Artificial Intelligence, vol. 35, pp. 10487–10495 (2021)
26. Yang, Z., et al.: Global interpretable graph-level anomaly detection via prototype. In: Proceedings of the 31st ACM SIGKDD International Conference on Knowledge Discovery and Data Mining (2025)
27. You, Y., Chen, T., Sui, Y., Chen, T., Wang, Z., Shen, Y.: Graph contrastive learning with augmentations. Adv. Neural Inf. Process. Syst. (2020)
28. Zhang, G., et al.: Dual-discriminative graph neural network for imbalanced graph-level anomaly detection. Adv. Neural. Inf. Process. Syst. **35**, 24144–24157 (2022)
29. Zhang, X., Qin, W., Huang, T., Gao, J.: X-GAD: explainable graph-level anomaly detection via inter-graph anomalies. Expert Syst. Appl. (2025)
30. Zhao, L., Akoglu, L.: On using classification datasets to evaluate graph outlier detection: peculiar observations and new insights. Big Data **11**(3), 151–180 (2023)
31. Zhou, Z., Ahmad, J.M., Liu, X., He, X., Xia, J.: Graph-level anomaly detection of brain connectivity with structural interpretation and knowledge distillation. In: Proceedings of the IEEE International Conference on Bioinformatics and Biomedicine (2025)

Explanation of Similarities in Temporal Case-Based Reasoning by Visualization

Roman Schander[1,2], Alexander Schultheis[1,2](✉), and Ralph Bergmann[1,2]

[1] Artificial Intelligence and Intelligent Information Systems, Trier University, Trier 54296, Germany
{s4rnscha,Alexander.Schultheis,bergmann}@uni-trier.de

[2] German Research Center for Artificial Intelligence (DFKI), Branch Trier University, Behringstraße 21, 54296 Trier, Germany
{Roman.Schander,Alexander.Schultheis,Ralph.Bergmann}@dfki.de,
http://www.wi2.uni-trier.de

Abstract. *Temporal Case-Based Reasoning* (TCBR) relies on time series similarity measures whose global similarity values emerge from multiple local contributions, making the development, validation, and maintenance of similarity models difficult for knowledge engineers. This paper investigates visualization-based explanations for mapping-based time series similarity measures that illustrate how such values are composed. To this end, a systematic literature study on visualization approaches for time series similarities is conducted, and a requirements catalog for similarity visualizations in TCBR is derived. Existing techniques are then assessed against these requirements. Based on the results, an extended point mapping visualization is presented that makes mappings between time series entries explicit and complements them with interactive tools for exploration and inspection. The concept is implemented in the ProCAKE framework and was evaluated in an exploratory user study. The results suggest that the approach is perceived as interpretable and practically useful for supporting the understanding of time series similarity values and their local composition in TCBR.

Keywords: Visualization · Temporal Case-Based Reasoning · Mapping-Based Time Series Similarity · Explainable Case-Based Reasoning

1 Introduction

Similarity is a central concept in *Case-Based Reasoning* (CBR), as it determines which collected cases are most useful for a new problem [6]. Accordingly, several similarity measures exist to identify the most useful case for a case representation. In *Temporal Case-Based Reasoning* (TCBR), relevant case information is often represented as time series data [22,37]. Such time series occur in settings including complex sensor streams in *Industrial Internet of Things* (IIoT) environments for classification and fault detection, as well as medical and

L. Malburg and K. Bach (Eds.): ICCBR 2026, LNAI 16780, pp. 169–186, 2027.
https://doi.org/10.1007/978-3-032-33865-5_11

energy-consumption contexts [22]. Time series similarity can be assessed by different approaches, including direct comparison methods and approaches based on transformed, abstracted, or learned representations [18,22,37,47]. This paper focuses on mapping-based similarity measures, i.e., measures aligning elements or local regions of two time series, e.g., *Smith-Waterman-Algorithm* (SWA) [44] or *Dynamic Time Warping* (DTW) [32]. Many mapping-based measures follow the local-global principle [6, pp. 106–107], such that multiple local similarity calculations contribute to a similarity value [33]. This makes the resulting similarity difficult to interpret and creates a need for explanation support.

For good retrieval results, the development, validation, and maintenance of similarity measures remain knowledge-intensive and error-prone tasks for knowledge engineers, especially for complex temporal patterns [38]. In TCBR, this challenge is pronounced for mapping-based similarity measures, because a single similarity value may arise from different alignments, heterogeneous local similarity values, and parameter settings of the underlying measure. Consequently, knowledge engineers frequently struggle to understand why a query-case pair yields a similarity value, how the induced mappings affect this value, and which local regions contribute most to it. Within *Explainable Artificial Intelligence* (XAI), explanations are used to support transparency and trust. The subfield of *Explainable Case-Based Reasoning* (XCBR) also addresses explanations of CBR systems, including retrieval results and thus the similarity value [34,38,45]. However, knowledge engineers need tool support to inspect and interpret the internal composition of similarity values [38]. Existing work demonstrates that visualization can facilitate this in CBR applications based on other case representations [3,24,38]. However, corresponding visualization approaches for explaining time series similarities in TCBR are not yet available.

To address this gap, this paper investigates visualization-based explanations for mapping-based time series similarities in TCBR to make similarity values and their local composition more accessible to knowledge engineers. To this end, a systematic literature study is conducted to identify, structure, and assess existing visualization approaches for time series similarities for mapping-based measures. Based on this, a requirements catalog for similarity visualizations in TCBR is derived, grounded in explainability goals [45] and established principles of information visualization [8,42,43]. Existing techniques are assessed against these requirements. From these results, a visualization concept centered on explicit point-to-point correspondences is designed and implemented in the ProCAKE framework [7], and its suitability is examined in an exploratory user study.

The paper is structured as follows. Section 2 provides foundations of TCBR, time series visualization approaches, and related work. Section 3 presents the literature study on visualization approaches for time series similarity, and Sect. 4 derives requirements for such a visualization in TCBR. Section 5 examines applicable literature approaches and adapts them for usage in TCBR. Section 6 evaluates the extended approach by a user study based on a prototypical implementation. Section 7 concludes and discusses future work.

2 Foundations and Related Work

This section provides the necessary background for this research. First, the research field of TCBR is introduced in Sect. 2.1, with a particular focus on time series as case representations and on the role of similarity measures. Subsequently, Sect. 2.2 introduces foundations from information visualization and the visualization of time series as a basis for explaining time series similarities. Finally, Sect. 2.3 discusses related work in XCBR and existing visual approaches relevant to the explanation of time series similarity values.

2.1 Temporal Case-Based Reasoning

TCBR is a subfield of CBR dealing with representing and processing temporal relationships within the CBR cycle [22]. In practice, especially in *Internet of Things* (IoT) applications, temporal case knowledge is frequently captured as multivariate sensor streams, which makes time series the most established case representation form in TCBR [22,37]. A time series is an ordered sequence of measured values associated with specific points in time, for example, originating from manufacturing sensors as well as from medical monitoring or energy-consumption recordings [22,37,40]. While alternative temporal representations such as episodes, graphs, or event sequences exist, time series enable a direct use of original sensor data and can be integrated as local attributes within a higher-level case description [22]. To reduce data volume and complexity, temporal abstraction techniques can aggregate observations to higher-level patterns. However, this comes with a trade-off between compactness and detail, which may be undesirable for fine-grained analyses [37,41].

Table 1. The Three Categories of Syntactic Mapping-Based Similarity Measures for Time Series (according to Malburg et al. [22]).

Category 1	Category 2	Category 3
Similarity measures that can only be applied to time series of the same length, comparing only the values at the corresponding times.	Similarity measures that can be applied to time series of different lengths, considering the values and the time points.	Similarity measures, like those in Cat. 2, but that can detect stretching and compression in addition.
List Mapping [22]	*Smith-Waterman-Algorithm* [44]	*Dynamic Time Warping* [32]

Retrieval in TCBR crucially depends on time series similarity measures [22]. Following the local-global principle [6, pp. 106–107], local similarities between time points (or local structures) are aggregated to a global similarity on the time series level and, if multiple series exist, further combined to an overall case similarity. Common syntactic measures include several mapping-based approaches, such as List Mapping [22], SWA [44], and DTW [32]. Among these, DTW additionally compensates stretching and compression effects [22,33]. Many widely used measures are knowledge-poor in the sense that they compare syntactic patterns without incorporating domain semantics [46]. Although knowledge-intensive semantic measures have been proposed, they are rarely used in TCBR practice, where syntactic measures dominate [22]. Table 1 summarizes a common categorization of syntactic measures [22], ranging from Cat. 1 to Cat. 3. This increasing complexity also creates a need for suitable explanation support, in particular for understanding how local contributions give rise to the resulting similarity value.

2.2 Visualization of Time Series

Visualizations are a promising means for supporting the understanding of complex issues such as time series similarities. Information visualization studies the computer-supported and interactive visual representation of abstract data, with the primary goal of enabling insight rather than merely producing graphics [8]. By reducing search effort, supporting pattern recognition, and enabling interactive exploration, visualizations can make complex data structures more accessible [43]. In the context of XAI, information visualization can contribute to transparency and trust [21]. Similarly, in XCBR, visual comparisons can support the communication of explanations, e.g., by contrasting a query with retrieved cases [45]. A widely used design guideline in this field is Shneiderman's Visual Information-Seeking Mantra, i.e., "overview first, zoom and filter, then details-on-demand" [42].

The visualization of time series constitutes a broad and heterogeneous research area [1]. Across many application contexts - including IIoT sensor analytics, medical monitoring, and energy-consumption analysis - time series visualizations serve two recurring purposes: (1) providing an interpretable depiction of temporal dynamics and (2) enabling the identification of relevant intervals, events, or anomalies for subsequent analysis. Surveys highlight that time-oriented data can be visualized either as explicit time series or as time-dependent attributes embedded into a broader data representation [2,10,27,43]. For explicit time series, coordinate-based representations such as line charts remain the dominant baseline due to their readability and expressiveness for continuous temporal change [1]. Beyond this baseline, more specialized and often more compact techniques exist, for example, circular, calendar-based, point-based, or matrix-based representations [2,10,27]. These alternatives can highlight periodicity, dense observations, or structural patterns, but often trade direct temporal traceability for compactness. Independent of the chosen encoding, interactive components are key to effective time series analysis. Common interaction patterns include filtering and focus mechanisms, linking multiple coordinated views, and providing details-on-demand to inspect specific time points or intervals without cluttering the overall display [10,43]. Overall, surveys consistently conclude that coordinate-based visualizations remain the practical default for time series, as they provide an intuitive overview and a robust basis for interactive inspection [1,10]. This is particularly relevant for visualization-based explanations of mapping-based time series similarities, where temporal context and local correspondences must remain visually accessible.

2.3 Visualizations as Explanations in Case-Based Reasoning

XCBR is a subtopic of XAI that focuses on CBR systems which explain their own output by providing additional explanations, for example through visual components [34]. In this context, XCBR differs from case-based explanations that use CBR to explain other *Artificial Intelligence* (AI) systems. Such case-based explanations are thematically related to this work, but address a different goal and are therefore not considered further here. Some publications use CBR to explain other AI approaches, for example, in work by Kenny and Keane [17], or Recio-García et al. [29]. Other XCBR work applies visualizations to explain similarity measures or their configuration, as in Batyrshin et al. [4]. In contrast, this work does not aim to visualize the composition of the similarity value based on the similarity measure. Instead, it focuses on mapping-based time series similarity measures, since they induce explicit or reconstructable correspondences that can serve as visual explanation objects. Furthermore, visualizations are used to depict similarity distributions in case bases or support retrieval-result inspection, for example in Rostami et al. [31] or Namee and Delany [28], and in approaches that visualize retrieval behavior over time [24].

Furthermore, several visualization approaches are related to this work. In CBR research, Massie et al. [25] extend CBR explanations beyond returning a case and a similarity value by using coordinate-based diagrams for cases represented as lists of numerical values. Bach and Mork [3] discuss how visual representations can support the development and inspection of similarity models during retrieval, particularly for computations following the local-global principle. In previous work [38], visualization-based explanations of similarities in *Process-Oriented Case-Based Reasoning* (POCBR) [26] were investigated by deriving a requirements catalog and designing three concepts for cases represented as workflow graphs. Although time series could in principle be encoded as graph structures, transferring these process-oriented visualizations to TCBR would add structure not needed for explaining time series similarity values and would clutter the view with information irrelevant to alignment-based sequence comparison, analogous to Weich et al. [47]. Interactive tools such as SimViz support similarity inspection and maintenance in structured, attribute-based CBR applications [14–16], but they do not support time series as case representations.

Beyond CBR-specific approaches, interactive systems for time series analysis also exist. TimeSearcher [12] and ChronoLenses [49] support exploratory search and transformation of time series data. In these systems, similarity is mainly used for filtering and navigation rather than for explaining similarity values computed by time series similarity measures in TCBR [12,49].

3 Systematic Literature Study on Visualization Approaches for Time Series Similarities

To provide a basis for selecting and designing a suitable visualization approach for explaining time series similarity values in TCBR, established guidelines for systematic literature studies were followed [30,48]. The study aims to identify concrete visualization techniques that explicitly address similarity between time series, particularly for mapping-based measures. As a result, the following four relevant approaches are identified.

Gogolou et al. [11] characterize similarity visualization for temporal data as covering both point-based and higher-level structural comparisons. A key observation is that the visualization strongly depends on the underlying similarity measure. In this context, two techniques are emphasized. **(1) Point Mapping Approaches** explicitly highlight correspondences between time points for mapping-based measures such as DTW. Matching points are connected by mapping lines, making local contributions and alignment effects visually accessible. **(2) Normalization Techniques** transform time series to compensate for amplitude differences or vertical shifts by rescaling the values relative to their mean and variability, which makes structural patterns more comparable in a coordinate-based visualization. While this does not change the underlying similarity measure, it makes structural patterns easier to compare visually.

Kumar et al. [19] propose a fundamentally different representation by converting time series into bitmap-like patterns. Their approach first discretizes time series using symbolic aggregate approximation and then maps frequency-based structural properties to a colored raster. Thus, **(3) Bitmap Patterns** enable efficient comparison and browsing of large collections because structurally similar time series yield similar patterns. However, the bitmap abstraction limits interpretability for individual query-case pairs, since relating specific color regions back to original time intervals and local structures becomes difficult. Finally, Chen et al. [9] introduce a **(4) Matching Matrix** for visualizing similar structures between two time series in the context of the spatial assembling distance measure. The matrix places both series on its axes using local pattern representations rather than raw values and marks local pattern matches as diagonal structures. The distribution of these matches provides a visual indication of where and how local patterns correspond across the two sequences.

4 Requirements for Similarity Visualization

To select and design a suitable visualization approach for explaining time series similarities in TCBR, a dedicated requirements catalog is needed. These requirements provide a basis for reviewing existing approaches and for extending them toward the goals of this work. A substantial part of these requirements builds on requirements previously derived for visualization-based explanations in POCBR [38], where knowledge engineers in a focus group were interviewed and the findings were discussed together. In this work, these requirements are examined for their transferability to TCBR, adapted where necessary, and complemented by established principles of information visualization [8,42,43], findings from time series visualization research [1,2,10,27], XCBR-related explainability goals such as justification of results [34,45], and related work [14]. Overall, seven requirements are defined as follows:

Req. 1 Representation of the Underlying Data: The visualization must support time series as the underlying data representation in TCBR [22]. For this work, the focus is restricted to discrete, linear, univariate time series without branching temporal structures or spatial context [1]. The visualization should support primitive local data types, including numerical values, Boolean attributes, and textual strings with an inherent or explicitly defined order, and it should support every mapping-based time series similarity measure.

Req. 2 Explainability of Computed Similarities: The visualization should represent computed time series similarities and their composition in a comprehensible way and provide an explanation for the resulting similarity value. This requirement adapts the explainability requirement from POCBR [38] and is grounded in the justification goal described by Sørmo et al. [45].

Req. 3 Visualization From the Query's Perspective: The explanation should be provided from the query's perspective. In TCBR, queries may cover only a relevant subset of a case, e.g., the pre-failure interval in predictive maintenance scenarios [18]. Attributes or intervals irrelevant to the query should therefore not dominate the visualization and should be visually de-emphasized or excluded.

Req. 4 Task- and Goal-Oriented Representation: The visualization interface should support common tasks of knowledge engineers focussing on time series and their similarities in TCBR. In particular, it should support the cognitively demanding and error-prone modeling and refinement of similarity measures [38]. The interface should facilitate both exploratory search and confirmatory analysis workflows [1] while following Shneiderman's Visual Information-Seeking Mantra [42].

- **Req. 4a Support of Exploratory Search**: The visualization should enable exploratory search without prior hypotheses by providing an overview and interaction mechanisms such as filtering and zooming.
- **Req. 4b Support of Confirmatory Analysis**: The visualization should support hypothesis-driven analysis by enabling comparisons, rankings, and associations between relevant data and similarity values.

Req. 5 Interaction Capabilities: The visualization should not be limited to a static representation of time series and similarity values but should integrate interactive elements that support analysis and model refinement [10,38].

- **Req. 5a Filter Functions for Time Series Attributes**: It should be possible to hide or filter individual time series attributes or values in order to focus on relevant aspects of similarity inspection [10].
- **Req. 5b Interactive Adaptation of Similarity Measures**: The interface should allow interactive changes to similarity measures on the global and local level to assess their influence on the resulting similarity value [38].

- **Req. 5c Dynamic Queries on Given Time Series**: It should be possible to formulate and execute new queries based on the current visualization, e.g., by selecting subsequences or applying transformations, to investigate their impact on retrieval and similarity values [38].

Req. 6 Relation Between Cases: Similarity explanations should be provided pairwise by comparing the query with one retrieved time series to ensure traceability. In addition, the visualization should support parallel comparison of multiple pairwise similarity visualizations and place the resulting similarity value in the context of the case base similarities [38].

Req. 7 Scalability of Time Series: The visualization must consider large time series with many data points, which are common in practice and pose visual as well as technical challenges [22,43]. Since non-specialized approaches may hide local structures or cause detail loss [49], the visualization should provide mechanisms for focusing on sub-intervals and reducing the number of visible data points, e.g., by defining a maximum number of rendered elements [13,16].

5 Visualization Approach for Time Series Similarity

This section presents the visualization approach investigated in this work for explaining mapping-based time series similarity values in TCBR. To this end, Sect. 5.1 identifies a suitable visualization method based on the requirements, which is then conceptually expanded in Sect. 5.2.

5.1 Selection of Suitable Visualization Approach

Based on the requirements defined in Sect. 4, the four approaches for visualizing time series similarities presented in Sect. 3 are evaluated. On a conceptual level, all approaches can be embedded into a pairwise visualization setting and thus address Req. 6. Similarly, Req. 2 and Req. 4 cannot be fully assessed from the visualization technique alone, since task- and goal-oriented support as well as explainability depend on the concrete user interface and therefore require evaluation. Nevertheless, the approaches allow deriving boundary conditions for these requirements. Bitmap patterns are not suitable in this work, since their strong abstraction does not expose explicit correspondences and therefore does not support explaining how a similarity value emerges from local contributions. This conflicts with Req. 2 and limits task-oriented analysis in Req. 4. While bitmap patterns are scalable and support compact comparisons across many cases, they do not allow tracing similarity-relevant structures back to concrete time intervals and value constellations, which is essential for Req. 1 in TCBR. The matching matrix can indicate local correspondences and is therefore related to Req. 2, but it places local pattern abstractions on its axes instead of directly displaying the compared time series and their induced mappings. This weakens traceability regarding Req. 1. This also limits the query-focused perspective required by Req. 3 and complicates interactive refinements such as formulating dynamic queries from the visual representation in line with Req. 5. In contrast, normalization techniques and point mapping approaches retain a coordinate-based view of the compared time series and therefore align more naturally with Req. 1. Both approaches can be aligned with Req. 3 and support typical interaction primitives such as filtering, zooming, and details-on-demand, including interval-focused inspection and dynamic queries in line with Req. 5. However, achieving scalability for long time series (Req. 7) requires additional mechanisms such as restricting the display to sub-intervals. Overall, coordinate-based approaches require only minimal extensions within the scope of this work. Therefore, point mapping is preferred, since it makes induced correspondences explicit and treats them as the primary explanation object, whereas normalization only supports visual comparison indirectly.

5.2 Conceptual Approach

Based on the selected point mapping approach, the extended concept for the visualization of mapping-based time series similarity is presented in the following. Several requirements, derived in Sect. 4, are translated into concrete user interface elements and interaction mechanisms as an extension of point mapping. The concept is described independent of a specific framework so that it can be transferred to different TCBR environments and complemented with application-specific details. As a guiding principle for structuring the interface, the Visual Information-Seeking Mantra by Shneiderman [42] is followed. Therefore, the user interface provides an overview of the relevant information, then enables zooming and filtering for exploration, and finally supports details-on-demand when inspecting local contributions. Whether the overall interface is task- and goal-oriented in the sense of Req. 4 and whether the explanations are perceived as sufficiently informative in the sense of Req. 2 must be validated by evaluation. The following design choices operationalize these requirements at the interface level.

Interface Overview. Fig. 1 illustrates the conceptual interface by the prototype implementation. The interface components are distributed in three sections: 1) a main visualization area with navigation controls (①, ②, ③), 2) a section for displaying information (④, ⑤), and finally, 3) an expandable tool section (⑥). The central idea of the chosen point mapping approach is to treat the mapping itself as the primary explanation object [11]. Instead of only juxtaposing two time series, the visualization makes correspondences induced by a mapping-based similarity measure explicit through mapping lines between query and case points. Each mapping line corresponds to one local comparison that contributes to the resulting similarity value. The overall set of mapping lines provides an immediate visual summary of alignment effects, e.g., shifts, repetitions, and many-to-one or one-to-many correspondences. In this sense, the coordinate system provides temporal context, while the mapping lines convey why specific regions are considered similar. Furthermore, local similarity values are encoded along the mapping

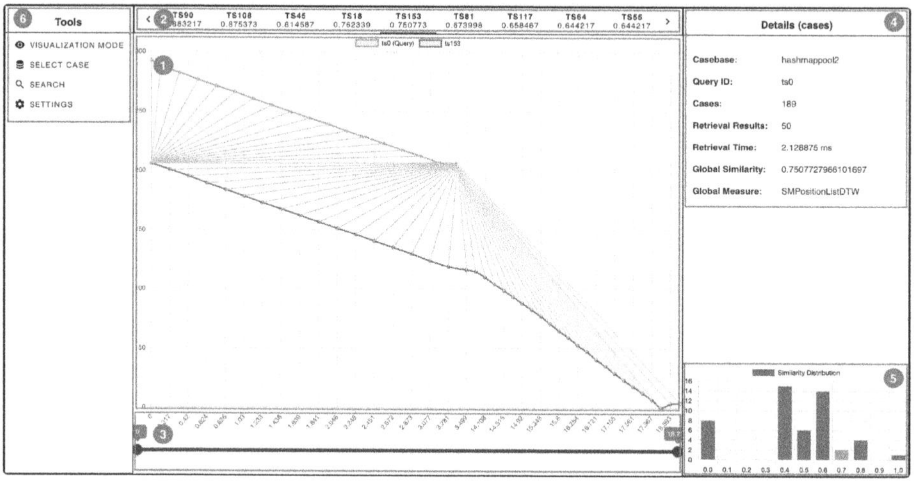

Fig. 1. The Conceptualized User Interface Illustrated by the Implementation.

using a color range and annotated values. Such encodings remain configurable to avoid clutter and keep the visualization usable for exploratory inspection. This design targets Req. 2 by making local contributions and their aggregation into a similarity value accessible at the level of individual mapping pairs.

Coordinate System Visualization. Query and case are displayed in a two-dimensional coordinate system for time series (see ①, Fig. 1) whose entry values are either numerical or can be mapped to an ordinal scale. If the entries contain Boolean values, both series are shown in two vertically stacked coordinate systems, since otherwise the two value states overlap too frequently, especially for very similar time series. In general, the x-axis represents the time attribute, which can be either a timestamp or a numeric value (e.g., time passed since the beginning of the measured event [22]). The y-axis represents the time series values. Use cases for time series whose entry values cannot be represented numerically or mapped to an ordinal scale have not been reported so far [22] and are therefore not considered in this approach. If query and case series have incompatible representations, the interface can fall back to separate displays of both series and communicate that point mapping is not available for the selected pair. The point mapping visualization follows a pairwise explanation setting aligned with Req. 6. The visualization is designed from the query's perspective as required by Req. 3. The query acts as the reference, and the mappings are interpreted as contributions explaining why the retrieved case is similar to the query. Case entries irrelevant for the query should not dominate the explanation so they can be visually de-emphasized, made non-selectable, or hidden by filter mechanisms.

Interaction and Details-on-Demand. Interaction is a core element of the concept and addresses Req. 5. The central view supports inspection of time series points and their mappings. Hover interactions reveal tooltips summarizing time, query value, case value, and the local similarity value. Clicking a point or mapping triggers a details-on-demand workflow by populating an information area with the corresponding local context. The information area (see ④, Fig. 1) supports an overview mode with context about the case base and the retrieval, as well as a detail mode for the selected mapping pair. In detail mode, the interface presents attribute-time-value pairs for query and case entries together with the local similarity value. If the underlying system provides further information about the local similarity computation, the detail mode can offer an entry point to inspect it.

Scalability and Interval Control. Scalability for large time series is addressed by restricting the visualized range to a configurable sub-interval (see ③, Fig. 1), as required by Req. 7. A time slider below the visualization enables users to select lower and upper bounds of the displayed interval. Adjusting this interval updates both time series and the visible mappings immediately. To prevent visual overload, the interface can enforce a maximum number of rendered points and reduce the displayed resolution when needed. This reduction is reflected in the displayed bounds so that users remain aware of the current level of detail. The maximum selectable interval spans the full temporal range of both series, including cases where query and case intervals do not overlap.

Comparison and Case Base Context. To support rapid comparison of multiple query-case pairs, the concept includes a compact selection component for switching between the most similar retrieved cases (see ②, Fig. 1). The component lists cases in descending order, highlights the current selection, and enables comparison without losing context. This supports Req. 6 and can be extended to parallel visualizations when comparing multiple similarity calculations side by side. To place the current similarity value in the context of the case base, the concept further includes an element for visualizing the similarity distribution over the case base (see ⑤, Fig. 1). A histogram-like view allows users to assess whether the current similarity value is typical or exceptional and whether similarity values are concentrated or well separated. This design is adapted from the similarity distribution component used in earlier visualization work [38].

Tool Support and Configuration. Finally, a compact tool palette (see ⑥, Fig. 1) provides additional functions without consuming central screen space. It supports directed search for points, intervals, or attribute conditions, as well as filtering mechanisms to hide irrelevant parts of the visualization, thereby contributing to Req. 4 and Req. 5. The palette also provides configuration options for the similarity visualization itself, such as showing or hiding mappings and enabling similarity color ranges. It further acts as an entry point for interactive similarity-model adjustments and re-running retrieval based on the current configuration, which targets Req. 5 and its subrequirements.

6 Experimental Evaluation

The evaluation investigates whether the proposed visualization is perceived as supporting knowledge engineers in understanding mapping-based time series similarity values, their local composition, and the effects of changes to similarity measures and parameters. Such understanding is an important prerequisite for the refinement and maintenance of similarity models. First, the evaluation setup is presented (see Sect. 6.1), followed by the results and their discussion (see Sect. 6.2).

6.1 Experimental Setup

As a foundation for the evaluation, the conceptual design was implemented as a prototype based on the ProCAKE framework [5,7]. The framework provides several similarity measures and exemplary datasets for TCBR applications [37, 39,47]. The implementation is integrated into ProCAKE Studio, which provides a web-based graphical user interface on top of ProCAKE[1].

The evaluation was conducted as an exploratory user study in which participants interacted with the visualization component and assessed the proposed approach against the requirements defined in Sect. 4 as well as by an overall suitability rating. Thus, the requirements serve as an assessment lens for examining whether the transferred and adapted design goals are perceived as addressed by the approach. For the study, a case base [22,40,47] from a Fischertechnik Smart Factory in the IoT Lab Trier[2] [23] was used. The case base consists of 189 time series cases with numeric or Boolean entry values, containing between 1 and 59 entries. Numerical time series contain 12.19 entries on average (median 3), whereas Boolean time series contain 1.49 entries on average (median 1). This results from a compact storage variant in which only value changes are represented [22]. This compact representation makes differences between the measure categories visible, for example, whether compression is accounted for by DTW as a Cat. 3 measure. This is particularly relevant because similarity measures from all three categories (see Sect. 2.1) were available in the evaluation and could be selected for visualization. Participants performed guided inspection tasks on example query-case pairs and explored several features of the point mapping visualization. After completing the tasks, they rated the approach using structured questionnaires aligned with the requirements and provided qualitative feedback on strengths, limitations, and desired extensions. Overall, eleven

[1] A demo video illustrating the implementation based on the presented concept for similarity visualization is available at the following link: https://procake.s.gy/procake-studio-time-series-visualization-demo.

[2] https://iot.uni-trier.de/.

participants with prior experience in the knowledge-engineering tasks of configuring or analyzing similarity measures as well as prior knowledge of TCBR and the ProCAKE framework took part in the study.

6.2 Experimental Results and Discussion

The evaluation results are primarily reported regarding the requirements defined in Sect. 4. Figure 2 summarizes the participants' ratings of how well the conceptual visualization approach addresses the requirements. Overall, the concept was assessed as addressing the core requirements for explaining mapping-based time series similarity values to a large extent. The ratings for Req. 2 suggest that the mapping lines and the details-on-demand workflow provide meaningful explanation cues at the level of local contributions. Requirements related to workflows and usability, in particular Req. 4, were evaluated positively, although with more heterogeneous ratings. This is consistent with the fact that task- and goal-oriented support depends not only on the visualization principle itself but also on the concrete interface realization and the users' familiarity with the domain. Scalability aspects (Req. 7) were rated as addressable by the concept, mainly due to the interval-based focus mechanism, while still suggesting a need for careful implementation decisions for large time series. In addition to the conceptual evaluation, participants also assessed the prototype. The implementation ratings were largely consistent with the conceptual assessment in Fig. 2, indicating that the implemented user interface preserves the main properties of the concept. Beyond the requirements-based assessment, the point mapping concept received an average school grade of 1.8 (median 2.0), providing a compact overall indicator of perceived suitability.

The results suggest that point mapping is perceived as a suitable approach for explaining mapping-based time series similarity values in TCBR. Participants reported clear agreement that the concept addresses Req. 1, Req. 3, Req. 5, and Req. 7. In addition, the previously open non-functional requirements Req. 2 and Req. 4 are largely perceived as addressed. In particular, this suggests that the mapping lines and the details-on-demand workflow support understanding of how a similarity value emerges from local contributions. Since such understanding is a prerequisite for refining and maintaining similarity models, the results indicate that the proposed visualization can provide useful support for knowledge engineers in TCBR. At the same time, the results indicate that requirements related to comparison and scalability are most sensitive to prototype completeness rather than to the conceptual approach alone. Ratings for Req. 6 are more heterogeneous, which aligns with participants' feedback that parallel comparison of multiple cases would be beneficial beyond the current pairwise focus. Similarly, more neutral ratings for interaction and scalability requirements point to missing prototype features, such as interactive similarity-model adaptation, dynamic queries, and reduction of visible data points. Detail view and gradient-based mapping are frequently perceived as helpful, whereas the global similarity distribution is rated less useful, likely because its role in the workflow is passive and would benefit from more interactive linking to retrieval results. A limitation

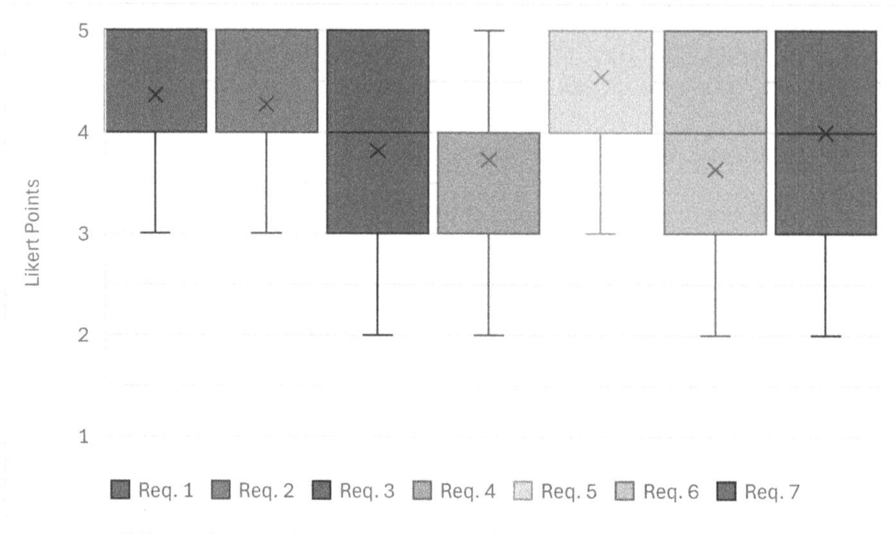

Fig. 2. Results of the Requirement Assessment for the Point Mapping Approach.

of the evaluation is that the prototype is not assessed across a wider range of time series lengths and that the study focuses on perceived suitability rather than objective performance measures. Larger series can increase visual clutter and reduce the explanation clarity provided by the point mappings.

7 Conclusion and Future Work

In this paper, visualization-based explanations for mapping-based time series similarities in TCBR are investigated to make similarity values and their local composition more accessible to knowledge engineers. To this end, existing visualization techniques for time series similarities were consolidated and assessed against a requirements catalog tailored to similarity visualization in TCBR. Based on this, point mapping was identified as the most suitable basis and extended toward a concrete visualization concept for TCBR, which was prototypically implemented on top of the ProCAKE framework. The current concept is restricted to mapping-based similarity measures for discrete, linear, univariate time series. An exploratory user study provides initial evidence that the point mapping concept is perceived as supporting the explainability goal and that the transferred and adapted requirements provide a useful assessment lens for this setting. Overall, the results suggest that explicit visualization of induced mappings is a promising way to support the inspection of how mapping-based similarity values emerge from local contributions in TCBR. The empirical findings are limited by the exploratory nature of the user study.

Future work should address scalability. The evaluation is conducted on comparatively small time series, and future studies should therefore investigate how the visualization behaves for substantially larger series and whether the explanation effect remains stable under higher visual density. Beyond this, the approach can be extended to support multivariate time series, which would require concepts that enable attribute-level inspection and comparison while keeping the explanation of similarity values comprehensible. Dependencies between such multivariate time series within cases, as well as higher-level dependencies across cases, can also be considered, especially if they are relevant for similarity computation (see Kumar et al. [20]). Further, the explanation can be extended by investigating dedicated visualizations of local similarity computations, for example, by providing textual or numerical views. This is particularly relevant because local similarities constitute the basis of the resulting similarity value and could serve as a complementary view to the point mapping representation. Moreover, the approach can be adapted to users without deep CBR expertise. The evaluation indicates that participants with limited prior knowledge of the specific similarity measures still experience some difficulties in understanding them. Future work should therefore introduce explanatory meta-levels for similarity measures in addition to the main visualization. An assistant component based on a large language model could provide context-sensitive explanations of the similarity measures, mappings, and parameters, allowing knowledge engineers or other users to ask questions about the observed similarity patterns. Finally, the approach can be explored in a twin-system setting [17], in which mapping-based similarity measures and their visual explanations serve as an interpretable explanatory layer for more complex methods. For example, such a setting could be used to explain deep-learning-based predictive maintenance classifications [18,35] or to investigate other, non-mapping-based similarity measures through mapping-based explanatory variants.

Acknowledgments. This work is funded by the Federal Ministry of Research, Technology and Space under grant No. 01MD22002C *EASY* [36].

Declaration on Generative AI. During the preparation of this work, the author(s) used ChatGPT and LanguageTool to: Paraphrase and reword, improve writing style, Grammar and spelling check, peer review simulation, and content enhancement. After using this tool/service, the author(s) reviewed and edited the content as needed and take(s) full responsibility for the publication's content.

References

1. Aigner, W., Miksch, S., Schumann, H., Tominski, C.: Visualization of Time-Oriented Data, 2nd edn. Human-Computer Interaction Series. Springer, London (2023). https://doi.org/10.1007/978-1-4471-7527-8
2. Ali, M., Alqahtani, A., Jones, M.W., Xie, X.: Clustering and classification for time series data in visual analytics: a survey. IEEE Access **7**, 181314–181338 (2019). https://doi.org/10.1109/ACCESS.2019.2958551
3. Bach, K., Mork, P.J.: On the explanation of similarity for developing and deploying CBR systems. In: 33rd FLAIRS, Florida, pp. 413–416 (2020)
4. Batyrshin, I.Z., Kubysheva, N., Solovyev, V., Villa-Vargas, L.A.: Visualization of similarity measures for binary data and 2x2 tables. CyS **20**(3), 345–353 (2016). https://doi.org/10.13053/cys-20-3-2457

5. Bergmann, R., et al.: ProCAKE Framework (7.0.0) (2024). https://doi.org/10.5281/zenodo.14020042
6. Bergmann, R.: Experience Management. LNCS, vol. 2432. Springer, Heidelberg (2002). https://doi.org/10.1007/3-540-45759-3
7. Bergmann, R., Grumbach, L., Malburg, L., Zeyen, C.: ProCAKE: a process-oriented case-based reasoning framework. In: 27th ICCBR Workshop Proceedings, vol. 2567, pp. 156–161. CEUR-WS.org (2019)
8. Card, S.K., Mackinlay, J.D., Shneiderman, B.: Readings in Information Visualization: Using Vision to Think. Academic Press (1999)
9. Chen, Y., Nascimento, M.A., Ooi, B.C., Tung, A.K.H.: SpADe: on shape-based pattern detection in streaming time series. In: 23rd ICDE Proceedings, pp. 786–795. IEEE Computer Society (2007). https://doi.org/10.1109/ICDE.2007.367924
10. Fang, Y., Xu, H., Jiang, J.: A survey of time series data visualization research. IOP Conf. Ser. Mater. Sci. Eng. **782**, 022013 (2020). https://doi.org/10.1088/1757-899X/782/2/022013
11. Gogolou, A., Tsandilas, T., Palpanas, T., Bezerianos, A.: Comparing similarity perception in time series visualizations. IEEE Trans. Vis. Comput. Graph. **25**(1), 523–533 (2019). https://doi.org/10.1109/TVCG.2018.2865077
12. Hochheiser, H., Shneiderman, B.: Dynamic query tools for time series data sets: timebox widgets for interactive exploration. Inf. Vis. **3**(1), 1–18 (2004). https://doi.org/10.1057/PALGRAVE.IVS.9500061
13. Holtz, S., Valle, G., Howard, J., Morreale, P.: Visualization and pattern identification in large scale time series data. In: LDAV 2011 Proceedings, pp. 129–130. IEEE Computer Society (2011). https://doi.org/10.1109/LDAV.2011.6092333
14. Jiménez-Díaz, G., Díaz-Agudo, B.: Visualization of similarity models for CBR comprehension and maintenance. In: Recio-Garcia, J.A., Orozco-del-Castillo, M.G., Bridge, D. (eds.) 32nd ICCBR Proceedings. LNCS, vol. 14775, pp. 67–80. Springer, Cham (2024). https://doi.org/10.1007/978-3-031-63646-2_5
15. Jiménez-Díaz, G., Díaz-Agudo, B.: SimViz: interactive visualizations to analyze similarity measures. SoftwareX **32**, 102454 (2025). https://doi.org/10.1016/J.SOFTX.2025.102454
16. Jiménez-Díaz, G., Lenz, M., Malburg, L., Díaz-Agudo, B., Bergmann, R.: A framework for supporting the iterative design of CBR applications. In: 33rd ICCBR Proceedings, LNCS, vol. 15662, pp. 252–266. Springer, Cham (2025). https://doi.org/10.1007/978-3-031-96559-3_17
17. Kenny, E.M., Keane, M.T.: Twin-systems to explain artificial neural networks using case-based reasoning: comparative tests of feature-weighting methods in ANN-CBR twins for XAI. In: 28th IJCAI, pp. 2708–2715 (2019). https://doi.org/10.24963/ijcai.2019/376
18. Klein, P., Weingarz, N., Bergmann, R.: Enhancing Siamese neural networks through expert knowledge for predictive maintenance. In: Gama, J., et al. (eds.) ITEM/IoT Streams -2020. CCIS, vol. 1325, pp. 77–92. Springer, Cham (2020). https://doi.org/10.1007/978-3-030-66770-2_6
19. Kumar, N., Lolla, V.N., Keogh, E.J., Lonardi, S., Ratanamahatana, C.A.: Time-series bitmaps: a practical visualization tool for working with large time series databases. In: SDM 2005 Proceedings, pp. 531–535. SIAM (2005). https://doi.org/10.1137/1.9781611972757.55
20. Kumar, R., Schultheis, A., Malburg, L., Hoffmann, M., Bergmann, R.: Considering inter-case dependencies during similarity-based retrieval in process-oriented case-based reasoning. In: 35th FLAIRS Proceedings, Florida, OJ (2022). https://doi.org/10.32473/flairs.v35i.130680

21. Longo, L., Goebel, R., Lecue, F., Kieseberg, P., Holzinger, A.: Explainable artificial intelligence: concepts, applications, research challenges and visions. In: Holzinger, A., Kieseberg, P., Tjoa, A.M., Weippl, E. (eds.) CD-MAKE 2020. LNCS, vol. 12279, pp. 1–16. Springer, Cham (2020). https://doi.org/10.1007/978-3-030-57321-8_1
22. Malburg, L., Schultheis, A., Bergmann, R.: Modeling and using complex IoT time series data in case-based reasoning: from application scenarios to implementations. In: 31st ICCBR Workshop Proceedings, vol. 3438, pp. 81–96 (2023)
23. Malburg, L., Seiger, R., Bergmann, R., Weber, B.: Using physical factory simulation models for business process management research. In: Del Río Ortega, A., Leopold, H., Santoro, F.M. (eds.) BPM 2020. LNBIP, vol. 397, pp. 95–107. Springer, Cham (2020). https://doi.org/10.1007/978-3-030-66498-5_8
24. Marín-Veites, P., Bach, K.: Explaining CBR systems through retrieval and similarity measure visualizations: a case study. In: 30th ICCBR. LNCS, vol. 13405, pp. 111–124. Springer, Cham (2022). https://doi.org/10.1007/978-3-031-14923-8_8
25. Massie, S., Craw, S., Wiratunga, N.: Visualisation of case-base reasoning for explanation. In: 7th ECCBR Proceedings, pp. 135–144 (2004)
26. Minor, M., Montani, S., Recio-García, J.A.: Process-oriented case-based reasoning. Inf. Syst. **40**, 103–105 (2014)
27. Müller, W., Schumann, H.: Visualization for modeling and simulation: visualization methods for time-dependent data - an overview. In: 35th WSC Proceedings, pp. 737–745. IEEE Computer Society (2003). https://doi.org/10.1109/WSC.2003.1261490
28. Namee, B.M., Delany, S.J.: CBTV: visualising case bases for similarity measure design and selection. In: Bichindaritz, I., Montani, S. (eds.) ICCBR 2010. LNCS (LNAI), vol. 6176, pp. 213–227. Springer, Heidelberg (2010). https://doi.org/10.1007/978-3-642-14274-1_17
29. Recio-García, J.A., Parejas-Llanovarced, H., Orozco-del-Castillo, M.G., Brito-Borges, E.E.: A case-based approach for the selection of explanation algorithms in image classification. In: Sánchez-Ruiz, A.A., Floyd, M.W. (eds.) ICCBR 2021. LNCS (LNAI), vol. 12877, pp. 186–200. Springer, Cham (2021). https://doi.org/10.1007/978-3-030-86957-1_13
30. Ridley, D.: The Literature Review. SAGE (2012)
31. Rostami, M.A., Saeedi, A., Peukert, E., Rahm, E.: Interactive visualization of large similarity graphs and entity resolution clusters. In: 21th EDBT, pp. 690–693. OpenProceedings.org (2018)
32. Sakoe, H., Chiba, S.: Dynamic programming algorithm optimization for spoken word recognition. IEEE Trans. Aco. Sp. Sig. Proc. **26**(1), 43–49 (1978)
33. Schake, E., Grumbach, L., Bergmann, R.: A time-series similarity measure for case-based deviation management to support flexible workflow execution. In: Watson, I., Weber, R. (eds.) ICCBR 2020. LNCS (LNAI), vol. 12311, pp. 33–48. Springer, Cham (2020). https://doi.org/10.1007/978-3-030-58342-2_3
34. Schoenborn, J.M., Weber, R.O., Aha, D.W., Cassens, J., Althoff, K.D.: Explainable case-based reasoning: a survey. In: AAAI-21 Workshop Proceedings (2021)
35. Schultheis, A.: Exploring a hybrid case-based reasoning approach for time series adaptation in predictive maintenance. In: 32nd ICCBR Workshop Proceedings, vol. 3708, pp. 230–235. CEUR-WS.org (2024)
36. Schultheis, A., et al.: EASY: energy-efficient analysis and control processes in the dynamic edge-cloud continuum for industrial manufacturing. Künstl. Intell. (2024). https://doi.org/10.1007/s13218-024-00868-3

37. Schultheis, A., Bertrand, Y., Grüger, J., Malburg, L., Bergmann, R., Serral Asensio, E.: Case-based data quality management for IoT logs: a case study focusing on detection of data quality issues. IoT **6**(4) (2025). https://doi.org/10.3390/iot6040063
38. Schultheis, A., Hoffmann, M., Malburg, L., Bergmann, R.: Explanation of similarities in process-oriented case-based reasoning by visualization. In: Massie, S., Chakraborti, S. (eds.) 31st ICCBR Proceedings. LNCS, vol. 14141, pp. 53–68. Springer, Cham (2023). https://doi.org/10.1007/978-3-031-40177-0_4
39. Schultheis, A., Zeyen, C., Bergmann, R.: An overview and comparison of case-based reasoning frameworks. In: Massie, S., Chakraborti, S. (eds.) 31st ICCBR Proceedings. LNCS, vol. 14141, pp. 327–343. Springer, Cham (2023). https://doi.org/10.1007/978-3-031-40177-0_21
40. Seiger, R., Schultheis, A., Bergmann, R.: Case-based activity detection from segmented internet of things data. In: Bichindaritz, I., López, B. (eds.) 33rd ICCBR Proceedings. LNCS, vol. 15662, pp. 438–453. Springer, Cham (2025). https://doi.org/10.1007/978-3-031-96559-3_29
41. Shahar, Y.: A framework for knowledge-based temporal abstraction. Artif. Intell. **90**(1–2), 79–133 (1997)
42. Shneiderman, B.: The eyes have it: a task by data type taxonomy for information visualizations. In: Proceedings of IEEE Symposium on Visual Languages, pp. 336–343. IEEE Computer Society (1996)
43. Silva, S.F., Catarci, T.: Visualization of linear time-oriented data: a survey. In: 1st WISE Proceedings, pp. 310–319. IEEE Computer Society (2000). https://doi.org/10.1109/WISE.2000.882407
44. Smith, T.F., Waterman, M.S.: Identification of common molecular subsequences. JMB **147**(1), 195–197 (1981)
45. Sørmo, F., Cassens, J., Aamodt, A.: Explanation in case-based reasoning - perspectives and goals. Artif. Intell. Rev. **24**(2), 109–143 (2005). https://doi.org/10.1007/s10462-005-4607-7
46. Stahl, A.: Learning of knowledge-intensive similarity measures in case-based reasoning. University of Kaiserslautern. Ph.D. thesis (2004)
47. Weich, J., Schultheis, A., Hoffmann, M., Bergmann, R.: Integration of time series embedding for efficient retrieval in case-based reasoning. In: 33rd ICCBR Proceedings. LNCS, vol. 15662, pp. 328–344. Springer, Cham (2025). https://doi.org/10.1007/978-3-031-96559-3_22
48. Wohlin, C.: Guidelines for snowballing in systematic literature studies and a replication in software engineering. In: 18th EASE Proceedings, pp. 38:1–38:10. ACM (2014). https://doi.org/10.1145/2601248.2601268
49. Zhao, J., Chevalier, F., Pietriga, E., Balakrishnan, R.: Exploratory analysis of time-series with ChronoLenses. IEEE Trans. Vis. Comput. Graph. **17**(12), 2422–2431 (2011). https://doi.org/10.1109/TVCG.2011.195

Explaining AlignLLM: Case Alignment in LLM-as-a-Judge Systems

Ramitha Abeyratne(✉), Nirmalie Wiratunga, Kyle Martin, and Ikechukwu Nkisi-Orji

Robert Gordon University, Aberdeen, Scotland
{r.abeyratne,n.wiratunga,k.martin3,i.nkisi-orji}@rgu.ac.uk

Abstract. The emergence of ensemble LLM-as-a-Judge systems has enabled reference-free, multi-model evaluation frameworks for question-answering tasks. However, the interpretability of their evaluation processes and outputs remains underexplored. In this work, we propose an explainability methodology grounded in case-based reasoning to analyse evaluation with LLM judges. Our approach combines Explainable Artificial Intelligence metrics with Integrated Gradients attribution to better understand their behaviour. To evaluate system outputs, we employ geometry-aware metrics that capture semantic concentration, dispersion, and cross-space consistency. We further apply these metrics to the AlignLLM framework, which models question–answer evaluation as a case-alignment problem, enabling a deeper analysis of semantic agreement across judges. Our findings indicate that judge agreement is primarily driven by semantic concentration within the solution space. Among the evaluated signals, Mean Answer Similarity emerges as the most stable indicator across different model architectures and datasets. Moreover, we introduce a novel approach using attribution analysis to understand the evaluation process of LLM judges, incorporating a parameter for controlled strictness, and revealing inter-judge agreement. This agreement is stronger for answers than for questions and is more consistent across general datasets than specialised ones, suggesting an emerging trend toward semantic convergence. Overall, our study provides a foundation for interpretable and geometry-aware evaluation of ensemble LLM-as-a-Judge systems, highlighting the emergence of consistent semantic alignment across judges.

Keywords: LLMs-as-Judges · Case alignment · Explainable AI

1 Introduction

As Large Language Models (LLMs) are increasingly deployed as evaluators, the reliability of automated judgement has become a central research concern.[1] Recent paradigms that treat LLMs as evaluators replace or supplement human

[1] Code available at https://github.com/RAbeyratne/alignllm-explainability.

L. Malburg and K. Bach (Eds.): ICCBR 2026, LNAI 16780, pp. 187–202, 2027.
https://doi.org/10.1007/978-3-032-33865-5_12

annotation by prompting models to assess the quality of candidate responses. While this approach reduces cost and improves scalability, individual judges often exhibit instability, biases, and sensitivity to prompt phrasing. These limitations motivate the use of multiple LLM judges, whose assessments are aggregated to produce more robust evaluations.

However, aggregating multiple judges introduces a new challenge: how should their reasoning be aligned and compared? Simply averaging scalar scores discards the rich semantic structure embedded in judge explanations. Recent work has begun to address this issue by modeling evaluation as a semantic agreement process across multiple judges, but there is still limited research on interpreting these systems.

To address these challenges, we introduce eXplainable AI (XAI) methods within the AlignLLM framework as a case study. AlignLLM formulates evaluation as a case-alignment problem inspired by Case-Based Reasoning (CBR), where problem–solution representations reconstructed from judge responses are embedded and compared within a shared latent space. The resulting alignment scores in this setting serve as an unsupervised proxy for answer quality, enabling reference-free evaluation when gold annotations are limited. Despite its conceptual elegance, the explainability of this process remains underexplored, particularly in understanding how different LLMs behave and how their reasoning converges to a final judgement.

In this work, we introduce a methodology for analysing the behaviour of multiple LLM judge systems using eXplainable AI techniques. We evaluate outputs using established explainability metrics and analyse the process of generating evaluations in multi-judge systems through attribution analysis. To demonstrate the approach, we apply our methodology to AlignLLM as a representative case-alignment framework for multi-LLM evaluation.

Our contributions are as follows:

- We investigate the relationship between alignment scores and existing explanation metrics under controlled response degradation to understand multi-judge evaluation output.
- We introduce a methodology for ensemble LLM judges by using attribution-based explanations to understand the evaluation process.
- We demonstrate the proposed methodology using AlignLLM as a case study across multiple datasets and LLM architectures.

Section 2 surveys the existing literature. Section 3 introduces the proposed explanation methodology. Section 4 presents the experimental evaluation. Finally, Sect. 5 summarises the conclusions of the paper.

2 Related Work

2.1 Case Alignment-Based Ensemble Evaluation

Case-Based Reasoning forms the foundation of the AlignLLM framework, which conceptualises evaluation as an alignment process between reconstructed problem representations and generated solutions [3]. In CBR, new problems are solved by adapting solutions from prior cases [1], and AlignLLM models each question–answer pair as a case. It constructs both problem and solution spaces using an ensemble of general-purpose LLMs augmented with Retrieval-Augmented Generation (RAG) [3]. The problem-space is generated through reverse generation, where a representative question is produced from a candidate answer, while the solution space is formed by generating answers to this reconstructed question. This bidirectional process enables AlignLLM to evaluate responses by measuring their alignment with plausible question–answer pairs, improving robustness and interpretability. The final evaluation score quantifies alignment between the problem and solution spaces (using case alignment principles), acting as a proxy for correctness without requiring reference answers.

Initially developed for domains with limited gold-standard annotations, such as legal question answering, AlignLLM advances unsupervised evaluation by aggregating judgements from multiple LLMs. Empirical results show that it outperforms single-model baselines and other unsupervised approaches, achieving stronger correlations with ground-truth metrics [3]. The CBR-based paradigm is further supported by its applications in low-supervision domains, including legal and general, demonstrating its suitability for open-domain question answering [4]. A subsequent study [2] provides deeper empirical analysis. Results show that contextual grounding improves evaluation accuracy, while assigning greater weight to the solution space (9:1) yields the best performance. For the Weighted ILRAlign metric, exponential decay aggregation of judge responses performs best. Experiments on representation depth of decoders for embedding generation indicate that 100% model depth achieves the highest accuracy, while 40% offers a favourable trade-off between performance and computational cost.

Despite these advances, the explainability of AlignLLM remains largely unexplored for both outputs and the generation processes of ensemble judges. Given its multi-component architecture and statistical aggregation mechanisms [3], understanding its internal dynamics is crucial for developing more stable, interpretable, and transparent evaluation systems [2].

2.2 Explainability Metrics for Alignment Output Interpretation

Quantifying and interpreting alignment behaviour in neural evaluation systems has been studied from multiple perspectives. Representation similarity measures such as cosine similarity, Representational Similarity Analysis (RSA) [13], and Centered Kernel Alignment (CKA) [12] are widely used to analyse the geometric structure of embedding spaces and compare representations across models. These methods reveal how semantic information is organised within neural architectures. In ensemble settings, dispersion-based measures—including predictive variance, entropy, and KL-divergence—are commonly used to estimate uncertainty and disagreement among model outputs [9]. However, these metrics operate mainly at the output-distribution level rather than the embedding-geometry level that our evaluation targets.

Beyond proximity and dispersion, alternative approaches can analyse alignment mechanisms. Graph-based similarity measures can characterise structural cohesion in similarity networks [22]. Procrustes alignment error quantifies geometric mismatch between representation spaces under linear transformation [10], while similarity-matrix correlations measure structural correspondence across spaces, as in RSA [13]. Mutual information provides a theoretically grounded measure of cross-space dependency [7], though it may be unstable in high-dimensional settings. Attribution-level agreement metrics—such as cosine similarity between gradient-based saliency maps [20,21] or rank correlation of token importance—enable fine-grained reasoning consistency analysis. Despite their usefulness, many of these methods introduce additional computational complexity, rely on strong statistical assumptions, or do not directly reflect the alignment mechanism.

Since AlignLLM evaluates responses by reconstructing and aligning problem and solution spaces through ensemble generation [3], representation geometry lies at the core of its mechanism. We therefore adopt metrics that capture geometric coherence, dispersion, and cross-space consistency without external supervision, consistent with prior work on geometric representation analysis [12]. Mean Question Similarity and Mean Answer Similarity measure semantic proximity within reconstructed problem and solution spaces, indicating inter-judge coherence [17]. While proximity typically reflects shared task understanding in the problem-space, applying it to the solution space reveals the consistency of independently generated answers and the transfer of reasoning from problem to solution. Question Variance and Answer Variance capture dispersion within each space, indicating ensemble stability and disagreement, consistent with variance-based uncertainty estimation in deep ensembles [14]. Finally, the Reasoning Transfer Inconsistency Gap (RTIG) measures discrepancies between problem- and solution-space alignment, probing bidirectional reasoning consistency and relating conceptually to cross-view representation alignment in multi-view learning [5].

These metrics are well suited for explaining alignment outputs because they directly operationalise the geometric principles underlying AlignLLM in a transparent and unsupervised manner. Unlike entropy or calibration-based measures that mainly reflect confidence, they quantify how semantic structure forms, stabilises, and transfers across reconstructed spaces. By combining proximity, dispersion, and cross-space inconsistency signals, this framework provides an interpretable and computationally stable basis for analysing alignment behaviour in multi-judge ensemble evaluation systems.

2.3 Attribution and Interpretability in LLM Evaluators

Attribution-based explanation techniques aim to quantify the contribution of individual input features to a model's output, enabling analysis of the evaluation process. Among these methods, Integrated Gradients (IG) [21] has emerged as a principled and theoretically grounded approach for feature attribution in deep neural networks. IG computes token-level importance scores by integrating gradients along a path from a baseline input to the actual input, satisfying desirable axioms such as sensitivity and implementation invariance. This makes it particularly suitable for analysing transformer-based LLMs, where decisions arise from complex nonlinear interactions across tokens.

Prior work demonstrates the effectiveness of IG for identifying salient linguistic patterns, detecting biases, and uncovering shortcut behaviours in neural NLP models [8]. Compared to alternative explanation techniques—such as attention-based analysis [11], Layer-wise Relevance Propagation (LRP) [15], and DeepLIFT [19]—IG provides a favourable balance between theoretical guarantees, interpretability granularity, and computational efficiency. Unlike raw attention weights, which may not faithfully reflect feature importance, gradient-based methods capture the sensitivity of outputs to input perturbations.

In this work, we apply Integrated Gradients to the LLM judges within AlignLLM to analyse how individual tokens influence alignment scores, enabling fine-grained examination of the evaluation process and inter-judge agreement. While reasoning traces have been used to interpret individual LLM responses [16], they provide only a partial view of model behaviour and do not capture the collective dynamics of multi-judge systems. By linking alignment-based scores to interpretable linguistic features through attribution, our approach provides deeper insight into the behaviour of multi-judge evaluation systems.

3 Methodology

3.1 Alignment Metrics Based on Inter-LLM Reconstruction

We adopt the Inter-LLM Reconstruction framework from AlignLLM [3] to quantify semantic alignment between problem and solution spaces. Given an input question Q, a generator model produces an answer A from a simulated RAG context (snippet) S. A set of N judge models then reconstruct reverse questions Q'_i from A, and corresponding reconstructed answers A'_i are generated from Q'_i. This produces reconstructed pairs (Q'_i, A'_i) intended to preserve the semantic relationship of the original pair (Q, A).

The contextual representations are generated by feeding Q, A, Q'_i, and each A'_i into the generator model $m(\cdot)$. We extract embeddings from selected intermediate transformer layers, denoted by $m_l(\cdot)$, where l specifies the layer index. Accordingly, we define:

$$\boldsymbol{E}_Q = m_{l_Q}(Q), \quad \boldsymbol{E}_A = m_{l_A}(A), \quad \boldsymbol{E}_{Q'_i} = m_{l_Q}(Q'_i), \quad \boldsymbol{E}_{A'_i} = m_{l_A}(A'_i),$$

where l_Q and l_A correspond to the transformer layers selected to encode questions (including reverse-generated questions) and answers, respectively. These are represented in two separate spaces. All similarities for the metrics are computed using cosine similarity.

Inter-LLM Reconstruction Alignment (ILRAlign) score combines problem-space similarity and solution-space similarity with equal weighting:

$$\text{ILRAlign} = \frac{1}{N}\sum_{i=1}^{N} \left(\text{Sim}(\boldsymbol{E}_Q, \boldsymbol{E}_{Q'_i}) + \text{Sim}(\boldsymbol{E}_A, \boldsymbol{E}_{A'_i})\right), \qquad (1)$$

Weighted ILRAlign (WILRAlign) reduces impact of inconsistent judges by assigning weights based on normalised problem-space similarity ($\alpha : \beta = 1 : 1$):

$$w_i = \frac{\mathrm{Sim}(\boldsymbol{E}_Q, \boldsymbol{E}_{Q'_i})}{\sum_{j=1}^{N} \mathrm{Sim}(\boldsymbol{E}_Q, \boldsymbol{E}_{Q'_j})}. \quad (2)$$

$$\mathrm{WILRAlign} = \sum_{i=1}^{N} w_i \left(\alpha\, \mathrm{Sim}(\boldsymbol{E}_Q, \boldsymbol{E}_{Q'_i}) + \beta\, \mathrm{Sim}(\boldsymbol{E}_A, \boldsymbol{E}_{A'_i})\right), \quad (3)$$

Tuned-WILRAlign emphasises solution-space ($\alpha : \beta = 1 : 9$) and judge weights are computed using inverse-distance based on the findings from [2]:

$$w_i = \frac{\frac{1}{1 - \mathrm{Sim}(\boldsymbol{E}_Q, \boldsymbol{E}_{Q'_i}) + 10^{-6}}}{\sum_{j=1}^{N} \frac{1}{1 - \mathrm{Sim}(\boldsymbol{E}_Q, \boldsymbol{E}_{Q'_j}) + 10^{-6}}}. \quad (4)$$

This formulation increases the influence of judges whose reconstructed problems are closest to the original question while prioritising answer-space influence for alignment in the final score.

3.2 Alignment Explainability Metrics

To analyse alignment output behaviour across reconstructed cases, we consider a target embedding pair $(\boldsymbol{E}_Q, \boldsymbol{E}_A)$ and a case base of N reconstructed pairs.

Mean Question Similarity (MQSim) measures the average semantic proximity between the current question embedding and historical question embeddings:

$$\mathrm{MQSim} = \frac{1}{N} \sum_{j=1}^{N} \mathrm{Sim}(\boldsymbol{E}_Q, \boldsymbol{E}_Q^{(j)}). \quad (5)$$

Higher values indicate stronger geometric coherence within the reconstructed problem-space.

Mean Answer Similarity (MASim) quantifies semantic proximity within the solution space:

$$\mathrm{MASim} = \frac{1}{N} \sum_{j=1}^{N} \mathrm{Sim}(\boldsymbol{E}_A, \boldsymbol{E}_A^{(j)}). \quad (6)$$

Question Variance (QVar) captures dispersion within the problem-space by measuring the variance of cosine similarities:

$$\mathrm{QVar} = \frac{1}{N} \sum_{j=1}^{N} \left(\mathrm{Sim}(\boldsymbol{E}_Q, \boldsymbol{E}_Q^{(j)}) - \mathrm{MQSim}\right)^2. \quad (7)$$

Lower values indicate greater structural stability among reconstructed problem representations.

Answer Variance (AVar) captures dispersion within the solution space:

$$\text{AVar} = \frac{1}{N}\sum_{j=1}^{N}\left(\text{Sim}(\boldsymbol{E}_A, \boldsymbol{E}_A^{(j)}) - \text{MASim}\right)^2. \tag{8}$$

Reasoning Transfer Inconsistency Gap (RTIG) assesses cross-space consistency, we compute the discrepancy between question–answer similarity in the current case and that of past cases. Let $\gamma = \text{Sim}(\boldsymbol{E}_Q, \boldsymbol{E}_A)$ denote the intrinsic problem–solution similarity of the current case, and let $\gamma^{(j)} = \text{Sim}(\boldsymbol{E}_Q^{(j)}, \boldsymbol{E}_A^{(j)})$ denote the corresponding similarity for past cases. RTIG is defined as:

$$\text{RTIG} = \frac{1}{N}\sum_{j=1}^{N}\left|\gamma - \gamma^{(j)}\right|. \tag{9}$$

Lower values indicate more consistent reasoning transfer between problem and solution spaces across reconstructed cases, while higher values suggest misalignment or instability in bidirectional semantic structure.

3.3 Layer-Wise Saliency and Cross-Model Agreement Analysis

To analyse how input tokens influence the evaluation process and alignment metric across representational depth, we employ a layer-specific attribution framework based on Integrated Gradients [21]. This enables us to quantify how strongly each token embedding contributes to the hidden representations at a given transformer layer, which are subsequently used in the alignment computation.

Let layer l process a token sequence $T = \{t_1, \ldots, t_n\}$ with embeddings $\mathbf{E} = \{\mathbf{e}_1, \ldots, \mathbf{e}_n\}$, producing hidden states $\mathbf{H}^{(l)}(\mathbf{E}) = m_l(\mathbf{E})$; since gradients are taken in embedding space, we define the scalar attribution function $F_l(\mathbf{E}) = \sum_{j=1}^{n} \|\mathbf{h}_j^{(l)}(\mathbf{E})\|_2$ to measure the layer-l activation magnitude.

Given a baseline embedding sequence $\mathbf{E}'$, the Integrated Gradient attribution of embedding $\mathbf{e}_i$ at layer l is defined as

$$\text{IG}_i^{(l)} = (\mathbf{e}_i - \mathbf{e}'_i)\int_0^1 \frac{\partial F_l(\mathbf{E}' + \alpha(\mathbf{E} - \mathbf{E}'))}{\partial \mathbf{e}_i}\, d\alpha. \tag{10}$$

The integral is approximated via finite-step interpolation between baseline and input embeddings. The resulting score $\text{IG}_i^{(l)}$ measures the contribution of token t_i (through its embedding) to the layer-l activation magnitude.

Since alignment is computed from neighbourhood structures induced by these representations, the IG scores provide an indirect explanation of token-level influence on alignment. Comparing attributions across layers further reveals how representational depth affects alignment sensitivity and inter-judge agreement.

Word-Level Aggregation. Since transformer models operate on subword tokens, we aggregate token-level IG scores to obtain word-level saliency values. Let a word w consist of k subword tokens $\{t_{i_1}, \ldots, t_{i_k}\}$.

We define three aggregation strategies for a token group $w = \{i_1, \ldots, i_k\}$: $S_{\text{sum}}(w) = \sum_{j=1}^{k} \text{IG}_{i_j}$, $S_{\text{avg}}(w) = \frac{1}{k}\sum_{j=1}^{k} \text{IG}_{i_j}$, and $S_{\max}(w) = \max_{j\in\{1,\ldots,k\}} \text{IG}_{i_j}$.

Only words present in the original text are retained, and stop words are excluded from further analysis.

Top-ρ Selection.
For a given aggregation method $a \in \{\text{sum}, \text{avg}, \text{max}\}$, let $\mathcal{W}(T)$ denote the set of eligible words in the input. The token cutoff ratio (strictness parameter) is

$$\rho \in \{0.1, 0.2, 0.3, 0.4, 0.5, 0.6, 0.7, 0.8, 0.9\}.$$

If $|\mathcal{W}(T)| = M$, we select the top $K = \lceil \rho M \rceil$ words ranked by $S_a(w)$ in descending order, denoting the resulting salient set as $\mathcal{K}_a^{(\rho)}(T)$.

Cross-Model Saliency Agreement. To measure consistency of salient words across models, let $\mathcal{K}_{a,m}^{(\rho)}(T)$ be the selected word set from model m. Given M models, we compute a Jaccard-based intersection score:

$$\text{IAA}_a^{(\rho)}(T) = \frac{\left|\bigcap_{m=1}^{M} \mathcal{K}_{a,m}^{(\rho)}(T)\right|}{\left|\bigcup_{m=1}^{M} \mathcal{K}_{a,m}^{(\rho)}(T)\right|}. \tag{11}$$

We compute this score separately for question and answer texts. Finally, for each dataset, aggregation method a, and token cutoff ratio ρ, we report the mean intersection agreement across all instances.

This unified procedure provides a systematic analysis of layer-wise token influence on alignment representations, robustness of salient word selection across aggregation strategies, and cross-model consistency of attribution patterns.

4 Evaluation

The objective of the first experiment is to evaluate the robustness of the proposed (existing) explainer-based metrics under controlled variations in response quality, and to compare their behaviour with alignment-based metrics. The second experiment aims to analyse the evaluation process by examining the overlap in the input focus of individual LLM judges in order to identify areas of agreement.

4.1 Alignment Methods Against Explainer Metrics

We adopt a temperature-based perturbation strategy inspired by [3], specifically tailored to assess explanation-driven evaluation. We construct multiple versions of each dataset by regenerating model responses at progressively increasing temperature levels. Starting from a baseline temperature, we incrementally raise the temperature for each generation round. As observed and used in [3] for the same settings, higher temperatures introduce greater variability and noise into the outputs, thereby inducing controlled degradation in response quality.

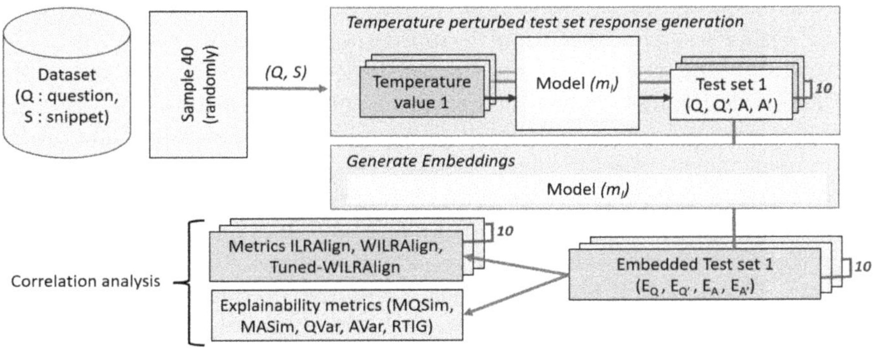

Fig. 1. Evaluation pipeline for explainer metrics.

As illustrated in Fig. 1, we randomly select 40 question–snippet–ground-truth answer triplets (Q, S, G) from each dataset. For each temperature setting, model m regenerates answers to the same 40 questions, producing 10 sets with varying response quality. This results in 400 generated responses per dataset (40 instances $\times$ 10 temperature levels). Each generated response is then used to reverse-generate a potential question and its corresponding answer using judge LLMs. All textual elements are subsequently converted into embeddings using the hidden layer l of a decoder model m.

For every generated response, we compute the proposed explainer metrics described in Sect. 3. Since temperature serves as a proxy for quality degradation, we analyse how sensitively each metric reflects this controlled variation to alignment measures by computing the correlation between temperature levels and the corresponding metric scores. A strong correlation indicates that the metric reliably tracks systematic changes in response quality.

We evaluate this methodology on three datasets previously used in [3] and [2]: the Australian Legal Question Answering (ALQA) dataset [6], the Sri Lankan Supreme Court (SLSC) dataset, and the NewsQA dataset. Each dataset consists of question–answer pairs accompanied by a supporting text snippet containing the evidence required to answer the question. ALQA and SLSC represent two distinct legal domains with different legal systems and linguistic characteristics, whereas NewsQA is a general-domain dataset derived from news articles. This selection ensures coverage of diverse textual structures and reasoning patterns.

We employ the same four open-source large language models as in [3]: the 7B variants of Llama 2-Chat, Falcon, Gemma, and Mistral v0.2. Each model is used both as a response generator and, under a leave-one-out way, as part of an ensemble of evaluators. When one model generates responses, the remaining three act as judges. For consistency, we use the same generation prompts in [3].

Using the embeddings of the temperature-perturbed generations, reverse-generated questions, and corresponding answers at 100% model depth, we apply ILRAlign, WILRAlign, and Tuned-WILRAlign. We then compute the Pearson's correlation [18] for all 400 test instances per dataset between the alignment metrics and the explainer metrics. Table 1 reports the resulting correlation coefficients, along with statistical significance testing ($p < 0.05$) conducted after applying Fisher's Z-transformation to approximate normality.

Across all three datasets, the alignment-based methods exhibit consistently strong and statistically significant correlations with the semantic similarity metrics MQSim and MASim. Even though MASim is mathematically different from the alignment mechanism [3], which uses two spaces, MASim demonstrates comparatively high correlations across all models and datasets, often exceeding 0.92. This trend holds across all models, indicating that alignment-based scoring tends to align closely with similarity-driven explanation metrics in the solution space. As expected, Tuned-WILRAlign further amplifies MASim correlations across nearly all settings, reflecting the increased weighting assigned to the solution space during tuning.

In contrast, correlations with QVar and AVar are generally weaker and predominantly negative, with substantial variation across models and datasets. On ALQA and SLSC, Gemma and Mistral exhibit moderately strong negative correlations under ILRAlign and WILRAlign, while Falcon shows consistently large negative correlations with AVar across all datasets. Tuned-WILRAlign often reduces the magnitude of these negative correlations and, in some cases (e.g., Llama on SLSC and NewsQA), even shifts QVar to small positive values. This suggests that tuning attenuates sensitivity to variance-based metrics, potentially trading variance-related robustness for stronger similarity alignment.

RTIG exhibits consistently strong negative correlations across nearly all models and datasets, frequently below -0.7 and in several cases approaching -0.9. This pattern is particularly pronounced for Llama and Mistral under Tuned-WILRAlign. The stability of this negative association indicates that higher alignment scores systematically correspond to lower RTIG values, suggesting a consistent inverse relationship between the two. Importantly, this effect is robust across datasets, reinforcing the generalisability of the observed relationship.

Overall, the most consistent and discriminative signal across methods is provided by MASim. While MQSim also shows positive and frequently significant correlations, MASim exhibits uniformly high and near-ceiling correlations across all models, datasets, and alignment variants, including the tuned setting. By contrast, QVar and AVar display model and dataset dependent behaviour with weaker and less stable associations, and RTIG—although strongly correlated—primarily captures an inverse relationship that does not substantially differenti-

Table 1. Correlation analysis across datasets (ALQA, SLSC, NewsQA) for alignment methods against explainer metrics.

Dataset	Model(m)	Alignment	MQSim	MASim	QVar	AVar	RTIG
ALQA	Llama	ILRAlign	0.7409*	0.9452*	-0.3127*	-0.0547	-0.8635*
		WILRAlign	0.7325*	0.9477*	-0.2743*	-0.0624	-0.8695*
		Tuned-WILRAlign	0.5170*	0.9975*	-0.2484*	-0.0454	-0.9141*
	Falcon	ILRAlign	0.2160*	0.9844*	-0.1713*	-0.4983*	-0.5498*
		WILRAlign	0.2160*	0.9844*	-0.1712*	-0.4983*	-0.5498*
		Tuned-WILRAlign	0.0904	0.9862*	-0.1377*	-0.5026*	-0.5365*
	Gemma	ILRAlign	0.8528*	0.7688*	-0.4234*	-0.2847*	-0.6406*
		WILRAlign	0.8455*	0.7763*	-0.3889*	-0.2784*	-0.6483*
		Tuned-WILRAlign	0.4051*	0.9687*	-0.0724	-0.2882*	-0.7511*
	Mistral	ILRAlign	0.6545*	0.9236*	-0.3713*	-0.1986*	-0.7324*
		WILRAlign	0.6322*	0.9291*	-0.2860*	-0.1671*	-0.7484*
		Tuned-WILRAlign	0.3495*	0.9871*	-0.1954*	-0.1190*	-0.8453*
SLSC	Llama	ILRAlign	0.6718*	0.9258*	-0.0247	-0.0318	-0.7769*
		WILRAlign	0.6562*	0.9296*	0.0483	-0.0079	-0.7894*
		Tuned-WILRAlign	0.3990*	0.9928*	0.0759	0.0188	-0.8287*
	Falcon	ILRAlign	0.1857*	0.9805*	-0.0508	-0.5291*	-0.6764*
		WILRAlign	0.1853*	0.9805*	-0.0500	-0.5291*	-0.6765*
		Tuned-WILRAlign	0.0154	0.9865*	0.0403	-0.4990*	-0.6828*
	Gemma	ILRAlign	0.9150*	0.7269*	-0.3999*	-0.3258*	-0.5837*
		WILRAlign	0.9087*	0.7344*	-0.3527*	-0.3041*	-0.5842*
		Tuned-WILRAlign	0.4915*	0.9407*	-0.0215	-0.2511*	-0.5389*
	Mistral	ILRAlign	0.4443*	0.9226*	-0.1878*	-0.2636*	-0.7682*
		WILRAlign	0.4270*	0.9228*	-0.0822	-0.2269*	-0.7754*
		Tuned-WILRAlign	0.1080*	0.9891*	-0.0791	-0.1968*	-0.8400*
NewsQA	Llama	ILRAlign	0.5880*	0.9350*	0.0216	0.0765	-0.6153*
		WILRAlign	0.5732*	0.9374*	0.0948	0.0922	-0.6113*
		Tuned-WILRAlign	0.3100*	0.9975*	0.0593	0.0315	-0.5973*
	Falcon	ILRAlign	0.4346*	0.9588*	-0.4097*	-0.3580*	-0.4022*
		WILRAlign	0.4336*	0.9591*	-0.4080*	-0.3575*	-0.4029*
		Tuned-WILRAlign	0.1690*	0.9897*	-0.1881*	-0.2951*	-0.4697*
	Gemma	ILRAlign	0.7115*	0.6720*	-0.1698*	-0.1008*	-0.8363*
		WILRAlign	0.7095*	0.6739*	-0.1546*	-0.1029*	-0.8364*
		Tuned-WILRAlign	0.0815	0.9880*	0.0253	-0.2047*	-0.5071*
	Mistral	ILRAlign	0.4136*	0.9295*	-0.1250*	-0.1266*	-0.6509*
		WILRAlign	0.4048*	0.9308*	-0.0716	-0.0990*	-0.6604*
		Tuned-WILRAlign	0.0860	0.9973*	-0.0825	-0.1081*	-0.7183*

ate between alignment strategies. ILRAlign and WILRAlign remain highly similar across all metrics, whereas Tuned-WILRAlign is most clearly characterised by its substantially elevated MASim correlation. Therefore, MASim emerges as the most reliable explainer metric for characterising alignment-based methods in our experiment setting. If a single metric is to be used for evaluation of ensemble output, MASim provides the most stable, interpretable, and method-sensitive signal across architectures and datasets.

4.2 Integrated Gradients Evaluation on Judge Agreement

In addition to the temperature-based experiments, we conduct a separate attribution-focused evaluation using Integrated Gradients to analyse the evaluation process of the ensemble judges. This experiment uses the original 40 question–answer pairs without any temperature perturbation. Each instance consists of a question (Q) and its corresponding ground-truth answer (G).

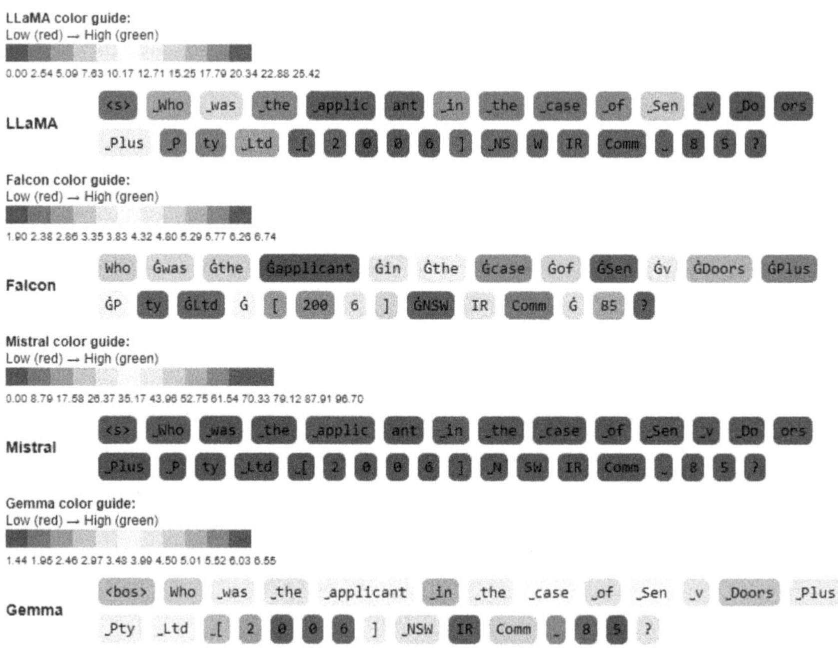

Fig. 2. Raw IG values for a sample question from ALQA at 40% model layer depth.

For each instance, we compute attribution scores over the input tokens using Integrated Gradients to analyse how the model's predictions are influenced by both the question and the answer independently. Unlike the temperature-controlled setup, this evaluation does not introduce synthetic degradation; instead, it examines the model's intrinsic explanatory behaviour on the original dataset. We then analyse attribution alignment patterns and measure their overlap to assess agreement across models. Integrated Gradients is computed for the selected language models using representations from the 40% and 100% layer depths of each model m, producing attribution scores assigned to byte-pair tokens, as illustrated by a sample question from ALQA dataset in Fig. 2.

Notably, the individual judges focus on different tokens in the question and answer, and the resulting attribution scores vary in scale. The byte-pair tokens are subsequently aggregated to the word level. The words are then ranked in descending order according to their aggregated scores, and predefined cut-off ratios are applied to compute overlap scores and maintain the strictness of evaluation.

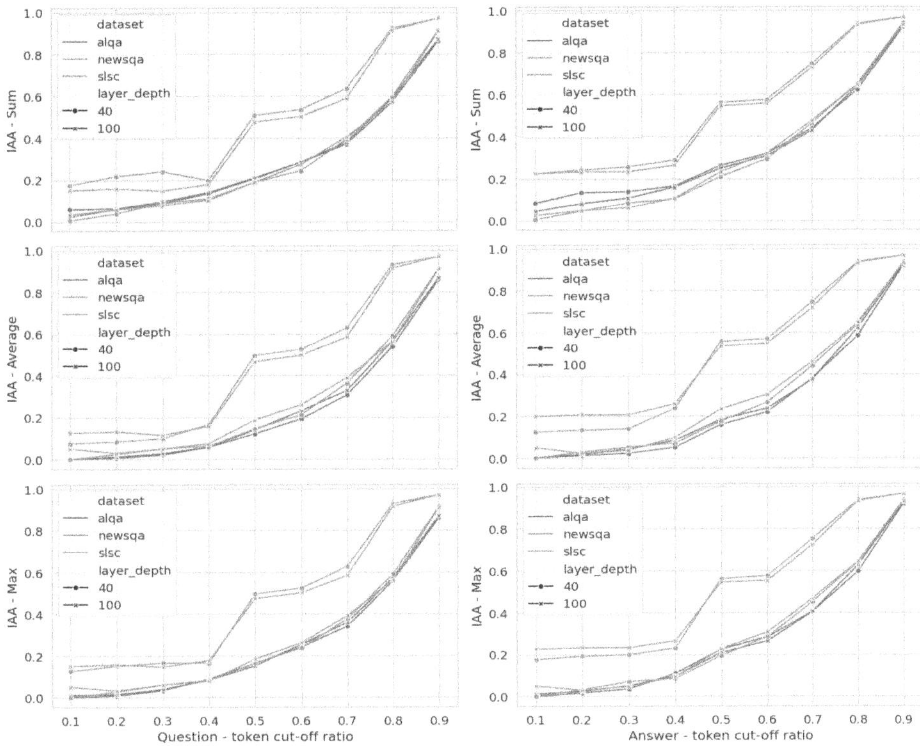

Fig. 3. IG based IAA overlap for judge LLMs using sum, average and max aggregation strategies on byte-pieces to form tokens.

Based on the results shown in Fig. 3, across all three datasets the overlap scores derived from aggregated Integrated Gradients reveal consistent and interpretable patterns. In general, overlap scores for answers are higher than for questions due to the more focused nature of answer spans, which constrains model attributions and leads to stronger cross-model agreement.

The overall trends are consistent across all token aggregation strategies (sum, average, and max) and for both questions and answers. Across datasets,

NewsQA exhibits the highest agreement among individual judges. This likely arises because NewsQA represents a more general-domain dataset, while the judge LLMs used in this study are primarily trained on broad, general-domain corpora. In contrast, the specialised datasets ALQA and SLSC show comparatively lower agreement, particularly at smaller cut-offs, indicating greater divergence in the highest-ranked tokens across models.

A notable pattern is the step change observed between the 0.4 and 0.5 token cut-off ratios for NewsQA across all aggregation strategies, where the overlap increases sharply. This suggests that a larger portion of cross-model agreement emerges once a slightly broader set of salient tokens is considered. This behaviour is not observed in the specialised datasets ALQA and SLSC, likely because domain-specific content leads to more dispersed attribution patterns across models. More generally, overlap increases steadily as the token cut-off ratio increases, indicating that cross-model agreement is concentrated across a wider set of important tokens rather than only within the very top-ranked tokens. Separately, we note that attribution overlap reflects cross-model agreement rather than faithfulness to the underlying reasoning process; therefore, high overlap does not necessarily imply correctness of attribution.

Examining layer depth, the results show small but consistent differences between the 40% and 100% representations. In many cases, the 100% layer depth produces slightly higher overlap values, although the overall trends remain very similar across depths. Thus, deeper layers do not substantially change the agreement pattern but tend to yield marginally stronger attribution alignment.

Overall, model agreement in attribution is governed by the selected token cut-off threshold. This can be tuned to manipulate the strictness of the overlap analysis. Empirically, a mid-to-high cut-off in the range of 0.6–0.8 balances strictness and robustness, capturing broader agreement while reducing sensitivity to divergence among the top-ranked tokens.

5 Conclusion

This paper introduced an explainability-oriented perspective for understanding LLM-as-a-Judge systems. Using AlignLLM as a case study, we applied representation level similarity metrics to study how alignment signals emerge in multi-judge evaluation to form outputs. Results suggest alignment can be interpreted as geometric coherence in representation space. Across legal and general-domain datasets, Mean Answer Similarity emerged as the most stable and discriminative metric, indicating that alignment scores are closely linked to semantic concentration in the solution space. In contrast, variance-based measures showed weaker, model-dependent behaviour, while the Reasoning Transfer Inconsistency Gap showed consistent inverse correlations with alignment. Complementary attribution analysis of individual judge LLMs, aimed at understanding ensemble behaviour, used layer-wise Integrated Gradients with a strictness parameter to reveal agreement patterns. Attribution overlap remained stable across depths, with only minor differences between the 40% and 100% layer representations.

Answer representations showed higher attribution overlap than question representations, suggesting stronger consistency in generated outputs.

Overall, these findings demonstrate how explainability methods provide insight into agreement mechanisms in LLM-as-a-Judge systems and support the development of more transparent evaluation frameworks in low-supervision settings. Future work will examine dynamic structure across layers and develop causal explanations for judges. We will also explore judge specialisation to assess whether more targeted evaluators yield stronger alignment signals.

Acknowledgments. The authors acknowledge support from Robert Gordon University and collaborators who contributed feedback during the development of this research.

Declaration on Generative AI. Large Language Models were employed in this study as a central component of the experimental framework, specifically to perform the text generation tasks required to achieve the research objectives. In addition, AI-based tools were used solely for minor linguistic editing, such as spell checking and formatting adjustments. All substantive content, analyses, and interpretations were conducted manually, independently reviewed, and verified by the authors, who assume full responsibility for the accuracy and integrity of the manuscript.

References

1. Aamodt, A., Plaza, E.: Case-based reasoning: foundational issues, methodological variations, and system approaches. AI Commun. **7**(1), 39–59 (1994)
2. Abeyratne, R., Wiratunga, N., Martin, K., Nkisi-Orji, I.: Design principles for alignment-based evaluation of large language models in reference-scarce domains (2026). https://doi.org/10.2139/ssrn.6153652
3. Abeyratne, R., Wiratunga, N., Martin, K., Nkisi-Orji, I., Jayawardena, L.: Align-LLM: alignment-based evaluation using ensemble of LLMs-as-Judges for Q&A. In: Bichindaritz, I., López, B. (eds.) Case-Based Reasoning Research and Development: 33rd International Conference, ICCBR 2025, Biarritz, France, June 30–July 3, 2025, Proceedings, pp. 21–36. Springer-Verlag, Berlin, Heidelberg (2025). https://doi.org/10.1007/978-3-031-96559-3_2
4. Ahmed, M., Begum, S., Olsson, E., Xiong, N., Funk, P.: Case-based reasoning for medical and industrial decision support systems. In: Montani, S., Jain, L.C. (eds.) Successful Case-based Reasoning Applications – I. Studies in Computational Intelligence, vol. 305, pp. 7–52. Springer, Berlin, Heidelberg (2010). https://doi.org/10.1007/978-3-642-14078-5_2
5. Andrew, G., Arora, R., Bilmes, J., Livescu, K.: Deep canonical correlation analysis. In: Dasgupta, S., McAllester, D. (eds.) Proceedings of the 30th International Conference on Machine Learning. Proceedings of Machine Learning Research, vol. 28, pp. 1247–1255. PMLR, Atlanta, Georgia, USA (2013)
6. Butler, U.: Open Australian legal QA (2023). https://doi.org/10.57967/hf/1479
7. Cover, T., Thomas, J.: Elements of Information Theory. Wiley-Interscience (2006)
8. Enguehard, J.: Sequential integrated gradients: a simple but effective method for explaining language models. In: Findings of the ACL 2023, pp. 7555–7565. ACL, Toronto, Canada (2023). https://doi.org/10.18653/v1/2023.findings-acl.477

9. Gal, Y., Ghahramani, Z.: Dropout as a Bayesian approximation: representing model uncertainty in deep learning. In: Balcan, M.F., Weinberger, K.Q. (eds.) Proceedings of The 33rd International Conference on Machine Learning. Proceedings of Machine Learning Research, vol. 48, pp. 1050–1059. PMLR, New York, New York, USA (2016)
10. Gower, J.C.: Generalized procrustes analysis. Psychometrika **40**(1), 33–51 (1975)
11. Hao, Y., Dong, L., Wei, F., Xu, K.: Self-attention attribution: interpreting information interactions inside transformer. In: AAAI Conference on Artificial Intelligence (2020)
12. Kornblith, S., Norouzi, M., Lee, H., Hinton, G.E.: Similarity of neural network representations revisited. In: Proceedings of the 36th International Conference on Machine Learning. Proceedings of Machine Learning Research, vol. 97, pp. 3519–3529. PMLR (2019)
13. Kriegeskorte, N., Mur, M., Bandettini, P.A.: Representational similarity analysis - connecting the branches of systems neuroscience. Front. Syst. Neurosci. **2** (2008). https://doi.org/10.3389/neuro.06.004.2008
14. Lakshminarayanan, B., Pritzel, A., Blundell, C.: Simple and scalable predictive uncertainty estimation using deep ensembles. In: Proceedings of the 31st International Conference on Neural Information Processing Systems, NIPS'17, pp. 6405–6416. Curran Associates Inc., Red Hook, NY, USA (2017)
15. Lapuschkin, S., Binder, A., Montavon, G., Müller, K.R., Samek, W.: The LRP toolbox for artificial neural networks. J. Mach. Learn. Res. **17**(114), 1–5 (2016)
16. Lee, J., Hockenmaier, J.: Evaluating step-by-step reasoning traces: a survey. In: Christodoulopoulos, C., Chakraborty, T., Rose, C., Peng, V. (eds.) Findings of the Association for Computational Linguistics: EMNLP 2025, pp. 1789–1814. Association for Computational Linguistics, Suzhou, China (2025). https://doi.org/10.18653/v1/2025.findings-emnlp.94, https://aclanthology.org/2025.findings-emnlp.94/
17. Reimers, N., Gurevych, I.: Sentence-BERT: sentence embeddings using siamese BERT-networks. In: Inui, K., Jiang, J., Ng, V., Wan, X. (eds.) Proceedings of the 2019 Conference on Empirical Methods in Natural Language Processing and the 9th International Joint Conference on Natural Language Processing (EMNLPIJCNLP), pp. 3982–3992. Association for Computational Linguistics, Hong Kong, China (2019). https://doi.org/10.18653/v1/D19-1410
18. Schober, P., Boer, C., Schwarte, L.A.: Correlation coefficients: appropriate use and interpretation. Anesth. Analg. **126**(5) (2018)
19. Shrikumar, A., Greenside, P., Kundaje, A.: Learning important features through propagating activation differences. In: Proceedings of the 34th International Conference on Machine Learning - Volume 70, ICML'17, pp. 3145–3153. JMLR.org (2017)
20. Simonyan, K., Vedaldi, A., Zisserman, A.: Deep inside convolutional networks: visualising image classification models and saliency maps. CoRR **abs/1312.6034** (2013)
21. Sundararajan, M., Taly, A., Yan, Q.: Axiomatic attribution for deep networks. In: Proceedings of the 34th International Conference on Machine Learning - Volume 70, ICML'17, pp. 3319–3328. JMLR.org (2017)
22. Watts, D.J., Strogatz, S.H.: Collective dynamics of 'small-world' networks. Nature **393**(6684), 440–442 (1998)

Component-Aware Case Retrieval for Professional Ethics with Ontology-Constrained LLM Extraction

Christopher B. Rauch(✉) and Rosina O. Weber

Drexel University, Philadelphia, PA 19104, USA
{cr625,rw37}@drexel.edu

Abstract. Professional ethics boards determine whether conduct conforms to established codes by comparing fact patterns against prior opinions and ethical code provisions, but identifying relevant precedents in a growing archive remains predominantly a manual process. Even when opinions are available in electronic form, text search is unlikely to surface complex ethical relationships between cases, and similarity scores based on embeddings provide no explanation for which aspects of two cases are related. We describe ProEthica, an applied CBR system that uses ontology-constrained LLM extraction to transform NSPE Board of Ethical Review cases into structured representations with nine components drawn from the computational ethics literature. The extraction produces named ontology entities for each component, embedded independently for retrieval, so similarity scores are traceable to the specific entities that produced them. Users can examine shared Principles, analogous Roles, differing Actions, or any combination of the nine components across retrieved precedents. Ground truth validation across 119 cases shows that structured methods recover cited precedents at 3 to 8 times the random baseline, outperforming section-based embedding.

Keywords: case-based reasoning · professional ethics · ontology-constrained extraction · component-aware retrieval · LLM knowledge acquisition

1 Introduction

Professional ethics boards determine whether professional conduct conforms to established codes by evaluating it against prior board opinions and code provisions. The National Society of Professional Engineers (NSPE) Board of Ethical Review (BER) has published over 600 advisory opinions since 1954, each applying the NSPE Code of Ethics to a specific fact pattern and citing prior board decisions as precedent [26]. A board member reviewing a new case, whether real or hypothetical, identifies the relevant professional roles, determines which code provisions apply, evaluates what actions were taken and what alternatives

L. Malburg and K. Bach (Eds.): ICCBR 2026, LNAI 16780, pp. 203–219, 2027.
https://doi.org/10.1007/978-3-032-33865-5_13

existed, and compares the situation to prior cases with analogous features. This process follows the precedent-based adjudication model of common law reasoning [4,21], where structured comparison of prior decisions guides evaluation of new situations. It parallels the CBR cycle of retrieving, reusing, and revising prior cases [31].

NSPE BER opinions follow a five-section template [26]. Facts gives the chronological narrative with named parties. Discussion presents the board's analysis with citations to NSPE Code provisions and prior decisions. Questions states the normative issues, and Conclusions and References close the opinion. The paper refers to these sections by name throughout.

CBR has been applied to ethical analysis with structured case representations [5,24], but populating those representations from published board opinions remains a manual process. McLaren's [24] SIROCCO system demonstrated that case-based comparison of extensionally defined principles can predict which principles and precedents are relevant to new engineering ethics situations. SIROCCO predates modern language models and requires hand-authored case representations (Sect. 2.1).

ProEthica [28,30][1] is an applied CBR system for professional ethics analysis. The system uses ontology-constrained LLM extraction to decompose NSPE BER opinions into nine typed components that the computational ethics literature [35,40] identifies as essential to representing an ethical case (Sect. 3). A domain ontology provides formal definitions that constrain LLM output during extraction, and domain experts may review proposed ontology entities before they enter the shared vocabulary. Figure 1 sketches the three-step extraction pipeline. A representative case, NSPE BER 22-9, presents an engineer offering self-serving advice to a public client and serves as the running example (Sect. 3.6).

The paper makes two contributions. First, we formalize a nine-component case representation (Sect. 3.1) and populate it from NSPE BER opinions through an ontology-constrained LLM extraction pipeline that produces named, typed entities grounded in a domain ontology. Similarity scores are traceable because each component embedding is generated directly from these entities. A high Principles similarity between two cases corresponds to specific Principle entities that users can inspect, compare across cases, and trace to the source text. Second, we evaluate the representation through a retrieval experiment comparing three embedding strategies under a shared weight configuration on 119 NSPE BER cases. Structured methods outperform section-based embedding, the two D-tuple aggregation strategies produce nearly identical rankings, and a divergent-case analysis shows that the most discriminative component varies by case.

Section 2 reviews related work. Section 3 describes the case representation and extraction pipeline. Section 4 presents the retrieval evaluation. Section 5 discusses implications and limitations. Section 6 concludes.

[1] Live similarity network at https://proethica.org.

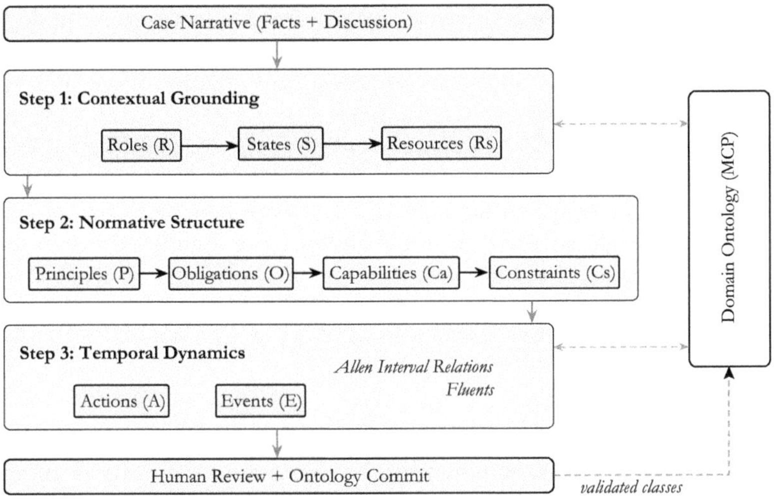

Fig. 1. Three-step extraction pipeline with dependency ordering. Solid arrows show extraction dependencies within and between steps. Dashed arrows show ontology queries (definitions injected before extraction) and the feedback loop where validated classes enter the shared ontology.

2 Background and Related Work

2.1 Professional Ethics and Precedent-Based Reasoning

Ashley and McLaren [5] developed Truth-Teller, a CBR system for practical ethics that compared pairs of cases by enumerating reasons for and against the action under evaluation, then identifying which reasons applied to both cases, applied more strongly in one, or applied to only one. McLaren [24] extended this work with SIROCCO, which defined ethical principles extensionally through case examples and encoded the associations between factual features and principles for retrieval based on normatively relevant characteristics. Both systems relied on manual knowledge engineering to construct case representations, a labor-intensive process that limited the size of their case bases.

2.2 CBR in Ethical and Legal Domains

Case-based approaches to ethical and legal reasoning require cases represented at a level of granularity that supports meaningful comparison on normatively relevant features. Ashley's HYPO system [4] established the dimension-based reasoning tradition in legal CBR, where cases are indexed by legally significant dimensions rather than textual features alone. Bench-Capon and Sartor [7] extended this line of work by incorporating theories and values into case comparison, and their framework supports formal reasoning about the relative strength of competing arguments.

Recent work shows the analytical value of formal structure in legal case analysis. Van Woerkom et al. [39] apply the theory of precedential constraint to datasets interpreted as collections of cases, and characterize which datasets exhibit the logical structure the formalism requires. Sun et al. [33] augment semantic legal case retrieval with neuro-symbolic logic rules at the case and law-article level, and improve performance over the semantic baseline. Mumford et al. [25] find a complementary limitation. LLMs applied to European Court of Human Rights cases perform better on broad outcome prediction than on structured keyword classification, but even outcome prediction shows limited absolute performance.

2.3 CBR and LLMs

The CBR-LLM Research Manifesto [6] identifies knowledge acquisition as a long-standing challenge in CBR and a primary opportunity for LLM integration. Ghazouani et al. [17] use LLMs to populate case bases by extracting entities from unstructured texts, while Brand et al. [11] demonstrate that LLMs can act as knowledge engineers to construct CBR knowledge containers by extrapolating from existing structured examples.

A recurring concern across this literature is output fidelity. Wilkerson and Leake [37] document that LLMs can hallucinate the contents of cases provided to them, altering case features in generated outputs. Ge and Xu [16] implement the full 4R cycle for expense fraud detection and address the same concern through case-based verification of LLM-generated rules. The present work takes a complementary approach, constraining LLM output through ontology definitions (Sect. 3) with optional human review of proposed ontology entities.

2.4 CBR, RAG, and Structured Retrieval

Retrieval-augmented generation (RAG) [22] has become the dominant approach for grounding LLM output in external knowledge, but standard implementations embed entire documents or passages as single vectors and lose the internal case structure. Wiratunga et al. [38] address this limitation in their CBR-RAG model for legal question answering by formalizing CBR's role in RAG and combining text embeddings with structured similarity metrics in a weighted multi-factor scoring function. Their results show that CBR-driven context selection improves answer quality compared to direct LLM responses without retrieval. Lenz et al. [20] compare three LLM-based approaches to similarity assessment, finding that LLM-driven configuration of similarity measures aligns with expert-defined rankings while direct LLM-generated scores do not. Bergmann et al. [9] propose EXAR, a unified architecture that integrates persistent Long-Term Memory with agent coordination via Short-Term Memory, generalizing both CBR and RAG within a single experience-grounded reasoning framework.

3 Case Representation and Ontology-Constrained Extraction

Professional ethics cases pose a representation challenge for CBR systems. Each case narrative incorporates professional roles, ethical standards, situational context, and temporal sequences of actions and events. McLaren [24] found that detailed case representations in SIROCCO supported retrieval and explanation but required a constrained transcription language and manual encoding that limited the size of the case base. This section presents a formal case representation and an ontology-constrained extraction pipeline that populates it from unstructured case narratives at scale.

The framework draws on several theoretical traditions. Oakley and Cocking [27] establish that professional roles generate distinct ethical requirements. Dennis et al. [13] formalize how abstract ethical principles translate into context-sensitive plan-selection rules, completing the chain from Roles to Principles to Obligations that forms the normative backbone of the representation. The professional standard of care in the Restatement (Second) of Torts § 299A [2] reflects the same role-dependent principle in legal doctrine. Berreby et al. [10] present a modular framework that distinguishes ethics-free contextual models from an ethical over-layer, an approach we adapt by separating normative components (Principles, Obligations, Capabilities, Constraints) from contextual ones (Roles, States, Resources). Allen's interval algebra [1], standardized through OWL-Time [12], provides the formal basis for temporal relations between Actions and Events.

3.1 The Nine-Component D-Tuple

We define a professional ethics case as a D-tuple:

$$D = (R, P, O, S, Rs, A, E, Ca, Cs) \quad (1)$$

The framework synthesizes nine concepts identified across the computational ethics literature into a unified case representation [30]. Each component has a formal definition in the ProEthica core ontology, which constrains what the LLM extracts from case narratives. The components group by extraction step. Step 1 (Contextual Grounding) covers Roles R (positions that generate ethical obligations [19]), States S (conditions affecting ethical decisions [10]), and Resources Rs (knowledge artifacts informing analysis [14,24]). Normative components in Step 2 include Principles P (ethical guidelines establishing professional ideals [24]), Obligations O (required actions or restraint derived from codes [13]), Capabilities Ca (competencies that enable actions and fulfill obligations [35]), and Constraints Cs (limitations on permissible actions [15]). Temporal Dynamics in Step 3 include Actions A (volitional interventions by an identified agent [32]) and Events E (occurrences outside agent control that affect evaluation [10]). Cross-component linkages established in the ontology extend the $R \to P \to O$ chain to include $S \to O$, $Ca \to A$, $A \to O$, $E \to Cs$, and $E \to S$. Each step builds on entities from prior steps. Normative extraction references the roles and states from Step 1, and temporal extraction links actions to the obligations and capabilities from Step 2.

The extraction pipeline classifies each entity as exactly one component type. Some component pairs are inherently disjoint through mappings to the Basic Formal Ontology (BFO) [3]. Ontology definitions enforce the distinction when components share a BFO parent class, and optional human review (Sect. 3.4) can validate the classification. Each extraction step queries the ontology server (Sect. 3.3) to retrieve existing class definitions before the LLM processes the case narrative. The LLM then provides a match decision for each entity, marking it as either an existing class or a novel discovery.

Extraction operates at two levels. Classes represent reusable concept types that apply across cases (e.g., "Disclosure Obligation" as a category). Individuals represent case-specific instances of those classes (e.g., Engineer A's obligation to disclose structural concerns to the municipal review board during the permit phase). New classes proposed by the LLM are flagged for optional review before entering the ontology. Individuals are grounded in specific case text with identified actors and temporal references.

3.2 Three-Step Extraction Methodology

The extraction pipeline transforms unstructured case narratives into the nine-component D-tuple through three sequential steps (Fig. 1). All three steps query the ontology server for existing class definitions before extraction begins.

Step 1 (Contextual Grounding) processes Roles first because both States and Resources reference the professional positions that Roles establish, then extracts States and Resources concurrently.

Step 2 (Normative Structure) processes Principles first, then Obligations, then Capabilities and Constraints concurrently. This ordering follows the $P \rightarrow O$ transformation from Dennis et al. [13] and Oakley and Cocking's [27] analysis of role-generated obligations.

Step 3 (Temporal Dynamics) formalizes temporal relations between Actions and Events through Allen's [1] interval algebra, mapped to OWL-Time [12]. Actions are evaluated against the Obligations identified in Step 2, and Events are linked to the States and Constraints they activate or transform.

3.3 Ontology Integration via Model Context Protocol

Unconstrained LLM extraction from professional ethics narratives risks producing inconsistent ethical concepts. Schema-guided extraction constrains output format but not conceptual vocabulary. ProEthica controls both by exposing a layered domain ontology to the LLM through the Model Context Protocol (MCP) at extraction time and applying a confidence-calibrated matcher at commit time.

The domain ontology is organized in three layers. A *core* layer specifies the nine D-tuple components and the formal relations among them [29]. An *intermediate* layer supplies BFO-grounded subclass taxonomies. An *extended* layer accumulates subclasses contributed by prior case extractions and grows monotonically as the case base expands. Per-case ontologies hold only individuals. OntServe,[2] a dedicated ontology server, indexes all three layers and serves them through MCP as a set of callable tools.

Duplicate prevention spans extraction and commit. Before each extraction step, the pipeline retrieves natural-language class definitions for the relevant component type from the intermediate and extended layers, prioritized over core, and injects them into the LLM prompt so extraction begins anchored in the existing vocabulary. During extraction, the LLM may issue additional MCP calls to verify candidates, retrieving the URI, definition, parent class, and source layer of any candidate label. The LLM uses each response to select between reusing an established class and proposing a new one.

The extraction prompt elicits a structured `match_decision` per entity, with confidence anchored to three rubric bands. *High* (0.85–1.0) marks candidates that name the same concept as an existing class. *Medium* (0.70–0.85) covers variants matched to a parent class. Lower confidences indicate novel concepts. The commit-time matcher auto-links entities at confidence 0.90 or above, links with a review flag between 0.75 and 0.90, and treats anything below 0.75 as a novel-class proposal subject to a cascaded duplicate check before insertion.

The cascaded check runs exact and substring label comparison against the cached class vocabulary, and on failure issues a cosine query over embeddings of the candidate label and definition with a 0.70 acceptance threshold. Type-level consistency across the growing vocabulary is verified separately through OWL-DL reasoning, described in a companion paper [29]. The confidence bands and commit-time cuts rely on LLM self-reported confidence. Elicitation and calibration of LLM confidence in RLHF-tuned models are active research areas [18,34]. Empirical calibration of the bands, cuts, and cosine threshold against expert similarity judgments is planned future work.

3.4 Case Synthesis and Review

After the three extraction steps produce the nine-component representation, a synthesis phase analyzes the Questions, Conclusions, and References sections of each NSPE BER case using the extracted entities as structured context. Synthesis links the case to applicable NSPE Code provisions and prior precedents and maps the board's reasoning across Questions and Conclusions onto the extracted components.

The pipeline supports two execution modes. In fully automated mode, all proposed entities and ontology classes are accepted, and extraction through synthesis completes without intervention. A step-by-step mode exposes an entity review interface where domain experts can accept or reject proposed classes

[2] https://github.com/cr625/OntServe.

before they are committed, a workflow designed primarily for initial ontology construction when practitioners integrate existing ontologies with imported ethical guidelines.

Accepted classes are written to the OntServe ontology and become available as vocabulary for all subsequent extractions, so the case base and ontology co-evolve as cases are processed.

3.5 Embedding Construction

The extraction pipeline calls the Anthropic API with concept-specific prompt templates. Per-component embeddings are stored in a pgvector-backed PostgreSQL database.

For each component type in a case, the label and definition of every extracted entity of that type are concatenated and encoded as an L2-normalized vector. Component-specific extraction-field attributes (for example `obligation_type` for Obligations or `persistence_type` for States) are preserved as structured metadata but are not included in the embedding. The per-component similarity computation (Sect. 4) uses these vectors directly. A weighted average using the component weights of Table 1 produces the combined D-tuple vector.

3.6 Example: NSPE BER 22-9

Case 14 (NSPE BER 22-9, *Providing Incomplete, Self-Serving Advice*) illustrates the pipeline on a single case. The Facts section reports that Engineer A, asked by a City Administrator to recommend a project delivery method for a wastewater system, identified only two of the four funding-agency-approved methods in the advisory memo and recommended the one under which Engineer A's firm could compete.

Extraction produced 117 typed entities across the nine components, including 21 Obligations. Of these, 10 matched existing classes (5 auto-linked, 5 flagged for review) and 11 entered as novel proposals. The individual *Faithful Agent Obligation Engineer A City B Advisory* auto-linked at confidence 0.95 to the existing class *Faithful Agent Obligation*, originally proposed during the extraction of Case 8. The class *Complete Comparative Advisory Analysis Obligation* matched at confidence 0.82, in the review-flagged band of Sect. 3.3. The constraint class *Self-Serving Partial Analysis Prohibition Constraint* entered the subclass taxonomy as a novel proposal.

Per-component retrieval against the remaining 118 cases returned Case 71 (NSPE BER 95-5, *Failure to Include Information in Engineering Report*) at rank 1 with similarity 0.584, and Case 85 (NSPE BER 99-8) at rank 6. The strongest channels were Principles (cosine 0.67), Roles (0.60), and Constraints (0.57). Actions and Events contributed least (0.24 each), the divergent pattern reported in Sect. 4.5. The Discussion section of Case 14 cites both BER 95-5 and BER 99-8 as relevant precedent, so per-component retrieval recovered the same prior decisions the Board itself relied on. Figure 2 shows the live Precedents view for this case.

4 Component-Aware Case Retrieval

Embedding-based retrieval offers scalability for case comparison, but the effectiveness of embeddings for retrieving professional ethics cases has not been validated against expert-authored citation patterns. This section evaluates whether the multi-factor similarity approach in ProEthica recovers cases that NSPE board members cite as precedent in their published opinions, whether replacing document-level embeddings with component-aware embeddings improves retrieval by preserving the D-tuple structure, and whether the resulting component-level similarity profiles capture domain-relevant variation across case topics.

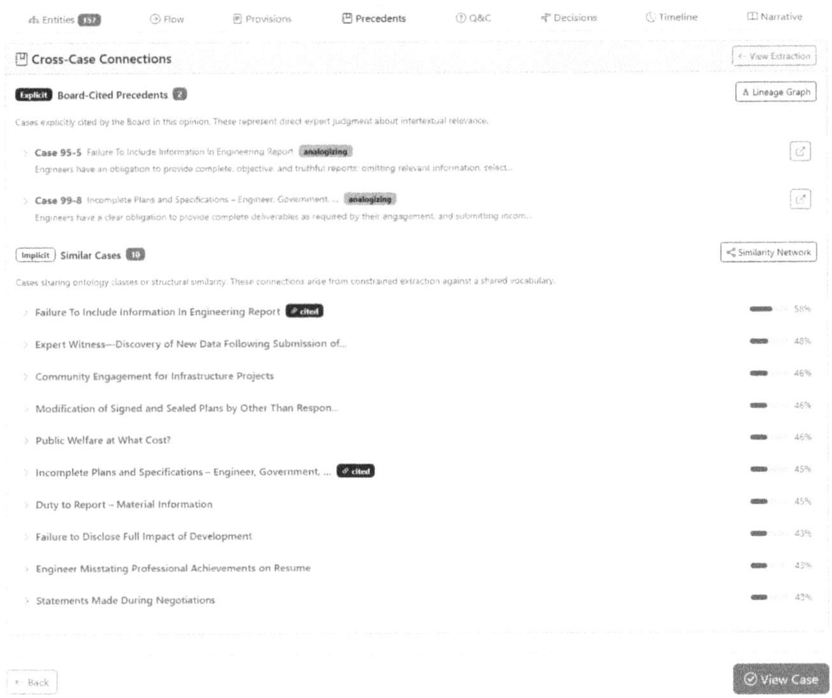

Fig. 2. Live Precedents view for Case 14 (NSPE BER 22-9). The two cases in the Explicit Board-Cited Precedents block (Case 95-5, *Failure to Include Information*; Case 99-8, *Incomplete Plans and Specifications*) are drawn from the case's References section. The Implicit Similar Cases block shows the top-10 ranking from per-component retrieval, with both board-cited cases recovered and tagged `cited`. Percentages are overall multi-factor scores per Eq. 2. The per-component channel cosines reported in the text are computed via Eq. 3.

4.1 Set-Based Features and Weight Allocation

ProEthica computes case similarity through a weighted multi-factor formula combining text-based embedding and set-based feature comparisons. All three embedding strategies share the same multi-factor scoring formula, with 40% of the overall score allocated to text-based embedding and 50% to three set-based features:

$$sim(D_i, D_j) = 0.40 \cdot sim_{\text{text}} + 0.25 \cdot sim_{\text{prov}} + 0.15 \cdot sim_{\text{out}} + 0.10 \cdot sim_{\text{tag}} \quad (2)$$

where sim_{text} is one of the three embedding strategies (Sect. 4.2) and the three set-based similarities use Jaccard overlap, except sim_{out}. Provision overlap ($w = 0.25$) uses Jaccard over cited NSPE Code sections and establishes the most direct normative link between cases. Outcome alignment ($w = 0.15$) is a ternary indicator over ethical, unethical, and mixed outcomes and provides a coarser signal of board agreement. Tag overlap ($w = 0.10$) captures a weaker structured signal. Composite scores are bounded by 0.90. The set-feature allocation weights explicit normative content over textual narrative similarity. NSPE boards anchor their analysis in cited code provisions and identified obligations [23,26]. The remaining 0.40 captures textual semantics. Calibration against expert similarity judgments is future work. The comparison across embedding strategies is unaffected by this choice because the set-feature contribution is shared across all three methods.

4.2 Three Embedding Strategies

Section-Based Embedding (Baseline). The Facts and Discussion sections together carry nearly all of the substantive content of a BER opinion, and embedding them as two vectors provides the strongest text-only alternative to D-tuple structure. The baseline embeds the two sections of each case separately using all-MiniLM-L6-v2 [36], producing two 384-dimensional vectors per case. Cosine similarity between corresponding section embeddings yields two scores, weighted at 0.15 (Facts) and 0.25 (Discussion), for a combined textual contribution of 0.40.
Combined D-Tuple Embedding. The combined method uses the single L2-normalized vector per case constructed in Sect. 3.5. A single cosine similarity between these vectors occupies the 0.40 embedding allocation. This method captures the D-tuple formalization (entities are extracted and typed by component) but collapses component-level distinctions into a single embedding space before comparison.
Per-Component Embedding. The per-component method preserves component independence through retrieval. Using the per-component vectors constructed in Sect. 3.5, nine independent cosine similarities are combined by weighted sum:

$$sim_{comp}(D_i, D_j) = \frac{\sum_{k=1}^{9} w_k \cdot \cos(\mathbf{e}_{i,k}, \mathbf{e}_{j,k})}{\sum_{k=1}^{9} w_k} \quad (3)$$

where w_k is the weight assigned to component k and $\mathbf{e}_{i,k}$ is the embedding vector for component k of case i. Each component occupies an independent semantic channel, so that high similarity in Principles paired with low similarity in Events is preserved rather than averaged away. The resulting per-component score occupies the same 0.40 embedding allocation as the combined method.

The weights in Table 1 are initial estimates based on the assumed salience of each component type in professional ethics evaluation. Principles and Obligations rank highest because they carry the most directly normative content for precedent comparison [14,23]. Roles place third because role identity establishes who carries those obligations [27]. States, Resources, and Actions occupy the middle range as case-specific contextual components [10]. Constraints, Events, and Capabilities rank lower as boundary, background, or competency features less likely to differentiate precedents. As Sect. 4.5 will show, this ranking does not hold uniformly across cases. Learning weights from expert similarity judgments is planned future work.

Table 1. Component weights for per-component similarity. Weights are baseline heuristics. Calibration against expert judgments is future work.

Component	Weight	Component	Weight
Principles (P)	0.20	Resources (Rs)	0.10
Obligations (O)	0.15	Actions (A)	0.10
Roles (R)	0.12	Constraints (Cs)	0.08
States (S)	0.10	Events (E)	0.08
		Capabilities (Ca)	0.07

When either case in a pair lacks entities for a component type, that component is skipped and the remaining weights are renormalized to sum to 1.0. Component text is truncated at 2,000 characters before embedding. All three methods use the same embedding model to isolate the effect of embedding granularity from model choice.

4.3 Citation Ground Truth Validation

NSPE BER opinions routinely cite prior board decisions as precedent. These expert-authored citations provide ground truth for evaluating retrieval quality. We extracted citation edges from the 119-case pool, yielding 228 directed citation links across 93 source cases (mean 2.5 citations per case). The remaining 26 cases predate the board's practice of citing prior opinions and contain no outgoing citation edges. For each source case, we ranked the remaining 118 candidates by the multi-factor similarity score and measured the rank positions of the expert-cited cases. Mean Reciprocal Rank (MRR) measures how early the first cited case appears. Recall@K measures the fraction of cited cases recovered within the top K results.

Table 2. Citation ground truth retrieval across 93 source cases with 228 citation edges (118 candidates per query). All methods share the same multi-factor formula (Eq. 2). Only the embedding computation differs.

Metric	Section	Combined	Per-comp.	Random
MRR	0.380	**0.407**	0.403	0.086
Recall@5	0.286	0.324	**0.331**	0.042
Recall@10	0.420	**0.463**	0.442	0.085
Recall@20	0.536	**0.577**	0.554	0.169

All three methods recover cited precedents at 3 to 8 times the random baseline, depending on the metric (Table 2). Both D-tuple methods outperform the section baseline across all four metrics. The two D-tuple aggregation strategies perform comparably, with combined achieving the highest R@10 (0.463) and per-component the highest R@5 (0.331). These metrics are conservative lower bounds because board members cite the most salient precedents, not all related cases.

Citation Text Ablation. BER Discussion sections describe cited precedents, which could inflate section-based similarity. An ablation that strips citation-containing sentences (326 of 3,932 sentences) and re-embeds yields no systematic inflation. Scored with section embedding alone (set-based features zeroed), the stripped condition achieves R@10 of 0.397 versus 0.387 for the original, with mixed per-edge effects (107 edges improved, 80 worsened, 41 unaffected). D-tuple methods are less susceptible to this confound because they embed extracted entity content, not raw case text.

Embedding Isolation Ablation. Because all three methods share 50% of their score from identical set-based features, the observable embedding effect is compressed. An ablation that scores cases using only the embedding component (set-based features zeroed) reveals a larger D-tuple advantage. Per-component embedding alone achieves Recall@10 of 0.568, compared to 0.387 for section-based embedding alone ($\Delta = +0.181$). Set-based features alone achieve 0.387. Set features raise section-based Recall@10 from 0.387 to 0.420 but lower per-component Recall@10 from 0.568 to 0.442 (Table 2). The 0.50 set-feature weight dilutes the D-tuple embedding signal at this configuration.

4.4 Rank Correlation Analysis

To assess how the three methods relate beyond citation retrieval, we computed pairwise Spearman rank correlation and top-10 overlap for all 119 cases across the full 118-candidate rankings (Table 3).

The two D-tuple methods produce nearly identical rankings ($\rho = 0.991$, Overlap@10 = 91.5%). The D-tuple extraction formalization is the primary contributor to retrieval quality, not the aggregation strategy. Both D-tuple methods diverge from section-based ranking by a similar degree ($\rho \approx 0.93$, Over-

Table 3. Pairwise agreement across 119 NSPE BER cases. Spearman ρ is averaged across per-case rank correlations over the full 118-candidate ranking. Overlap@10 measures the fraction of shared cases in the top-10 results.

Metric	Sec. vs Comb.	Sec. vs Comp.	Comb. vs Comp.
Mean Spearman ρ	0.929	0.935	0.991
Mean Overlap@10	76.9%	78.3%	91.5%

lap@10 $\approx$ 77–78%). The transition from section text to D-tuple content produces a consistent shift in how cases are ranked.

4.5 Analysis of Divergent Cases

The three cases with the lowest section-vs-per-component ρ are Case 19 (Duty to Report Misconduct, $\rho = 0.711$), Case 105 (Reviewing Work of Another Engineer, $\rho = 0.785$), and Case 141 (Selection of Firm, $\rho = 0.821$). Per-component similarity profiles for the top-10 neighbors of each case reveal which components drive the ranking disagreement.

Case 19 illustrates the pattern. Actions shows the highest variance among top-10 neighbors (std = 0.105, range 0.30–0.72), while Constraints shows the lowest (std = 0.038). A case about reporting misconduct shares general ethical constraints with many cases, but the professional actions taken vary widely among neighbors. Across all three divergent cases, Actions is consistently among the highest-variance components (std = 0.073–0.105) and Capabilities among the lowest (std = 0.025–0.060), but the most discriminative component varies. Actions dominates in Case 19, Roles in Case 105, Principles in Case 141. Section-based embedding collapses these component-level distinctions into two monolithic vectors. The per-component method preserves them, and the ranking divergences occur in cases where the discrimination pattern is most case-specific.

5 Discussion

5.1 Implications

The embedding allocation underweights the D-tuple signal. The embedding-isolation ablation (Sect. 4.3) shows that the 0.50 set-feature weight raises section-based recall but dilutes the per-component embedding signal. The current allocation reflects domain-informed heuristics (Sect. 4.1) rather than tuning against professional-ethics retrieval data. Recalibration against expert similarity judgments in professional ethics is future work.

Component-level embedding produces an explanation property that section embedding cannot. Users can examine which components two cases share and which they differ on, rather than reading a single opaque score. The divergent-case analysis (Sect. 4.5) shows how per-component similarity exposes which component drives ranking disagreement in each case. Component-level representation also enables targeted queries that a monolithic embedding cannot express, for example retrieval of cases with similar Obligations but different temporal profiles.

These results align with prior structured-retrieval findings in legal CBR [33, 38]. The choice to present users with examinable component profiles rather than aggregate verdicts also fits the hypothesis-driven presentation paradigm of Benk and Miller [8]. In their framework, decision support surfaces evidence for examination rather than recommending an outcome.

Richter and Weber's four knowledge containers of CBR (vocabulary, similarity, case base, and adaptation) [31] each have a distinct realization in ProEthica. Vocabulary is encoded in the layered ontology, externalized through OntServe as a queryable resource rather than implicit in the case representation. Similarity uses the multi-factor formula (Eq. 2) and the per-component cosines (Eq. 3), and the case base holds 119 typed D-tuple representations. ProEthica does not address adaptation. The system retrieves precedents and leaves any adaptation of board reasoning to the human reviewer. Retain operates on vocabulary as well as on the case base. A committed extraction adds typed individuals to the case base and may expand the class taxonomy when a novel-class proposal passes the duplicate check, so vocabulary co-evolves with the cases (Sect. 3.4).

5.2 Limitations

The 228 citation edges across 93 source cases provide a meaningful evaluation signal, but the pool remains small relative to the full NSPE archive (over 600 cases). The component weights are domain-informed heuristics. The divergent-case analysis suggests that discriminative power varies across components in ways the current weights do not reflect. The embedding model (all-MiniLM-L6-v2) is a general-purpose sentence transformer, not fine-tuned for ethics or legal text. The traceability of similarity scores to extracted entities has not been evaluated with domain experts. Calibration of the weight configuration and the embedding model against expert similarity judgments is future work. Extracted class labels accumulate as compound forms that prioritize disambiguation over reuse. Canonicalization via embedding-based matching at commit is in active development.

6 Conclusion and Future Work

Precedent identification in the NSPE archive remains a manual process. ProEthica converts the archive into a structured retrieval problem by decomposing each case into a nine-component D-tuple through ontology-constrained LLM extraction. The resulting representation outperforms section-based embedding on cited-precedent recovery, and the per-component method produces a similarity profile that names which components two cases share rather than a single aggregate score. The two D-tuple strategies produce nearly identical rankings (Sect. 4.4). The extraction formalization itself drives retrieval quality. Aggregation choice has negligible effect.

The same pipeline addresses the manual encoding cost that limited earlier ethics CBR systems and produces a vocabulary of typed ethical entities that grows with the case base. Future work includes empirical calibration of retrieval weights, the embedding model, and the duplicate-detection thresholds against expert similarity judgments, evaluation of component-level profiles with domain experts, extension to education and legal ethics domains, and scenario analysis for user-supplied vignettes.

Acknowledgments. The NSPE Board of Ethical Review cases used in this study are publicly available through the NSPE Ethics Resources website.

Declaration on Generative AI. During the preparation of this work, the authors used Claude (Anthropic) to assist with manuscript editing and experiment analysis scripts. After using this tool, the authors reviewed and edited the content as needed and take full responsibility for the publication's content.

Disclosure of Interests. The authors have no competing interests to declare.

Data and Code Availability. Experiment data, analysis scripts, and the ProEthica source code are available at https://github.com/cr625/proethica (tag: `iccbr-2026-experiments`).

References

1. Allen, J.F.: Maintaining knowledge about temporal intervals. Commun. ACM **26**(11), 832–843 (1983)
2. American Law Institute: Restatement of the Law Second, Torts §299A, American Law Institute Publishers (1965)
3. Arp, R., Smith, B., Spear, A.D.: Building Ontologies with Basic Formal Ontology, MIT Press (2015)
4. Ashley, K.D.: Reasoning with cases and hypotheticals in HYPO. Int. J. Man Mach. Stud. **34**(6), 753–796 (1991)
5. Ashley, K.D., McLaren, B.M.: A CBR knowledge representation for practical ethics. In: Advances in Case-Based Reasoning, pp. 180–197. Springer (1995)
6. Bach, K., Bergmann, R., Brand, F., Caro-Martínez, M., Eisenstadt, V., et al.: Case-based reasoning meets large language models: A research manifesto for open challenges and research directions. https://hal.science/hal-05006761 (2025)
7. Bench-Capon, T.J.M., Sartor, G.: A model of legal reasoning with cases incorporating theories and values. Artif. Intell. **150**(1–2), 97–143 (2003)
8. Benk, M., Miller, T.: Same performance, hidden bias: Evaluating hypothesis- and recommendation-driven AI, (2026). arXiv:2603.15824 arXiv preprint
9. Bergmann, R., Brand, F., Lenz, M., Malburg, L.: EXAR: A unified experience-grounded agentic reasoning architecture. In: Case-Based Reasoning Research and Development, pp. 3–17. Springer (2025)
10. Berreby, F., Bourgne, G., Ganascia, J.G.: A declarative modular framework for representing and applying ethical principles. In: 16th Conference on Autonomous Agents and MultiAgent Systems, pp. 96–104. (2017)
11. Brand, F., Malburg, L., Bergmann, R.: Large language models as knowledge engineers. In: ICCBR 2024 Workshop Proceedings (2024)

12. Cox, S., Little, C.: OWL-Time: Time ontology in OWL. W3c recommendation, W3C (2017)
13. Dennis, L.A., Fisher, M., Slavkovik, M., Webster, M.: Formal verification of ethical choices in autonomous systems. Robot. Auton. Syst. **77**, 1–14 (2016)
14. Frankel, M.S.: Professional codes: Why, how, and with what impact? J. Bus. Ethics **8**(2–3), 109–115 (1989)
15. Ganascia, J.G.: Ethical system formalization using non-monotonic logics. In: Proceedings of the Annual Meeting of the Cognitive Science Society, vol. 29 (2007)
16. Ge, X., Xu, J.: Integrating case-based reasoning with LLM for expense fraud detection. In: Case-Based Reasoning Research and Development, pp. 52–66. Springer (2025)
17. Ghazouani, F., Giustozzi, F., Le Ber, F.: LLM-driven case-base populating for structuring and integrating restoration experiences. In: Case-Based Reasoning Research and Development, pp. 67–80. Springer (2025)
18. Kadavath, S., et al.: Language models (mostly) know what they know. arXiv preprint arXiv:2207.05221 (2022)
19. Kong, K.C.C., Lam, P.W.Y., Cheng, W.: Corpus-based empirical approach to professionalism: Identifying interactional roles and dispositions in professional codes of ethics. J. Appl. Linguist. Profess. Pract. **14**(1), 3–28 (2017)
20. Lenz, M., Hoffmann, M., Bergmann, R.: LLsiM: Large language models for similarity assessment in case-based reasoning. In: Case-Based Reasoning Research and Development, pp. 126–141. Springer (2025)
21. Levi, E.H.: An Introduction to Legal Reasoning, University of Chicago Press (1949)
22. Lewis, P., et al.: Retrieval-augmented generation for knowledge-intensive NLP tasks. In: Advances in Neural Information Processing Systems, vol. 33, pp. 9459–9474 (2020)
23. Martin, M.W., Schinzinger, R.: Ethics in Engineering, McGraw-Hill (2005)
24. McLaren, B.M.: Extensionally defining principles and cases in ethics: an ai model. Artif. Intell. **150**(1–2), 145–181 (2003)
25. Mumford, J., Atkinson, K., Bench-Capon, T.: Unravelling the ECHR: Components of legal case analysis. In: JURIX 2024, vol. 395, pp. 107–118. (2024)
26. National Society of Professional Engineers: Board of ethical review case archive. https://www.nspe.org/career-growth/ethics/board-ethical-review-cases (2025). Accessed Mar 2026
27. Oakley, J., Cocking, D.: Virtue Ethics and Professional Roles, Cambridge University Press (2001)
28. Rauch, C.B.: Precedent-based professional role ethics for AI decision analysis. In: Proceedings of the AAAI/ACM Conference on AI, Ethics, and Society (AIES), vol. 8, pp. 2921–2923 (2025)
29. Rauch, C.B.: An ontology-grounded representation for defeasible professional ethics analysis (2026). manuscript submitted for publication
30. Rauch, C.B., Weber, R.O.: ProEthica: A professional role based ethical analysis tool using LLM-orchestrated, ontology supported case based reasoning. In: Proceedings of the AAAI Conference on Artificial Intelligence, vol. 40, pp. 41673–41675 (2026). https://doi.org/10.1609/aaai.v40i48.42377
31. Richter, M.M., Weber, R.O.: Case-Based Reasoning: A Textbook, Springer (2013). https://doi.org/10.1007/978-3-642-40167-1
32. Sarmiento, C., Bourgne, G., Inoue, K., Ganascia, J.G.: Action languages based actual causality in decision making contexts. In: PRIMA 2022: Principles and Practice of Multi-Agent Systems, pp. 243–259. Springer (2023)

33. Sun, Z., Zhang, K., Yu, W., Wang, H., Xu, J.: Logic rules as explanations for legal case retrieval. In: LREC-COLING 2024, pp. 10747–10759. ELRA and ICCL (2024)
34. Tian, K., et al.: Just ask for calibration: Strategies for eliciting calibrated confidence scores from language models fine-tuned with human feedback. In: Proceedings of the 2023 Conference on Empirical Methods in Natural Language Processing, pp. 5433–5442 (2023)
35. Tolmeijer, S., Kneer, M., Sarasua, C., Christen, M., Bernstein, A.: Implementations in machine ethics: a survey. ACM Comput. Surv. **53**(6), 132:1–132:38 (2020)
36. Wang, W., Wei, F., Dong, L., Bao, H., Yang, N., Zhou, M.: MiniLM: deep self-attention distillation for task-agnostic compression of pre-trained transformers. In: Advances in Neural Information Processing Systems, vol. 33, pp. 5776–5788. (2020)
37. Wilkerson, K., Leake, D.: Case hallucinations and steps toward repair. In: CBR-LLM Workshop at ICCBR 2025, pp. 43–54 (2025)
38. Wiratunga, N.: CBR-RAG: Case-based reasoning for retrieval augmented generation in LLMs for legal question answering. In: Case-Based Reasoning Research and Development, pp. 445–460 Springer (2024)
39. van Woerkom, W., Grossi, D., Prakken, H., Verheij, B.: A fortiori case-based reasoning: from theory to data. J. Artif. Intell. Res. **81**, 401–441 (2024)
40. Zhong, T., Song, Y., Limarga, R., Pagnucco, M.: Computational machine ethics: a survey. J. Artif. Intell. Res. **82**, 1581–1628 (2025)

GenWriter 2.0: A Hybrid Case-Based and LLM Rewriting Approach for Mitigating Implicit Gender Cues in Text

Shweta Soundararajan(✉) and Sarah Jane Delany

Technological University Dublin, Dublin, Ireland
shweta.x.soundararajan@mytudublin.ie, sarahjane.delany@tudublin.ie

Abstract. Gendered language is the use of words or phrases that indicate an individual's gender. Although useful in some contexts, gendered language can reinforce gender stereotypes and introduce bias, particularly in machine learning models for tasks involving people such as recruitment or occupation classification. When textual content about individuals, such as biographies, contain gender cues, models can learn spurious associations between gender and other characteristics of individuals, such as profession, potentially resulting in unfair outcomes such as reduced hiring opportunities for women.

To address this challenge, we propose GenWriter 2.0, a hybrid approach that integrates Case-Based Reasoning (CBR) with Large Language Models (LLMs) to rewrite textual content about people in a manner that reduces implicit gender cues while preserving semantic meaning. We aim to mitigate bias at its source by transforming the text people write, enabling the generation of content that obscures gender and can also serve as less biased training data for machine learning systems. GenWriter 2.0 retrieves semantically similar content describing people of a different gender from a casebase and uses an LLM for adaptation to generate controlled, context-aware rewrites.

We evaluate GenWriter 2.0 by measuring gender bias in an occupation classification task, before and after rewriting the biographies used for training the occupation classification model. Results show that models trained on GenWriter 2.0-rewritten biographies achieve higher classification accuracy (up to 98.85%) and significantly reduce gender bias by 78% in nurse and 63% in surgeon biographies, while preserving semantic consistency and maintaining balanced lexical variation. In contrast, LLM-only rewriting, despite introducing greater lexical variation, leads to lower accuracy and smaller bias reduction in all cases. Further analysis demonstrates that moderate casebase reduction and increased casebase diversity preserve the performance of GenWriter 2.0, with casebase reduction improving rewriting efficiency and casebase diversity enhancing rewriting coverage. Overall, GenWriter 2.0 provides a robust and effective approach for rewriting text to mitigate gender bias at the source, achieving a strong balance between gender bias reduction, classification performance, semantic preservation and lexical variation.

L. Malburg and K. Bach (Eds.): ICCBR 2026, LNAI 16780, pp. 220–235, 2027.
https://doi.org/10.1007/978-3-032-33865-5_14

Keywords: Case-Based Reasoning · Large Language Models · Casebase Reduction · Casebase Diversity · Gender Bias

1 Introduction

Gendered language refers to language that explicitly or implicitly conveys the gender of an individual [4]. Explicit gender cues appear through words such as pronouns or gendered nouns (e.g., he, she, mother, man), while implicit cues arise through descriptions of roles, behaviours, or characteristics that are culturally associated with particular genders. Research has shown that such implicit cues often reflect societal stereotypes, where women are described using communal traits (e.g., caring, supportive) and men using agentic traits (e.g., ambitious, assertive) [14]. These linguistic patterns are widely observed in various forms of textual content including biographies [10], job advertisements [14], recommendation letters [23], and media articles [26].

The presence of gendered language in text can lead to unfair treatment of an individual based on their gender, identifiable through the content itself. It becomes a serious issue when the presence of gendered language in text leads to harmful consequences when used in machine learning systems. For example, models trained on textual data may learn correlations between gender-associated language patterns and occupational roles, leading to biased predictions in downstream tasks. Prior work has demonstrated that occupation classification systems trained on biographies may misclassify individuals due to gendered language patterns, such as predicting "nurse" more frequently for women and "doctor" for men [10]. Similarly, an AI-powered recruitment model in Amazon showed gender bias against female applicants [31]. Such biases can contribute to allocational harms [5], reinforcing gender stereotypes and potentially influencing opportunities in domains such as recruitment or recommendation systems.

Existing work on rewriting text to reduce gender cues has explored techniques for generating gender-neutral text [12,22,37] or replacing gendered expressions with neutral alternatives [2,29]. However, many of these approaches rely solely on neural models or rule-based transformations, which may fail to capture deeper contextual biases, specifically implicit biases and stylistic signals or unintentionally alter the meaning of the original text [17,27,36].

In this work, we present GenWriter 2.0[1], an approach that combines Case-Based Reasoning (CBR) with Large Language Models (LLMs) to rewrite texts about people in a way that reduces implicit gender cues while preserving semantic content. In this framework, sentences are stored as cases in a casebase representing prior experiences. When rewriting a new sentence, the system retrieves semantically similar cases with the opposite gender and uses them as solutions to guide the rewriting process. An LLM is then used to adapt these solutions to the specific content of the query case, producing a revised solution.

[1] GenWriter 2.0 introduces a slightly modified case representation; see [36] for the earlier version.

Although prior research has addressed gender bias, particularly explicit gender cues at the model level [6,21,46] and in training data [10], we aim to mitigate bias by focusing on the textual content people write, helping them produce content that doesn't reveal their gender, which may later also serve as training data for machine learning systems. The focus is on reducing implicit gender indicators in the text, rather than explicit, which are often fixed, necessary, or not meaningful to alter, particularly in domains such as biographies.

Despite the remarkable text generation capabilities of LLMs, recent studies have highlighted that LLM-generated text itself can contain gender stereotypes and biased language patterns [20,34]. These biases may manifest through word choices, descriptive attributes, or narrative framing that systematically associate particular traits or roles with specific genders [35,41].

CBR, a problem-solving paradigm, supports text generation by leveraging solutions from similar past cases to address new problems. However, adapting these solutions remains challenging due to the variability and complexity of natural language. To address this, CBR can be combined with LLMs to leverage both prior examples and generative language capabilities [43]. CBR provides structured examples that guide the rewriting process and reduce the likelihood of uncontrolled generation of gender bias and stereotypical content by the LLM. Meanwhile, LLMs facilitates flexible adaptation of retrieved cases to new contexts and support knowledge-intensive aspects of the CBR process, enabling applications in domains where formal knowledge representation is limited, costly, or difficult to construct, thereby expanding the applicability of CBR.

As the focus is on rewriting text about individuals, biographies provide an appropriate application domain to demonstrate our approach. To evaluate the effectiveness of GenWriter 2.0, we assess the impact of rewriting biographies on a downstream occupation classification task. We show that the rewritten biographies reduce gender cues, as a classifier trained on these texts exhibits lower gender bias in its predictions while maintaining classification performance and the rewritten biographies preserve semantic similarity with the original biographies. We also explore the impact on GenWriter 2.0's performance of reducing the size of the casebase and introducing diversity in the casebase.

2 Related Work

CBR has been applied to various automated text generation tasks such as generation of obituaries [39], sports summaries [40], product reviews [7], product descriptions [42], weather forecast [1], multilingual dialogue [30], and many more [13,16].

Recent work has increasingly explored the integration of CBR with LLMs for text generation across various domains. In these approaches, CBR is used to retrieve relevant prior examples, which are then incorporated into LLM prompts to guide the generation process. For example, Minor et al. [25] leverages CBR to retrieve cases that are used within prompts to generate explanations for business process models. Similarly, Wiratunga et al. [44] improves legal question answering by retrieving relevant legal cases and incorporating them into LLMs through Retrieval-Augmented Generation (RAG). Building on this, Marom [24] extends the approach to multimodal settings by transforming non-textual case components into textual representations to enhance retrieval and enrich LLM inputs. Likewise, Yang [45] applies this hybrid framework in healthcare and legal domains, where LLMs utilize retrieved cases to process queries and generate more accurate and actionable insights.

This integration of CBR and LLMs has also been applied to a range of explanation and decision-support tasks. For example, Bastardo-Rojas et al. [3] retrieves past image cases and their explanations to guide LLM-based visual question answering systems, while Ge et al. [15] leverages past fraud cases to support expense analysis. In knowledge-based question answering, Hu et al. [18] use a similarity-based CBR approach to retrieve and adapt reasoning patterns for few-shot generation, and Tel et al. [38] combine CBR with LLMs to generate process-related explanations grounded in retrieved cases.

3 Approach: GenWriter 2.0

The goal is to rewrite the text in a way that suggests it was authored by someone of a different gender, making the gender of the described person less obvious in the rewritten version. We create a casebase of sentences describing individuals which are retrieved and adapted to rewrite texts to remove implicit gender cues. The LLM serves a dual role in this framework: it supports the creation of cases and the adaptation of solutions from retrieved cases to the specifics of the current problem.

Case Representation: Each case in the casebase corresponds to a sentence describing a particular aspect of an individual. The case representation includes ***gender***, denoting the gender of the individual described in the sentence and a ***generalized sentence***, a sentence describing an individual in which pronouns and specific entities such as the individual's name, locations, organizations, educational institutions, dates and times, numerical values, occupation, and areas of expertise/specialization, are replaced with context-based placeholders to ensure entity generalization. The generalized sentence is generated through few-shot prompting [8] with an LLM. Table 1 shows the core instruction prompted to the LLM along with representative few-shot examples of sentences such as those in a biography. Table 2 presents examples of cases created from a biography using GPT-4o.

Case Retrieval: To solve a new problem, the most similar problem (the nearest neighbor), which is the case that has the opposite gender and the highest semantic similarity between its generalized sentence and that of the query case, is retrieved. Semantic similarity between sentences is measured by computing the cosine similarity between their Sentence-BERT (all-mpnet-base-v2) embeddings. To ensure retrieved cases are sufficiently relevant and meaningful to be used in rewriting the query sentence/case, a similarity threshold is set. Only cases with similarity scores above this threshold are retrieved, while those below it are excluded, and the query case remains unchanged (i.e., it is not rewritten).

Table 1. Core instruction and representative few-shot examples used to prompt the LLM to generate generalized sentence.

Instruction Prompt
Transform the input sentence into a generalized template by replacing pronouns and specific entities with descriptive placeholders, while preserving grammatical structure and using consistent placeholders throughout.
Few-shot Examples
Input 1: Dr. Dilip Nadkarni is an Orthopedic surgeon specialized in Arthroscopic or Key-hole surgery for the Knee Joint. Output 1: Dr. [Name of the Person] is an [Occupation] specialized in [Specialisation]. Input 2: Dr. Crow graduated from University of Arkansas for Medical Sciences College of Medicine in 1966 and has been in practice for 51 years. Output 2: Dr. [Name of the Person] graduated from [University] in [Year] and has been in practice for [Duration].

Table 2. Cases created from sentences in the following example biography, using GPT-4o: *Kristin Burnette is a Nurse Practitioner Specialist in Knoxville, Tennessee. She graduated with honors in 2013. Having more than 3 years of diverse experiences, especially in Nurse Practitioner, Kristin Burnette affiliates with Fort Sanders Regional Medical Center.*

Gender	Generalized Sentence
Female	[Name of the Person] is a [Occupation] in [Location].
Female	[He/She] graduated with honours in [Year].
Female	Having more than [Duration] of diverse experiences, especially in [Occupation], [Name of the Person] affiliates with [Hospital].

Case Reuse and Adaptation: Adaptation uses an LLM which populates the placeholders in the generalized sentences with relevant details like entities and pronouns available from the query case, while preserving sentence structure and retaining placeholders where information is unavailable. Example query cases rewritten using GenWriter with GPT-4o are included in Table 5 (column 3).

4 Evaluation

We evaluate the effectiveness of rewriting a set of biographies by measuring classification accuracy and gender bias in an occupation classification task. Different classification models are built on a training set of original biographies and on that training set rewritten by GenWriter. Each model is evaluated using the same test set. The expectation is that a reduction in gender bias in the model trained on rewritten biographies without any impact on classification accuracy suggests that the rewritten biographies contain fewer gender cues and are less influenced by content that signals a particular gender. We also rewrite the original training set of biographies using an LLM to see the impact on classification accuracy and gender bias of a model trained on LLM-only rewritten biographies.

Classification performance is measured using the average class classification accuracy (ACA), to account for potential class imbalance across classes in the test set.

The gender bias of a classification model is captured by the difference in a model's performance across genders at the class level and is quantified using the *True Positive Rate Gap* (TPR_{gap}) [28], which is the absolute difference in true positive rates between male and female instances for each class. $TPR_{\text{gap}}(c)$ for class c is defined as $TPR_{\text{gap}}(c) = TPR_{c,\text{male}} - TPR_{c,\text{female}}$, where TPR_{c,g_i} denotes the *True Positive Rate* for class c and gender g_i. A positive TPR_{gap} indicates bias toward males, meaning the model predicts that class more accurately for male instances and makes more errors for female instances. A negative value indicates bias toward females, and a value of zero indicates no gender bias.

Semantic and lexical similarity are also measured between the original and rewritten biographies to estimate meaning preservation. Similar to the similarity function in the CBR retrieval phase, semantic similarity is measured as the cosine similarity of their embeddings. The semantic similarity ranges from -1 to 1, where 1 indicates that the rewritten biography fully preserves the meaning of the original, 0 indicates no semantic similarity, and -1 indicates opposite meaning. The lexical similarity measures the degree of word-level overlap between the original and rewritten biographies and is computed using term frequency (TF)-based weighted Jaccard similarity [19]. Unlike standard Jaccard similarity, which treats all words equally, TF-based weighting accounts for the frequency of each word within a biography. Words that appear frequently (e.g., "worked," "graduated," or occupation terms such as "surgeon" or "nurse") carry core meaning; changes to these words are weighted more heavily. This ensures that edits affecting important words are reflected more accurately in the similarity score. The TF-weighted Jaccard similarity score ranges from 0 to 1, where lower values indicate greater lexical variation and higher values indicate stronger retention of the original phrasing.

High semantic similarity combined with lower lexical similarity indicates that the biographies have been rewritten using different wording while preserving the original meaning.

4.1 Dataset

To evaluate GenWriter, we use the BiasBios dataset [10], which contains 397,340 biographies across 28 occupations, each biography having a specified gender (male or female). We focus on biographies of surgeons and nurses, an occupational pair known to exhibit substantial gender bias [10]. From BiasBios, we randomly extract two independent datasets, each containing equal numbers of male and female surgeons and nurses: D_{train} with 300 biographies, to serve as training data for the occupation classification task and D_{cb} with 500 biographies used to build the casebase used for rewriting. For evaluation, we use the official

BiasBios test set of 9,764 biographies which is imbalanced across both occupation and gender. The size and distributions of these datasets are shown in the first three rows of Table 3.

Table 3. Distribution of biographies in train, test set and datasets D_{cb} and $D_{cb_{cd}}$, used to build casebases CB_O (original casebase) & CB_{CD}, respectively. *Other occupations include accountant, professor, software engineer, architect.

Dataset	Occupation	Gender		#Size (%)
		#Male (%)	#Female (%)	
D_{train}	Nurse	75 (50)	75 (50)	150 (50)
	Surgeon	75 (50)	75 (50)	150 (50)
D_{test}	Nurse	502 (12.5)	5116 (89.1)	5618 (57.5)
	Surgeon	3519 (87.5)	627 (10.9)	4146 (42.5)
D_{cb}	Nurse	125 (50)	125 (50)	250 (50)
	Surgeon	125 (50)	125 (50)	250 (50)
$D_{cb_{cd}}$	Nurse	50 (16.7)	50 (16.7)	100 (16.7)
	Surgeon	50 (16.7)	50 (16.7)	100 (16.7)
	Other Occupations*	50 (16.7) × 4*	50 (16.7) × 4*	100 (16.7) × 4*

4.2 Evaluation Approach

A casebase CB_O, is built using D_{cb}. Each biography is divided into sentences and a case is created for each sentence. The value for the gender feature for each case is taken from the original biography. Exact duplicates, defined as cases with the same gender and generalized sentences with identical wording, are removed from the casebase, resulting in a 33% reduction in casebase size. This results in reductions of 35% and 30% in male and female cases respectively.

This casebase is then used to rewrite all the original biographies in our training set, D_{train}, with a similarity threshold of 0.75 for retrieving the most similar cases. The retrieved generalized sentences for each sentence in a query biography are concatenated into a revised biography and the adaptation phase replaces the placeholders. The original biographies in D_{train} are also rewritten using a powerful LLM, GPT-4o, using a prompt with the core instruction below [36]:

> Given an original biography that describes a <*gender_1*>, produce a revised version of the original biography in a way that a <*gender_2*> would write it, without changing the person's name and gendered pronouns.

Here, < *gender_1* > and <*gender_2*> denote *male* and *female*, respectively, when the query biography describes a male, and vice versa when it describes a female. The prompt is designed to be comparable to the biography transformation performed by GenWriter of rewriting as if it was written by someone of a different gender. Example query cases rewritten using the LLM-only approach are shown in column 4 of Table 5.

4.3 Evaluation Results

The three versions of the training data, the original biographies, the biographies rewritten by GenWriter and the biographies rewritten by an LLM, were used to build occupation classification models. The transformer-based model, BERT, with hyperparameter tuning using a 20% stratified split of the training set, was used to build all models. To prevent the classifier from exploiting explicit cues that could reveal the occupation, occupation names, professional titles (e.g., Dr.), and academic qualifications (e.g., MD, MBBS) were removed from all biographies in both the training and test sets. Table 4 reports the results of the evaluation including the average class accuracy (ACA) and gender bias in the occupation classification task and the average semantic and lexical similarity for the three versions of the training biographies.

Table 4. Results for different versions of training set biographies–Original, LLM rewritten, and GenWriter rewritten using casebase CB_O. The LLM used was GPT-4o.

Training data	ACA (%)	Bias in Nurse	Bias in Surgeon	Avg. Sem. Similarity	Avg. Lex. Similarity
Original	89.55	−0.09	0.08	–	–
LLM	85.11	−0.05	0.07	0.97	0.56
GenWriter	98.85	−0.02	0.03	0.96	0.74

The results show substantial gender bias in the original biographies for both nurses (0.09) and surgeons (0.08). Across all three training sets, the models consistently associate nurse with females and surgeon with males, as shown by the negative TPR_{gap} values for nurse and positive values for surgeon. Biographies rewritten using only the LLM produces smaller bias reductions in the resulting model–44% for nurse biographies (from 0.09 to 0.05) and 13% for surgeon biographies (from 0.08 to 0.07), and also lead to a notable decrease in classification accuracy of about 4%. In contrast, GenWriter rewritten data substantially improves performance, increasing classification accuracy by 10% and further reducing gender bias by 78% for nurse biographies (from 0.09 to 0.02) and by 63% for surgeon biographies (from 0.08 to 0.03).

While both approaches preserve semantic similarity (0.96–0.97), the lower lexical similarity of the LLM (0.56 vs. 0.74 for GenWriter) suggests more aggressive rewriting, which may contribute to its lower accuracy and weaker bias reduction. Overall, GenWriter provides a better balance between bias reduction, classification performance, and content preservation than the LLM-only approach.

Table 5 shows examples of rewriting using GenWriter and the LLM-only approach, with differences shown in bold. The LLM-only approach tends to introduce additional descriptive gendered terms, such as "skilled", "distinguished", "dedicated" (see examples 3 and 5), commonly found in gender lexicons [9,14] and use positive phrases more often for males than females (see example 6). This

Table 5. Example query cases rewritten using GenWriter and LLM-only approach, with gender & occupation indicated (M/F: male/female; N/S: nurse/surgeon). *Original* denotes the query sentence, while *GenWriter* & *LLM* denote the sentences rewritten by GenWriter using casebase CB_O & the LLM, respectively.

No.	Original	GenWriter	LLM
1	FN - Rayelle acquired her Master of Science in Nursing from the University of South Alabama.	After completing her **undergraduate studies at [University]**, Rayelle Jiles **earned** her Masters of Science in Nursing **Specializing in [Specialisation]** at the University of South Alabama.	Her **advanced expertise is backed** by a Master of Science in Nursing from the University of South Alabama.
2	FS - Dr. Datinderjeet Singh Tulla completed MBBS, MS - General Surgery and M.Ch.	Dr. Datinderjeet Singh Tulla **attended [University], graduating with an** MBBS in **[Field of Study]**, an MS - General Surgery and then an M.Ch.	Dr. Tulla's **impressive educational credentials include** an MBBS, an MS in General Surgery, and an M.Ch.
3	FN - Sue McKechnie is a Registered Nurse with broad experience within the health and aged care industry.	Sue McKechnie is a Registered Nurse with **over [Duration]** experience in the health and aged care industry.	Sue McKechnie is a **distinguished** Registered Nurse with **extensive experience** in the health and aged care industry.
4	MN - Brian holds a B.S. in nursing and is completing a master's degree in health policy and law.	Brian R. Jones **received** a B.S. in nursing **from [University]** and is completing a master's degree in health policy and law **from [University]**.	With a B.S. in nursing, he is **furthering his education** by completing a master's degree in health policy and law.
5	MS - Dr. Brian Gengler is an orthopedic surgeon with advanced training in spinal surgery.	Dr. Brian Gengler is an orthopedic surgeon with **expertise** in spinal surgery.	Dr. Brian Gengler is a **highly skilled** orthopedic surgeon specializing in spinal surgery.
6	MN - Since September 2015, he holds the position of Head Nurse in the Elderly Care Unit Aktios and Aktios Alzheimer Unit in Agia Paraskevi.	**He worked in [Field] at [Organization] from [Year] to [Year],** and has been working as a Head Nurse at the Elderly Care Unit Aktios and Aktios Alzheimer Unit since September of 2015.	He has been serving as the Head Nurse in the Elderly Care Unit Aktios and Aktios Alzheimer Unit in Agia Paraskevi since September 2015, **where he continues to make a positive impact**.

may signal a particular gender and could influence the model's predictions. In contrast, GenWriter does not introduce gendered terms and instead replaces or adds words that reflect language patterns typical of the opposite gender (examples 1, 2, and 6). GenWriter also introduces placeholders (see examples 1, 2, 4, and 6) to represent elements typical of biographies of the opposite gender that are not explicitly present in the original text. Overall, GenWriter generates more controlled and bias-aware rewrites than the LLM-only approach by avoiding added gendered terms and offering suggestions through placeholders to guide rewriting when contextual details are missing in the original text.

Inspired by De-Arteaga et al. [10], and as a sanity check, we perform gender prediction using a BERT model trained on the same training sets and tested with the same test set. Prior to training, gendered pronouns (e.g. he, she, him, her), gender-specific honorifics (e.g. Mr., Ms., Sir, Ma'am), and person names are scrubbed from the biographies. As shown in Table 6, the accuracy for female and male biographies drops by 9% and 11%, respectively, with GenWriter, compared to only 6% and 8% with the LLM, indicating that the model fails to identify the person's gender, suggesting that gender is less evident in the text. Moreover, the accuracy values for the GenWriter rewritten data are closer to 50%, indicating that the model cannot reliably determine whether the biography corresponds to a male or female individual suggesting that the biographies have been rewritten to more effectively obscure gender.

Table 6. Class accuracy for gender prediction of biographies across different training set versions–Original, LLM rewritten, and GenWriter rewritten using casebase CB_O. The LLM used was GPT-4o.

Training data	Female Class Accuracy (%)	Male Class Accuracy (%)
Original	54	65
LLM	51	60
GenWriter	49	58

4.4 Impact of Casebase Reduction

In CBR systems, the size of the casebase directly affects both computational cost and retrieval efficiency. A large casebase may contain many redundant or highly similar cases, which increases retrieval time without necessarily improving the quality of the retrieved solutions. It is also important to maintain coverage of the problem space so that the system retains sufficient knowledge to solve new problems effectively. The goal is therefore to maintain a small but competent casebase [33].

The aim of this experiment is to evaluate whether a reduced casebase can maintain the effectiveness of GenWriter in rewriting biographies while reducing gender bias and preserving classification performance. By systematically removing cases with high similarity scores, we investigate how different levels of casebase reduction affect the ability of the system to retrieve useful cases and generate coherent rewritten biographies.

Evaluation. We use the original casebase CB_O (described in Sect. 4.2). Near-duplicates, defined as cases of the same gender whose generalized sentences are closely semantically similar to another case, are removed. The resulting casebase $\text{CB}_{CR(p)}$ is one where cases that have a semantic similarity score of greater than p% to another case in the casebase, are removed. We construct reduced casebases $\text{CB}_{CR(0.9)}$, $\text{CB}_{CR(0.8)}$, $\text{CB}_{CR(0.7)}$ and $\text{CB}_{CR(0.6)}$ by applying different similarity thresholds. FAISS[2] is used for efficient similarity search over sentence embeddings [47]. The data distribution of these casebases is shown in Table 7. Each casebase is used to independently rewrite the biographies in the training set

[2] https://faiss.ai/.

D_{train}. The performance of the occupation classification model trained on these rewritten biographies is measured and compared with the original biographies and the biographies rewritten using the LLM alone. Results are displayed in Table 8 which also includes the *rewrite rate*, the extent to which training set biographies are modified by the rewriting method. Rewrite rate is computed as the ratio of the number of sentences rewritten to the total number of sentences in the training set. Rewrite rate is not reported for the LLM-only approach, due to lack of sentence-level tracking, as it generates fully rewritten biographies in a single step.

Table 7. Distribution of cases in the casebases after removing near-duplicates at different similarity thresholds.

Casebase	Size	Nurse		Surgeon		Reduction in Size (%)
		#Male	#Female	#Male	#Female	
CB_O	1438	306	312	404	416	–
$CB_{CR(0.9)}$	922	209	219	236	258	35.9
$CB_{CR(0.8)}$	553	150	143	125	135	61.5
$CB_{CR(0.7)}$	282	84	83	48	67	80.4
$CB_{CR(0.6)}$	108	48	25	13	22	92.5

Table 8. Results for different training sets of biographies–Original, LLM rewritten, GenWriter-rewritten using CB_O and $CB_{CR(i)}$, the reduced casebases obtained by removing near-duplicate cases at similarity threshold i, where $i \in \{0.9, 0.8, 0.7, 0.6\}$. The LLM used was GPT-4o.

Training data	ACA (%)	Bias in Nurse	Bias in Surgeon	Rewrite Rate (%)	Avg. Sem. Similarity	Avg. Lex. Similarity
Original	89.55	-0.09	0.08	–	–	–
LLM	85.11	-0.05	0.07	–	0.97	0.56
CB_O	98.85	-0.02	0.03	78	0.96	0.74
$CB_{CR(0.9)}$	98.72	-0.02	0.03	71.48	0.95	0.54
$CB_{CR(0.8)}$	95	-0.01	0.07	23.41	0.87	0.51
$CB_{CR(0.7)}$	93.67	-0.01	0.11	0.71	0.99	0.92
$CB_{CR(0.6)}$	87.87	-0.01	0.16	0.08	1	0.98

The results show that moderate casebase reduction can significantly decrease the casebase size without substantially affecting system performance. In particular, removing near-duplicate cases with a similarity threshold of 0.9 reduces the casebase size by 35.9% (see Table 7) while maintaining nearly the same classification accuracy (98.72%) and gender bias as the original casebase CB_O (see

Table 8). Although the rewrite rate for $CB_{CR(0.9)}$ is slightly lower than CB_O, the reduced lexical similarity (0.54 vs. 0.74) indicates greater lexical variation, while still preserving performance. Compared to the LLM, while both exhibit similar semantic and lexical similarity, $CB_{CR(0.9)}$ achieves substantially higher classification accuracy and lower gender bias.

In contrast, more aggressive reduction thresholds lead to noticeable performance degradation. As the threshold decreases from 0.8 to 0.6, the classification accuracy drops and the gender bias increases, particularly for surgeon biographies. At the same time, the rewrite rate decreases substantially, indicating that the system is unable to find sufficiently similar cases for effective rewriting. For example, at a threshold of 0.6, the rewrite rate drops to 0.08%, indicating insufficient coverage for the rewriting task, as the casebase becomes too small, retaining only 7.5% of its original size (see Table 7). Additionally, the lexical similarity increases at lower thresholds, implying that fewer sentences are being rewritten and the resulting biographies remain closer to the original text.

Overall, these results demonstrate that while moderate casebase reduction can remove redundancy without affecting performance, excessive reduction reduces case diversity and negatively impacts the system's ability to retrieve useful cases for rewriting. Among the evaluated thresholds, $CB_{CR(0.9)}$ provides the best balance between reducing casebase size and gender bias & maintaining rewriting effectiveness and classification performance.

4.5 Impact of Casebase Diversity

The performance of a CBR system depends not only on the size of the casebase but also on the diversity and coverage of the cases. A casebase constructed from a limited set of domains or occupations may contain repetitive linguistic patterns, which can restrict the system's competence and reduce the likelihood of retrieving useful cases for adaptation. Previous work in casebase maintenance has shown that maintaining an appropriate balance between casebase size, diversity, and competence is important for effective problem solving [32,33].

Evaluation. To examine the impact of casebase diversity, we add biographies from other occupations to the casebase. We construct two casebases: CB'_O, a baseline, containing 200 biographies (100 nurses and 100 surgeons, balanced across gender) randomly selected from CB_O; and CB_{CD} which extends this set by adding 100 biographies, gender-balanced, each from four additional occupations—accountant, professor, software engineer, and architect—from the BiasBios dataset. The distribution of these biographies is shown in Table 3 (row 4).

Exact duplicate cases are removed from both casebases. These casebases are then used independently to rewrite all the biographies in our training set, D_{train}. The performance of the classification model trained on these rewritten biographies is measured and compared with both the original biographies and the biographies rewritten solely by the LLM, results are shown in Table 9. To assess GenWriter's adaptability across LLMs, we used GPT-5 instead of GPT-4o to evaluate generalizability and consistency of performance trends. It's worth noting that the same test set is used as for the occupation classification task which only includes nurse and surgeon biographies.

Table 9. Results for different training sets of biographies–Original, LLM rewritten, GenWriter rewritten using CB'_O and CB_{CD}. The LLM used was GPT-5. CB'_O denotes the nurse–surgeon casebase, while CB_{CD} denotes the diverse casebase containing biographies from multiple occupations.

Training data	ACA (%)	Bias in Nurse	Bias in Surgeon	Rewrite Rate (%)	Avg. Sem. Similarity	Avg. Lex. Similarity
Original	89.55	-0.09	0.08	–	–	–
LLM	94.9	-0.01	0.08	–	0.96	0.58
CB'_O	96.76	-0.05	0.04	77.06	0.97	0.79
CB_{CD}	98.69	-0.02	0.03	79.65	0.97	0.78

Both CB'_O and CB_{CD} achieve higher classification accuracy and lower gender bias than rewriting with the LLM, with CB_{CD} performing best (98.69% ACA, 0.02 and 0.03 bias in nurse and surgeon biographies, respectively). Although the LLM shows lower lexical similarity (0.58), reflecting greater lexical variation, this leads to a trade-off with lower classification accuracy and higher gender bias.

The rewrite rate increases slightly with the more diverse casebase, rising from 77.06% with CB'_O to 79.65% with CB_{CD}. This suggests that the diverse casebase provides better coverage for retrieving similar cases, allowing more sentences to be successfully rewritten. Importantly, the semantic similarity between the original and rewritten biographies remains high (0.97 for both casebases), indicating that the meaning of the biographies is preserved. At the same time, lexical similarity remains relatively lower (0.79 and 0.78), demonstrating that the rewritten biographies use different wording while maintaining the original semantics.

After removing exact duplicates, the size of CB'_O and CB_{CD} reduces by 28% and 11%, respectively. The lower percentage of duplicates removed in CB_{CD} suggests that incorporating additional occupations introduces different sentence structures and linguistic patterns into the casebase, thereby increasing case diversity. In contrast, the higher duplicate removal rate in CB'_O indicates that biographies within the same occupations tend to exhibit more repetitive sentence structures.

For CB'_O, most retrieved cases come from the same occupation as the target biography (86.4% for nurses and 91.2% for surgeons). In contrast, CB_{CD} incorporates cases from other occupations (15.3% for nurses and 12.5% for surgeons), while slightly increasing the rewrite rate (by 5% for nurses and 2% for surgeons) and reducing the use of same-occupation cases by 13% for nurses and 11% for surgeons.

Overall, these results suggest that increasing casebase diversity improves the ability of GenWriter to retrieve useful cases and generate effective rewrites. A diverse casebase provides richer linguistic patterns that enhance both rewriting coverage and classification performance while further reducing gender bias in the occupation classification task.

5 Conclusion and Future Work

In this paper, we presented GenWriter 2.0, a hybrid approach that combines CBR with LLMs to rewrite biographies in a way that reduces gender cues while preserving meaning. We aim to mitigate bias at its source by targeting the text people write, enabling them to produce content in which gender is less evident. The effectiveness of GenWriter is evaluated by measuring classification accuracy and gender bias of a occupation classification model trained on both the original biographies and the rewritten versions of the biographies. We showed that a reduction in gender bias while maintaining the classification accuracy across the models indicates that the biographies were effectively rewritten, with gender being less evident. The model trained on GenWriter rewritten biographies achieved an ACA of 98.85%, representing an improvement of approximately 10.4%, while substantially reducing gender bias by 78% in nurse and 63% in surgeon biographies. In contrast, rewriting the biographies using an LLM results in smaller reductions in gender bias and lower classification accuracy in all cases, despite introducing lexical variation.

The biographies rewritten with GenWriter also maintain high semantic similarity with the original text while introducing lexical variation, indicating that the meaning of the biographies is preserved. Furthermore, gender prediction experiments show that the rewritten biographies make it more difficult for a model, trained on the rewritten biographies, to infer gender, demonstrating that gender cues have been effectively reduced.

Our experiments also show that moderate casebase reduction can significantly reduce casebase size while maintaining performance of Genwriter (98.72% ACA, gender bias reduction of 78% in nurse and 63% in surgeon biographies), whereas excessive reduction negatively affects rewriting effectiveness. Furthermore, introducing greater casebase diversity improves classification accuracy (by 10%) and reduces gender bias (by 78% in nurse and 63% in surgeon biographies) by providing a wider range of linguistic patterns for retrieval and reuse.

Overall, the findings demonstrate that GenWriter, which integrates CBR with LLMs, provides an effective strategy for rewriting text to mitigate gender bias while preserving relevant information.

As an initial step toward rewriting text, we focus on nurse and surgeon biographies to maintain a controlled setting, and on binary gender identities due to limited availability of datasets with sufficient non-binary representation [11]. Future work will extend this approach to other domains, evaluate its use as a writing aid to reduce gender cues through a usability study, and incorporate non-binary identities to support more inclusive and representative outcomes.

Acknowledgments. This research was funded by Technological University Dublin through the TU Dublin Scholarship–Presidents Award.

Declaration on Generative AI. ChatGPT was used for text polishing. The authors reviewed and edited the content and take full responsibility for the publication.

References

1. Adeyanju, I.: Generating weather forecast texts with CBR. Int. J. Comput. Appl. **975**, 8887 (2012)
2. Amrhein, C., et al.: Exploiting biased models to de-bias text: a gender-fair rewriting model. In: 61st ACL (Vol. 1: Long Papers), pp. 4486–4506 (2023)
3. Bastardo-Rojas, Á., Caro-Martínez, M.: VQA to generate case-based explanations for image classification. In: ICCBR, pp. 37–51. Springer (2025)
4. Bigler, R.S., Leaper, C.: Gendered language: psychological principles, evolving practices, and inclusive policies. PIBBS **2**(1), 187–194 (2015)
5. Blodgett, S.: Language (technology) is power: a critical survey of "bias" in NLP. In: 58th ACL, pp. 5454–5476 (2020)
6. Bolukbasi, T.: Man is to computer programmer as woman is to homemaker? Debiasing word embeddings. In: NeurIPS, vol. 29 (2016)
7. Bridge, D., Healy, P.: GhostWriter-2.0: product reviews with case-based support. In: SGAI, pp. 467–480. Springer (2010)
8. Brown, T., et al.: Language models are few-shot learners. NeurIPS **33**, 1877–1901 (2020)
9. Cryan, J.: Detecting gender stereotypes: Lexicon vs. supervised learning methods. In: CHI, pp, 1–11 (2020)
10. De-Arteaga, M.: Bias in bios: a case study of semantic representation bias in a high-stakes setting. In: FAccT, pp, 120–128 (2019)
11. Dev, S.: Harms of gender exclusivity and challenges in non-binary representation in language technologies. In: EMNLP, pp. 1968–1994 (2021)
12. Dinan, E.: Queens are powerful too: mitigating gender bias in dialogue generation. In: EMNLP, pp, 8173–8188 (2020)
13. Fan, Y.: A CBR approach for speech corpus generation. In: IJCNLP (2005)
14. Gaucher, D., et al.: Evidence that gendered wording in job ads exists and sustains gender inequality. J. Pers. Soc. Psychol. **101**(1), 109 (2011)
15. Ge, X., Xu, J.: Integrating CBR with LLM for expense fraud detection. In: ICCBR, pp. 52–66. Springer (2025)
16. Gervás, P.: Story plot generation based on CBR. In: SGAI-AI, pp. 33–46. Springer (2004)
17. He, Z.: Detect and perturb: neutral rewriting of biased and sensitive text via gradient-based decoding. In: EMNLP Findings, pp. 4173–4181 (2021)
18. Hu, X., et al.: Fuzzy symbolic reasoning for few-shot KBQA: a CBR-inspired generative approach. In: ICCBR, pp. 96–110. Springer (2025)
19. Ioffe, S.: Improved consistent sampling, weighted minhash and l1 sketching. In: IEEE International Conference on Data Mining, pp. 246–255. IEEE (2010)
20. Kotek, H.: Gender bias and stereotypes in LLMs. In: ACM Collective Intelligence Conference, pp. 12–24 (2023)
21. Lu, K.: Gender bias in neural natural language processing. In: Logic, language, and security, pp. 189–202. Springer (2020)
22. Ma, X.: PowerTransformer: unsupervised controllable revision for biased language correction. In: EMNLP, pp, 7426–7441 (2020)

23. Madera, J., et al.: Gender and letters of recommendation for academia: agentic and communal differences. J. Appl. Psychol. **94**(6), 1591 (2009)
24. Marom, O.: A general RAG framework for multimodal CBR applications (2025). arXiv preprint arXiv:2501.05030
25. Minor, M., Kaucher, E.: RAG with LLMs for explaining business process models. In: ICCBR, pp. 175–190. Springer (2024)
26. Van der Pas, D., et al.: Gender differences in political media coverage: a meta-analysis. J. Commun. **70**(1), 114–143 (2020)
27. Piergentili, A.: Gender-neutral rewriting in Italian: models, approaches, and trade-offs. In: CLiC-it, pp. 899–910 (2025)
28. Prost, F.: Debiasing embeddings for reduced gender bias in text classification. In: 1st GeBNLP Workshop, pp. 69–75 (2019)
29. Pryzant, R.: Automatically neutralizing subjective bias in text. In: AAAI Conference on Artificial Intelligence, vol. 34, pp. 480–489 (2020)
30. Salazar, V., et al.: A case based reasoning model for multilingual language generation in dialogues. Expert Syst. Appl. **39**(8), 7330–7337 (2012)
31. Simaki, V.: Sociolinguistic features for author gender identification: From qualitative evidence to quant. analysis. J. Quant. Linguistics **24**(1), 65–84 (2017)
32. Smyth, B.: Case-base maintenance. In: IEA/AIE, pp. 507–516. Springer (1998)
33. Smyth, B., McKenna, E.: Building compact competent case-bases. In: ICCBR, pp. 329–342. Springer (1999)
34. Soundararajan, S., et al.: Using ChatGPT to generate gendered language. In: 31st AICS, pp. 1–8. IEEE (2023)
35. Soundararajan, S., Delany, S.J.: Investigating gender bias in large language models through text generation. In: 7th ICNLSP, pp. 410–424 (2024)
36. Soundararajan, S., Delany, S.J.: GenWriter: reducing gender cues in biographies through text rewriting. In: 6th GeBNLP Workshop, pp. 347–357 (2025)
37. Sun, T.: They, them, theirs: rewriting with gender-neutral English (2021). arXiv preprint arXiv:2102.06788
38. Tel, T., Minor, M.: Utilizing the structure of process models for guided generation of explanatory texts. In: ICCBR, pp. 157–171. Springer (2025)
39. Upadhyay, A.: Case-based approach to automated NLG for obituaries. In: 28th ICCBR, Proceedings 28, pp. 279–294. Springer (2020)
40. Upadhyay, A.: A case-based approach to data-to-text generation. In: 29th ICCBR, Proceedings, vol. 29, pp. 232–247. Springer (2021)
41. Wan, Y., et al.: "Kelly is a warm person, Joseph is a role model": gender biases in LLM-generated reference letters. In: ACL Findings, EMNLP, pp. 3730–3748 (2023)
42. Waugh, A., Bridge, D.: An evaluation of the ghostwriter system for case-based content suggestions. In: 20th AICS, pp. 262–272. Springer (2010)
43. Wilkerson, K., Leake, D.: On implementing CBR with LLMs. In: ICCBR, pp. 404–417. Springer (2024)
44. Wiratunga, N., et al.: CBR-RAG: CBR for RAG in LLMs for legal question answering. In: ICCBR, pp. 445–460. Springer (2024)
45. Yang, R.: CaseGPT: a case reasoning framework based on language models and RAG, (2024). arXiv preprint arXiv:2407.07913
46. Zhao, J.: Gender bias in coreference resolution: evaluation and debiasing methods. NAACL, pp, 15–20 (2018)
47. Zoupanos, S., et al.: Efficient comparison of sentence embeddings. In: 12th SETN, pp. 1–6 (2022)

Top-Down Hyperbolic Case Retrieval for Few-Shot Hierarchical Ordinal Text Classification

Vihanga Ashinsana Wijayasekara(✉), Kyle Martin, and Nirmalie Wiratunga

Robert Gordon University, Aberdeen, UK
{v.wijayasekara,k.martin3,n.wiratunga}@rgu.ac.uk

Abstract. Case-Based Reasoning (CBR) for natural language processing usually relies on Euclidean embedding spaces, which struggle to represent complex hierarchical taxonomies due to their limited capacity for exponential volume growth, resulting in distant nodes to become indistinguishable from closely related ones. Hyperbolic geometry naturally captures these hierarchical structures and offers a promising solution but its potential in CBR remains largely underexplored. To address this gap, we propose a novel **Top-Down Hyperbolic Case Retrieval Framework** designed specifically for few-shot settings where annotated hierarchical data is scarce. Our approach embeds cases into the hyperbolic space and abstracts them using a dual-level prototype strategy, computing generalised parent and child prototypes via hyperbolic weighted midpoints. To use this non-Euclidean hierarchy during retrieval, we introduce a Top-Down Filtered Inference approach. Rather than committing to a single parent prediction, our approach selects the top-k candidate parent categories by hyperbolic distance, masking out all child tasks not belonging to either candidate. This provides robustness against borderline queries near category boundaries, while still eliminating the vast majority of irrelevant child branches and preventing the severe cross-domain misclassifications. Evaluation of the Care Robotics Task Utterance Dataset and Restructured Amazon Dataset shows that our model outperforms Euclidean baselines. By enforcing taxonomic consistency, our framework eliminates the severe out-of-domain misclassifications, providing a structure aware retrieval system tailored for ordinal aware complex taxonomies.

Keywords: Few-Shot Learning · Hyperbolic Geometry · Ordinal Hierarchical Text Classification · Case-Based Reasoning

1 Introduction

Modern Textual Case-Based Reasoning (TCBR) methods often harness semantic representations from word embeddings for case vocabulary [14,22]. Subsequently, case retrieval is typically performed in high-dimensional embedding

L. Malburg and K. Bach (Eds.): ICCBR 2026, LNAI 16780, pp. 236–251, 2027.
https://doi.org/10.1007/978-3-032-33865-5_15

spaces, where geometric distance is measured as a proxy for semantic similarity. Optimising text embeddings to improve similarity-based retrieval has therefore been widely explored in TCBR research [1,10,12,21]. Often, these approaches harness Deep Metric Learning (DML) algorithms, which learn an embedding function optimised for similarity-based return through training on iterative comparisons of instances [17].

Most existing DML approaches map representations into a Euclidean space. Since the Euclidean geometry is fundamentally flat (with constant sectional curvature equal to zero), it behaves polynomially and is well suited for general-purpose vector relationships. However in complex expertise-driven domains such as clinical coding [13], financial document analysis [2], and engineering [11], textual structures can be enhanced with taxonomic knowledge [15]. The hierarchical structure of taxonomies facilitate richer case representations, with parent-child relationships modeling domain-relevant knowledge. However, reliance on Euclidean comparisons means that existing DML algorithms are poorly suited to complex hierarchical structures. Since the Euclidean distance scales polynomially, the distances between specific leaf node cases become artificially compressed. Consequently, the similarity metric becomes distorted; two highly specific child cases in a hierarchical tree may appear geometrically closer to each other than to their parent node.

To overcome these limitations, this paper proposes structuring the casebase on a hyperbolic manifold. Hyperbolic geometry characterised by constant negative curvature, often visualised locally as a saddle-like shape. A comparison between different manifold types are shown in Fig. 1. Euclidean space follows a flat space (curvature = 0), and Sphere has a positive curvature while Hyperbolic space has a negative curvature.

Fig. 1. Different Manifold Types.

Recent works have successfully applied hyperbolic embeddings to complex taxonomies in domains like biological classification [16]. However, despite embedding data in this hierarchy aware space, existing hyperbolic metric learning approaches still generally perform "flat" retrieval during inference; meaning they search across all leaf node cases simultaneously without exploiting the hierarchy to narrow the search space. To address this gap, we do not just embed data in hyperbolic space; we propose a novel **Top-Down Hyperbolic Case Retrieval** system that actively exploits this geometry during the matching process. Our contributions are:

- To the best of our knowledge, this is the **first approach** of its kind that uses multi-level prototypical networks based on hyperbolic space for textual taxonomies in CBR.
- **A hierarchical prototypical network (ProtoFlooNetwork)** approach that leverages hyperbolic space for ordinal, hierarchical, text-based taxonomic datasets, and incorporates a hybrid hierarchical loss function that dynamically abstracts cases into generalised prototypes at both parent and child levels using only a few support examples.
- **A Top-Down Filtered Inference Strategy** that explicitly exploits the hyperbolic hierarchy by predicting the parent category first, and systematically masking out invalid child cases during retrieval.

This paper is structured as follows. In Sect. 2 we discuss relevant literature, while in Sect. 3 we describe background concepts important for understanding the difference between Euclidean and hyperbolic space. In Sect. 4 we describe our top-down hyperbolic case retrieval framework. In Sect. 5 we describe our evaluation on 2 public datasets, while in Sect. 6 we discuss the outcomes. Finally, in Sect. 7 we offer some conclusions.

2 Related Work

In this section we discuss relevant literature in deep metric learning and hyperbolic geometry.

2.1 Deep Metric Learning in Euclidean Spaces

DML algorithms have been widely explored for optimising representations of word embeddings for similarity-based retrieval in Euclidean spaces [1,12,21,22]. Such algorithms use iterative comparisons of instances to train a neural embedding function based on distance-based loss functions [17,20]. A significant value of these algorithms is that they typically facilitate few-shot training (i.e. training on limited data) due to the rich knowledge that can be mined from instance comparisons [21]. A recurring theme of these works is the benefits of similarity-optimised embeddings, typically offering improvements beyond general purpose embeddings for case retrieval. In [1], the authors demonstrate improvement on top-3 and top-7 retrieval of help-desk tickets. Both [12] and [21] demonstrate that embeddings from DML algorithms can improve similarity-based classifications. Importantly, these findings scale to large architectures, as [22] demonstrated that metric-based language models produce better embeddings for retrieval augmented generation (and improved generative responses).

Prototypical Networks [17] are a DML algorithm which compute a *prototype* by taking the mean of a set of support cases to act as a generalised representative for a subset of the casebase (i.e., a class, or coverage set), which is then used as a comparator for query cases. However, there is a fundamental geometric catch when performing this abstraction in a non-Euclidean manifold. A standard arithmetic mean (Euclidean average) is mathematically invalid on a curved manifold [16]. To abstract cases properly, a valid hyperbolic centroid, or a practical approximation of one, must be used in place of the Euclidean arithmetic mean.

2.2 Hyperbolic Representation Learning for Hierarchical Labels

Hyperbolic geometry has been widely adopted for modeling hierarchical structures due to its ability to represent tree-like relationships efficiently. HyperIM [3] embeds both words and labels in a shared hyperbolic space, using the inherent tree-like geometry of hyperbolic space to represent label taxonomies. The model learns document embeddings that align with their corresponding labels through hyperbolic interactions, enabling effective hierarchical representation learning.

Similarly, [9] employs hyperbolic geometry to capture hierarchical label dependencies and introduce a hierarchy-aware negative sampling strategy to improve representation learning in hyperbolic space. HypEmo [4] further demonstrates the effectiveness of hyperbolic embeddings in fine-grained emotion classification. In this work, emotion labels exhibit natural hierarchical relationships, and embedding them in hyperbolic space allows the model to capture these relationships more effectively than Euclidean representations.

Beyond text classification, hyperbolic embeddings have also been applied to tasks involving complex hierarchical structures in other domains. For instance, [16] propose a Hyperbolic Prototypical Network designed to capture hierarchical relationships between plant species in the PlantCLEF dataset. While the dataset itself contains a hierarchical taxonomy, the classification task is formulated as a flat classification problem that predicts fine-grained species-level labels using hyperbolic distances.

Similarly, the HAPPI framework proposed by [19] introduces a hierarchical part-prototypical network for fine-grained image recognition. Visual features naturally exhibit hierarchical organisation, where general features capture overall class characteristics while more specific features help differentiate between visually similar classes. Prototypical Part Networks leverage this structure by representing each class using multiple prototypes corresponding to discriminative object parts (e.g., for the class Red-winged Blackbird, prototypes may represent features such as wing shape or the distinctive red wing patch).

Despite the growing body of work on hyperbolic representation learning for hierarchical classification, existing approaches primarily focus on modeling label hierarchies rather than incorporating ordinal relationships within those hierarchies. In many real world tasks, class labels are not only hierarchical but also inherently ordinal, meaning that the relative ordering between labels carries semantic significance. To address this limitation, our work introduces ordinality aware hierarchical text classification in hyperbolic space. In addition, we use the

Care Robotics Task-Priority Utterance Dataset, which also exhibits a dual-level hierarchy with ordinal relationships.

3 Background

In modern TCBR, textual cases are represented as high-dimensional dense embeddings. In these approaches, the geometry of the embedding space (i.e., the manifold), has a significant impact on case relationships and case retrieval.

3.1 Case Representation in Non-Euclidean Manifolds

The majority of deep learning and traditional CBR methods map cases into Euclidean space. Because Euclidean space has a constant sectional curvature of zero, it is fundamentally flat, meaning its volume grows only polynomially. While Euclidean geometry is suitable for general purpose relationships, it struggles to encode highly structured or taxonomy based data. Hierarchical taxonomies such as data structures with parent-child relationships exhibit an exponential growth in the number of nodes as the depth increases. Attempting to embed this exponentially growing structure into a polynomially growing Euclidean space results in a fundamental mismatch in volume growth. Consequently, highly specific leaf-node cases are heavily compressed and distorted, artificially inflating their geometric similarity.

To overcome this, many existing works use Hyperbolic space, a non-Euclidean geometry characterised by a constant negative curvature. The hyperbolic space can be conceptualised as a saddle shape (Fig. 1) where the available volume expands exponentially as the distance from the origin is further away. This exponential expansion naturally accommodates the branching structure of tree-like data with minimal distortion (Fig. 2). To the best of our knowledge, hyperbolic space has not been widely explored in the Case-Based Reasoning domain.

In Fig. 4a, the Euclidean projection compresses distinct parent categories in the Care Robotics Task-priority Utterance Dataset (CaRTUD) parent categories, such as Emergency and Medical, into overlapping regions, causing queries "like Alert someone, I lost my balance" to risk matching a Medical task instead of an Emergency one. 4b shows that hyperbolic geometry better separates parent categories while keeping child tasks close to their correct prototypes. This matters in elder care, where such errors could leave urgent falls unaddressed, motivating geometry that preserves parent-level taxonomic separability.

3.2 The Poincaré Ball and Hyperbolic Similarity

While hyperbolic space accommodates the exponential growth of hierarchical data, true hyperbolic space is a theoretical and infinite manifold. However, deep learning networks require a concrete mathematical coordinate system to perform calculations. To bridge this gap, existing work harness the Poincaré ball model,

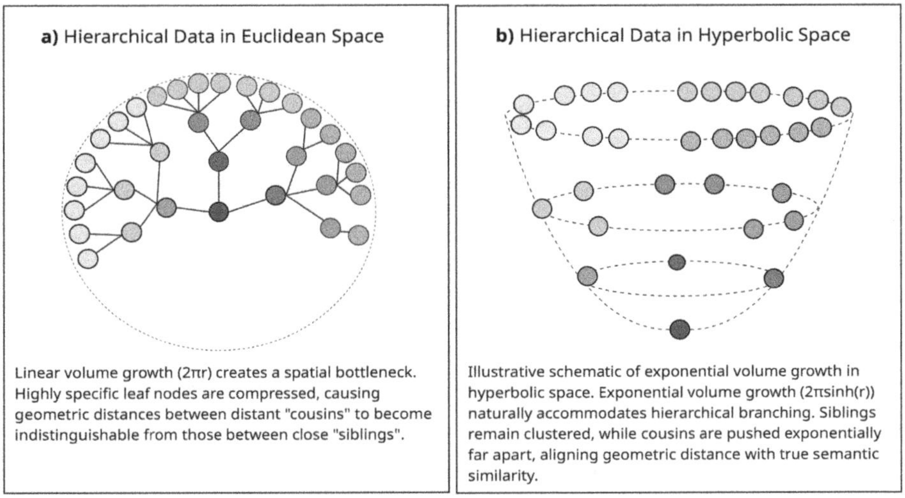

Fig. 2. How hierarchical data lies in Euclidean vs. hyperbolic spaces.

which is an isometric model of hyperbolic space that maps infinite space within a finite Euclidean ball. The Poincaré ball is defined as:

$$\mathcal{P}_c^d = \{x \in \mathbb{R}^d : c\|x\|^2 < 1\} \tag{1}$$

where $c \geq 0$ represents the negative curvature of the space. It preserves the exact structural knowledge of true hyperbolic space while remaining computationally viable.

Feature Mapping: Initially, high-dimensional cases extracted by standard neural networks exist as flat Euclidean vectors. To properly transition these cases into the curved manifold, these vectors are treated as residing in the Euclidean tangent space at the origin ($\mathcal{T}_0\mathcal{P}_c^d \cong \mathbb{R}^d$). An **Exponential Map** is then applied to project these flat vectors into the curved manifold of the Poincaré ball [6].

$$\text{expmap}_0^c(v) = \tanh(\sqrt{c}\|v\|)\frac{v}{\sqrt{c}\|v\|} \tag{2}$$

Similarity Measurement: Traditional CBR methods often rely on distance metrics such as Euclidean and Cosine distances to measure the similarity between a query and an existing case. However, these metrics assume flat space. In curved spaces such as the Poincaré ball, these metrics no longer reflect true distances. In this space, the similarity is calculated using Hyperbolic Distance (Eq. 3).

$$d_c(\mathbf{x}, \mathbf{y}) = \frac{2}{\sqrt{c}} \cdot \text{arctanh}\big(\sqrt{c} \cdot \|-\mathbf{x} \oplus_c \mathbf{y}\|\big) \tag{3}$$

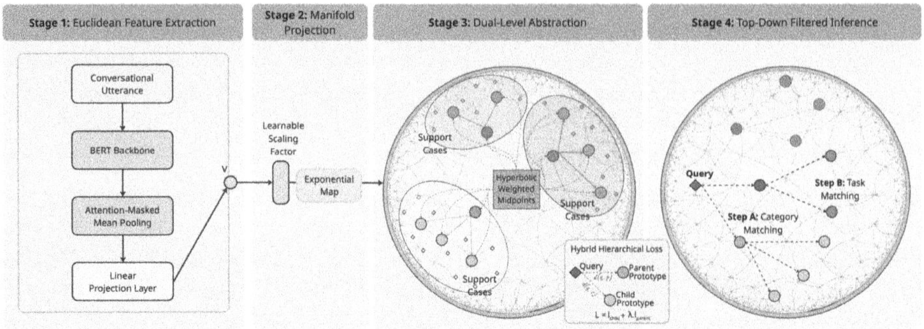

Fig. 3. High-Level Architecture of ProtoFlooNetwork.

4 Methodology: Hierarchical Hyperbolic Case Retrieval

We propose a Top-Down Hierarchical Case Retrieval framework called ProtoFlooNetwork, tailored for complex, ordinal text taxonomies. As illustrated in Fig. 3, the high-level architecture of our proposed approach consists of four key stages: Euclidean Feature Extraction via a pre-trained language model, Manifold Projection into the negatively curved Poincaré ball, Dual-Level case extraction using hyperbolic weighted midpoints, and finally, a Top-Down filtering inference strategy during retrieval. The following subsections outline each stage's formulation.

4.1 Case Representation (Feature Extraction)

To convert text into word embeddings for retrieval, we employ a pretrained bert-base-uncased language model. To prevent overfitting in the few-shot setting while still allowing the model to adapt to the task, we freeze the lower layers of the backbone and only fine-tune the top two transformer encoder layers alongside the pooling mechanisms.

For a given input utterance, the backbone outputs a sequence of token embeddings which then go through an attention masked mean pooling operation over the entire sequence of the last hidden state to aggregate the token representations into a single, dense Euclidean vector (Stage 1 of Fig. 3). Near the origin in the Poincaré ball, the space behaves very much like flat Euclidean space. As one moves closer to the edge, the "volume" of the space grows exponentially. If the Euclidean vectors are too small, all the embeddings will cluster near the origin, completely ignoring the benefit of using hyperbolic space. If they are too large, these vectors will be pushed to the extreme boundary of the ball, leading to numerical instability. By using a learnable scaling parameter, the model can dynamically figure out the optimal spread for the embeddings to best capture the hierarchical structure of the dataset. The learnable scaling parameter scales the Euclidean vectors before they are mapped into the hyperbolic space via the exponential map (Stage 2 of Fig. 3).

Because Euclidean representations suffer from severe distortion when modeling hierarchical taxonomies, we map these BERT representations into the Poincaré ball model ($\mathcal{P}_c^d$). We then project this scaled vector onto the hyperbolic manifold using the exponential map at the origin, as defined in Eq. 2. This results in a fully hyperbolic case representation which naturally encodes the hierarchical relationships of the data.

4.2 Generalised Case Abstraction (Class Prototypes)

A critical limitation of existing hierarchical and hyperbolic metric learning models is their focus on single-level abstractions. For instance, while methods applied to taxonomies successfully embed hierarchical data into the Poincaré ball, they aggregate prototypes and perform predictions solely at the finest, leaf node level [16]. Other recent methods, such as HAPPI [19], extract multiple hierarchical prototypes (generic and specific), but define these based on spatial, part-to-whole relationships within individual visual images, rather than explicit semantic label taxonomies. To explicitly capture the semantic taxonomy of our data, we introduce a novel dual-level dynamic abstraction strategy (Stage 3 of Fig. 3).

For every episodic training fold (or inference batch), we dynamically compute prototypes at *both* the coarse-grained parent level and the fine-grained child level. Given a support set $\mathcal{S}$ of hyperbolic embeddings $z_i \in \mathcal{P}_c^d$, let $y_{task}^{(i)}$ and $y_{cat}^{(i)}$ denote their corresponding task and category labels. The generalised task prototypes $p_{task}^{(t)}$ and parent prototypes $p_{cat}^{(c)}$ are dynamically computed as the hyperbolic weighted midpoints of their respective sets:

$$p_{task}^{(t)} = \text{WeightedMidpoint}(\{z_i \in \mathcal{S} \mid y_{task}^{(i)} = t\}) \tag{4}$$

$$p_{cat}^{(c)} = \text{WeightedMidpoint}(\{z_i \in \mathcal{S} \mid y_{cat}^{(i)} = c\}) \tag{5}$$

While the Fréchet mean is the theoretically rigorous hyperbolic centroid, it has no closed form and requires costly iterative optimisation; we therefore use the hyperbolic weighted midpoint, a fully differentiable approximation implemented via [8]. By dynamically computing abstractions at both taxonomic tiers simultaneously, our model does not merely memorise fine grained intents. Instead, it maintains a generalised, geometric representation of the broader domains (e.g., establishing a "Banking" parent prototype distinct from a "Travel" parent prototype). This dual level abstraction is what directly enables our subsequent hybrid hierarchical loss function and top-down filtered retrieval mechanisms.

4.3 Hybrid Similarity Learning (Training Objective)

The Hybrid Hierarchical Loss in the algorithm is calculated by simultaneously optimising for both the fine-grained child intents and the broader parent intents. It does this by combining two distinct cross-entropy loss components based on hyperbolic distances:

Category-Level Loss (Parent Loss): The algorithm calculates the hyperbolic distance between the input case embeddings and the generalised parent category prototypes. These negative distances are scaled by a temperature parameter and passed through a cross-entropy loss function against the true category labels.

Task-Level Loss (Child Loss): The algorithm calculates the hyperbolic distance between the input embeddings and the specific child task prototypes. To maintain stability, this is done using a Leave-One-Out (LOO) logic, meaning the input sample being evaluated is excluded from the calculation of its own task prototype. The negative distances are then passed through a cross-entropy loss function against the true task labels.

Total Hybrid Loss: Finally, the overall loss is computed by adding the task-level loss to the category-level loss, with the category-level loss scaled by a specific weighting hyperparameter. Mathematically, this is expressed as:

$$\mathcal{L}_{total} = \mathcal{L}_{task} + \lambda_{cat}\mathcal{L}_{cat} \tag{6}$$

4.4 Top-Down Filtered Case Retrieval (Inference)

In traditional flat classification, the model compares the query/test instance with every fine grained class (leaf nodes) and select the closest one as the predicted one. Here the model ignores the implicit information about the task's classes' parents information. In our approach we use top-down filtered case retrieval. The Top-Down Filtered approach facilitates a two-step "filter-then-classify" process that strictly enforces the Category → Task hierarchy (Stage 4 of Fig. 3).

Unlike existing hyperbolic models such as [16] which do a softmax over all classes simultaneously, the proposed approach actively prunes the search space. The HAPPI model [19] combines hierarchical features by calculating separate logits for "generic" and "specific" features and then averaging them together to make a "joint decision", but in our approach, we replace this averaging approach with **hard logical mask**, mathematically guaranteeing that the model cannot predict a specific task (leaf node) if it fundamentally misunderstands the broad category (parent class). By filtering out entire branches of the taxonomy, this approach eliminates the most severe misclassifications seen in flat classifiers where a query is matched to a task from a completely unrelated parent category. The top-down mask structurally prevents any such predictions. Errors are therefore constrained to within-category confusions between sibling tasks at worst.

5 Evaluation

We perform a comparative evaluation to measure the performance of ProtoFlooNetwork across 2 datasets.

5.1 Dataset

Care Robotics Task-Priority Utterance Dataset (CaRTUD). CaRTUD is a hierarchical textual utterance dataset designed to support few-shot task routing and planning in elder care robotics[1]. The dataset has been evaluated by healthcare professionals and older adults across several criteria. The dataset offers hierarchical text classification on user utterances. For a given user utterance such as "Alert someone, I lost my balance", the utterance is mapped with a respective elder care robotic task (*Detecting falls and calling for help*) and its category (*Emergency*). The dataset is intentionally designed for few-shot and low resource evaluation settings, which has 760 user utterances that belong to 36 tasks grouped into 6 categories. One of the novelties in this dataset is both levels have an ordinal nature, which means parent categories have an order based on priority and the tasks have localised order.

Restructured Amazon Dataset (RAD). Due to the limited availability of hierarchical ordinal text classification datasets, we restructured the Amazon dataset [7] into a hierarchical format. Due to the larger size of the dataset and our focus on low-data settings, we selected a sample of reviews from the following categories: Appliances, Handmade Products, Health and Personal Care. This restructured dataset shows a partial ordinal nature; the parent nodes follow a nominal nature while child nodes follow an ordinal nature. The resulting hierarchical label structure is shown below:

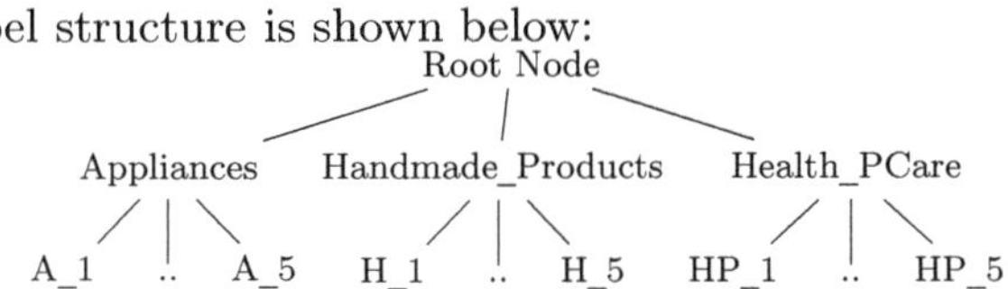

5.2 Baselines for Comparison

We benchmarked ProtoFlooNetwork against several Euclidean space-based baselines and one hyperbolic baseline. The Euclidean baselines include Deep Metric Learning approaches (Matching Networks/MatchNets [20], Prototypical Networks/ProtoNets [17]), existing work on Hierarchical Text Classification (Hierarchical Attention Prototypical Networks ($HAPN$) [18]), fine-tuned traditional models ($bert-base-uncased$ [5]), and traditional instance-based classifiers (kNN, $ProtoKNN$). To ensure a strictly fair comparison, all deep learning baselines use the same pre-trained $bert-base-uncased$ backbone and project representations into an embedding space of the exact same dimensionality ($d = 128$).

Furthermore, we also implemented a hyperbolic variant of flat Prototypical Networks ($HyperFPN$) as a direct geometric baseline. By comparing $HyperFPN$ to $ProtoNets$, we can measure the isolated impact of manifold selection on overall performance, and further we can measure the isolated impact of our hybrid loss function and Top-Down filtered retrieval approach by comparing $HyperFPN$ to $ProtoFlooNetwork$.

[1] https://huggingface.co/datasets/VihangaAW/CaRTUD.

Table 1. Results for different models and n-shots - CaRTUD Dataset

Model	QWK			
	Task		Category	
	5	10	5	10
KNN	0.5841 ± 0.0979	0.6601 ± 0.0836	0.5649 ± 0.1416	0.6409 ± 0.0997
ProtoKNN	0.6412 ± 0.0836	0.6780 ± 0.0761	0.6305 ± 0.0907	0.6793 ± 0.0996
BERT-base	0.0089 ± 0.1025	0.0370 ± 0.0824	0.0461 ± 0.1061	0.0564 ± 0.1110
HAPN	0.7402 ± 0.0786	0.8060 ± 0.0567	0.7332 ± 0.0768	0.8003 ± 0.0622
ProtoNets	0.7261 ± 0.0685	0.8078 ± 0.0598	0.7246 ± 0.0752	0.8061 ± 0.0681
MatchNets	0.6076 ± 0.1582	0.7910 ± 0.0804	0.6364 ± 0.1276	0.7902 ± 0.0818
HyperFPN	0.7594 ± 0.0927	0.8124 ± 0.0575	0.7530 ± 0.0931	0.8069 ± 0.0666
ProtoFlooNetwork	**0.7750 ± 0.0697**	**0.8253 ± 0.0551**	**0.7689 ± 0.0733**	**0.8213 ± 0.0581**
	F1-Macro			
	Task		Category	
	5	10	5	10
KNN	0.4518 ± 0.0513	0.5270 ± 0.0461	0.6589 ± 0.0647	0.7182 ± 0.0549
ProtoKNN	0.5303 ± 0.0556	0.6140 ± 0.0571	0.7119 ± 0.0487	0.7726 ± 0.0563
BERT-base	0.0101 ± 0.0079	0.0189 ± 0.0135	0.1156 ± 0.0417	0.1646 ± 0.0597
HAPN	0.5698 ± 0.0572	0.6496 ± 0.0470	0.7405 ± 0.0605	0.7904 ± 0.0484
ProtoNets	0.5633 ± 0.0477	0.6494 ± 0.0449	0.7381 ± 0.0504	0.8066 ± 0.0454
MatchNets	0.3545 ± 0.1931	0.6380 ± 0.0532	0.6551 ± 0.0701	0.7910 ± 0.0554
HyperFPN	**0.6001 ± 0.0441**	**0.6838 ± 0.0389**	0.7595 ± 0.0601	**0.8147 ± 0.0518**
ProtoFlooNetwork	0.5833 ± 0.0537	0.6605 ± 0.0419	**0.7814 ± 0.0461**	0.8102 ± 0.0488

5.3 Training and Hyperparameter Details

Experiments were conducted using few-shot paradigm on CaRTUD, evaluating on 5-shot and 10-shot configurations across 10-fold stratified cross-validation split. Because few-shot datasets can be highly sensitive to the random sampling of the support set, we adapted our random seed strategy based on dataset size. Due to the smaller size of the CaRTUD dataset, all baselines and proposed models were run across two random seeds (42 and 10) to reduce the variance while 10-fold stratified cross-validation was used for the experiments in Restructured Amazon Dataset. Based on empirical experiments, the category loss weighting hyperparameter was set to $\lambda = 0.5$.

6 Results and Discussion

To evaluate our proposed Top-Down Hierarchical Case Retrieval System, we benchmarked our ProtoFlooNetwork method with several Euclidean and Hyperbolic baselines across both CaRTUD and RAD datasets. F1-Macro treats all misclassifications equally, while QWK penalises errors according to their ordinal distance. This is important in hierarchical elder care tasks, where confusing an

Table 2. Results for different models and n-shots - Restructured Amazon Dataset

Model	QWK			
	Task		Category	
	5	10	5	10
KNN	0.5390 ± 0.0481	0.5649 ± 0.0540	0.6302 ± 0.0426	0.6462 ± 0.0546
ProtoKNN	**0.5600 ± 0.0331**	**0.5657 ± 0.0654**	**0.6491 ± 0.0361**	**0.6491 ± 0.0685**
BERT-base	0.0274 ± 0.0271	0.0646 ± 0.0541	0.0256 ± 0.0346	0.0747 ± 0.0702
HAPN	0.4265 ± 0.0871	0.4669 ± 0.0552	0.4815 ± 0.1073	0.5322 ± 0.0613
ProtoNets	0.4000 ± 0.0901	0.4769 ± 0.0649	0.4681 ± 0.0921	0.5492 ± 0.0644
MatchNets	0.4682 ± 0.0535	0.4781 ± 0.0684	0.5325 ± 0.0556	0.5304 ± 0.0743
HyperFPN	0.4443 ± 0.0338	0.5108 ± 0.0628	0.5187 ± 0.0431	0.5703 ± 0.0710
ProtoFlooNetwork	0.4912 ± 0.0708	0.5348 ± 0.0657	0.5770 ± 0.0647	0.6068 ± 0.0624
	F1-Macro			
	Task		Category	
	5	10	5	10
KNN	0.1502 ± 0.0187	0.1697 ± 0.0202	0.6504 ± 0.0372	0.6759 ± 0.0275
ProtoKNN	0.1689 ± 0.0240	0.1863 ± 0.0238	**0.6708 ± 0.0315**	**0.6938 ± 0.0417**
BERT-base	0.0220 ± 0.0155	0.0316 ± 0.0189	0.2138 ± 0.0992	0.2603 ± 0.1056
HAPN	0.1536 ± 0.0213	0.1665 ± 0.0279	0.5590 ± 0.0559	0.5947 ± 0.0432
ProtoNets	0.1416 ± 0.0221	0.1662 ± 0.0244	0.5494 ± 0.0485	0.5954 ± 0.0445
MatchNets	0.1695 ± 0.0272	0.1744 ± 0.0236	0.5921 ± 0.0264	0.5971 ± 0.0473
HyperFPN	0.1605 ± 0.0160	0.1778 ± 0.0222	0.5735 ± 0.0423	0.6095 ± 0.0470
ProtoFlooNetwork	**0.1812 ± 0.0194**	**0.1886 ± 0.0257**	0.6318 ± 0.0481	0.6491 ± 0.0364

Emergency with a Social task is more severe than predicting a sibling task within the same parent category.

Performance on CaRTUD Dataset: The results on the CaRTUD dataset (Table 1) demonstrate that ProtoFlooNetwork consistently outperforms all Euclidean and hyperbolic baselines across both 5-shot and 10-shot settings in QWK. In the specific context of the CaRTUD dataset, category prediction is essential due to its real world severity. Flat classifiers evaluate all leaf nodes simultaneously, ignoring the semantic hierarchy, which frequently causes leaf-level errors to cascade into severe parent-level misclassifications. Since QWK penalises these cross-category errors most heavily, flat Euclidean baselines score considerably lower. ProtoFlooNetwork avoids this by predicting the parent category first (*top-k*) and masking invalid child branches, achieving a QWK of 0.7750 in the 5-shot task setting.

Performance on Restructured Amazon Dataset: The evaluation on the Restructured Amazon Dataset further validates the robustness of our framework in different hierarchical environments (Table 2). Consistent with the CaRTUD

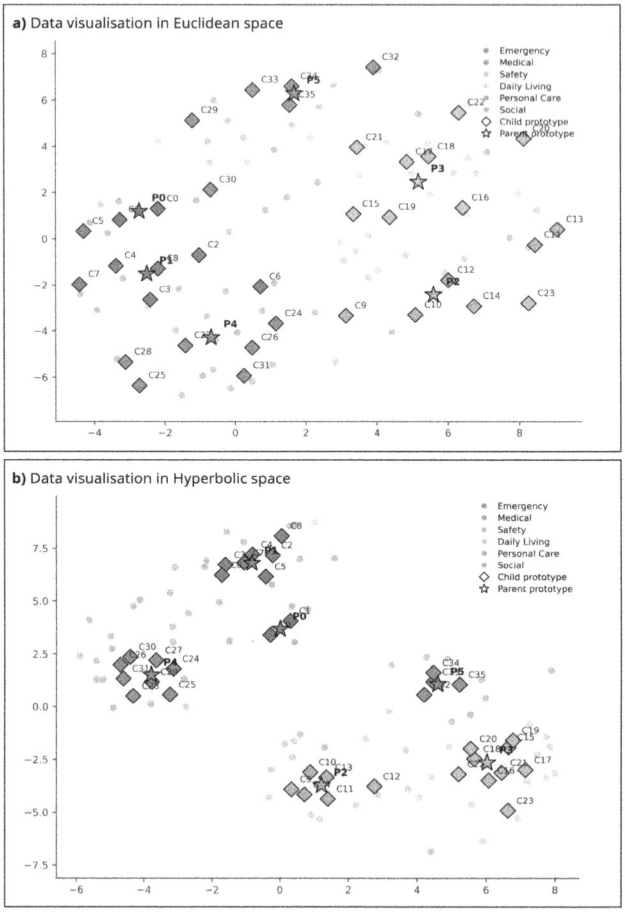

Fig. 4. This figure shows parent and child prototypes in the embedding space, using t-SNE on CaRTUD embeddings.

results, ProtoFlooNetwork outperforms both standard Euclidean models and hierarchical baselines. For example, in the 5-shot task configuration shown in Table 2, ProtoFlooNetwork achieves a QWK of 0.4912, noticeably surpassing Euclidean baselines such as ProtoNets (0.4000) and HAPN (0.4265). This pattern holds for standard classification accuracy as well, where ProtoFlooNetwork achieves the highest Task and Category F1-Macro compared to all the baselines.

QWK results from both datasets shows that ProtoFlooNetwork outperforms all baselines. While the architecture is optimised for hierarchical taxonomy rather than the explicit ordinal nature of the task, a Top-Down filtered inference approach acts as a strict guardrail against large ordinal misclassifications. By geometrically separating parent classes (Fig. 4) and masking out out-of-domain branches, the model implicitly follows ordinal priority, resulting in state-of-the-art QWK performance. The framework captures ordinal structure through a two-stage design: category-level loss establishes coarse membership, and the top-down mask keeps fine-grained predictions consistent with it. The resulting QWK improvements empirically validate that this hierarchical enforcement produces ordinality consistent predictions.

6.1 Ablation Study: The Geometric Impact on Latent Space

To isolate the impact of the underlying manifold, we conducted an ablation study comparing our proposed ProtoFlooNetwork against a Euclidean variant of the same approach. Both models used the same Bert backbone, hybrid hierarchical loss function and top-down filtered retrieval strategy, differing only in the geometry of their embedding space. The hybrid loss and top-down inference are co-dependent: the category level loss forms parent prototypes needed by the top-down filter. Without it, filtering becomes flat classification.

Figure 4 visualises the latent spaces of both models using t-SNE. In the Euclidean manifold (Fig. 4a), limited volume capacity causes distinct taxonomic branches to compress, so samples and prototypes from different parent categories appear close together and their class boundaries overlap. In contrast, the hyperbolic manifold (Fig. 4b) uses exponential volume growth to accommodate hierarchical branching, forming clearer clusters. Sibling tasks remain close to their parent prototypes, while parent categories are pushed farther apart, creating larger geometric margins.

This visualisation shows that while top-down classification provides the logical filter, it is the negatively curved hyperbolic geometry that provides the spatial capacity to truly separate hierarchal domains resulting high QWK performance.

7 Conclusion

Modern Textual Case-Based Reasoning methods commonly rely on flat euclidean spaces, which fundamentally struggle to model complex hierarchical taxonomies due to their polynomial volume capacity. To overcome this fundamental limitation, we introduced **Top-Down Hyperbolic Case Retrieval** framework, which uses the hyperbolic space through the Poincaré ball to embed textual taxonomies. To properly aggregate cases in this curved space, we proposed a dual-level dynamic abstraction strategy that geometrically averages support cases into explicit parent and child class representations. It employs a top-down retrieval model during inference, by predicting the parent categories first to mask out irrelevant child class representations to minimise the search space. Evaluation on the CaRTUD dataset and Restructured Amazon Dataset show that the proposed approach outperforms all of its Euclidean counterparts. Furthermore, an ablation study shows the geometric impact on the latent space in hierarchical domain. Ultimately, this work paves the way for the adoption of non-Euclidean curved manifolds for representing hierarchical structures in Case-Based Reasoning.

Acknowledgments. This research is supported by the Artificial Intelligence & Reasoning (AIR) Research Group and the Personalised Artificial Intelligence Technologies for Health (PATH) Research Centre at Robert Gordon University, UK.

Declaration on Generative AI. During the preparation of this work, the authors used ChatGPT in order to: Paraphrase and reword, improve writing style, and Grammar and spelling check. After using this tool, the author reviewed and edited the content as needed and take full responsibility for the publication's content.

References

1. Amin, K., Lancaster, G., Kapetanakis, S., Althoff, K.-D., Dengel, A., Petridis, M.: Advanced similarity measures using word embeddings and siamese networks in CBR. In: Bi, Y., Bhatia, R., Kapoor, S. (eds.) IntelliSys 2019. AISC, vol. 1038, pp. 449–462. Springer, Cham (2020). https://doi.org/10.1007/978-3-030-29513-4_32
2. Araci, D.: FinBERT: financial sentiment analysis with pre-trained language models. arXiv preprint arXiv:1908.10063 (2019)
3. Chen, B., Huang, X., Xiao, L., Cai, Z., Jing, L.: Hyperbolic interaction model for hierarchical multi-label classification. In: Proceedings of the AAAI Conference on Artificial Intelligence, vol. 34, pp. 7496–7503 (2020)
4. Chen, C.Y., Hung, T.M., Hsu, Y.L., Ku, L.W.: Label-aware hyperbolic embeddings for fine-grained emotion classification. In: Proceedings of the 61st Annual Meeting of the Association for Computational Linguistics (Volume 1: Long Papers), pp. 10947–10958 (2023)
5. Devlin, J., Chang, M.W., Lee, K., Toutanova, K.: BERT: pre-training of deep bidirectional transformers for language understanding. In: Proceedings of the 2019 Conference of the North American Chapter of the Association for Computational Linguistics: Human Language Technologies, Volume 1 (Long and Short Papers), pp. 4171–4186 (2019)
6. Ganea, O., Bécigneul, G., Hofmann, T.: Hyperbolic neural networks. In: Advances in Neural Information Processing Systems, vol. 31 (2018)
7. Hou, Y., Li, J., He, Z., Yan, A., Chen, X., McAuley, J.: Bridging language and items for retrieval and recommendation. arXiv preprint arXiv:2403.03952 (2024)
8. Kochurov, M., Karimov, R., Kozlukov, S.: Geoopt: riemannian optimization in pytorch (2020)
9. Kumar, A., Toshniwal, D.: Hyilr: hyperbolic instance-specific local relationships for hierarchical text classification. In: Proceedings of the 63rd Annual Meeting of the Association for Computational Linguistics (Volume 4: Student Research Workshop), pp. 872–883 (2025)
10. Lamontagne, L.: Textual CBR authoring using case cohesion. In: Proceedings of 3rd Textual Case-Based Reasoning Workshop at the 8th European Conference on CBR, pp. 33–43 (2006)
11. Litzinger, T., Lattuca, L.R., Hadgraft, R., Newstetter, W.: Engineering education and the development of expertise. J. Eng. Educ. **100**(1), 123–150 (2011)
12. Martin, K., Wiratunga, N., Sani, S.: Locality sensitive batch selection for triplet networks. In: 2020 International Joint Conference on Neural Networks (IJCNN), pp. 1–8. IEEE (2020)

13. Mullenbach, J., Wiegreffe, S., Duke, J., Sun, J., Eisenstein, J.: Explainable prediction of medical codes from clinical text. In: Walker, M., Ji, H., Stent, A. (eds.) Proceedings of the 2018 Conference of the North American Chapter of the Association for Computational Linguistics: Human Language Technologies, Volume 1 (Long Papers), pp. 1101–1111. Association for Computational Linguistics, New Orleans, Louisiana (2018). https://doi.org/10.18653/v1/N18-1100, https://aclanthology.org/N18-1100/
14. Naqvi, S.M.R., Ghufran, M., Meraghni, S., Varnier, C., Nicod, J.M., Zerhouni, N.: CBR-based decision support system for maintenance text using NLP for an aviation case study. In: 2022 Prognostics and Health Management Conference (PHM-2022 London), pp. 344–349. IEEE (2022)
15. Recio-Garcia, J.A., Wiratunga, N.: Taxonomic semantic indexing for textual case-based reasoning. In: Bichindaritz, I., Montani, S. (eds.) ICCBR 2010. LNCS (LNAI), vol. 6176, pp. 302–316. Springer, Heidelberg (2010). https://doi.org/10.1007/978-3-642-14274-1_23
16. Shah, M.: Hyperbolic few-shot learning for taxonomic plant classification. In: NeurIPS 2025 Workshop for Imageomics: Discovering Biological Knowledge from Images Using AI (2025)
17. Snell, J., Swersky, K., Zemel, R.: Prototypical networks for few-shot learning. In: Advances in Neural Information Processing Systems, vol. 30 (2017)
18. Sun, S., Sun, Q., Zhou, K., Lv, T.: Hierarchical attention prototypical networks for few-shot text classification. In: Proceedings of the 2019 Conference on Empirical Methods in Natural Language Processing and the 9th International Joint Conference on Natural Language Processing (EMNLP-IJCNLP), pp. 476–485 (2019)
19. Vaseli, H., et al.: HAPPI: hyperbolic hierarchical part prototypes for image recognition. In: Proceedings of the IEEE/CVF International Conference on Computer Vision, pp. 685–694 (2025)
20. Vinyals, O., Blundell, C., Lillicrap, T., Wierstra, D.: Matching networks for one shot learning. In: Advances in Neural Information Processing Systems, vol. 29 (2016)
21. Wijayasekara, V.A., Martin, K., Wiratunga, N., Massie, S., Wijekoon, A.: Few-shot essay grading: weighted prototypical networks for ordinal text classification. Front. Artif. Intell. Appl. (2025)
22. Wiratunga, N., et al.: CBR-RAG: case-based reasoning for retrieval augmented generation in LLMs for legal question answering. In: Recio-Garcia, J.A., Orozco-del-Castillo, M.G., Bridge, D. (eds.) International Conference on Case-Based Reasoning. ICCBR 2024. Lecture Notes in Computer Science(), vol. 14775, pp. 445–460. Springer, Cham (2024). https://doi.org/10.1007/978-3-031-63646-2_29

LLM-Based CBR: Prompting, Adaptation, and Generation

Case-Based Prompt Learning for SO_2 Pump Scheduling

Hongyu Cui[1], Jiarui Wang[2], Guanghua Tang[2], and Abdoul Fatakhou Ba[2](✉)

[1] School of Information and Electronics, Beijing Institute of Technology, Beijing 100081, China

[2] Nanjing Innointel Technology, Zhujiang Road, Xuanwu District, Nanjing 699, China

{wjr,tgh,bfd}@innointel.cn

Abstract. Wet flue gas desulfurization (WFGD) plants must schedule circulation pumps to keep outlet SO_2 within limits while limiting auxiliary power and equipment wear. This supervisory task is difficult because measurements are noisy, operating conditions drift, and every action must satisfy hard plant rules. Existing rule-based controllers are easy to certify but adapt poorly, whereas fine-tuned models require repeated retraining and provide limited operational justification. We address this gap with **Case-Based Prompt Learning (CBPL)**, a case-based decision framework in which a large language model serves as the adaptation engine rather than the memory itself. CBPL stores each decision episode as a case, retrieves semantically similar operating precedents to ground the next action, and updates a Lesson Guidebook that consolidates repeatedly supported adaptations without modifying model weights. This design preserves the core CBR properties of precedent-based reuse, revision, and auditability because each recommendation can be traced to retrieved cases, explicit safety rules, and consolidated lessons. On 1,714 decision episodes distilled from roughly 3 million 10-second measurements from three WFGD units, CBPL improves action accuracy by 17.8% points over a rule-based baseline and by 6.3% points over PID, while maintaining 98.7% rule compliance and reducing switch rate by 54.4% relative to PID.

Keywords: Case-Based Reasoning · Large Language Models · Prompt Learning · Emission Control · Explainable AI

1 Introduction

Industrial decision support systems often react to the current state without explicitly accumulating reusable operational experience. As a result, they may perform acceptably under nominal conditions yet degrade when sensing becomes noisy, local operating practice changes, or the plant enters a regime that was seen before but not encoded as an explicit rule. What is missing is not just more data,

L. Malburg and K. Bach (Eds.): ICCBR 2026, LNAI 16780, pp. 255–269, 2027.
https://doi.org/10.1007/978-3-032-33865-5_16

but a mechanism that converts past episodes into compact guidance that can be reused when conditions recur.

Wet flue gas desulfurization (WFGD) pump scheduling is a representative instance of this problem [15,24]. Circulation-pump decisions determine SO_2 removal, auxiliary power consumption, and equipment wear. They also operate under hard supervisory constraints, including minimum pump counts, pH guards, and one-step action limits. A useful controller must therefore do more than predict a label: it must adapt to changing operating conditions while remaining auditable and rule compliant.

Existing approaches address only part of this requirement. Rule-based controllers are transparent and easy to certify, but they are labor-intensive to maintain and often brittle when conditions drift. Classical and learning-based controllers can improve adaptation, yet supervisory pump scheduling is discrete, context dependent, and safety constrained, which makes pure feedback control or static model training insufficient on their own. Large language models (LLMs) are appealing because they can reason over heterogeneous context [3,14,27], but their usable memory is limited to the prompt, and prompt-only systems forget experience once it falls outside the context window.

Our starting insight is that WFGD supervision already resembles a case-based activity: operators recall comparable operating windows, reuse prior actions, and refine them after observing outcomes. Case-Based Reasoning (CBR) formalizes exactly this loop through retrieve–reuse–revise–retain [1,11]. In this setting, the central design question is therefore not whether to use memory, but how to represent operational episodes, retrieve functionally similar precedents, and revise behavior without losing traceability. Classical CBR provides this structure, but it leaves open how to perform flexible adaptation over heterogeneous textual summaries. LLM prompting offers that adaptation capacity, yet by itself it does not preserve experience across episodes.

We therefore propose **Case-Based Prompt Learning (CBPL)**, a framework that couples a persistent case memory with prompt-level strategy consolidation. CBPL follows the CBR cycle explicitly: it represents each supervisory episode as a case, retrieves semantically similar episodes, uses the LLM to adapt retrieved precedent to the current state, revises the outcome with expert feedback when needed, and retains both episodic and consolidated knowledge for future decisions. By promoting lessons only after repeated support, CBPL reduces sensitivity to noisy one-off outcomes while preserving traceability through explicit cases, rules, and revisions.

Our contributions are:

- We introduce CBPL, a CBR-oriented framework for WFGD pump scheduling in which an LLM performs case adaptation over retrieved operational precedents.
- We design a lightweight lesson consolidation mechanism that extends the retain step with add/edit/upgrade/downgrade operators, turning repeated revisions into stable prompt-level guidance without changing model weights.

- On 1,714 logged episodes from three WFGD units, CBPL improves action accuracy by 17.8% points over a rule-based policy while maintaining 98.7% rule compliance; ablations isolate the contributions of retrieval, revision, and lesson consolidation.

The code and data are available at https://github.com/bafatah/CBPL-code-paper.

2 Background and Related Work

Emission-control decisions in thermal power plants directly affect both environmental compliance and operating cost [26]. Wet flue gas desulfurization (WFGD) is the dominant technology for removing SO_2 from flue gas, and its effectiveness depends strongly on circulation flow and slurry alkalinity [5,24]. In practice, industrial WFGD units are controlled through a layered architecture: low-level loops regulate continuous variables, while supervisory logic selects discrete pump configurations under hard safety constraints [22,23]. This supervisory layer must simultaneously meet emission targets, limit auxiliary power, and avoid unstable switching under noisy and non-stationary operating conditions.

Rule-based procedures and interlocks remain common because they are transparent and certifiable, but they are difficult to maintain as operating regimes drift and they provide limited support when several constraints interact. Classical control methods such as PID and MPC offer principled feedback when adequate models and measurements are available [2,18], yet direct application to supervisory pump scheduling is nontrivial because the actions are discrete and strongly context dependent. Learning-based alternatives, including reinforcement learning, can optimize long-horizon trade-offs, but they require substantial interaction budgets and careful safety engineering in high-stakes settings [6,25]. Model-based optimization for WFGD circulation pumps has also been studied [26], but these methods typically depend on calibrated surrogates and do not naturally expose experience-grounded justifications.

CBR provides a pragmatic alternative in domains where operators already reason by analogy. The retrieve–reuse–revise–retain cycle supports experience reuse and makes decisions explainable through explicit precedents [1,11,20]. Prior fielded deployments suggest that explicit case memory can preserve expert knowledge and improve auditability in operational environments [4,17]. From a CBR perspective, the important issue is not only storing episodes, but deciding what should count as a case, how similarity should be defined, and how revisions should be retained without destabilizing future reuse.

In parallel, LLMs have shown strong ability to reason over heterogeneous context via prompting and in-context examples [3,14,27], but they do not retain experience beyond the context window. Retrieval-augmented generation addresses this limitation by grounding generation in external memory [13]; lexical methods such as BM25 remain useful baselines, while dense retrieval better captures semantic similarity in heterogeneous descriptions [10,21]. Recent CBR–LLM hybrids suggest that combining structured episodic memory with language-based reasoning can improve robustness and explanation quality [7,12,28,29]. CBPL builds on this line with three case-based commitments: structured episodes with outcomes and corrections, retrieval over operationally summarized states, and consolidation of repeated revisions into a lightweight guidebook.

3 Problem Formulation

We model circulation-pump recommendation as a discrete-time decision process with steps $t \in \{1, \ldots, T\}$. At each step, the controller observes a multivariate history window

$$W_t = \{o_{t-L+1}, \ldots, o_t\}, \quad o_t = (\mathrm{SO}_2^{\mathrm{in}}{}_t, \mathrm{SO}_2^{\mathrm{out}}{}_t, \mathrm{load}_t, \mathrm{pH}_t, q_t, n_t, \xi_t), \tag{1}$$

where q_t is slurry flow, n_t is the active pump count, and ξ_t aggregates auxiliary variables. To avoid saturating the context window, we convert W_t into a compact textual state $s_t = \mathcal{T}(W_t)$ that preserves the full outlet SO_2 sequence and summarizes other channels by statistics (min/max/mean/std), trend, and current value.

Actions are incremental pump adjustments $\mathcal{A} = \{-1, 0, +1\}$ (decrease, keep, or increase by one). CBPL augments this decision process with experience. The controller produces a proposed action together with a short explanation, then records an outcome after a feedback window:

$$\begin{aligned} \mathrm{outcome}_t &= \big(\mathrm{SO}_2^{\mathrm{out}}{}_{t+1},\ \mathrm{pH}_{t+1},\ P(n_t + a_t),\ y_{t+1}\big), \\ y_{t+1} &= \begin{cases} 1, & \text{if } \mathrm{SO}_2^{\mathrm{out}}{}_{t+1} \le \tau \text{ and } \mathrm{pH}_{\min} \le \mathrm{pH}_{t+1} \le \mathrm{pH}_{\max}, \\ 0, & \text{otherwise.} \end{cases} \end{aligned} \tag{2}$$

Here τ is the outlet SO_2 regulatory threshold, $\mathrm{pH}_{\min}$ and $\mathrm{pH}_{\max}$ are plant-defined slurry-pH safety bounds, and $P(n_t + a_t)$ denotes auxiliary power in kW for the resulting pump configuration, obtained from measured plant curves. If an episode fails ($y_{t+1} = 0$), an expert correction $a_t^{\star}$ is stored as feedback. Cases are embedded and retrieved by cosine similarity, and the retrieved neighborhood is used to ground the next decision. Figure 1 and Algorithm 2 summarize the overall method.

4 Methodology

Operational expertise in WFGD emerges from repeated observe–act–feedback cycles: operators assess the current state, adjust pumps, and interpret the system response. CBPL mirrors this practice with an explicit experience loop. At each decision point, it summarizes recent plant sensor data into a textual state

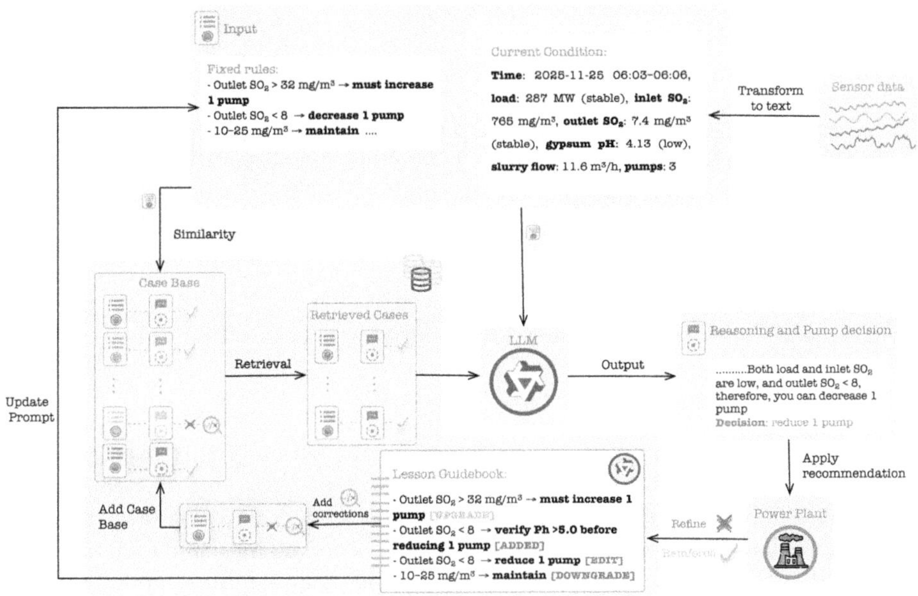

Fig. 1. CBPL architecture and data flow across plant sensor data, retrieval, prompt-guided decision-making, feedback, and lesson consolidation.

representation, retrieves similar episodes, adapts them to the current state, and consolidates feedback into stable strategies. In CBR terms, the LLM is used inside the reuse/revise stages, while the case base and Lesson Guidebook provide the persistent memory. Unlike methods that update behavior after every action, CBPL promotes strategies only after repeated support, reducing sensitivity to noisy outcomes while keeping decisions auditable without parameter updates. The LLM weights are fixed throughout; adaptation is performed in the prompt using retrieved cases and guidebook lessons, while the four CBR steps are realized by retrieval, prompt-based reuse, feedback revision, and retention in the case base and guidebook.

4.1 Overview and Key Components

CBPL maintains two memory artifacts: a case base $\mathcal{C}$ that stores episodic records and a Lesson Guidebook $\mathcal{G}$ that stores consolidated strategies. The pipeline consists of six components: state summarization and fixed rules, case memory, retrieval, LLM decision, revision and retention, and lesson consolidation.

State Summarization and Fixed Rules. The raw sensor stream is a multivariate time series $W_t = \{o_{t-L+1}, \ldots, o_t\}$ that can exceed prompt budgets. We represent W_t compactly as $s_t = \mathcal{T}(W_t)$, preserving the full outlet SO_2 series while summarizing the other channels (inlet SO_2, load, pH, slurry flow) with statistics:

$$\phi(x_{t-L+1:t}) = \big(x_t, \min(x), \max(x), \mu(x), \sigma(x), \mathrm{slope}(x)\big). \tag{3}$$

The summary includes the current pump configuration and flags missing or out-of-range values, allowing the controller to default to conservative actions when data quality is low. We also prepend a small set of fixed rules, i.e., standard operating practices that generally work. Because these defaults may be overly strict when plant conditions or local policies differ, retrieval and the Lesson Guidebook allow CBPL to adapt beyond them.

Case–Based Memory. Each episode is stored as a case:

$$c_i = (s_i, a_i, e_i, o_i, a_i^\star), \tag{4}$$

where s_i is the state summary, a_i is the proposed action with reasoning e_i, o_i contains the post-action measurements and success label, and $a_i^\star$ is an expert correction when the episode fails. This representation makes the case structure explicit: problem (s_i), proposed solution (a_i, e_i), observed outcome (o_i), and revision signal ($a_i^\star$). Keeping outcomes and corrections makes failure modes explicit: the memory records not only what was done, but also when it failed and how it was corrected. To avoid over-representing routine regimes, we retain redundant cases only if they introduce a new outcome or correction.

Retrieval. Retrieval is performed over the problem/state part of each case, not over the action, outcome, correction, or fixed rules. Given s_t, we compute a vector embedding $v_t = f(s_t) \in \mathbb{R}^d$ and retrieve by cosine similarity

$$\mathrm{sim}(v_t, v_i) = \frac{v_t^\top v_i}{\|v_t\|\,\|v_i\|}, \qquad \mathcal{N}_t = \mathrm{topk}_{c_i \in \mathcal{C}}\ \mathrm{sim}(v_t, v_i). \tag{5}$$

The retrieved neighborhood $\mathcal{N}_t$ contains the five prior episodes ($k = 5$) whose summarized operating states are most similar to the current state; we do not use a similarity threshold. The state summary follows a fixed schema and includes the pump configuration, full outlet SO_2 trajectory, and summarized inlet SO_2, load, pH, and slurry-flow statistics; we do not assign manual feature weights during retrieval. Instead, cosine similarity over dense embeddings serves as a first-stage approximation of functional similarity, so that states with comparable behavior can remain close even when their textual summaries differ lexically [10,19]. Since each case stores an action, its reasoning, the observed outcome, and an expert correction when needed, retrieval provides more than raw context: it provides grounded precedents about what was tried, what worked, and how failures were revised. These retrieved cases are formatted into the prompt and used to anchor the next decision in comparable operating conditions, while hard configuration and safety constraints remain explicit in the downstream rule gate. We use FAISS for kNN/ANN search; standard implementations rely on scalable indexing ideas such as product quantization and graph-based search [8,9,16]. CBPL is embedding-agnostic.

LLM Decision. The adaptive prompt concatenates a fixed seed (role and safety rules), the evolving guidebook $\mathcal{G}_t$, the retrieved neighborhood $\mathcal{N}_t$, and the current state s_t:

$$P_t = \text{concat}\big(p_{\text{seed}}, \mathcal{G}_t, \text{format}(\mathcal{N}_t), s_t\big), \tag{6}$$

$$(\tilde{a}_t, e_t) = \textsc{Decide}(P_t), \tag{7}$$

$$a_t = \Pi(\tilde{a}_t; s_t) = \arg\min_{a \in \mathcal{A}(s_t)} |a - \tilde{a}_t|. \tag{8}$$

Here $\textsc{Decide}(\cdot)$ denotes a call to Qwen3-8B (temperature 0.2), and $\Pi(\cdot)$ projects proposals to the nearest admissible pump adjustment under plant rules (one-step changes plus pH and minimum-pump guards). Algorithm 1 specifies the guidebook update used during retention.

Here $\mathcal{A}(s_t)$ is the admissible action set under safety constraints, and $\Pi(\cdot)$ projects a proposal to the nearest legal action. This keeps the decision module compatible with LLM prompting while guaranteeing rule compliance. Figure 2 shows a concrete prompt instance used to produce a pump adjustment together with an auditable rationale.

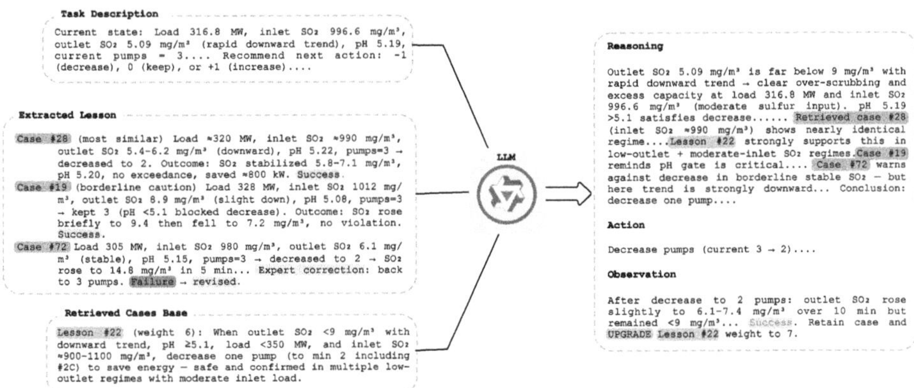

Fig. 2. Example CBPL prompt instance assembled from (i) seed safety rules, (ii) the Lesson Guidebook, (iii) retrieved cases, and (iv) the current state summary, together with the expected structured output (reasoning, action, and post-action observation).

Revision and Retention. After applying a_t, we monitor a fixed feedback window and label success/failure using outlet SO_2 and pH-stability criteria. Successful episodes are retained as new cases. Human intervention is therefore not required for every routine decision; it is triggered for failed or ambiguous episodes. In the offline replay used here, historical expert/operator actions provide the correction signal, while in deployment the same field would be populated by operator review. Failed episodes receive the expert operation correction $a_t^\star$ plus a concise diagnostic note before being added. To make failures actionable,

CBPL contrasts the failed episode with a retrieved successful neighbor, highlighting differences in state and action that explain the divergence. The contrastive note is stored in the case and used to update the guidebook.

Algorithm 1 Lesson Update Procedure

Input: Episode $(s_t, a_t, o_t, a_t^\star)$, guidebook $\mathcal{G} = \{(\ell_j, w_j)\}$
Ensure: Updated guidebook $\mathcal{G}$
extract candidate lesson ℓ (success pattern or failure correction)
choose operation $\textsc{op} \in \{\text{ADD}, \text{EDIT}, \text{UPGRADE}, \text{DOWNGRADE}\}$
if $\textsc{op} = \text{ADD}$ **then**
    $\mathcal{G} \leftarrow \mathcal{G} \cup \{(\ell, 2)\}$
else if $\textsc{op} = \text{EDIT}$ on (ℓ_j, w_j) **then**
    $\ell_j \leftarrow \text{edit}(\ell_j, \ell)$; $w_j \leftarrow w_j + 1$
else if $\textsc{op} = \text{UPGRADE}$ on (ℓ_j, w_j) **then**
    $w_j \leftarrow w_j + 1$
else if $\textsc{op} = \text{DOWNGRADE}$ on (ℓ_j, w_j) **then**
    $w_j \leftarrow w_j - 1$
end if
remove lessons with $w_j \leq 0$ and keep top lessons by w_j

Algorithm 2 CBPL Decision Cycle

Input: Current window $\mathbf{x}_{1:L}$, case base $\mathcal{C}$, guidebook $\mathcal{G}$
Ensure: Pump action a_t
$s_t \leftarrow \text{summarize}(\mathbf{x}_{1:L})$
$\mathcal{N}_t \leftarrow \text{retrieveTopK}(s_t, \mathcal{C})$
$P_t \leftarrow \text{composePrompt}(p_{\text{seed}}, \mathcal{G}, \mathcal{N}_t, s_t)$
$(\tilde{a}_t, e_t) \leftarrow \textsc{Decide}(P_t)$
$a_t \leftarrow \Pi(\tilde{a}_t; s_t)$ ▷ rule gate projects to admissible action
apply a_t, observe outcome o_t
if o_t is successful **then**
    retain case (s_t, a_t, e_t, o_t) in $\mathcal{C}$
    update $\mathcal{G}$ via Alg. 1
else
    obtain expert correction $a_t^\star$, store revision in $\mathcal{C}$
    update $\mathcal{G}$ via Alg. 1
end if

Lesson Guidebook Consolidation. The Lesson Guidebook summarizes recurring patterns that lead to success or failure. From each episode, CBPL extracts a candidate lesson and applies one of four operators: ADD, EDIT, UPGRADE, DOWNGRADE. Each lesson carries a weight w_j (initialized to 2); UPGRADE/EDIT increment w_j, DOWNGRADE decrements it, and lessons are removed when $w_j \le 0$. From a CBR perspective, this extends retain from simple case accumulation to lightweight case-derived knowledge consolidation: stable revisions are promoted into reusable guidance, whereas weak or contradicted lessons are demoted. This mechanism filters unstable rules without retraining the model.

Algorithm 2 summarizes the CBPL decision cycle.

5 Experiments

5.1 Experimental Setup

We evaluate CBPL in offline replay on 1,714 decision episodes distilled from roughly 3 million 10-second timesteps in WFGD logs collected from three plant units. Episodes are extracted around supervisory events where pump changes occurred, were likely, or were explicitly avoided to preserve negative examples. We split the data into training (80%) and testing (20%) partitions to reduce temporal leakage. The training partition is used to construct the case memory and Lesson Guidebook, while the test partition is held out for evaluation. All reported results come from this single split with a fixed deterministic seed and should be interpreted as offline evidence rather than a deployment claim.

Implementation Details. We use Qwen3-8B as the base LLM. Retrieval uses 1024-dimensional semantic embeddings with top-$k = 5$. For the supervised fine-tuning (SFT) baseline, we fine-tune Qwen3-8B using LoRA (rank 128, scaling 256) with learning rate 10^{-4} for 10 epochs. All inference runs use temperature 0.2 under the fixed seed. Preliminary temperature-0 trials produced less robust structured outputs, while temperature 0.2 preserved stable action choices under the fixed seed.

Dataset Statistics. The dataset reflects typical industrial operations with high variance in key process variables (Table 1). Because episodes are sampled around pump-change and near-change situations, the label distribution (Table 2) is intentionally enriched for informative transitions even though KEEP remains the largest class (48.43%).

Table 1. Summary of key process variables (full dataset, pre-split).

Variable	Mean ± Std	Min	Max
Inlet SO_2 (mg/m^3)	1501.67 ± 556.23	1.53	2923.45
Outlet SO_2 (mg/m^3)	15.88 ± 11.17	0.12	97.83
Load (MW)	431.46 ± 120.33	0.31	650.12
Slurry pH	5.00 ± 0.45	4.01	9.18
Pump count	3.44 ± 0.83	2	6

Table 2. Decision distribution (full dataset).

Decision	Count	Percent (%)
Increase	524	30.57
Decrease	360	21.00
Keep	830	48.43

Baselines. We compare CBPL with representative baselines under the same split and evaluation protocol to isolate the benefits of case-based reasoning and iterative skill consolidation.

- **Rule-Based:** A hard-coded strategy reflecting current operating practice, with threshold-based pump changes and a 5-minute cooldown.
- **PID (Discrete):** A classical feedback controller with gains $K_p = 1.2, K_i = 0.05, K_d = 0.2$, SO_2 target 20 mg/m^3, and deadband ± 2 mg/m^3.
- **RAG-Case:** Semantic retrieval ($k = 5$) over raw cases without the Lesson Guidebook.
- **DeepSeek-R1 (Prompt-Only):** Zero-shot prompting with no episodic memory or lesson consolidation.
- **Qwen3-8B SFT:** A supervised fine-tuned model without case retrieval.

Metrics. We report four metrics: (1) **Accuracy** $\uparrow$ (alignment with expert actions), (2) **Rule Compliance** $\uparrow$ (safety constraints), (3) **Average Power** $\downarrow$ (operational cost), and (4) **Control Stability** $\downarrow$ (switch and chatter rates).

5.2 Main Results

Superior Action Alignment with Safety Guarantees. CBPL achieves the best overall action alignment among the compared methods. It improves accuracy by 17.8% points over the Rule-Based controller, by 6.3% points over PID, and by 23.0% points over DeepSeek-R1. On safety, CBPL improves rule compliance by 35.1 percentage points over PID while remaining within 1.3 percentage points of the fully rule-constrained Rule-Based controller.

Enhanced Control Stability. CBPL cuts switch rate by 54.4% relative to PID and by 14.0% relative to Qwen3-8B SFT, while also achieving the lowest chatter rate among the learning-based methods. This pattern is consistent with the role of the Lesson Guidebook in stabilizing repeated adaptations.

Operational Efficiency Trade-Offs. CBPL also achieves a favorable efficiency profile among the data-driven methods. It lowers average power by 107.7 kW (3.3%) relative to DeepSeek-R1 and by 43.4 kW (1.3%) relative to Qwen3-8B SFT, suggesting that retrieved precedents help avoid overly aggressive pump increases. Figure 3 summarizes the main comparison across action agreement, rule compliance, control stability, and power consumption.

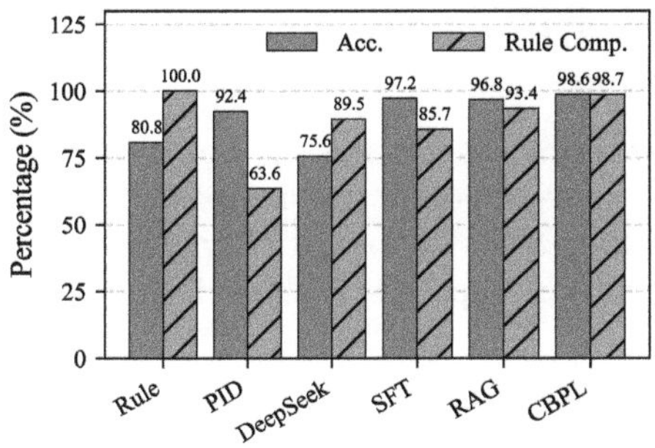

(a) Action agreement and rule compliance.

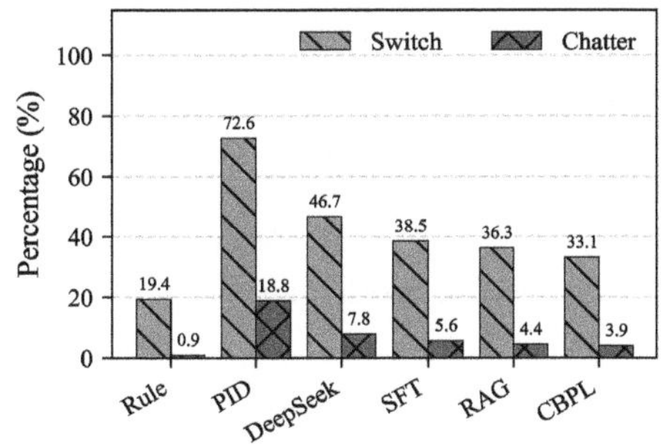

(b) Switch and chatter rates.

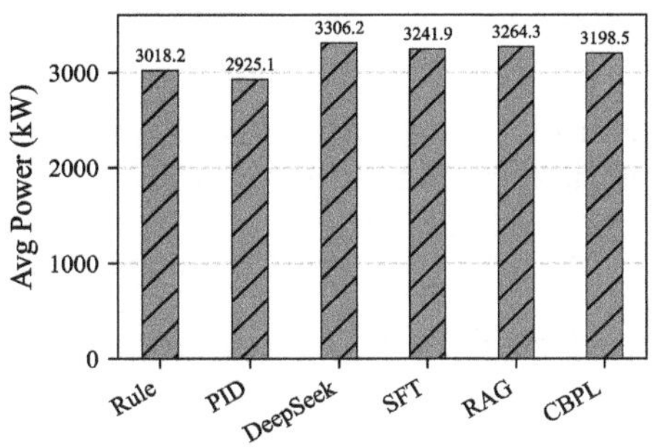

(c) Average power consumption.

Fig. 3. Performance comparison across the six evaluated methods: Rule-Based, PID, DeepSeek-R1, Qwen3-8B SFT, RAG-Case, and CBPL. (a) CBPL achieves the highest accuracy while maintaining safety. (b) CBPL substantially reduces control instability. (c) CBPL lowers power consumption relative to other learning methods.

5.3 Ablation Studies

We ablate core CBPL components to verify their contribution (Table 3).

Semantic Retrieval Captures Functional Similarity. Using semantic embeddings with $k=5$ yields the best balance, capturing functional state similarity (e.g., rising SO_2 under high load) that lexical matching can miss. Because

Table 3. Ablation study of CBPL components.

Method	Acc. ↑ (%)	Comp. ↑ (%)	Power ↓ (kW)	Switch ↓ (%)	Chatter ↓ (%)
CBPL (Full)	98.64	98.70	3198.47	33.12	3.94
No Revision	80.82	100.00	3018.20	19.40	0.92
No Lesson Guidebook	96.78	93.40	3264.33	36.28	4.41
No Retrieval	82.74	100.00	3160.57	35.60	4.36

the rule gate still enforces admissible moves, the main impact appears in action alignment and stability rather than compliance.

Lesson Guidebook is Pivotal for Efficiency. Removing the Lesson Guidebook (Row 3) reduces accuracy by 1.9 percentage points and increases average power by 65.9 kW. It also raises switch rate by 8.7% and chatter by 10.7% relative to the full model, showing that consolidation improves both decision quality and efficiency.

Case Retrieval Grounds the Agent. Removing retrieval reduces accuracy by 15.9 percentage points relative to the full model. It also increases switch rate by 7.0% and chatter by 9.6%, even though rule compliance remains high because the rule gate still enforces admissible actions. This shows that the Lesson Guidebook alone is too coarse.

Iterative Revision Enables Learning. The "No Revision" variant loses 17.8 percentage points of accuracy relative to the full model and collapses to the Rule-Based controller by construction.

6 Limitations and Safety Considerations

CBPL is validated only in offline replay on historical logs from three units, so the results should be interpreted as evidence for decision support rather than readiness for autonomous plant deployment. The framework is intended for episodic, discrete supervisory tasks with recurring situations, explicit safety constraints, and available correction signals, rather than arbitrary continuous control. Any deployment would require staged validation, plant-specific re-tuning of safety bounds, and verification of the rule gate against local interlocks and operating procedures. We also treat dense cosine retrieval as a practical first-stage similarity mechanism rather than a complete substitute for domain-weighted or configuration-aware similarity metrics, which remain important future extensions.

7 Conclusion

In this paper, we presented CBPL, a framework for adaptive WFGD pump scheduling that combines case retrieval, LLM-based case adaptation, revision, and prompt-level lesson consolidation without parameter updates. In offline replay on 1,714 decision episodes distilled from roughly 3 million 10-second measurements from three plant units, CBPL improves action accuracy by 17.8 percentage points over a rule-based baseline, improves rule compliance by 35.1 percentage points over PID, and reduces switch rate by 54.4% relative to PID while maintaining 98.7% overall compliance. These results suggest that a case-based architecture can use LLMs as flexible adaptation modules while preserving the auditability and reuse structure valued in industrial decision support.

Future work includes staged validation under plant-specific safety constraints, broader tests across units and sites, and studying how stable strategies captured in the Lesson Guidebook can be consolidated into model-weight updates while preserving explicit retrieval and rule gating.

Declaration on Generative AI. During the preparation of this work, the authors used Qwen in order to: Grammar and spelling check. After using this tool, the authors reviewed and edited the content as needed and take full responsibility for the publication's content.

Disclosure of Interests. The authors have no competing interests to declare that are relevant to the content of this article.

References

1. Aamodt, A., Plaza, E.: Case-based reasoning: foundational issues, methodological variations, and system approaches. AI Commun. **7**(1), 39–59 (1994). https://doi.org/10.3233/AIC-1994-7104
2. Åström, K.J., Hägglund, T.: The future of PID control. Control. Eng. Pract. **9**(11), 1163–1175 (2001). https://doi.org/10.1016/S0967-0661(01)00062-4
3. Brown, T.B., et al.: Language models are few-shot learners. In: Advances in Neural Information Processing Systems, vol. 33, pp. 1877–1901. Curran Associates, Inc. (2020). https://proceedings.neurips.cc/paper/2020/hash/1457c0d6bfcb4967418bfb8ac142f64a-Abstract.html
4. Cheetham, W., Watson, I.: Fielded applications of case-based reasoning. Knowledge Eng. Rev. **20**(3), 321–323 (2005). https://doi.org/10.1017/S0269888906000580
5. Dou, B., Pan, W., Jin, Q., Wang, W., Li, Y.: Prediction of SO_2 removal efficiency for wet flue gas desulfurization. Energy Convers. Manage. **50**(10), 2547–2553 (2009). https://doi.org/10.1016/j.enconman.2009.06.012
6. Garcia, J., Fernández, F.: A comprehensive survey on safe reinforcement learning. J. Mach. Learn. Res. **16**(42), 1437–1480 (2015). https://jmlr.org/papers/v16/garcia15a.html
7. Ghazouani, F., Giustozzi, F., Le Ber, F.: LLM-Driven case-base populating for structuring and integrating restoration experiences. In: Case-Based Reasoning Research and Development (ICCBR 2025). Lecture Notes in Computer Science, vol. 15662, pp. 67–80. Springer (2025). https://doi.org/10.1007/978-3-031-96559-3_5
8. Jégou, H., Douze, M., Schmid, C.: Product quantization for nearest neighbor search. IEEE Trans. Pattern Anal. Mac. Intell. **33**(1), 117–128 (2011). https://doi.org/10.1109/TPAMI.2010.57
9. Johnson, J., Douze, M., Jégou, H.: Billion-scale similarity search with GPUs. IEEE Trans. Big Data **7**(3), 535–547 (2021). https://doi.org/10.1109/TBDATA.2019.2921572
10. Karpukhin, V., et al.: Dense passage retrieval for open-domain question answering. In: Proceedings of the 2020 Conference on Empirical Methods in Natural Language Processing (EMNLP), pp. 6769–6781. Association for Computational Linguistics, Online (2020). https://doi.org/10.18653/v1/2020.emnlp-main.550. https://aclanthology.org/2020.emnlp-main.550/
11. Kolodner, J.L.: Case-Based Reasoning. Morgan Kaufmann, San Mateo, CA (1993)

12. Lenz, M., Hoffmann, M., Bergmann, R.: LLsiM: large language models for similarity assessment in case-based reasoning. In: Case-Based Reasoning Research and Development (ICCBR 2025). Lecture Notes in Computer Science, vol. 15662, pp. 126–141. Springer (2025). https://doi.org/10.1007/978-3-031-96559-3_9
13. Lewis, P., et al.: Retrieval-augmented generation for knowledge-intensive NLP tasks. In: Advances in Neural Information Processing Systems. vol. 33, pp. 9459–9474. Curran Associates, Inc. (2020). https://proceedings.neurips.cc/paper_files/paper/2020/hash/6b493230205f780e1bc26945df7481e5-Abstract.html
14. Liu, P., Yuan, W., Fu, J., Jiang, Z., Hayashi, H., Neubig, G.: Pre-train, prompt, and predict: a systematic survey of prompting methods in natural language processing. ACM Comput. Surv. **55**(9), 1–35 (2023). https://doi.org/10.1145/3560815
15. Liu, S., Sun, L., Zhu, S., Li, J., Chen, X., Zhong, W.: Operation strategy optimization of desulfurization system based on data mining. Appl. Math. Model. **81**, 144–158 (2020). https://doi.org/10.1016/j.apm.2019.12.004
16. Malkov, Y.A., Yashunin, D.A.: Efficient and robust approximate nearest neighbor search using hierarchical navigable small world graphs. IEEE Trans. Pattern Anal. Mach. Intell. **42**(4), 824–836 (2020). https://doi.org/10.1109/TPAMI.2018.2889473
17. Marling, C., Rissland, E., Aamodt, A.: Integrations with case-based reasoning. Knowledge Eng. Rev. **20**(3), 241–245 (2005). https://doi.org/10.1017/S026988890600066X
18. Qin, S.J., Badgwell, T.A.: A survey of industrial model predictive control technology. Control. Eng. Pract. **11**(7), 733–764 (2003). https://doi.org/10.1016/S0967-0661(02)00186-7
19. Reimers, N., Gurevych, I.: Sentence-BERT: sentence embeddings using Siamese BERT-Networks. In: Proceedings of the 2019 Conference on Empirical Methods in Natural Language Processing and the 9th International Joint Conference on Natural Language Processing (EMNLP-IJCNLP), pp. 3982–3992. Association for Computational Linguistics, Hong Kong, China (2019). https://doi.org/10.18653/v1/D19-1410. https://aclanthology.org/D19-1410/
20. Richter, M.M., Weber, R.O.: Case-Based Reasoning: A Textbook. Springer, Berlin, Heidelberg (2013)
21. Robertson, S., Zaragoza, H.: The probabilistic relevance framework: BM25 and beyond. Found. Trends Inf. Retr. **3**(4), 333–389 (2009). https://doi.org/10.1561/1500000019
22. Seborg, D.E., Edgar, T.F., Mellichamp, D.A., Doyle, F.J.: Process Dynamics and Control, 3rd edn. Wiley, Hoboken, NJ (2010)
23. Skogestad, S., Postlethwaite, I.: Multivariable Feedback Control: Analysis and Design, 2nd edn. Wiley, Chichester (2005)
24. Srivastava, R.K., Jozewicz, W.: Flue gas desulfurization: The state of the art. J. Air & Waste Manage. Assoc. **51**(12), 1676–1688 (2001). https://doi.org/10.1080/10473289.2001.10464387
25. Sutton, R.S., Barto, A.G.: Reinforcement Learning: An Introduction, 2nd edn. MIT Press, Cambridge, MA (2018)
26. Trojan, M., Wielgus, S., Taler, J., Dzierwa, P., Kaczmarski, K., Granda, M.: Optimization of the operation of circulation pumps in the wet flue gas desulphurisation system. Energy **325**, 136209 (2025). https://doi.org/10.1016/j.energy.2025.136209
27. Wei, J., et al.: Chain-of-Thought prompting elicits reasoning in large language models. In: Advances in Neural Information Processing Systems. vol. 35, pp. 24824–24837. Curran Associates, Inc. (2022). https://proceedings.neurips.cc/paper_files/paper/2022/hash/9d5609613524ecf4f15af0f7b31abca4-Abstract-Conference.html

28. Wilkerson, K., Leake, D.: On implementing case-based reasoning with large language models. In: Case-Based Reasoning Research and Development (ICCBR 2024). Lecture Notes in Computer Science, vol. 14775, pp. 404–417. Springer (2024). https://doi.org/10.1007/978-3-031-63646-2_26
29. Wiratunga, N., et al.: CBR-RAG: case-based reasoning for retrieval augmented generation in LLMs for legal question answering. In: Case-Based Reasoning Research and Development (ICCBR 2024). Lecture Notes in Computer Science, vol. 14775, pp. 445–460. Springer (2024). https://doi.org/10.1007/978-3-031-63646-2_29

Hallucinations Considered Helpful: Increasing Case Base Competence with LLM-Hallucinated Cases

Kaitlynne Wilkerson and David Leake(✉)

Luddy School of Informatics, Computing, and Engineering, Indiana University, Bloomington, IN 47408, USA
{kwilker,leake}@iu.edu

Abstract. Hallucinations are a common problem for Large Language Models (LLMs). Hallucinations are generally seen as errors, leading to unsupported, inaccurate, or nonsensical output. This has motivated research on hallucination repair. However, recent research on implementing case-based reasoning with LLMs revealed a surprising result about LLM hallucinations affecting cases: A policy of removing hallucinated cases could harm overall performance, compared to enforcing case correctness. This raised questions about the assumption that case hallucinations degrade accuracy and how retention of hallucinated cases affects competence, and about whether selective retention of hallucinated cases could improve system competence. This paper reports on three experiments conducted to address these questions. First, solidifying the previous results, we illustrate that the result that blanket removal of hallucinated cases can be harmful holds across multiple LLMs. Next, we provide a detailed analysis of the competence of captured hallucinated cases, which shows that not only are hallucinated cases often capable of solving problems, but some can make strong competence contributions. Finally, we show that a simple strategy of retaining hallucinated cases that are suspected to be valuable to competence can increase the accuracy for a testbed system. This suggests that selective retention of hallucinated cases may be a useful case acquisition strategy for LLM-based CBR systems.

1 Introduction

The extensive capabilities of Large Language Models (LLMs) have prompted great interest in CBR-LLM integrations [1]. An appealing opportunity is for LLMs to perform steps of the CBR process, such as similarity assessment [9] and case adaptation [8], or even to implement the full CBR cycle. In previous work, we conducted initial experiments on implementing the CBR process with large language models [18]. In these experiments, a case or entire case base was provided to an LLM, with prompts guiding the LLM to perform CBR for classification. Our motivation was to increase both accuracy and explainability compared to the original LLM process, by grounding LLM decisions in real cases.

L. Malburg and K. Bach (Eds.): ICCBR 2026, LNAI 16780, pp. 270–284, 2027.
https://doi.org/10.1007/978-3-032-33865-5_17

The studies were encouraging for accuracy benefits but revealed an unexpected LLM behavior: Rather than reliably applying the provided cases, the LLMs often reported basing their reasoning on versions of the cases in which hallucinations changed case details [19].

Hallucinations are a common problem for Large Language Models, and have prompted much concern and study [2,21]. Their occurrence is tied to the statistical nature of LLM reasoning and the lossy encoding of data during LLM training [4,13], making hallucination an intrinsic issue for LLMs. Consequently, research on hallucinations primarily focuses on how to identify and remove hallucinations in responses [3,5,7,13,21]. These methods have been shown to provide benefits, and after noting the prevalence of hallucinations affecting cases in our LLM-based CBR implementation, we applied related methods to remove hallucinated cases in our testbed system [19]. However, to our surprise, the system's accuracy decreased despite a concurrent decrease in observed hallucinations, raising interesting questions about why hallucinated cases may add value in a CBR system and how hallucinated cases may affect a case base. We suspected that some of these hallucinated cases served as useful synthetic data—a form of "ghost cases" [6] that improved system performance despite not capturing real episodes. This suggested that identifying and capturing these hallucinated ghost cases in real time could improve the competence of the CBR-LLM system. This paper proposes and demonstrates a method for determining which hallucinated cases to retain, based on notions from research on case-base competence (e.g., [15]).

In this paper, we first present experiments examining the prevalence of problem-useful hallucinated cases for a testbed CBR process implemented using a range of LLMs. Next, we present an analysis of the competence of observed case hallucinations. Finally, we present and evaluate a case-based method, using similarity of hallucinated cases to known competent cases, for identifying, storing, and re-using potentially competent hallucinated cases in real time. The results of these experiments demonstrate that in our test domain, problem-useful hallucinated cases are generated by multiple LLMs and that many of the hallucinated cases are competence-important, sometimes providing more competence than the original cases. Finally, we showed that selectively allowing use of hallucinated cases expected to be competence-important increased the accuracy of the LLM-implemented CBR system, compared to relying on the original cases from which the hallucinations were generated.

The paper begins with an overview of related work, next summarizes our previous work on implementing CBR with LLM, and then presents the research questions to be addressed, the experimental design to address them, and the experimental results. It closes with a discussion of future research questions.

2 Related Work

The work in this paper relates to research on CBR-LLM integrations, research on case-base competence, and research on generating "ghost cases," artificial cases to increase case-base competence.

Using LLMs to Support the CBR Process. LLM-based methods to support CBR are an active research area, with opportunities for tasks including knowledge engineering, similarity assessment, adaptation, maintenance, and results presentation [1,9]. This paper examines LLM use both for similarity assessment and adaptation, and as part of an end-to-end LLM-driven CBR process (cf. [14]).

Retrieval Augmented Generation. Providing LLMs with external knowledge has been shown to improve LLM accuracy, with the most common method being Retrieval Augmented Generation (RAG) [3,10]. RAG assesses similarity between chunked text and a query and returns problem-relevant factual statements to augment input to an LLM. CBR-RAG enhances the RAG process by using CBR retrieval to more effectively match potential solution cases to current problems [20]. Our work focuses on providing cases as inputs to the LLM.

Case-Based Competence. Case base competence refers to the range of problems that the system can solve based on cases in the case base [15–17]. Competence measurements can assess both the overall problem-solving power of the case base and individual case contributions to problem-solving.

Under the "representativeness assumption" [15] that problems in the current case base are representative of future problems the system will solve, contributions to competence can be derived by computing competence groups, sets of cases that can solve each other and are isolated from other groupings. The isolation of a competence group from other competence groups within the case space indicates that the group makes a unique competence contribution because it can solve cases that no other group can.

Individual competence-important cases can be identified by calculating the relative coverage of the case or by identifying whether the case belongs to the footprint set of the coverage group [17]. Relative coverage (RC) calculates the comparative competence contributions of a case, crediting for the cases that it can solve, inversely weighted by the ability of other cases to solve them. Specifically, Smyth and McKenna define relative coverage by:

$$RelativeCoverage(c) = \sum_{c' \in CoverageSet(c)} \frac{1}{|ReachabilitySet(c')|} \tag{1}$$

A high RC score is indicative of a case highly valuable for competence. The footprint set identifies cases that make positive competence contributions to a competence group. Footprint cases may often overlap with cases with high RC scores [16,17].

Ghost Cases. The generation of artificial "ghost cases" to augment the case base was proposed by Schack and Leake [6] for case-base maintenance, to increase case base compression effectiveness with an "expansion-contraction" case base compression strategy. The solutions of those ghost cases were generated using case adaptation knowledge. Case base compression was then applied to the new case base. This approach could be seen as a knowledge container transfer strategy, from case adaptation knowledge to the case base. This paper focuses on ghost cases generated by a different method: By harvesting hallucinated cases that have proven useful at solving problems.

3 Our Previous Work on Implementing CBR with LLMs

The experiments discussed in this paper build on our previous work. This section briefly summarizes the techniques and results from that work to provide the motivations and foundational techniques for the current experiments.

3.1 Implementing CBR with LLMs

Wilkerson and Leake [18] introduced a method for implementing the CBR process with LLMs, using cases representing feature value-pairs in textual form. Their model provided an LLM with individual cases, or sets of cases, as a form of external knowledge to the LLM. Their motivation for using an LLM to perform CBR processes was twofold: to benefit CBR by reducing knowledge acquisition, and to benefit LLMs by reducing errors, as well as making LLM reasoning more transparent by grounding the LLM reasoning process in the CBR cycle. Three prompts were used to assess the effect of providing cases on accuracy and the ability of LLMs to perform similarity assessment and adapt cases.

- **Direct Solution**: only given problem and asked to solve.
- **Implicit CBR (ICBR)**: given problem; k-NN provides LLM with one or more prior cases; asks for adaptation of problem using provided case(s).
- **Explicit CBR (ECBR)**: given problem; k-NN provides 10 most similar cases to the problem; asks for similarity assessment of provided cases and adaptation of problem using selected case(s).

The ICBR and ECBR prompts were tested on three different conditions for the cases provided to the LLM: nearest neighbor only (1NN), the top two nearest neighbors (2NN), and the nearest neighbor and nearest unlike neighbor (NUN). This aimed to assess whether the LLM performed best with certain types or amounts of information. Testing used ChatGPT 3.5 and Llama2 70B on a medical triage domain. ChatGPT was used to assess performance with a state-of-the-art commercial model at that point in time (as of March 2024), and Llama2 tests provided replicability. The case base contained 100 randomly selected cases, while the test set contained 25 randomly selected cases. This experiment and its results will be referred to throughout this paper as the Original results or experiments. The primary system illustrated in Fig. 1 was developed to support these tests.

Performance of the ECBR and ICBR prompts equalled or surpassed the Direct Solution baseline (28%) for both models. The best performing prompt was ICBR 1NN, with 60% accuracy for ChatGPT and 56% for Llama2. When compared to unweighted and weighted 1NN systems, ECBR and ICBR mostly

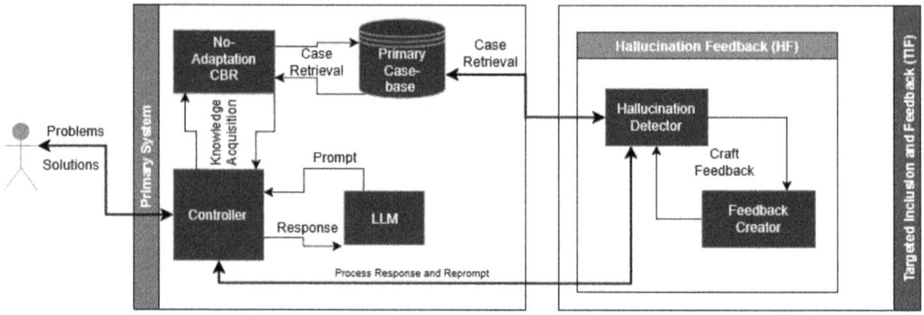

Fig. 1. System design and workflow for the experiments. Arrows depict interactions and the flow of information.

outperformed the unweighted system and, in a few instances, performed at or above the weighted system.

These results were encouraging for benefits of prompting the LLM to perform CBR, due to the accuracy improvement with provided cases and, in some instances, with LLM guided similarity assessment and adaptation. This suggested that this hybrid approach could be useful for LLMs; it also facilitates application of CBR by obviating the need for traditional knowledge acquisition.

3.2 Repairing Case Hallucinations

Follow-up tests on hybrid systems using Llama3 70B revealed an unexpected behavior: that LLM hallucinations sometimes changed details of the provided cases [19]. In what follows, a "case hallucination", or "hallucinated case", describes an instance in which at least one feature value of the case listed in the LLM response conflicts with provided case. The prevalence of case hallucinations depended on the LLM. In our tests, Llama2 and ChatGPT had effectively no case hallucinations (see Wilkerson and Leake [19] for an exact breakdown). Typically, hallucinations could be eliminated by re-prompting without change to the prompt, but Llama3 was resistant to this method.

To control case hallucinations, we applied a Hallucination Feedback module (see Fig. 1) that scanned newly generated responses for case hallucinations and generated feedback prompts with instructions to fix the hallucinated case. The module significantly reduced, and sometimes completely eliminated, hallucinated cases. However, to our surprise, it also reduced system accuracy. This decrease was later determined not to be statistically significant ($p = .232$, $t = .748$) via a Paired Samples t-Test. However, the initial observation and confirmation of lack of statistically significant harm from using hallucinated cases motivated the study in this paper. In the rest of this paper, we will refer to this experiment as the "Hallucination Feedback" (HF) experiment.

4 Research Questions

The prevalence of case hallucinations for some LLMs, combined with the surprising result that removing case hallucinations could decrease accuracy, prompted us to try to better understand this phenomenon and assess whether case hallucinations might be a useful source of ghost cases to add to the case base to benefit system competence. We conducted experiments focusing on three primary questions:

1. Do high hallucination rates and statistically significant decreases in accuracy from hallucination removal occur for other LLMs?
2. What is the competence of the hallucinated cases? This determines whether adding to the case base hallucinated cases that lead to correct solutions could be expected to have broad benefit to overall problem-solving.
3. Can problem-useful hallucinated cases with high contributions to competence be selected for addition to the case base, to improve accuracy? Not all hallucinated cases would be expected to be equally useful, even when they lead to accurate solutions for the current problem. A successful selection strategy would increase competence while controlling case-base growth. Selective retention is also desirable if accuracy of selected cases will be verified by human vetting, as selectivity decreases vetting cost.

We consider a hallucinated case problem-useful if the baseline LLM generated an incorrect solution but solved the problem correctly when provided with the hallucinated case. The following sections discuss the experiments and hypotheses used to address these questions.

5 Experimental Design

We performed three experiments exploring the usefulness of case hallucinations. Experiment 1 extends our prior tests on implementing CBR with LLMs and repairing case hallucinations to additional LLMs. This is done to assess the generalizability of initial observations concerning the problem-usefulness of LLM-hallucinated cases. Experiment 2 analyzes all observed case hallucinations to assess their competence and problem-usefulness. Problem-useful hallucinated cases are compared to not-yet-useful hallucinated cases to determine whether any group has higher competence than the other. Finally, Experiment 3 examines whether competent hallucinated cases can be captured in real-time and used to improve accuracy. This section discusses the setup and procedures for each experiment.

5.1 Experimental Setup

Dataset. All experiments in this paper used the Kaggle medical triage dataset used in our previous experiments.[1] Experiments 1 (generalizability) and 2 (competence analysis) reuse the case base from previous experiments, composed of

[1] https://www.kaggle.com/datasets/ilkeryildiz/emergency-service-triage-application.

100 randomly-selected cases. Experiment 3 (targeted inclusion) uses this case base combined with competent hallucinated cases found during Experiment 2.

Llama3 70B was tested on the original 25 test cases from previous experiments, while the other models were tested on 75 cases composed of the original 25 and an additional randomly selected 50 cases from unused data. The change in number of test cases for later models was done to generate an equivalent number of hallucinated cases for competence analysis as Llama3 70B had previously undergone temperature testing (i.e., re-running the experiment at different internal temperatures) and had generated a sizable number of hallucinated cases, all of which were used for competence analysis. The original 25 test cases were not capable of generating the same number of hallucinated cases for other models, and since temperature testing produced no worthwhile results, this discrepancy was solved by using additional test cases for other LLMs.

Large Language Models. For Experiment 1 (generalizability), five LLMs were added: Llama3.1 8B Instruct, Gemma 3 4B Instruct, MedGemma 4B Instruct, Gemma 2 9B Instruct and Mistral 7B Instruct. All are open-source and were set to a temperature of 0 for reproducibility. Experiments 2 (competence analysis) and 3 (targeted inclusion) used the same models plus Llama3 70B.

System Design. Experiment 1 (generalizability) relies solely on the initial system and Hallucination Feedback module developed for the experiments described in Sects. 3 and 3.2 (see Fig. 1). Experiment 3 (targeted inclusion) relies on the primary system and a new module called Targeted Inclusion and Feedback, which uses the Hallucination Feedback module as a component. Figure 1 covers the entire workflow for Experiment 3. Experiments 1 and 3 reused the ECBR and Hallucination Feedback prompts without change.

Experiment 2 does not rely on the system shown in Fig. 1. It relies on the Smyth and McKenna competence modeling algorithm (see Sect. 2.3 for a brief discussion or [16] for specific equations). This algorithm depends on a "solve predicate" that assesses whether a case can solve another. As basis for the solve predicate for our test domain of medical triaging decisions, we built a computational model of triaging based on publicly available documents from the U.S. Centers for Disease Control (CDC)[2], the American College of Surgeons (ACS)[3,4], and the Emergency Nurses Association[5] [11,12].

Hallucination Generation. Hallucinations generated by Llama3 70B were captured during the experiments in [18,19] and were used in our analysis. The

[2] https://www.cdc.gov/mmwr/pdf/rr/rr6101.pdf.

[3] https://www.facs.org/quality-programs/trauma/systems/field-triage-guidelines/.

[4] https://www.stritch.luc.edu/lumen/meded/surgery/traumaii.pdf.

[5] https://californiaena.org/wp-content/uploads/2023/05/ESI-Handbook-5th-Edition-3-2023.pdf.

remaining five models generated hallucinations during Experiment 1 (generalizability), which were reused in Experiments 2 (competence analysis) and 3 (targeted inclusion).

5.2 Procedure and Analysis

Experiment 1: Model Generalizability. We performed two rounds of testing on each of the newly added LLMs: one using the primary system alone (i.e., the original experiment) and one where the Hallucination Feedback (HF) module was enabled. Both rounds of testing used the 75 case test set.

Hypotheses
The primary purpose of this experiment is to assess the prevalence of hallucinated cases and their usefulness, and whether the experimental trends observed in our initial work hold more generally. We tested two hypotheses:

1.1. The test models hallucinate cases at high rates.
1.2. Removing hallucinated cases from case selection responses, thus ensuring the use of only real case knowledge in decisions, decreases the accuracy of the system.

Experiment 2: Competence Analysis. Competence analysis was conducted on six combined case bases, one for each LLM tested, consisting of the original case base plus all hallucinations cataloged for that specific model. Hallucinated cases required for correct solutions (i.e., problem-useful hallucinated cases) were tagged as useful. To assess competence contributions at a global and individual level, eight measures were used, based on competence groups, footprint sets, and relative coverage (RC) scores:

1. The number of competence groups and their composition, including total hallucinations and the proportion of problem-useful hallucinations.
2. The number of footprints and their composition.
3. The average RC score of cases in the combined case base.
4. The average and standard deviation of RC scores for original cases.
5. The average and standard deviation of RC scores for hallucinated cases.
6. The number of original cases above the average RC score and their average.
7. The number of hallucinated cases above the average RC score and their average.
8. The number of standard deviations above average for the groups in items 6 and 7.

The number of competence groups and footprint sets, and their composition, indicates the overlap in coverage between hallucinated cases and their original dataset counterparts. This reflects the extent to which hallucinated cases are competent to solve known problems in the domain. The composition of the footprint set and individual competence contributions given by RC score provide a finer grained indication of the competence contributions of hallucinated cases by directly comparing their contributions to the original dataset. Equivalent or greater averages in competence contribution for hallucinated cases demonstrate concrete examples of cases highly valuable for competence hallucinated cases. If a hallucinated case belongs to the same competence groups as original cases, exists in the footprint set, or has a higher than average RC score, it can be considered a candidate for a useful ghost case. We expect that problem-useful hallucinated cases will meet more of these criteria than not-yet-useful hallucinated cases.

Experiment 3: Targeted Inclusion of Hallucinated Cases. This experiment tests a method for selecting which hallucinated cases to retain and the effects of retention. For this, we added to the system a new module, Targeted Inclusion and Feedback (TIF). TIF operates with a modified case base containing cases with the highest competence (e.g., either cases from the footprint set or with very high RC scores as described in Sect. 6.2) from the combined case base from Experiment 2. When a hallucinated case is detected in an LLM response, TIF retrieves a similar case [18] from the modified case base, with the goal of using known competent cases as a proxy for identifying hallucinated cases that are potentially valuable for competence. If a newly hallucinated case is "sufficiently similar" to a known competence-important case, it is allowed to bypass reduction and will be retained for future use. For the experiments, the threshold for "sufficiently similar" was set to the average similarity of cases in the combined case bases (here, .57). We believe that an expansion-contraction maintenance strategy could be used in the future to manage this growing set of cases [6].

Hypotheses
To assess whether similar, previously-seen, competence-important hallucinated cases can be used as a proxy for predicting competence of a newly detected case, and whether such hallucinated cases are useful to retain, this experiment tests one hypothesis:

3.1. When suspected competence-important hallucinated cases are retained and applied, accuracy is improved.

6 Results

6.1 Experiment 1: Model Generalizability

Hypothesis 1.1: Other LLMs Have High Case Hallucination Rates. - Supported
Table 1 displays the recorded hallucination rates for each of the models and knowledge formulations tested. Although Llama3 70B was not tested during this experiment, it was included in the table as a reference for the high hallucination rate found in the previous Hallucination Feedback experiments [19]. The table displays two different percentages for 2NN and NUN because the LLM was required to make two different selections during prompting.

Table 1. LLM case hallucination rates. The ECBR 2NN and NUN rows have two different values because two selections (i.e., two cases need to be selected for this prompt) are made by the LLM: NN (first selection) and 2NN or NUN (second selection).

Prompt Types		Llama3 70B	Llama3 8B	Gemma 2 9B	Gemma 3 4B	Med Gemma 4B	Mistral 7B
ECBR 1NN		32%	64%	90.6%	44%	84%	82.6%
ECBR 2NN	NN	32%	64%	96%	44%	98%	82.6%
	2NN	68%	74.6%	88%	66.6%	2.6%	97.3%
ECBR NUN	NN	32%	69.3%	89%	92%	97.3%	90.6%
	NUN	44%	93.3%	86%	84%	74.6%	97.3%

With the exception of MedGemma 4B 2NN second selection (see Table 1), the new models hallucinated at rates equivalent to or higher than Llama3 70B. In many cases, Llama3 70B has lower case hallucination rates than its peers on the same task. Accordingly, this hypothesis is considered to be supported by the data.

Hypothesis 1.2: Removing Hallucinated Cases from Responses Decreases the Accuracy of the System. - Not Supported
Table 2 provides information on the accuracy of each model on the original and HF experiments, with the final column displaying the total change in accuracy. Again, Llama3 70B is included in this table as a reference point. A Paired Samples t-Test found that no statistically significant decreases ($p = .464$, $t = .748$) in accuracy occurred for any of the models tested. Despite this, a majority of the 18 results in the table experienced negative impacts from the removal of hallucinated cases. This is consistent with the previous experiments on Llama3 70B.

6.2 Experiment 2: Competence Analysis

Competence Groups: For each of the six combined case bases tested, only one competence group was generated. This indicates that in a case base where hallucinated cases generated by each model are included with original cases, the hallucinated cases are capable of solving the original cases and vice versa.

Footprint Sets: The second to last column in Table 3 displays the percentage of hallucinated cases belonging to the footprint set. With the exception of Gemma 2 9B, hallucinated cases constituted the majority of the footprints for each model's competence group. This demonstrates that hallucinated cases not only play a role in the problem-solving power of the case base, but are primary contributors.

Relative Coverage Scores: The average RC score for each of the six combined case bases was close to 1.0. When hallucinated cases were separated from the original cases, the average RC score of hallucinated cases tended to be slightly lower and the variance slightly higher than their original dataset counterparts.

Table 2. Accuracy Rates for the Original Experiment and the Hallucination Feedback Experiment, organized by prompt type and model.

Model	Prompt Type	Original Accuracy	Hallucination Feedback Accuracy	Change
Llama 3 70B	ECBR 1NN	40%	28%	-12%
	ECBR 2NN	36%	32%	-4%
	ECBR NUN	36%	32%	-4%
Llama 3.1 8B	ECBR 1NN	34.6%	21.3%	-13.3%
	ECBR 2NN	36%	33%	-3%
	ECBR NUN	36%	41.3%	+5.3%
Gemma 2 9B	ECBR 1NN	37.3%	41.3%	+4%
	ECBR 2NN	40%	38.6%	-2.4%
	ECBR NUN	40%	36%	-4%
Gemma 3 4B	ECBR 1NN	36%	36%	0%
	ECBR 2NN	14.6%	36%	+21.4%
	ECBR NUN	8%	6.6%	-2.4%
Med Gemma 4B	ECBR 1NN	36%	42.6%	+6.6%
	ECBR 2NN	29.3%	37.3%	+8%
	ECBR NUN	29.3%	21.3%	-8%
Mistral 7B	ECBR 1NN	34.6%	21.3%	-13.3%
	ECBR 2NN	21.3%	20%	-1.3%
	ECBR NUN	20%	13.3%	-6.7%

Table 3. The total number of unique (i.e., no duplicates) hallucinated cases ("Hals") generated by each model and size of footprint set of each model. The final two columns describe footprint set composition.

Model	No. of Hals Generated	No. of Footprints	Hals in Footprint Set (%)	Useful Hals in Footprint Set (%)
Llama3 70B	280	143	74%	41.5%
Llama3 8B	119	14	64%	11%
Gemma 2 9B	85	9	44.4%	0%
Gemma 3 4B	115	13	61.5%	0%
MedGemma 4B	62	4	75%	0%
Mistral 7B	122	10	50%	40%

Interestingly, when the ranges of RC scores for each group were examined, hallucinated cases tended to have higher RC maximums. Table 4 lists the proportion of cases with above average RC scores for both the hallucinated and original cases. For each of the models tested, the proportion of above average hallucinated cases was quite small. When combined with the greater variance, this likely caused the lower RC average for all hallucinated cases.

Given the potential desirability of harvesting competence-important cases, Table 4 provides further analysis on the portion of above average cases for each group. The average RC scores for the hallucinated group tend to be larger than and are at least one standard deviation above the RC scores for the original dataset. This means that, on average, the richest hallucinated cases tend to make greater unique contributions to competence than the richest cases from the original dataset. Furthermore, the rate at which these cases are generated and the standard deviation differences argue that while competence-important hallucinated cases occur less frequently, they tend to be especially valuable.

Table 4. Proportion of cases above average with the composition of problem-useful hallucinated cases ("Hals"). Averages (avg.) and standard deviations (sd) above average are listed.

Model	Hals Above Avg.	Problem Useful Hals	Avg. RC Score	SD Above Avg.	Originals Above Avg.	Avg. RC Score	SD Above Avg.
Llama3 70B	2.8%	75%	1.93	> 3	7%	1.93	> 3
Llama3 8B	11.8%	50%	2.76	> 2	43%	2.12	> 1
Gemma 2 9B	18.8%	31%	2.16	> 2	43%	1.76	> 1
Gemma 3 4B	13.9%	18.7%	2.47	> 2	43%	2.07	1
MedGemma 4B	17.7%	54.5%	2.28	> 2	43%	1.6	1
Mistral 7B	18.8%	50%	1.84	> 2	43%	2.17	> 1

Proportion of Problem-Useful Hallucinated Cases: Table 3 lists the proportions of problem-useful hallucinated cases in the footprint sets for each model. None of these proportions reached 50%, and half of the models tested had no problem-useful hallucinated cases in the footprint set. Interestingly, this trend is reversed for the proportion of problem-useful hallucinated cases with above average RC scores (see Table 4). Two-thirds of the models tested had 50% or more problem-useful hallucinated cases. Thus, although problem-useful hallucinated cases are not strongly represented among footprint cases, they provide competence contributions that should be considered during retention.

6.3 Experiment 3: Targeted Inclusion of Hallucinated Cases

Hypothesis 3.1: When suspected competence-important hallucinated cases are allowed to bypass reduction and reused in the case base, system accuracy is improved. - Supported

Significance of results was assessed using two Wilcoxon Signed Rank tests to determine whether any statistically significant increases occurred between (1) the original system and the system with the TIF module and (2) the use of the HF and TIF modules. The Wilcoxon Signed Rank test is a non-parametric alternative to the Paired Samples t-Test and was used because both groups had significant Shapiro-Wilk test results ($p=.002$ and $p=.028$, respectively) indicating non-normality in the data distribution. Because these hypotheses do not directly consider the impact of knowledge formulations (1NN, 2NN, NUN), each pairing of an LLM and knowledge formulation is considered an individual measurement ($N=18$). Significance was set at 0.05.

The Wilcoxon Signed Rank tests revealed statistically significant increases by the TIF module over both the original system ($p = 0.017$, $z = -2.395$) and the HF module ($p = 0.01$, $z = -2.587$). A closer inspection of the accuracy results (see Table 5) shows that 14 of the 18 LLM and knowledge formulation pairings have increased accuracy over the original system and 12 of the 18 have increased accuracy over the HF module. Accuracy improvements were at or over 10% for 6 of the 14 improvements over the original system and 4 of the 12 improvements over the HF module; the majority of these improvements were over 20%.

These results not only support this specific hypothesis, but point to a larger claim regarding the potential usefulness of hallucinated cases. The improvements demonstrated by the TIF module suggest that the *strategic* usage of hallucinated cases is more effective for raising accuracy than leaving hallucinations unchecked (i.e., the policy of the original system) and than the blanket removal of hallucinated cases (i.e., the policy of the HF module). Furthermore, the statistical significance of these improvements validates the competence modeling results from Experiment 2 by providing practical evidence that for our testbed task, hallucinated cases are not only competent in theory.

Table 5. Accuracy for baseline, Feedback, and Targeted Inclusion tests and the Original and Hallucination Feedback tests, followed by accuracy changes.

Model	Prompt Type	Original Accuracy	Hallucination Feedback Accuracy	Targeted Inclusion Feedback Accuracy	Change Over Original	Change Over Hallucination Feedback
Llama 3 70B	ECBR 1NN	40%	28%	84%	+44%	+56%
	ECBR 2NN	36%	32%	64%	+28%	+32%
	ECBR NUN	36%	32%	76%	+40%	+44%
Llama 3.1 8B	ECBR 1NN	34.6%	21.3%	45.3%	+10.7%	+24%
	ECBR 2NN	36%	33%	40%	+4%	+7%
	ECBR NUN	36%	41.3%	40%	+4%	-1.3%
Gemma 2 9B	ECBR 1NN	37.3%	41.3%	41.3%	+4%	0%
	ECBR 2NN	40%	38.6%	42.6%	+2.6%	-4%
	ECBR NUN	40%	36%	37.3%	-2.7%	+1.3%
Gemma 3 4B	ECBR 1NN	36%	36%	36%	0%	0%
	ECBR 2NN	14.6%	36%	33%	+18.4%	-3%
	ECBR NUN	8%	6.6%	10.6%	+2.6%	+4%
Med Gemma 4B	ECBR 1NN	36%	42.6%	40%	+4%	-2.6%
	ECBR 2NN	29.3%	37.3%	44%	+14.7%	+6.7%
	ECBR NUN	29.3%	21.3%	13.3%	-16%	-10%
Mistral 7B	ECBR 1NN	34.6%	21.3%	29.3%	-5.3%	+8%
	ECBR 2NN	21.3%	20%	29.3%	+8%	+9.3%
	ECBR NUN	20%	13.3%	22.6%	+2.6%	+9.3%

7 Conclusions

This paper investigated two surprising observations from previous early research on an LLM-based CBR system: that hallucinations affecting provided cases were common and that removal of hallucinated cases could actually reduce system accuracy. Experiment 1 (generalizability) supported that high rates of hallucinated cases are common among the tested models and that accuracy suffers when the hallucinations are removed from responses. Experiment 2 (competence analysis) revealed that while the hallucinated cases tested are capable of solving problems, their coverage of the case base varies; a subset of hallucinated cases is competence-important and those cases tend to be abnormally so when compared to their original dataset counterparts. Furthermore, problem-useful hallucinated cases tended to be overrepresented among these abnormally competence-important cases, which demonstrates applicability of the problem-useful hallucinated cases beyond the problem they were originally able to solve. Not-yet-useful hallucinated cases with similar competence might be useful for future problems. Experiment 3 (targeted inclusion) showed that the strategic use of hallucinated cases statistically improves accuracy over situations where hallucinated cases are left in responses or removed entirely. The results from these three experiments support that hallucinated cases can provide competent, synthetic data—promising candidate ghost cases—generated during processing by the LLM, and that when used, they can improve the ability of an LLM-based CBR system to solve problems.

The experiments in this paper have three primary limitations to address in future research. First, because the experiments use a single dataset, tests are needed to study domain generalizability of the results and whether certain dataset properties lead to more beneficial hallucinated cases. Second, because the experiments focus on the competence of individual cases, study is needed on the impact of retaining hallucinated cases on overall case-base competence and total competence gain over a series of problems. Finally, human subject testing is needed to assess how hallucinated cases affect perceived trustworthiness of explanations of solutions. Experiments for additional domains and total competence gain are planned for the near future.

Acknowledgments and Declaration on Generative AI. This work was funded by the US Department of Defense (Contract W52P1J2093009). This research was supported in part by Lilly Endowment, Inc., through its support for the Indiana University Pervasive Technology Institute. The authors did not use any generative AI for the preparation of this paper.

References

1. Bach, K., et al.: Case-Based Reasoning Meets Large Language Models: A Research Manifesto For Open Challenges and Research Directions (2025). https://hal.science/hal-05006761
2. Bang, Y., et al.: A Multitask, Multilingual, Multimodal Evaluation of ChatGPT on Reasoning, Hallucination, and Interactivity. In: Proceedings of the 13th International Joint Conference on Natural Language Processing and the 3rd Conference of the Asia-Pacific Chapter of the Association for Computational Linguistics (volume 1: Long papers), pp. 675–718 (2023)
3. Gao, Y., et al.: Retrieval-Augmented Generation for Large Language Models: A Survey. arXiv preprint arXiv:2312.10997 (2023)
4. Hammond, K., Leake, D.: Large Language Models Need Symbolic AI. In: Proceedings of the 17th International Workshop on Neural-Symbolic Learning and Reasoning, La Certosa di Pontignano, Siena, Italy. vol. 3432, pp. 204–209 (2023)
5. Kang, H., Ni, J., Yao, H.: Ever: Mitigating Hallucination in Large Language Models Through Real-Time Verification and Rectification. arXiv preprint arXiv:2311.09114 (2023)

6. Leake, D., Schack, B.: Exploration vs. exploitation in case-base maintenance: leveraging competence-based deletion with ghost cases. In: Cox, M.T., Funk, P., Begum, S. (eds.) ICCBR 2018. LNCS (LNAI), vol. 11156, pp. 202–218. Springer, Cham (2018). https://doi.org/10.1007/978-3-030-01081-2_14
7. Lei, D., et al.: Chain of Natural Language Inference for Reducing Large Language Model Ungrounded Hallucinations. arXiv preprint arXiv:2310.03951 (2023)
8. Lenz, M., Bergmann, R.: Case-Based Adaptation of Argument Graphs with WordNet and Large Language Models. In: Case-Based Reasoning Research and Development, ICCBR 2023, pp. 263–278. Springer (2023)
9. Lenz, M., Hoffmann, M., Bergmann, R.: LLSim: Large Language Models for Similarity Assessment in Case-based Reasoning. In: Case-Based Reasoning Research and Development ICCBR 2025, pp. 126–141. Springer (2025)
10. Liu, J., et al.: Generated Knowledge Prompting for Commonsense Reasoning. arXiv preprint arXiv:2110.08387 (2021)
11. Lupton, J.R., et al.: Under-triage and over-triage using the field triage guidelines for injured patients: a systematic review. Prehosp. Emerg. Care **27**(1), 38–45 (2023)
12. Newgard, C.D., et al.: National guideline for the field triage of injured patients: recommendations of the national expert panel on field triage, 2021. J. Trauma Acute Care Surg. **93**(2), e49–e60 (2022)
13. Peng, B., et al.: Check Your Facts and Try Again: Improving Large Language Models with External Knowledge and Automated Feedback. CoRR abs/2302.12813 (2023)
14. Regulagedda, R., Krupashankar, N., Leake, D.: Keep adaptation simple: Implicit vs. explicit adaptation for LLM-based CBR. In: Case-Based Reasoning Research and Development, ICCBR 2026. Springer (2026). in press
15. Smyth, B., Keane, M.: Remembering to forget: a competence-preserving case deletion policy for case-based reasoning systems. In: Proceedings of the Thirteenth International Joint Conference on Artificial Intelligence, pp. 377–382. Morgan Kaufmann, San Mateo (1995)
16. Smyth, B., McKenna, E.: Building compact competent case-bases. In: International Conference on Case-Based Reasoning, pp. 329–342. Springer (1999)
17. Smyth, B., McKenna, E.: Competence models and the maintenance problem. Comput. Intell. **17**(2), 235–249 (2001)
18. Wilkerson, K., Leake, D.: On Implementing Case-Based Reasoning with Large Language Models. In: International Conference on Case-Based Reasoning, pp. 404–417. Springer (2024)
19. Wilkerson, K., Leake, D.: Case Hallucinations and Steps Toward Repair. In: Proceedings of the Workshops at the 33rd International Conference on Case-Based Reasoning (ICCBR-WS 2025) co-located with the 33rd International Conference on Case-Based Reasoning (ICCBR 2025), Biarritz, France, 30 June 2025. CEUR Workshop Proceedings, CEUR-WS.org (2025)
20. Wiratunga, N., et al.: CBR-RAG: Case-Based Reasoning for Retrieval Augmented Generation in LLMs for Legal Question Answering. In: Case-Based Reasoning Research and Development, ICCBR 2024, pp. 445–460. Springer (2024)
21. Xu, Z., Jain, S., Kankanhalli, M.: Hallucination is Inevitable: An Innate Limitation of Large Language Models. arXiv preprint arXiv:2401.11817 (2024)

Keep Adaptation Simple: Implicit vs. Explicit Adaptation for LLM-Based CBR

Ravi Regulagedda[1](✉), Nischal Bangalore Krupashankar[2], and David Leake[1]

[1] Luddy School of Informatics, Computing, and Engineering, Indiana University, Bloomington, IN 47408, USA
{raregul,leake}@iu.edu
[2] PamirAI Incorporated, San Francisco, CA 94109, USA
nischal@pamir.ai

Abstract. The remarkable capabilities of large language models (LLMs) have prompted interest in LLM-based support for the case-based reasoning (CBR) process, including LLM implementations of each step of the CBR cycle. However, CBR research showing the tight coupling of retrieval and adaptation suggests potential benefits of a more unified approach. This paper presents an LLM-based CBR architecture and uses it to compare the performance explicitly guiding the model to perform adaptation versus having adaptation arise implicitly within LLM processing. It tests four architectures varying along two dimensions–retrieval mechanism (explicit multi-stage, with separate LLM calls for retrieval sub-tasks, vs. unified, with a single LLM call for all retrieval reasoning) and adaptation mechanism (explicit multi-stage, with prompting steps guiding adaptation, vs. implicit, with a single LLM call)—across six LLM models from three families, on GSM8K and MATH data sets. Performance of the case-based unified retrieval architecture, which presents the retrieved cases and the problem in a single context window, matches published few-shot chain-of-thought benchmarks without requiring curated few-shot examples. In contrast, explicit multi-stage adaptation consistently degrades accuracy. A failure analysis identifies fourteen distinct ways in which multi-stage adaptation may destroy information. Our results suggest the *simple adaptation hypothesis*: In LLM-based CBR systems for such domains, adaptation should be implicitly performed by the LLM rather than by explicit multi-stage prompting.

1 Introduction

Large Language Models (LLMs) provide remarkable capabilities over a broad range of tasks but remain unreliable at structured, multi-step reasoning, with failure modes including hallucinated intermediate steps and inconsistent rule application [8,17]. CBR, by bringing to bear specific prior examples, offers a natural complement to the generalization of LLMs, which has prompted much

R. Regulagedda and N. Bangalore Krupashankar—contributed equally.

L. Malburg and K. Bach (Eds.): ICCBR 2026, LNAI 16780, pp. 285–300, 2027.
https://doi.org/10.1007/978-3-032-33865-5_18

interest in how CBR can support LLMs, and vice versa [2]. One such area is LLM-based implementations of the entire CBR process [18].

A natural approach to such implementations is to apply LLM-based reasoning to successive steps of the CBR process. However, previous CBR research presents evidence for tight coupling between steps of the CBR process (e.g., [10,14]). This suggests the question of whether LLM-based CBR should implement phases of the CBR process through explicit guidance for each step or in a more unified way, as an effect of prompting the LLM to apply a case to a new problem.

This paper presents a general LLM-based architecture for CBR and applies it to four testbed systems for reasoning in a mathematical problem-solving domain. These systems vary along two dimensions. The first is *retrieval mechanism*: an *explicit retrieval pipeline* in which separate LLM calls handle similarity assessment, case ranking, and new case construction from retrieved documents; versus a *unified retrieval* approach in which a single LLM call performs all retrieval reasoning. The second is *adaptation mechanism*: *explicit adaptation*, in which dedicated LLM stages implement adaptation by generating a reasoning chain that applies this approach to the new problem, and performing an error analysis that checks the adapted solution for consistency before producing a final answer; versus *implicit adaptation*, in which the retrieved case is passed directly to the solver and adaptation arises naturally from the LLM's internal processing over the combined context.

We evaluate the system variants on two mathematical reasoning datasets across three LLM families. In these tests, unified retrieval with implicit adaptation achieves high accuracy across all models above 10B parameters, while explicit multi-stage adaptation consistently degrades performance. The performance effects of retrieval and adaptation design dominate those of model choice, with implicit retrieval resulting in large performance gains on grade-school-level problems but not reliably on competition-level problems, revealing limits of surface-similarity retrieval on competition-level problems.

The paper makes the following contributions:

1. It presents a domain-agnostic LLM-based CBR architecture implemented with two variants for retrieval (explicit and unified) and adaptation (implicit and explicit), applicable to any case base, available as a community resource[1]. This repository also contains all experiment code.
2. It presents an evaluation across three model families, at multiple scales, and two benchmarks, providing evidence that architecture design dominates model choice for LLM-based CBR across model families: mid-size and large models converge to ~92% accuracy on GSM8K under unified retrieval, comparable to published 8-shot chain-of-thought results without curated examples.
3. It develops a failure taxonomy for explicit case adaptation, identifying fourteen distinct failure types across ~6000 failure cases. The types suggest that the issue in the multi-step process is post-retrieval processing, not retrieval itself, and that explicit adaptation can degrade quality as each adaptation

[1] https://github.com/raregul/keeping-adaptation-simple.

stage compounds errors by treating its predecessor's output as authoritative without cross-referencing the original problem.

2 Related Work

Reasoning in Large Language Models. Much recent work on LLM reasoning traces back to chain-of-thought (CoT) prompting [17], which showed that asking a model to produce intermediate reasoning steps can lead to large performance gains on arithmetic and commonsense tasks. Recent work includes self-consistency decoding, which samples multiple reasoning paths and takes a majority vote [16], tree-of-thought prompting, which explores branching solution paths [20], and least-to-most prompting, which decomposes hard problems into simpler sub-problems [21]. However, models can still produce chains that contain logical errors or struggle with problems that require combining familiar reasoning steps in new ways [6]. In our approach, rather than building reasoning chains from scratch, reasoning steps in retrieving solved cases serve as implicit CoT examples, for the model to ground its reasoning in demonstrated solutions.

Retrieval-Augmented Generation: RAG [12], which retrieves related facts to augment queries, is a standard technique for grounding LLM outputs in external knowledge. RAG has demonstrated effectiveness in multiple domains. However, even strong embedding models struggle to retrieve structurally similar problems, suggesting that standard embeddings match on surface features rather than reasoning structure [15]. Recent work on solution-guided retrieval [3,5,13] trains retrievers to match on solution structure; integrating such retrievers into CBR pipelines is a promising direction we discuss in Sect. 7.

Integrating Case-Based Reasoning with LLMs: CBR-LLM integrations have recently gained traction; a community paper [2] lays out a research agenda and argues that the relationship is symbiotic: LLMs can help CBR, for example by automating case acquisition, learning similarity measures, and proposing adaptation rules or directly performing case adaptation, while CBR can help LLMs, for example, by structuring retrieval, planning reasoning chains, and grounding outputs in concrete precedents. Initial empirical research has tested LLM capabilities for CBR sub-tasks such as similarity assessment [11] and fuller CBR processing [18]. That work found accuracy improvements but also the need for careful prompt design and risk of case hallucinations.

CBR-RAG [19] applies CBR retrieval to structure Retrieval-Augmented Generation, for legal question answering. It uses indexing vocabulary and similarity knowledge to select contextually relevant cases, and is shown to provide better answer quality than standard RAG. This work suggests the promise of CBR in imposing a useful structure on what would otherwise be a generic retrieval step. The work in this paper applies a similar perspective to mathematical reasoning.

Table 1. System configurations. MN = Multi-Node, UR = Unified Retrieval, RO = Retrieval-Only, FA = Full-Architecture (explicit adaptation).

Config	Retrieval	Adaptation	LLM Calls	Description
LLM-BL	None	None	1	Direct prompting baseline
MN-RO	Multi-node	Minimal	6–9+	Multi-stage retrieval, case → solver
MN-FA	Multi-node	Explicit 3-stage	9–12+	Multi-stage retrieval + explicit adaptation
UR-RO	Unified	Minimal	2	Single retrieval call, case → solver
UR-FA	Unified	Explicit 3-stage	4	Single retrieval call + explicit adaptation

3 An Architecture for LLM-Based CBR and Variants

We have designed, implemented, and evaluated a general architecture for CBR-augmented reasoning using LLMs. The design is domain-agnostic: It can be applied to any domain with a case base of solved problems simply by providing it to the system.

Based on this architecture, we developed four testbeds varying along two independent dimensions: the *retrieval mechanism*—how cases are found and validated, and the *adaptation mechanism*—how retrieved cases are processed before answer generation. Crossing these two dimensions yields four configurations, which we compared to a zero-shot baseline with no retrieval. Table 1 summarizes the five configurations. No model fine-tuning is performed, and all reasoning is done through zero-shot prompting.

We consider a *case* to be a structured representation that contains the problem statement, a step-by-step reasoning chain and the solution. The case base provided to the system contains this information in a textual form. During retrieval, a structured case is generated with solution strategies and supporting facts from retrieved documents, which is then passed to the adaptation process to generate the reasoning chain and the solution. Both retrieval variants construct these structured cases, either through a sequence of prompts (explicit, multi-stage) or with a single prompt (implicit). This structured case allows us to transfer a unified solution strategy from the retrieved cases to the adaptation mechanism, letting that phase focus solely on problem-solving from the retrieved information (Fig. 1).

3.1 Retrieval Variants

The retrieval mechanism has two variants, multi-node and unified.

Multi-node (MN) Pipeline: The *explicit multi-stage retrieval* pipeline consists of the following stages:

1. **Front-end**: Extracts keywords and structures the query for retrieval.
2. **Retrieve**: Performs vector similarity search over the case base.

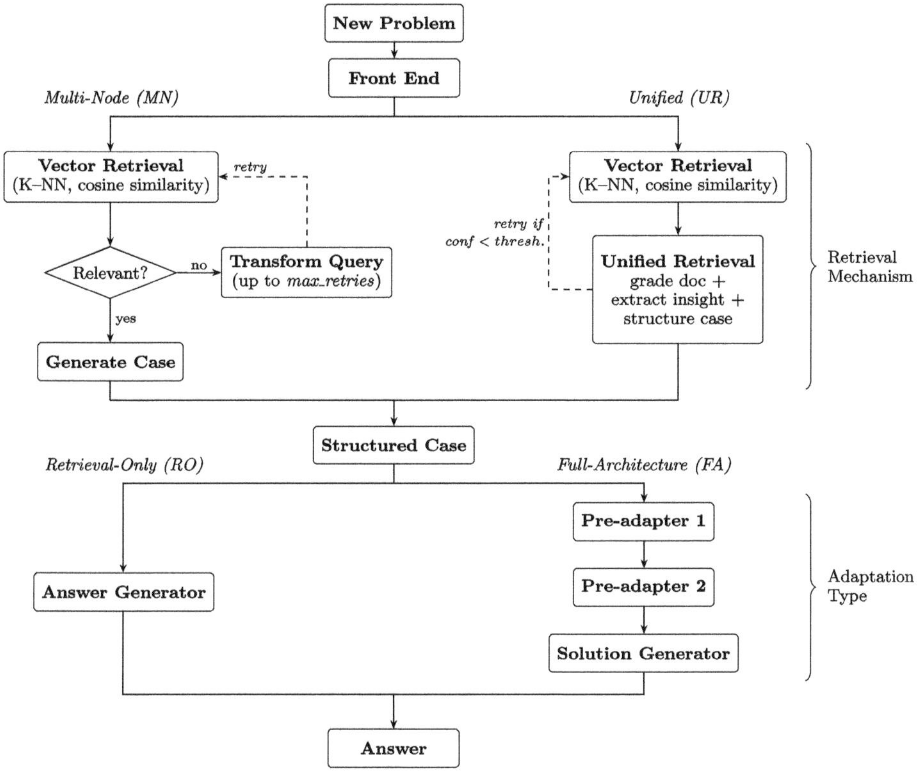

Fig. 1. System architecture, varying along two independent dimensions: *retrieval mechanism* (Multi-Node vs. Unified) and *adaptation mechanism* (Retrieval-Only vs. Full-Architecture).

3. **Grade documents**: An LLM call judges each retrieved document for relevance, filtering out cases that match on surface features but not reasoning structure.
4. **Transform query** (loop, max 3 iterations): If grading rejects all documents, the query is reformulated and retrieval is retried.
5. **Generate case**: Structures the approved documents into a case representation containing relevance summaries, problem breakdowns, supporting facts, and solution approaches.
6. **Generate answer**: Adaptation module produces the final answer using the structured case.

This pipeline requires 6–9+ LLM calls per question, depending on the number of retrieval retries. When all retrieval attempts fail, a fallback mechanism routes directly to LLM answer generation without case context.

Unified Retrieval (UR) Pipeline: The *unified retrieval* pipeline collapses the multi-node pipeline into a single LLM call. After vector retrieval returns a set of K candidate documents, one LLM call performs document grading, relevance assessment, hallucination checking, fact extraction, and case structuring within a single context window. The output is a structured case representation identical to that produced by the multi-node pipeline, but generated in a single pass.

A confidence-based retry mechanism (max 2 retries) generates alternatives if the model is uncertain about the quality of the generated case. The LLM is prompted to rate how well the constructed case can guide a solution to the current problem, producing a confidence score in [0, 1]. If confidence is below a set threshold, retrieval and case generation are repeated.

The multi-node and unified approaches reflect a potential trade-off: isolated calls could in principle allow each stage to specialize and validate intermediate outputs, while a single integrated context allows the LLM to act on all information at the hidden-representation level. Our experiments test which of these benefits dominates in practice.

3.2 Adaptation Variants

Each retrieval mechanism is paired with either of two adaptation strategies:

Retrieval-Only (RO): The structured case from retrieval is passed directly to a final answer generator. The LLM receives the original question plus the case and produces an answer. This represents *implicit adaptation*, in which the LLM is prompted to adapt retrieved patterns through its attention mechanism.

Full-Architecture (FA): After case generation, three *explicit adaptation* stages process the case before answer generation:

1. **Pre-adapter 1**: Analyzes the case to identify relevant solution patterns, analogies, and potential pitfalls.
2. **Pre-adapter 2**: Refines the identified patterns and generates specific transformation guidelines for the current problem.
3. **Solution generator**: Produces a step-by-step solution using the adapted case information.

4 Experimental Questions and Design

Our experiments address four questions:

1. **Implicit vs. explicit adaptation**: When retrieval is held constant, does implicit or explicit adaptation produce better results?
2. **How can adaptation fail?** What types of issues cause either type of adaptation to break down?
3. **Architecture vs. model scale**: Does architecture choice or model choice matter more for these systems?
4. **Is retrieval the problem?** Do adaptation failures stem more from poor retrieval quality, or from the adaptation process itself?

Table 2. Models evaluated are instruction-tuned variants without fine-tuning.

Family	Model	Parameters
Qwen 2.5	Qwen2.5-7B-Instruct	7B
	Qwen2.5-14B-Instruct	14B
	Qwen2.5-32B-Instruct	32B
Gemma 3	gemma-3-12b-it	12B
	gemma-3-27b-it	27B
Llama 3.1	Llama-3.1-8B-Instruct	8B

Experimental Setup: We set the number K of documents retrieved initially to 4 and the confidence threshold for the unified retriever (UR) variant to 0.3.

Models: We evaluate six instruction-tuned LLMs from three model families, spanning 7B to 32B parameters (Table 2). No fine-tuning is performed; all models are used with zero-shot prompting.

Datasets: We evaluate on two mathematical reasoning benchmarks. **GSM8K** [4] contains 7,473 training and 1,319 test problems requiring grade-school level mathematical reasoning (arithmetic, fractions, word problems). Answers are integers, enabling exact-match evaluation. **MATH** [7] contains 7,500 training and 5,000 test problems spanning seven subjects (algebra, geometry, number theory, counting and probability, intermediate algebra, precalculus, prealgebra) at competition level. Answers are LaTeX expressions (fractions, radicals, symbolic expressions), requiring symbolic equivalence checking.

Our baseline (LLM-BL) uses zero-shot direct prompting, which differs from published benchmarks that typically use 8-shot chain-of-thought [17]. This makes our baselines deliberately weaker to isolate the effect of retrieval augmentation. Published GSM8K results for Qwen 14B and 32B are 94.8% and 95.9% respectively under 8-shot CoT; our zero-shot baselines for the same models are 38.1% and 37.2%. Under unified retrieval, these same models recover to ~92% accuracy, nearly matching 8-shot CoT. Our experiments use the train split as the case base and automatically retrieve relevant cases for each test example.This suggests that much of the benefit of 8-shot CoT can be recovered by retrieving examples from a broad in-domain case base, without needing manually curated few-shot examples.

Evaluation Metrics: GSM8K solution quality is evaluated by exact numeric match after extracting the final numerical answer from model output. MATH solution quality is evaluated by a three-tier comparison. The primary strategy parses the model answer and ground truth as LaTeX expressions and checks whether their symbolic difference simplifies to zero; when that fails, it falls back to numeric evaluation within tolerance. Its final fallback is to compare normalized string representations. All configurations are evaluated on the full test sets.

Table 3. GSM8K accuracy (%) across models and configurations. Best in **bold**. †Llama 8B results are affected by systematic formatting errors.

Model	LLM-BL	MN-RO	MN-FA	UR-RO	UR-FA
Qwen 7B	80.21	66.57	22.29	**80.06**	23.88
Qwen 14B	38.13	73.92	28.89	**92.04**	27.90
Qwen 32B	37.23	47.08	14.56	**91.89**	15.62
Gemma 12B	22.37	85.75	22.67	**91.28**	37.76
Gemma 27B	30.33	90.45	47.16	**92.95**	58.15
Llama 8B†	**42.76**	29.80	14.48	33.81	18.50

Retrieval Quality Tests: Because performance of later steps depends on upstream performance as well, before attributing downstream performance differences to architecture design, we test retrieval quality. Using an LLM-based document grader (the same method used in our multi-stage pipeline), we evaluate retrieval quality across both datasets. Dense retrieval with Nomic Embed v1.5 achieves a 78.5% document approval rate on GSM8K (97.6% coverage, which is the proportion of queries with at least one relevant retrieved case) and 71.4% on MATH (93.9% coverage). These rates confirm that the retrieval pipeline provides relevant cases for the vast majority of queries. We analyze retrieval quality and its implications further in Sect. 6.4.

5 Experimental Results

5.1 GSM8K Results

Table 3 presents accuracy across all 30 model–configuration combinations on GSM8K. Several patterns emerge:

Unified Retrieval Dominates for 12B+ Models. UR-RO achieves 91–93% for Qwen 14B/32B and Gemma 12B/27B, a remarkably tight range given that these models' baselines span 22–38%. In these tests, architecture design eliminates the 16-percentage-point gap between model families.

Multi-node Retrieval Helps, But Inconsistently. MN-RO produces large gains for Gemma (85–90%) but mixed results for Qwen (47–74%). The multi-node pipeline's 6–9 sequential LLM calls create opportunities for error propagation that the unified approach avoids.

Explicit Adaptation is Consistently Harmful. Both MN-FA and UR-FA degrade accuracy relative to their retrieval-only counterparts, with degradations ranging from 33 to 76 percentage points. The effect is particularly stark for UR-FA: starting from the same high-quality retrieval that produces 92% accuracy under UR-RO, adding three adaptation stages drops accuracy to 15–28% for Qwen and 38–58% for Gemma. This is the central finding of our work.

Table 4. MATH accuracy (%) across models and configurations. Best in **bold**.

Model	LLM-BL	MN-RO	MN-FA	UR-RO	UR-FA
Qwen 7B	**57.82**	18.38	6.90	29.16	11.76
Qwen 14B	24.84	7.90	16.92	12.76	**24.86**
Qwen 32B	**37.55**	7.98	24.70	12.22	29.78
Gemma 12B	21.54	75.62	26.40	**77.64**	34.64
Gemma 27B	36.58	81.14	34.94	**82.92**	41.74
Llama 8B	5.52	10.10	6.96	**10.20**	8.70

Small Models Hit a Capacity Ceiling. Qwen 7B achieves ~80% regardless of configuration, suggesting that at 7B parameters, the model's intrinsic reasoning capacity is the binding constraint. Llama 8B generated systematic formatting failures that prevent fair evaluation of retrieval benefits.

5.2 MATH Results

To test whether these patterns generalize beyond grade-school mathematics, we evaluate on the MATH dataset competition-level problems. Table 4 presents accuracy across all five configurations. Results suggest the following observations:

Unified Retrieval Still Outperforms Multi-node. UR-RO matches or exceeds MN-RO for every model: Qwen 7B (+10.8%), Qwen 14B (+4.9%), Qwen 32B (+4.2%), Gemma 12B (+2.0%), and Gemma 27B (+1.8%). The advantage of unified context persists on harder problems.

Retrieval Helps Gemma But Hurts Qwen. The baseline results reveal a model-family split. Qwen models achieve strong baselines (Qwen 7B: 57.82%, Qwen 32B: 37.55%) that retrieval-augmented configurations cannot match; Qwen 7B's best retrieval result (UR-RO, 29.16%) is half its baseline. In contrast, Gemma models see large gains from retrieval: Gemma 12B from 21.54% to 77.64% under UR-RO (+56%), and Gemma 27B from 36.58% to 82.92% (+46%). This contrasts with GSM8K, where retrieval helped all models above 10B.

Explicit Adaptation Remains Harmful. MN-FA and UR-FA consistently underperform their retrieval-only counterparts for Gemma models on MATH. Gemma 27B falls from 82.92% to 41.74% (−41%) and Gemma 12B from 77.64% to 34.64% (−43%) when adding explicit adaptation to UR-RO. For Qwen 14B and 32B, UR-FA outperforms UR-RO (+12% and +18% respectively), but neither exceeds the zero-shot baseline for Qwen 32B, and Qwen 14B's best retrieval result (UR-FA, 24.86%) only matches its baseline (24.84%).

5.3 Cross-Dataset Comparison

Comparing GSM8K and MATH results shows which findings apply across both:

Generalized Conclusions. Two conclusions hold across both datasets. Unified retrieval consistently outperforms multi-node retrieval, confirming that consolidated context is preferable to sequential processing regardless of problem difficulty. Explicit adaptation is harmful across both datasets for models where retrieval helps, with the same failure mechanisms identified in Sect. 6.2.

Dataset-Dependent Conclusions. The tight convergence under UR-RO seen on GSM8K (91–93% for all 12B+ models) breaks down on MATH. Gemma models benefit enormously from retrieval (Gemma 12B: 21.54% to 77.64%, Gemma 27B: 36.58% to 82.92%), while Qwen models are actively harmed by it (Qwen 7B: 57.82% to 29.16%, Qwen 32B: 37.55% to 12.22% under the same UR-RO architecture). On grade-school problems, surface-similar retrieved cases reliably share solution structure, so retrieval helps universally. On competition-level problems, surface similarity no longer guarantees solution relevance and models that cannot filter out misleading cases are worse off than with no retrieval at all. This points to a fundamental limitation of embedding-based retrieval for harder reasoning tasks, which we discuss further in Sect. 7.

6 Analysis

6.1 Question: Implicit vs. Explicit Adaptation

The contrast between UR-RO and UR-FA provides a clean test of implicit versus explicit adaptation. Both use identical retrieval (same unified retrieval call, same retrieved cases, same structured case). The only difference is what happens next: UR-RO passes the case directly to the solver, while UR-FA routes through three adaptation stages first.

On GSM8K, this difference is dramatic: UR-RO achieves 91–93% for 12B+ models, while UR-FA drops to 15–28% for Qwen and 38–58% for Gemma. The 430 failure cases all involve questions where the same retrieval input produced a correct answer under UR-RO but an incorrect one under UR-FA.

We interpret this as evidence that LLMs perform adaptation more effectively through their attention mechanism, operating over a unified context, than through explicit multi-stage token generation. When the model sees the question and retrieved cases together, it can selectively attend to relevant solution patterns, numerical details, and structural cues. When forced to generate an explicit adaptation plan across multiple stages, information is lost at each handoff.

This has implications for how we think about the "Revise" step in LLM-based CBR. Classical CBR assumes explicit adaptation is necessary to transfer solutions between cases. Our results suggest that for LLMs, the Revise step should be *implicit* and performed by the model's internal reasoning over unified context rather than externalized as a multi-stage pipeline.

6.2 Question: How Explicit Adaptation Degrades Performance

To understand why explicit adaptation degrades performance, we conducted a systematic analysis of failure cases. We identified 430 questions on GSM8K for

Table 5. Failure taxonomy for explicit adaptation across both datasets. Each row is a candidate where UR-RO succeeded but UR-FA failed under identical retrieval. *Italicized* codes appear in both datasets and represent mechanisms that transfer; non-italicized codes are dataset-specific.

GSM8K (n=430)				MATH (n=5,552)			
Code	Failure Mode	n	%	Code	Failure Mode	n	%
MAE	Minor Arithmetic Error	101	23.5	MTY	Mismatched Type	1,150	20.7
MFT	Missing Final Transformation	99	23.0	AIR	Answer In Reasoning	1,068	19.2
TSC	Temporal Semantic Confusion	53	12.3	WAF	Wrong Answer Form	395	7.1
CCH	Complete Context Hallucination	44	10.2	*MFT*	Missing Final Transformation	387	7.0
MC	Magnitude Confusion	24	5.6	*MC*	Magnitude Confusion	284	5.1
APE	Arithmetic Propagation Error	16	3.7	SCM	Symbolic Computation Mistake	216	3.9
NDS	Numerical Detail Stripping	8	1.9	UEX	Unevaluated Expression	196	3.5
EAIE	Error Analysis Introduces Error	7	1.6	*NDS*	Numerical Detail Stripping	158	2.8
				MAE	Minor Arithmetic Error	157	2.8
				AR	Adapter Refusal	34	0.6
	Unclassified	78	18.1		Unclassified	1,507	27.1

which UR-RO answered correctly but UR-FA answered incorrectly, with identical retrieval and only adaptation different. Using a heuristic rule-based classifier combining NLTK tokenization with numerical analysis, we classified 352 of these (81.9%) into eight failure modes. We then ran a parallel analysis on MATH (5,552 UR-RO-correct / UR-FA-wrong candidates), extending the classifier with six MATH-specific detectors to handle MATH's diverse answer space (symbolic expressions, intervals, tuples, LaTeX-formatted values). The unified taxonomy across both datasets is shown in Table 5.

The top three failure modes—Minor Arithmetic Error, Missing Final Transformation, and Temporal Semantic Confusion—account for 253 of 430 failures (59%) in GSM8K. These represent different ways in which information loss can occur:

Minor Arithmetic Error (MAE, 23.5%): The adaptation pipeline produces a solution that is on-topic and uses the right approach, but contains a small calculation error. For example, correctly identifying all prices and quantities but computing 7.5 instead of 5.5 in one intermediate step.

Missing Final Transformation (MFT, 23.0%): The pipeline solves most of the problem correctly but omits a final conversion or transformation step. A typical case: computing 80 legs correctly but failing to convert to "pairs" by dividing by 2. The unified solver, with the full problem visible, catches this; the adapter pipeline, having abstracted the problem across three stages, loses track of what the question actually asks.

Temporal Semantic Confusion (TSC, 12.3%): The fact extraction stage conflates time-related quantities (e.g., interpreting "$300/week" as "monthly

$300"), and subsequent stages propagate this error without cross-checking the original question.

A notable model-specific pattern: Complete Context Hallucination (CCH) is heavily concentrated in Qwen 14B, which accounts for 39 of 44 cases (89%). In these failures, the adaptation stages solve an unrelated retrieved case problem instead of the target question.

The common thread across all failure modes is that each adaptation stage treats its predecessor's output as authoritative, without cross-referencing the original question, even when it has access to the full information at every step. The unified approach avoids this by keeping all information in a single context upon which the model's attention mechanism freely operates.

MATH Surfaces a New Class of Failure: Presentation-Stage Breakdowns. The MATH analysis adds 5,552 candidates from six models, but only four of the eight GSM8K modes transfer (MAE, MFT, MC, NDS). The remaining MATH candidates concentrate in six new modes that do not exist on GSM8K. Two are dominant: *Mismatched Type* (MTY, 20.7%): the pipeline returns an answer of the wrong mathematical shape (e.g., a scalar when the ground truth is an interval, a coordinate point when an equation is expected, an integer when a decimal is expected), and *Answer In Reasoning* (AIR, 19.2%): the pipeline produces an answer that matches ground truth during the reasoning phases, but the final extraction stage fails to surface it cleanly. Together with *Wrong Answer Form* (WAF) and *Unevaluated Expression* (UEX), these four account for 50.5% of MATH failures. They are not new reasoning errors; they are the failures of a downstream stage that is supposed to deliver the answer in canonical form, and they exist on MATH only because MATH's answer space is heterogeneous enough to expose them.

Model-Specific Concentrations Differ Between Datasets. On GSM8K, CCH is concentrated in Qwen 14B (39/44). On MATH, AIR is concentrated in Gemma 12B and 27B (849/1,068) indicating the Gemma models reason toward the right answer but ramble in their final output. AR is essentially Gemma-only (30/34 on Gemma 12B), reflecting these models' tendency to commit to uncertainty rather than guessing. Qwen 14B's MATH candidate pool is smaller (420) and, as noted in Sect. 5.2, UR-FA outperforms UR-RO on this model at the aggregate level; a model-specific exception to the broader pattern.

Caveats. The taxonomy is heuristic and illustrative rather than exhaustive; the unclassified failures (18.1% on GSM8K, 27.1% on MATH) reflect heterogeneous failures rather than a single missing mode. The broader message is that multi-stage adaptation breaks down in many ways, and any single benchmark can indicate only the subset its answer structure permits; GSM8K and MATH together give a more complete picture than either alone.

6.3 Question: Architecture vs Model Scale

A striking finding across both datasets is that architecture design dominates model choice. On GSM8K, four models from two different families (Qwen

Table 6. Retrieval quality evaluation. Approval rate is proportion of retrieved documents judged relevant by LLM grader. Coverage is proportion of queries with at least one relevant document.

Configuration	GSM8K		MATH	
	Approval	Coverage	Approval	Coverage
Dense (Nomic, 137M)	78.5%	97.6%	71.4%	93.9%
Dense (Qwen3, 8B)	85.0%	98.6%	86.9%	98.5%
Hybrid+Rerank (Nomic)	77.7%	97.0%	65.8%	92.3%
Hybrid+Rerank (Qwen3)	79.0%	97.0%	69.8%	94.3%

14B (92.04%), Qwen 32B (91.89%), Gemma 12B (91.28%), and Gemma 27B (92.95%)) converge to a 1.7-percentage-point range under UR-RO, despite baseline performances ranging from 22% to 38%. The 58-percentage-point gap between Gemma 12B's baseline (22.37%) and Qwen 7B's baseline (80.21%) is eliminated: under UR-RO, Gemma 12B (91.28%) substantially outperforms Qwen 7B (80.06%).

Models around 7–8B parameters appear to hit a capacity ceiling. Qwen 7B achieves ~80% regardless of architecture, suggesting its intrinsic reasoning capacity cannot be overcome by retrieval alone. This defines a practical "retrieval breakpoint": below ~10B parameters, the model's internal capabilities are the binding constraint; above it, architecture design determines performance.

On MATH, the convergence is less tight with Gemma models outperforming Qwen models even under UR-RO. This suggests that on harder problems, model-specific capabilities play a larger role. Still, the core pattern holds: a 12B Gemma model with good architecture (77.64%) dramatically outperforms a 32B Qwen model with the same architecture (12.22%).

We noted an asymmetry the results: The same Dense Nomic retrieval that lifts Gemma 12B from 21.54% to 77.64% under UR-RO drops Qwen 32B from 37.55% to 12.22%, with retrieval quality identical for both families (Sect. 6.4). Our experiments aim to isolate architecture from retrieval quality; the mechanisms of each model's attention layers and internal representation work on the same retrieved cases. Whether the pipeline succeeds for one model but fails for another depends on their internal model architecture. Our analysis is external and behavioral; we evaluate across six models from three families to have the breadth to enable detecting model-level effects such as this asymmetry. Retrieval helps one family by 56% and hurts another by 25% under identical input, showing a model-family effect that tempers any expectation that retrieval augmentation transfers uniformly across model families.

6.4 Question: Is Retrieval Quality the Problem

A possible hypothesis is that adaptation failures stem from poor retrieval, due to retrieved cases not being sufficiently relevant to be useful. We test this using a separate retrieval quality evaluation comparing four retrieval configurations across both datasets (Table 6). Several findings emerge:

Retrieval Quality is Adequate. Our production configuration (Dense Nomic) achieves 78.5% approval on GSM8K and 71.4% on MATH, with 94–98% coverage. The vast majority of queries receive at least one relevant case.

Embedding Model Quality is the Dominant Factor for Initial Retrieval. Upgrading from Nomic (137M parameters) to Qwen3 Embedding (8B parameters) yields +6.5% on GSM8K and +15.5% on MATH which exceeds any pipeline-level improvement.

BM25 Hurts for Math. Adding BM25 keyword matching (via Reciprocal Rank Fusion) *degrades* retrieval quality: −0.8% on GSM8K and −5.6% on MATH for Nomic, and −6.0%/−17.1% for Qwen3. The errors increase with complexity. This contradicts general-domain RAG results [1], where hybrid retrieval reduces failures. For mathematical reasoning, keyword matching will retrieve problems with similar vocabulary but not similar answer structure.

The Bottleneck is Post-retrieval, Not Retrieval Itself. Dense Nomic achieves 78.5% approval and powers UR-RO to 92% accuracy but the same retrieval under UR-FA produces only 15–28% accuracy. The 430 UR-FA failure cases analyzed in Sect. 6.2 all have the same high-quality retrieval. That is not the bottleneck; what happens *after* retrieval determines success.

7 Conclusion

We evaluated four LLM-based CBR architectures for mathematical reasoning across six models and two benchmarks. In our tests, explicit adaptation consistently and often dramatically harms performance compared to implicit adaptation. An analysis of failure cases identified fourteen mechanisms across two datasets by which explicit adaptation destroys information, with arithmetic errors, missed transformations, and semantic confusion accounting for most.

In contrast, unified retrieval with implicit adaptation achieves high accuracy on GSM8K for all models above 10B parameters, regardless of model family. This supports the *simple adaptation hypothesis* that for such domains, adaptation should be implicitly performed by the LLM rather than by explicit multi-stage prompting, with the LLM's attention mechanism handling adaptation implicitly. Our results also show that architecture design dominates model choice on GSM8K. On MATH, however, retrieval benefits depend on the model family. This suggests that surface-similarity retrieval reaches its limits on competition-level problems.

Our evaluation is limited to two mathematical reasoning benchmarks, so solidifying these results as a general principle and delineating its scope of application will require broader testing. The principle that implicit adaptation outperforms explicit adaptation may not hold for domains where the adaptation step involves genuinely novel transformations not present in the retrieved cases.

This suggests the need for a solution-aware retrieval process, in which cases are matched by the reasoning strategies they require rather than by surface features of the problem statement—a modern manifestation of the classic CBR indexing problem [9].

Acknowledgments and Declaration on Generative AI. This research was supported in part by Lilly Endowment, Inc., through its support for the Indiana University Pervasive Technology Institute. The authors did not use any generative AI for the preparation of this paper.

References

1. Anthropic: Contextual retrieval. Eng. Anthropic (blog) (2024). https://www.anthropic.com/engineering/contextual-retrieval
2. Bach, K., et al.: Case-based reasoning meets large language models: a research manifesto for open challenges and research directions (2025). HAL Archives, hal-05006761
3. Chen, J., Lan, J., Li, C., Lian, D., Liu, Z.: Reasonembed: enhanced text embeddings for reasoning-intensive document retrieval. arXiv preprint arXiv:2510.08252 (2025)
4. Cobbe, K., et al.: Training verifiers to solve math word problems (2021). https://arxiv.org/abs/2110.14168
5. Das, D., O'Nuallain, S., Rahimi, R.: RaDeR: reasoning-aware dense retrieval models. In: Proceedings of the 2025 Conference on Empirical Methods in Natural Language Processing (EMNLP), pp. 19970–19997. ACL (2025)
6. Dziri, N., et al.: Faith and fate: Limits of transformers on compositionality. In: Advances in Neural Information Processing Systems, pp. 70293–70332. Curran, Red Hook (2023)
7. Hendrycks, D., et al.: Measuring mathematical problem solving with the math dataset. In: Thirty-fifth Conference on Neural Information Processing Systems Datasets and Benchmarks Track (Round 2) (2021)
8. Huang, J., Chang, K.C.C.: Towards reasoning in large language models: a survey. In: Findings of ACL, pp. 1049–1065. ACL (2023)
9. Kolodner, J., Leake, D.: A tutorial introduction to case-based reasoning. In: Leake, D. (ed.) Case-Based Reasoning: Experiences, Lessons, and Future Directions, pp. 31–65. AAAI Press, Menlo Park, CA (1996)
10. Leake, D., Ye, X.: Harmonizing case retrieval and adaptation with alternating optimization. In: Case-Based Reasoning Research and Development, ICCBR 2021, pp. 125–139. Springer (2021)
11. Lenz, M., Hoffmann, M., Bergmann, R.: Llsim: large language models for similarity assessment in case-based reasoning. In: Case-Based Reasoning Research and Development - 33rd International Conference, ICCBR 2025, pp. 126–141. Springer (2025)
12. Lewis, P., et al.: Retrieval-augmented generation for knowledge-intensive NLP tasks. In: Proceedings of the 34th International Conference on Neural Information Processing System (NeurIPS), pp. 9459–9474 (2020)
13. Shao, R., et al.: ReasonIR: training retrievers for reasoning tasks. arXiv preprint arXiv:2504.20595 (2025)

14. Smyth, B., Keane, M.: Adaptation-guided retrieval: questioning the similarity assumption in reasoning. Artif. Intell. **102**(2), 249–293 (1998)
15. Su, H., et al.: BRIGHT: a realistic and challenging benchmark for reasoning-intensive retrieval. In: 13th International Conference on Learning Representations, ICLR 2025 (Spotlight) (2025)
16. Wang, X., et al.: Self-consistency improves chain of thought reasoning in language models. In: 11th International Conference on Learning Representations, ICLR 2023 (2023)
17. Wei, J., et al.: Chainof-thought prompting elicits reasoning in large language models. In: Proceedings of the 36th International Conference on Neural Information Processing System (NeurIPS), pp. 24824–24837 (2022)
18. Wilkerson, K., Leake, D.: On Implementing Case-Based Reasoning with Large Language Models. In: Case-Based Reasoning Research and Development - 32nd International Conference, ICCBR 2024, Merida, Mexico, 1–4 July 2024, Proceedings. Lecture Notes in Computer Science, vol. 14775, pp. 404–417. Springer (2024)
19. Wiratunga, N., et al.: CBR-RAG: case-based reasoning for retrieval augmented generation in LLMs for legal question answering. In: CaseBased Reasoning Research and Development, ICCBR-24. Springer (2024)
20. Yao, S., et al.: Tree of thoughts: deliberate problem solving with large language models. In: Proceedings of the 37th International Conference on Neural Information Processing Systems, pp. 11809–11822 (2023)
21. Zhou, D., et al.: Least-to-most prompting enables complex reasoning in large language models. In: 11th International Conference on Learning Representations, ICLR 2023 (2023)

TextBFGS: A Case-Based Reasoning Approach to Code Optimization via Error-Operator Retrieval

Zizheng Zhang[1(✉)], Yuyang Liao[1], Chen Chen[3], Jian He[1], Dun Wu[1], Qianjin Yu[1], Yanqin Gao[1], Jin Yang[2], Kailai Zhang[2], Eng Siong Chng[3], and Xionghu Zhong[4]

[1] Zhongxing Telecom Equipment (ZTE), Shenzhen, China
zzz128@alumni.pku.edu.cn
[2] China Mobile, Beijing, China
[3] Nanyang Technological University (NTU), Singapore, Singapore
[4] Hunan University, Hunan, China
https://github.com/TzuchengChang

Abstract. Iterative code generation with Large Language Models (LLMs) can be viewed as an optimization process guided by textual feedback. However, existing LLM self-correction methods predominantly operate in a stateless, trial-and-error manner akin to first-order search, failing to leverage past problem-solving experiences. To bridge this gap, we introduce TextBFGS, a Case-Based Reasoning (CBR) framework inspired by the Quasi-Newton optimization method. Instead of retrieving raw, unstructured textual instances, TextBFGS maintains a dynamic Case Base of historical "Error-to-Operator" correction trajectories to approximate the semantic curvature (inverse Hessian matrix) of the task. Specifically, given a textual error feedback (the target problem), TextBFGS retrieves analogous historical correction patterns (Retrieve) and applies these abstract operators to refine the current code (Reuse/Revise). Furthermore, successful adaptations are continuously retained back into the Case Base (Retain), enabling a self-evolving system. Empirical evaluations on Python code optimization tasks (HumanEval, MBPP) demonstrate that TextBFGS significantly outperforms stateless baselines. It achieves superior pass rates with fewer model calls, establishing an efficient, experience-driven paradigm for LLM-based code optimization.

Keywords: Case-Based Reasoning · Large Language Models · Code Optimization · Retrieval Augmented Generation · Experience Reuse

1 Introduction

Large Language Models (LLMs) have demonstrated remarkable capabilities, particularly in code generation and automated optimization [14,19]. However, their

L. Malburg and K. Bach (Eds.): ICCBR 2026, LNAI 16780, pp. 301–316, 2027.
https://doi.org/10.1007/978-3-032-33865-5_19

performance heavily relies on iterative refinement rather than a single forward pass. Consequently, code optimization has evolved from a manual trial-and-error process into a systematic optimization problem. Early works such as OPRO [27] and MIPRO [18] explored automatic prompt generation using LLMs as meta-optimizers. While TextGrad [28], have formalized this paradigm by treating LLM-generated textual error feedback as "gradients" (∇), enabling the optimization of discrete code variables through iterative backpropagation.

Despite these advancements, existing textual optimizers still predominantly operate as first-order methods, conceptually equivalent to Stochastic Gradient Descent (SGD) [2]. While effective in simple scenarios, first-order approaches in the discrete semantic space suffer from significant limitations. First, they are stateless: each optimization run begins tabula rasa, failing to leverage past problem-solving experiences (i.e., historical cases). Second, they neglect the semantic curvature of the optimization landscape. In numerical optimization, the Hessian matrix describes local geometry, indicating how aggressively parameters should be updated. In code optimization, naive gradient descent treats all errors with uniform step logic, often leading to inefficient "zig-zagging"—where the model operates without addressing the underlying misconceptions—or requiring excessive token consumption to converge.

To address the statelessness of SGD, recent frameworks like REMO [24] have attempted to incorporate case-based memory modules by retrieving successful correction traces. However, these methods typically rely on input similarity for retrieval (e.g., retrieving similar code problems). We argue that this surface-level retrieval limits generalization. A "boundary error" in a sorting algorithm shares the same structural defect as one in a pathfinding algorithm, even if their problem descriptions are textually disjoint. By binding retrieval to surface-level content rather than the error dynamics, existing memory-augmented methods fail to facilitate effective transfer learning across different task domains.

In this paper, we introduce TextBFGS, a Case-Based Reasoning (CBR) framework for code optimization, conceptually inspired by the Quasi-Newton optimization method, which approximates the inverse Hessian matrix using historical gradient differences. TextBFGS approximates semantic curvature via a novel Gradient-Operator retrieval mechanism. Instead of retrieving input based on problem similarity, we construct a dynamic Case Base mapping specific feedback patterns (gradients) to abstract modification strategies (operators). Crucially, TextBFGS operates in a One-Pass manner. Upon receiving feedback (the target problem), it retrieves high-order correction operators from its trajectory memory (Retrieve) and fuses the gradient generation (perception) and variable modification (update) into a single inference step (Reuse/Revise). This design not only injects second-order guidance to accelerate convergence but also significantly reduces the computational overhead compared to multi-step pipelines.

Our contributions are summarized as follows:

- **Gradient-Operator Retrieval:** We bridge the gap between numerical second-order optimization and Case-Based automated code optimization, proposing TextBFGS and a robust baseline TextBFGS-REMO, adapting the existing input-based retrieval method into our efficient One-Pass architecture to enable a rigorous comparison between different retrieval paradigms.

- **One-Pass Update & Case Retention:** We propose the One-Pass update mechanism, which unifies feedback diagnosis and operator application into a single LLM inference step, significantly reducing computational overhead. This is coupled with a Case Retention loop where successful optimization trajectories, consisting of gradients and abstract operators, are dynamically injected back into the memory. This allows the optimizer to continuously refine its Case Base.
- **Empirical Superiority & Efficiency:** Experiments on rigorous code optimization benchmarks demonstrate the superiority and efficiency of TextBFGS. It achieves superior pass rates (+20.5% in MBPP) with fewer token counts (-50.6% in HumanEval) compared to TextGrad-based approaches and exhibits strong cross-domain transferability (+16.2% in MBPP) compared to input-based retrieval, effectively applying debugging logic learned from one Case Base to another Case Base.

2 Related Work

2.1 Zero-Order Approaches: Stateless Heuristic Search

Early approaches treated LLMs as black-box functions, navigating the optimization landscape through iterative mutation and selection without explicit directional guidance (gradients). OPRO [27] pioneered using LLMs as meta-optimizers to generate prompts based on the scalar trajectory of past scores. DSPy [9] introduced a declarative programming model where the MIPRO [18] optimizer employs Bayesian-inspired search strategies. These methods, including PromptBreeder [6] and EvoPrompt [8], rely fundamentally on blind trial-and-error. They suffer from high sample complexity because they lack a diagnostic mechanism to explain why a candidate failed, relying solely on scalar rewards to guide the search, entirely lacking the ability to reuse past debugging experiences.

2.2 First-Order Approaches: Feedback-Driven Debugging

To introduce directionality, recent works [16] formalize the use of natural language feedback as Textual Gradients [28], treating the LLM's critique of an output as a gradient (∇), conceptually updating the code variable akin to SGD [2].

Although originally framed as evolutionary, AlphaEvolve [17] and GEPA [1] also fall under this feedback-driven paradigm. Unlike blind mutation, they utilize feedback to guide its genetic crossover and mutation operations, effectively performing population-based gradient descent. While these methods introduce directionality, they remain strictly first-order and stateless.

Besides, TextGrad's "momentum" variant is a simple linear aggregation of past critiques, lacking the geometric interpretation of curvature found in code optimization. Consequently, first-order methods treat the semantic landscape as Euclidean and flat, often leading to inefficient "zig-zagging" in complex code debugging tasks where the descent direction does not point to the global optimum.

2.3 Memory-Augmented Optimization: Towards Case-Based Reasoning

Addressing the statelessness of gradient descent, recent research integrates memory (conceptually akin to a Case Base in CBR) to approximate higher-order geometric information. In numerical optimization, the Hessian matrix (curvature) captures the relationship between parameter updates (Δx) and gradient changes (Δg). In the semantic space, historical optimization trajectories—tuples of mistakes and their successful corrections—serve as cases (problem-solution pairs) that proxy this curvature information.

Reflexion [20], REVOLVE [30], and HessianGrad [29] utilize short-term memory or meta-prompt optimization [21] to avoid repeating immediate errors. However, it limits the fidelity of Hessian approximation. If the optimization stagnates early or fails to discover valid paths, the history remains sparse. Consequently, the optimizer cannot derive curvature information from an empty buffer, leaving it blind to the landscape's geometry.

To overcome this limitation, REMO [24] couples TextGrad with a Retrieval-Augmented Generation (RAG) [10] module acting as a preliminary Case Base. By retrieving past corrections, REMO implicitly approximates the inverse Hessian, guiding the optimizer with historical structural wisdom. However, REMO relies on *input semantic similarity* for retrieval, restricting generalization across domains. Our TextBFGS bridges this gap by shifting the retrieval paradigm from surface-level inputs to *error dynamics (gradients)*, enabling experience-driven code optimization with robust cross-task transferability.

3 Methodology

In this section, we formalize the problem of code optimization and introduce TextBFGS as a Case-Based Reasoning (CBR) system. We first briefly review the stateless first-order search to highlight its limitations in the semantic space, and then derive our Retrieval-Approximated Quasi-Newton update rule, explicitly mapping it to the classic CBR cycle, as shown in Figure 1 and Algorithm1.

3.1 Problem Formulation: Error Feedback as Target Problem

We consider the optimization of a discrete executable variable x (e.g., a code snippet) to maximize an objective function $f(x)$, which represents the performance score on a downstream task (e.g., unittest passrate). Since $f(x)$ is non-differentiable with respect to discrete tokens, we adopt the Textual Gradient [28].

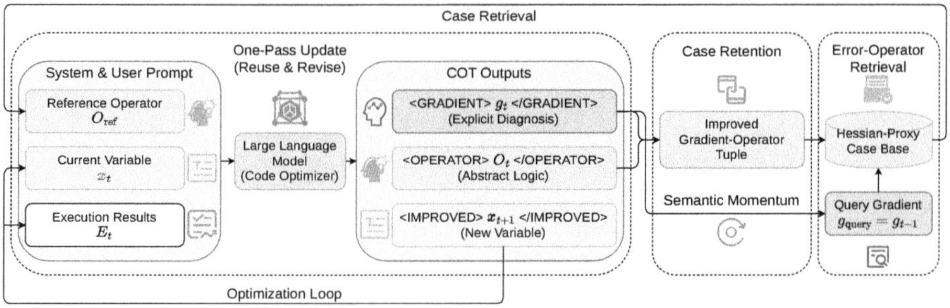

Fig. 1. The schematic overview of the proposed TextBFGS framework, explicitly mapped to the Case-Based Reasoning (CBR) cycle. (1) **Case Retrieval (Retrieve):** Instead of retrieving based on input similarity, TextBFGS retrieves abstract optimization operators $\mathcal{O}_{\text{ref}}$ based on error/gradient similarity from the Case Base. (2) **One-Pass Update (Reuse & Revise):** The LLM receives the current variable x_t, execution results E_t, and retrieved operators $\mathcal{O}_{\text{ref}}$ to simultaneously generate an explicit diagnosis (<**GRADIENT**>), a general correction rule (<**OPERATOR**>), and the improved variable (<**IMPROVED**>) in a single inference step. (3) **Case Retention (Retain):** Upon successful validation (Evaluation), the new error-operator case is injected back into the Case Base, allowing the system to self-evolve and accumulate debugging wisdom.

Let g_t be the error feedback signal generated by an LLM-based evaluator, which serves as the negative gradient $\nabla f(x_t)$. In the context of CBR, g_t functions as the *Target Problem Description* that needs to be resolved. In standard TextGrad, the update follows a stateless SGD scheme:

$$x_{t+1} = \text{LLM}_{\text{update}}(x_t, g_t) \tag{1}$$

where $\text{LLM}_{\text{update}}$ is an LLM call that applies the feedback to the variable without consulting any historical memory.

3.2 Semantic Curvature and the Newton Step as Case Adaptation

A critical limitation of the SGD update above is its assumption of an isotropic optimization landscape. In reality, the semantic space of code debugging exhibits high curvature [5]. First-order methods, lacking knowledge of this geometry and past experiences, often overshoot or oscillate, as shown in Fig. 2.

In numerical optimization, Quasi-Newton methods such as BFGS [12] approximate the inverse Hessian matrix to capture local curvature information, enabling faster convergence. Drawing inspiration from BFGS, we conceptually adapt this philosophy to design our CBR system for discrete semantic domain.

To accelerate convergence, we aim to perform a Quasi-Newton step:

$$x_{t+1} = \text{LLM}_{\text{update}}(x_t, H_t^{-1}, g_t) \tag{2}$$

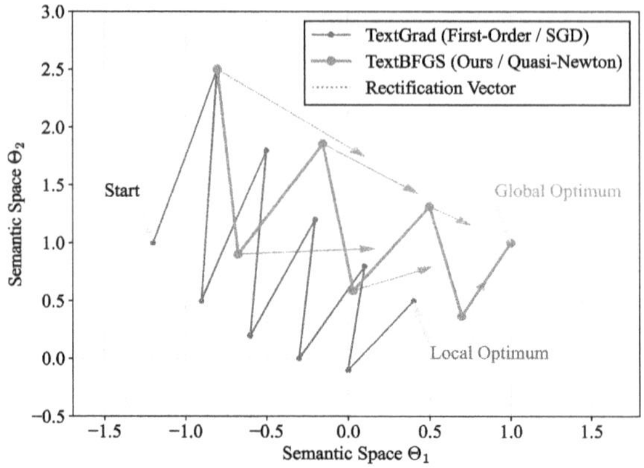

Fig. 2. Schematic visualization of debugging trajectories in a semantic space. TextGrad (Red) operates as a stateless first-order optimizer, exhibiting inefficient oscillation and getting trapped in a local optimum. In contrast, TextBFGS (Blue) adopts a Quasi-Newton inspired CBR approach. It utilizes prior error dynamics to query the Hessian-Proxy Case Base for historical adaptation rules. This case reuse acts as a structural rectification mechanism (Green), allowing TextBFGS to bypass superficial edits, dampen oscillations, and converge faster to a robust solution. (Color figure online)

where H_t^{-1} represents the inverse Hessian matrix. In numerical optimization, H_t^{-1} acts as a geometric transformation matrix. In our discrete code optimization, explicitly calculating this matrix is mathematically intractable. Instead, we propose that a *Case Base* of historical optimization operators acts as a conceptual approximation of the inverse Hessian.

We justify this conceptual approximation through functional equivalence. Just as numerical BFGS accumulates past gradient differences and step updates to estimate curvature, our Case Base accumulates historical errors (g) and successful abstract operators ($\mathcal{O}$). Retrieving an operator for a specific error applies a structural transformation to the code edit, analogous to how H^{-1} rotates a gradient to correct for landscape geometry. Furthermore, if a current problem exactly matches a historical case, reusing its operator perfectly reconstructs the successful update, effectively satisfying a discrete analog of the Quasi-Newton secant condition ($H\Delta g = \Delta x$).

Since the current gradient g_t is unknown prior to generation, we utilize the "Semantic Momentum" derived from the previous step (g_{t-1}) to estimate this curvature matrix, assuming that error directions exhibit local persistence [5]:

$$H_t^{-1} \approx \mathcal{T}(g_{t-1}; \mathcal{M}) \tag{3}$$

Here, $\mathcal{T}$ denotes the retrieval-based transformation function and $\mathcal{M}$ denotes the Hessian-Proxy Case Base. Unlike standard RAG which retrieves raw text, our $\mathcal{T}$ retrieves a *successful adaptation rule* (operator) based on historical error dynamics. Consequently, the inference of TextBFGS can be formalized as:

Algorithm 1. TextBFGS Case-Based Optimization Loop

Input: Initial variable x_0, Objective metric $f(\cdot)$, Hessian-Proxy Case Base $\mathcal{M}$
Output: Optimized variable x_{best}

for step $t = 0, 1, \ldots, T$ **do**
  if $t > 0$ **then**
    Query Error/Gradient: $g_t^{\text{query}} \leftarrow g_{t-1}$
  end if
  Execute: Run $f(x_t)$ to get execution results E_t.
  # CBR Phase 1: Retrieve
  Case Retrieval:
    $\mathcal{O}_{\text{ref}} \leftarrow \text{Retrieve}(\mathcal{M}, \text{query} = g_t^{\text{query}}, \text{num} = k)$
  # CBR Phase 2 & 3: Reuse and Revise
  One-Pass Update:
    Prompt $\leftarrow \mathcal{P}(x_t, E_t, \mathcal{O}_{\text{ref}})$
    $g_t, \mathcal{O}_t, x_{t+1} \leftarrow \text{LLM(Prompt)}$
  if $f(x_{t+1})$ is better than $f(x_t)$ **then**
    # CBR Phase 4: Retain
    Case Retention:
      $\mathcal{M} \leftarrow \mathcal{M} \cup \{(g_t, \mathcal{O}_t)\}$
  end if
end for
return Optimized variable x_{best}

$$\Delta x_t \approx \underbrace{\mathcal{T}(g_{t-1})}_{\text{Hessian Proxy / Case Retrieval}} \otimes \underbrace{g_t}_{\text{Current Target Problem}} \tag{4}$$

where $\otimes$ represents the LLM's internal reasoning process that applies the retrieved abstract operator ($\mathcal{T}$) to the specific current diagnosis (g_t) to generate the final variable update.

3.3 Approximating Hessian via Error-Operator Retrieval

TextBFGS approximates H_t^{-1} using a Case-Based retrieval mechanism [7]. We construct a Hessian-Proxy Case Base (HPCB), denoted as $\mathcal{M}$, which stores pre-learned successful optimization trajectories as cases (tuples):

$$\mathcal{M} = \{(g_i, \mathcal{O}_i)\}_{i=1}^{N} \tag{5}$$

Here, g_i is the textual gradient (the historical error description / Problem), and $\mathcal{O}_i$ is the Optimization Operator—the abstract logic used to resolve g_i (the adaptation rule / Solution), rather than the raw code difference.

The Retrieval Process: We utilize the previous gradient g_{t-1} as the current query g_t^{query} based on Semantic Momentum, facilitating One-Pass inference. We then query $\mathcal{M}$ to find the k nearest neighbors based on error similarity:

$$\begin{aligned} \mathcal{O}_{\text{ref}} &= \text{Retrieve}(\mathcal{M}, g_t^{\text{query}}, k) \\ &= *Top\text{-}k_{(g_i,\mathcal{O}_i)\in\mathcal{M}} \left(\text{CS}(\text{Embed}(g_t^{\text{query}}), \text{Embed}(g_i))\right) \end{aligned} \tag{6}$$

where Embed(·) is a vector embedding, and CS(·) denotes cosine similarity.

Why this Matters: Unlike REMO [24] which retrieves based on *input* similarity ($\text{sim}(x_t, x_i)$), TextBFGS retrieves based on *gradient/error* similarity ($\text{sim}(g_t, g_i)$). For instance, an "Index Error" gradient in a sorting algorithm can retrieve a "Boundary Check" operator originally learned from a string parsing task, effectively transferring debugging logic across distinct coding domains.

3.4 One-Pass Update Loop (Reuse and Revise)

To ensure efficiency, TextBFGS fuses gradient generation and variable modification into a single LLM inference step, explicitly mirroring the **Reuse** and **Revise** phases of CBR. We design a specialized prompt structure forcing the LLM to explicitize the error and operator.

Let $\mathcal{P}$ be the system prompt. The update rule is formally:

$$g_t, \mathcal{O}_t, x_{t+1} = \text{LLM}(\mathcal{P}(x_t, E_t, \mathcal{O}_{\text{ref}})) \tag{7}$$

where E_t is the execution result. The model performs the following internal Chain of Thought (CoT) [23]:

1. **Gradient Analysis** (g_t): The model analyzes the error pattern between the current output and the expectation (identifying the target problem).
2. **Operator Application** ($\mathcal{O}_t$): The model generates the hybrid operator from g_t and the retrieved set $\mathcal{O}_{\text{ref}}$, **Reusing** the historical case solutions.
3. **Newton Update** (x_{t+1}): The model applies this operator to x_t, **Revising** the code to resolve the error.

This mechanism reduces computational cost by 50% compared to standard methods [25] while injecting experience-driven second-order guidance.

3.5 Case Retention: Self-evolving Case Base

TextBFGS mimics the self-correcting nature of Quasi-Newton methods by dynamically updating its HPCB during optimization, which corresponds to the **Retain** phase in CBR. In numerical optimization, BFGS achieves self-correction by iteratively refining its Hessian approximation using historical changes. TextBFGS transfers this principle: its HPCB continuously self-improves through accumulating error-operator pairs, making the curvature estimation increasingly accurate.

Upon a successful update (e.g., $f(x_{t+1}) > f(x_t)$), the system abstracts the specific transformation into a generalized operator $\mathcal{O}_t$. The resulting case tuple $(g_t, \mathcal{O}_t)$ is then retained into the HPCB. This continuous retention enriches the case coverage, transforming the optimizer into a self-evolving agent that progressively masters the debugging landscape [15].

4 Experiments

We empirically evaluate TextBFGS on the task of code optimization, where code serves as the executable text, demanding rigorous logic and structural correctness. We focus on cases where the base model fails initially, to strictly measure the optimizer's ability to turn failure into success through experience reuse.

4.1 Experimental Setup

Base Model and Initialization. We employ Qwen3-235B-A22B [26] as the backbone model for the optimizer, Qwen3-Embedding-8B [31] as the retrieval model, and ChromaDB[1] as the Case Base (CB), with the number of iterations limited to 20 per optimization task. To simulate a challenging debugging landscape and eliminate interference from internal reasoning traces, we disable the reasoning mode by setting enable-thinking to False, forcing the model to rely solely on explicit error feedback (gradients) rather than its internal latent reasoning. Additionally, we set the backbone model's temperature to 0.7, top-p to 0.95, and an appropriate max-tokens to ensure responses are not truncated. Other experimental details such as prompt implementation can be found in our *code repository*[2].

Benchmarks and Metrics. We employ EvalPlus[3] [13] as the evaluation toolkit, which incorporates two standard benchmarks: HumanEval [4] and MBPP [3]. To ensure the robustness of our results, we report the following metrics:

- **Base Pass Rate:** The average pass rate of tasks on the standard test cases of HumanEval or MBPP.
- **Plus Pass Rate:** The average pass rate on the augmented test cases provided by EvalPlus. These represent a more rigorous set of tasks designed to detect overfitting and evaluate the model's capability in handling edge cases.

We filtered the datasets to retain only the problems where Qwen3-235B-A22B scored 0 in the initial Pass@1 attempt for further optimization. The filtered subsets are as follows:

- **HumanEval-Hard:** 45 tasks (filtered from 164 tasks).
- **MBPP-Hard:** 117 tasks (filtered from 378 tasks).

Unless otherwise specified, HumanEval or MBPP mentioned in subsequent experiments refer to the above hard subsets of HumanEval or MBPP, and a task is considered failed if it fails to pass even a single testcase.

---

[1] https://github.com/chroma-core/chroma.
[2] https://github.com/TzuchengChang/TextBFGS.
[3] https://github.com/evalplus/evalplus.

Baselines. To rigorously evaluate the effectiveness of TextBFGS, we compare it against three categories of approaches:

- **TextGrad** and **TextGrad-Momentum**[4] [28]: The mainstream stateless feedback-driven textual optimization frameworks. TextGrad performs memoryless updates. TextGrad-Momentum extends this by aggregating a buffer of historical feedback to smooth the update trajectory, though it remains unaware of the global semantic geometry and lacks a persistent Case Base.
- **TextBFGS (w/o CB)**: An ablation variant of our framework where the Hessian-proxy case retrieval module is disabled. This baseline utilizes the same efficient One-Pass inference architecture to generate errors and updates simultaneously but operates without access to the Case Base.
- **TextBFGS-REMO:** A TextBFGS reproduction of REMO [24], the latest memory-augmented textual optimization framework. Since the official implementation is unavailable, we replicate it using the TextBFGS backbone and One-Pass architecture. Crucially, it employs problem-based retrieval: it queries the Case Base using the semantic similarity of the target problem input, simulating standard RAG-enhanced generation.

Case Base Construction. To populate the Hessian-proxy Case Base with high-quality data, we employ a bootstrapping procedure using the stateless variant, TextBFGS (w/o CB). We execute it on both HumanEval-Hard and MBPP-Hard with 3 optimization learning epochs per task.

For each successful optimization step, we store a case tuple containing 4 components: the pre-optimization text (x_t), the error description/gradient (g_t), the abstract adaptation rule/operator ($\mathcal{O}_t$), and the post-optimization text (x_{t+1}). This unified schema supports both our method (which queries via g_t) and the TextBFGS-REMO baseline (which queries via the surface-level problem x_t).

This process yields a concentrated repository of 39 case trajectories for the HumanEval domain and 245 for the MBPP domain. During inference, we retrieve the top-k ($k = 3$) most similar entries. The choice of $k = 3$ aligns exactly with the TextGrad-Momentum baseline, which maintains a context window of the three most recent optimization records, ensuring a fair comparison of context length and information capacity.

4.2 Ablation Study: Impact of CBR Components

To dissect the contribution of each module in TextBFGS, we conduct a component-wise analysis on both HumanEval-Hard and MBPP-Hard. For consistency in this ablation, both tasks utilize the Case Base (CB) from MBPP, which contains richer cases than HumanEval. The results are presented in Tables 1 and 2.

[4] https://github.com/zou-group/textgrad.

Table 1. Ablation on HumanEval-Hard (using MBPP CB). Case Base integration yields substantial gains. Notably, retrieving based on error gradients (TextBFGS) outperforms problem-based retrieval (TextBFGS-REMO) by +2.22% in both Pass Rate

Method	Base Pass	Plus Pass
TextGrad	91.11%	82.22%
TextGrad-Momentum	91.11%	86.67%
TextBFGS (w/o CB)	91.11%	82.22%
TextBFGS-REMO	95.56%	91.11%
TextBFGS	**97.78%**	**93.33%**

Table 2. Ablation on MBPP-Hard (using MBPP CB). When the case source strictly aligns with the target task, problem-based retrieval (TextBFGS-REMO) performs slightly better, though error-based retrieval (TextBFGS) remains highly competitive.

Method	Base Pass	Plus Pass
TextGrad	85.47%	48.72%
TextGrad-Momentum	88.89%	58.12%
TextBFGS (w/o CB)	85.47%	48.72%
TextBFGS-REMO	**95.73%**	**78.63%**
TextBFGS	94.02%	74.36%

Impact of Momentum. Comparing standard TextGrad with TextGrad-Momentum, we observe that aggregating historical feedback consistently improves robustness. Especially on MBPP-Hard (Table 2), momentum yields a boost of +9.4% in Plus pass rate (from 48.72% to 58.12%). This confirms that recording the update direction helps prevent the optimizer from oscillating in complex solution spaces.

Impact of Case Base Augmentation. The most significant performance leap stems from the integration of the Hessian-Proxy Case Base. Regardless of the retrieval strategy, retrieval methods drastically outperform stateless baselines. For instance, on HumanEval-Hard, the Plus pass rate improved by up to **+6.66%** compared with Momentum (from 86.67% to 93.33%), while on MBPP-Hard, the Plus pass rate showed a maximum increase of **+20.51%** compared with Momentum (from 58.12% to 78.63%). This validates our premise that accessing historical successful cases is essential for solving hard instances.

4.3 Cross-Domain vs. In-Domain Retrieval

To strictly evaluate the generalization capability of different retrieval methods, we compare performance when the Case Base (CB) is populated with data from the same domain (In-Domain) versus a disjoint domain (Cross-Domain). This

Table 3. Performance of TextBFGS-REMO (problem-based retrieval) degrades significantly in Cross-Domain scenarios. Notably, on MBPP using the HumanEval CB, the robust Plus metric drops -20.51%, indicating poor transferability.

Target Task & Case Source	Base Pass	Plus Pass
HumanEval (w/o CB)	91.11%	82.22%
MBPP (w/o CB)	85.47%	48.72%
HumanEval (HumanEval CB, In)	**99.39%**	**97.56%**
HumanEval (MBPP CB, Cross)	95.56%	91.11%
MBPP (MBPP CB, In)	**95.73%**	**78.63%**
MBPP (HumanEval CB, Cross)	91.45%	58.12%

Table 4. Performance of TextBFGS (error-based retrieval) maintains high accuracy across domains. Crucially, when optimizing MBPP using HumanEval CB, TextBFGS significantly outperforms TextBFGS-REMO by +16.24% on the Plus.

Target Task & Case Source	Base Pass	Plus Pass
HumanEval (w/o CB)	91.11%	82.22%
MBPP (w/o CB)	85.47%	48.72%
HumanEval (HumanEval CB, In)	**99.39%**	**96.34%**
HumanEval (MBPP CB, Cross)	97.78%	93.33%
MBPP (MBPP CB, In)	94.02%	74.36%
MBPP (HumanEval CB, Cross)	**94.02%**	**74.36%**

experiment tests whether the system relies on memorizing task-specific code snippets or learning transferable debugging logic. We split the results by retrieval strategy into Tables 3 and 4 for clarity.

Analysis. As shown in Table 3, the problem-based retrieval (TextBFGS-REMO) exhibits signs of surface-level case overfitting. While it performs slightly better in In-Domain settings (e.g., 97.56% vs. 96.34% on HumanEval) by retrieving near-identical historical examples, it fails to transfer knowledge across disjoint tasks. Specifically, when solving MBPP tasks using HumanEval cases, the Plus pass rate collapses to 58.12%, barely improving over the baseline (48.72%).

In contrast, Table 4 demonstrates the superior generalization of TextBFGS. By retrieving cases based on error dynamics (gradients) rather than surface problem descriptions, TextBFGS successfully identifies shared failure modes even when the task contexts differ. Consequently, on the challenging MBPP benchmark with HumanEval cases, TextBFGS maintains a high Plus pass rate of 74.36%, outperforming the input-based baseline by a substantial margin of **+16.24%**. This confirms that optimization logic, encapsulated as adaptation operators in the case base, is more transferable than specific code instances.

Table 5. Efficiency on HumanEval-Hard (Cross-Domain). Using MBPP CB, TextBFGS achieves the best trade-off, demonstrating superior efficiency in transferring debugging logic across domains.

Method	Calls/Task	Tokens/Call	Tokens/Task
TextGrad	35.8	**863.9**	30.9k
TextGrad-Momentum	29.8	1464.2	43.7k
TextBFGS (w/o CB)	17.0	1481.3	25.2k
TextBFGS-REMO	13.9	1594.4	22.2k
TextBFGS	**13.6**	1581.7	**21.6k**

Table 6. Efficiency on MBPP-Hard (In-Domain). In-Domain retrieval results in higher token consumption per call compared to Table 5 due to the retrieval of more detailed, context-heavy specific experiences, but it sharply reduces the number of calls.

Method	Calls/Task	Tokens/Call	Tokens/Task
TextGrad	36.6	**727.3**	26.6k
TextGrad-Momentum	34.0	1114.1	37.9k
TextBFGS (w/o CB)	18.2	1330.2	24.2k
TextBFGS-REMO	**7.1**	2262.0	**16.1k**
TextBFGS	8.2	2103.9	17.2k

4.4 Efficiency Analysis

We assess the computational cost on both datasets and utilize the Case Base (CB) from MBPP to evaluate efficiency under cross-domain and in-domain settings. We employ an early-stopping mechanism. Consequently, a stronger solver that finds solutions faster will lead to faster convergence, naturally resulting in fewer average API calls. The results are presented in Tables 5 and 6. We summarize the key observations below:

One-Pass Inference Reduces API Overhead. A distinct advantage of our framework is the One-Pass architecture. Methods like TextGrad and REMO operate in a two-stage manner: one API call to compute the error diagnosis (gradient) and a second separate call to apply the update. In contrast, TextBFGS integrates the diagnosis computation (via internal CoT) and the operator execution into a single inference step.

As shown in Table 5, although TextGrad has the lowest tokens per call (863.9), it requires significantly more API calls (35.8). While both TextBFGS (w/o CB) and TextGrad achieve identical performance (82.22%), TextBFGS (w/o CB) achieves an **18.4%** cost reduction compared to TextGrad (25.2k vs. 30.9k), proving that One-Pass inference saves substantial overhead.

Token Consumption and Retrieval Granularity. We analyze the trade-off using Tokens/Task. As shown in Table 5 and Table 6, two distinct patterns emerge:

- **Inefficiency of Stateless Momentum:** While TextGrad-Momentum improves pass rates over vanilla TextGrad, it incurs the highest computational cost (43.7k). This is because Momentum simply concatenates the optimization history. Since this history is stateless and unfiltered, it may contain irrelevant or redundant information that bloats the context without proportionally reducing the number of iterations.
- **Efficiency via Case-Retrieval:** In contrast, although retrieving cases increases the input size, the injected operators are highly relevant "high-utility" adaptation priors that guide the model to the correct solution much faster. This drastically cuts the iteration count (e.g. down to 13.6), achieving higher performance (from 86.67% to 93.33%), resulting in the lowest total token consumption (21.6k), effectively saving a total of **50.6%** tokens compared to Momentum.

Furthermore, we observe a granularity preference across domains. Case-retrieval methods consume obviously fewer tokens per call on HumanEval (Cross-Domain, 1582 tokens) than on MBPP (In-Domain, 2104 tokens). We attribute this to the nature of case matching: In-domain queries tend to fetch lengthy, task-specific snippets, whereas cross-domain queries retrieve shorter, more abstract structural logic. This suggests that in cross-domain scenarios, generalizable debugging experiences matter most, and our system naturally adapts its retrieval granularity, maintaining efficiency even when transferring knowledge across disjoint domains.

5 Case Study

We present a concrete example from our real optimization logs: `HumanEval/127`. This case directly illustrates that TextBFGS can turn a persistent failure mode into a fully correct solution under the same backbone model.

Initial Code (Before Optimization).

```
print(intersection((1, 2), (2, 3)))       # Output: "NO"
print(intersection((-1, 1), (0, 4)))      # Output: "NO"
print(intersection((-3, -1), (-5, 5)))    # Output: "YES"
```

TextGrad result (still fails).

```
length = intersect_end - intersect_start + 1  # Inclusive interval
...
return "YES" if is_prime(length) else "NO"
```

TextBFGS result (passes all tests).

```
length = overlap_end - overlap_start  # corrected difference
...
return "YES" if is_prime(length) else "NO"
```

Compared with TextGrad, TextBFGS retrieves and applies a more precise correction pattern for this boundary-sensitive logic. As a result, it fixes the off-by-one error and achieves full pass on both base and plus test suites.

6 Conclusion and Future Work

We introduced TextBFGS, a Case-Based Reasoning (CBR) framework inspired by Quasi-Newton methods to overcome the stateless inefficiencies of first-order code optimization. By retrieving historical error-operators instead of surface-level problems, TextBFGS conceptually approximates semantic curvature, enabling the robust cross-domain transfer of debugging logic. Coupled with efficient One-Pass updates and Case Retention, it establishes a highly effective, experience-driven paradigm for LLM self-correction. Future work will explore extending this framework beyond code generation to broader reasoning tasks and dynamic agentic workflows.

Disclosure of Interests. The authors have no competing interests to declare that are relevant to the content of this paper.

Declaration on Generative AI. We utilized Large Language Models (DeepSeek [11] and Gemini [22]) solely for grammatical refinement and polishing of the text. All scientific claims and experimental results are the authors' own work.

References

1. Agrawal, L.A., et al.: Gepa: reflective prompt evolution can outperform reinforcement learning. arXiv preprint arXiv:2507.19457 (2025)
2. Amari, S.I.: Backpropagation and stochastic gradient descent method. Neurocomputing **5**(4-5), 185–196 (1993)
3. Austin, J., et al.: Program synthesis with large language models. arXiv preprint arXiv:2108.07732 (2021)
4. Chen, M.: Evaluating large language models trained on code. arXiv preprint arXiv:2107.03374 (2021)
5. Ethayarajh, K.: How contextual are contextualized word representations. Comparing the geometry of BERT, ELMo, and GPT-2 Embeddings 2 (2019)
6. Fernando, C., Banarse, D., Michalewski, H., Osindero, S., Rocktäschel, T.: Promptbreeder: self-referential self-improvement via prompt evolution. arXiv preprint arXiv:2309.16797 (2023)
7. Gao, B., et al.: The devil is in the prompts: retrieval-augmented prompt optimization for text-to-video generation. In: Proceedings of the Computer Vision and Pattern Recognition Conference, pp. 3173–3183 (2025)
8. Guo, Q., et al.: Connecting large language models with evolutionary algorithms yields powerful prompt optimizers. arXiv preprint arXiv:2309.08532 (2023)
9. Khattab, O., et al.: Dspy: compiling declarative language model calls into self-improving pipelines (2024)
10. Lewis, P., et al.: Retrieval-augmented generation for knowledge-intensive NLP tasks: Adv. Neural. Inf. Process. Syst. **33**, 9459–9474 (2020)
11. Liu, A., et al.: Deepseek-v3 Technical report. arXiv preprint arXiv:2412.19437 (2024)
12. Liu, D.C., Nocedal, J.: On the limited memory BFGS method for large scale optimization. Math. Program. **45**(1), 503–528 (1989)

13. Liu, J., Xia, C.S., Wang, Y., Zhang, L.: Is your code generated by chatGPT really correct? Rigorous evaluation of large language models for code generation. In: Thirty-seventh Conference on Neural Information Processing Systems (2023). https://openreview.net/forum?id=1qvx610Cu7
14. Ma, X., Lin, C., Zhang, Y., Tresp, V., Ma, Y.: Agentic neural networks: self-evolving multi-agent systems via textual backpropagation. arXiv preprint arXiv:2506.09046 (2025)
15. Madaan, A., Tandon, N., Clark, P., Yang, Y.: Memory-assisted prompt editing to improve GPT-3 after deployment. arXiv preprint arXiv:2201.06009 (2022)
16. Madaan, A., et al.: Self-refine: iterative refinement with self-feedback. Adv. Neural. Inf. Process. Syst. **36**, 46534–46594 (2023)
17. Novikov, A., et al.: Alphaevolve: a coding agent for scientific and algorithmic discovery. arXiv preprint arXiv:2506.13131 (2025)
18. Opsahl-Ong, K., et al.: Optimizing instructions and demonstrations for multi-stage language model programs. arXiv preprint arXiv:2406.11695 (2024)
19. Sahoo, P., Singh, A.K., Saha, S., Jain, V., Mondal, S., Chadha, A.: A systematic survey of prompt engineering in large language models: techniques and applications. arXiv preprint arXiv:2402.07927 (2024)
20. Shinn, N., Cassano, F., Gopinath, A., Narasimhan, K., Yao, S.: Reflexion: language agents with verbal reinforcement learning. Adv. Neural. Inf. Process. Syst. **36**, 8634–8652 (2023)
21. Suzgun, M., Kalai, A.T.: Meta-prompting: enhancing language models with task-agnostic scaffolding. arXiv preprint arXiv:2401.12954 (2024)
22. Team, G., et al.: Gemini: a family of highly capable multimodal models. arXiv preprint arXiv:2312.11805 (2023)
23. Wei, J., et al.: Chain-of-thought prompting elicits reasoning in large language models. Adv. Neural. Inf. Process. Syst. **35**, 24824–24837 (2022)
24. Wu, C., Qu, Z.: Reflection-enhanced meta-optimization integrating textgrad-style prompt optimization with memory-driven self-evolution. arXiv preprint arXiv:2508.18749 (2025)
25. Xu, G., Yuksekgonul, M., Guestrin, C., Zou, J.: metatextgrad: automatically optimizing language model optimizers. arXiv preprint arXiv:2505.18524 (2025)
26. Yang, A., et al.: Qwen3 Technical report. arXiv preprint arXiv:2505.09388 (2025)
27. Yang, C., et al.: Large language models as optimizers. In: The Twelfth International Conference on Learning Representations (2023)
28. Yuksekgonul, M., et al.: Textgrad: automatic differentiation via text. arXiv preprint arXiv:2406.07496 (2024)
29. Zhang, P., et al.: Hessiangrad: optimizing AI systems with hessian-aware textual gradients (2024)
30. Zhang, P., et al.: Revolve: optimizing AI systems by tracking response evolution in textual optimization. arXiv preprint arXiv:2412.03092 (2024)
31. Zhang, Y., et al.: Qwen3 embedding: advancing text embedding and reranking through foundation models. arXiv preprint arXiv:2506.05176 (2025)

NegLLM: Enhancing Strategic LLM Negotiation Agents with Case-Based Reasoning

Ruoke Wang[1,2], Tianzi Ma[1,2], Yulin Wu[1,2], Jiajia Zhang[1,2], and Xuan Wang[1,2](✉)

[1] Harbin Institute of Technology, Shenzhen, China
{24s151159,tianzima}@stu.hit.edu.cn,
{yulinwu,wangxuan}@cs.hitsz.edu.cn, zhangjiajia@hit.edu.cn
[2] Guangdong Provincial Key Laboratory of Novel Security Intelligence Technologies, Shenzhen, China

Abstract. Negotiation is a critical interaction of conflict resolution and resource distribution in human society. While Large Language Models (LLMs) show potential as negotiation agents, they face challenges in balancing strategic reasoning with conversational flexibility. In this paper, we propose NegLLM, a novel framework that integrates the Case-Based Reasoning (CBR) paradigm to enhance the strategic capabilities of LLM-based negotiators. Specifically, NegLLM employs a multi-dimensional action generation method to ensure utterance diversity. This process is then utilized in a tree search guided by the Pareto front to explore negotiation trajectories, from which it retrieves cases that represent optimal strategic decisions. Next, after retrieving multiple negotiation trees, NegLLM extracts action-level cases with high immediate utility and long-term reward. These cases are then internalized in the Llama3-8B-Instruct model via a specially designed fine-tuning loss function, aligning with the optimal action distribution. During deployment, NegLLM operates without online search, extra prompts, or auxiliary modules, reflecting its self-sufficiency in negotiating independently. Experimental results demonstrate that NegLLM improves 27.58% in individual utility and 44.11% in Pareto efficiency over the baseline. Furthermore, NegLLM outperforms four LLM-based agents, including ChatGPT and DeepSeek, by 15.87% on average in individual utility. These results highlight the potential of enhancing lightweight models, like Llama3-8B-Instruct, with the CBR paradigm to surpass huge LLMs in complex negotiation tasks. The code is available at https://github.com/Requalvia/NegLLM.

Keywords: Case-based reasoning · Large Language Models · Negotiation agents · Game theory · Generative AI

1 Introduction

Negotiation is a fundamental form of social interaction in human society, playing a role in conflict resolution and resource allocation [24]. It is a communicative process

R. Wang and T. Ma—Contributed equally to this work.

L. Malburg and K. Bach (Eds.): ICCBR 2026, LNAI 16780, pp. 317–333, 2027.
https://doi.org/10.1007/978-3-032-33865-5_20

in which negotiators must balance their own utility with concessions to reach an agreement acceptable to all parties. Recent advancements have established Large Language Models (LLMs) as negotiation agents due to their superior dialogue understanding and reasoning capabilities [15], exhibiting human-like persuasive behaviors with built-in general prior knowledge [2].

The principle of Case-Based Reasoning (CBR) is solving new problems based on the solutions of similar past problems [1]. Negotiation is a dynamic strategic game that relies heavily on skill and experience, which the CBR paradigm can augment by transposing past solutions to new problem instances. CBR has been widely applied in LLM research [31], demonstrating its potential in enhancing the performance of LLM agents. However, LLM-based negotiation agents still face challenges. Despite the linguistic fluency, LLM agents lack autonomous strategic reasoning, leading to an inconsistency between tactical intent and dialogue. Current approaches often bridge this gap through external offer-generation modules, which limit their adaptability in fluid negotiations. Furthermore, while episodic memory can be provided via in-context prompts, this approach results in contextual overhead and response latency during deployment. A more fundamental challenge is how to integrate these strategic cases into the model's intrinsic policy, rather than merely appending them as external, transient references.

To address these challenges, we propose NegLLM, a novel framework that integrates the CBR paradigm to enhance strategic LLM negotiation agents. Specifically, NegLLM employs multi-dimensional modeling of negotiation dialogues to generate actions with diverse strategies and negotiation styles. This approach is then implemented in self-play negotiations where both parties are Language Models, guided by the Pareto front for an extensive tree search throughout the negotiation process. After retrieving a set of negotiation trees, instead of using the entire negotiation history as context, NegLLM focuses on extracting action-level cases with high immediate utility and long-term outcomes for refinement. Finally, NegLLM fine-tunes the Language Models using a specially designed loss function, aligning the model's output probability distribution with the target policy. Since the selected cases are internalized into the model's parameters, NegLLM operates without online searches or auxiliary modules during deployment, enabling efficient and deployable negotiation agents in complex scenarios.

Our contributions are summarized as follows:

- We introduce NegLLM, a framework for enhancing the strategic capabilities of LLM negotiation agents. Following the CBR paradigm, NegLLM empowers LLM-based negotiation agents to improve negotiation capabilities autonomously from past experiences.
- We propose a multi-dimensional modeling method to generate diverse actions, a Pareto-guided tree search to explore different strategies, and extract action-level cases for revision. NegLLM then fine-tunes the Llama3-8B-Instruct model with a designed loss function to internalize successful cases.
- NegLLM improves individual utility by **27.58%** and Pareto efficiency by **44.11%** compared to the base Llama3-8B-Instruct. Crucially, NegLLM outperforms four state-of-the-art LLM-based negotiation agents (including ChatGPT and DeepSeek)

by **15.87%** on average in individual utility, demonstrating that the CBR-based internalization enables lightweight LLMs to surpass huge LLMs in negotiations.

2 Related Work

CBR solves new problems by retrieving and reusing similar past cases [1,8], and is therefore particularly suitable for complex tasks that are difficult to formalize completely but depend heavily on accumulated experience [30]. Negotiation is a dynamic, time-limited, and highly strategic interaction in which decisions often depend on the experience of similar situations, making it inherently well-suited to the CBR paradigm. Early work demonstrated that negotiation can benefit from CBR-supported persuasive argumentation and strategy generation [6,28,29]. With the rise of LLMs, CBR has regained relevance in addressing LLMs' limitations in structured reasoning and experience reuse. Recent work has implemented CBR to LLM agents in solving complex tasks iteratively [12], retrieval-augmented generation [32], and automated similarity assessment [16]. These studies suggest that CBR serves as an effective framework for equipping LLM agents with experiential knowledge, reliable reasoning, and long-horizon decision-making.

Automated negotiation focuses on enabling autonomous agents to reach agreements through strategic decision-making, concession control, and opponent modeling. It has been widely applied in domains such as e-commerce and conflict resolution [4,7,33]. Existing research has developed a variety of negotiation methods, including fuzzy, rule-based, and learning-based approaches [19,20]. With the rapid advancement of LLMs, recent work has established them as capable negotiation agents by exploiting their superior dialogue understanding and reasoning capabilities [5]. Research demonstrates that LLMs can handle negotiation tasks through prompt engineering [25], dialogue planning [34,35], self-reflection [17], and psychological tactics [22,26]. Existing studies mainly improve negotiation performance through inference-time reasoning, while the reuse and retention of negotiation experiences remain relatively underexplored.

3 Preliminary

Negotiations. A negotiation involves two negotiators, denoted by p_1 and p_2. The negotiation proceeds in a turn-based manner, where two negotiators take actions alternately. An action consists of three components: $action = (\textit{thought}, \textit{utterance}, o)$, where *thought* represents the agent's private internal reasoning process, which is not observable by the opponent; *utterance* denotes the natural language utterance communicated to the opponent; and o is a structured offer.

Issues and Offers. Let the negotiation involve n issues, denoted by $\mathcal{I} = \{I_1, \ldots, I_n\}$. Each issue I_k is associated with a finite outcome space, and an outcome for issue I_k is denoted by $i_k \in I_k$, where $k \in \{1, \ldots, n\}$. The joint outcome space is defined as the Cartesian product of all issue-level outcome spaces: $\mathcal{O} = I_1 \times \cdots \times I_n$. An offer $o \in \mathcal{O}$ therefore corresponds to a complete assignment over all issues.

Utility Functions. Each negotiator $p \in \{p_1, p_2\}$ is associated with a utility function $u_p : \mathcal{O} \rightarrow [0, 1]$, which maps a complete offer $o \in \mathcal{O}$ to a utility value, where higher values indicate better preferences. The utility function captures the negotiator's private preferences over all issues and is not observable by the opponent.

Negotiation Process. The negotiation is conducted over a finite horizon of $2N_\mathrm{r}$ rounds. In round i, the active negotiator p first decides whether to accept the opponent's most recent offer with probability α_p^i, leading to immediate termination with an agreement; otherwise, the negotiator proceeds to take an action consisting of thought, utterance, and a new offer. This alternation continues until reaching an agreement or the maximum number of rounds. For simplicity, α_p^i denotes the conditional probability of accepting the offer in round i, given that the negotiation has not terminated before round i.

The offer made by negotiator p in round k is denoted as o_p^k. The expected utility $\mathbb{E}(p)$ for negotiator p consists of two components: (i) the utilities obtained when the opponent accepts p's offers, and (ii) the utilities obtained when p accepts the opponent's offers. Accordingly, the expected utility is:

$$\mathbb{E}(p) = \sum_{k=0}^{N_r-1} u_p(o_{p_1}^{2k}) \cdot \alpha_{p_2}^{2k+1} + \sum_{i=k}^{N_r-1} u_p(o_{p_2}^{2k-1}) \cdot \alpha_{p_2}^{2k}. \tag{1}$$

Pareto Front. Given the utility functions u_{p_1} and u_{p_2}, the quality of a negotiated outcome can be characterized from a game-theoretic perspective. An offer $o \in \mathcal{O}$ is Pareto optimal if there exists no other offer $o' \in \mathcal{O}$ such that

$$u_{p_1}(o') \geq u_{p_1}(o) \quad \text{and} \quad u_{p_2}(o') \geq u_{p_2}(o), \tag{2}$$

with at least one inequality being strict. The set of all Pareto-optimal offers forms the Pareto front, denoted as $\mathcal{P}$. Offers in the Pareto front mean that it is impossible to improve the utility of one negotiator without reducing the utility of the other [21,23].

Pareto Efficiency. The Pareto efficiency [13] of an offer o, denoted as $V_{\mathrm{PE}}(o) \in [0, 1]$, measures how close the offer is to the Pareto-optimal set. The distance $d(o)$ from offer o to the Pareto front is defined as:

$$d(o) = \min_{o' \in \mathcal{P}} \sqrt{(u_{p_1}(o) - u_{p_1}(o'))^2 + (u_{p_2}(o) - u_{p_2}(o'))^2} \tag{3}$$

The Pareto efficiency is $V_{\mathrm{PE}}(o) = \frac{d_{\max} - d(o)}{d_{\max} - d_{\min}}$, where $d_{\max}$ and $d_{\min}$ are the maximum and minimum distances. A higher $V_{\mathrm{PE}}(o)$ indicates an offer closer to the Pareto front.

Negotiation Trees. We extend the linear negotiation process into a tree structure. In negotiation trees, each node represents a single *action* by a negotiator. Before each negotiation, a main viewer $mv \in \{p_1, p_2\}$ is assigned. Only the main viewer is allowed to have multiple possible actions at a single node, while the opponent's action is sampled once. We alternate the main viewer between the two negotiators across different negotiations to promote capability for both sides. $\mathcal{T}$ denotes a negotiation tree. $\mathcal{A}(n)$ denotes the set of all children nodes at node n, and $\mathrm{par}(n)$ denotes the parent of node n.

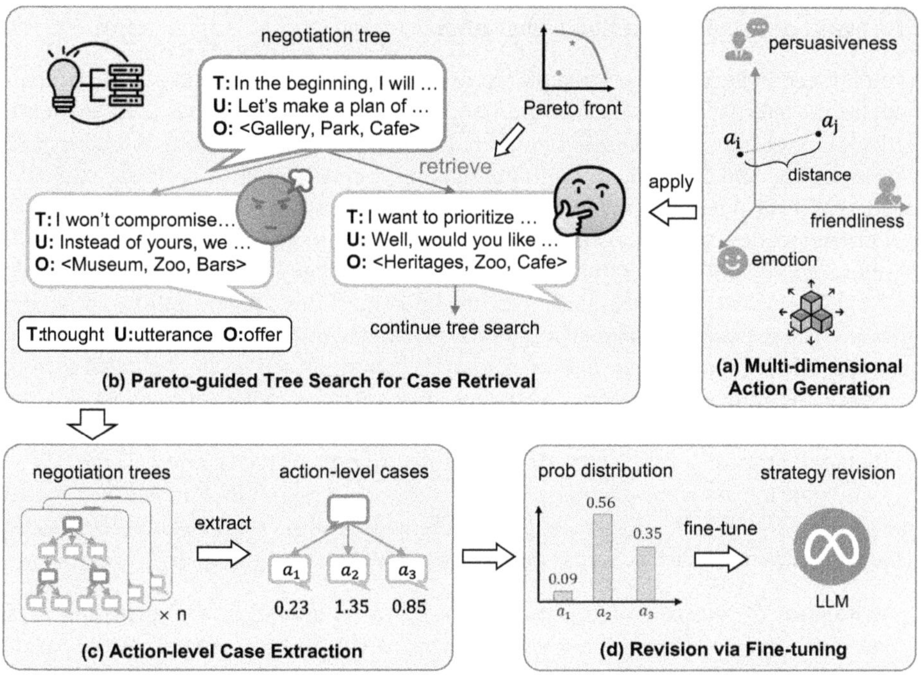

Fig. 1. Overview of the NegLLM framework. **(a) Multi-dimensional Action Generation (Sect.** 4.1). NegLLM maps negotiation actions into a multi-dimensional space and selects a distinct set of candidates based on the semantic distance to ensure strategy diversity. **(b) Pareto-guided Tree Search for Case Retrieval (Sect.** 4.2). NegLLM constructs negotiation trees to explore diverse trajectories, balancing the Pareto front with individual utility. **(c) Action-level Case Extraction (Sect.** 4.3). NegLLM extracts action-level cases from the negotiation trees using a recursive value function to capture actions with high values. **(d) Revision via Fine-tuning (Sect.** 4.4). NegLLM normalizes these values into a target probability distribution, fine-tuning the LLM to align its policy toward this target.

4 Method

In this section, we introduce NegLLM, a framework for enhancing the capacity of negotiation agents. The architecture of NegLLM is shown in Fig. 1. It is a self-refining framework to enhance LLM negotiation agents through strategic self-play. Specifically, multi-dimensional modeling is employed to generate diverse candidate actions. Then NegLLM constructs multiple negotiation trees to retrieve high-quality trajectories. From these trees, NegLLM retrieves strategic cases and calculates action values. Finally, the LLM revises its policy by adjusting its output to align with the normalized probability distribution of actions, internalizing the case-based reasoning strategies into LLM parameters. We conduct all experiments using Llama3-8B-Instruct [3] as the base Language Model and for fine-tuning.

4.1 Multi-dimensional Action Generation

As mentioned in Sect. 3, an action consists of $thought$, $utterance$, and offer o. Because thoughts are internal reasoning and offers are structured expressions, we focus primarily on the styles of utterances at this step. In negotiations, the space of possible utterances is unstructured and theoretically infinite, making it challenging to optimize strategies based solely on natural language. To characterize the strategic nature of utterances, it is crucial to define the semantic dimensions behind them. Subsequently, NegLLM samples a set of candidate actions that exhibit diverse strategies and styles.

NegLLM restricts the negotiation history to at most three recent actions, reflecting the bounded memory in human negotiations. The first action is obtained by querying the Language Model for *thought*, *utterance*, and the offer o based on the bounded history. To obtain the remaining actions, we adopt an iterative exploration method. At each iteration, the previously generated actions are included in the prompt, and the LLM is instructed to propose a new action that is distinct from the existing ones.

Although the iterative diversification method generates sufficient actions, it may still produce stylistically similar utterances. To address this, we measure the semantic distance between utterances across three dimensions according to [9]:

- **Vagueness** d^v measures the semantic clarity of an utterance. We query the LLM multiple times to classify it as clear (1) or vague (0), and compute $d^v \in [0, 1]$ as the average of the responses.
- **Persuasiveness** d^p measures the tone strength of an utterance. We query the LLM multiple times to classify it as high (1) or low (0), and compute $d^p \in [0, 1]$ as the average of the responses.
- **Emotion** d^e measures the emotional profile of an utterance. We query the LLM multiple times over K emotion labels and aggregate the results into a probability vector $d^e \in [0, 1]^K$.

For two utterences utt_1 and utt_2, the distance D is calculated by:

$$D(utt_1, utt_2) = \sqrt{(d_1^v - d_2^v)^2 + (d_1^p - d_2^p)^2 + JSD(d_1^e \parallel d_2^e)^2}, \tag{4}$$

where vagueness and persuasiveness are measured using squared differences, and emotion is measured by the Jensen-Shannon divergence [18], which is suitable for calculating the distance between two vectors.

We compute the semantic distance between actions, and actions with overly similar utterances are then pruned. We explicitly specify the dimension labels (ensuring sufficient distance from all existing utterances) and instruct the Language Model to generate new actions based on these style combinations to ensure diversity.

4.2 Pareto-Guided Tree Search for Case Retrieval

We introduce Pareto-guided tree search for case retrieval (PGTS-CR), a method with Monte Carlo Tree Search to retrieve relevant negotiation cases based on past negotiation trajectories. The search process is guided by Pareto efficiency, empirical rewards, and the exploration of new possibilities, with the goal of retrieving the most promising case to continue the negotiation. PGTS-CR leverages the generative capabilities of LLMs without relying on any predefined negotiating tactics.

Selection. At the beginning of each PGTS-CR iteration, selection starts at the root and recursively descends the negotiation tree to identify a non-terminal (i.e., ongoing) leaf node for further negotiation. At main viewer nodes, the selection proceeds deterministically to the single child, since the opponent is restricted to a single action at each step. At opponent nodes, multiple candidate continuations generated by the main viewer are evaluated and compared.

At an opponent node, children nodes are ranked according to the following formula, which balances empirical rewards, Pareto efficiency of the proposed offer, and visit counts. Specifically, for a node n, the selection score $V_{\text{score}}(n)$ is defined as

$$V_{\text{score}}(n) = \lambda_{d_n} \bar{R}(n) + (1 - \lambda_{d_n}) V_{\text{PE}}(o_n) + \beta_t \sqrt{\frac{2 \ln N(\text{par}(n))}{N(n) + 1}}, \tag{5}$$

where d_n denotes the negotiation round of node n, $\bar{R}(n)$ denotes the mean empirical reward accumulated from previous roll-outs passing through n. The last term with $N(n)$ and $N(\text{par}(n))$ denotes visit counts of node n and its parent, respectively.

The depth-dependent weight λ_{d_n} is designed to shift the emphasis from Pareto efficiency gradually to empirical rewards, as the negotiation rounds increase:

$$\lambda_{d_n} = \frac{2}{\pi} \cdot \arctan\left(1 + \left\lfloor \frac{d_n}{2} \right\rfloor\right). \tag{6}$$

This design encourages PGTS-CR to prioritize offers closer to the Pareto front in earlier rounds, while gradually shifting the focus toward maximizing the main viewer's utility in later rounds.

To further regulate exploration over the course of PGTS-CR, the exploration coefficient β_t is scheduled to decay smoothly with the number of PGTS-CR iteration t:

$$\beta_t = \beta_{\min} + (\beta_{\max} - \beta_{\min}) \cos^2\left(\frac{\pi t}{2N_{\text{iter}}}\right), \tag{7}$$

where $\beta_{\max}$ and $\beta_{\min}$ denote the initial and final exploration coefficients respectively. The selection favors broader exploration in early iterations and increasingly exploits high-quality branches as PGTS-CR goes on.

During selection, this recursive process guarantees that PGTS-CR selects an opponent leaf node that is suitable for expansion from the main viewer's perspective.

Expansion. In the expansion step, we query the Language Model several times to compute α, the probability of accepting the opponent's last offer. If the last offer is rejected, PGTS-CR generates a set of N_c candidate actions at the selected leaf node with the method introduced in Sect. 4.1.

Roll-out. In the roll-out step, PGTS-CR simulates the continuation of the negotiation from the newly expanded node until a terminal state is reached or the maximum negotiation depth $2N_r$. Both negotiation agents take only one action at a single node during

Algorithm 1. Pareto-guided tree search for case retrieval

Require: Negotiation depth $2N_r$, Number of candidate actions N_c, Number of PG-MCTS iterations N_{iter}, Main viewer $mv \in \{p_1, p_2\}$, Language Model $\mathcal{LM}$
Ensure: Negotiation tree $\mathcal{T}$ with estimated utilities for mv

Initialize negotiation tree $\mathcal{T}$ with root node $root$
for $t = 1$ to N_{iter} **do**
  $n \leftarrow root$
  while n is non-terminal **do**
    if Role$(n) \neq mv$ **then**
      $n \leftarrow \arg\max_{n' \in \mathcal{A}(n)} V_{\text{score}}(n')$
    else
      $n \leftarrow$ the single child of n
    end if
  end while
  $\mathcal{A}(n) \leftarrow \text{GENCANDIDATES}(\mathcal{LM}, n, N_c)$
  $n \leftarrow \arg\max_{n' \in \mathcal{A}(n)} V_{\text{score}}(n')$
  $\mathbb{E}(mv) \leftarrow \text{ROLLOUT}(\mathcal{LM}, n, 2N_r)$
  while $n \neq root$ **do**
    if Role$(n) = mv$ **then**
      VisitCount$(n) \leftarrow$ VisitCount$(n) + 1$
      ValueSum$(n) \leftarrow$ ValueSum$(n) + \mathbb{E}(mv)$
    end if
    $n \leftarrow$ par(n)
  end while
end for
return $\mathcal{T}$

the roll-out. After the roll-out terminates, the expected utility of the main viewer $\mathbb{E}(mv)$ along the simulated trajectory is computed for the backpropagation step.

Backpropagation. In the backpropagation step, PGTS-CR propagates the expected utility of the main viewer $\mathbb{E}(mv)$ back along the path from the expanded node to the root. For each main viewer's node on this path, the visit count is incremented, and the empirical reward is updated accordingly.

In conclusion, PGTS-CR constructs a negotiation tree through repeated iterations. The tree records negotiation trajectories, along with their associated value estimates, enabling the retrieval of the most relevant historical cases. By systematically exploring various negotiation paths, PGTS-CR identifies promising cases for guiding the current negotiation, ensuring that past experiences inform the decision-making process effectively. The pseudo-code of PGTS-CR is summarized in Algorithm 1.

4.3 Action-Level Case Extraction

After constructing a collection of negotiation trees using PGTS-CR, we extract high-quality action-level supervision negotiation cases. Each case contains at most three historical actions to reflect the bounded memory in human negotiations, along with the current action.

Value Evaluation of Actions. Each action of the main viewer is assigned a scalar score that reflects both its immediate utility and the expected outcome of continuing the negotiation. We evaluate the future value of every action via a depth-first traversal.

The immediate reward of taking action a at node n is defined as

$$R(a) = \alpha_n \cdot u_{mv}(o_{\text{par}(n)}), \tag{8}$$

where α_n denotes the probability that the offer proposed at the parent node of n is accepted at node n, and u_{mv} denotes the utility of the main viewer.

The future value of a main-viewer's action $a \in \mathcal{A}(n)$ at an opponent node n is computed recursively as

$$V(n, a) = \begin{cases} R(a), & \text{if } a \text{ is leaf,} \\ R(a) + \gamma(1 - \alpha_n)V(a, b), & \text{otherwise,} \end{cases} \tag{9}$$

where b is the single child of a (because there is only one opponent node beneath each main viewer node), and γ is the discount factor. This evaluation assigns each main viewer's action a scalar score that captures both its immediate utility and its expected long-term outcome.

Case Extraction. Given the action-level value estimates, NegLLM extracts negotiation cases by traversing the negotiation tree recursively and retaining sufficiently competitive actions. For an opponent node n, we identify the set of high-quality actions as

$$\mathcal{A}_{\text{HQ}}(n) = \{a \in \mathcal{A}(n) \mid V(n, a) \geq \tau \max_{a' \in \mathcal{A}(n)} V(n, a')\}, \tag{10}$$

where $\tau \in (0, 1)$ is a relative threshold.

The case extraction process proceeds recursively along the successor nodes induced by the retained actions, preserving a set of near-optimal actions, while filtering out low-value actions.

4.4 Revision via Fine-Tuning

While fine-tuning the Language Model towards the optimal solution is possible, NegLLM instead aligns the model's output with a probability distribution, enhancing dynamic adaptability in negotiation tasks.

Normalization. To ensure fair comparison and eliminate the effect of value scale differences, the action values are normalized and transformed into a probability distribution as follows:

$$\rho_{\text{HQ}}(a|n) = \frac{V(n, a)}{\sum_{a' \in \mathcal{A}_{\text{HQ}}(n)} V(n, a')}. \tag{11}$$

This equation first normalizes the high-quality action values $V(n, a)$ to the range $[0, 1]$ and then converts them into a probability distribution.

The Loss Function. The fine-tuning objective is minimizing the Kullback-Leibler (KL) divergence [14] between the Language Model's output probability distribution and the target normalized probability distribution:

$$\min_{\pi_\phi} \mathbb{E}_{(n,a)} \left[D_{\mathrm{KL}} \Big(\pi_\phi(a|n) \parallel \rho_{\mathrm{HQ}}(a|n) \Big) \right], \tag{12}$$

where $\pi_\phi(a|n)$ represents the Language Model's output probability distribution over action a given the input n.

NegLLM revise the parameters of the Language Model by fine-tuning with the probability distribution of the high-quality negotiation cases. As a result, the model can operate effectively without the need for online search during deployment, allowing for faster and more efficient decision-making in real-world applications.

Note that, all stages (in PGTS-CR and in evaluation) of the prompts querying Language Models, and all the cases for fine-tuning do not include any information about the Pareto front or the opponent's private information. The Pareto front is only used as a guiding signal in the PGTS-CR selection step, and is not reflected in the prompts. All $thoughts$ in actions are not observable by the opponent.

5 Experiments

In this section, we conduct a comprehensive evaluation of NegLLM to assess its effectiveness in negotiations. Section 5.1 introduces the experimental scenarios, settings, and metrics. Section 5.2 evaluates whether NegLLM leads to better performance compared to the original model. Section 5.3 evaluates the performance of NegLLM on scenarios that are not included during training. Section 5.4 compares NegLLM against other negotiation agents and state-of-the-art LLMS. Section 5.5 conducts the ablation studies.

5.1 Experimental Setup

Scenarios. We evaluate NegLLM across three negotiation scenarios with substantially different characteristics: Antique Trade (AT), Travel Plan (TP), and City Management (CM). These scenarios vary in terms of the number of issues, the size of the outcome space, the structure of utility functions, and the degree of competitiveness versus cooperativeness between agents. We introduce randomness in every scenario initialization. This prevents Language Models from relying on memories, ensuring that the actions reflect the reasoning in negotiations.

Table 1 shows the differences among the three scenarios under the number of issues, outcome space, cooperation or competition, and the structure of the utility function.

Experimental Settings. In PGTS-CR, the number of search iterations is $N_{iter} = 80$, the negotiation depth is limited to $2N_r = 16$, and the number of candidate actions is $N_c = 5$. We generate 50 negotiation trees for each scenario. All cases for fine-tuning are extracted from those negotiation trees.

Table 1. Comparative analysis of three scenarios.

Scenario	AT	TP	CM
Number of issues	2	3	4
Outcome space	6561	27	10000
Cooperation or competition	competitive	mixed	mixed
Structure of utility function	weighted sum	weighted sum	complex

All experiments are conducted on a machine running Ubuntu 20.04.3 LTS, equipped with two Intel Xeon E5-2640 v4 processors, 251 GB of RAM, and one NVIDIA A100 GPU with 40 GB of memory. The revision via fine-tuning process takes 8.7 h.

Evaluation Metrics. In the evaluation, we denote the original and fine-tuned negotiation agents as p and p' respectively. To evaluate the effectiveness of NegLLM, we consider three negotiation settings: *baseline* (two original models), *single* (one original model and one fine-tuned model), and *dual* (two fine-tuned models). We run 300 negotiations for each setting (100 negotiations each scenario).

We evaluate the performance using four metrics: individual utility, Pareto efficiency, negotiation rounds, and social welfare.

- **Individual utility** u_p and $u_{p'}$ represent the individual utility of the original model and NegLLM, respectively.
- **Pareto efficiency** V_{PE} measures how close the agreement is to the Pareto front.
- **Social welfare** sw is the sum of the utilities of all negotiators: $sw = u_{p_1} + u_{p_2}$ [10]. We measure the change of sw to evaluate whether NegLLM enhances the overall sum of individual utilities.
- **Agreement rounds** rounds is the number of negotiation rounds reaching an agreement. We measure the change of rounds to observe how NegLLM affects negotiation efficiency.

5.2 Evaluation with the *baseline* Setting

The evaluation results of NegLLM's performance are shown in Table 2. Within the implementation of fine-tuned negotiation agents, NegLLM improves individual utilities by **27.58%** and Pareto efficiency by **44.11%** compared to the *baseline* setting. In terms of social welfare, the average improvement compared to the *baseline* is **19.71%**. Additionally, the number of agreement rounds decreased by **18.18%**, indicating that NegLLM improves outcome quality and enhances negotiation efficiency, resulting in fewer rounds to reach agreement.

Table 2. Evaluation results for NegLLM across different settings and scenarios.

Scenario	Setting	u_p	$u_{p'}$	V_{PE}	sw	Rounds
AT	*baseline*	0.4375	–	0.4470	0.8749	13.0122
	single	0.4456	**0.5708**	0.7018	1.0163	10.6427
	dual	–	**0.5241**	**0.8285**	**1.0482**	**9.1480**
TP	*baseline*	0.5973	–	0.5947	1.1945	14.8210
	single	0.5423	**0.8143**	0.6835	1.3565	13.2824
	dual	–	**0.7114**	**0.7143**	**1.4227**	**12.2817**
CM	*baseline*	0.4646	–	0.4221	0.9292	15.7583
	single	0.5074	**0.6154**	0.5859	1.1228	13.5976
	dual	–	**0.5983**	**0.6266**	**1.1967**	**12.6118**

In *single* settings, there is an improvement in the utility of NegLLM side as well as an increase in Pareto efficiency. Due to the scenario potentially exhibiting cooperation or competition, as well as the pressure from NegLLM on the original model in negotiations, the utility of the original model side may either increase or decrease. In *dual* settings, the utility of the NegLLM side is lower than in the *single* setting because the two NegLLM counterbalance each other. However, other metrics all improve further.

5.3 Performance on Unseen Scenarios

A natural question is how NegLLM would perform in a scenario without being fine-tuned on cases from that scenario. To address this, we fine-tuned three additional models, each excluding cases from one of the scenarios (AT, TP, or CM), and evaluated their performance on the excluded scenario.

The result for NegLLM in unseen scenarios is shown in Table 3. With the implementation of fine-tuned negotiation agents, NegLLM improves individual utilities by an average of **23.46%** and Pareto efficiency by **21.93%** across unseen scenarios compared to the *baseline*. The social welfare increases by **11.23%**, and the agreement rounds decrease by **9.92%**. Although these improvements are smaller than those observed in Sect. 5.2, NegLLM still achieves consistent improvements over the *baseline* in unseen scenarios.

Overall, NegLLM preserves a substantial portion of its effectiveness in unseen scenarios, demonstrating transferable negotiation strategies rather than merely overfitting to scenario-specific patterns.

Table 3. Evaluation results for NegLLM on unseen negotiation scenarios.

Scenario	Setting	u_p	$u_{p'}$	V_{PE}	sw	Rounds
AT	*baseline*	0.4375	–	0.4470	0.8749	13.0122
	single	0.4025	**0.5834**	0.5788	**0.9859**	**11.7457**
	dual	–	**0.4918**	**0.5851**	0.9836	12.9765
TP	*baseline*	0.5973	–	0.5947	1.1945	14.8210
	single	0.4600	**0.7773**	0.6365	1.2372	13.4061
	dual	–	**0.5263**	**0.6645**	**1.3304**	**12.5702**
CM	*baseline*	0.4646	–	0.4221	0.9292	15.7583
	single	0.4626	**0.5588**	0.5018	1.0214	14.4965
	dual	–	**0.5453**	**0.5638**	**1.0906**	**13.1110**

Table 4. Evaluation results for NegLLM against four LLM negotiation agents.

Scenario	AT		TP		CM	
Utility	NegLLM	Opponent	NegLLM	Opponent	NegLLM	Opponent
ChatGPT	**0.60** ± 0.18	0.43 ± 0.18	**0.78** ± 0.13	0.68 ± 0.14	**0.61** ± 0.14	0.58 ± 0.09
DeepSeek	**0.52** ± 0.15	0.49 ± 0.17	0.72 ± 0.13	**0.73** ± 0.15	**0.61** ± 0.14	0.57 ± 0.10
GDP-Zero	**0.59** ± 0.13	0.42 ± 0.15	**0.80** ± 0.13	0.62 ± 0.23	**0.62** ± 0.11	0.47 ± 0.04
OG-Narrator	**0.58** ± 0.13	0.43 ± 0.14	**0.80** ± 0.13	0.59 ± 0.21	**0.62** ± 0.14	0.47 ± 0.06

Note: **Bold** values indicate higher utilities in each pair. Each opponent is evaluated with 300 negotiations with NegLLM (100 negotiations each scenario). The data in the table represents the average values with the standard deviations, i.e., $\mu \pm \sigma$.

5.4 Comparison with Existing LLM-Based Negotiation Agents

We compare NegLLM with two commercial LLMs (ChatGPT [27] and DeepSeek [11]) and two existing negotiation agents (GDP-Zero and OG-Narrator). GDP-Zero [35] employs prompt-based online Monte Carlo Tree Search for planning dialogues. OG-Narrator [34] utilizes an external offer generator for bargaining. Although the prior works were originally built on GPT-3.5/4, we implement both GDP-Zero and OG-Narrator using GPT-5.2 as the backbone in our experiments.

The evaluation results are shown in Table 4. It shows that NegLLM outperforms the opponent agents by **15.87%** in terms of utility across the three scenarios. Except for NegLLM's utility in the TP scenario, which is 1.37% lower when negotiating with DeepSeek, NegLLM's utility is higher than that in all other cases.

GDP-Zero and OG-Narrator perform well in AT, but their performance is relatively poor in TP and CM. One possible explanation is that AT is a near-zero-sum negotiation about price bargaining, whereas TP and CM allow for some degree of cooperation. These two negotiation agents are likely better suited for handling zero-sum bargaining situations, but less effective in identifying favorable agreements in cooperative negotiation scenarios.

Table 5. Ablation study on fine-tuning, guidance from Pareto, and the number of tree branches.

Setting	u_{OG}	u_{setting}	V_{PE}	sw	Rounds	Time(s)
OG	–	0.4998	0.4879	0.9995	14.5305	2.38
w/oFt	0.5213	0.6341	0.6456	1.1754	13.6522	57.81
w/oPG	0.5126	0.5250	0.5424	0.9671	15.1505	2.33
w/oTS	0.4717	0.6153	0.6593	1.0776	13.5039	**2.31**
NegLLM	0.4984	**0.6668**	**0.7231**	**1.2225**	**11.3472**	2.34

Note: Time refers to the average response time for making an action, measured in seconds. "-" refers to the results of both sides of OG in this setting, which is equivalent to the self-play of OG. Each setting is evaluated with 300 negotiations with OG (100 negotiations each scenario).

Overall, the results suggest that NegLLM outperforms existing negotiation agents and state-of-the-art LLMs. Notably, NegLLM is based on fine-tuned Llama3-8B-Instruct, a lightweight Large Language Model, demonstrating that even smaller models can achieve competitive performance in complex negotiation tasks. This underscores the efficiency and potential of enhancing smaller Language Models for negotiations.

5.5 Ablation Study

In the ablation study, we investigate and evaluate the contribution of crucial components to NegLLM. Specifically, we conduct five settings:

- *OG*: The original Llama3-8B-Instruct model.
- *w/oFt*: This setting utilizes Llama3-8B-Instruct with online PGTS-CR, without the process of case extraction and revision via fine-tuning.
- *w/oPG*: During PGTS-CR, there is no guidance from the Pareto front, i.e., $\lambda_{d_n} \equiv 1$ in Eq. 5.
- *w/oTS*: During PGTS-CR, the tree search is disabled; consequently, the model explores a linear structure instead of tree branches, i.e., $N_c \equiv 1$ in Algorithm 1.
- NegLLM: the final negotiation agent we propose.

The result of the ablation study is shown in Table 5. In addition to the metrics mentioned above, the average response time is also recorded.

The results indicate that the *w/oFt* setting can improve utility, and that other metrics are comparable to those of NegLLM. However, due to the reliance on online search, its response time is much higher than that of the other four settings.

In the *w/oPG* setting, the absence of Pareto signals fails to improve performance. This is likely because the agent focuses too much on its own utility during case retrieval. As a result, it refuses to make concessions, leading to a mutually detrimental outcome.

In the *w/oTS* setting, the performance improves compared to *OG*, but still falls short of NegLLM. This is likely because, although some high-quality cases are used for fine-tuning, the absence of tree structures prevents multi-dimensional action generation from exploring more valuable actions, limiting the potential of the *w/oTS* setting.

The ablation study proves the importance and necessity of crucial components in NegLLM. It shows that these components contribute to improving utility and social welfare and to reducing response time, thereby building an effective negotiation agent.

6 Limitations and Future Work

Real-world Negotiation Workflow. The negotiation process of NegLLM is a structured protocol of real-world negotiations. However, real-world negotiations are not strictly turn-based. They often lack explicit utility functions and do not require offers at every step. The assumptions in this work simplify learning and evaluation but may limit the applicability of our results to real-world settings. Future work could explore asynchronous communication and preference ambiguity to handle real-world negotiations.

Problem Scale and Utility Diversity. While NegLLM supports multi-issue negotiations with utility functions to reflect preferences, the diversity of utility patterns is more constrained compared to the field of automated negotiation. In this work, we ensure that the negotiation scenarios and utility functions are aligned with real-world decision-making contexts and intuitive human behaviors. This design improves the tractability, but may limit generalization to negotiations with larger or more irregular preference structures. Future work could investigate how LLM agents adapt to larger outcome spaces and highly non-linear utility functions.

7 Conclusion

We propose NegLLM, a novel framework for enhancing and self-improving LLM negotiation agents with the Case-Based Reasoning paradigm. NegLLM integrates Pareto-guided tree search for case retrieval with multi-dimensional action generation, exploring negotiation trajectories that balance individual utility with Pareto efficiency. Then NegLLM extracts high-quality action-level cases and fine-tunes Llama3-8B-Instruct to retain these cases within LLM parameters. Experimental results demonstrate that NegLLM achieves notable improvements and outperforms existing LLMs in negotiation capabilities. These findings open up new possibilities for developing more sophisticated LLM-based negotiation agents with the CBR paradigm.

Acknowledgments. This study was funded by National Natural Science Foundation of China General Program (No. 62376073), and Shenzhen Natural Science Foundation General Program (No. JCYJ20250604145644060), and Colleges and Universities Stable Support Project of Shenzhen, (No. GXWD20220811170225001).

Declaration on Generative AI. During the preparation of this work, the authors used ChatGPT to: Improve writing style, and grammar and spelling check. After using this tool, the authors review and edit the content as needed and take full responsibility for the publication's content.

References

1. Aamodt, A., Plaza, E.: Case-based reasoning: foundational issues, methodological variations, and system approaches. AI Commun. **7**(1), 39–59 (1994)
2. Abdelnabi, S., Gomaa, A., Sivaprasad, S., Schönherr, L., Fritz, M.: Cooperation, competition, and maliciousness: LLM-stakeholders interactive negotiation. Adv. Neural. Inf. Process. Syst. **37**, 83548–83599 (2024)
3. AI@Meta: Llama 3 model card (2024). https://github.com/meta-llama/llama3/blob/main/MODEL_CARD.md
4. Bagga, P., Paoletti, N., Alrayes, B., Stathis, K.: Anegma: an automated negotiation model for e-markets. Auton. Agent. Multi-Agent Syst. **35**(2), 27 (2021)
5. Bianchi, F., Chia, P.J., Yuksekgonul, M., Tagliabue, J., Jurafsky, D., Zou, J.: How well can LLMs negotiate? negotiationarena platform and analysis. In: Proceedings of the 41st International Conference on Machine Learning, pp. 3935–3951 (2024)
6. Bouslama, R., Ayachi, R., Amor, N.B.: A new generic framework for argumentation-based negotiation using case-based reasoning. In: International Conference on Information Processing and Management of Uncertainty in Knowledge-Based Systems, pp. 633–644. Springer (2018)
7. Cao, M., Luo, X., Luo, X.R., Dai, X.: Automated negotiation for e-commerce decision making: a goal deliberated agent architecture for multi-strategy selection. Decis. Support Syst. **73**, 1–14 (2015)
8. De Mantaras, R.L., et al.: Retrieval, reuse, revision and retention in case-based reasoning. Knowl. Eng. Rev. **20**(3), 215–240 (2005)
9. Duerr, S., Gloor, P.A.: Persuasive natural language generation-a literature review. arXiv:2101.05786 arXiv preprint (2021)
10. Endriss, U., Maudet, N., Sadri, F., Toni, F.: Negotiating socially optimal allocations of resources. J. Artifi. Intell. Res. **25**, 315–348 (2006)
11. Guo, D., et al.: Deepseek-r1 incentivizes reasoning in LLMs through reinforcement learning. Nature **645**(8081), 633–638 (2025)
12. Guo, S., Deng, C., Wen, Y., Chen, H., Chang, Y., Wang, J.: Ds-agent: automated data science by empowering large language models with case-based reasoning. In: Proceedings of the 41st International Conference on Machine Learning, pp. 16813–16848 (2024)
13. Hansson, S.O.: Welfare, justice, and pareto efficiency. Ethical Theory Moral Pract **7**(4), 361–380 (2004)
14. Kullback, S., Leibler, R.A.: On information and sufficiency. Ann. Math. Stat. **22**(1), 79–86 (1951)
15. Kwon, D., Weiss, E., Kulshrestha, T., Chawla, K., Lucas, G., Gratch, J.: Are LLMs effective negotiators? systematic evaluation of the multifaceted capabilities of LLMs in negotiation dialogues. In: Findings of the Association for Computational Linguistics: EMNLP 2024, pp. 5391–5413 (2024)
16. Lenz, M., Hoffmann, M., Bergmann, R.: Llsim: large language models for similarity assessment in case-based reasoning. In: International Conference on Case-Based Reasoning, pp. 126–141. Springer (2025)
17. Li, J., et al.: Reflectevo: improving meta introspection of small LLMs by learning self-reflection. In: Findings of the Association for Computational Linguistics: ACL 2025, pp. 16948–16966 (2025)
18. Lin, J.: Divergence measures based on the shannon entropy. IEEE Trans. Inf. Theory **37**(1), 145–151 (2002)
19. Luo, X., Li, Y., Huang, Q., Zhan, J.: A survey of automated negotiation: human factor, learning, and application. Comput. Sci. Rev. **54**, 100683 (2024)

20. Memon, M.A., Scoccia, G.L., Autili, M.: A systematic mapping study on automated negotiation for autonomous intelligent systems. Autom. Softw. Eng. **32**(2), 1–46 (2025)
21. Nash, J.F., et al.: The bargaining problem. Econometrica **18**(2), 155–162 (1950)
22. Noh, S., Chang, H.C.H.: LLMs with personalities in multi-issue negotiation games. arXiv:2405.05248 arXiv preprint (2024)
23. Rubinstein, A.: Perfect equilibrium in a bargaining model. Econometrica: J. Econometric Soc. 97–109 (1982)
24. Sandholm, T.: Automated negotiation. Commun. ACM **42**(3), 84–85 (1999)
25. Schneider, J., Haag, S., Kruse, L.C.: Negotiating with LLMs: prompt hacks, skill gaps, and reasoning deficits. In: International Conference on Computer-Human Interaction Research and Applications, pp. 238–259. Springer (2024)
26. Shea, R., Kallala, A., Liu, X.L., Morris, M.W., Yu, Z.: Ace: a LLM-based negotiation coaching system. In: Proceedings of the 2024 Conference on Empirical Methods in Natural Language Processing, pp. 12720–12749 (2024)
27. Singh, A., et al.: Openai gpt-5 system card. arXiv preprint arXiv:2601.03267 (2025)
28. Soh, L.K., Tsatsoulis, C.: Agent-based argumentative negotiations with case-based reasoning. In: AAAI Fall Symposium Series on Negotiation Methods for Autonomous Cooperative Systems, pp. 16–25. North Falmouth, Mass (2001)
29. Sycara, K.P.: Persuasive argumentation in negotiation. Theor. Decis. **28**(3), 203–242 (1990)
30. Watson, I.: Case-based reasoning is a methodology not a technology. Knowl.-Based Syst. **12**(5–6), 303–308 (1999)
31. Wilkerson, K., Leake, D.: On implementing case-based reasoning with large language models. In: International Conference on Case-Based Reasoning, pp. 404–417. Springer (2024)
32. Wiratunga, N., et al.: CBR-RAG: case-based reasoning for retrieval augmented generation in LLMs for legal question answering. In: International Conference on Case-Based Reasoning, pp. 445–460. Springer (2024)
33. Wollkind, S., Valasek, J., Ioerger, T.: Automated conflict resolution for air traffic management using cooperative multiagent negotiation. In: AIAA Guidance, Navigation, and Control Conference and Exhibit, p. 4992 (2004)
34. Xia, T., et al.: Measuring bargaining abilities of LLMs: a benchmark and a buyer-enhancement method. In: Findings of the Association for Computational Linguistics: ACL 2024, pp. 3579–3602 (2024)
35. Yu, X., Chen, M., Yu, Z.: Prompt-based monte-carlo tree search for goal-oriented dialogue policy planning. In: Proceedings of the 2023 Conference on Empirical Methods in Natural Language Processing, pp. 7101–7125 (2023)

Beyond Trajectory: Explicit Case-Based Memory for Decision-Making in Multimodal GUI Agents

Yongkang Zhang[1(✉)] and Ai Zheng[2]

[1] Huazhong Agricultural University, Wuhan, China
yongkangzhang273@gamil.com
[2] Tsinghua University, Beijing, China

Abstract. Multimodal GUI agents increasingly depend on prior experience to solve complex interactive tasks. However, many existing memory mechanisms treat prior experience as raw trajectory retrieval, leaving reuse implicit and difficult to control. We present an explicit case-based memory framework for offline decision-making in multimodal GUI-agent tasks. It organizes prior interactions as structured cases and supports reuse through similarity-based retrieval, candidate shaping, and selective revision. We evaluate it on AndroidWorld and OSWorld under held-out protocols across heterogeneous backbones, and further examine semantic-action transfer on GUI Odyssey. Across these settings, explicit case representation and controlled reuse consistently improve over benchmark-matched no-memory baselines. Additional attribution analyses show that the gains are driven primarily by structured retrieval and candidate-space shaping, not by arbitrary retrieval or revision-heavy repair.

Keywords: Case-Based Reasoning · Multimodal GUI Agents · Agent Memory · Case Retrieval and Reuse

1 Introduction

Case-based reasoning (CBR) views intelligent behavior as a cycle of retrieving prior cases, reusing them in a new context, revising imperfect reuses, and retaining new experience [1,6,10,24,25]. This perspective is increasingly relevant for multimodal GUI agents, where a previously completed workflow or manipulation pattern can often be reused when a later task shares similar app structure, action families, or operational constraints [3,4,9,14,18,19,27,28,33,34].

In practice, prior experience in retrieval-enhanced agents is often represented as raw text chunks, loosely related demonstrations, or opaque trajectory snippets [11,15,16,21,22,26,28,30,32,33]. This makes it difficult to tell whether

Y. Zhang and A. Zheng—These authors contributed equally.

L. Malburg and K. Bach (Eds.): ICCBR 2026, LNAI 16780, pp. 334–353, 2027.
https://doi.org/10.1007/978-3-032-33865-5_21

a gain comes from semantic similarity, app compatibility, action-family reuse, benchmark-schema alignment, or later repair [15,21,32].

This ambiguity is especially consequential in GUI benchmarks [3,4,12,18, 27,34]. Unlike generic document retrieval, GUI decision prediction is organized around benchmark-specific label spaces and app-dependent action constraints. A useful prior interaction is therefore not just a similar trace, but a reusable *case* whose relevance can be interpreted through goal, app context, action family, and downstream decision support [1,10,24,25].

In this paper, we study memory for multimodal GUI agents as an *explicit case-based reuse* problem. Rather than treating memory as unstructured retrieved text, we represent prior interaction records as structured cases and implement a four-stage controller: case representation, similarity retrieval, adaptation with candidate shaping, and conservative revision. The key point is that structured retrieval and lightweight adaptation reshape the candidate decision space through app-compatible routing, schema alignment, and task-appropriate choice control.

A further complication is that GUI benchmarks are not difficult in the same way. In our study, AndroidWorld [18,19] is primarily coverage-limited, whereas OSWorld [27] is more directly schema-sensitive. These differences imply that reuse must remain task- and schema-aware.

To study this question conservatively, we adopt an offline evaluation setting centered on AndroidWorld and OSWorld, and examine whether the same reuse signal generalizes across multiple backbone models. We focus on a simpler question: can an explicit case-memory formulation outperform raw trajectory retrieval while making reuse more interpretable?

Our results support this framing. Across AndroidWorld and OSWorld, structured case reuse achieves the strongest mean performance, outperforming both raw trajectory retrieval and structured retrieval without adaptation. The same reuse signal also transfers across multiple backbones under task-native decision regimes, and the most stable explanation is decision-space reshaping through structured retrieval, app-compatible routing, and schema-aware choice control.

Our contributions are as follows:

- We formulate memory for multimodal GUI agents around **structured cases** rather than opaque retrieved trajectory chunks, making the reusable memory unit itself explicit and inspectable.
- We present a **four-stage case-memory controller**—case representation, similarity retrieval, adaptation with candidate shaping, and conservative revision—that maps naturally onto explicit case-based retrieve–reuse–revise reasoning.
- We provide a **task- and schema-aware offline evaluation protocol** spanning AndroidWorld and OSWorld, supplemented with a transfer check on GUI Odyssey.
- We show that the strongest gains arise from **candidate shaping, schema alignment, and app-compatible routing**, together with attribution, revision, and split-isolation controls.

2 Related Work

Multimodal GUI Agents and Grounded Interaction. Recent multimodal GUI-agent research has shifted evaluation from text-only reasoning to grounded interaction under app-specific action constraints, spatial interface structure, and task-specific label spaces. Representative benchmarks include MIND2WEB, WEBARENA, OSWORLD, ANDROIDWORLD, and WORKARENA, together with complementary datasets such as WEBSHOP, SCREENSPOT, GUI ODYSSEY, and MEMGUI-BENCH [2–4,12,14,18,27,29,34]. Models such as COGAGENT, APPAGENT, MOBILE-AGENT, and WEBVOYAGER further demonstrate the feasibility of multimodal control in realistic web, desktop, and mobile environments [7,8,23,31]. These settings matter not only because they increase realism, but also because they make reuse more structured than in generic text tasks: a useful prior interaction must align not only with instruction semantics, but also with the relevant app family, action schema, and evaluator semantics. This is precisely why memory for multimodal GUI agents cannot be treated as generic text retrieval alone.

Memory, Reflection, and Trajectory Retrieval in LLM Agents. A second line of work studies how agents benefit from memory, reflection, and iterative repair. Frameworks such as REACT, REFLEXION, and SELF-REFINE show that feedback, self-correction, and iterative revision can improve downstream behavior [15,21,30]. Longer-horizon agent systems such as VOYAGER, MEMGPT, and EXPEL explore experience accumulation, skill reuse, and context management across extended interaction histories [16,22,32]. Related directions also study trajectory-level prompting and memory for computer control or open-ended agents, including SYNAPSE, auto-scaling memory for GUI agents, and broader agent benchmarks and tool-use settings [13,17,20,26,33,35]. Collectively, these works establish that prior experience can help. However, in many such systems, reuse remains implicit: prior interaction is stored as summaries, prompt-side memories, demonstrations, or raw trajectory snippets, making the boundary between retrieval, reuse, and repair difficult to observe directly. Our work is motivated by this gap. Rather than asking whether memory helps in general, we ask how prior GUI interaction should be represented if reuse itself is to remain explicit, inspectable, and analyzable under task and schema constraints.

Case-based Reasoning and Explicit Reuse. This question is naturally aligned with classical Case-Based Reasoning (CBR), which organizes problem solving around the explicit cycle of *retrieve–reuse–revise–retain* and places case representation and adaptation at the center of the method [1,10]. Recent work has increasingly connected CBR with modern LLM-based systems, arguing that explicit case vocabularies, structured similarity, and controlled adaptation can improve interpretability and alignment beyond standard retrieval-augmented generation [5,6,11,24,25]. For example, CBR-RAG-style formulations improve retrieval alignment in knowledge-intensive domains such as legal question answering [25], while other work explores how LLMs can assist specific parts of the CBR cycle or formalizes the broader relationship between CBR and LLM agents [6,24]. These studies validate the relevance of explicit case structure, but they mostly focus on text-based or domain-specific question answering. Much less is known about how explicit case structures should be designed for multimodal GUI agents, where visual states, app-specific constraints, and task-specific action schemas directly determine what counts as reusable experience.

Position of this Work. Our work is closest in spirit to retrieval-based GUI agents, memory-augmented LLM agents, and recent CBR–LLM integrations, but its claim is narrower and more explicit. We do not study memory as generic prompt augmentation, nor do we treat revision-heavy reflection as the main source of gain. Instead, we formulate prior GUI experience as an explicit structured case and study how similarity retrieval and lightweight adaptation reshape the candidate decision space through app-compatible routing, schema-aware filtering, and benchmark-matched decoding control [28]. In this sense, our contribution is not simply stronger retrieval, but a more explicit case-based account of how prior GUI experience can be represented, reused, and analyzed in multimodal GUI agents.

3 Method

3.1 Overview

We study memory for multimodal GUI agents as explicit *case-based reuse* [10]. As shown in Fig. 1, the controller consists of four stages: case representation, similarity retrieval, adaptation with candidate shaping, and conservative revision. In classical CBR terms, the reuse core remains similarity, adaptation, and revision [1]; the added representation stage makes both the query episode and prior interactions explicit enough for controlled retrieval and audit.

Given a query episode, the controller converts both the query and prior interactions into structured cases, retrieves a local neighborhood, reshapes the candidate decision space using compatibility cues, and applies revision only when the adapted prediction remains low-confidence or inconsistent. The framing is narrower than generic retrieval-augmented generation [11]: we study benchmark decision prediction on GUI tasks and ask how prior experience should be represented and reused so that reuse remains explicit and testable.

3.2 Structured Case Representation

A remaining challenge in GUI memory is that prior experience is often stored as raw trajectories or loosely formatted demonstrations, which makes reuse difficult to interpret and control. We address this by making the memory unit explicit.

Each prior interaction record is encoded as a structured case

$$c_i = (u_i, s_i, r_i, y_i, a_i, v_i, o_i),$$

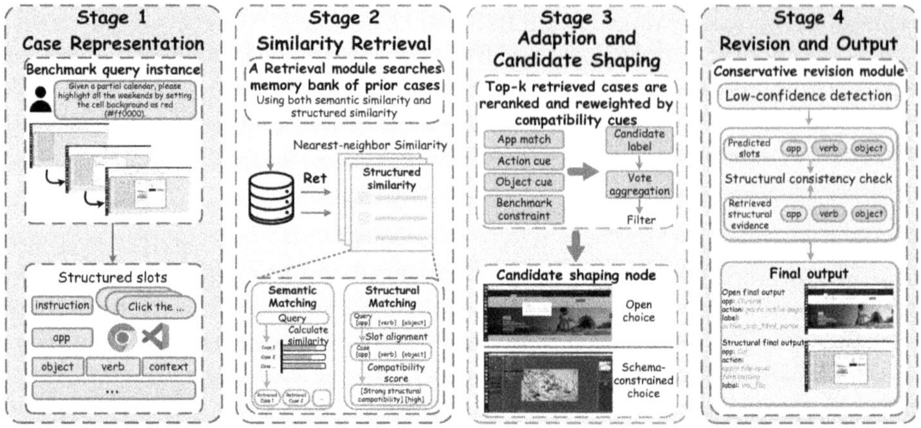

Fig. 1. Four-stage method overview for explicit case-based reuse. Stage 1 converts the query episode and prior interactions into structured cases. Stage 2 retrieves reusable neighbors with both semantic and structural matching. Stage 3 reranks retrieved support into a task- and schema-aware candidate space using app, action, object, and schema cues. Stage 4 applies conservative revision only for low-confidence or structurally inconsistent drafts, then emits a task-native final output together with a logged reuse trace.

where u_i is the instruction, s_i is the benchmark-specific structured context, r_i is an optional raw serialized record, y_i is the canonical decision label, a_i is the app or environment identity, v_i is a normalized verb or action-family cue, and o_i is a lightweight object cue. These fields are constructed with lightweight rule-based normalization rather than a learned parser.

The exact structured context is benchmark-specific. On AndroidWorld, task names are split into app, verb, and object cues, and s_i concatenates those cues with the official difficulty and metadata tags. On OSWorld, s_i concatenates the snapshot app, evaluator result type, and normalized verb/object cues from the instruction. The label schema is also benchmark-specific: AndroidWorld uses `app::verb`, whereas OSWorld uses `app::result_type`. All knowledge comes from benchmark metadata and normalized instruction fields; stored training-case labels provide supervision, and the query gold label is never used.

This representation exposes the fields that matter most for GUI reuse while keeping later stages grounded in explicit compatibility signals.

3.3 Similarity Retrieval

Instruction-level similarity alone is insufficient for GUI reuse, because semantically similar tasks may still belong to different apps or evaluator schemas. We therefore retrieve cases using both semantic and structured signals.

For a query

$$q = (u, s, a, v, o)$$

the similarity between the query and a stored case c_i is computed as

$$S(q, c_i) = \beta_{\text{inst}} \cdot \text{sim}(u, u_i) + \beta_{\text{struct}} \cdot \text{sim}(s, s_i)$$

where $\text{sim}(\cdot, \cdot)$ denotes a text similarity function over the corresponding fields. We weight β_{struct} more heavily than β_{inst}, since benchmark structure and app context are more predictive of reusable decisions than instruction text alone.

For our primary evaluation, we use TF-IDF bigram similarity over instruction and structured text with weights 0.6 and 0.4, retrieve a top-5 neighborhood, and expose the top k = 3 cases to the prompt. The weighted retrieval score is used only to form a candidate neighborhood, not to directly determine the final decision. Potential conflicts between instruction-level and structural similarity are handled in the adaptation stage, where app, verb, object, and schema compatibility are rechecked before candidate aggregation. Thus, semantically similar but structurally incompatible cases may enter the neighborhood, but they are down-weighted during candidate shaping.

3.4 Adaptation via Candidate Shaping

Retrieval alone does not guarantee reusable support. Even among nearby cases, some labels may be incompatible with the current app, action family, or evaluator schema, so we use an explicit adaptation stage to reshape the candidate decision space. Adaptation applies compatibility-sensitive reweighting with additive verb and object boosts of 0.12 and 0.06, using app identity, normalized verb and object cues, evaluator-result schema information, and benchmark metadata already present in the query description. The goal is to rerank retrieved support so that structurally compatible labels become more likely while incompatible labels are suppressed. On GUI Odyssey, retrieved cases remain contextual hints and the final decision still ranges over the full benchmark label space.

3.5 Conservative Revision and Audit

A final challenge is that even after adaptation, some predictions remain unreliable. We therefore retain revision as an explicit stage for auditability, but use it only as a selective repair mechanism rather than as the main source of gain. Revision is triggered when the adapted top-1 margin is small or when the predicted app prefix is inconsistent with the query, with a threshold of 0.005 set on validation margins. The reviser is a logistic regression model trained on sparse instruction and structured-text features, and each run logs retrieved cases, compatibility flags, vote scores, margins, and revision triggers.

3.6 Scope of the Method

Our study focuses on offline decision-level reuse rather than online memory retention or trajectory editing. We do not attempt full trajectory rewriting, continual memory maintenance, or long-horizon online adaptation. Instead, we ask how prior GUI experience should be represented and reused so that the process remains explicit, task- and schema-aware, and empirically testable.

4 Experimental Setup

We evaluate our method along three complementary axes: AndroidWorld and OSWorld provide the primary offline decision-level results under benchmark-matched decoding, GUI Odyssey serves as a transfer-oriented semantic-action test, and evaluation logs support mechanism analysis. Because all three evaluations operate on logged offline episodes rather than full online execution, they isolate decision-level reuse more directly than end-to-end agent rollouts.

4.1 Implementation Details and Fairness

To ensure reproducible evaluation, we standardize the protocol across benchmarks. Retrieval uses TF-IDF bigrams over instruction and structured text with weights 0.6 and 0.4, retrieving a top-5 neighborhood from which the prompt receives the top $k = 3$ cases. During adaptation, we apply additive verb and object boosts of 0.12 and 0.06, and revision is triggered when the top-1 margin falls below 0.005. The reviser is a logistic regression model trained on sparse instruction and structured-text features from the training split. Memory cases are constructed from the training split only, and decoding uses vLLM with temperature 0.0 and top-$p = 0.9$.

Across all variants, we keep the same structured fields, retrieval stack, and decoder, changing only whether memory retrieval is enabled and how the final decision space is constrained. On AndroidWorld, the official matrix uses the benchmark-matched open no-memory baseline. On OSWorld, we use the app-schema no-memory baseline because the label space is naturally app-scoped and the open baseline degrades sharply. Accordingly, structured case reuse uses open final choice on AndroidWorld and closed app-schema choice on OSWorld. On GUI Odyssey, retrieved labels serve as contextual hints rather than hard answer-space pruning.

This setup is intentionally conservative with respect to scope. The paper studies whether explicit reusable cases improve offline decision prediction under task-native interfaces; it does not claim gains for fully online execution, continual retention, or long-horizon trajectory correction.

When diagnostic comparisons are available, we additionally compare against no retrieval, raw trajectory retrieval, semantic nearest-neighbor retrieval, and structured retrieval without adaptation. Semantic nearest-neighbor retrieval denotes instruction-only TF-IDF retrieval without structural adaptation. AndroidWorld and OSWorld use success rate as the primary metric. For detailed analysis, AndroidWorld is further broken down into its official difficulty levels (Easy, Medium, Hard), while OSWorld follows the official category groups (OS, Office, Daily, Professional, Workflow). Unless stated otherwise, all slice analyses keep the original benchmark metadata rather than new regroupings introduced here.

5 Results

5.1 Cross-Model Evaluation

Table 1 reports the main evaluation results across ten backbone models under the benchmark-matched settings described above.

Table 1. Joint AndroidWorld/OSWorld official local slice matrix on the official held-out local protocol. Each backbone occupies benchmark-matched Base and default Ours rows on the same held-out rows. AndroidWorld columns follow the official difficulty strata (61 Easy, 36 Medium, 19 Hard) plus Overall. OSWorld columns follow the official category groups (24 OS, 117 Office, 78 Daily, 49 Professional, 101 Workflow) plus Overall.

Model	Method	AndroidWorld				OSWorld					
		Easy	Med.	Hard	All	OS	Off.	Daily	Prof.	Work.	All
Qwen2.5-3B	Base	1.64	2.78	0.00	1.72	66.67	87.18	35.90	22.45	38.61	53.12
	Ours	81.97	77.78	57.89	**76.72**	66.67	95.73	52.56	73.47	66.34	**73.71**
Qwen2.5-7B	Base	9.84	0.00	0.00	5.17	54.17	60.68	41.03	28.57	36.63	45.26
	Ours	83.61	77.78	89.47	**82.76**	66.67	95.73	43.59	75.51	68.32	**72.63**
Qwen2.5-14B	Base	29.51	38.89	15.79	30.17	58.33	17.95	34.62	14.29	24.75	25.47
	Ours	90.16	80.56	89.47	**87.07**	66.67	95.73	50.00	71.43	69.31	**73.71**
Qwen2.5-32B	Base	11.48	11.11	0.00	9.48	50.00	19.66	37.18	18.37	25.74	26.83
	Ours	95.08	97.22	94.74	**95.69**	62.50	95.73	43.59	69.39	67.33	**71.27**
Qwen3-VL-4B	Base	21.31	13.89	21.05	18.97	62.50	92.31	37.18	22.45	34.65	53.66
	Ours	93.44	83.33	78.95	**87.93**	66.67	96.58	52.56	73.47	64.36	**73.44**
Qwen3-VL-8B	Base	19.67	25.00	5.26	18.97	66.67	88.89	35.90	30.61	40.59	55.28
	Ours	85.25	80.56	78.95	**82.76**	58.33	96.58	47.44	69.39	68.32	**72.36**
Qwen3-32B	Base	21.31	36.11	0.00	22.41	54.17	55.56	50.00	16.33	31.68	42.55
	Ours	93.44	97.22	94.74	**94.83**	66.67	96.58	51.28	67.35	67.33	**73.17**
InternVL3-8B	Base	18.03	13.89	10.53	15.52	58.33	40.17	42.31	30.61	47.52	42.55
	Ours	78.69	66.67	89.47	**76.72**	70.83	95.73	48.72	75.51	69.31	**74.25**
InternVL3-14B	Base	16.39	16.67	5.26	14.66	62.50	24.79	46.15	14.29	39.60	34.42
	Ours	95.08	91.67	94.74	**93.97**	58.33	95.73	46.15	67.35	68.32	**71.54**
Mistral-Small-3.1-24B	Base	21.31	27.78	5.26	20.69	62.50	58.97	39.74	26.53	34.65	44.17
	Ours	65.57	63.89	73.68	**66.38**	66.67	95.73	51.28	71.43	68.32	**73.71**

Across all ten backbones, structured case reuse consistently improves over the benchmark-matched baselines on both AndroidWorld and OSWorld. On AndroidWorld, performance gains are broad across the Easy, Medium, and Hard tiers, with the most pronounced improvements observed on smaller-scale foundational baselines. On OSWorld, the gains remain stable across Office, Professional, and Workflow categories, while the limited 24-row OS slice exhibits expected statistical variance due to its size. Overall, the benefit of structured reuse remains consistent across both benchmark protocols, although its magnitude depends on benchmark difficulty and candidate-space structure.

5.2 Semantic Action Transfer on GUI Odyssey

GUI Odyssey provides a complementary zero-shot transfer evaluation across its six task categories: Tool, Information, Shopping, Media, Social, and Multi-Apps. We evaluate the models using a standardized offline semantic-action prediction protocol on this dataset. Table 2 reports the held-out-device performance across a representative subset of backbone models. By operating on identical episodes and candidate label sets, this setup yields a direct measure of memory-driven action alignment.

Table 2. GUI Odyssey held-out-device semantic-action matrix. Each backbone is evaluated with paired Base and Ours rows on the same held-out-device episodes. Columns follow the official six GUI Odyssey task categories (Tool, Information, Shopping, Media, Social, Multi-Apps) plus Overall, and report semantic-action accuracy. Ours keeps retrieved cases as contextual hints while preserving the full global label space at decision time.

Model	Method	Tool	Information	Shopping	Media	Social	Multi-Apps	Overall
Qwen2.5-3B	Base	41.68	35.62	47.19	38.06	33.25	38.60	38.48
	Ours	57.79	43.18	49.21	40.90	53.75	48.07	**49.45**
Qwen2.5-VL-7B	Base	59.83	53.49	59.10	59.81	60.55	58.18	58.28
	Ours	62.19	54.75	58.43	56.50	66.15	57.61	**59.34**
Qwen2.5-32B	Base	71.86	64.38	72.81	69.98	73.30	71.70	70.69
	Ours	79.16	74.80	70.56	76.36	77.83	78.58	**77.03**
Qwen3-VL-4B	Base	72.40	66.67	71.24	70.45	67.82	68.92	69.32
	Ours	82.38	78.24	76.85	80.38	78.55	78.46	**79.17**
Qwen3-VL-8B	Base	74.65	68.38	70.34	74.00	74.14	69.99	71.61
	Ours	81.95	76.98	74.38	79.91	77.71	77.57	**78.21**
Qwen3-32B	Base	71.32	55.90	70.79	67.85	67.94	57.68	63.55
	Ours	79.16	66.09	62.25	65.25	71.99	69.30	**70.04**
InternVL3-8B	Base	44.47	38.03	51.91	40.19	43.38	43.65	43.23
	Ours	57.14	45.48	47.64	45.63	58.40	44.60	**49.67**
InternVL3-14B	Base	70.14	52.58	67.19	61.94	61.62	58.56	61.19
	Ours	77.87	68.61	69.89	69.74	73.78	70.75	**72.03**
LLaVA-v1.6-Mistral-7B	Base	40.39	32.53	40.45	35.70	31.82	35.94	35.87
	Ours	54.35	39.29	42.25	38.77	51.85	42.77	**45.41**

Under this isolated protocol, explicit case memory demonstrates consistent empirical benefits. Treating retrieved cases as structural contextual evidence rather than rigid candidate gates yields positive gains across the evaluated models. The most substantial improvements emerge on schema-sensitive foundational models (e.g., Qwen2.5-3B, LLaVA-v1.6-Mistral-7B, and InternVL3-14B), indicating that explicit memory effectively compensates for weaker native GUI priors. Meanwhile, highly optimized architectures like Qwen3 and Qwen2.5-VL also register clear, positive performance deltas, confirming that the retrieval mechanism provides additive value even for strong baselines.

5.3 Ablation and Sensitivity

Figure 2 summarizes three auxiliary checks. Panel (a) reports official 5-seed robustness on three representative backbones: Qwen2.5-14B, Qwen3-VL-8B, and InternVL3-14B. In all three cases, structured case reuse remains above the benchmark-matched baseline across seeds on AndroidWorld, and the mean gain remains positive on OSWorld.

Panels (b) and (c) vary the retrieval budget k under the same app-filtered local controller and measure end-to-end accuracy on five representative backbones from four families: Qwen2.5-3B, GUI-Owl-7B, Qwen2.5-14B, Qwen3-VL-4B, and InternVL3-14B.

On AndroidWorld, sensitivity is visible but not unstable: several models improve from top-1 to top-2, while larger neighborhoods often plateau or degrade. On OSWorld, the same sweep is flatter, with accuracy concentrated within a narrow band from top-1 to top-3 and softening only at top-5. Taken together, the figure shows that the main result is robust across seeds, and that retrieval depth matters more on AndroidWorld than on OSWorld.

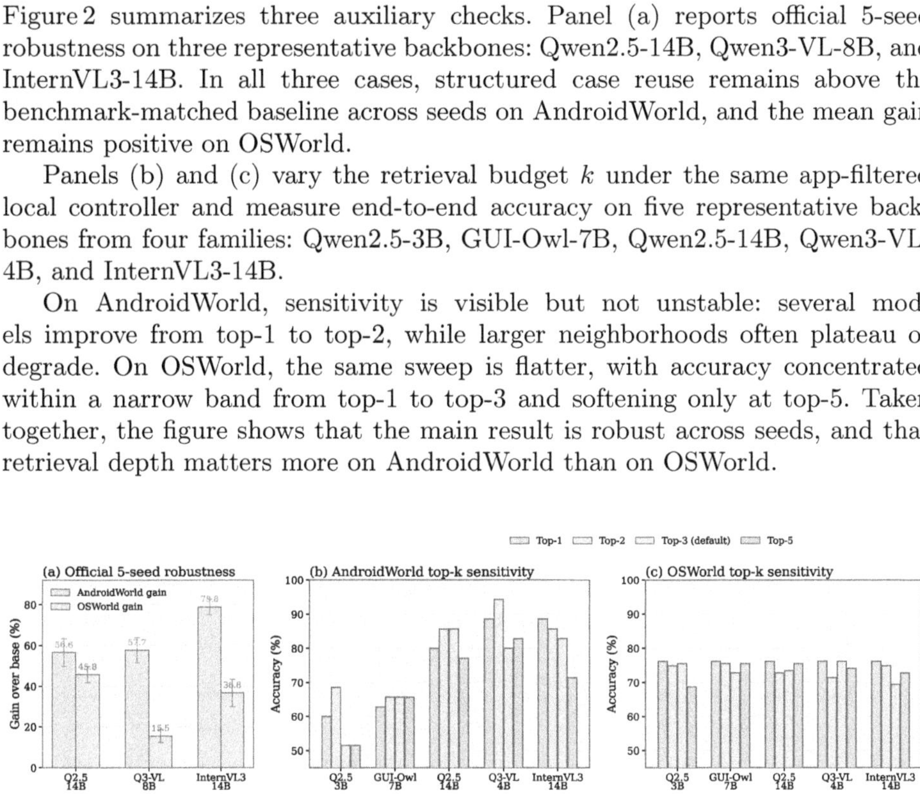

Fig. 2. Robustness and retrieval-budget sensitivity summary. Panel (a) reports official 5-seed robustness on three representative backbones, showing mean full-over-base gain with standard-deviation bars on AndroidWorld and OSWorld. Panels (b) and (c) report app-filtered top-k sensitivity under the local benchmark-matched controller on five representative backbones from four families, using top-3 as the main default and comparing it against shallower and deeper retrieval budgets. The resulting pattern is benchmark-specific but not brittle: AndroidWorld is more sensitive to retrieval depth and often peaks around top-2 or top-3, while OSWorld stays comparatively stable across top-1 to top-3 and softens only at top-5.

5.4 Mechanism Analysis

The benchmark results establish that the method improves decision prediction. We next examine whether retrieval consistently places useful cases in the local neighborhood and whether the controller changes model decisions in a measurable way. Figure 3 addresses the first question through retrieval coverage and choice-regime sensitivity. Figure 4 addresses the second through probability reshaping and prompt-state drift.

Figure 3 shows a clear benchmark asymmetry. The coverage panel aggregates 16 stratified split seeds, yielding 560 AndroidWorld and 2352 OSWorld held-out exposures. Under app-filter retrieval, AndroidWorld reaches 45.18/49.46/50.54 top-1/top-3/top-5 gold coverage, whereas OSWorld reaches 74.32/88.86/90.60. This leaves substantially less downstream room for recovery on AndroidWorld than on OSWorld.

The choice-regime panels follow the same pattern. On AndroidWorld, open-choice case memory improves substantially over the weak open baseline, but the advantage shrinks once the baseline is strengthened with app-constrained choice. On OSWorld, the benchmark-matched app-schema baseline remains relatively weak, open-choice memory helps, and closed-choice memory improves further across the retained backbone sweep.

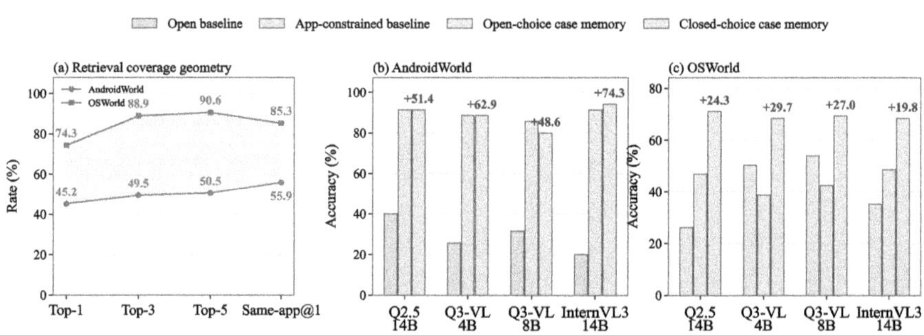

Fig. 3. Broader mechanism overview of retrieval coverage and task-native decision regimes. Panel (a) reports pooled coverage under app-filter retrieval (16 split seeds; 560 AndroidWorld and 2352 OSWorld held-out exposures), measured by whether the gold case appears within top-1, top-3, or top-5. Panels (b) and (c) report matched held-out split-7 choice-regime sweeps for four selected backbones. AndroidWorld compares the open baseline, an app-constrained baseline, and open-choice structured reuse; OSWorld compares the app-constrained baseline, open-choice reuse, and schema-constrained reuse. The overall pattern is benchmark-specific: AndroidWorld is more coverage-limited and baseline-sensitive, whereas OSWorld more clearly reveals the benefit of schema-aware candidate-set control.

Figure 4 turns to the internal probe and again separates the two benchmarks. The left panel focuses on a representative subset of six benchmark-model pairs. These are drawn from three diverse backbones selected to span different model

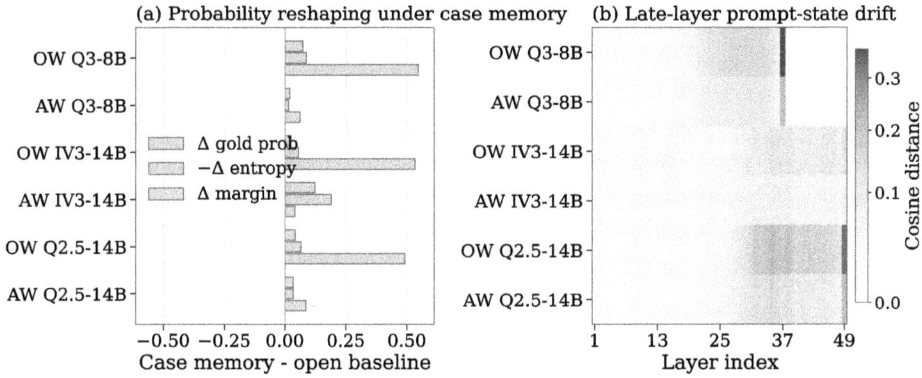

Fig. 4. Internal probe on benchmark-model pairs. Both panels compare structured case reuse with the open no-memory baseline on six representative rows from three probe backbones, shown with compact 'AW/OW + model code' tags. Panel (a) reports signed probability-level deltas: Δ gold-label probability and Δ margin are reuse minus open baseline, while $-\Delta H$ denotes entropy reduction. Panel (b) reports count-weighted layerwise mean cosine distance between prompt states under the two settings, where darker values indicate larger internal state displacement. OSWorld shows larger gold-probability gains and stronger late-layer drift, while AndroidWorld remains closer to the boundary where retrieved cases provide weaker additional control.

families and scaling behaviors: Qwen2.5-14B, Qwen3-VL-8B, and InternVL3-14B. For gold-label probability and top-1 margin, we plot Δ = case memory − open baseline; for entropy, we plot $-\Delta H = H_{\text{open}} - H_{\text{case}}$, so that a positive bar indicates a sharper output distribution under case memory.

The strongest signal is the shift in gold-label probability. Every displayed OSWorld row shows a large positive gain, whereas the AndroidWorld rows move in the same direction but by smaller amounts. This asymmetry survives beyond the displayed slice: across the wider pool of seven locally traced probe models, OSWorld shows positive Δ gold probability on all seven, whereas AndroidWorld does so on only four.

The remaining probability metrics are secondary. Margin and entropy need not improve monotonically even when the gold label becomes more likely, because retrieved cases can redistribute probability mass among several plausible labels. The drift panel provides a complementary state-level view. For each layer, we compute the cosine distance between prompt states under the open baseline and under structured case reuse, then average those distances within each benchmark-model pair. OSWorld again shows the clearer late-layer pattern, especially for Qwen3-VL-8B and InternVL3-14B, while AndroidWorld shows weaker or more heterogeneous drift.

Taken together, the two mechanism figures indicate that the method behaves differently across the two benchmarks: OSWorld demonstrates a more consistent behavioral improvement for coverage, candidate control, and internal reshaping, while AndroidWorld remains closer to the boundary where retrieval often provides weaker downstream leverage.

5.5 Attribution and Control Analyses

The appendix makes the central attribution claim explicit at the table level. As shown in Table 3, random or semantic-only retrieval yields only partial gains, raw trajectory retrieval helps but remains below structured case reuse, and the strongest gains appear once retrieved evidence is converted into compatibility-weighted candidate support. Tables 4, 5 and 6 show that this pattern remains stable under repeated seeds and coverage-bucket diagnostics, while Table 10 shows that alternative routing and truncation choices usually tie or underperform the tuned controller.

6 Discussion

Taken together, the results support a case-based, constraint-sensitive view of reuse for multimodal GUI agents. The attribution analyses make the claim sharper: raw trajectory retrieval and semantic-only retrieval provide only partial gains, while the largest improvement appears when structured cases are converted into compatibility-weighted candidate support. Revision remains useful, but only as a selective repair mechanism rather than the dominant source of improvement. AndroidWorld is constrained primarily by retrieval coverage, whereas OSWorld more cleanly reveals the benefit of schema-compatible candidate control.

Beyond these benchmark-specific observations, the results suggest broader lessons for memory-augmented agents. Useful memory should be represented as structured reusable cases rather than as undifferentiated context snippets, and retrieval should be judged by whether it constrains the downstream decision space in a task-compatible way. These lessons may extend beyond GUI benchmarks to embodied, tool-use, and workflow agents.

7 Limitations

The evaluation is conducted in an offline decision-level setting rather than full online deployment. As a result, we do not study continual memory updates, trajectory-level adaptation, or long-horizon error propagation. The current study also depends on task-specific label spaces and schema information, so it does not yet establish how the same controller transfers to less structured or fully open-ended settings. Large-scale online deployment and broader dense or hybrid retrieval baselines remain future work.

8 Conclusion

We presented an explicit case-based memory framework for multimodal GUI agents and evaluated it in an offline setting spanning model results, transfer checks, and mechanism analysis. Across these settings, case memory helps primarily through candidate shaping—via structured retrieval, schema alignment, and app-compatible routing—rather than through revision-heavy repair. More broadly, useful agent memory may depend less on retrieving longer trajectories than on representing prior experience in a reusable form that can shape the downstream decision space.

Disclosure of Interests. The authors have no competing interests to declare that are relevant to the content of this article.

Use of AI Tools. The authors used AI-assisted tools only for language polishing, grammar checking, and improving the clarity of the manuscript.

Appendix A. Retrieval Attribution and Candidate Shaping

As shown in Table 3, the attribution analysis separates retrieval quality from the later candidate-shaping step. Random retrieval and semantic-only retrieval provide only limited gains, raw trajectory retrieval improves over these weaker controls but remains below structured case reuse, and the largest improvements appear when retrieved evidence is converted into compatibility-weighted candidate support. This pattern supports the interpretation that memory is useful not merely because similar trajectories are placed in the prompt, but because the retrieved cases are made compatible with the benchmark action schema.

Table 3. Retrieval attribution analysis across the main AndroidWorld/OSWorld pair and corrected GUI Odyssey splits. Values are percentages. The table reports the marginal effect of moving from no retrieval to raw trajectory retrieval, semantic nearest-neighbor retrieval, structured retrieval without adaptation, and structured case reuse with revision.

	AndroidWorld-116		OSWorld-300		GUI Odyssey Random		GUI Odyssey Device		Mean	
Method	Acc.	Macro-F1	Acc.	Macro-F1	Acc.	Macro-F1	Acc.	Macro-F1	Acc.	Macro-F1
No retrieval	8.57	0.56	19.73	0.65	32.29	3.75	36.22	4.83	24.20	2.45
Raw trajectory retrieval	40.00	21.79	61.22	32.95	58.77	35.74	57.12	34.25	54.28	31.18
Semantic nearest-neighbor retrieval	37.14	20.61	34.01	13.59	55.98	31.53	56.04	30.88	45.79	24.15
Structured retrieval without adaptation	42.86	22.50	83.67	56.49	44.13	22.55	48.30	23.86	54.74	31.35
Ablation: without revision	42.86	22.50	85.71	60.09	43.90	22.43	47.83	23.42	55.07	32.11
Structured case reuse	42.86	25.96	87.07	63.88	78.28	43.63	80.34	50.89	72.14	46.09

Appendix B. Revision Contribution and Robustness

As shown in Table 4, repeated-seed evaluation keeps the same qualitative ordering between the no-memory baseline and structured case reuse, indicating that the main result is not a single-seed artifact. Table 5 further shows that gains concentrate in buckets where the gold case is retrieved reliably, while Table 6 summarizes how coverage and revision interact. Together, these tables indicate that revision acts as a selective repair stage rather than the dominant source of improvement.

Table 4. Five-seed robustness summary on fixed AndroidWorld and OSWorld subsets. Values are mean ± standard deviation over seeds 3, 7, 13, 29, and 47. These rows are controller-level stability checks rather than multi-backbone reruns: AndroidWorld and OSWorld use fixed 116-item and 300-item subsets with 1000 held-out items per seed.

Benchmark	Items/seed	Structured case reuse	Structured-case F1	No revision	Structured only
AndroidWorld-116	1000	0.4171 ± 0.0779	0.2783 ± 0.0690	0.4229 ± 0.0816	0.3829 ± 0.0758
OSWorld-300	1000	0.8467 ± 0.0361	0.5557 ± 0.0524	0.8511 ± 0.0278	0.8511 ± 0.0278

Table 5. Coverage-bucket diagnostic on the OSWorld proxy set. Rows partition test examples by the first position at which the gold case appears in the tuned retrieval list. The table shows that OSWorld benefits when the gold evidence appears within the top-3 neighborhood, and that revision provides limited but positive recovery on a small subset of difficult cases.

Bucket	n	Share	Struct.	Full	Gain	Rev. trig.
Top-1 hit	103	70.07	95.15	98.06	+2.91	0.00
Top-3 only	25	17.01	72.00	84.00	+12.00	0.00
Top-5 only	4	2.72	0.00	0.00	+0.00	25.00
Miss@5	15	10.20	0.00	13.33	+13.33	26.67

Table 6. Mechanism summary on the primary OSWorld proxy set. Coverage columns use the app-filtered retrieval setting; revision columns report rates under structured case reuse.

Benchmark	Coverage			Accuracy			Revision/lift		
	Top-1	Top-3	Top-5	Same-app@1	Structured	Structured case reuse	Gain	Trigger	Changed
OSWorld	76.19	85.03	87.76	83.67	78.91	84.35	+5.44	3.40	3.40

Appendix C. Split Isolation and Leakage Control

The split-isolation protocol is included as a procedural control for the tables above. All memory cases are constructed strictly from the training split, and no held-out instruction, trajectory, label, or evaluation target is inserted into the memory bank. Retrieval candidates are additionally generated without direct duplication of evaluation rows or benchmark-specific answer templates. These controls rule out direct leakage and exact-template matching as primary explanations for the main effect, while leaving the broader online-deployment question open.

Appendix D. Representative Benchmark-Matched Comparisons

As shown in Table 7, the representative benchmark-matched comparisons expose the same baseline-versus-case-memory contrast on a compact subset of backbone-level results. This table is intended as an inspectable bridge between the headline results and the larger benchmark matrices: each row keeps the comparison protocol explicit so that gains are not conflated with a weaker controller baseline.

Table 7. Representative benchmark-matched comparisons on a compact subset of backbone-level results. The table highlights a small number of local cases that are sufficient to inspect the strongest benchmark-matched gains without consulting the larger matrices.

Benchmark	Model	Baseline regime	Baseline	Case reuse	Gain	Tier
AndroidWorld	GUI-Owl-7B	app-schema	0.5429	0.6571	+0.1142	Headline
AndroidWorld	Qwen3-VL-8B	open	0.6286	0.8857	+0.2571	Headline
OSWorld	GUI-Owl-7B	app-schema	0.3333	0.7347	+0.4014	Headline
OSWorld	Qwen3-VL-8B	app-schema	0.3537	0.7483	+0.3946	Headline
AndroidWorld	Qwen2.5-32B	app-schema	0.5429	0.8286	+0.2857	Secondary
AndroidWorld	Qwen3-VL-4B	app-schema	0.5429	0.9429	+0.4000	Secondary

Appendix E. Per-Model Benchmark Summary

As shown in Table 8, the per-model summary compresses the benchmark-level results into one view of baseline performance, structured case reuse, and mean gain across AndroidWorld and OSWorld. The table is useful for checking whether the main conclusion depends on a single backbone or whether the effect appears across multiple local model families.

Table 8. Per-model benchmark summary under the benchmark-matched comparison protocol. AndroidWorld reports the official no-memory baseline versus structured case reuse with open final choice. OSWorld reports the app-schema no-memory baseline versus structured case reuse with schema-constrained final choice. The final column averages the benchmark-level gains across the two primary benchmarks.

Model	AndroidWorld Base	AndroidWorld Structured Reuse	OSWorld Base	OSWorld Structured Reuse	Mean Gain
Qwen2.5-3B	1.72	76.72	53.12	73.71	+22.80
Qwen2.5-7B	5.17	82.76	45.26	72.63	+52.48
Qwen2.5-14B	30.17	87.07	25.47	73.71	+52.57
Qwen2.5-32B	9.48	95.69	26.83	71.27	+65.33
Qwen3-VL-4B	18.97	87.93	53.66	73.44	+44.37
Qwen3-VL-8B	18.97	82.76	55.28	72.36	+40.44
Qwen3-32B	22.41	94.83	42.55	73.17	+51.52
InternVL3-8B	15.52	76.72	42.55	74.25	+46.45
InternVL3-14B	14.66	93.97	34.42	71.54	+58.22

Appendix F. Top-k Sensitivity

As shown in Table 9, the retrieval-budget sweep studies how many retrieved cases should be exposed to the adaptation stage. The results indicate that performance is not monotonic in neighborhood size: smaller neighborhoods are often sufficient, whereas larger neighborhoods can introduce noise, especially on AndroidWorld. This supports the choice of a conservative default retrieval budget rather than simply increasing top-k.

Table 9. Top-k sensitivity summary across the five representative backbones used in Fig. 2. Each cell reports the mean accuracy (%) across the same five-model subset under the same controller, varying only the number of retrieved cases exposed to the adaptation stage.

Retrieved neighborhood	AndroidWorld mean	OSWorld mean
Top-1	82.38	76.19
Top-2	83.24	73.88
Top-3 (default)	77.94	73.47
Top-5	75.71	73.13

Appendix G. Controller Sensitivity Analysis

As shown in Table 10, the controller sensitivity analysis varies one routing or revision component at a time while holding the remaining settings fixed. The comparison helps separate the main mechanism from implementation-specific choices: most alternatives either tie the tuned controller or underperform it, which supports the use of the default structured-reuse configuration in the main experiments.

Table 10. Meaning of the main local controller switches used in Appendix G. Because these settings affect comparability, they are reported explicitly rather than inferred from filenames.

Switch	Meaning	Main effect
`app`	retrieval keeps only same-app cases	tighter, benchmark-matched candidate set
`noapp`	retrieval may use cross-app cases	broader recall, higher drift risk
`choice`	decode from retrieved/schema candidates only	strict closed-choice control
`choice_open`	retrieved candidates are hints, not a hard set	open-choice reuse under incomplete coverage
`schema app`	no-retrieval baseline sees only same-app labels	fair app-constrained baseline
`top-`k	number of retrieved cases exposed to the controller	coverage versus noise trade-off

References

1. Aamodt, A., Plaza, E.: Case-based reasoning: foundational issues, methodological variations, and system approaches. AI Commun. **7**(1), 39–59 (1994)
2. Cheng, K., Sun, Q., Chu, Y., Xu, F., Li, Y., Zhang, J., Wu, Z.: SeeClick: harnessing GUI grounding for advanced visual GUI agents. In: Proceedings of the 62nd Annual Meeting of the Association for Computational Linguistics (Volume 1: Long Papers), pp. 9313–9332. Association for Computational Linguistics (2024). https://doi.org/10.18653/v1/2024.acl-long.505
3. Deng, X., et al.: Mind2Web: towards a generalist agent for the web. In: Advances in Neural Information Processing Systems (NeurIPS) (2023)
4. Drouin, A., et al.: WorkArena: how capable are web agents at solving common knowledge work tasks? In: Proceedings of the 41st International Conference on Machine Learning. Proceedings of Machine Learning Research, vol. 235, pp. 11642–11662. PMLR (2024)
5. Gao, Y., et al.: Retrieval-augmented generation for large language models: a survey. arXiv preprint arXiv:2312.10997 (2023)
6. Hatalis, K., Christou, D., Kondapalli, V.: Review of case-based reasoning for LLM agents. In: Theoretical Foundations, Architectural Components, and Cognitive Integration arXiv:2504.06943 arXiv preprint (2025)
7. He, H., et al.: WebVoyager: building an end-to-end web agent with large multimodal models. In: Proceedings of the 62nd Annual Meeting of the Association for Computational Linguistics (Volume 1: Long Papers), pp. 6864–6890. Association for Computational Linguistics (2024). https://doi.org/10.18653/v1/2024.acl-long.371
8. Hong, W., et al.: CogAgent: a visual language model for GUI agents. In: Proceedings of the IEEE/CVF Conference on Computer Vision and Pattern Recognition (CVPR), pp. 14281–14290 (2024)
9. Kim, G., Baldi, P., McAleer, S.: Language models can solve computer tasks. In: Advances in Neural Information Processing Systems (NeurIPS) (2023)
10. Kolodner, J.L.: Case-Based Reasoning. Morgan Kaufmann (1993)
11. Lewis, P., et al.: Retrieval-augmented generation for knowledge-intensive NLP tasks. In: Advances in Neural Information Processing Systems (NeurIPS). vol. 33, pp. 9459–9474 (2020)
12. Liu, G., et al.: MemGUI-Bench: benchmarking memory of mobile GUI agents in dynamic environments. arXiv preprint arXiv:2602.06075 (2026)
13. Liu, X., et al.: AgentBench: evaluating LLMs as agents. In: International Conference on Learning Representations (ICLR) (2024)

14. Lu, Q., et al.: GUIOdyssey: a comprehensive dataset for cross-app GUI navigation on mobile devices. In: Proceedings of the IEEE/CVF International Conference on Computer Vision (ICCV), pp. 22404–22414 (2025)
15. Madaan, A., et al.: Self-refine: iterative refinement with self-feedback. In: Advances in Neural Information Processing Systems (NeurIPS) (2023)
16. Packer, C., et al.: MemGPT: towards LLMs as operating systems. arXiv:2310.08560 arXiv preprint (2023)
17. Park, J.S., O'Brien, J.C., Cai, C.J., Morris, M.R., Liang, P., Bernstein, M.S.: Generative agents: interactive simulacra of human behavior. In: Proceedings of the 36th Annual ACM Symposium on User Interface Software and Technology, pp. 1–22 (2023)
18. Rawles, C., et al.: AndroidWorld: a dynamic benchmarking environment for autonomous agents. arXiv preprint arXiv:2405.14573 (2024)
19. Rawles, C., Li, A., Rodriguez, D., Riva, O., Lillicrap, T.: Android in the wild: a large-scale dataset for Android device control. In: Advances in Neural Information Processing Systems (NeurIPS) (2023)
20. Schick, T., et al.: Toolformer: language models can teach themselves to use tools. In: Advances in Neural Information Processing Systems (NeurIPS) (2023)
21. Shinn, N., Cassano, F., Gopinath, A., Narasimhan, K., Yao, S.: Reflexion: language agents with verbal reinforcement learning. In: Advances in Neural Information Processing Systems (NeurIPS) (2023)
22. Wang, G., et al.: Voyager: an open-ended embodied agent with large language models. arXiv:2305.16291 arXiv preprint (2023)
23. Wang, J., et al.: Mobile-agent: autonomous multi-modal mobile device agent with visual perception. arXiv:2401.16158 arXiv preprint (2024)
24. Wilkerson, K., Leake, D.: On implementing case-based reasoning with large language models. In: Case-Based Reasoning Research and Development, pp. 404–417. Lecture Notes in Computer Science, Springer Nature Switzerland (2024). https://doi.org/10.1007/978-3-031-63646-2_26
25. Wiratunga, N., et al.: CBR-RAG: case-based reasoning for retrieval augmented generation in LLMs for legal question answering. In: Case-Based Reasoning Research and Development, pp. 445–460. Lecture Notes in Computer Science, Springer Nature Switzerland (2024). https://doi.org/10.1007/978-3-031-63646-2_29
26. Wu, W., et al.: Auto-scaling continuous memory for GUI agent. arXiv preprint arXiv:2510.09038 (2025)
27. Xie, T., et al.: OSWorld: benchmarking multimodal agents for open-ended tasks in real computer environments. In: Advances in Neural Information Processing Systems (NeurIPS) (2024)
28. Xu, R., et al.: Retrieval-augmented GUI agents with generative guidelines. In: Proceedings of the 2025 Conference on Empirical Methods in Natural Language Processing, pp. 17866–17875. Association for Computational Linguistics (2025). https://doi.org/10.18653/v1/2025.emnlp-main.902
29. Yao, S., Chen, H., Yang, J., Narasimhan, K.: WebShop: towards scalable real-world web interaction with grounded language agents. In: Advances in Neural Information Processing Systems (NeurIPS) (2022)
30. Yao, S., et al.: ReAct: synergizing reasoning and acting in language models. In: International Conference on Learning Representations (ICLR) (2023)
31. Zhang, C., et al.: AppAgent: multimodal agents as smartphone users. In: Proceedings of the 2025 CHI Conference on Human Factors in Computing Systems, pp. 1–20. ACM (2025). https://doi.org/10.1145/3706598.3713600

32. Zhao, A., Huang, D., Xu, Q., Lin, M., Liu, Y.J., Huang, G.: ExpeL: LLM agents are experiential learners. arXiv preprint arXiv:2308.10144 (2023)
33. Zheng, L., Wang, R., Wang, X., An, B.: Synapse: trajectory-as-exemplar prompting with memory for computer control. In: International Conference on Learning Representations (ICLR) (2024)
34. Zhou, S., et al.: WebArena: a realistic web environment for building autonomous agents. In: International Conference on Learning Representations (ICLR) (2024)
35. Zhu, X., et al.: Ghost in the minecraft: generally capable agents for open-world environments via large language models with text-based knowledge and memory. arXiv:2305.17144 arXiv preprint (2023)

Retrieving Precedents, Adapting Tool Plans, and Revising Judgments: Case-Based Reasoning for Zero-Shot Multimodal Harmful Content Detection

Jianyu Zhou(✉) and Zhanyi Zhou

Hohai University, Nanjing, China
{2361010312,2304010512}@hhu.edu.cn

Abstract. Multimodal harmful content detection is challenging in zero-shot settings because novel memes highlight two key limitations: 1) **contextual void**, where retrieved similar memes lack rationale-based grounding for evolving cultural context; and 2) **static reasoning rigidity**, where fixed reasoning templates struggle with subtle cross-modal incongruities. To address this problem, we propose RAMTA, a case-based reasoning framework for zero-shot harmful content detection and open-world multimodal moderation. RAMTA implements three CBR-aligned strategies: 1) **retrieval**, by fetching rationale-enriched precedents rather than raw similar memes; 2) **adaptation**, by redefining case reuse as tool-plan adaptation, using retrieved cases to select a tailored subset of reasoning tools rather than directly transferring labels; and 3) **revision**, by employing a Dialectical Consensus Adjudicator to cross-examine multi-view evidence and synthesize the final verdict. Experiments on three benchmarks show that RAMTA achieves strong zero-shot results, including a +3.67% accuracy gain over MIND on HarM and a +10.45% gain over Gemini-2.0-Flash (CoT) with the same backbone, suggesting that case-guided adaptation is an effective CBR paradigm for multimodal moderation, highlighting the value of CBR in LLM agentic systems.

Keywords: Case-Based Reasoning · Harmful Content Detection · LLM Agents · Tool Adaptation

1 Introduction

Harmful content detection has become an increasingly important problem for online content moderation, as multimodal memes are widely used to spread hate, stereotypes, and social division. It is especially challenging in zero-shot settings, as it relies on subtle cross-modal incongruities, evolving cultural references, and episodic contextual knowledge. To address this challenge, existing methods generally fall into two categories. The first category focuses on Multimodal Large Language Models (MLLMs) [2,15], which attempt to convert multimodal signals to perform joint image-text modeling [10]. The second category explores

L. Malburg and K. Bach (Eds.): ICCBR 2026, LNAI 16780, pp. 354–370, 2027.
https://doi.org/10.1007/978-3-032-33865-5_22

LLM-based multi-agent frameworks, which decompose the detection task into manageable steps to enhance evidence acquisition [9,18]. However, they still suffer from two major cognitive gaps when facing novel memes. First is the *Contextual Void of Logic*: although recent systems retrieve similar memes [9], they fetch raw labels without underlying rationales, failing to comprehend highly contextual memes (Fig. 1a). Second is *Static Reasoning Rigidity*: existing frameworks process immensely diverse memes using fixed, one-size-fits-all reasoning templates. This static rigidity forces irrelevant analytical dimensions upon a meme, ultimately trapping the system in decision confusion when confronting deep cross-modal conflicts (Fig. 1b).

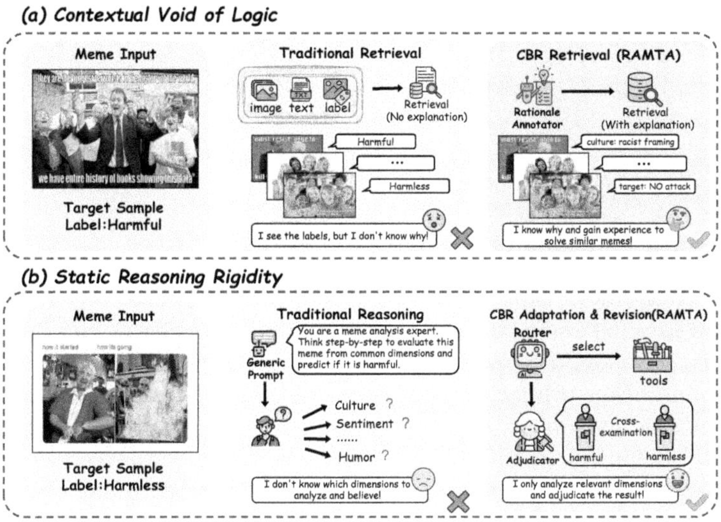

Fig. 1. Why zero-shot harmful content detection requires case-based reasoning. (a) **Contextual Void**: RAMTA uses CBR Retrieval to fetch rationale-enriched precedents instead of raw labels. (b) **Static Rigidity**: RAMTA applies CBR Adaptation and Revision, using precedents to guide Router for tool selection and conflict resolution.

These limitations suggest that zero-shot harmful content detection is a case-grounded reasoning problem: interpreting a new meme requires recalling similar prior cases, examining how they were resolved, and adapting their reasoning patterns to the current instance rather than copying their labels. This makes the task a natural fit for case-based reasoning (CBR), where prior cases provide reusable interpretive context for open-world multimodal moderation. Motivated by this view, we propose RAMTA (**R**etrieval-**A**ugmented **M**ulti-**T**ool **A**gentic reasoning), a CBR-inspired framework that uses prior cases not as static in-context examples, but as precedents for guiding case-specific evidence acquisition and conflict-aware judgment revision.

Our main contributions are summarized as follows:

- To the best of our knowledge, this work is among the first to formulate zero-shot harmful content detection as an explicit case-based reasoning framework, extending the principles of case-based planning to dynamically orchestrate multi-agent tool workflows.
- We operationalize the CBR retrieval and adaptation stages by introducing a *Retrieval-as-Experience* mechanism to fetch rationale-enriched precedents, and redefining case reuse as *tool-plan adaptation.* Retrieved precedents act as a Router to dynamically route queries to a tailored subset of tools.
- We instantiate the CBR revision stage by designing a Dialectical Consensus Adjudicator (DCA) to resolve cross-modal conflicts via evidence-grounded cross-examination.
- Extensive experiments on three benchmark datasets demonstrate that RAMTA consistently outperforms competitive zero-shot baselines, achieving an absolute +3.67% accuracy gain over MIND on the HarM dataset, and rivals heavily parameterized proprietary APIs like GPT-4o.[1]

2 Related Work

2.1 Harmful Content Detection

Harmful content detection requires interpreting complex cross-modal incongruities and implicit socio-cultural references [20]. Large-scale benchmarks have significantly accelerated research in this domain [7].

Early approaches primarily relied on two-stream fusion or fine-tuned vision-language models for joint region-text alignment [23]. As Large Language Models (LLMs) advanced, a paradigm shift occurred towards converting multi-modal signals into textual evidence to leverage the reasoning capabilities of instruction-tuned LLMs [11]. Recently, researchers have explored zero-shot LLM agents, retrieval-augmented reasoning, and domain-aware multi-view modeling for open-world harmful content analysis [14,18,19], while rationale-based methods improve interpretability [24].

2.2 Case-Based Reasoning with Large Language Models

Case-based reasoning (CBR) solves new problems by retrieving similar prior cases, reusing and adapting their solutions, and revising proposed answers [1]. Recent work has connected CBR with large language models: Wilkerson and Leake study case-augmented LLM reasoning [27]; Ge and Xu integrate CBR with LLMs for expense fraud detection [8]; and Lenz et al. investigate LLM-based similarity assessment for case retrieval [13]. These studies show the potential of LLM-supported case reuse, but they do not address zero-shot multimodal harmful content detection, where retrieved cases must guide tool adaptation and conflict-aware revision.

[1] **Reproducible code is available:** https://github.com/luoli-z/cbr-for-meme.

Related case-based intuitions have also appeared in moderation settings, including fake-news verification [30], hate-speech rationale generation [29], policy-grounded RAG [28], and example-based meme explanation [16]. However, these efforts mainly use cases for explanation, auxiliary retrieval, or policy grounding, whereas RAMTA formulates multimodal harmful content detection as a CBR process with retrieval, tool-plan adaptation, and conflict-aware revision.

3 Methodology

We propose RAMTA, a zero-shot framework that explicitly formulates multimodal harmful content detection as a Case-Based Reasoning (CBR) process, which introduces a dynamically routed architecture to adapt tool plans based on historical precedents. As illustrated in Fig. 2, RAMTA orchestrates a three-stage pipeline that aligns with the core CBR process: **retrieving** contextual cases to provide experiential priors (CAR); **adapting** these priors by dynamically routing queries to a tailored subset of orthogonal tools (TED); **revising** the judgment by weighing multi-view evidence through dialectical adjudication to reach a consensus (DCA).

3.1 Problem Definition and CBR Formulation

Let a query meme be denoted as $Q = (I_q, T_q)$, where I_q represents the image and T_q denotes the accompanying text, including caption and embedded scene

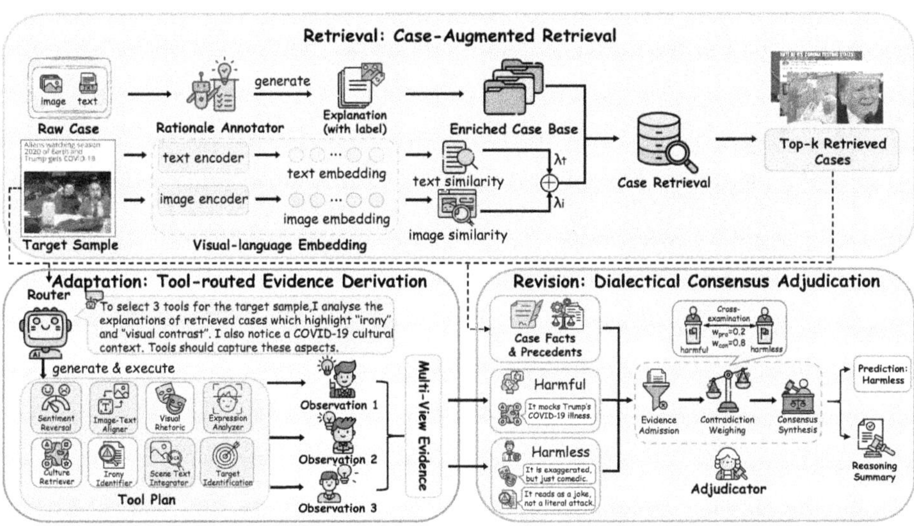

Fig. 2. The overall architecture of RAMTA under the case-based reasoning formulation. CAR retrieves rationale-enriched prior cases, TED adapts them to derive a case-specific tool plan and collect multi-view evidence, and DCA revises conflicting evidence to produce the final verdict and rationale.

text. The objective of harmful content detection is to assign a discrete label $\hat{y} \in \{\text{harmful}, \text{harmless}\}$ to the query meme under a zero-shot setting, where training samples are used only as an unlabeled case archive.

We cast this task as a case-based reasoning (CBR) problem. Instead of treating a meme as an isolated multimodal classification instance, we view it as a query case that should be interpreted with reference to previously resolved precedents. Each stored case is represented as:

$$c_j = (I_j, T_j, Y_j, E_j), \tag{1}$$

where I_j and T_j denote the meme image and text, Y_j is the LLM-generated label, and E_j is a rationale explaining the basis of the decision. Collectively, these cases form an enriched case base:

$$\mathcal{C} = \{(I_j, T_j, Y_j, E_j)\}_{j=1}^{|\mathcal{C}|}, \tag{2}$$

whose offline construction is described in Sect. 3.2.

Under this formulation, RAMTA performs inference over both the query meme and the case base:

$$(\hat{y}, \mathcal{R}) = \mathcal{F}_{\text{RAMTA}}(Q, \mathcal{C}), \tag{3}$$

where $\mathcal{R}$ denotes the final reasoning summary.

Mapping to the CBR Cycle. RAMTA follows the CBR cycle in an internal decision-support setting: retrieval identifies rationale-enriched precedents, adaptation converts them into a query-specific tool plan, and revision resolves conflicts among multi-view evidence before prediction.

3.2 Retrieval: Case-Augmented Retrieval (CAR)

To address contextual voids in zero-shot multimodal harmful content detection, CAR augments classical similarity-based retrieval with LLM-generated rationales. Inspired by similar-meme retrieval [18] and rationale-enhanced retrieval [26], CAR first builds a rationale-enriched case base offline and then retrieves top-k precedents online, providing both similar instances and reusable explanatory context for adaptation.

Offline Rationale Enrichment. The process begins with a raw case archive consisting of image-text pairs (I_j, T_j). To transform this basic archive into a rationale-enriched case base, we employ an advanced large language model as an offline *Rationale Annotator* LLM_{RA}. For each pair (I_j, T_j), the annotator systematically analyzes how the visual and textual modalities jointly inform the decision, and produces both an LLM-generated judgment and its corresponding rationale. Formally, the rationale E_j and label Y_j are generated as:

$$(Y_j, E_j) = \text{LLM}_{\text{RA}}(I_j, T_j \mid \mathcal{P}_{\text{dim}}) \tag{4}$$

where $\mathcal{P}_{\text{dim}}$ denotes the prompt template specifically guiding the analysis to cover 8 orthogonal cognitive dimensions. By design, these dimensions directly correspond to the 8 cognitive tools defined in our downstream library. By augmenting each raw pair with the generated label and rationale, we construct a rationale-enriched case base $\mathcal{C}$.

Online Case Retrieval. During inference, CAR retrieves the top-k most relevant precedents from the enriched case base $\mathcal{C}$. Given a query meme Q, we employ a dual-encoder architecture (CLIP) to extract visual embeddings $\mathbf{e}_q^i$ and textual embeddings $\mathbf{e}_q^t$. The relevance score between Q and the j-th case is computed via a weighted cosine similarity:

$$s(Q,j) = \lambda_t \cdot \cos(\mathbf{e}_q^t, \mathbf{e}_j^t) + \lambda_i \cdot \cos(\mathbf{e}_q^i, \mathbf{e}_j^i), \tag{5}$$

where $\lambda_t, \lambda_i \geq 0$ are modality weights satisfying $\lambda_t + \lambda_i = 1$. The top-$k$ case set is retrieved as $\mathcal{A}_k(Q) = \underset{\mathcal{A}\subset\mathcal{C},|\mathcal{A}|=k}{\arg\max} \sum_{j\in\mathcal{A}} s(Q,j)$. The retrieved cases provide rationale-enriched precedents that ground subsequent adaptation in previously resolved logic patterns.

3.3 Adaptation: Tool-Routed Evidence Derivation (TED)

As the adaptation stage of RAMTA, the **TED** module reuses retrieved precedents to derive a case-specific tool plan for the current meme. Rather than invoking all available tools indiscriminately, TED selects a tailored subset of tools to reduce reasoning noise and improve evidence relevance. Inspired by recent advances in tool-augmented multimodal agents such as Toolformer [25], and by dynamic tool subset selection in T^2 Agent [5], TED implements *retrieval-guided meta-planning* for adaptive evidence derivation.

Retrieval-Guided Router. The planner operates as an autonomous controller agent π. Instead of following a rigid chain-of-thought template, it analyzes the retrieved precedent set $\mathcal{A}_k(Q)$ and their rationales E_j to infer which reasoning dimensions are most relevant for the target meme Q.

To balance reasoning diversity with computational efficiency, π formulates a tailored execution plan by selecting a fixed-size subset of tools $S \subset \mathcal{T}$ ($|S| = N$, empirically set to 3). The agent autonomously evaluates a utility score $U_t = \text{LLM}_\pi(t \mid Q, \mathcal{A}_k(Q), \mathcal{P}_{\text{route}})$ for each tool via prompt-guided reasoning. Consequently, the routing process is formalized as a utility-maximization problem: $S = \arg\max_{S\subset\mathcal{T},|S|=N} \sum_{t\in S} U_t$. In this way, TED instantiates CBR adaptation by transforming retrieved precedents into a tailored tool-use strategy.

Orthogonal Cognitive Tools. The tool library $\mathcal{T}$ consists of 8 orthogonal cognitive tools, each acting as an adaptation specialist for addressing case-specific

Table 1. Cognitive tool library $\mathcal{T}$ used in adaptation. Each tool operationalizes a reasoning dimension for case-specific evidence derivation.

Tool	Dimension & Function
Sentiment Reversal Detector	**Text–Visual Disparity**: Detects mismatches between literal text polarity and visual semantics.
Image-Text Aligner	**Visual Grounding**: Verifies whether textual entities align with visual objects and attributes.
Visual Rhetoric Decoder	**Imagery Analysis**: Identifies exaggeration, caricature, and juxtaposition in images.
Micro-Expression Analyzer	**Facial Affect**: Detects conflicts between facial expression and caption tone.
Culture Retriever	**External Knowledge**: Retrieves background knowledge on celebrities, events, and cultural memes.
Pragmatic Irony Identifier	**Linguistic Modality**: Detects sarcasm markers such as puns and over-politeness.
Scene Text Integrator	**OCR Semantics**: Combines embedded text with captions to detect semantic conflict.
Target Identification	**Target Attribution**: Identifies the meme target to distinguish self-deprecation from attack.

reasoning needs. Upon selection, these tools execute concurrently to generate multi-view evidence. Details are provided in Table 1.

Each selected tool $t \in S$ outputs an observation $o_t = (\mathbf{v}_t, c_t, r_t)$, where $\mathbf{v}_t$ is a structured evidence vector, $c_t \in [0, 1]$ is a self-assessed confidence score explicitly produced by the tool during inference, and r_t is a concise natural-language justification. The aggregated evidence set is $\mathcal{O} = \{o_t\}_{t \in S}$, which serves as the input to the subsequent revision stage.

3.4 Revision: Dialectical Consensus Adjudication (DCA)

As the revision stage of RAMTA, the **DCA** module resolves conflicts among the multi-view evidence derived during adaptation. Inspired by multi-agent debate protocols [3], the Adjudicator performs a three-step, evidence-grounded revision process over the target meme Q, the collected evidence $\mathcal{O}$, and the retrieved case set $\mathcal{A}_k(Q)$. DCA performs internal evidence-grounded revision by checking consistency among tool outputs, query facts, and retrieved precedents, without relying on external feedback.

Evidence Admission. The Adjudicator first parses the observation set $\mathcal{O}$ and filters out unreliable or irrelevant evidence, including speculative observations whose self-assessed confidence c_t falls below a reliability threshold of 0.5 and observations judged by the Adjudicator to be insufficiently grounded in the target meme Q and the retrieved case set $\mathcal{A}_k(Q)$.

Contradiction Weighing. To revise conflicts among the adaptation-derived observations, the Adjudicator places competing observations into a dialectical comparison and cross-examines their natural-language justifications (τ_i, τ_j). This comparison is grounded in the target meme Q as the current case facts and the retrieved case set $\mathcal{A}_k(Q)$ as prior resolved precedents. Based on its consistency with the current case facts, support from retrieved precedents, and robustness under cross-examination, the Adjudicator assigns a soft logical precedence weight $w_t \in [0, 1]$ to each core piece of evidence, yielding the weight set $W = \{w_t\}_{t \in S}$. These weights quantify the case-grounded validity of each tool output.

Consensus Synthesis. Finally, the Adjudicator synthesizes the weighted evidence into a case-grounded consensus. Rather than simple voting, it jointly considers the target instance Q, the retained observations $\mathcal{O}$, the logical precedence weights W, and the retrieved cases $\mathcal{A}_k(Q)$. Evidence that is both highly weighted and consistent with the current case facts is prioritized, while weaker or conflicting observations are contextualized or overridden. The consensus produces the final label $\hat{y}$ and a natural-language rationale $\mathcal{R}$.

The revision process is formalized as:

$$(\hat{y}, \mathcal{R}) = \mathrm{LLM}_{\mathrm{adj}}\big(Q, \mathcal{O}, W, \mathcal{A}_k(Q) \mid \mathcal{P}_{\mathrm{adj}}\big), \tag{6}$$

where $\mathcal{P}_{\mathrm{adj}}$ denotes the adjudication prompt that instructs the agent to reconcile the weighted evidence under the current case facts and retrieved precedents. This synthesis instantiates the revision stage of CBR, while retention is left as an optional future extension in which solved cases with final adjudication confidence above 0.8 may be added to the case base.

3.5 Algorithm Overview

The overall zero-shot CBR process of RAMTA is summarized in Algorithm 1.

4 Experiments

To evaluate RAMTA as a case-based reasoning framework for zero-shot harmful content detection, we assess the effectiveness of the full framework, the roles of retrieval, adaptation, and revision, and the robustness and interpretability of its case-based mechanism as reflected in the following research questions (RQs):

RQ1: How does RAMTA perform against state-of-the-art zero-shot baselines? **RQ2:** How do retrieval, adaptation, and revision individually contribute

Algorithm 1 RAMTA: A Zero-shot Case-Based Reasoning Framework

Require: Target sample $Q = (I_q, T_q)$, Enriched Case Base $\mathcal{C}$, Tool Library $\mathcal{T}$
Ensure: Predicted label $\hat{y}$, Natural-language rationale $\mathcal{R}$
Retrieval: Case-Augmented Retrieval (CAR)
Extract dual-modality embeddings $\mathbf{e}_q^t, \mathbf{e}_q^i$ via VLM encoder
Retrieve cases $\mathcal{A}_k(Q) \leftarrow \arg\max_{A \subset \mathcal{C}, |A|=k} \sum_{j \in A} s(Q, j)$
Adaptation: Tool-Routed Evidence Derivation (TED)
Generate plan $S \leftarrow \text{Router}_\pi(Q, \mathcal{A}_k(Q))$ ▷ Reuse precedents to select N tools
$\mathcal{O} \leftarrow \emptyset$
for each tool $t \in S$ **in parallel do**
  $o_t \leftarrow \text{ExecuteTool}(t, Q)$ ▷ Yields observation $(\mathbf{v}_t, c_t, \tau_t)$
  $\mathcal{O} \leftarrow \mathcal{O} \cup \{o_t\}$
end for
Revision: Dialectical Consensus Adjudicator (DCA)
Weights $W \leftarrow \text{WeighEvidence}(\mathcal{O}, \mathcal{A}_k(Q))$ ▷ Dialectical cross-examination
$(\hat{y}, \mathcal{R}) \leftarrow \text{Adjudicate}(Q, \mathcal{O}, W, \mathcal{A}_k(Q))$ ▷ Synthesize case-grounded consensus
return $\hat{y}, \mathcal{R}$

to performance? **RQ3:** How do the number of retrieved cases and the number of adapted tools affect performance? **RQ4:** Is the case-based mechanism of RAMTA robust across different MLLM backbones? **RQ5:** How does RAMTA retrieve, adapt, and revise prior cases when interpreting complex memes?

4.1 Experimental Setup

Datasets. We evaluate RAMTA on three widely used multimodal meme datasets: Facebook Hateful Memes (FHM) [12], Harmful Memes (HarM) [23], and Multimedia Automatic Misogyny Identification (MAMI) [7]. Following previous studies [18], we reformulate HarM as a binary task by merging "very harmful" and "partially harmful" into a single "harmful" class. Dataset statistics are summarized in Table 2.

Table 2. Statistical distributions of the datasets used for evaluation.

Dataset	Theme	Train		Test	
		Harmful	Harmless	Harmful	Harmless
FHM	Hate Speech	3,050	5,450	250	250
HarM	COVID-19	1,064	1,949	124	230
MAMI	Misogyny	5,000	5,000	500	500

Baselines. We compare RAMTA with three categories of methods: **(1) MLLMs & Chain-of-Thought (CoT):** general-purpose MLLMs including open-source MLLMs *InstructBLIP-13B* [6], *LLaVA-NeXT-34B* [15], and

Qwen2.5-VL-32B [2], as well as closed-source APIs *Gemini-2.0-Flash* [4] and *GPT-4o* [21] (both evaluated with CoT prompting). **(2) Task-specific Methods:** *Evolver* [10], and *U-CoT+* [22]. **(3) Agentic Frameworks:** *LOREHM* [9], *Ask, Acquire, Understand (AAU)* [17], and *MIND* [18]. Among these baselines, MIND is the most closely aligned with RAMTA in terms of resource assumptions, since both avoid using human-annotated target-task labels for task-specific adaptation.

Evaluation Metrics. Following previous studies in multimodal meme detection [18], we adopt Accuracy (Acc) and Macro-F1 (M-F1) as our primary evaluation metrics. Macro-F1 serves as a crucial indicator to evaluate robustness against inherent label imbalances.

Implementation Details. We implement RAMTA in PyTorch and use Gemini-2.0-Flash as the primary MLLM-based agent. Unless otherwise stated, the retrieval size and tool subset size are set to $k = 5$ and $N = 3$, respectively, based on the sensitivity analysis in Sect. 4.4. The case base is constructed from the training split of each dataset. For case retrieval, we use FAISS over frozen CLIP `ViT-L/14@336px` image-text features, with modality weights $\lambda_i = 0.8$ and $\lambda_t = 0.2$. Selected tools are executed in parallel through prompt-specialized agent calls on the same multimodal backbone. For closed-source baselines, we fixed temperature to 0 for all evaluated models. All local experiments are conducted on a single NVIDIA RTX 4090 GPU. Detailed prompt templates and runnable code are provided in GitHub repository.

4.2 Main Results (RQ1)

Table 3 reports the overall zero-shot performance on FHM, HarM, and MAMI. We draw the following observations:

(O1) Case-based reasoning improves over direct MLLM prediction. Compared with general-purpose MLLMs, RAMTA achieves stronger and more consistent results across all three datasets. In particular, it surpasses the strongest open-source MLLM, Qwen2.5-VL-32B, by 3.60% Accuracy on FHM (72.20% vs. 68.60%) and by 5.93% on HarM (71.47% vs. 65.54%). This suggests that single-pass multimodal prediction is insufficient for harmful meme detection, where interpretation often requires contextual grounding beyond surface semantics.

(O2) Retrieved cases are most effective when reused for adaptation and revision. MIND is the strongest prior reasoning baseline, yet RAMTA still improves Accuracy by 1.80%, 3.67%, and 1.40% on FHM, HarM, and MAMI, respectively. This indicates that retrieved cases are more useful as reasoning precedents for adaptation and revision than as static in-context examples.

(O3) RAMTA remains competitive with stronger proprietary APIs. RAMTA achieves the best overall results on FHM. On MAMI, although

Table 3. Overall zero-shot performance comparison on FHM, HarM, and MAMI datasets. The best results are in **bold**, and the second-best are <u>underlined</u>. † indicates our reproduction. For a fair comparison, all reproduced baselines (†) and our RAMTA framework utilize Gemini-2.0-Flash as the backbone MLLM.

Category	Method	FHM		HarM		MAMI	
		Acc	M-F1	Acc	M-F1	Acc	M-F1
MLLMs & CoT	InstructBLIP-13B	55.40	51.89	64.97	49.61	60.10	57.97
	LLaVA-NeXT-34B	64.80	64.63	66.38	62.53	74.10	73.61
	Qwen2.5-VL-32B	68.60	63.49	65.54	62.93	75.90	75.79
	Gemini-2.0-Flash (CoT)	69.20	64.33	61.02	57.14	77.80	77.57
	GPT-4o (CoT)	<u>71.80</u>	<u>70.23</u>	66.67	65.74	**80.80**	<u>80.52</u>
Task-specific Methods	Evolver (2025)†	67.80	67.14	65.25	64.37	72.30	71.48
	U-CoT+ (2026)†	71.20	68.45	67.51	65.59	78.60	78.32
Agentic Frameworks	LOREHM (2024)†	67.40	64.77	63.28	61.50	71.50	70.46
	AAU (2025)†	68.80	63.19	67.23	63.29	78.30	77.90
	MIND (2025)†	70.40	69.68	<u>67.80</u>	<u>66.15</u>	79.20	78.89
CBR	RAMTA	**72.20**	**72.12**	**71.47**	**69.25**	<u>80.60</u>	**80.60**

GPT-4o attains slightly higher Accuracy (80.80% vs. 80.60%), RAMTA surpasses it in Macro-F1 (80.60% vs. 80.52%), indicating slightly better robustness under label imbalance. This suggests that case-based retrieval and reuse can partly compensate for differences in model capacity.

(O4) Case-based reasoning is especially beneficial in contextual domains. The largest improvement appears on HarM, where RAMTA reaches 71.47% Accuracy, compared with 61.02% for Gemini-2.0-Flash (CoT) using the same backbone. This gap highlights the value of retrieved prior cases when harmfulness depends more on contextual interpretation than on surface semantics.

4.3 Ablation Study (RQ2)

To evaluate the contribution of each CBR stage in RAMTA, we design five ablation variants: (1) **w/o CAR**: Replaces rationale-enriched case retrieval with rationale-free retrieval. (2) **w/o V-CAR**: Uses text-only retrieval, excluding visual similarity from precedent retrieval. (3) **w/o Case-guided Routing**: Retains the Router but removes retrieved cases from tool planning, so tool selection depends only on the query. (4) **w/o Router**: Retains tool execution but invokes all 8 tools indiscriminately, removing case-specific tool selection. (5) **w/o Adjudicator**: Uses simple majority voting, removing conflict-aware revision.

Table 4 presents the ablation results across the three datasets. We draw the following observations:

(O1) Retrieval is necessary, and effective case retrieval must be multimodal. Removing CAR causes clear performance drops on all three

Table 4. Ablation study of RAMTA across FHM, HarM, and MAMI.

Model Variant	FHM		HarM		MAMI	
	Acc	M-F1	Acc	M-F1	Acc	M-F1
RAMTA (Full Model)	72.20	72.12	71.47	69.25	80.60	80.60
w/o CAR (Rationale-free Retrieval)	67.80	67.65	68.08	66.82	76.50	76.43
w/o V-CAR (Text-only Retrieval)	70.20	70.18	69.21	67.33	78.90	78.78
w/o Case-guided Routing (Query-only)	68.60	68.49	65.54	64.12	77.20	77.16
w/o Router (All 8 Tools)	69.40	69.31	64.97	63.48	78.40	78.35
w/o Adjudicator (Majority Voting)	71.00	70.84	67.23	65.59	79.50	79.46

datasets, e.g., −4.40% Acc on FHM and −4.10% on MAMI. Replacing multimodal retrieval with text-only retrieval also reduces performance, e.g., by 2.00% Acc on FHM. This shows that harmful meme detection benefits from prior cases, and that relevant case matching requires joint image-text retrieval rather than textual similarity alone.

(O2) Adaptive reuse is crucial for fully exploiting retrieved cases. Removing tool-based adaptation leads to substantial degradation, with Accuracy drops of 3.60% and 5.93% on FHM and HarM, respectively, indicating that retrieved cases must be transformed into case-specific evidence rather than used as static context. Meanwhile, executing all tools indiscriminately also underperforms the full model, with a particularly large drop of 6.50% Acc on HarM. This suggests that case reuse should remain selective and adaptive, since indiscriminate tool execution introduces irrelevant or conflicting evidence.

(O3) DCA demonstrates the advantage of conflict-aware revision over naive aggregation. Replacing DCA with simple majority voting consistently reduces performance; on HarM, for example, Accuracy and Macro-F1 drop by 4.24% and 3.66%, respectively. This shows that final prediction cannot rely on naive aggregation when different tools provide competing interpretations. Instead, the evidence must be revised under the current case context before a reliable decision can be made.

4.4 Parameter Sensitivity (RQ3)

In this section, we evaluate RAMTA's sensitivity to two hyperparameters across FHM, HarM, and MAMI: the number of retrieved cases (k) and adapted tools (N). We vary one parameter while fixing the other at its optimum.

Impact of Retrieved Cases (k). We vary $k \in \{1, 3, 5, 7, 9\}$ to examine how precedent support affects performance. As shown in Fig. 3(a), performance consistently peaks at $k = 5$. Before this point, increasing k improves contextual grounding by expanding precedent coverage: for example, FHM rises from 67.8% at $k = 1$ to 72.12% at $k = 5$, while MAMI improves from 76.5% to 80.60%. Beyond $k = 5$, performance generally declines, indicating that overly broad retrieval introduces noisy or weakly relevant precedents. This suggests

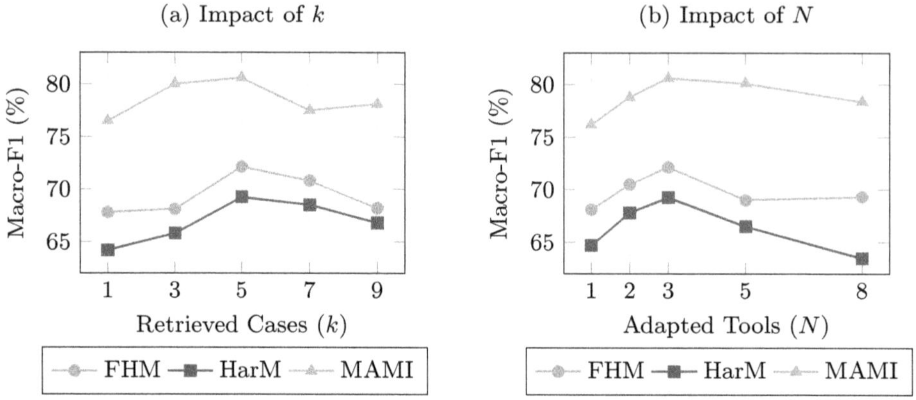

Fig. 3. Sensitivity analysis of hyperparameters k and N.

that effective CBR depends on retrieving a precedent set that is both sufficiently informative and sufficiently selective.

Impact of Adapted Tools (N). We vary $N \in \{1, 2, 3, 5, 8\}$ to examine how adaptation breadth affects performance. Figure 3(b) shows that $N = 3$ provides the best overall balance. Performance improves sharply from $N = 1$ to 3, suggesting that a small set of complementary tools is sufficient to derive useful case-specific evidence. However, performance degrades once too many tools are executed. On FHM, the score falls from 72.12% at $N = 3$ to 69.31% at $N = 8$; on HarM, it drops more severely to 63.48%. These results indicate that adaptive reuse benefits from a limited number of well-matched tools, whereas overly broad tool execution introduces irrelevant or conflicting evidence.

4.5 MLLM Backbone Robustness (RQ4)

Table 5. Performance improvements of our proposed framework across different MLLM backbones spanning 4B to closed-source APIs. Numbers in green indicate absolute improvements over original models.

MLLM Backbone	HarM				FHM				MAMI			
	Accuracy		Macro-F_1		Accuracy		Macro-F_1		Accuracy		Macro-F_1	
	ori.	RAMTA	ori.	RAMTA	ori.	RAMTA	ori.	RAMTA	ori.	RAMTA	ori.	RAMTA
Phi-3-Vision (4B)	53.67	57.63 (+3.96)	46.52	51.34 (+4.82)	50.20	52.80 (+2.60)	42.16	45.21 (+3.05)	48.50	51.70 (+3.20)	44.53	48.65 (+4.12)
LLaVA-1.5 (7B)	59.32	62.43 (+3.11)	49.44	54.12 (+4.68)	53.80	55.40 (+1.60)	45.51	48.04 (+2.53)	52.90	54.80 (+1.90)	41.53	44.78 (+3.25)
Qwen2.5-VL (7B)	61.02	63.84 (+2.82)	55.61	59.17 (+3.56)	57.00	59.20 (+2.20)	55.34	57.63 (+2.29)	58.80	61.50 (+2.70)	57.42	60.12 (+2.70)
LLaVA-1.5 (13B)	62.15	66.38 (+4.23)	50.45	58.76 (+8.31)	58.20	61.80 (+3.60)	56.12	60.45 (+4.33)	60.10	65.20 (+5.10)	55.52	61.84 (+6.32)
Qwen2.5-VL (32B)	65.54	70.34 (+4.80)	62.93	68.14 (+5.21)	68.60	71.00 (+2.40)	68.49	71.20 (+2.71)	75.90	78.80 (+2.90)	75.79	78.43 (+2.64)
Gemini-1.5-Flash	66.10	68.36 (+2.26)	64.18	66.82 (+2.64)	60.20	63.40 (+3.20)	58.93	62.15 (+3.22)	76.40	78.10 (+1.70)	74.29	76.84 (+2.55)
GPT-4o	66.67	68.64 (+1.97)	65.74	68.12 (+2.38)	71.80	73.20 (+1.40)	70.23	71.85 (+1.62)	80.80	81.90 (+1.10)	80.52	81.63 (+1.11)

To further investigate the robustness of RAMTA across different MLLM sizes and types, we evaluate it with seven representative backbones ranging from 4B to 32B parameters (e.g., Phi-3-Vision, LLaVA-1.5, and Qwen2.5-VL), together with strong closed-source APIs. The results are reported in Table 5.

CBR Effectiveness Generalizes Across Backbones. RAMTA consistently improves over the corresponding original backbone across all tested models, indicating that its gains do not rely on a particular model family or size. This suggests that the benefit of RAMTA comes from a transferable case-based mechanism, retrieving relevant prior cases and reusing them through adaptation and revision, rather than from backbone-specific biases alone. This advantage also extends to smaller models: for example, Qwen2.5-VL (7B) with RAMTA reaches 63.84% Accuracy on HarM, surpassing the zero-shot result of the much larger LLaVA-1.5 (13B), which achieves 62.15%.

Stronger Backbones Better Exploit the CBR Process. Within the Qwen2.5-VL series, the gains from RAMTA grow with model scale, suggesting that stronger backbones can better exploit retrieved precedents and the subsequent adaptation and revision stages. On HarM, for example, the Macro-F1 gain increases from +3.56% for Qwen2.5-VL (7B) to +5.21% for Qwen2.5-VL (32B). At the same time, RAMTA remains effective on strong proprietary APIs: when applied to GPT-4o, it achieves the best overall results on FHM and MAMI. These results show that RAMTA is broadly compatible with diverse MLLMs while preserving its effectiveness as a case-based reasoning framework.

4.6 Case Study (RQ5)

To understand how RAMTA handles complex multimodal memes, we analyze three representative cases from MAMI, HarM, and FHM (Fig. 4), focusing on retrieval quality and precedent-guided reasoning.

We observe that: **(1) Retrieved cases provide diagnostically useful precedents rather than superficial matches.** In Fig. 4(a), the retrieved cases identify the *Mean Girls* template as an anti-feminist sarcasm trope. In Fig. 4(b), they point to political criticism rather than explicit hate content. In Fig. 4(c), they reveal that seemingly mild wording becomes harmful when paired with historically charged imagery. These examples show that RAMTA retrieves contextually relevant precedents rather than merely similar memes.

(2) Retrieved precedents guide tool selection and final revision. In Fig. 4(a), they make cultural framing and pragmatic irony the most relevant evidence sources. In Fig. 4(b), they shift attention toward target attribution and pragmatic interpretation. In Fig. 4(c), they highlight image-text conflict and racist wordplay, which then drive the final harmful judgment. Overall, RAMTA uses prior cases not as static demonstrations, but as precedents that guide adaptation and support revision under the CBR formulation.

Fig. 4. Examples of correctly predicted memes by our RAMTA framework in (a) MAMI, (b) HarM, and (c) FHM datasets.

5 Conclusion

In this paper, we introduced RAMTA, a zero-shot framework that formulates harmful content detection as a case-based reasoning process. RAMTA retrieves rationale-enriched prior cases, adapts them into case-specific tool plans, and revises conflicting evidence through dialectical adjudication. In this way, it addresses contextual voids and static reasoning rigidity in open-world meme interpretation. Experiments on three benchmarks show that RAMTA achieves strong zero-shot performance. Further results confirm the contributions of retrieval, adaptation, and revision, as well as robustness across different MLLM backbones and hyperparameter settings. Overall, RAMTA provides an interpretable and effective CBR blueprint for future multimodal agentic moderation.

Declaration on Generative AI. During the preparation of this work, the authors used ChatGPT and Writefull for grammar and spelling checks, paraphrasing, and writing-style improvement. The authors reviewed and edited the content as needed and take full responsibility for the publication's content.

References

1. Aamodt, A., Plaza, E.: Case-based reasoning: Foundational issues, methodological variations, and system approaches. AI Commun. **7**(1), 39–59 (1994). https://doi.org/10.3233/AIC-1994-7104
2. Bai, S., et al.: Qwen2.5-VL technical report. arXiv preprint arxiv:2502.13923 (2025)
3. Chen, J.C.Y., Saha, S., Bansal, M.: Reconcile: Round-table conference improves reasoning via consensus among diverse llms. In: Proceedings of the 62nd Annual Meeting of the Association for Computational Linguistics (ACL) (2024)

4. Comanici, G., et al.: Gemini 2.5: Pushing the frontier with advanced reasoning, multimodality, long context, and next generation agentic capabilities. arXiv preprint arXiv:2507.06261 (2025). https://doi.org/10.48550/arXiv.2507.06261
5. Cui, X., Zou, Y., Li, Z., Li, P., Xu, X., Liu, X., Huang, H.: T^2agent: A tool-augmented multimodal misinformation detection agent with monte carlo tree search. In: Proceedings of the AAAI Conference on Artificial Intelligence (2026), to appear
6. Dai, W., et al.: Instructblip: Towards general-purpose vision-language models with instruction tuning. arXiv preprint arXiv:2305.06500 (2023). https://doi.org/10.48550/arXiv.2305.06500
7. Fersini, E., et al.: Proceedings of the 16th International Workshop on Semantic Evaluation (SemEval-2022), pp. 533–549. (2022). SemEval-2022 Task 5: Multimedia Automatic Misogyny Identification (MAMI)
8. Ge, X., Xu, J.: Integrating Case-Based Reasoning with LLM for Expense Fraud Detection. In: Case-Based Reasoning Research and Development. Lecture Notes in Computer Science, vol. 15662, pp. 52–66. Springer, Cham (2025). https://doi.org/10.1007/978-3-031-96559-3_4
9. Huang, J., Lin, H., Liu, Z., Luo, Z., Chen, G., Ma, J.: Towards low-resource harmful meme detection with lmm agents. In: Proceedings of the 2024 Conference on Empirical Methods in Natural Language Processing (EMNLP), pp. 2269–2293 (2024). https://doi.org/10.18653/v1/2024.emnlp-main.136
10. Huang, J., Pan, J., Wan, Z., Lyu, H., Luo, J.: Evolver: Chain-of-evolution prompting to boost large multimodal models for hateful meme detection. In: Proceedings of the 31st International Conference on Computational Linguistics (COLING), pp. 7321–7330 (2025). https://dblp.org/rec/conf/coling/HuangPWL025
11. Ji, J., Lin, X., Naseem, U.: Capalign: Improving cross modal alignment via informative captioning for harmful meme detection. In: Proceedings of the ACM Web Conference 2024 (WWW), pp. 4585–4594 (2024)
12. Kiela, D., Firooz, H., Mohan, A., Goswami, V., Singh, A., Ringshia, P., Testuggine, D.: The hateful memes challenge: Detecting hate speech in multimodal memes. In: Advances in Neural Information Processing Systems (NeurIPS), vol. 33, pp. 2611–2624 (2020)
13. Lenz, M., Hoffmann, M., Bergmann, R.: LLsiM: Large Language Models for Similarity Assessment in Case-Based Reasoning. In: Case-Based Reasoning Research and Development. Lecture Notes in Computer Science, vol. 15662, pp. 126–141. Springer, Cham (2025).https://doi.org/10.1007/978-3-031-96559-3_9
14. Li, C., Lu, W.: Decoding the market's pulse: Context-enriched agentic retrieval augmented generation for predicting post-earnings price shocks. In: Proceedings of the 19th Conference of the European Chapter of the Association for Computational Linguistics (Volume 1: Long Papers). pp. 3055–3073 (2026)
15. Li, F., et al.: Llava-next-interleave: Tackling multi-image, video, and 3d in large multimodal models. arXiv preprint arXiv:2407.07895 (2024). https://doi.org/10.48550/arXiv.2407.07895
16. Lin, H., Luo, Z., Gao, W., Ma, J., Wang, B., Yang, R.: Towards explainable harmful meme detection through multimodal debate between large language models. In: Proceedings of the ACM Web Conference 2024, pp. 1379–1390. Association for Computing Machinery (2024). https://doi.org/10.1145/3589334.3645381
17. Lin, X., Jia, C., Ji, J., Han, H., Naseem, U.: Ask, acquire, understand: A multimodal agent-based framework for social abuse detection in memes. In: Proceedings of the ACM Web Conference 2025 (WWW), pp. 4734–4744 (2025)

18. Liu, Z., Fan, C., Lou, H., Wu, Y., Deng, K.: Mind: A multi-agent framework for zero-shot harmful meme detection. In: Proceedings of the 63rd Annual Meeting of the Association for Computational Linguistics (ACL), pp. 923–947 (2025)
19. Lu, W., Tong, Y., Ye, Z.: DAMMFND: Domain-aware multimodal multi-view fake news detection. In: Proceedings of the AAAI Conference on Artificial Intelligence, pp. 559–567 (2025)
20. Lu, W., Zhao, Z., Li, Y., He, H.: Mm-stancedet: Retrieval-augmented multi-modal multi-agent stance detection. arXiv preprint arXiv:2604.27934 (2026)
21. OpenAI: Gpt-4o system card. arXiv preprint arXiv:2410.21276 (2024). https://doi.org/10.48550/arXiv.2410.21276
22. Pan, F., Wu, X., Quan, T., Luu, A.T.: Read as you see: Guiding unimodal llms for low-resource explainable harmful meme detection. In: Proceedings of the ACM Web Conference 2026 (2026). https://arxiv.org/abs/2506.08477, to appear
23. Pramanick, S., Sharma, S., Dimitrov, D., Akhtar, M.S., Nakov, P., Chakraborty, T.: Momenta: A multimodal framework for detecting harmful memes and their targets. In: Findings of the Association for Computational Linguistics: EMNLP, pp. 4439–4455. (2021). https://doi.org/10.18653/v1/2021.findings-emnlp.379
24. Rizwan, N., Swain, S., Bhaskar, P., Aryan, G., Shah Khan, S., Mukherjee, A.: See, explain, and intervene: A few-shot multimodal agent framework for hateful meme moderation. arXiv preprint arxiv:2601.04692 (2026)
25. Schick, T., et al.: Toolformer: Language models can teach themselves to use tools. In: Advances in Neural Information Processing Systems (NeurIPS) (2023)
26. Wei, Z., Chen, W.L., Meng, Y.: Instructrag: Instructing retrieval-augmented generation via self-synthesized rationales. In: International Conference on Learning Representations (ICLR) (2025)
27. Wilkerson, K., Leake, D.: On Implementing Case-Based Reasoning with Large Language Models. In: Case-Based Reasoning Research and Development. Lecture Notes in Computer Science, vol. 14775, pp. 404–417. Springer, Cham (2024). https://doi.org/10.1007/978-3-031-63646-2_26
28. Willats, R., Pennington, J., Mohan, A., Vidgen, B.: Classification is a rag problem: A case study on hate speech detection. arXiv preprint arXiv:2508.06204 (2025)
29. Yang, Y., Kim, J., Kim, Y., Ho, N., Thorne, J., Yun, S.Y.: HARE: Explainable hate speech detection with step-by-step reasoning. In: Findings of the Association for Computational Linguistics: EMNLP 2023, pp. 5490–5505 (2023)
30. Yang, Y., Zhou, Y., Zhu, Z., Qian, Z., Zhang, X., Li, S.: Roe-fnd: A case-based reasoning approach with dual verification for fake news detection via llms. arXiv preprint arXiv:2506.11078 (2025)

Case-Based Calibration of Adaptive Reasoning and Execution for LLM Tool Use

Renning Pang, Tian Lan, Leyuan Liu[✉], Piao Tong, Sheng Cao, and Xiaosong Zhang

University of Electronic Science and Technology of China, Chengdu 611731, China
{prn,piaot}@std.uestc.edu.cn,
{lantian1029,leyuanliu,caosheng,johnsonzxs}@uestc.edu.cn

Abstract. Tool use extends large language models beyond parametric knowledge, but reliable execution requires balancing appropriate reasoning depth with strict structural validity. We approach this problem from a case-based perspective to present CAST, a case-driven framework that treats historical execution trajectories as structured cases. Instead of reusing raw exemplar outputs, CAST extracts case-derived signals to identify complexity profiles for estimating optimal reasoning strategies, alongside failure profiles to map likely structural breakdowns. The framework translates this knowledge into a fine-grained reward design and adaptive reasoning, enabling the model to autonomously internalize case-based strategies during reinforcement learning. Experiments on BFCLv2 and ToolBench demonstrate that CAST improves both schema-faithful execution and task-level tool-use success while reducing unnecessary deliberation. The approach achieves up to 5.85 percentage points gain in overall execution accuracy and reduces average reasoning length by 26%, significantly mitigating high-impact structural errors. Ultimately, this demonstrates how historical execution cases can provide reusable adaptation knowledge for calibrated tool use.

Keywords: Case-Based Reasoning · Large Language Models · Tool Use · Reinforcement Learning · Reasoning Budget Calibration

1 Introduction

Tool use has become a central mechanism for extending large language models (LLMs) beyond parametric knowledge, and recent surveys identify tool invocation, planning, and action coordination as core components of LLM-agent systems [4,6,21,25]. At the same time, benchmark-oriented studies suggest that reliable function calling remains far from solved, especially in settings that require memory, dynamic decision-making, and long-horizon reasoning rather than single-turn text generation alone [22]. Representative frameworks such as Toolformer [26], ReAct [29], and ToolLLM [24] further show that the key challenge is no longer simply whether LLMs can call tools, but whether they can

L. Malburg and K. Bach (Eds.): ICCBR 2026, LNAI 16780, pp. 371–387, 2027.
https://doi.org/10.1007/978-3-032-33865-5_23

allocate reasoning effort and execute structured tool actions in a stable and task-sensitive manner.

This challenge arises because tool use places two simultaneous demands on the model. Different queries require different amounts of intermediate reasoning: some can be solved with little deliberation, whereas others require additional reasoning to verify constraints, normalize arguments, or compose multi-step tool calls. Recent work on adaptive chain-of-thought (CoT) and efficient tool calling suggests that treating all inputs with the same reasoning policy is often inefficient and can even be counterproductive [19,20,27]. At the same time, tool execution is governed by strict structural constraints, while standard reinforcement learning (RL) often provides only coarse end-task feedback, making it difficult to identify whether failure originates from tool selection, parameter coverage, type mismatch, schema violation, or value construction. The central difficulty in tool use is therefore to calibrate reasoning depth and execution structure jointly under heterogeneous task demands.

We approach this problem from a modern Case-Based Reasoning (CBR) perspective on tool-use adaptation in LLMs. In our setting, historical execution trajectories are treated as cases that record how a task was solved, how much reasoning preceded action, whether the tool invocation succeeded, and what kinds of failures arose when it did not. This view is consistent with classical CBR [1] and with subsequent work emphasizing adaptation bottlenecks and case-base maintenance [7,11]. Recent studies further suggest that LLMs can support several stages of the CBR process, including case adaptation, similarity assessment, and experience-grounded agent reasoning [3,13,14,18]. Together, these developments motivate the use of historical execution cases as structured sources of calibration knowledge for tool use. In this paper, we formulate tool use as a case-based adaptation problem and introduce **C**ase-driven **A**daptation for **S**chema-faithful **T**ool use (CAST), a case-driven framework that extracts two forms of case-derived signals from past trajectories. Specifically, it derives a complexity profile to estimate the necessary reasoning depth and a failure profile to map likely structural breakdowns. As shown in Figure 1, rather than imposing a static reasoning limit or a uniform chain-of-thought policy, CAST translates this case-derived knowledge into a fine-grained reward design that supports adaptive reasoning. In particular, the model learns to shorten deliberation for easy cases while preserving sufficient reasoning steps for cases that require constraint verification, argument normalization, or multi-step tool composition. This approach enables the model to internalize historical case experiences during reinforcement learning, empowering it to autonomously orchestrate the model's reasoning budget and execute schema-faithful tool actions. Experiments on BFCLv2 and ToolBench show that CAST improves both schema-faithful execution and task-level tool-use success while reducing unnecessary reasoning, with especially strong gains on more complex cases and clear reductions in high-impact structural failures.

The remainder of this paper is organized as follows. Section 2 reviews related work on CBR for LLMs and agents, adaptive reasoning, and tool-use alignment. Section 3 formulates tool use as a case-based adaptation problem. Section 4

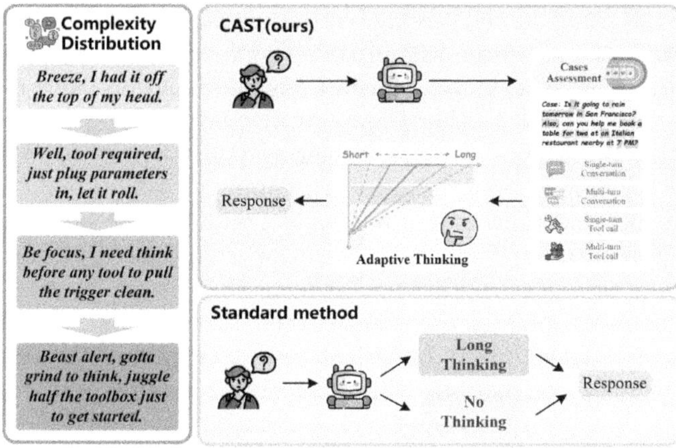

Fig. 1. Comparison of reasoning workflows with and without a case-based mechanism.

presents the CAST framework. Section 5 reports the experimental results and analyses. Section 6 concludes the paper and discusses limitations and future work.

2 Related Work

Case-based reasoning (CBR) addresses new problems by reusing and adapting solutions from similar prior cases through retrieval, reuse, revision, and retention [1]. In recent years, this perspective has increasingly intersected with large language models and agentic systems. Prior work has explored the use of LLMs for case adaptation in argumentative reasoning [13], while more recent studies investigate how LLMs can support similarity assessment in case retrieval [14]. Other work extends case-based ideas to reinforcement learning and agent settings, for example through case-based knowledge distillation for reinforcement learning [18], and unified experience-grounded agentic reasoning architectures [3]. Recent work has also examined how LLMs can support case-base population from unstructured sources [10] and how CBR can be integrated with LLMs in practical decision-support settings such as fraud detection [9]. Taken together, these studies suggest that LLMs can support multiple stages of the CBR process, including similarity assessment, adaptation, case acquisition, and the use of structured prior experience in agent reasoning.

A related line of research studies how to regulate the amount of reasoning generated by large language models. Existing methods seek to shorten, compress, or selectively trigger chain-of-thought in order to improve efficiency while maintaining competitive task performance [19,20]. This line of work is directly relevant to our setting because it recognizes that different inputs may require different amounts of intermediate reasoning. In parallel, another line of work focuses on tool use and reasoning–acting behavior in LLMs. Toolformer shows that language models can learn when and how to invoke external tools [26], while ReAct demonstrates the value of interleaving reasoning traces with external actions [29]. Tool-use research has also been accompanied by increasingly realistic evaluation settings, including large-scale API benchmarks and function-calling leaderboards [22,24]. More recent work further improves invocation discipline and efficiency, for example through meta-cognitive triggering [15], alignment for efficient tool calling [27], or token-level policy gradient reshaping for tool-use LLMs [16]. These studies substantially advance reasoning control and tool-use alignment, but they generally treat reasoning depth and execution structure as separate concerns rather than as jointly case-conditioned aspects of the same problem.

Our work is motivated by the gap between these directions. Existing CBR-oriented research suggests that historical cases can provide reusable structure for future reasoning and action, while adaptive reasoning and tool-alignment research shows that both reasoning cost and execution discipline must be carefully controlled. What remains underexplored is how historical execution cases can be used to derive calibration signals for these two aspects jointly. CAST is a case-driven framework in which historical execution cases provide case-derived complexity and failure signals, designed to explicitly internalize the case-based experience that calibrates reinforcement learning through reasoning-budget control and schema-faithful tool optimization.

3 Problem Formulation

Given a user query q and a tool set $\mathcal{T}$, tool use requires a model to generate a trajectory $\tau = (r, c)$, where r denotes the reasoning trace and $c = \text{call}(f, z)$ denotes a structured tool invocation with function f and arguments z. We formulate this problem from a case-based adaptation perspective: historical execution trajectories are treated as execution cases, $\xi_i = (q_i, r_i, c_i, o_i, \phi_i)$, where q_i is the input query, r_i is the reasoning trace, c_i is the executed tool call, o_i is the execution outcome, and $\phi_i = (h_i, e_i)$ is the case profile consisting of a complexity profile h_i and a failure profile e_i. Under this formulation, historical executions are not treated merely as supervision traces, but as structured cases from which case-derived calibration signals can be obtained for reasoning-budget control and schema-faithful tool use. The objective is therefore to learn a policy π_θ calibrated by these historical cases, such that the generated trajectory $\tau \sim \pi_\theta(\cdot \mid q, \mathcal{T})$ produces tool actions that are both semantically appropriate and structurally executable.

4 Method

Figure 2 illustrates the overall architecture of CAST. From a case-based perspective, CAST organizes historical tool-use trajectories as structured execution cases, derives case-derived complexity and failure signals from these cases, and uses them to guide two coordinated adaptation processes: reasoning-budget calibration and schema-faithful tool optimization. In implementation, CAST is

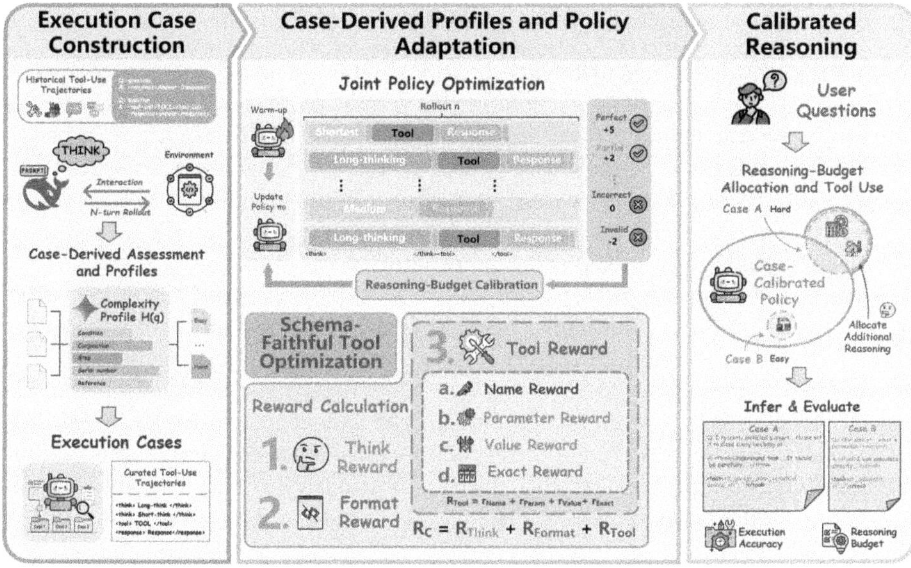

Fig. 2. Overview of CAST. Historical tool-use trajectories are organized as execution cases. These case signals guide two coordinated adaptation processes: reasoning-budget calibration and schema-faithful tool optimization. Reinforcement learning serves as the optimization mechanism for this case-based adaptation framework.

trained with a supervised warm-up stage followed by reinforcement learning calibrated by these case-derived signals. In this sense, reasoning-budget calibration model is encouraged to vary its deliberation depth according to case complexity before producing a schema-faithful tool action. Under this formulation, reinforcement learning serves as the optimization mechanism, while the methodological core lies in case-driven capability assessment and adaptation.

4.1 Execution Case Construction

CAST first converts historical tool-use trajectories into execution cases. Unlike ordinary supervision pairs, an execution case preserves not only the input query and target tool call, but also the intermediate reasoning process and the observed execution outcome. This allows historical trajectories to function as structured experience rather than isolated input–output examples. Formally, each case is represented as $\xi_i = (q_i, r_i, c_i, o_i, \phi_i)$, where q_i is the user query, r_i is the reasoning trace, c_i is the structured tool invocation, o_i is the execution outcome, and ϕ_i is the case profile defined in Sect. 4.2. In practice, we bootstrap the case base from tool-augmented reasoning trajectories distilled from DeepSeek-R1, normalize all tool interactions into a unified function-schema format, and filter malformed or unverifiable traces during preprocessing.

4.2 Case Representation: Complexity and Failure Profiles

After constructing the execution case base, CAST represents each case through a profile $\phi_i = (h_i, e_i)$, where h_i is a complexity profile and e_i is a failure profile. The complexity profile characterizes how much intermediate reasoning is typically required before action, whereas the failure profile characterizes where execution is most likely to break, such as function selection, argument construction, type mismatch, or schema violation. Together, these profiles provide the case-derived calibration signals used in the subsequent adaptation stages.

We estimate case complexity from the base model's observed execution behavior rather than from a manually specified heuristic. For each historical query-target pair (q, a), we sample a trajectory $y \sim \pi_{\text{base}}(\cdot \mid q)$ and evaluate it with the verifier V. If the generated tool call is fully correct and schema-faithful, the case is assigned zero hardness. Otherwise, the failed trajectory is assessed by an external rubric-guided judge using reference examples of simple and difficult cases. In our implementation, this judge is instantiated with Gemini-Pro. We define the resulting hardness score as

$$H(q) = \begin{cases} 0, & V(y,a) = 1, \\ 1 - S_{\text{judge}}(q, y), & V(y,a) = 0, \end{cases} \tag{1}$$

where $S_{\text{judge}}(q, y) \in [0, 1]$ denotes the judged adequacy of the failed trajectory with respect to logical coherence, parameter construction, and schema adherence. We use this score as an operational proxy for reasoning demand, and partition the case base into D_{easy} and D_{hard} for curriculum scheduling while retaining the continuous score for finer-grained analysis.

The failure profile is derived from the mismatch between the generated tool call and the reference execution. For each failed case, we record the principal failure dimensions involved in the mismatch, including function-name errors, parameter-key omissions, type mismatches, constraint violations, and value mismatches, and summarize them as

$$e_i = (e_i^{\text{name}}, e_i^{\text{key}}, e_i^{\text{type}}, e_i^{\text{constraint}}, e_i^{\text{value}}). \tag{2}$$

Each component indicates whether the corresponding failure pattern is present in the trajectory.

4.3 Case-Based Adaptation for Reasoning-Budget Calibration

The adaptation problem in tool use is to determine how much reasoning should precede action for a given case. A uniform reasoning policy is inadequate because different cases require different amounts of intermediate deliberation: simple cases may suffer from unnecessary verbosity. CAST addresses this problem by using the case complexity profile to internalize historical execution strategies into the model's policy. Through a fine-grained reward design, the model learns to autonomously produce appropriately short or long CoT traces, mirroring the successful adaptation patterns found in similar prior cases.

Concretely, the complexity profile introduced in Sect. 4.2 is operationalized by the hardness score $H(q) \in [0, 1]$, where smaller values indicate easier cases and larger values indicate more difficult ones. We discretize $H(q)$ into a small number of difficulty bands $d(q)$ only for estimating stable empirical length baselines, while retaining the continuous value $H(q)$ itself as the control signal for reward shaping. Let $r_a \in [-2, 2]$ denote the final answer score and L the response length. We define a difficulty-conditioned length baseline as:

$$L_{emp}^{d(q)}(t) = L_{max}^{d(q)} - \left(L_{max}^{d(q)} - L_{target}^{d(q)}\right) \cdot \min\left(1, \frac{t}{T_{warmup}}\right), \tag{3}$$

where $L_{max}^{d(q)}$ is the initial relaxed length limit for difficulty band $d(q)$, $L_{target}^{d(q)}$ is the target concise length, and T_{warmup} is the curriculum duration.

We then define the excess-length ratio

$$\rho(q, L) = \max\left(0, \frac{L}{L_{emp}^{d(q)}} - 1\right), \tag{4}$$

which measures how much the current response exceeds the expected reasoning budget, and the complexity-sensitive gating weight

$$\lambda(q) = 1 - H(q), \tag{5}$$

so that easy cases are more strongly penalized for unnecessary overthinking, whereas difficult cases are less sensitive to length and remain primarily correctness-driven.

The shaping coefficient is defined as

$$\alpha(q, r_a, L) = \begin{cases} \max(0, 1 - \lambda(q)\rho(q, L)), & r_a > 0, \\ 1 + \lambda(q)\rho(q, L), & r_a < 0, \\ 1, & r_a = 0, \end{cases} \tag{6}$$

and the reasoning-side reward is

$$\mathcal{R}_{\text{Think}} = \alpha(q, r_a, L) \cdot r_a. \tag{7}$$

Under this formulation, the same complexity signal plays two roles. Through $d(q)$, it provides a stable empirical baseline for expected reasoning length; through $H(q)$, it determines how strongly overlong reasoning should be penalized. As a result, easy cases are encouraged to remain concise, while difficult cases preserve a larger reasoning workspace and are optimized primarily with respect to answer correctness.

4.4 Failure-Profile-Grounded Optimization for Schema-Faithful Tool Use

While reasoning-budget calibration governs how much deliberation precedes action, a complementary challenge remains: ensuring that the final tool action is structurally executable. Even when a reasoning trace appears semantically plausible, execution can still fail because of errors in function names, argument keys, types, constraints, or values. CAST therefore treats tool optimization as a separate but coordinated objective grounded in the failure profile $e_i = (e_i^{\text{name}}, e_i^{\text{key}}, e_i^{\text{type}}, e_i^{\text{constraint}}, e_i^{\text{value}})$. Let $\mathcal{G}$ and $\mathcal{P}$ denote the ground-truth and predicted collections of tool calls. To handle multi-call settings, we align them by maximum-weight bipartite matching:

$$\mathcal{J} = \arg \max_{M \in \mathcal{M}(\mathcal{G},\mathcal{P})} \sum_{(G,P) \in M} s_{\text{match}}(G, P), \tag{8}$$

where $s_{\text{match}}(G, P) = \delta(\text{name}(G), \text{name}(P)) + \frac{|K^G \cap K^P|}{|K^G \cup K^P|}$, and K^G, K^P are the parameter-key sets of G, P. Repeated tool calls remain distinct nodes in the matching graph.

We then define a six-dimensional structural reward vector:

$$\mathbf{r}_{\text{tool}} = (r_{\text{name}}, r_{\text{key}}, r_{\text{type}}, r_{\text{constraint}}, r_{\text{value}}, r_{\text{exact}})^{\top}. \tag{9}$$

Let N_G, N_P be the overall function-name sets of $\mathcal{G}, \mathcal{P}$. The name score is the Jaccard overlap $r_{\text{name}} = \frac{|N_G \cap N_P|}{|N_G \cup N_P|}$. The key score averages parameter-key overlap over aligned calls: $r_{\text{key}} = \frac{1}{|\mathcal{J}|} \sum_{j \in \mathcal{J}} \frac{|K_j^G \cap K_j^P|}{|K_j^G \cup K_j^P|}$ when $|\mathcal{J}| > 0$, and 0 otherwise; when $K_j^G = K_j^P = \varnothing$, the corresponding overlap term is set to 1. We define $r_{\text{type}}, r_{\text{constraint}}, r_{\text{value}}$ as the average indicator matches over overlapping keys, with default value 0 when the number of overlapping keys is zero. The exact-match term is $r_{\text{exact}} = V_{\text{AST}}(\mathcal{P}, \mathcal{G}) \in \{0, 1\}$, where AST denotes Abstract Syntax Tree matching. The raw structural score is:

$$R_{\text{raw}} = r_{\text{name}} + r_{\text{key}} + r_{\text{type}} + r_{\text{constraint}} + r_{\text{value}} + r_{\text{exact}}. \tag{10}$$

Since each component is bounded in $[0, 1]$, the global maximum is $S_{\text{max}} = 6$. We therefore define the final tool-side reward as

$$\mathcal{R}_{\text{Tool}} = 2 \cdot \frac{R_{\text{raw}}}{S_{\text{max}}} - 1 \in [-1, 1]. \tag{11}$$

As a result, CAST provides dense and interpretable credit assignment for schema-faithful tool use without hand-tuned gating rules or query-dependent scaling constants.

4.5 Training Objective and Optimization

Given a query q and a tool set $\mathcal{T}$, the model generates a trajectory $\tau = (r, c)$. To guide the optimization securely and prevent degenerate behaviors, we formulate a composite reward that provides feedback at three complementary levels of abstraction:

$$\mathcal{R}_C = \mathcal{R}_{\text{Think}} + \mathcal{R}_{\text{Format}} + \mathcal{R}_{\text{Tool}}. \tag{12}$$

The first term, $\mathcal{R}_{\text{Think}}$, is derived from the complexity profile and aligns the model toward adaptive reasoning by calibrating the intermediate deliberation budget for each case. (Section 4.3). The second, $\mathcal{R}_{\text{Format}}$, is a rule-based guardrail that enforces valid tag encapsulation. The third, $\mathcal{R}_{\text{Tool}}$, relies on the failure profile to evaluate fine-grained schema-faithful accuracy (Sect. 4.4).

In practice, we first initialize the model using SFT on curated tool-augmented trajectories with the standard next-token prediction loss:

$$\mathcal{L}_{\text{SFT}} = -\frac{1}{|\mathcal{D}_{\text{SFT}}|} \sum_{(x,y)\in\mathcal{D}_{\text{SFT}}} \sum_{t=1}^{|y|} \log \pi_\theta(y_t \mid x, y_{<t}). \tag{13}$$

After initialization, we optimize the policy π_θ using a Group Relative Policy Optimization (GRPO)-based procedure augmented with the case-derived composite reward $\mathcal{R}_C$, which replaces the standard scalar reward with our decomposed complexity- and failure-conditioned signals. To stabilize the learning dynamics, we organize the RL training following an Easy-to-Hard curriculum based on the difficulty subsets partitioned by the complexity profile. For each query q, we sample a group of G trajectories $\{\tau_1, \ldots, \tau_G\}$. The group-relative advantage for the i-th trajectory is computed by normalizing the composite rewards within the group:

$$A_i = \frac{\mathcal{R}_C(\tau_i) - \mu_{\mathcal{R}}}{\sigma_{\mathcal{R}} + \epsilon_{\text{stab}}}, \tag{14}$$

where $\mu_{\mathcal{R}}$ and $\sigma_{\mathcal{R}}$ are the mean and standard deviation of the group rewards, and ϵ_{stab} is a small constant for numerical stability. The policy is then updated by maximizing the clipped surrogate objective augmented with a KL divergence penalty:

$$\begin{aligned}\mathcal{J}_{\text{CAST}}(\theta) = \mathbb{E}_{q,\{\tau_i\}_{i=1}^{G}} \Big[&\min\Big(\rho_i A_i, \text{clip}\big(\rho_i, 1-\epsilon, 1+\epsilon\big) A_i\Big) \\ &- \beta \cdot D_{\text{KL}}\Big(\pi_\theta(\cdot \mid q) \parallel \pi_{\text{ref}}(\cdot \mid q)\Big)\Big],\end{aligned} \tag{15}$$

where $\rho_i = \frac{\pi_\theta(\tau_i|q)}{\pi_{\theta_{\text{old}}}(\tau_i|q)}$ is the probability ratio, ϵ is the clipping margin, β controls the KL penalty strength, and π_{ref} is the reference policy. Under this formulation, SFT provides warm-up initialization and the GRPO-based procedure serves as the optimization engine, while the methodological core of CAST lies in representing historical executions as structured cases, deriving complexity and failure profiles, and translating them into the decomposed case-derived signals that drive the GRPO updates.

5 Experiments

5.1 Experimental Setup

We evaluate CAST on BFCLv2, including 5,551 instances covering single-turn, parallel, multi-step, and irrelevance-detection scenarios, and on ToolBench with diverse queries mapping to REST APIs across 49 categories. Model-level baselines include the original backbones alongside their SFT and GRPO variants. We primarily use Qwen2.5-7B-Instruct, adding Qwen2.5-Coder-7B-Instruct and Llama-3.2-8B-Instruct to examine cross-backbone robustness, and report closed models (GPT-4o [12], Qwen-Max [28], DeepSeek-V3 [17]) for context. Method-level comparisons feature Toolformer [26], ReAct [29], ToolAlign [5], CoT-Valve [20], OTC [8], Granite [2], and Gorilla [23] evaluated under identical protocols. We utilize CAST via Megatron with an 8K maximum response length and evaluate inference using SGLang. To balance exploration and warm-up, we train for 2 epochs during the SFT phase. For RL training, we sample a group of $G = 8$ rollouts per query at a temperature of 0.9. The policy is optimized using AdamW with a peak learning rate of 1×10^{-6}, a cosine learning rate scheduler, and a weight decay of 0.01. To stabilize the reinforcement learning dynamics, we apply a KL divergence penalty coefficient of $\beta = 0.01$.

5.2 Overall Performance and Efficiency

Table 1 reports the main results on BFCLv2 and ToolBench. On BFCLv2, CAST consistently improves over both SFT and GRPO across all three open-source

Table 1. Main results on BFCLv2 and ToolBench. We report execution accuracy on BFCLv2 (Non-Live AST, Live, and Overall) and task success on ToolBench (Pass and Win).

Category	Model/Method	Non-Live AST	Live	Overall	**Pass**	Win
		BFCLv2 (%)			ToolBench (%)	
Closed Source	GPT-4o	86.83	78.92	82.88	64.43	67.63
	Qwen-Max	84.97	80.85	82.91	70.93	71.83
	DeepSeek-V3	86.37	75.28	80.83	70.73	72.93
Open Source	Llama-3.2-8B-Instruct-SFT	83.14	73.82	78.48	70.63	45.83
	Llama-3.2-8B-Instruct-GRPO	82.18	75.21	78.73	71.23	45.23
	Llama-3.2-8B-Instruct-CAST	83.95	76.84	80.43	75.93	47.23
	Qwen2.5-Coder-7B-Instruct-SFT	86.07	74.92	80.86	67.84	65.37
	Qwen2.5-Coder-7B-Instruct-GRPO	86.51	75.07	80.79	71.13	67.82
	Qwen2.5-Coder-7B-Instruct-CAST	87.12	82.43	84.70	80.61	79.14
	Qwen2.5-7B-Instruct-SFT	86.23	78.90	82.58	68.67	65.23
	Qwen2.5-7B-Instruct-GRPO	87.05	80.29	83.67	72.71	68.23
	Qwen2.5-7B-Instruct-CAST	88.24	87.40	88.43	80.67	79.43
Other	Granite	86.17	79.19	84.71	68.47	50.17
	Gorilla	86.02	80.44	82.21	62.27	46.29
	Toolformer	76.11	59.47	67.07	48.92	22.11
	ReAct	73.58	58.43	66.08	43.37	18.22
	ToolAlign	77.26	61.47	71.16	46.78	22.36
	OTC	82.64	71.28	78.33	65.49	36.12

backbones, indicating that case-derived calibration transfers across different model families and pretraining styles. The strongest result is obtained with Qwen2.5-7B-Instruct, where CAST reaches 88.43% overall, gaining 5.85 points over SFT and 4.76 points over GRPO. The narrow 0.84-point gap between Non-Live AST and Live scores suggests that the gains transfer from offline schema matching to actual tool execution. The same trend is visible on the other open-source backbones. On Llama-3.2-8B-Instruct, CAST improves BFCLv2 Overall from 78.48% under SFT and 78.73% under GRPO to 80.43%. On Qwen2.5-Coder-7B-Instruct, CAST reaches 84.70% overall, with especially large gains on Live execution, rising from 74.92% and 75.07% to 82.43%. Together, these results suggest that CAST is particularly effective when evaluation places stricter weight on execution validity. On ToolBench, the transfer pattern is also consistently positive. CAST achieves the strongest ToolBench results among CAST-trained models with Qwen2.5-7B-Instruct, reaching 80.67% Pass and 79.43% Win, both substantially above its SFT and GRPO counterparts. Llama-3.2-8B-Instruct shows a similar trend. Notably, the updated results on Qwen2.5-Coder-7B-Instruct now reveal a strong monotonic improvement as well: ToolBench Pass increases from 67.84% under SFT and 71.13% under GRPO to 80.61% under CAST, while Win rises from 65.37% and 67.82% to 79.14%. Rather than indicating a trade-off between schema-faithful calibration and end-to-end task success, the coder backbone now provides additional evidence that case-derived calibration transfers beyond local structural correctness and yields substantial gains on task-level tool-use performance.

5.3 Evidence for Case-Conditioned Adaptation

We evaluate CAST through ablations, budget sensitivity, and training stability. Figure 3 shows that removing any major component consistently lowers average reward across backbones, indicating that CAST depends on the interaction between reasoning-side and tool-side adaptation. Table 2 confirms this on BFCLv2. The dynamic-only variant, which keeps the adaptive reasoning-budget component without the full schema-level reward, reduces average length from 236.9 to 164.7 tokens while reaching 85.50 Non-Live AST. This confirms that the adaptive reasoning component alone can suppress unnecessary deliberation, although schema-faithful optimization is still needed for the best execution accuracy. Combining both gives the best result 88.24% Non-Live AST at 175.4 tokens. Table 3 shows the importance of budget control. Removing the cap increases average length to 486.2 tokens and lowers BFCLv2 Overall to 86.3%. A strict 50th-percentile cap shortens outputs to 140.8 tokens but drops ToolBench Pass to 76.5%. The 80th-percentile setting achieves the best overall trade-off across BFCLv2 and ToolBench, supporting case-conditioned reasoning budgets for heterogeneous tool-use tasks.

Figure 4 shows that CAST also stabilizes RL training. Its normalized advantage variance decreases from 0.48 to 0.10, while GRPO remains around 0.21, indicating cleaner credit assignment and fewer oscillations between overthinking and underthinking.

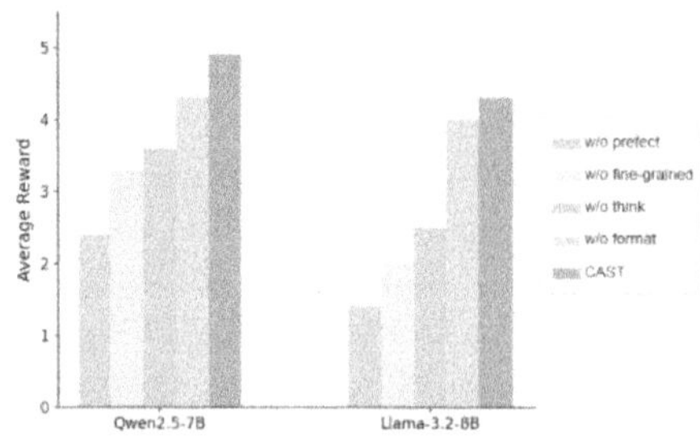

Fig. 3. Ablation study of the major adaptation components.

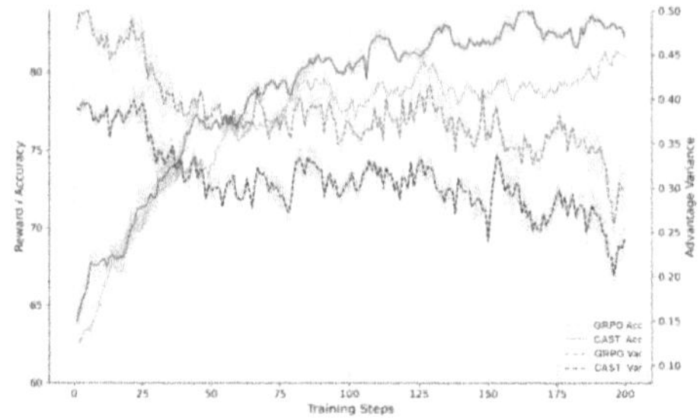

Fig. 4. Training accuracy and normalized advantage variance.

Table 2. Ablation of reasoning-side and tool-side adaptation on BFCLv2.

Variant	Non-Live AST ↑	Avg. Reasoning Length (tok) ↓
base-GRPO	87.05	236.9
dynamic-only	85.50	164.7
schema-only	86.59	214.5
CAST	88.24	175.4

5.4 Case Complexity and Failure Profiles

To verify that the case-derived profiles operate as intended, we analyze their impact across three dimensions: instance-level budget allocation, structural error suppression, and global curriculum organization.

Adaptive Budget Allocation via Complexity Profiles. Fig. 5 reports execution accuracy across fine-grained difficulty levels. If the complexity profile merely acted as a length penalty, its effect would be roughly uniform across buckets or even harmful on harder cases. Instead, CAST yields only small gains on easy instances, where budget control mainly reduces verbosity, but substantially larger gains as difficulty increases. This pattern suggests that the complexity profile enables adaptive reasoning allocation: CAST shortens reasoning when additional deliberation is unnecessary, but preserves or expands the reasoning budget when compositional reasoning is required.

Table 3. Impact of varying reasoning length budgets on task accuracy and schema alignment.

Threshold	BFCLv2 (Overall)	ToolBench (Pass)	ToolBench (Win)	Length
0 (no cap)	86.3	69.9	65.7	486.2
100th (loose)	87.5	80.3	79.6	240.9
80th (default)	**88.43**	**80.67**	**79.43**	**175.4**
50th (strict)	86.8	76.5	73.1	140.8

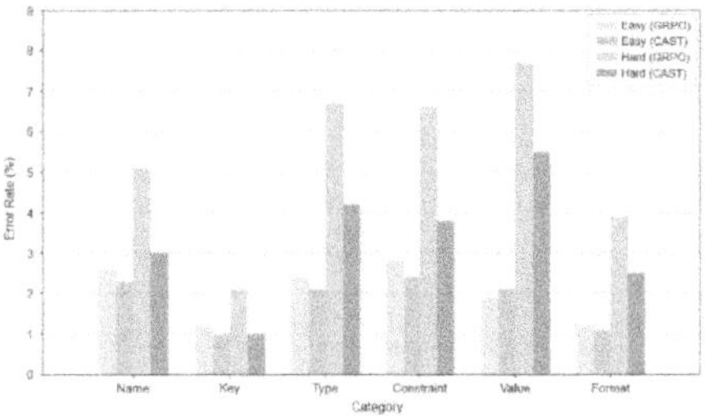

Fig. 5. Performance across fine-grained difficulty levels.

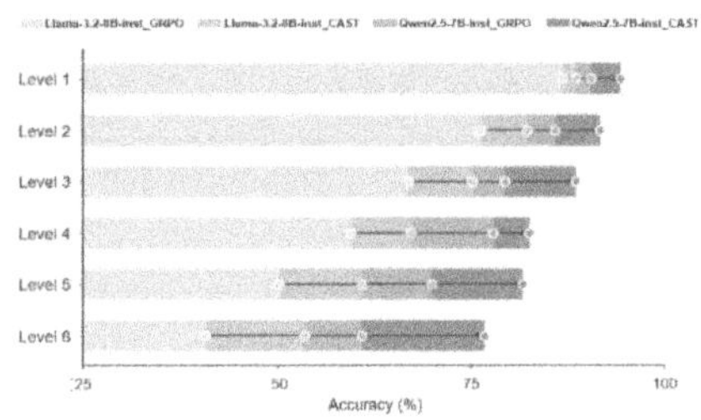

Fig. 6. Error-rate distribution by category.

Structural Error Suppression via Failure Profiles. We next study whether schema-faithful tool optimization targets specific failure modes. Figure 6 separates execution errors into structural violations and localized content errors. As shown in the Reward Calculation module of Fig. 2, $\mathcal{R}_{\text{Tool}}$ explicitly penalizes structural deviations. Accordingly, CAST reduces structural failures much more than the GRPO baseline, leaving most residual errors in localized value prediction. This result indicates that CAST improves the conversion of free-form reasoning into schema-compliant tool execution.

Table 4. Effect of curriculum strategy on ToolBench.

Method	Pass (%)	Win (%)	Length
No Selection	73.2	69.5	2417.3
Two Stage	76.8	74.2	297.3
Hard to Easy	68.5	64.3	426.3
Easy to Hard	**80.7**	**79.4**	**175.4**

At the training level, Table 4 tests whether the case-derived complexity score $H(q)$ provides a useful curriculum signal. The easy-to-hard schedule achieves the best accuracy and the shortest outputs, with an average generation length of 175.4 tokens. In contrast, the hard-to-easy schedule performs worst and produces much longer outputs (426.3 tokens on average), suggesting that early exposure to difficult cases encourages unstable trial-and-error behavior and persistent overthinking. Overall, case-derived complexity serves as an effective signal for both local budget control and global curriculum design.

5.5 Case Study

Figures 7 and 8 illustrate CAST's adaptive reasoning-execution boundary. In the easy weather-query case, GRPO produces redundant deliberation about rate limits and execution order, whereas CAST directly emits the necessary tool calls.

Easy Instance Case

Query: Could you check the current weather conditions in Beijing and New York City for me?

SFT	The user asks for weather in Beijing and New York City. I should use get_current_weather for each location. Two calls, one for Beijing, one for NYC.	`get_current_weather (location='Beijing') get_current_weather (location='NYC')`	✓
GRPO	The query involves retrieving weather for two cities. I have access to get_current_weather. Since both Beijing and NYC are mentioned, I should invoke this for each city. No single API returns multiple cities. Wait, let me pause. Is parallel execution safe? While it reduces latency, there is a non-zero probability of hitting a 429 error if I trigger both at the same millisecond. Should I introduce a micro-delay? Or execute sequentially? Sequential adds latency but guarantees safety. However, the user likely values speed. No complex transformation needed, just passing city names. To maximize efficiency, I will call the function twice in parallel.	`get_current_weather (location='Beijing') get_current_weather (location='NYC')`	✓
CAST	The user wants weather for Beijing and NYC. The simplest approach is to call the weather function for each city. I will use get_current_weather twice, one for each city, possibly in parallel. No further reasoning needed, the task is straightforward.	`get_current_weather (location='Beijing') get_current_weather (location='NYC')`	✓

Fig. 7. Easy case.

Hard Instance Case

Query: Calculate density (mass=50kg, volume=10m3), future value ($5000 at 5% for 10 years), Apple stock price, and Amazon rating (ASIN: B08PPDJWC8)

SFT	The request involves multiple tasks: density, future value, stock price, and product rating. I will tackle them in order. For density, I have calculate_density with mass=50, volume=10. For future value, calculate_future_value with present_value=5000, interest_rate=5, periods=10. Then Apple stock with get_stock_price, and Amazon rating with get_rating_by_ASIN.	`calculate_density (mass=50, volume=10) calculate_future_value (5000, 5, 10) get_stock_price ('Apple') get_rating_by_ASIN ('B08PPDJWC8')`	✗
GRPO	The user requests four independent results. The safest plan is to map each task to one tool call and validate arguments. For density: mass=50, volume=10, straightforward. For future value: present_value=5000, interest_rate=5%, periods=10. I need to decide how to encode 5%. Many functions expect decimal 0.05, but some accept 5. I'll use 5, keeping closer to surface form. For Apple stock: the tool likely expects ticker symbol AAPL, not company name. For ASIN: pass B08PPDJWC8 exactly.	`calculate_density (mass=50, volume=10) calculate_future_value (5000, 5, 10) get_stock_price ('AAPL') get_rating_by_ASIN ('B08PPDJWC8')`	✗
CAST	The request comprises four diverse tasks requiring careful handling. I will approach each methodically. Density: calculate_density(mass=50, volume=10), straightforward. Future value: Must be precise with interest_rate. 5% = 0.05 decimal. Crucial to pass 0.05, not integer 5. Stock price: Safest to use ticker symbol AAPL, not company name. Amazon rating: Pass ASIN exactly as given.	`calculate_density (mass=50, volume=10) calculate_future_value (5000, 0.05, 10) get_stock_price ('AAPL') get_rating_by_ASIN ('B08PPDJWC8')`	✓

Fig. 8. Hard case.

In the harder compositional case, SFT and GRPO copy the surface form of 5% into the tool arguments, while CAST preserves enough reasoning to normalize it to 0.05 and keeps the remaining calls structurally valid. This shows that CAST shortens reasoning when execution is straightforward and preserves it when semantic normalization is required.

6 Conclusion

This paper revisits tool use from a case-based reasoning perspective and proposes CAST, a framework that uses signals distilled from past execution cases to guide reinforcement learning. Specifically, CAST summarizes historical trajectories through complexity and failure profiles, and uses them to regulate reasoning length and supervise schema-level tool execution. Experiments on BFCLv2 and ToolBench show that this case-conditioned calibration improves execution accuracy, transfers to end-to-end tool-use success, and reduces unnecessary reasoning, with the largest gains on more complex cases. Long-horizon planning remains challenging, but the results suggest that case-derived supervision provides a practical basis for improving both reliable tool calling and downstream task completion. A natural next step is to extend this framework to richer case memories, stronger retrieval and reuse, and more interactive agent settings.

Acknowledgments. This work was partially supported by the National Natural Science Foundation of China (U2336204), Chengdu Industrial Chain Collaborative Innovation Project (Grant No. 2025-XT00-00017-GX) and the Open bidding for selecting the best candidates of Sichuan Provincial Department of Science and Technology (2024YFCY0003).

Generative AI Disclosure. LLMs were used exclusively for stylistic refinement of the manuscript. All textual content was initially drafted in full by the authors and subsequently polished with the assistance of LLM-based tools, including ChatGPT and Gemini. All scientific contributions, technical methods, ideas, and core results presented in this work are entirely the original work of the authors.

References

1. Aamodt, A., Plaza, E.: Case-based reasoning: foundational issues, methodological variations, and system approaches. AI Commun. **7**(1), 39–59 (1994)
2. Abdelaziz, I., Basu, K., Agarwal, M., Kumaravel, S., Stallone, M., Panda, R.: Granite-function calling model: Introducing function calling abilities via multi-task learning of granular tasks. In: Proceedings of the 2024 Conference on Empirical Methods in Natural Language Processing: Industry Track, pp. 1131–1139. (2024)
3. Bergmann, R., Brand, F., Lenz, M., Malburg, L.: Exar: A unified experience-grounded agentic reasoning architecture. In: International Conference on Case-Based Reasoning, pp. 3–17. Springer (2025)
4. Chen, J., Wu, H., Pang, J., Wang, Y., Zhang, D., Sun, C.: Tool learning with language models: a comprehensive survey of methods, pipelines, and benchmarks. Vicinagearth **2**(1), 16 (2025)
5. Chen, Z.Y., Shen, S., Shen, G., Zhi, G., Chen, X., Lin, Y.: Towards tool use alignment of large language models. In: Proceedings of the 2024 Conference on Empirical Methods in Natural Language Processing, pp. 1382–1400 (2024)
6. Chowa, S.S., Alvi, R., Rahman, S.S., Rahman, M.A., Raiaan, M.A.K., et al.: From language to action: a review of large language models as autonomous agents and tool users. Artif. Intell. Rev.(2026)

7. Craw, S., Wiratunga, N., Rowe, R.C.: Learning adaptation knowledge to improve case-based reasoning. Artif. Intell. **170**(16–17), 1175–1192 (2006)
8. El-Tantawy, S., Abdulhai, B.: Towards multi-agent reinforcement learning for integrated network of optimal traffic controllers (marlin-otc). Transport. Letters **2**(2), 89–110 (2010)
9. Ge, X., Xu, J.: Integrating case-based reasoning with LLM for expense fraud detection. In: International Conference on Case-Based Reasoning, pp. 52–66. Springer (2025)
10. Ghazouani, F., Giustozzi, F., Le Ber, F.: LLM-driven case-base populating for structuring and integrating restoration experiences. In: International Conference on Case-Based Reasoning, pp. 67–80. Springer (2025)
11. Hanney, K., Keane, M.T.: The adaptation knowledge bottleneck: How to ease it by learning from cases. In: Leake, D.B., Plaza, E. (eds.) ICCBR 1997. LNCS, vol. 1266, pp. 359–370. Springer, Heidelberg (1997). https://doi.org/10.1007/3-540-63233-6_506
12. Hurst, A., et al.: GPT-4o system card (2024). arXiv:2410.21276 arXiv preprint
13. Lenz, M., Bergmann, R.: Case-based adaptation of argument graphs with wordnet and large language models. In: International Conference on Case-Based Reasoning, pp. 263–278. Springer (2023)
14. Lenz, M., Hoffmann, M., Bergmann, R.: LLsiM: large language models for similarity assessment in case-based reasoning. In: International Conference on Case-Based Reasoning, pp. 126–141. Springer (2025)
15. Li, W., et al.: Adaptive tool use in large language models with meta-cognition trigger. In: Proceedings of the 63rd Annual Meeting of the Association for Computational Linguistics (Volume 1: Long Papers), pp. 13346–13370 (2025)
16. Lin, Z., Wang, X., Cao, J., Chai, J.: Rest: Reshaping token-level policy gradients for tool-use large language models. In: ICLR 2026 Conference Proceedings, (2026)
17. Liu, A., et al.: Deepseek-v3 technical report (2024). arXiv:2412.19437 arXiv preprint
18. Liu, H., Liu, Q., Wu, L., Shi, M., Cui, Z.: Offline-to-online: Case-based knowledge distillation with large language models for reinforcement learning. In: ICCBR 2025. LNCS, vol. 15662, pp. 142–156. Springer (2025)
19. Lou, C., et al.: Adacot: Pareto-optimal adaptive chain-of-thought triggering via reinforcement learning (2025). arXiv:2505.11896 arXiv preprint
20. Ma, X., Wan, G., Yu, R., Fang, G., Wang, X.: Cot-valve: Length-compressible chain-of-thought tuning. In: Proceedings of the 63rd Annual Meeting of the Association for Computational Linguistics (Volume 1: Long Papers), pp. 6025–6035 (2025)
21. Mohammadi, M., Li, Y., Lo, J., Yip, W.: Evaluation and benchmarking of LLM agents: a survey. In: Proceedings of the 31st ACM SIGKDD Conference on Knowledge Discovery and Data Mining V. 2, pp. 6129–6139. (2025)
22. Patil, S.G., Mao, H., Yan, F., Ji, C.C.J., Suresh, V., Stoica, I., Gonzalez, J.E.: The berkeley function calling leaderboard (BFCL) (2025)
23. Patil, S.G., Zhang, T., Wang, X., Gonzalez, J.E.: Gorilla: Large language model connected with massive apis. In: Advances in Neural Information Processing Systems, vol. 37 (NeurIPS 2024) (2024)
24. Qin, Y., et al.: Toolllm: Facilitating large language models to master 16000+ real-world apis. In: The Twelfth International Conference on Learning Representations (ICLR) (2024)
25. Ruan, J., et al.: Tptu: Task planning and tool usage of large language model-based AI agents. In: NeurIPS 2023 Foundation Models for Decision Making Workshop (2023)

26. Schick, T., et al.: Toolformer: language models can teach themselves to use tools. Adv. Neural. Inf. Process. Syst. **36**, 68539–68551 (2023)
27. Xu, H., et al.: Alignment for efficient tool calling of large language models. In: Proceedings of the 2025 Conference on Empirical Methods in Natural Language Processing, pp. 17787–17803 (2025)
28. Yang, A., et al.: Qwen2.5 technical report (2025). https://arxiv.org/abs/2412.15115
29. Yao, S., et al.: React: Synergizing reasoning and acting in language models. In: The Eleventh International Conference on Learning Representations (2022)

ProtoCase: Case-Based Repair for LLM-Generated Security Protocol Models

Shicong Zhang(✉)

School of Cryptology, University of Chinese Academy of Sciences, Beijing, China
zhangshicong20@mails.ucas.ac.cn

Abstract. Recent pipelines use LLMs to generate Tamarin/SAPIC+ security protocol models from natural language, and the resulting models frequently contain structural and semantic defects that compromise verification and require systematic repair. We identify four conditions under which case-based reasoning can control the repair of such models: a finite operator space, decomposable adaptation, bounded LLM delegation, and deterministic verifier feedback. We present ProtoCase, a framework that instantiates these conditions in three phases: deterministic preconditioning, a single LLM call guided by a retrieved case, and deterministic cleanup. A quality-gated retain step feeds verified repairs into the case base so that subsequent retrievals return format-matched cases. In leave-one-out experiments on 18 benchmark protocols, single-pass repair produces models whose security properties match hand-crafted references for 11 of 18 protocols (from a baseline of 8 of 18), and retention raises this to a median of 15 of 18 over five random case-base orderings, outperforming a RAG baseline at 5 of 18. Results hold across five LLM backends.

Keywords: case-based reasoning · security protocols · formal verification · large language models · adaptation operators

1 Introduction

Translating security protocols into verifier-ready formal models [2,4,7,17] requires deep domain expertise, including cryptographic primitives, message-flow structure, and tool-specific modelling idioms, making formal modelling labour-intensive and error-prone. Recent work addresses this bottleneck by using LLMs to automate the translation [8,14,16], but the resulting models frequently contain structural defects (syntax errors, misused primitives, missing security-critical annotations) that compromise verification. In our experiments across 18 protocols and five LLM backends, we find that these defects fall into ten recurring error classes. Each class has a characteristic syntactic signature, making it possible to match new errors to previously solved cases. This regularity makes

L. Malburg and K. Bach (Eds.): ICCBR 2026, LNAI 16780, pp. 388–404, 2027.
https://doi.org/10.1007/978-3-032-33865-5_24

repair amenable to *Case-Based Reasoning* (CBR): retrieve a past case from the same error class and adapt its stored solution to the current model.

Existing LLM-aided pipelines treat the verifier as a pass/fail oracle after generation and ignore error regularity. A natural alternative is *retrieval-augmented generation* (RAG), widely used in code-generation tasks: retrieve a similar correct model and prompt the LLM to rewrite the faulty one. Without structural decomposition, the LLM decides what to preserve and what to rewrite. In our experiments with a straightforward RAG formulation, the LLM destroys process structure during rewriting, producing models with fewer correct security properties than the unrepaired originals.

The alternative is to let CBR control the repair loop and confine the LLM to a bounded subtask. We identify four conditions (C1–C4, Sect. 3.2) under which this is possible. Two observations make this possible. First, the errors that LLM-generated models exhibit are regular enough that most repair steps can be carried out by deterministic operators, leaving the LLM a single bounded rewrite guided by a retrieved case. Second, the verifier pinpoints each error precisely enough to select the right operator without LLM interpretation. When both hold, CBR orchestrates an otherwise deterministic repair loop in which the LLM executes one step.

We present ProtoCase, a case-based repair framework for LLM-generated Tamarin models that instantiates this architecture. Our contributions are:

1. **CBR-as-Controller conditions.** We propose four design conditions (C1–C4) under which CBR can orchestrate LLM-aided repair, and show empirically that all four hold in the protocol-modelling domain.
2. **Three-phase adaptation with error-driven retrieval.** We instantiate the architecture as ProtoCase, with formally specified deterministic operators bracketing a single case-guided LLM rewrite. Error-driven retrieval selects the most similar case via error-type and structural similarity.
3. **Quality-gated retention.** Validated repairs re-enter the case base through an event-structural match gate. Retained cases are in SAPIC+ process format, closing the format mismatch between rule-style references and LLM-generated output.
4. **Cross-backend validation.** In leave-one-out experiments on the 18-protocol benchmark of [16], the three-phase pipeline alone raises the property match rate from 8/18 to 11/18. With quality-gated retention, the median reaches 15/18. Both configurations outperform a RAG baseline (5/18). The pipeline generalises across five LLM backends without modification.

2 Background and Related Work

2.1 Protocol Modelling and Verification

Tamarin [17] is a symbolic protocol verifier that analyses security protocols under the Dolev–Yao attacker model, in which the adversary has full control over the network but cannot break cryptographic primitives. A Tamarin theory specifies protocol behaviour via *action facts*, named events (such as `Running`, `Commit`, `Secret`) that mark security-relevant steps of a protocol. Security properties are stated as first-order *lemmas* over traces, sequences of these events over which Tamarin searches. ProtoCase compares models by the security-relevant events each emits per role.

SAPIC+ [12] extends Tamarin with a process calculus: protocols are written as concurrent processes with channels and let-bindings, then compiled into Tamarin rules. Tamarin's parse and well-formedness checks produce structured error messages that identify the offending construct and its location. ProtoCase generates and repairs models in SAPIC+.

2.2 Case-Based Reasoning

CBR [1] solves new problems by retrieving similar past cases and adapting their solutions. ProtoCase builds on operator-based adaptation [11,19], which structures adaptation as a sequence of discrete operators with defined preconditions and effects. The central challenge in operator-based adaptation is selecting and sequencing operators. Existing approaches derive this selection from case-difference analysis: comparing the new problem to the retrieved case to determine which operators apply [6,10,11,19]. ProtoCase replaces case-difference analysis with verifier feedback. Because each verifier error maps to exactly one operator, the operator sequence is determined without comparing the query to the retrieved case.

EXAR [3] also combines CBR with LLM generation, but gives the LLM the orchestrator role: the LLM decides how to use the retrieved case. ProtoCase inverts this relationship. CBR orchestrates the repair loop, and the LLM executes a single bounded subtask. We are not aware of prior work that combines CBR with formal verification feedback for model repair.

2.3 Automated Modelling and Repair

The systems closest to ProtoCase all close the gap between natural-language protocol descriptions and verified formal models, but differ in how much control the LLM retains over the repair.

Several recent pipelines use LLMs to generate Tamarin models from natural-language protocol descriptions [8,14,16]. All three treat the verifier as a pass/fail oracle after generation, with no iterative repair loop. We use AutoSM [16] as the upstream generator. ProtoCase operates as a post-processing layer on its output. The structural defects these pipelines produce recur across backends.

Baldur [9], Laurel [18], and Clover [20] close the verifier feedback loop for Isabelle/HOL, Dafny, and Dafny respectively, but all three give the LLM full responsibility for interpreting verifier feedback and generating the repair. ProtoCase removes both responsibilities: deterministic operators handle feedback interpretation, and the LLM executes only a bounded rewrite.

Like ICEBAR and ATR, ProtoCase exploits the structural regularity of specification errors. ICEBAR [5] and ATR [22] propose feedback-driven and template-based repair for Alloy specifications, but derive patches from the specification under repair, making each repair episode self-contained. ProtoCase retrieves solutions from an external case base, enabling cross-protocol reuse of repair experience.

In automated program repair (APR), GenProg [21] and TBar [15] apply genetic and template-based patches guided by test-suite feedback. RAG-Verus [23] applies the retrieval-augmented generation paradigm [13] to guide LLM-based program verification, but gives the LLM full freedom over rewrite scope. ProtoCase bounds the LLM to a single rewrite step, with all other repair steps handled deterministically.

3 The ProtoCase Framework

3.1 Problem Formulation and Structural Match

Given a model M_{gen} produced by an LLM-aided modelling pipeline, ProtoCase produces a repaired model M' that is syntactically valid and preserves the security properties of a hand-crafted reference M_{ref}. We approximate property preservation by comparing the action-fact events each model emits per role.

Verified protocol models are most widely available in Tamarin's rule style, but the LLM pipeline and ProtoCase both target SAPIC+. We call this the *cross-format gap*. It affects Phase 2's rewrite quality: the LLM must translate between two syntactic formats when rewriting the model.

The case base contains 18 verified models from the Tamarin example repository [17], all in rule style. A case is a tuple $c = \langle M_{ref},\ meta,\ Err \rangle$, where *meta* records the protocol's builtins, cryptographic primitives, role count, and action-fact signatures, and $Err \subseteq \{E_1, \ldots, E_{10}\}$ is the error vector computed from the protocol's LLM-generated model. Retrieval uses the error vector to find cases with similar defects. *meta* and *Err* are extracted in a one-time preprocessing step that runs the upstream pipeline on each protocol.

We compare models by extracting the set of *action facts per role* from each model. For SAPIC+ models, each top-level process definition corresponds to a role. For rule-style references, roles are identified by naming convention (e.g., rules prefixed with `I_` or `R_`). All 18 reference models satisfy this convention. For each role, we collect tuples (e, n) where e is an event name and n its occurrence count. Infrastructure events not specific to the protocol's security goals (`KeyGen`, `Reveal`, `RevLtk`, `LtkReveal`, `Compromise`, `Register`, `OnlyOnce`, `Honest`, `Eq`) are filtered out.

Definition 1 (Event-Structural Match). $\text{ESM}(M', M_{ref}) = true$ *iff for every role* r *and every event* e, $\text{count}(e, r, M') \geq \text{count}(e, r, M_{ref})$.

The inequality ($\geq$ instead of $=$) is deliberate: the LLM may insert redundant events that do not affect the protocol's security properties, and requiring exact

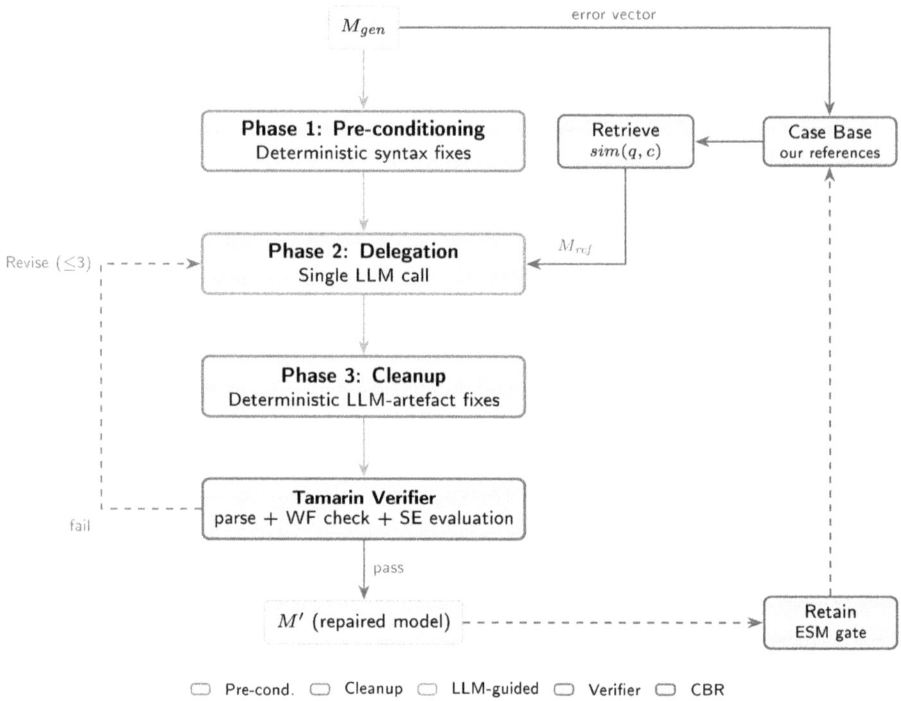

Fig. 1. The ProtoCase pipeline. Given M_{gen}, the system retrieves a structurally similar case from the case base (right). Repair proceeds in three phases: deterministic pre-conditioning (Phase 1, blue), a single LLM call guided by the retrieved case (Phase 2, orange), and deterministic cleanup (Phase 3, teal). The Tamarin verifier closes the loop with machine-parseable feedback. Repairs that pass the ESM gate are retained in the case base for future retrieval.

equality would reject such repairs unnecessarily. ProtoCase uses ESM as a quality gate for retention and failure diagnosis, since it operates at the structural level and runs instantly. Semantic equivalence (SE) evaluation requires Tamarin's theorem prover and is used only in the final evaluation stage.

3.2 CBR-As-Controller Architecture

We identify four conditions (C1–C4) under which CBR can control the repair loop, confining the LLM to a single bounded subtask. Table 1 summarises each condition with its ProtoCase realisation and ablation evidence.

C1: Finite Operator Space. Repair must draw from a finite set of operators, each with a well-defined trigger and transformation. ProtoCase uses 17 regex/AST-based operators.

C2: Decomposable Adaptation. Operators must divide into independent phases that run in sequence. Errors fixed in one phase should not reappear in another.

Table 1. Conditions for CBR-as-controller, with instantiation in ProtoCase and empirical evidence. Phases refer to the pipeline in Fig. 1.

Condition	Instantiation in ProtoCase	Evidence
C1: Finite operator space	Regex/AST-based operators triggered by model text or verifier output	Without LLM rewrite: SE drops from 15 to 8 (Table 5)
C2: Decomposable adaptation	Phase 1 handles syntax, Phase 2 handles semantics, Phase 3 handles cleanup	Without Phase 1: SE drops from 15 to 9 (Table 5)
C3: Bounded delegation	Fixed input: cleaned model + retrieved case. Fixed task: rewrite primitives, add tags, insert events	With RAG-style delegation: SE is only 5 (Table 5)
C4: Deterministic verifier feedback	Tamarin parse/WF errors are fragment-level and machine-parseable, each mapping to exactly one operator	10 error types fire across all 18 protocols with no manual disambiguation (Tables 2, 5)

C3: Bounded Delegation. The LLM's task must be narrow and well-defined. In ProtoCase, the LLM is restricted to three actions: rewrite cryptographic primitives, add message tags to encrypted terms, and insert action facts.

C4: Deterministic Verifier Feedback. The verifier must produce machine-parseable errors that each map to exactly one operator. Otherwise the LLM would need to interpret error messages, which defeats C3. Across all 18 protocols, every Tamarin parse or well-formedness error maps to exactly one operator.

3.3 Error-Driven Retrieval (Retrieve)

Through manual analysis of the 18 LLM-generated models, we identified ten recurring error types that follow from SAPIC+'s well-formedness rules. Table 2 summarises their distribution across three phases.

Table 2. Repair phases and error types.

Phase	Control	Error types
1: Pre-conditioning	Deterministic	E1: `id()` misuse, E2: double binding, E3: builtin errors, E4: dead code
2: Delegation	LLM-guided	E5: crypto primitive errors, E6: missing message tags
3: Cleanup	Deterministic	E7: missing action facts, E8: process–event mismatch, E9: undefined references, E10: arity errors

Given M_{gen}, the system computes an error vector $Err \subseteq \{E_1, \ldots, E_{10}\}$ from these error types and retrieves the case with highest composite similarity:

$$sim(q, c) = 0.4 \cdot Jaccard_w(Err_q, Err_c) + 0.6 \cdot struct(q, c)$$

where $Jaccard_w$ is a weighted Jaccard over error types with per-type weights w_{E5}=3, w_{E6}=2, w_{E1}=w_{E2}=1, w_{E3}=w_{E4}=0.5, and w_{E7-E10}=0 (Phase 3 errors appear in every protocol and carry no discriminative power). The second component, *struct*, is a weighted combination of three features:

$$struct(q, c) = 0.5 \cdot J_{crypto} + 0.3 \cdot J_{builtin} + 0.2 \cdot \frac{\min(r_q, r_c)}{\max(r_q, r_c)}$$

where J_{crypto} and $J_{builtin}$ are Jaccard similarities over crypto primitives and builtins, respectively. All weights were set by manual analysis of error distributions across the 18 protocols.

3.4 Three-Phase Adaptation (Reuse)

Phase 1: Pre-conditioning. Eight deterministic operators remove syntax-level noise so that the LLM receives a parseable model. For instance, one operator replaces LLM-generated `id(X)` function calls with string-constant public names, a pattern that appears in over half the generated models and always causes a parse failure. Another normalises variable names that collide with Tamarin reserved words. A third removes dead-code blocks that reference undefined processes.

Phase 2: Delegation. Phase 2 operates in one of two modes. If Phase 1's output parses, the system first attempts *targeted insertion*: a single LLM call that adds only the missing events to the existing model. If either targeted insertion or Phase 1's output fails to parse, the system falls back to a *full rewrite*: a single LLM call that rewrites the model guided by the retrieved case.

In both modes, the prompt includes a *case template*: a structured header derived from the case's *meta*, listing builtins, primitives, role count, and required action-fact signatures. The prompt instructs the LLM to fix cryptographic-primitive errors, add message tags to encrypted terms, and insert action facts (`Running`, `Commit`, `Secret`) at appropriate positions. The complete prompt template is available in the source repository.

Phase 3: Deterministic Cleanup. Nine regex-based operators correct recurring LLM output artefacts. For example, LLMs routinely place `Commit` events before the corresponding verification step. A dedicated operator relocates `Commit` to after the nearest `verify`/`if` statement. In all 18 generated models, `Commit` appears before the verification step. Other Phase 3 operators handle undeclared variable references, arity mismatches, and process–event binding conflicts.

3.5 Iterative Repair (Revise) and Quality-Gated Retention (Retain)

Iterative Repair. After Phase 3, Tamarin's parse check determines whether the model is syntactically valid. On failure, the system re-enters Phase 2 with updated context and runs Phase 3 again. Phase 1 is skipped in subsequent rounds, as its operators are idempotent. The loop runs for at most $N=3$ rounds. Each round is a deterministic operator application (C4). It maps to one Reuse–Revise pass in the CBR cycle.

Quality-Gated Retain. When $\text{ESM}(M', M_{ref}) = \textit{true}$ (Definition 1), the repaired model enters the case base. The system records the original error vector and per-role event comparison as metadata.

In our experiments ESM serves as the retention gate. A retained case is in the same SAPIC+ format the LLM generates, so it closes the cross-format gap between rule-style references and process output. When a downstream protocol retrieves a retained SAPIC+ case, the LLM receives a template whose process structure and event placement match the target format. For example, in single-pass mode Denning-Sacco fails SE because the LLM places a `Secret` event at the wrong position, and the rule-style reference does not show where to place it. When Kao-Chow's retained SAPIC+ case is available, Phase 2 receives a format-matched template and SE passes (5/5).

4 Evaluation

4.1 Experimental Setup

We use the 18-protocol benchmark from AutoSM [16], covering symmetric-key, public-key, and Diffie-Hellman-based protocols ranging from 2 to 4 roles. Each protocol comes with a natural-language description and two reference models: (i) a hand-crafted SAPIC+ model containing ground-truth security lemmas, used for SE evaluation (below), and (ii) a rule-style Tamarin model, used as the case base for retrieval. The case base uses rule-style models because verified SAPIC+ models exist for only a subset of the 18 protocols.

The initial model M_{gen} is produced by an LLM-generation pipeline with DeepSeek-V3 (`deepseek-chat`) as the backend. In this step, we also populate each case's error vector *Err* (Sect. 3.1). All experiments use the same set of 18 generated models as input. All experiments use *leave-one-out* cross-validation: when repairing protocol p, the case base contains the 17 reference models for the remaining protocols. This ensures that the system never has access to the ground truth for the protocol under repair. The repair backend is also DeepSeek-V3, with maximum repair rounds $N=3$. Cross-model experiments use four additional LLMs: Llama-3.3-70B-Instruct, Mistral-Large-2512, Kimi-K2-Instruct, and Qwen2.5-72B-Instruct.

Metrics. Following [16], we say two models are *semantically equivalent (SE)* with respect to a property φ iff φ holds in both or fails in both. We operationalise this as follows. Security lemmas (encoding secrecy, authentication, and executability properties) are extracted from the ground-truth SAPIC+ reference model and injected into the repaired model. Tamarin `--prove` then determines whether each lemma is verified or falsified. A protocol receives **SE** iff every lemma result in the repaired model matches the ground-truth result exactly, including executability lemmas that guard against vacuous satisfaction.

Lemma injection requires that the repaired model uses event names and argument structures compatible with the reference lemmas, a prerequisite enforced by the Phase 2 and Phase 3 operators. SE evaluation is semi-automated: Tamarin verification runs without intervention, and a manual check confirms that injected lemmas bind to the intended events. This check involves inspecting event names and arities and takes under one minute per protocol. SE follows the evaluation criterion of [16]. We also report Parse Success (PS): Tamarin accepts the model with `--parse-only`. PS is a prerequisite for SE and confirms that the model is syntactically valid.

Conditions.

- **No-repair (baseline)**: the AutoSM output is evaluated directly, serving as a lower bound.
- **RAG**: the same retrieved reference model is included in the LLM prompt together with the generated model, and the LLM is asked to produce a corrected version. The prompt provides no Phase 1/3 operators, no error taxonomy, and no structural constraints. The LLM decides what to preserve and what to rewrite.
- **ProtoCase (single-pass)**: full CBR pipeline (Phases 1–3), each protocol repaired independently.
- **ProtoCase + Retain (full)**: full pipeline with quality-gated case retention. Validated repairs are added to the case base for subsequent protocols.

Research Questions.

RQ1 How effective is ProtoCase's full pipeline at repairing protocols to semantic equivalence?
RQ2 What does each pipeline component contribute to repair effectiveness?
RQ3 Does the pipeline generalise across LLM backends?

4.2 Repair Effectiveness (RQ1)

We evaluate ProtoCase under the four conditions defined above. Table 3 summarises the results. With the full pipeline including quality-gated retention, ProtoCase achieves a median SE of 15/18 across five random protocol-processing orderings (range 13–15), up from 8/18 without repair. Each ordering determines which retained cases are available for subsequent protocols. Without retention (single-pass mode), the median is 11/18 (range 10–12). The RAG baseline's low SE (5/18) stems primarily from the LLM's unconstrained rewrite scope: random retrieval (Table 5) still yields SE 9, higher than RAG's 5, because the Phase 1/2/3 operators continue to constrain the rewrite. The −Phase 1 ablation confirms the same on a different axis: removing pre-conditioning still yields SE 9.

Table 3. Main results across conditions (18 protocols). SE reports median over 5 runs.

Condition	PS	SE
No-repair (baseline)	15/18	8/18
RAG	9/18	5/18
ProtoCase (single-pass)	17/18	11/18
ProtoCase + Retain (full)	17/18	**15/18**

In single-pass mode, three protocols (`CCITT-X509`, `Denning-Sacco`, `EDHOC`) fail in all five runs due to systematic event-placement errors caused by the cross-format gap. Retention recovers all three from 0/5 to 5/5 and improves a fourth.

Table 4 lists all 18 protocols with their SE results and median repair time (Phases 1–2 only, excluding Tamarin verification).

Table 4. Per-protocol SE results and cost (DeepSeek-V3). $|\varphi|$ = ground-truth security lemmas. T_{rep} = median wall-clock time for Phases 1–2 over 5 orderings. T_{ver} = Tamarin **`--prove`** wall-clock time on the ground-truth SAPIC+ model (reference verification cost). (†) 9 protocols that achieve 5/5 in both configurations (Example protocol, Toy, NSPK, Otway-Rees, Woo-Lam, NSSK, Kao-Chow, Naxos, LAK06) are collapsed into one row.

Protocol	$\lvert\varphi\rvert$	T_{rep}(s)	T_{ver}(s)	Single-pass	+Retain
9 protocols (†)	3–9	0.4–45	1–185	5/5	5/5
SPLICE	7	0.8	167	2/5	3/5
Denning-Sacco	5	0.9	6	0/5	**5/5**
Example	4	9.6	1	4/5	5/5
CCITT-X509	4	17.9	9	0/5	**5/5**
Yahalom	7	25.5	22	4/5	4/5
EDHOC	10	41.4	38	0/5	**5/5**
Neuman-Stubb.	7	33.6	25	0/5	0/5
SSH	5	35.7	<1	0/5	0/5
KEMTLS	5	36.4	<1	0/5	0/5

Table 4 also reports T_{rep} and T_{ver}. Each repair episode requires approximately 1 LLM call (range 0–3). The median T_{rep} per protocol is 14 s, and all 18 protocols complete in under 6 min total. Tamarin verification is a separate step with protocol-dependent cost: most protocols verify in under 40 s, with three outliers (`NSPK`, `Otway-Rees`, `LAK06`) taking 1–3 min.

Section 4.3 opens with a repair trace on Denning-Sacco.

4.3 Component Analysis (RQ2)

We trace a repair episode on Denning-Sacco to ground the analysis. Denning-Sacco uses symmetric-key encryption with a trusted server (three roles, five security lemmas). The initial model M_{gen} parses successfully (PS) and passes Phase 1 with only minor normalisation (E1: one `id()` replacement). The core defect is a Phase 2 problem: the LLM-generated model encrypts the session key with a raw `senc()` call, missing the protocol's nested encryption structure, and omits the `Secret` event entirely.

Phase 2 retrieves the rule-style reference for Kao-Chow (score 0.53), whose symmetric-key architecture closely matches Denning-Sacco. Using the case template, the LLM rewrites the encryption structure and inserts `event Secret($A, $B, key)` after key acceptance. Phase 3 relocates `Commit` to after the decryption check (E7) and fixes an arity mismatch in `Running` (E10).

In single-pass mode, this repair achieves 2/5 SE. The `Secret` event placement is correct and authentication lemmas verify. The failing runs misplace the event's arguments (swapping sender and receiver). Retention resolves this ambiguity by supplying a format-matched SAPIC+ case.

Table 5 reports a component ablation on DeepSeek-V3. Each row removes one component. All Δ values are computed relative to the full system (15/18) for uniform comparison, even though – Retain's natural baseline is the single-pass system (11/18) and the remaining ablations operate in single-pass mode.

Table 5. Component ablation (DeepSeek-V3, SE out of 18). All Δ values are relative to the full system (15) for uniformity. Component ablations below – Retain are performed in single-pass mode.

Condition	SE	Δ
Full system (with Retain)	**15**	–
– Retain	11	−4
– Retrieval (random case)	9	−6
– Phase 1	9	−6
– Case template	11	−4
– LLM	8	−7
RAG baseline	5	−10

Removing the LLM (Δ=−7) reduces SE to the no-repair baseline (8/18). Deterministic operators resolve syntax-level and structural-placement errors and do not achieve semantic equivalence.

Retrieval (Δ=−6) and Phase 1 pre-conditioning (Δ=−6) are the next largest contributors, with equal magnitude and distinct mechanisms. When similarity-guided retrieval is replaced with a random case, the LLM loses its structural scaffold and must infer process structure from the protocol description alone. Removing Phase 1 preserves the scaffold and feeds the LLM syntactically noisy input, so the rewrite propagates pre-existing errors. The equal magnitude on this benchmark suggests that LLM rewrite quality degrades comparably whether the input or the guidance is deficient, though the coincidence of −6 in both cases may not generalise to larger benchmarks.

Coefficient Sensitivity. The retrieval formula in Sect. 3.3 contains 11 coefficients. We test whether their values are load-bearing by replacing them with two uniform variants: averaging the error-vector term and structural term (which changes 4/18 case selections) and setting the three sub-weights of *struct* to 1/3 each (which changes 3/18). Both variants reach single-pass SE 10/18, within one point of the default coefficients' 11/18. Because the size of our evaluation set is small, the influence of the retrieval coefficients seems inconclusive. A more thorough study is left to future work.

The case template (Δ=−4) provides explicit structural cues (primitives, builtins, expected events) that help the LLM focus its rewrite. Without the template, the LLM must extract this information from the raw reference model, and frequently omits or misspecifies required events. The template addresses *what* the LLM should insert. A separate bottleneck is the *format* of the retrieved case itself.

Retention Mechanism Analysis. Retention also contributes Δ=−4, targeting this format bottleneck. In the single-pass mode, three protocols (`CCITT-X509`, `Denning-Sacco`, `EDHOC`) fail because the LLM must translate the rule-style reference's multiset-rewriting structure into SAPIC+ process syntax. This translation is error-prone: the LLM transposes event arguments (e.g., swapping sender and receiver in a `Secret` event), producing models that parse and contain the right events, yet fail SE because argument order determines lemma binding.

Retention eliminates this translation step. When an earlier protocol's repair passes the ESM gate (Definition 1), the repaired SAPIC+ model enters the case base. Subsequent protocols that retrieve this case receive a template already written in SAPIC+ process syntax, with event arguments in the correct positions. Table 6 shows the four protocols that consistently pass the ESM gate: all are symmetric-key or simple DH protocols (2–3 roles, 3–9 lemmas) where Phase 2 reliably produces correct event placement. For instance, Naxos requires only a builtin typo fix (Phase 1) and one event insertion (Phase 2); the repaired model passes ESM in all five orderings and is subsequently retrieved by downstream protocols such as `KEMTLS`. `Kao-Chow_retained` is the most frequently reused (up to 7 retrievals per run). When `Denning-Sacco` retrieves it instead of the rule-style reference, the argument-ordering ambiguity noted in Sect. 4.2 disappears (2/5 → 5/5). Table 7 shows the per-ordering breakdown: median SE rises from

11 to 15, and the range narrows from 10–12 to 13–15. The benefit scales with how many retained cases are available early in the ordering.

Table 6. Retained protocols and their downstream impact. "Retained in" = orderings where the protocol passed ESM. "Retrieved by" = later protocols that used the retained SAPIC+ case.

Protocol	Retained in	Retrieved by (examples)
Naxos	5/5	Toy, KEMTLS
Kao-Chow	5/5	Yahalom, Otway-Rees, NSSK, Woo-Lam
Otway-Rees	5/5	Neuman-Stubb., NSSK, LAK06
Example	4/5	Toy, KEMTLS, NSPK

4.4 Cross-Model Generalisation (RQ3)

Table 8 reports SE for five LLM backends in the single-pass configuration. All backends repair the same 18 DeepSeek-V3-generated input models (no-repair SE = 8/18), so the no-repair baseline is identical across rows. The same pipeline configuration (Phase 1/3 operators, retrieval logic, and prompt) is applied to all five backends without modification.

Removing similarity-guided retrieval degrades every backend (median drop −3), showing that CBR retrieval helps across all five backends. Qwen2.5-72B is the least sensitive to retrieval (−1). One possible explanation is that Qwen's instruction-following strength may let it extract structural cues from the raw reference model even without similarity-guided selection.

Table 7. Retain per-ordering breakdown (DeepSeek-V3, 5 orderings).

Ordering	SE	Retained	Retrieved
1	15/18	4	7
2	14/18	4	6
3	13/18	3	1
4	15/18	4	5
5	15/18	4	10
Median	**15/18**	4	6

Table 8. Cross-model results (SE out of 18, single-pass). Random case: similarity-guided retrieval replaced with a random case from the case base.

Backend	Full	Random case
DeepSeek-V3	11	9
Llama-3.3-70B	15	11
Mistral-Large	14	11
Kimi-K2	13	8
Qwen2.5-72B	14	13

4.5 Discussion

Three failure modes and limitations merit discussion beyond the ablation (Table 5). The three persistently failing protocols (`Neuman-Stubblebine`, `KEMTLS`, `SSH`) all have initial models that deviate from the target at the message-flow level, beyond what the current operator set and bounded iterative repair can address. `Neuman-Stubblebine` requires restructuring its two-round message flow with correct forward references. `KEMTLS` and `SSH` would require regeneration of the protocol skeleton, which is outside the scope of operator-level repair.

`Yahalom`'s no-repair model already achieves SE, yet unconditional Phase 2 rewriting occasionally introduces a regression (4/5, Table 4). A pre-repair SE check could skip such protocols. We leave this to future work because the leave-one-out design ensures each protocol is repaired exactly once regardless of its initial status.

Threats to Validity. We analyse the 18 protocols in the AutoSM suite that have both verified reference models and LLM-generated counterparts. Larger protocols from the Tamarin example repository (TLS 1.3, 5G AKA, Signal) exceed current generation reliability, and end-to-end evaluation on these is left to future work. The ten error types in our taxonomy were observed across these 18 protocols and may not be exhaustive. The taxonomy itself follows from SAPIC+'s syntax and well-formedness rules (builtin errors, arity mismatches, missing actions), protocols beyond the suite could surface additional categories. The RAG baseline uses a minimal prompt without error messages or few-shot examples, because our comparison targets the effect of unstructured delegation, not the ceiling of retrieval-augmented approaches. A more carefully engineered RAG variant might narrow the gap. Cross-model experiments use the single-pass configuration with the same DeepSeek-V3-generated input models. Varying the generation backend or combining retention with other backends would test broader generalisability.

5 Conclusion

We have presented ProtoCase, a framework that uses CBR to orchestrate LLM-aided repair of security protocol models, confining the LLM to a single bounded rewrite within an otherwise deterministic loop. With quality-gated retention, the system matches hand-crafted references on all security properties for a median of 15/18 protocols (range 13–15 across five orderings), up from 8/18 without repair and 5/18 with a RAG baseline.

In prior operator-based adaptation work [6,10,11,19], the system computes how the new problem differs from the retrieved case and uses this difference to select or sequence operators. ProtoCase shows that when a verifier identifies exactly which construct is wrong, verifier feedback alone can drive operator selection: each error message maps to exactly one operator (condition C4), so the verifier output determines the full operator sequence without case-difference computation. This removes the search over operator sequences that case-difference analysis requires. The feedback-driven selection mechanism is not specific to

Tamarin. Alloy specification repair [5] and Dafny assertion generation [18] both use verifiers that identify specific errors, and condition C4 transfers directly to such domains. Whether their error spaces also satisfy the remaining conditions (finite operator set, independent phases, bounded LLM scope) is an open question. More broadly, ProtoCase inverts the role CBR plays in LLM-aided generation. In EXAR [3], retrieved cases guide an LLM orchestrator that decides how to use them. ProtoCase makes CBR the controller: it selects operators and bounds the LLM's rewrite, and the verifier determines what to fix next.

Quality-gated retention addresses a different challenge: the cross-format gap between rule-style hand-crafted references and LLM-generated SAPIC+ output. By storing validated repairs in the format the LLM generates, the retain stage shifts case-base composition toward format-matched cases, so that subsequent retrieval can return a case the LLM can directly imitate. The three-phase pipeline alone reaches a median of 11/18. Retention raises this to 15/18.

The benchmark contains only 18 protocols, so individual protocol characteristics influence aggregate scores. Quality-gated retention has been evaluated with one LLM backend only, and whether it generalises to other backends or to protocol families with different cryptographic structures remains open. The current operators are manually designed. Learning operators from repair traces, as explored by Craw *et al.* [6] and Müller & Bergmann [19] in other CBR domains, would reduce the effort required to extend the operator set.

Acknowledgments. This work is supported by the National Key R&D Program of China (Grant No.2023YFB3105803).

Data and Code Availability. The ProtoCase source code, benchmark data, and evaluation scripts are publicly available at https://github.com/WLeann/protocase-original.

Declaration on Generative AI. During the preparation of this work, the author used ChatGPT and Cursor only for language polishing, including grammar and spelling checks and minor improvements to clarity and fluency. After using this tool, the author reviewed and edited the content as needed and takes full responsibility for the publication's content.

References

1. Aamodt, A., Plaza, E.: Case-based reasoning: Foundational issues, methodological variations, and system approaches. AI Commun. **7**(1), 39–59 (1994). https://doi.org/10.3233/AIC-1994-7104
2. Basin, D.A., Dreier, J., Hirschi, L., Radomirovic, S., Sasse, R., Stettler, V.: A formal analysis of 5g authentication. In: CCS 2018, pp. 1383–1396. ACM (2018). https://doi.org/10.1145/3243734.3243846
3. Bergmann, R., Brand, F., Lenz, M., Malburg, L.: EXAR: A unified experience-grounded agentic reasoning architecture. In: Case-Based Reasoning Research and Development - 33rd International Conference, ICCBR 2025, pp. 3–17. Lecture Notes in Computer Science, Springer (2025). https://doi.org/10.1007/978-3-031-96559-3_1

4. Blanchet, B.: An efficient cryptographic protocol verifier based on prolog rules. In: CSFW-14 2001, pp. 82–96. IEEE Computer Society (2001). https://doi.org/10.1109/CSFW.2001.930138
5. Brida, S.G., et al.: ICEBAR: feedback-driven iterative repair of alloy specifications. In: 37th IEEE/ACM International Conference on Automated Software Engineering, ASE 2022, pp. 55:1–55:13. ACM (2022). https://doi.org/10.1145/3551349.3556944
6. Craw, S., Wiratunga, N., Rowe, R.: Learning adaptation knowledge to improve case-based reasoning. Artif. Intell. **170**(16–17), 1175–1192 (2006). https://doi.org/10.1016/J.ARTINT.2006.09.001
7. Cremers, C., Horvat, M., Hoyland, J., Scott, S., van der Merwe, T.: A comprehensive symbolic analysis of TLS 1.3. In: CCS 2017, pp. 1773–1788. ACM (2017). https://doi.org/10.1145/3133956.3134063
8. Curaba, C., D'Ambrosi, D., Minisini, A., Pérez-Campanero Antolín, N.: Cryptoformaleval: Integrating large language models and formal verification for automated cryptographic protocol vulnerability detection. Poster at the NeurIPS 2024 Workshop on System-2 Reasoning at Scale (2024). https://openreview.net/forum?id=hqvJT2pOxu
9. First, E., Rabe, M.N., Ringer, T., Brun, Y.: Baldur: Whole-proof generation and repair with large language models. In: ESEC/FSE 2023, pp. 1229–1241. ACM (2023). https://doi.org/10.1145/3611643.3616243
10. François, N., Lieber, J.: A knowledge representation approach for reasoning with adaptation rules. In: Case-Based Reasoning Research and Development - 33rd International Conference, ICCBR 2025, pp. 204–219. Lecture Notes in Computer Science, Springer (2025). https://doi.org/10.1007/978-3-031-96559-3_14
11. Hotz, M., Malburg, L., Bergmann, R.: Advanced search techniques for determining optimal sequences of adaptation rules in process-oriented case-based reasoning. In: Case-Based Reasoning Research and Development - 33rd International Conference, ICCBR 2025, pp. 236–251. Lecture Notes in Computer Science, Springer (2025). https://doi.org/10.1007/978-3-031-96559-3_16
12. Kremer, S., Künnemann, R.: Automated analysis of security protocols with global state. In: SP 2014, pp. 163–178. IEEE Computer Society (2014). https://doi.org/10.1109/SP.2014.18
13. Lewis, P., et al.: Retrieval-augmented generation for knowledge-intensive NLP tasks. In: NeurIPS 2020 (2020). https://proceedings.neurips.cc/paper/2020/hash/6b493230205f780e1bc26945df7481e5-Abstract.html
14. Li, Q., Han, J., Yuan, L., Li, X., Wang, X.: Constructing formal models of cryptographic protocols from alice&bob style specifications via LLM. Sci. Rep. **15**(1), 11866 (2025). https://doi.org/10.1038/s41598-025-93373-y
15. Liu, K., Koyuncu, A., Kim, D., Bissyandé, T.F.: Tbar: revisiting template-based automated program repair. In: ISSTA 2019, pp. 31–42. ACM (2019). https://doi.org/10.1145/3293882.3330577
16. Mao, Z., Wang, J., Sun, J., Qin, S., Xiong, J.: LLM-aided automatic modeling for security protocol verification. In: ICSE 2025, pp. 642–654. IEEE (2025). https://doi.org/10.1109/ICSE55347.2025.00197
17. Meier, S., Schmidt, B., Cremers, C., Basin, D.A.: The TAMARIN prover for the symbolic analysis of security protocols. In: CAV 2013 pp. 696–701. Lecture Notes in Computer Science, Springer (2013). https://doi.org/10.1007/978-3-642-39799-8_48

18. Mugnier, E., Gonzalez, E.A., Polikarpova, N., Jhala, R., Zhou, Y.: Laurel: unblocking automated verification with large language models. Proc. ACM Program. Lang. **9**(OOPSLA1), 1519–1545 (2025). https://doi.org/10.1145/3720499
19. Müller, G., Bergmann, R.: Learning and applying adaptation operators in process-oriented case-based reasoning. In: Case-Based Reasoning Research and Development - 23rd International Conference, ICCBR 2015, pp. 259–274. Lecture Notes in Computer Science, Springer (2015). https://doi.org/10.1007/978-3-319-24586-7_18
20. Sun, C., Sheng, Y., Padon, O., Barrett, C.W.: Clover: Closed-loop verifiable code generation. In: AI Verification - First International Symposium, SAIV 2024, pp. 134–155. Lecture Notes in Computer Science, Springer (2024). https://doi.org/10.1007/978-3-031-65112-0_7
21. Weimer, W., Nguyen, T., Le Goues, C., Forrest, S.: Automatically finding patches using genetic programming. In: ICSE 2009, pp. 364–374. IEEE (2009). https://doi.org/10.1109/ICSE.2009.5070536
22. Zheng, G., et al.: ATR: template-based repair for alloy specifications. In: ISSTA 2022, pp. 666–677. ACM (2022). https://doi.org/10.1145/3533767.3534369
23. Zhong, S.C., Si, X.: Towards repository-level program verification with large language models. In: Proceedings of the 1st ACM SIGPLAN International Workshop on Language Models and Programming Languages (LMPL '25), pp. 27–39. LMPL '25, ACM (2025). https://doi.org/10.1145/3759425.3763382

From Redundancy to Precision: Constructing a Compressed Tree-Based Experiential Case Base for LLMs

Mucun Xie[1], Yijia Xu[1], and Jian Li[1,2,3](✉)

[1] School of Artificial Intelligence, Beijing Normal University, Beijing, China
{202521081015,202311051007}@mail.bnu.edu.cn
[2] Engineering Research Center of Intelligent Technology and Educational Application, Ministry of Education, Beijing, China
[3] Beijing Key Laboratory of Artificial Intelligence for Education, Beijing, China
jli@mail.bnu.edu.cn

Abstract. Large Language Models (LLMs) have demonstrated impressive reasoning capabilities; however, effectively leveraging past experiential cases to enhance their performance on complex tasks still faces significant limitations. Existing case retrieval methods often grapple with the utility problem—where accumulating redundant raw cases leads to context window overload and scalability issues. Furthermore, existing methods treat all extracted experiences equally, lacking differentiation in case base maintenance. To address these limitations, we propose the Compressed Tree-based Experiential Repository (CTER) framework. CTER acts as a hierarchical case base constructed through a two-stage process: first, it builds a dynamic tree structure based on problem classification and extracts specific experiential cases guided by model feedback; subsequently, a dual-mode extraction strategy refines these instance-level specific cases into generalized cases based on their empirical utility. During inference, CTER retrieves contextually precise generalized cases from specific sub-nodes, providing low-noise guidance to the LLMs. Empirical evaluations on scientific and mathematical benchmark datasets demonstrate that CTER not only constructs a highly compact case base but also significantly mitigates retrieval noise, achieving state-of-the-art performance in complex reasoning tasks.

Keywords: Generative Case-Based Reasoning · Large Language Models · Case Base Maintenance · Complex Reasoning

1 Introduction

In recent years, Large Language Models (LLMs) have demonstrated impressive capabilities in reasoning and natural language understanding [6]. However, when tackling complex, multi-step tasks, relying solely on the static parametric knowledge acquired during pre-training often results in reasoning bottlenecks

L. Malburg and K. Bach (Eds.): ICCBR 2026, LNAI 16780, pp. 405–420, 2027.
https://doi.org/10.1007/978-3-032-33865-5_25

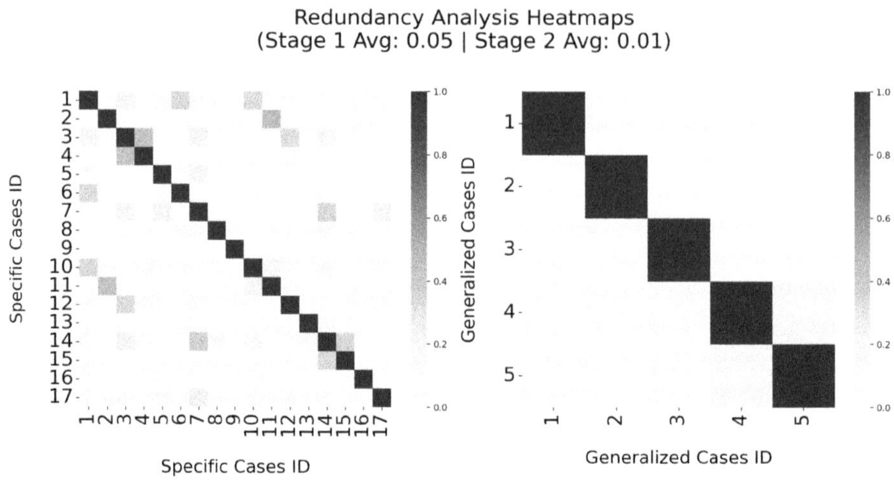

Fig. 1. Redundancy Analysis Heatmaps. The significant reduction in redundancy motivates the necessity of transitioning from raw, specific cases to compressed, generalized cases to mitigate context window overload.

or logical inconsistencies [22,29]. Explicitly equipping LLMs with an external, persistent memory of past experiential cases has proven critical for improving their adaptability. This paradigm, known as Generative Case-Based Reasoning (CBR), allows LLMs to autonomously synthesize and reuse historical reasoning strategies to guide novel problem-solving [26].

Despite its potential, integrating generative experiential case bases with LLMs currently faces two fundamental limitations. First, as highlighted by the redundancy analysis in Fig. 1, existing methods typically accumulate unstructured, raw experiential logs linearly. As the volume of generated cases grows, retrieving and appending these raw instances quickly exceeds the strict context window constraints of contemporary LLMs. This triggers the classical CBR utility problem—where the accumulation of redundant data overloads the context window, and the computational cost outweighs the benefits of retrieval [4]. Second, current frameworks treat all extracted experiences equally, lacking a differentiated approach to Case Base Maintenance (CBM). Ignoring this experiential differentiation results in a bloated case base filled with redundant information, failing to distill high-value knowledge [5,27].

Consequently, a critical research question arises: *How can we construct a scalable, highly condensed experiential case base that differentiates experience utility and provides precise generative guidance without overwhelming the LLM's context window?*

To address these limitations, we propose the **Compressed Tree-based Experiential Repository (CTER)** framework. CTER is designed to transition from unstructured redundancy to structured precision by organizing experiential knowledge into a hierarchical, compressed format. The construction of

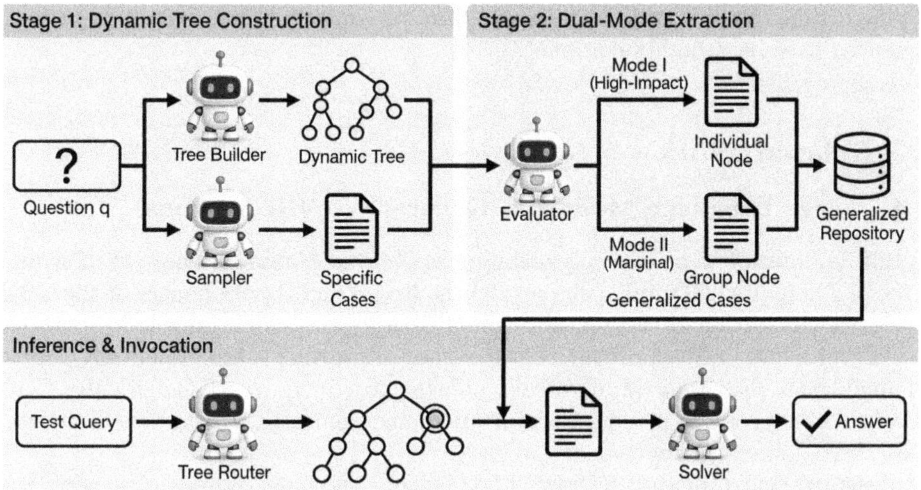

Fig. 2. The architectural overview of CTER.

CTER involves a novel two-stage generative Case Base Maintenance (CBM) process. First, to overcome the unstructured accumulation of cases, CTER establishes a dynamic tree structure rooted in problem classification. Within this hierarchy, the LLM engages in multi-round reasoning to extract specific Cases, explicitly capturing both positive strategies and negative pitfalls.

Second, to address the lack of experiential differentiation, we introduce a performance-driven dual-mode extraction strategy. By evaluating the empirical utility of each specific case, CTER handles them with differentiation: specific cases that demonstrate significant performance gains (high utility) are abstracted into standalone generalized cases, while those yielding marginal gains (low utility) are clustered and summarized collectively. This actively compresses instance-level redundancy and transforms fragmented experiences into a high-density, tree-based rule repository.

Empirical evaluations on complex reasoning benchmarks demonstrate that CTER constructs a significantly more compact case base compared to existing baselines, completely mitigating context overload while achieving state-of-the-art inference accuracy.

Our main contributions are summarized as follows:

- We propose CTER, a novel framework that dynamically constructs a hierarchical tree-based case base, extracting specific positive and negative experiences to avoid unstructured accumulation.
- We introduce a dual-mode CBM strategy based on empirical utility, treating high-utility and marginal-utility cases differently to compress redundancy and maximize context information density.
- We achieve substantial performance improvements across complex scientific and mathematical benchmarks (GPQA, Omni-MATH-Rule, AIME), exhibit-

ing strong generalization under distribution shifts while keeping the experiential case base highly compact.

2 Related Work

2.1 Large Language Models as Generative CBR Systems

While foundational prompting techniques such as Chain-of-Thought [23] and Tree of Thoughts [25] implicitly parallel the Reuse and Revise phases of the CBR cycle, they traditionally rely on the model's static parametric knowledge without persistent memory. Recognizing that few-shot prompting is fundamentally a form of analogical reasoning [2,9], recent efforts have introduced Generative CBR to the LLM ecosystem, enabling autonomous agents to synthesize their own experiential cases [7,26].

Despite this progress, current LLM agents struggle significantly with the Retain phase—a challenge reminiscent of early instance-based learning limitations [1]. They frequently store raw, unstructured textual logs that lack the formal representation required for scalable reuse. Our work explicitly formalizes the Retain phase for LLMs. By extracting structured experiential cases that explicitly differentiate between successful strategies (positive cases) and logical pitfalls (negative cases), the proposed CTER framework transforms ephemeral LLM interactions into a reusable, generative case base.

2.2 Case Base Organization: From Flat RAG to Hierarchical Indexing

Retrieval-Augmented Generation (RAG) has become the de facto standard for augmenting LLM memory, acting primarily as the Retrieve phase [11]. Standard RAG treats the case base as a flat repository relying on dense vector embeddings. While effective for factoid retrieval, this flat mechanism struggles with multi-step reasoning tasks, often leading to the "lost-in-the-middle" phenomenon where LLMs fail to extract logical structures from purely semantic, noisy contexts [12].

In classical CBR, hierarchical case organization is essential for retrieval efficiency and logical accuracy [3,16,17]. CTER adapts this fundamental principle to the LLM era. Unlike flat vector stores, CTER organizes experiential cases into a dynamic, tree-based hierarchy rooted in problem classification. This ensures retrieval is logically partitioned rather than merely semantic, significantly reducing noise and aligning modern LLM memory with classic structured CBR methodologies [24].

2.3 Case Base Maintenance and the Utility Problem in LLMs

The well-known "Utility Problem" in CBR—where uncontrolled case base growth degrades retrieval and reasoning performance [20]—manifests acutely in contemporary LLMs. Accumulating raw experiences linearly bloats memory buffers, exceeds strict context constraints, and overwhelms the LLM's attention mechanism with redundant instances [4].

While traditional Case Base Maintenance (CBM) relies on footprinting or competence models [10,21], most current LLM learning frameworks ignore CBM, treating all successful trials equally and naively appending them to prompts [19]. To address this, CTER introduces a performance-driven dual-mode extraction strategy as a generative CBM mechanism. By evaluating the empirical utility (ΔP) of each case, CTER distills high-impact instances into standalone generalized cases to preserve unique competence, while compressing marginal-impact instances into group cases. This explicitly compresses redundancy and extracts abstract rules, building a high-competence, low-footprint case base tailored for autonomous LLMs [14].

3 Methodology

In this section, we detail the proposed **Compressed Tree-based Experiential Repository (CTER)** framework. Conceptually, CTER redefines the traditional Case-Based Reasoning (CBR) cycle (Retrieve, Reuse, Revise, Retain) for the LLM era, transforming unstructured episodic memory into a strictly bounded, high-density hierarchical rule base. As illustrated in Fig. 2 and outlined in Algorithm 1, CTER operates in two primary stages: (1) Dynamic Tree Construction and Specific Case Extraction (corresponding to the revise phase), and (2) Performance-Driven Dual-Mode Knowledge Distillation (corresponding to the retain phase). The retrieve and reuse phases are subsequently handled during the inference stage via tree-based routing.

3.1 Problem Formalization

Let $\mathcal{Q}$ be the space of incoming queries and $\mathcal{A}$ be the target answer space. The LLM $\mathcal{M}$ acts as the reasoning agent, mapping $q \in \mathcal{Q}$ to a final response $r \in \mathcal{A}$ via an intermediate multi-step reasoning trajectory τ. Traditional generative CBR directly stores the raw episodic tuple (q, τ, r), leading to unstructured, linear accumulation.

In CTER, we aim to construct a directed hierarchical tree $\mathcal{T} = (\mathcal{V}, \mathcal{E})$, where each node $v \in \mathcal{V}$ corresponds to a dynamically determined problem category $c_i \in \mathcal{C} = \{c_1, \ldots, c_m\}$. Each node v stores a highly compressed, generalized rule set $\mathcal{C}_{gen}(v)$ rather than raw texts. The objective of CTER is to maximize the case base's problem-solving competence while strictly bounding the contextual token length during retrieval, transitioning from raw experience accumulation to principle abstraction.

3.2 Stage 1: Dynamic Tree Construction and Specific Case Extraction

This stage dynamically establishes the taxonomy of the tree $\mathcal{T}$ without relying on predefined labels, and captures instance-level specific cases through multi-round contrasting generation.

Dynamic Tag Generation. Instead of relying on a static, rigid taxonomy, we construct the hierarchy dynamically. For a question q routed to a parent node n_{parent}, we utilize the LLM's intrinsic zero-shot summarization capability to generate a hierarchical meta-tag t_q.
LLM-Assisted Tag Clustering. To form meaningful hierarchy levels and avoid generating a flat list of isolated tags, CTER employs a dynamic semantic clustering mechanism. We aggregate t_q with the tags of existing sub-nodes under n_{parent}. The LLM acts as a router: if the semantic overlap between t_q and an existing sub-node's scope is high, q is routed to that sub-node. If no sufficient match is found, a new sibling node is instantiated, dynamically expanding the breadth of $\mathcal{T}$.
Specific Case Derivation. Once q is mapped to its specific terminal node, $\mathcal{M}$ performs K independent reasoning trials using temperature scaling, yielding a trajectory set $\mathcal{S}_q = \{(\tau_j, r_j)\}_{j=1}^{K}$, where $r_j \in \{0,1\}$ denotes correctness. By explicitly contrasting successful and failed trajectories through a reflection meta-prompt ("*Why did trajectory A succeed while trajectory B failed?*"), we extract a **Specific Experiential Case** $C_{spec}(q)$:

$$C_{spec}(q) = \langle C_q^+, C_q^- \rangle \tag{1}$$

where C_q^+ (Positive Case) distills the essential, minimal correct reasoning path, and C_q^- (Negative Case) identifies the specific logical pitfalls or miscalculations that led to failure. This contrastive derivation explicitly isolates robust reasoning from random hallucinations.

3.3 Stage 2: Performance-Driven Dual-Mode Extraction

To fundamentally mitigate the CBR utility problem (bloated context windows and retrieval noise), specific cases must be evaluated and generalized. We define the Empirical Utility ΔP of a specific case $C_{spec}(q)$ as the net performance gain it provides over the zero-shot baseline model on a localized validation set $\mathcal{Q}_{local}$ (comprising analogous questions within the same node):

$$\Delta P = P(\mathcal{M} \text{ succeeds on } \mathcal{Q}_{local} \mid C_{spec}) - P(\mathcal{M} \text{ succeeds on } \mathcal{Q}_{local} \mid \emptyset) \tag{2}$$

Given a statistical significance threshold θ, CTER applies a Dual-Mode Extraction Strategy to transform $C_{spec}(q)$ into highly compressed generalized cases:

Mode I: Individual Summarization (High-Utility). If $\Delta P \geq \theta$, the specific case is distilled into a standalone Generalized Case C_{gen} stored at node n_{c_i}:

$$C_{gen} = \mathcal{F}_{distill}(C_{spec}(q)) \tag{3}$$

The distillation function $\mathcal{F}_{distill}$ is implemented via an abstraction prompt that systematically strips instance-specific variables and numerical constants, converting the episodic text into universal, symbolic reasoning rules or algorithmic checklists.

Algorithm 1 Construction and Inference Process of CTER

Require: Training set $\mathcal{Q}_{train}$, LLM $\mathcal{M}$, Trials K, Utility Threshold θ, Test query q_{test}
Ensure: Hierarchical Case Base $\mathcal{T}$, Test response r_{test}

% **Phase 1: Dynamic Tree Construction & Specific Case Extraction**
Initialize tree $\mathcal{T}$ with root node
for $q \in \mathcal{Q}_{train}$ **do**
  Route q to dynamic target node n_{c_i} via LLM tagging and similarity matching
  Sample K trajectories with temperature scaling to form Specific Case $C_{spec} = \langle C^+, C^- \rangle$
  Compute empirical utility ΔP using localized validation set $\mathcal{Q}_{local}$
  Store tuple $(C_{spec}, \Delta P)$ at node n_{c_i}
end for
% **Phase 2: Dual-Mode Case Base Maintenance (CBM)**
for each node $n_{c_i} \in \mathcal{T}$ **do**
  $\mathcal{P}_{marg} \leftarrow \emptyset$ ▷ Initialize marginal pool
  for each $(C_{spec}, \Delta P) \in n_{c_i}$ **do**
    if $\Delta P \geq \theta$ **then**
      Mode I: Store $C_{gen} \leftarrow \mathcal{F}_{distill}(C_{spec})$ ▷ High-Utility: Standalone Rule
    else
      Mode II: $\mathcal{P}_{marg} \leftarrow \mathcal{P}_{marg} \cup \{C_{spec}\}$ ▷ Marginal-Utility: Add to pool
    end if
  end for
  if $\mathcal{P}_{marg} \neq \emptyset$ **then**
    Store Group Case $C_{group} \leftarrow \mathcal{F}_{distill}(\mathcal{P}_{marg})$ at n_{c_i}
  end if
  Delete raw C_{spec} tuples from n_{c_i} ▷ Compress case base, retaining only rules
end for
% **Phase 3: Inference via Tree-based Routing**
Route q_{test} top-down in $\mathcal{T}$ to matched node n_{target}
Retrieve generalized context $C^* \leftarrow \bigcup_{C \in n_{target}} C$
Generate $r_{test} \leftarrow \mathcal{M}(q_{test} \oplus C^*)$
return $\mathcal{T}$, r_{test}

Mode II: Group Summarization (Marginal-Utility). If $\Delta P < \theta$, the individual case provides marginal utility, often containing redundant logic. To prevent case base bloating without discarding subtle edge-case nuances, we aggregate these low-impact instances $\{q'\}$ into a marginal pool $\mathcal{P}_{marg}$ under c_i, to form a Clustered Group Case:

$$C_{group} = \mathcal{F}_{distill}\left(\bigcup_{q' \in \mathcal{P}_{marg}} C_{spec}(q') \right) \tag{4}$$

In this mode, $\mathcal{F}_{distill}$ acts as a macro-summarizer, synthesizing a unified checklist of common pitfalls and generalized heuristics from the entire pool. This actively adheres to the Minimum Description Length (MDL) principle, ensuring structural sparsity.

3.4 Inference via Tree-Based Routing

During inference for an unseen test query q_{test}, CTER entirely bypasses flat, dense vector retrieval—which often introduces severe semantic noise. Instead, it performs a top-down logical traversal of the structured tree $\mathcal{T}$:

1. **Hierarchical Routing:** Starting from the root, $\mathcal{M}$ generates a meta-tag for q_{test} and evaluates which child node logically subsumes the query. This top-down routing continues until q_{test} reaches its specific, highly-aligned target node n_{target}.
2. **Direct Case Invocation:** We directly invoke and concatenate the aggregated generalized cases (both C_{gen} and C_{group}) natively stored at n_{target}:

$$C^* = \bigcup_{C \in \mathcal{C}(n_{target})} C \tag{5}$$

The dense, generalized context C^* is seamlessly prepended to the system prompt. Unlike conventional RAG that appends redundant instances, C^* acts as an explicit set of expert principles, providing the LLM with low-noise, highly-relevant experiential guidance to tackle the complex reasoning task.

4 Theoretical Analysis

To rigorously justify the proposed CTER framework, we formulate our theoretical analysis through the lens of Information Theory, mapping classic Case-Based Reasoning (CBR) concepts—such as the Utility Problem, Case Competence, and Retrieval Space—into mathematical constraints.

4.1 Hierarchical Indexing Mitigates Semantic Noise: An Entropy Perspective

In the Retrieve phase, conventional flat retrieval paradigms treat the case base $CB = \{c_1, c_2, \ldots, c_N\}$ as an unstructured set [18]. Given a target problem x, the retrieval process relies on calculating the marginal semantic similarity. We denote the retrieved context as a random variable C_{ret}. In a flat structure, the uncertainty of retrieving the logically correct case from a large, noisy case base is quantified by the conditional Shannon entropy $H(C_{ret} \mid x)$.

As the case base grows ($N \to \infty$), the semantic overlap among specific cases increases, leading to a high retrieval entropy $H(C_{ret} \mid x)$, which theoretically explains the "lost-in-the-middle" phenomenon and the degraded retrieval accuracy in the Utility Problem.

Proposition 1. *The hierarchical tree-based organization $\mathcal{T}$ in CTER effectively reduces the uncertainty of case retrieval compared to flat indexing.*

Proof. In CTER, cases are dynamically clustered into a hierarchical tree $\mathcal{T}$. The retrieval follows a top-down logical traversal path $P = \{v_1, v_2, \ldots, v_d\}$, where each node v_i represents a problem classification boundary. By injecting the hierarchical path P as prior structural knowledge, the new retrieval uncertainty is expressed as $H(C_{ret} \mid x, P)$.

According to the fundamental property of Information Theory that *conditioning reduces entropy*, we have:

$$H(C_{ret} \mid x, P) \leq H(C_{ret} \mid x) \tag{6}$$

The equality holds if and only if the structural path P is independent of the target problem x. However, since $\mathcal{T}$ is rooted in problem classification, P is highly correlated with x. Thus, the strict inequality $H(C_{ret} \mid x, P) < H(C_{ret} \mid x)$ holds. This proves that hierarchical indexing mathematically bounds the retrieval space, filtering out semantically similar but logically irrelevant noise, thereby guaranteeing higher logical accuracy in the Retrieve phase.

4.2 Generative CBM Enhances Case Competence: A Mutual Information Perspective

A core objective of Case Base Maintenance (CBM) is to enhance the problem-solving competence of the case base while significantly reducing its physical footprint (i.e., overcoming the Utility Problem) [13]. For LLMs, the footprint is strictly bounded by the context window limit L_{max}.

Let S be the underlying solution logic for a target distribution of problems. A key objective of CBM is to increase the Mutual Information $I(S; CB_{retained})$ subject to the constraint $\mathcal{L}(CB_{retained}) \leq L_{max}$, where $\mathcal{L}(\cdot)$ denotes the description length (token size).

Naive LLM agents append raw experiential cases unconditionally, increasing $\mathcal{L}(CB)$ linearly without ensuring a proportional increase in $I(S; CB)$, ultimately violating the L_{max} constraint and causing attention dilution.

Proposition 2. *CTER's dual-mode extraction strategy achieves an effective Information Bottleneck (IB) trade-off, preserving high case competence while reducing the memory footprint.*

Proof. CTER evaluates the empirical utility ΔP of each specific case c_i. The maintenance strategy is defined as a mapping $f_{CBM}(c_i)$:

1. **For high-utility cases ($\Delta P > \theta$):** These cases represent novel logical boundaries with high marginal mutual information $I(S; c_i \mid CB)$. CTER distills them into standalone generalized cases, preserving their distinct competence in the case base.
2. **For marginal-utility cases ($\Delta P \leq \theta$):** These cases offer highly redundant information $I(c_i; c_j) \gg 0$. CTER applies a compression strategy inspired by Minimum Description Length (MDL) principles, merging them into a group case c_{group}.

Mathematically, by abstracting shared logical rules and discarding redundant case-specific details, this compression ensures:

$$\mathcal{L}(c_{group}) \ll \sum_i \mathcal{L}(c_{i,redundant}) \tag{7}$$

while the mutual information regarding the solution logic is largely maintained:

$$I(S; c_{group}) \approx I(S; \bigcup_i c_{i,redundant}) \tag{8}$$

By actively compressing redundant experiential instances (reducing description length) and explicitly retaining generalized logical paths (preserving mutual information), CTER acts as a Generative CBM mechanism. It provides a theoretical basis for constructing a high-density, high-competence case base that strictly adheres to the LLM's context bottleneck, formally mitigating the Utility Problem in lifelong learning agents.

5 Experiments

We evaluate CTER across complex reasoning tasks on GPQA (physics, chemistry, biology) [15] and Omni-MATH-Rule (mathematics) [8].

5.1 Complex Scientific Reasoning (GPQA)

Experimental Setup. We evaluated CTER on graduate-level GPQA questions using Gemini-2.5-flash. We generated 16 independent trajectories, reporting mean@16 and pass@16. Baselines include zero-shot Base, standard RAG [11], unstructured experience agents LEAP [27] and ExpeL [28], and Training-free GRPO [5].

Main Results. Results are in Table 1. CTER significantly outperforms all baselines. Compared to Base, CTER achieves an absolute improvement of 12.2% in average mean@16. While LEAP and ExpeL provide marginal gains, they struggle with high noise inherent in flat retrieval. CTER mitigates this via its tree-based structure, ensuring only low-noise generalized principles are reused. Notably, CTER surpasses test-time scaling methods like TF-GRPO, proving that structured generative CBR provides more reliable anchors than purely online exploration.

Furthermore, to illustrate the efficacy of our case base compression strategy, Fig. 4 compares the total string character lengths and formula character counts before and after the Stage 2 processing across different GPQA domains. The substantial decline in both metrics confirms that CTER effectively compresses raw instance-level redundancy while abstracting specific formulas into concise generalized principles, thereby directly mitigating context window overload. Despite this significant reduction in context footprint, Fig. 3 demonstrates that the model successfully preserves key reasoning information during generalization, maintaining high semantic alignment scores before and after the rigorous compression phase.

Table 1. Performance comparison on the GPQA dataset using the Gemini-2.5-flash model. Models are evaluated across domains, reporting mean@16 and pass@16 metrics (%). TF-GRPO denotes Training-free GRPO. Best results are in **bold**.

Metric	Subject	Base	RAG [11]	LEAP [27]	ExpeL [28]	TF-GRPO [5]	**CTER (Ours)**
mean@16	Physics	51.3	50.9	50.8	52.1	63.2	**64.7**
	Chemistry	42.8	45.7	48.2	44.6	53.9	**55.2**
	Biology	70.3	71.5	74.5	72.6	76.6	**77.1**
	Average	48.5	49.8	51.2	49.9	59.4	**60.7**
pass@16	Physics	67.4	68.3	70.2	73.8	76.2	**78.9**
	Chemistry	58.5	61.5	63.1	62.2	72.4	**76.1**
	Biology	85.6	88.1	85.5	87.1	89.9	**91.2**
	Average	65.0	67.1	68.4	69.7	75.8	**78.8**

5.2 Mathematical Reasoning

Experimental Setup. We evaluated on the Omni-MATH-Rule dataset and conducted out-of-distribution (OOD) testing on the AIME 2024 and AIME 2025 competition problems. The training case base utilized 2,676 samples. All evaluation metrics in this section are reported as Mean@16 accuracy.

Main Results and Generalization Analysis. To evaluate the robustness of our framework, we analyzed both cross-dataset (OOD) generalization and cross-model generalization, as presented in Table 2.

On the Gemini-Flash-Lite model, CTER achieves an average of 40.2% (precisely 40.19%) on Omni-MATH-Rule, delivering a 12.45% absolute improvement over the zero-shot baseline. Furthermore, CTER demonstrates strong OOD generalization on the highly challenging AIME benchmarks, indicating that the abstracted generalized cases capture underlying mathematical properties rather than merely memorizing surface-level instances from the training set.

Crucially, CTER exhibits excellent cross-model generalization. Transferring the case base generated purely by Gemini-Flash-Lite directly to Grok-4 (denoted as CTER (GFL)) yields significant performance gains compared to Grok-4's baseline. This proves the model-agnostic versatility of our structured generalized case base.

Ablation Study. We conducted an ablation study on the Omni-MATH-Rule dataset, as detailed in Table 3, to quantify the contribution of each framework component:

(1) Intrinsic Value of Case Retrieval: Simply retrieving raw cases (w/o D.T.) surpasses the baseline, proving the fundamental value of experiential scaffolding.

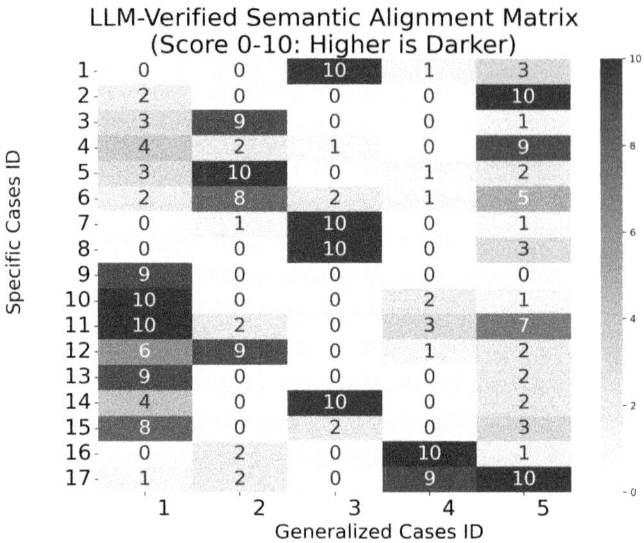

Fig. 3. LLM-based evaluation scores (out of 10) measuring the retention of critical case information before and after the Stage 2 compression. The results show that the model successfully preserves key reasoning information during generalization.

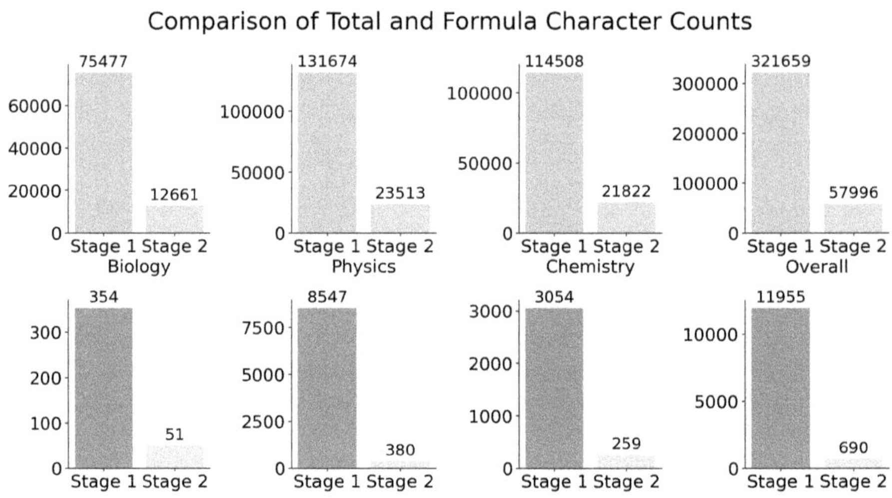

Fig. 4. Comparison of total and formula character counts between Stage 1 (specific cases) and Stage 2 (generalized cases) across different GPQA domains. The top row illustrates the reduction in total string character length, while the bottom row depicts the decrease in formula character counts. The substantial decline in both metrics demonstrates that CTER effectively compresses raw instance-level redundancy and abstracts specific formulas into concise generalized principles, thereby mitigating context window overload.

Table 2. Cross-model and cross-dataset generalization performance. Results cover the Omni-MATH-Rule dataset and out-of-distribution AIME competition problems. All metrics are reported as mean@16 accuracy (%).

Task/Dataset	Gemini-Flash-Lite		Grok-4		
	Base LLM	**CTER**	Base LLM	CTER (GFL)	**CTER**
Precalculus	25.2	**38.9**	28.5	35.1	**39.2**
Number Theory	32.5	**42.7**	35.1	40.2	**44.5**
Geometry	19.1	**27.1**	21.3	25.0	**28.3**
Discrete Math.	23.4	**40.5**	26.8	36.5	**41.8**
Calculus	33.1	**43.4**	36.0	41.5	**45.1**
Applied Math.	16.7	**28.9**	18.2	24.1	**30.1**
Algebra	44.2	**59.8**	48.1	56.6	**61.3**
Omni-MATH Avg.	27.7	**40.2**	30.6	37.0	**41.5**
AIME 2024	25.2	**32.7**	38.5	—	**47.2**
AIME 2025	14.8	**19.4**	29.6	—	**37.3**

Note: CTER (GFL) indicates transferring the case base generated by Gemini-Flash-Lite directly for evaluation on Grok-4, demonstrating cross-model case base compatibility.

Table 3. Ablation study of CTER components on the Omni-MATH-Rule dataset using the Gemini-Flash-Lite model. All metrics are reported as mean@16 accuracy (%).

Method/Task	Base LLM	w/o D.T.	w/o Ext.	w/o D.M.	**CTER**
Precalculus	25.2	30.2	33.4	34.0	**38.9**
Number Theory	32.5	35.1	37.8	38.2	**42.7**
Geometry	19.1	22.2	24.8	26.3	**27.1**
Discrete Math.	23.4	30.6	36.2	37.1	**40.5**
Calculus	33.1	36.4	37.8	39.2	**43.4**
Applied Math.	16.7	21.8	24.3	25.2	**28.9**
Algebra	44.2	50.8	55.4	57.2	**59.8**
Average	27.7	32.4	35.7	36.7	**40.2**

Note: D.T. = Dynamic Tree, Ext. = Extraction, D.M. = Dual-Mode.

(2) Dynamic Tree is Crucial for Logic Alignment: Without the tree organization, flat retrieval introduces severe semantic noise. The hierarchy ensures logical case matching.
(3) Extraction Enables Generalization: Ablating the extraction module (w/o Ext.) degrades performance. Reusing raw, specific instances is evidently less effective than applying distilled, generalized rules.
(4) Dual-Mode Extraction Manages the Utility Problem: The removal of the dual-mode mechanism (w/o D.M.) accounts for the final performance gap. Treating all cases equally leads to a bloated context that dilutes the model's attention.

The dual-mode strategy acts as an effective Case Base Maintenance (CBM) mechanism, clustering marginal cases to preserve sparsity and ensure high context density.

6 Conclusion

In this work, we presented the Compressed Tree-based Experiential Repository (CTER), a novel generative CBR framework that explicitly addresses the Utility Problem and retrieval noise in LLM agents. By dynamically structuring cases into a hierarchy and utilizing a performance-driven dual-mode CBM strategy, CTER successfully distills specific instance-level cases into highly dense, generalized rules. Extensive evaluations on scientific and mathematical reasoning datasets confirm that CTER achieves state-of-the-art performance, highlighting structured case base maintenance as a highly promising direction for lifelong learning in LLMs.

Acknowledgments. The work is supported partially by National Natural Science Foundation of China (No. 62576041, 62106257, 62437001), and supported by the Fundamental Research Funds for the Central Universities(No. 2253500001, No. 2251200169).

Disclosure of Interests. The authors have no competing interests to declare that are relevant to the content of this article.

Declaration on Generative AI. During the preparation of this work, the authors used Gemini-3 to improve writing style, paraphrase, and check grammar. After using these tools, the authors reviewed and edited the content as needed and take full responsibility for the publication's content.

References

1. Aha, D.W., Kibler, D., Albert, M.K.: Instance-based learning algorithms. Mach. Learn. **6**(1), 37–66 (1991)
2. Bach, K., et al.: Case-based reasoning meets large language models: A research manifesto for open challenges and research directions (2025)
3. Bergmann, R., Breen, S., Goker, M., Manago, M., Wess, S.: Developing Industrial Case-Based Reasoning Applications: The INRECA Methodology, Springer (1998)
4. Bulatov, A., Kuratov, Y., Burtsev, M.: Recurrent memory transformer. Adv. Neural. Inf. Process. Syst. **35**, 11079–11091 (2022)
5. Cai, Y., et al.: Training-free group relative policy optimization. arXiv preprint arXiv:2510.08191 (2025)
6. Cheng, F., Li, H., Liu, F., Van Rooij, R., Zhang, K., Lin, Z.: Empowering LLMs with logical reasoning: a comprehensive survey. arXiv preprint arXiv:2502.15652 (2025)
7. Du, P.: Memory for autonomous LLM agents: Mechanisms, evaluation, and emerging frontiers (2026). arXiv:2603.07670 arXiv preprint
8. Gao, B., et al.: Omni-math: A universal olympiad level mathematic benchmark for large language models, (2024). arXiv:2410.07985 arXiv preprint

9. Gentner, D.: Structure-mapping: a theoretical framework for analogy. Cogn. Sci. **7**(2), 155–170 (1983)
10. Leake, D.B., Wilson, D.C.: Remembering why to remember: Performance-guided case-base maintenance. Advances in Case-Based Reasoning, pp. 161–175 (2001)
11. Lewis, P., et al.: Retrieval-augmented generation for knowledge-intensive NLP tasks. In: Advances in Neural Information Processing Systems (NeurIPS), vol. 33, pp. 9459–9474 (2020)
12. Liu, N.F., et al.: Lost in the middle: How language models use long contexts. In: Proceedings of the 61st Annual Meeting of the Association for Computational Linguistics (ACL), vol. 1, pp. 1123–1143. (2023)
13. Lupiani, E., Juarez, J.M., Palma, J.: Evaluating case-base maintenance algorithms. Knowl.-Based Syst. **67**, 180–194 (2014)
14. McKenna, E., Smyth, B.: Competence-guided case discovery. In: Research and Development in Intelligent Systems XVIII: Proceedings of ES2001, the Twenty-first SGES International Conference on Knowledge Based Systems and Applied Artificial Intelligence, Cambridge, December 2001, pp. 97–108. Springer (2002)
15. Rein, D., et al.: GPQA: A graduate-level google-proof q&a benchmark. In: First Conference on Language Modeling (2024)
16. Richter, M.M.: The knowledge contained in similarity measures. In: Invited talk at the 1st International Conference on Case-Based Reasoning (1995) ICCBR-95
17. Schank, R.C.: Dynamic memory: A theory of reminding and learning in computers and people, Cambridge University Press (1982)
18. Shang, Y., Tang, H., Gao, L., Jia, C., Lin, Z.: Beyond flat retrieval: towards dynamic graph-augmented generation for complex question answering. In: 2025 IEEE 6th International Conference on Computer, Big Data, Artificial Intelligence (ICCBD+ AI), pp. 1–5. IEEE (2025)
19. Shinn, N., Cassano, F., Gopinath, A., Narasimhan, K., Yao, S.: Reflexion: Language agents with verbal reinforcement learning. Adv. Neural. Inf. Process. Syst. **36**, 8634–8652 (2023)
20. Smyth, B., Keane, M.T.: Remembering to forget: a competence-preserving case deletion policy for case-based reasoning systems. In: Proceedings of the 14th International Joint Conference on Artificial Intelligence (IJCAI), vol. 1, pp. 377–382 (1995)
21. Smyth, B., Keane, M.T.: Competence models and the maintenance problem. Comput. Intell. **17**(2), 258–274 (2001)
22. Sosa, R.U., Ramamurthy, K.N., Chang, M., Singh, M.: Reasoning about concepts with LLMs: Inconsistencies abound. In: First Conference on Language Modeling, (2024)
23. Wei, J., et al.: Chain-of-thought prompting elicits reasoning in large language models. In: Advances in Neural Information Processing Systems (NeurIPS), vol. 35, pp. 24824–24837. (2022)
24. Wess, S., Althoff, K.D., Derwand, G.: Using k-d trees to improve the retrieval step in case-based reasoning. In: European Workshop on Case-Based Reasoning (EWCBR), pp. 167–181. Springer (1993)
25. Yao, S., et al.: Tree of thoughts: Deliberate problem solving with large language models. In: Advances in Neural Information Processing Systems (NeurIPS), vol. 36, (2023)
26. Zhan, H., Wu, Y., Ding, J., Xu, B., Yang, L., Lin, H.: Case-based reasoning in generative agents: review and prospect. In: International Conference on Case-Based Reasoning, pp. 172–186. Springer (2025)

27. Zhang, T., et al.: -context principle learning from mistakes (2024). arXiv:2402.05403 arXiv preprint
28. Zhao, A., Huang, D., Xu, Q., Lin, M., Liu, Y.J., Huang, G.: Expel: LLM agents are experiential learners. In: Proceedings of the AAAI Conference on Artificial Intelligence, vol. 38, pp. 19632–19642 (2024)
29. Zhou, Y., et al.: Breaking the exploration bottleneck: rubric-scaffolded reinforcement learning for general LLM reasoning. arXiv preprint arXiv:2508.16949 (2025)

CBR for Dynamic Real-World Domains and Applications

InterruptSense: Uncertainty-Aware Multimodal CBR for Interruptibility Detection in Knowledge Work

Tim Haase and Jörg Cassens(✉)

Engineering Interactive Applications, University of Hildesheim, Hildesheim, Germany
cassens@cs.uni-hildesheim.de
https://www.uni-hildesheim.de/fb4/institute/ifi/enia/

Abstract. Interrupting colleagues in knowledge work is often beneficial or even necessary for the performance of the overall socio-technical system. Such interruptions can carry significant cognitive costs for the interrupted person, yet determining the right moment for interrupting a colleague remains a socially and contextually complex problem. In this paper, we present InterruptSense, a Case-Based Reasoning system that detects knowledge workers' interruptibility through multimodal biosensor fusion, communicating its assessment via an ambient LED interface. Cases combine physiological signals (heart rate), behavioural signals (keyboard and mouse activity, blink rate, gaze direction), and ambient context (illumination, noise, temperature, humidity) with a weighted similarity function. A key design principle is the option for uncertainty-aware output: rather than forcing a binary classification (interruptible vs. non-interruptible), InterruptSense can produce a three-tier signal reflecting the similarity distribution across retrieved cases. This shows the system's uncertainty and supports context-sensitive decision making. In high-risk environments or high-stakes situations, the externalised uncertainty can trigger human judgment; in low-risk contexts or low-stakes situations, a binary majority decision might suffice. A pre-study with five participants seeded the case base; a main study with twelve participants across two simulated work scenarios yielded 87% classification accuracy (sensitivity 90%, specificity 85%). User feedback was strongly positive, with nine of twelve participants indicating willingness to use the system in daily work. We discuss implications for CBR system design, particularly the value of exposing rather than concealing retrieval uncertainty in ambient, human-in-the-loop applications.

Keywords: Interruptibility Detection · Ambient Intelligence · Multimodal Sensing · Uncertainty-Aware Systems

1 Introduction

Knowledge workers are routinely interrupted during cognitively demanding tasks, with significant consequences for productivity, error rates, and subjective

L. Malburg and K. Bach (Eds.): ICCBR 2026, LNAI 16780, pp. 423–438, 2027.
https://doi.org/10.1007/978-3-032-33865-5_26

well-being [24,30]. The cost of poorly-timed interruptions in knowledge work is well documented, and users tend to defer interruptions during high cognitive workload [41]. Returning to interrupted tasks can be difficult, and while support strategies for returning to the original task exist [33], they are not universally supported. Recovery from interruptions can require significant time [2], and frequent interruptions increase stress, frustration, and error rates even if they potentially accelerate task execution speed [30].

However, interruptions are not uniformly harmful, and some reviews [18,37] point out that interruptions can provide timely information, facilitate knowledge exchange, and support collaborative problem-solving, particularly when they occur during periods of lower cognitive engagement. Interruptions can improve the overall performance of the organisation, for example, a quick question to a more experienced colleague could significantly shorten the time the interrupter spends on a specific task [20]. Essentially, not all interruptions are costly: a colleague catching a moment of relaxed browsing is qualitatively different from one breaking a state of deep concentration or "flow". In essence, we have both undesirable interruptions and desirable interactions, and the central challenge is not to eliminate interruptions, but to time them appropriately.

Traditional approaches to interruptibility detection typically frame the problem as binary classification (a user is either available or not) and report a single decision to potential interrupters [17]. Variations to this include tiered, multi-class definitions of interruptibility [23], potentially including an "unknown interruptibility" status [4]. Other approaches include probabilistic models of the duration of a worker's interruptibility status to allow the interrupter to time their interruptions better [43]. However, even systems that model uncertainty explicitly might only use it for internal purposes, like robots addressing a different person than originally planned or trying to get better input data [5]. Such framing withholds information that is epistemically significant from human users: a system that is genuinely uncertain about a user's state should communicate that uncertainty rather than hide it behind a forced decision. The appropriate response to that uncertainty is then context-dependent—in safety-critical or high-cost interruption scenarios, it should trigger caution or defer to human judgment; in low-stakes settings, a majority decision may suffice.

We present *InterruptSense* [19], a Case-Based Reasoning (CBR) system that detects knowledge workers' interruptibility through the fusion of physiological, behavioural, and ambient sensor streams, and communicates its assessment via an ambient LED interface. Its key design contribution is an *uncertainty-aware three-tier output*: rather than forcing a binary classification, the system exposes the distribution across the three nearest retrieved cases, yielding a transparent green/amber/red signal. This externalises the system's internal state and allows users in the deployment context to determine how uncertainty is handled.

In CBR terms, this means treating the *similarity distribution* of retrieved cases as a first-class output, not merely as an intermediate computation step. We argue that this is a principled design choice grounded in CBR's analogical epistemology: if the case base contains genuinely mixed evidence, the system *knows what it does not know*, and should say so.

We make the following contributions:

- A multimodal case representation for knowledge worker interruptibility, combining physiological signals (heart rate), behavioural signals (keyboard and mouse activity, blink rate, gaze direction), and ambient context (illumination, noise level, temperature, humidity).
- An uncertainty-aware output architecture for ambient CBR systems, supporting context-sensitive deployment across a spectrum from fully autonomous to human-in-the-loop decision making.
- A feedback-driven retain mechanism enabling per-user personalisation without requiring explicit labelling effort.
- An empirical evaluation with 12 participants across two simulated work scenarios, yielding 87% classification accuracy (sensitivity 90%, specificity 85%), with all results significant at $p < 0.001$.

Note that we use *multimodal* throughout this paper in the sense established in HCI and cognitive science research, referring to the integration of multiple sensory and physiological channels [14,35]. In particular, we differentiate between *modality* which is concerned with the sensory-motor system, *mediality* capturing the technical implementation of sensing and acting, and *codality* as the semiotic representation [32]. This differs from its use in e.g. NLP, where e.g. multimodality typically denotes the combination of text and image modalities.

The remainder of the paper is structured as follows. Section 2 introduces the theoretical background on interruptibility, CBR, and ambient intelligence. Section 3 describes the design of InterruptSense. Section 4 presents the evaluation study and results. Section 5 discusses the uncertainty-aware output as a CBR design principle. Section 6 concludes and outlines future work.

2 Background

Previous computational approaches to interruptibility detection used sensor data to predict user availability [16,25] or modelled the cost of interruption as a function of context [22]. These systems typically produce binary, multi-class, or probabilistic outputs without explicitly representing uncertainty in their output. Prior work has also explored ontology-based interruptibility inference in ambient settings [39,40] and the role of awareness systems in reducing unwanted interruptions [36]. These approaches differ in method but share a design assumption: uncertainty, where modelled at all, is consumed internally rather than communicated. InterruptSense inverts this—the three-tier output surfaces the retrieval distribution itself, making the system's uncertainty an interactional resource rather than a hidden intermediate quantity.

2.1 Case-Based Reasoning

CBR solves new problems by retrieving and adapting solutions from a case base of prior experience [1]. The canonical lazy-learning, four-phase cycle—retrieve, reuse, revise, retain [1]—makes CBR particularly suited to domains where (labelled) training data is scarce but individual cases can be accumulated incrementally. In dynamic, changing environments such as personal work contexts, CBR's ability to personalise through case retention offers a practical advantage over eagerly learned, batch-trained classifiers.

The similarity distribution across retrieved cases carries information beyond the top-ranked solution. In classification tasks, a unanimous top-3 retrieval signals high confidence whereas a 2:1 split signals genuine ambiguity. Making this distribution visible is the foundation of our uncertainty-aware output design.

2.2 Ambient Intelligence: Context Awareness and Context Sensitivity

Ambient intelligence (AmI) systems are embedded in the environment, perceiving context and acting on it in ways that are unobtrusive to users [11,13]. A useful analytical distinction separates *context awareness*—the ability to detect and represent the current situation—from *context sensitivity*—the ability to respond appropriately given that situation [29]. Ambient systems additionally embed these two different aspects of contextualisation in the (physical) world by means of sensors and actuators [10].

In InterruptSense, the CBR system provides context awareness: it detects the worker's interruptibility state from sensor data. Context sensitivity is a separate, deployment-level concern: the same three-tier output may warrant different responses depending on the stakes of the interruption. The implemented actuator can either signal a binary decision (e.g. a green or a red light), or it can expose the system's uncertainty to the observer (e.g. by adding an amber light). This ability to expose uncertainty—as evidenced by the different classifications suggested by the retrieved cases—rather than collapsing it into a binary decision is a direct consequence of the theoretical separation: the classification of the CBR component is context-aware; how it is acted upon is context-sensitive.

3 System Design

InterruptSense was designed to detect the interruptibility of a knowledge worker at their desk and communicate the result unobtrusively to colleagues in the immediate environment. The system comprises three integrated components: a multimodal sensor layer and client application, a myCBR server [3], and an ambient output module. Figure 1 gives an overview.

3.1 Case Representation

Each case encodes a snapshot of the user's state at a point in time. Cases are structured as feature vectors combining three signal categories.

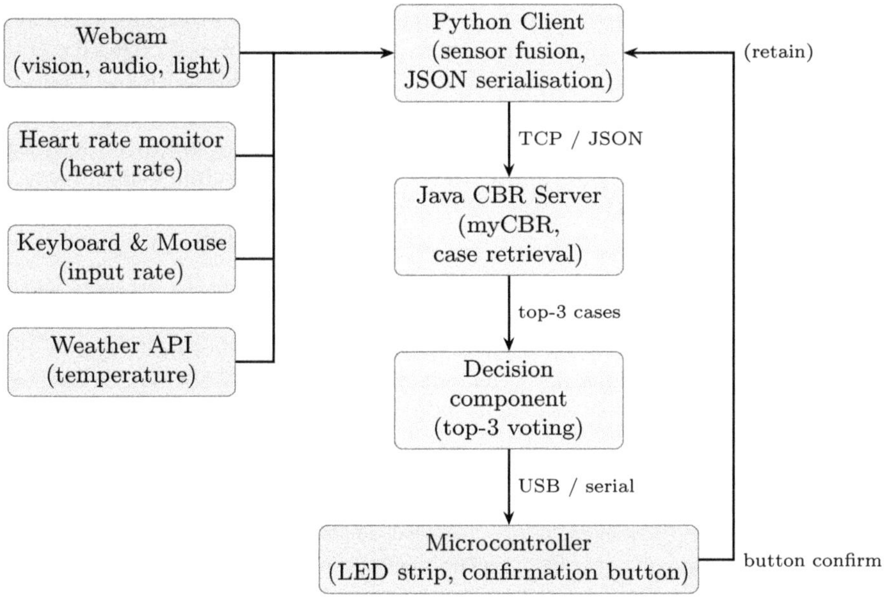

Fig. 1. System architecture of InterruptSense. Sensor data are fused by the Python client and transmitted to the Java myCBR server every 30 s via TCP. The server returns the three most similar cases; the decision component applies the chosen strategy, e.g. majority voting, and drives the LED strip via an Arduino microcontroller. A physical button attached to the Arduino triggers the retain step when the user confirms a correct classification.

Physiological Signals. Heart rate (HR) and heart rate as a percentage of age-predicted maximum (HR%) are captured via a chest strap with a heart rate monitor, a standard device often used in sports as well as in research (Polar H7), over Bluetooth. Elevated heart rate relative to personal baseline is a reliable indicator of cognitive load [34,47]. Both absolute and relative HR are included to support inter-individual comparison.

Behavioural Signals. Four behavioural streams are captured. Blink count and blink rate are derived from webcam footage using OpenCV [7] and dlib [28] facial landmark detection: the ratio of horizontal to vertical eye aperture determines blink events. Gaze direction (LEFT, CENTER, RIGHT) is estimated from the distribution of iris pixels across each eye. Keyboard and mouse activity is aggregated into an input count and input rate (events per minute), capturing the overall rhythm of interaction without recording content, thus minimising privacy intrusion.

Ambient Context Signals. Ambient illumination is estimated from the mean red-channel value of the webcam feed. Sound level is captured from the webcam's integrated microphone and converted to dB SPL. Outdoor temperature and humidity are retrieved from the Weatherbit.io API, providing contextual information about the broader environment that may influence cognitive state.

The full feature vector is summarised in Table 1, together with the similarity weights assigned to each attribute. Weights were assigned a priori according to a three-tier theoretical hierarchy derived from the literature indicated with each feature, reflecting each feature's directness and cross-individual reliability as an indicator of cognitive load.

Table 1. Case features and similarity weights used in InterruptSense. Weights reflect a literature-grounded hierarchy of signal reliability: physiological signals that are consistent across individuals receive the highest weights [34,47]; behavioural signals receive moderate weights due to higher inter-individual variability [21,27,31,44]; ambient context signals receive the lowest weights as indirect, contextualising factors [8,45].

Category	Feature	Weight	Rationale
Physiological	Heart rate (bpm)	5	Direct cognitive load indicator [34]
	Heart rate (% of max)	6	Cross-individually normalised; highest reliability [34]
Behavioural	Blink count	2	Trend indicator; high individual variation [21,31]
	Blink rate (blinks/min)	3	More informative than count alone [44]
	Gaze direction	2	Ambiguous signal; moderate weight [27]
	Input count	2	Activity proxy; task-type dependent
	Input rate (events/min)	3	Rate captures rhythm of engagement
Ambient	Ambient noise (dB)	2	Indirect; affects but does not indicate load [45]
	Luminance	1	Contextualising only [8]
	Temperature (° C)	1	Contextualising only
	Humidity	1	Contextualising only

The two physiological features receive the highest weights because heart rate provides the most consistent cross-individual signal of cognitive load [34], and the percentage of age-predicted maximum normalises for inter-individual baseline differences. Behavioural signals receive intermediate weights: blink rate is more diagnostic than raw count [44], while gaze direction receives a lower weight because its relationship to interruptibility is ambiguous—unfocused gaze can indicate either cognitive overload or relaxed availability [27]. Ambient signals receive the lowest weights as they provide context that may modulate but does not directly index cognitive state [8].

The specific numerical values within each tier reflect design judgment rather than empirical optimisation. Weight learning or sensitivity analysis on a larger case base would be a natural next step, noted as a limitation in Sect. 5.

3.2 The CBR Cycle

Retrieve. The client polls the CBR server every 30 s, transmitting the current feature vector as a JSON object. The server computes a weighted distance to all cases in the case base:

$$\text{dist}(A, B) = \sum_{i=1}^{n} \omega_i \cdot |A_i - B_i| \quad (1)$$

where A and B are two cases, ω_i is the weight of feature i, and $|A_i - B_i|$ is the absolute difference on the i-th attribute (normalised to $[0, 1]$ per feature). This weighted Manhattan distance serves as a dissimilarity measure: a lower score indicates higher similarity. The three cases with the smallest distance are returned to the client.

The 30-second polling interval is a deliberate design choice that balances responsiveness against signal stability: it gives potential interrupters a temporally stable signal to act on, long enough to notice and act on before it changes, while avoiding the confusion of rapid state oscillation. The interval is constrained by the usability of the output, not by the classification itself.

Reuse. Each of the three retrieved cases carries a solution label: `interruptible` or `not_interruptible`. These three labels are returned to the client, which applies one of three decision strategies (see Sect. 3.3).

Revise. Rather than detecting and correcting an erroneous solution after the fact, the system inverts the feedback polarity: users confirm *correct* decisions rather than flagging incorrect ones. When a user presses a physical button to indicate that the current classification is accurate, the current sensor data snapshot is submitted to the server as a new case. This feedback is optional and can be done when the user notices the indicated state by chance.

Retain. The confirmed case is added to the case base with its validated label. Over time, this incrementally personalises the case base to the individual user's physiological and behavioural patterns. The initial case base of 30 cases (seeded via pre-study, see Sect. 4) thus grows dynamically through use. New cases are accepted only when user-confirmed, ensuring that noise or misclassified states do not degrade the case base. We anticipate the necessity of case maintenance when used over a long period of time.

3.3 Uncertainty-Aware Output

A central design concept of InterruptSense is the treatment of retrieval uncertainty as a first-class output. The three retrieved cases may be unanimous (3:0) or split (2:1). Three decision strategies were implemented and evaluated:

Traffic light. The output reflects the full distribution: unanimous retrieval yields red (not interruptible) or green (interruptible); a 2:1 split yields amber. This directly exposes retrieval uncertainty to the observer.

Two-of-three majority. The amber state is resolved in favour of the majority label, collapsing uncertainty into a binary decision when a plurality exists.

Most similar case. Only the top-ranked case's label is used, ignoring the other two cases.

The amber signal in the traffic light strategy is not a failure mode but a *deliberate resource for human judgment.* The appropriate response to amber depends on the deployment context (Sect. 5). The three-tier scheme is deliberately chosen so that the system's epistemic state—confident availability, confident unavailability, or genuinely mixed evidence—maps onto a culturally established sign system the interrupter already reads without (or with little) instruction. This context-sensitive interpretation is enabled precisely because uncertainty is made visible rather than resolved internally.

This reflects the context awareness / context sensitivity distinction (Sect. 2): the CBR component is context-aware, while context-sensitive judgment is delegated to the human interrupter. This delegation is the system's core human-in-the-loop commitment: InterruptSense informs a decision rather than making one on the human's behalf.

3.4 Ambient Output Module

The system's decisions are communicated via an Arduino-based microcontroller system [6] driving a RGB LED strip. The LED strip can be placed in the user's peripheral visual field or on the outside of their office, visible to approaching colleagues but not foregrounded in the user's own attention. The same Arduino module provides the physical button for the retain feedback mechanism.

The communication is directed outwards, toward potential interrupters, and not towards the user themselves, who would be disrupted by attending to their own interruptibility signal. This design choice reflects the ambient intelligence principle of unobtrusiveness [11,13]. Note that the constraint to be unobtrusive applies to both the interrupter and the interrupted – EEG sensors, for example, would likely lead to better performance, but strapping EEG sensors to Knowledge workers constantly is (usually) not an option.

4 Evaluation

The evaluation tests two hypotheses.

Accuracy. InterruptSense's two-of-three majority strategy achieves classification accuracy significantly above chance, using a case base seeded from a general population of knowledge workers.

Calibration. When the three-tier traffic-light output exposes the retrieval distribution, unambiguous signals (red or green) coincide with markedly higher accuracy than ambiguous signals (amber), indicating that the system's own uncertainty is informative about its accuracy.

4.1 Pre-study: Seeding the Case Base

A pre-study with five knowledge workers established the initial case base of 30 cases. Participants completed two 10-minute sessions: one involving focused cognitive work at their own desk, and one involving free internet browsing. Sessions were labelled `not_interruptible` and `interruptible` respectively. The resulting 30 cases provided a balanced starting point for the main study.

Sensor data confirmed the theoretical signal rationale: heart rate was consistently higher during focused work across all participants, while blink rate showed individual variation consistent with the literature [21,44].

4.2 Main Study

Participants and Procedure. Twelve knowledge workers participated in the main study (same two-scenario design as the pre-study). Each scenario lasted 10 min; 20 sensor readings were captured per scenario per participant, yielding 480 decisions in total. Scenario 1 (not interruptible) used a custom cognitive challenge website comprising arithmetic tasks, a Stroop test, logic puzzles, and a memory sequence game. Scenario 2 (interruptible) instructed participants to browse freely between five self-chosen websites.

Ethical Considerations. Participants provided informed consent before data collection. All sensor data were anonymised; keyboard and mouse activity were captured as aggregate counts only, with no content recorded.

4.3 Results

Classification Accuracy. Table 2 summarises accuracy, sensitivity, and specificity across the three decision strategies. Figure 2 visualises the individual decisions returned by InterruptSense for every testcase.

Table 2. Classification performance across decision strategies (n = 480 decisions, 12 participants).

Strategy	Accuracy	Sensitivity	Specificity
Two-of-three majority	87%	90%	85%
Most similar case	86%	89%	84%
Traffic light (unanimous only)	24.5% clear correct	—	—

The two-of-three and most-similar-case strategies yielded very similar results. The traffic light strategy produced an unambiguous (red or green) signal in 24.5% of cases, with only 0.6% of unambiguous decisions being incorrect. The remaining 74.9% were amber, reflecting genuine case base ambiguity. The 0.6% error rate on unambiguous traffic-light outputs, compared to a 13% error rate on the two-of-three majority decisions across the same data, supports our hypothesis that the system's expressed certainty is calibrated to its accuracy.

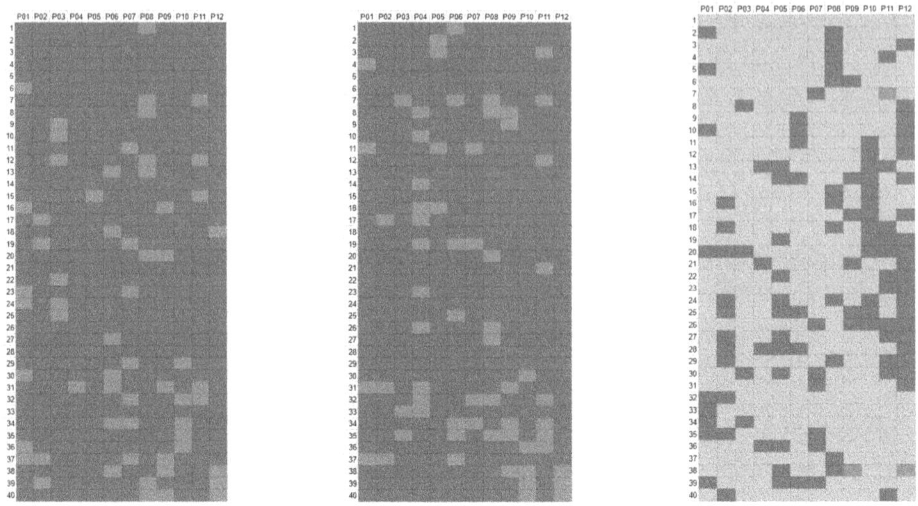

(a) Two-of-three (b) Most similar case (c) Traffic light

Fig. 2. Decision heatmaps for all three strategies across 12 participants (P01–P12) and 40 measurements (rows 1–20: Scenario 1, not interruptible; rows 21–40: Scenario 2, interruptible). **Dark blue** : correct decision; **light blue**: uncertain (amber, traffic light only); **orange**: incorrect decision. The traffic light heatmap (right) shows predominantly uncertain states, reflecting the system's appropriate epistemic caution rather than high error rates. (Color figure online)

Statistical Significance. The traffic light strategy uses three nominal output categories, so a chi-square goodness-of-fit test was used against a uniform null distribution (expected: 160 decisions per category under the assumption that the system performs no better than chance across three equally likely outcomes). The test yielded $\chi^2 = 412.59$, $df = 2$, $p = 2.56 \times 10^{-90}$. Since the two other strategies (majority vote and best case) only have two output categories, a binomial test against a 50% chance baseline was used. The two-of-three strategy yielded $p = 9.88 \times 10^{-67}$ (419 of 480 correct); the most-similar-case strategy yielded $p = 1.87 \times 10^{-63}$ (414 of 480 correct). All results are significant well beyond conventional thresholds.

We note that the 480 decisions are not fully independent: 40 measurements per participant are temporally ordered and share individual physiological baselines. Per-participant accuracy for the two-of-three strategy ranged from 80% to 97.5% (median 86.25%), confirming that the aggregate result is not driven by a small number of high-performing participants, but the effective degrees of freedom are lower than the raw n suggests. A mixed-effects analysis accounting for participant-level clustering would be a natural extension.

User Survey. A post-study questionnaire (12 respondents) assessed system acceptance. All 12 participants rated their experience as *satisfied* or *very satis-*

fied. Nine of twelve indicated willingness to use the system in daily work. Ten of twelve reported that they ceased to notice the sensors after initial habituation. Two participants raised data privacy concerns. Eleven of twelve expressed interest in a daily summary of their interruptibility patterns.

5 Discussion

We will now discuss the treatment of uncertainty in classification systems such as InterruptSense, deployment considerations, and limitations of our approach.

5.1 Uncertainty as a CBR Design Principle

The high amber rate (74.9%) might superficially appear as a weakness. We argue the opposite: it is an accurate reflection of the genuine difficulty of interruptibility classification from sensor data alone, and a consequence of the relatively small initial case base. Forcing a binary output would have obscured this uncertainty, potentially giving overconfident signals in precisely the situations where human judgment is most needed.

The CBR framework makes this principled rather than merely pragmatic. Similarity-based retrieval produces a distribution over the case base, and that distribution is meaningful. A 2:1 split among the three nearest cases means the retrieved evidence is genuinely mixed—the query case sits in a region of the case space where both interruptible and non-interruptible cases are plausibly close neighbours. Exposing this to the user is an act of *epistemic honesty* that aligns with emerging principles of explainable and transparent AI [9,12,15,42].

In terms of explanation goals [46], the three-tier output primarily serves the *transparency* goal: it makes the system's internal epistemic state visible to the user rather than hiding it behind a post-hoc rationalisation. Unlike justification-oriented explanations that argue *for* a particular decision, transparency-oriented communication reveals the evidential basis, including its limitations. The amber signal says "the retrieved evidence is mixed"—which is itself informative.

The uncertainty exposed by the amber state is, following Hüllermeier and Waegeman [26], primarily *epistemic*: it reflects the limited coverage of the case base rather than irreducible randomness in the phenomenon itself. As such, it is reducible through the retain mechanism—each confirmed case narrows the epistemic gap. This distinguishes the present approach from systems that model aleatoric uncertainty (e.g. inherent variability in physiological signals), which cannot be resolved by accumulating more data from the same user.

It is worth emphasising that the contribution here is not algorithmic but architectural: the underlying retrieval mechanism (weighted k-nearest-neighbour with $k = 3$) is deliberately simple. The novelty lies in the principled decision to *surface* the retrieval distribution rather than collapse it, and in grounding that decision in CBR's analogical epistemology and the context-awareness / context-sensitivity distinction. Any CBR system that retrieves multiple cases already computes a distribution; the design choice is whether to expose or suppress it. We argue that in ambient, human-in-the-loop applications, suppressing it discards epistemically valuable information.

We expect that, as the case base grows through personalised retain operations, the amber rate will decrease, since the case base will better cover the individual user's personal physiological and behavioural patterns. The amber state is thus also a developmental signal: it identifies regions of the case space that need more cases.

5.2 Context-Sensitive Deployment

The three-tier output supports a spectrum of deployment configurations. In safety-critical or high-interruption-cost contexts—where breaking a user's concentration carries significant consequences—the amber state can be treated as equivalent to red, yielding a conservative binary policy. In lower-stakes settings, the majority decision of the two-of-three strategy is appropriate. This separation of concerns—a context-aware signal whose context-sensitive interpretation is delegated to the deployment context (Sect. 2)—is a feature, not a limitation [10,29].

5.3 Limitations and Threats to Validity

Ecological Validity. The main study used controlled, simulated scenarios rather than ecological observation in actual office environments. The two scenarios (structured cognitive challenge vs. free browsing) represent relatively extreme points on the interruptibility spectrum; real knowledge work involves subtler intermediate states such as low-concentration administrative tasks, partially engaging meetings, or creative work with variable cognitive load. The controlled design was necessary for ground-truth labelling, but the system's performance on naturalistic, unlabelled work remains untested.

Sample and Case Base. The pre-study case base was seeded by five participants, including the first author; the twelve main-study participants were a separate group not involved in the pre-study. This separation mitigates the risk that the case base was tailored to participants who also served as test subjects, but the initial cases may still carry individual biases from the five pre-study contributors. Furthermore, the heatmaps in Fig. 2 reveal substantial inter-individual variation: some participants (e.g. P04, P05) show high accuracy across both scenarios, while others (e.g. P08) exhibit more errors, suggesting that the generic case base serves some individuals better than others. This underscores the importance of the personalisation-through-retain mechanism for long-term deployment.

Baseline Comparison. No comparison against a non-CBR baseline (e.g. a trained SVM or random forest on the same feature set) was conducted; such a comparison would help isolate the specific contribution of the CBR approach, particularly the incremental personalisation through retain. However, we note that the primary contribution of this work is the uncertainty-aware output architecture rather than classification performance per se.

Weight Assignment. The similarity weights in Table 1 were set a priori from literature and design judgment. Empirical weight optimisation through leave-one-out sensitivity analysis or learned feature weighting [38] is still open, but should reduce the amber rate by sharpening the similarity gradient between interruptible and non-interruptible regions of the case space. This is consistent with our interpretation of amber as a marker of case-base sparsity rather than inherent task ambiguity.

Data and Code Availability. The dataset combines heart-rate and behavioural traces with per-participant baselines and was collected under consent terms that preclude public release since the re-identification risk for longitudinal biosignal data is non-trivial in our sample. The core CBR component is implemented on top of myCBR [3], which is publicly available.

6 Conclusion and Future Work

We presented InterruptSense, a CBR-based system for interruptibility detection in knowledge work, and argued for uncertainty-aware output as a principled design choice for ambient CBR applications. Exposing the similarity distribution across retrieved cases—rather than collapsing it into a forced binary decision—enables context-sensitive deployment and maintains epistemic honesty about the limits of sensor-based inference. Empirical evaluation with 12 participants yielded 87% accuracy with the two-of-three strategy, with high user acceptance and low sensor obtrusiveness.

Ground-truth labelling for interruptibility trades fidelity against ecological validity: controlled tasks (as used here) yield reliable labels but lose naturalism, while in-situ self-reporting is itself an interruption. A posteriori video-based self-annotation offers a third, ecologically valid path. In future work, this could be used for a longitudinal field study that exercises the retain-driven personalisation mechanism in an authentic office environment.

In addition, the feature set could be extended with calendar context (scheduled meetings as a proxy for expected concentration) and richer physiological measures such as heart rate variability. Lastly, the contribution here is architectural rather than algorithmic: the retrieval mechanism is deliberately simple, and the novelty lies in surfacing the similarity distribution rather than collapsing it. The uncertainty-aware output developed here therefore deserves investigation as a general design pattern for CBR systems beyond the interruptibility domain.

Declaration on Generative AI. During the preparation of this work, the authors used Anthropic's Claude (Sonnet 4 and Opus 4 model families) for drafting the outline, paraphrasing text, content enhancement, and peer review simulation of the manuscript. We use these terms as defined in https://ceur-ws.org/GenAI/Taxonomy.html. All intellectual contributions, research design, evaluation, and editorial decisions are the authors' own. After using these tools, the authors reviewed and edited the text as needed and take full responsibility for the content.

References

1. Aamodt, A., Plaza, E.: Case-based reasoning: foundational issues, methodological variations, and system approaches. AI Commun. **7**(1), 39–59 (1994)
2. Altmann, E.M., Trafton, J.G., Hambrick, D.Z.: Momentary interruptions can derail the train of thought. J. Exp. Psychol. Gen. **143**(1), 215–226 (2014). https://doi.org/10.1037/a0030986
3. Bach, K., Sauer, C., Althoff, K.D., Roth-Berghofer, T.: Knowledge modeling with the open source tool myCBR. In: Proceedings of the 10th International Conference on Knowledge Engineering and Software Engineering, pp. 84–94. CEUR-WS.org, Aachen, DEU (2014)
4. Banerjee, S., Chernova, S.: Temporal models for robot classification of human interruptibility . In: Proceedings of the 16th Conference on Autonomous Agents and MultiAgent Systems, pp. 1350–1359 (2017)
5. Banerjee, S., Silva, A., Chernova, S.: Robot classification of human interruptibility and a study of its effects **7**(2) (2018). https://doi.org/10.1145/3277902
6. Banzi, M.: Getting Started with Arduino. O'Reilly, Sebastopol, CA (2008)
7. Bradski, G.: The OpenCV Library. Dr. Dobb's Journal of Software Tools (2000)
8. Cajochen, C., Zeitzer, J.M., Czeisler, C.A., Dijk, D.J.: Dose-response relationship for light intensity and ocular and electroencephalographic correlates of human alertness. Behav. Brain Res. **115**(1), 75–83 (2000). https://doi.org/10.1016/S0166-4328(00)00236-9
9. Cassens, J., Wegener, R.: Intrinsic, dialogic, and impact measures of success for explainable AI. In: Proceedings of the Twelfth International Workshop Modelling and Reasoning in Context (MRC 2021). No. 2995 in CEUR Workshop Proceedings (2021). http://ceur-ws.org/Vol-2995/#paper5
10. Cassens, J., Wegener, R.: Ambient explanations: ambient intelligence and explainable AI. In: Chatzigiannakis, I., Ruyter, B.D., Mavrommati, I. (eds.) Proceedings of AmI 2019 – European Conference on Ambient Intelligence, vol. LNCS. Springer, Rome, Italy (2019)
11. De Ruyter, B., Wegener, R., Cassens, J., Aarts, E.: Ambient Intelligence, pp. 1–32. Springer, Cham (2024). https://doi.org/10.1007/978-3-319-27648-9_32-1
12. Deuschel, J., Foltyn, A., Roscher, K., Scheele, S.: The role of uncertainty quantification for trustworthy AI. In: Unlocking artificial intelligence: from theory to applications, pp. 95–115. Springer (2024)
13. Ducatel, K., Bogdanowicz, M., Scapolo, F., Leijten, J., Burgelman, J.C.: ISTAG Scenarios for Ambient Intelligence in 2010. Tech. rep, IST Advisory Group (2001)
14. Dumas, B., Lalanne, D., Oviatt, S.: Multimodal interfaces: a survey of principles, models and frameworks 5440, 3–26 (2009). https://doi.org/10.1007/978-3-642-00437-7_1
15. Esposito, E.: Transparency versus explanation: the role of ambiguity in legal AI. J. Cross-disciplinary Res. Comput. Law **1**(2) (2022)
16. Fogarty, J., Hudson, S.E.: Toolkit support for developing and deploying sensor based statistical models of human situations. In: CHI 2007: Proceedings of the SIGCHI Conference on Human Factors in Computing Systems (2007)
17. Fogarty, J., et al.: Predicting human interruptibility with sensors. ACM Trans. Comput.-Hum. Interaction **12**(1), 119–146 (2005). https://doi.org/10.1145/1057237.1057243
18. Gross, T., Von Kalben, M.: A literature review on positive and negative effects of interruptions and implications for design. In: IFIP Conference on Human-Computer Interaction, pp. 373–379. Springer (2023)

19. Haase, T.: Behavioral Interfaces with Bio-Sensors to Optimize the Environment of Knowledge Workers. Master's thesis, University of Hildesheim (2024)
20. Harr, R., Kaptelinin, V.: Unpacking the social dimension of external interruptions. In: Field, M., Lohr, K. (eds.) GROUP 2007: Proceedings of the 2007 International ACM Conference on Supporting Group Work, pp. 399–408. ACM, New York, NY, USA (2007). https://doi.org/10.1145/1316624.1316686
21. Holland, M.K., Tarlow, G.: Blinking and mental load. Psychol. Rep. **31**(1), 119–127 (1972). https://doi.org/10.2466/pr0.1972.31.1.119
22. Horvitz, E., Apacible, J.: Learning and reasoning about interruption. In: Proceedings of the 6th International Conference on Multimodal Interfaces (ICMI), pp. 20–27. ACM (2004)
23. Horvitz, E., Koch, P., Apacible, J.: BusyBody: creating and fielding personalized models of the cost of interruption. In: Proceedings of the 2004 ACM Conference on Computer Supported Cooperative Work, pp. 507–510. CSCW 2004, ACM, New York, NY, USA (2004). https://doi.org/10.1145/1031607.1031690
24. Hudson, J.M., Christensen, J., Kellogg, W.A., Erickson, T.: i'd be overwhelmed, but it's just one more thing to do: availability and interruption in research management. In: CHI 2002: Proceedings of the SIGCHI Conference on Human factors in computing systems, pp. 97–104 (2002)
25. Hudson, S.E., et al.: Predicting human interruptibility with sensors: a wizard of oz feasibility study. In: Cockton, G., Korhonen, P. (eds.) CHI 2003: Proceedings of the SIGCHI Conference on Human Factors in Computing Systems, pp. 257–264. ACM (2003)
26. Hüllermeier, E., Waegeman, W.: Aleatoric and epistemic uncertainty in machine learning: an introduction to concepts and methods. Mach. Learn. **110**(3), 457–506 (2021). https://doi.org/10.1007/s10994-021-05946-3
27. Iqbal, S.T., Bailey, B.P.: Understanding and developing models for detecting and differentiating breakpoints during interactive tasks. In: CHI 2007: Proceedings of the SIGCHI Conference on Human Factors in Computing Systems, pp. 697–706. ACM (2007). https://doi.org/10.1145/1240624.1240732
28. King, D.E.: Dlib-ML: a machine learning toolkit. J. Mach. Learn. Res. **10**, 1755–1758 (2009)
29. Kofod-Petersen, A., Cassens, J.: Explanations and context in ambient intelligent systems. In: Modeling and Using Context – CONTEXT 2007. LNCS, vol. 4635, pp. 303–316. Springer, Roskilde, Denmark (2007). https://doi.org/10.1007/978-3-540-74255-5_23
30. Mark, G., Gudith, D., Klocke, U.: The cost of interrupted work: more speed and stress, pp. 107–110 (2008). https://doi.org/10.1145/1357054.1357072
31. Martins, R., Carvalho, J.: Eye blinking as an indicator of fatigue and mental load – a systematic review. Occupational Safety Hygiene **III**(10), 231–235 (2015)
32. Maybury, M., Wahlster, W.: Introduction to readings in intelligent user interfaces. Morgan Kaufmann (1998)
33. McFarlane, D.C.: Comparison of four primary methods for coordinating the interruption of people in human-computer interaction. Hum.-Comput. Interaction **17**(1), 63–139 (2002). https://doi.org/10.1207/S15327051HCI1701_2
34. Mulder, L.J.M.: Measurement and analysis methods of heart rate and respiration for use in applied environments. Biol. Psychol. **34**(2–3), 205–236 (1992)
35. Oviatt, S.: Multimodal interfaces. In: Jacko, J.A., Sears, A. (eds.) The Human Computer Interaction Handbook: Fundamentals, Evolving Technologies and Emerging Applications, pp. 286–304. Lawrence Erlbaum Associates (2002)

36. Petersen, S.A., Cassens, J., Kofod-Petersen, A., Divitini, M.: To be or not to be aware: Reducing interruptions in pervasive awareness systems. In: Proceedings of the Second International Conference on Mobile Ubiquitous Computing, Systems, Services and Technologies – UBICOMM 2008, pp. 327–332. IEEE Computer Society Press, Valencia, Spain (2008). https://doi.org/10.1109/UBICOMM.2008.35
37. Puranik, H., Koopman, J., Vough, H.C.: Pardon the interruption: an integrative review and future research agenda for research on work interruptions. J. Manag. **46**(6), 806–842 (2020)
38. Richter, M.M., Weber, R.O.: Case-Based Reasoning: A Textbook. Springer, Heidelberg (2016). https://doi.org/10.1007/978-3-540-71544-3
39. Ruge, L., Cassens, J., Kindsmüller, M.C., Herczeg, M.: Steps towards a system for inferring the interruptibility status of knowledge workers. In: Proceedings of the First International Conference on Intelligent Interactive Technologies and Multimedia – IITM 2010, pp. 250–253. ACM, New York, NY, USA (2010). https://doi.org/10.1145/1963564.1963608
40. Ruge, L., Kindsmüller, M.C., Cassens, J., Herczeg, M.: How about a mate for awareness in teams? In: Cassens, J., Wegener, R., Kofod-Petersen, A. (eds.) Proceedings of the Seventh International Workshop on Modelling and Reasoning in Context, pp. 58–69. Karlsruhe, Germany (2011)
41. Salvucci, D.D., Bogunovich, P.: Multitasking and monotasking: the effects of mental workload on deferred task interruptions. In: CHI 2010: Proceedings of the SIGCHI Conference on Human Factors in Computing Systems, pp. 85–88. ACM (2010). https://doi.org/10.1145/1753326.1753339
42. Schoenborn, J.M., Weber, R.O., Aha, D.W., Cassens, J., Althoff, K.D.: Explainable case-based reasoning: a survey. In: Proceedings for the Explainable Agency in AI Workshop at AAAI 2021. The Internet (2021)
43. Shiratori, S., Fujimoto, Y., Fujita, K.: Predicting uninterruptible durations of office workers by using probabilistic work continuance model. IEICE Trans. Inf. Syst. **E103.D**, 838–849 (2020). https://doi.org/10.1587/transinf.2019EDP7168
44. Siegle, G.J., Ichikawa, N., Steinhauer, S.: Blink before and after you think: blinks occur prior to and following cognitive load indexed by pupillary responses. Psychophysiology **45**(5), 679–687 (2008). https://doi.org/10.1111/j.1469-8986.2008.00681.x
45. Szalma, J.L., Hancock, P.A.: Noise effects on human performance: a meta-analytic synthesis. Psychol. Bull. **137**(4), 682–707 (2011). https://doi.org/10.1037/a0023987
46. Sørmo, F., Cassens, J., Aamodt, A.: Explanation in case-based reasoning - perspectives and goals. Artif. Intell. Rev. **24**(2), 109–143 (2005). https://doi.org/10.1007/s10462-005-4607-7
47. Woodard, K., Markwell, L., Beck, A., Porter, J.: Heart rate is distinctly influenced by complexity of instructions and direction of attentional focus. Int. J. Motor Control Learn. **4**(3), 1–4 (2022). https://doi.org/10.52547/ijmcl.4.3.1

IceCBR: Climate-Shift-Aware Case Adaptation for Non-stationary Arctic Sea-Ice Forecasting

Wei Wang[1], Weidong Yang[1(✉)], Xing Liu[1], Xing Xing[1], and Wenfang Cheng[2]

[1] School of Computer Science, Fudan University, Shanghai, China
wdyang@fudan.edu.cn
[2] Polar Research Institute of China, Shanghai, China

Abstract. Accurate and interpretable forecasting of Arctic sea ice remains challenging because temporal non-stationarity and evolving climate regimes can weaken forecasting strategies based on fixed historical relationships. Recent deep-learning approaches achieve competitive predictive skill, but they often lack transparency and may be less reliable under evolving climate conditions. Analogue-based methods offer a physically grounded alternative, yet most rely on static similarity and fixed reuse strategies. We present a case-based reasoning (CBR) framework that extends classical analogue forecasting with climate-state-aware retrieval, Climate-Shift-Aware Adaptation (CSA-Adapt) for reuse, a revise stage with case-specific reliability weighting, and an online retain strategy under bounded memory. Experiments on monthly Arctic sea ice concentration data show progressive improvements over standard statistical and analogue baselines across the staged CBR pipeline. Notably, the resulting system remains competitive with recent deep learning baselines on RMSE and ACC under aligned 6-month target coverage and climate-input design, while trailing the strongest deep-learning baseline on MAE and IIEE. Overall, the results indicate that carefully designed CBR systems can provide an interpretable forecasting framework under climate drift, offering a transparent alternative to black-box models without requiring claims of uniform superiority. Code and the forecast results are available at https://github.com/WeiWang31/ice_cbr.

Keywords: Case-based reasoning · Arctic sea-ice forecasting · analogue forecasting · climate non-stationarity

1 Introduction

Arctic sea-ice forecasting is a challenging prediction problem under non-stationarity. Long-term sea-ice decline, regionally heterogeneous change, and occasional extreme years mean that a historically similar month may still be associated with a future sea-ice field from the wrong climate background [11,20,23,24,30]. In this setting, the main difficulty is not merely to retrieve precedent, but to reuse it without introducing climate-shift bias.

L. Malburg and K. Bach (Eds.): ICCBR 2026, LNAI 16780, pp. 439–454, 2027.
https://doi.org/10.1007/978-3-032-33865-5_27

This problem exposes limitations at both ends of current practice. Black-box forecasting models and recent machine-learning correction models can achieve strong predictive skill, but often provide limited case-level interpretability [2,12,31,32]. Traditional analogue forecasting is transparent and naturally precedent-based, yet its reuse step is typically too coarse for a drifting Arctic climate. Even with global detrending, the correction is applied uniformly, while observed changes vary substantially across regions and seasons, especially near the ice edge [10]. This mismatch motivates a formulation in which adaptation, revision, and retention are treated as integral components rather than auxiliary adjustments.

We introduce IceCBR, a lifecycle-aware case-based system for non-stationary Arctic sea-ice forecasting. We predict sea ice concentration (SIC), the fraction of a grid cell covered by sea ice, at a future *target month* given the current *issue month*, with *lead time* denoting the months between them. From predicted SIC fields, we derive the ice edge as the 0.15 contour separating open water from ice-covered ocean. Building on *analogue forecasting*, which retrieves similar historical states and reuses their realized futures as evidence, we extend this into a full case-based reasoning cycle under climate drift. Retrieval uses similarity over SIC, climate context, and recent history. Reuse applies Climate-Shift-Aware Adaptation (CSA-Adapt) to shift retrieved fields toward query target-time means via region- and month-specific corrections. Revise down-weights unreliable cases when retrieval exhibits strong disagreement. Retain stores forecast-outcome episodes, enabling reuse of newer climate-regime experience in expanding-window evaluation.

We evaluate IceCBR with a monthly expanding-window protocol, where each issue month is predicted using only the historical prefix available at that time. Reported results are aggregated over the shared target-month window 2016/01–2023/12 and use the same target coverage, forecast horizon, and metrics as recent sea-ice benchmark work. Across the study, performance improves progressively as climate-shift-aware reuse, revise, and retain are added to the baseline analogue pipeline, with the largest CBR-stage gain appearing when coarse reuse is replaced by localized CSA-Adapt. Under matched target coverage and climate-input design, the resulting system shows a competitive trade-off against strong deep-learning baselines in the 6-month setting, with its strongest relative performance on RMSE and ACC rather than on MAE and IIEE.

Contributions.

- We cast Arctic sea-ice forecasting under climate drift as a full case-based reasoning problem, moving beyond retrieval-only analogue forecasting to a complete retrieve–reuse–revise–retain formulation.
- We propose IceCBR, a lifecycle-aware CBR framework centered on Climate-Shift-Aware Adaptation (CSA-Adapt), with disagreement-aware revision and online bounded-memory retention to support forecasting under non-stationarity.
- Under a monthly expanding-window evaluation, we show that these CBR stages progressively improve the analogue baseline, with the largest downstream CBR-stage gain appearing when coarse reuse is replaced by localized

CSA-Adapt, and the full system remaining competitive with strong deep-learning baselines at the 6-month horizon.

2 Related Work and Background

Case-based reasoning (CBR) formulates problem solving as a cycle of retrieval, reuse, revision, and retention [1,15,22]. In this framework, adaptation is central because retrieved cases often require modification before they can be applied to current conditions [7,33]. Prior work has also emphasized that retrieval may need to anticipate adaptation difficulty [26], and that retention and other case-base maintenance operations are important for preserving competence over time [14,25,27]. These issues become especially important under environmental drift, where historical cases may remain informative even as their stored solutions become progressively misaligned with present conditions.

Analogue forecasting has long been used in atmospheric and climate prediction [9,17], and remains attractive in Arctic sea-ice forecasting because it is transparent and directly grounded in historical precedent [16]. Strong reference systems include climatology, persistence, damped persistence [3], initialized seasonal forecasts [4,6,29], and more recent deep-learning or hybrid models [2,12,21,31,32]. Beyond the cryosphere, precedent-based methods demonstrate broader value for transparent decision support. For instance, Delaney et al. [8] combine k-NN augmentation with explanation-oriented forecasting in dairy production. However, most analogue and k-nearest-neighbor approaches remain largely retrieval-centric: they retrieve similar historical states and aggregate their associated futures, often with only coarse global adjustment. Under Arctic climate drift, this is restrictive because long-term sea-ice decline, regional and seasonal heterogeneity, and evolving ice-edge predictability mean that a precedent from an earlier climate regime may still encode a useful spatial pattern while its stored future is biased relative to the present background [5,10,20,24]. Recency weighting, global detrending, and heuristic preference for recent analogues only partly address this mismatch because the required correction is neither spatially nor seasonally uniform. Building on the success of such interpretable approaches, our work addresses this gap by formulating sea-ice forecasting as CBR under climate drift, where reuse requires explicit adaptation of historical solutions, revision moderates unreliable case contributions, and retention incorporates newly observed forecast–outcome episodes.

3 Problem Formulation and Case Representation

We study monthly Arctic sea-ice forecasting on the 25 km NSIDC Sea Ice Polar Stereographic North grid [18,19]. Let $Y_t \in [0,1]^{H\times W}$ denote the observed SIC field at month t, where H and W are the spatial dimensions. For an issue month t and a target lead time $\tau \in \{1,\dots,6\}$, the objective is to predict the future field $Y_{t+\tau}$.

We cast this task in a case-based reasoning (CBR) framework, where each historical episode links an issue-time state to its realized future. To balance spatial interpretability and computational efficiency, the issue-time state is represented by compact regional descriptors, while the stored solution remains the full SIC field.

Let $\mathcal{R}$ denote the set of sea-ice regions under the NSIDC-0780 scheme [18], and let $R = |\mathcal{R}|$. The problem description at issue time t is

$$P_t = \{z_{ice,t}^{(r)}, z_{bg,t}^{(r)}, h_t^{(r)}\}_{r=1}^{R}, \tag{1}$$

where for each region r, $z_{ice,t}^{(r)}$ and $z_{bg,t}^{(r)}$ are low-dimensional vectors encoding the current SIC state and auxiliary background-climate features, and $h_t^{(r)}$ summarizes recent temporal evolution.

The associated solution at lead τ is the realized future SIC field

$$S_{t,\tau} = Y_{t+\tau}. \tag{2}$$

A case is therefore defined as $C_{t,\tau} = (P_t, S_{t,\tau})$. Forecasting proceeds by matching the current query state against a case memory and reusing relevant historical precedents.

Climate Drift. The main difficulty in long-range Arctic forecasting is non-stationarity. Because sea ice has declined over time and the magnitude of change differs across regions and seasons [20,24,30], the relationship between issue-time conditions and future SIC fields is not stable. As a result, a historical case may remain similar to the current query in problem space while its stored solution reflects an outdated climate background. IceCBR is designed for this setting: historical precedents can still provide useful structural information, but their stored futures must be corrected for target-time climate-shift mismatch before reuse.

4 Method

4.1 Framework Overview

IceCBR treats monthly Arctic sea-ice forecasting as a full case-based reasoning process in which each historical episode links an issue-time state to the SIC field realized several months later. A case therefore contains a problem description, summarizing the sea-ice and climate background at the issue month, and a solution consisting of the observed future SIC field at the requested lead time. For each region, the problem description summarizes three complementary aspects of the issue-time state: the current sea-ice configuration, the large-scale atmospheric and oceanic background, and short recent temporal evolution. This regional organization keeps matching interpretable under heterogeneous Arctic drift while leaving the final output as a full gridded SIC forecast.

Figure 1 summarizes the workflow. On the left, each case is represented over the NSIDC-0780 sea-ice regions adopted here [18], which summarize issue-time

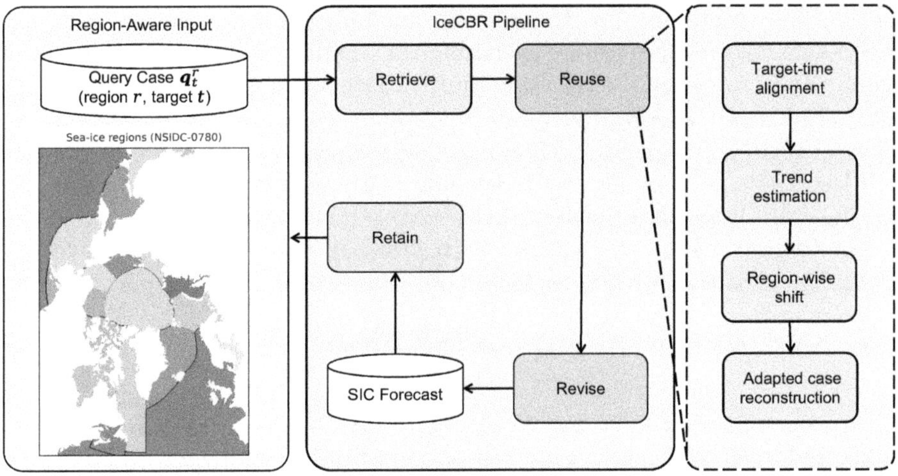

Fig. 1. IceCBR pipeline. A region-aware query is processed through retrieve, reuse, revise, and retain. The reuse stage performs target-time climate-shift-aware adaptation, while revise and retain adjust case weights and update the case base over time.

sea-ice conditions, climate background, and short recent history. On the right, IceCBR separates the full cycle into retrieval, target-time adaptation of retrieved solutions, disagreement-aware revision of the adapted case set, and online retention of newly verified forecast–outcome episodes in a bounded memory. The key methodological challenge is that under climate drift, a historically similar issue-time state does not guarantee that the future SIC field stored in that case remains directly reusable. This organization makes the method a complete CBR system rather than a static analogue model with a single correction layer, while preserving the explanation-oriented advantages usually associated with precedent-based reasoning [28].

4.2 Retrieval

Given a query Q_t at issue month t and lead τ, retrieval searches the case base for the K cases whose issue-time conditions most closely resemble Q_t. Each candidate C_i stores the observed state at its own issue time and the SIC field $S_{i,\tau}$ realized τ months later.

The Arctic domain is partitioned into predefined regions $\mathcal{R}$ (NSIDC-0780). For each region r, the similarity between Q_t and C_i combines three terms:

$$s_{i,r} = w_{\text{ice}}\ \phi_{\text{ice}}(Q_t, C_i, r) + w_{\text{bg}}\ \phi_{\text{bg}}(Q_t, C_i, r) + w_{\text{hist}}\ \phi_{\text{hist}}(Q_t, C_i, r). \tag{3}$$

The SIC term ϕ_{ice} and background term ϕ_{bg} are both cosine similarities computed in region-specific PCA spaces (5 and 3 retained components, respectively), where PCA bases are fitted on the expanding training prefix at each issue date.

The SIC representation uses the regional anomaly field; the background representation is formed by spatially averaging the auxiliary climate variables within region r and projecting the resulting multivariate anomaly onto a separate PCA basis. The history term $\phi_{\text{hist}} = 1/(1+|h_t^{(r)} - h_i^{(r)}|)$ compares trailing three-month slopes of regional mean SIC. All climatologies and projections are recomputed from the available training prefix, keeping retrieval leakage-free. Weights w_{ice}, w_{bg}, w_{hist} are listed in Table 1.

The case-level score averages across regions, $s_i = \frac{1}{|\mathcal{R}|}\sum_r s_{i,r}$, and the top-$K$ set $\mathcal{N}_K(Q_t, \tau)$ is converted to weights via softmax with temperature $\rho > 0$:

$$\alpha_i = \frac{\exp(\rho\, s_i)}{\sum_{C_j \in \mathcal{N}_K(Q_t,\tau)} \exp(\rho\, s_j)}. \tag{4}$$

The analogue forecast is $\hat{Y}_{t+\tau} = \sum_{C_i \in \mathcal{N}_K(Q_t,\tau)} \alpha_i\, S_{i,\tau}$, where $S_{i,\tau}$ is the full SIC field stored in C_i. This predictor is transparent but has a fundamental limitation under climate drift: a retrieved case may capture a useful spatial pattern while its stored future reflects an outdated climate mean. The reuse stage addresses this mismatch.

4.3 Reuse (CSA-Adapt)

The reuse component of IceCBR is Climate-Shift-Aware Adaptation (CSA-Adapt), a case-adaptation rule that adjusts retrieved solutions at the forecast target time. Retrieval is climate-state-aware because background variables guide case selection, whereas reuse is climate-shift-aware because it corrects long-term SIC drift. Under non-stationarity, a close match in problem space does not guarantee that the stored solution remains appropriate: a retrieved case may match the current issue-time state while its future reflects an earlier climate regime. IceCBR therefore adapts each retrieved future field toward the query target-time SIC mean state before aggregation, rather than correcting only the final forecast.

Instead of a coarse pan-Arctic detrend, CSA-Adapt performs a structured reuse procedure that aligns case and query target times, estimates region- and calendar-month-specific SIC trends, and applies a region-wise target-time shift. For each region r and month m, a linear SIC shift trend is fitted as

$$T^{(r,m)}(s) = a^{(r,m)} s + b^{(r,m)}, \tag{5}$$

where s denotes the target-time index. Trends are re-estimated from the expanding training prefix at each issue date to avoid look-ahead leakage.

For a query at time t with lead τ, let (s_q, m_q) denote the target-time index and month of $t + \tau$, and (s_i, m_i) those of a retrieved case C_i. Let $S_{i,\tau}^{(r)}$ be the regional subfield of the retrieved future. The adapted contribution in region r is

$$\tilde{S}_{i,\tau}^{(r)} = S_{i,\tau}^{(r)} - T^{(r,m_i)}(s_i) + T^{(r,m_q)}(s_q). \tag{6}$$

This removes the case-specific target-time mean state and adds the query-specific one. The same scalar offset is applied within each region, preserving intra-region spatial patterns while correcting region-level mean-state mismatch.

Applying this correction across regions yields the adapted full-field solution $\tilde{S}_{i,\tau}$, and the final forecast is

$$\hat{Y}_{t+\tau}^{\text{CSA-Adapt}} = \sum_{C_i \in \mathcal{N}_K(Q_t,\tau)} \alpha_i \, \tilde{S}_{i,\tau}. \tag{7}$$

CSA-Adapt thus preserves precedent-based interpretability while introducing explicit adaptation for reuse under climate drift.

4.4 Revise and Retain

Even after CSA-Adapt, retrieved cases need not be equally reliable. Revise therefore reweights adapted cases before final aggregation according to their internal disagreement over the active forecast domain. Let $\{\tilde{S}_{i,\tau}\}_{C_i \in \mathcal{N}_K(Q_t,\tau)}$ denote the adapted case solutions. IceCBR computes their variance map and defines a disagreement region $\Omega_{t,\tau}$ from the high-variance active cells. A consensus field is then formed by the median across adapted cases,

$$M_{t,\tau}(x) = \text{median}_{C_i \in \mathcal{N}_K(Q_t,\tau)} \, \tilde{S}_{i,\tau}(x), \tag{8}$$

and each case is scored by its mean absolute deviation from that consensus over $\Omega_{t,\tau}$:

$$d_i = \frac{1}{|\Omega_{t,\tau}|} \sum_{x \in \Omega_{t,\tau}} \left| \tilde{S}_{i,\tau}(x) - M_{t,\tau}(x) \right|. \tag{9}$$

This deviation is converted into a reliability factor

$$r_i = \exp\left(-\beta \frac{d_i}{\lambda_{t,\tau}} \right), \tag{10}$$

where $\lambda_{t,\tau}$ is a query-specific disagreement scale and β controls downweighting strength. The revised aggregation weights are

$$\alpha_i' = \frac{\alpha_i r_i}{\sum_j \alpha_j r_j}. \tag{11}$$

Revise thus acts as a local reliability-aware correction layer on top of reuse rather than as a separate predictive model.

Retain closes the CBR cycle once the verifying observation becomes available. Each verified forecast–outcome episode preserves the original issue-time case description together with the realized SIC field at the same lead time, and is assigned a usefulness score based on post-hoc quantities available at verification, including forecast error, disagreement level, recency, and adaptation magnitude. Retained episodes are managed separately for each lead time and can affect only later issue times in the expanding-window evaluation. IceCBR uses this score for bounded online case-base maintenance under climate drift, with representative replacement based on usefulness and recency; the detailed retention policy is summarized in Table 1.

Table 1. Key configuration for the main CBR experiments.

Group	Component	Setting
General	Lead times	1–6 months
	Training	Monthly expanding window
	Regions	NSIDC-0780
Retrieval	Neighbors K	7
	Weighting	Softmax ($\rho = 2.0$)
	Weights	Ice 0.5 / Background 0.3 / Hist 0.2
Representation	SIC PCA	5 per region
	Background PCA	3 per region
Reuse	Trend model	Linear (region $\times$ month)
	Evaluation time	Target month
Revise	Disagreement	Top 0.9 quantile (active cells)
	Downweight strength β	2.0
	Min reliability	0.05
Retain	Update	After verification (online)
	Representative memory	2 per lead
	Priority	0.7 usefulness + 0.3 recency
	Admission	Rank-based (no threshold)

5 Evaluation

Our target variable is monthly Arctic SIC from the NSIDC passive-microwave Climate Data Record (CDR), version 4, on the 25 km NSIDC Sea Ice Polar Stereographic North grid [19]. The record spans January 1979 through December 2023. To characterize the large-scale climate state at each issue time, we augment SIC with atmospheric reanalysis from ERA5 [13] and ocean reanalysis from ORAS5 [35]. The atmospheric variables describe circulation, temperature, radiation, and near-surface wind, while the ocean variables capture upper-ocean thermal conditions and mixed-layer structure.

We follow the 6-month SIC+Climate configuration used in IceMamba, where alternative input combinations are evaluated empirically, and keep the predictor set fixed across all methods to ensure comparability [31]. All auxiliary fields are regridded to the SIC grid, converted to anomalies using only past information available at each issue time, and normalized following the IceMamba preprocessing convention. These variables make retrieval climate-state-aware by informing case selection rather than prediction targets; the reuse-stage target-time adjustment in CSA-Adapt is instead driven by region- and month-specific SIC dynamics and is therefore climate-shift-aware.

5.1 Baselines and Variants

Table 2 summarizes all compared methods. We group them into three families: (i) statistical baselines (Climatology and Damped persistence), (ii) a staged analogue-to-CBR progression, and (iii) three deep-learning models (SICNet [21], IceDiff [34], and IceMamba [31]) evaluated at the shared 6-month SIC+Climate horizon. The analogue and CBR variants are arranged as controlled comparisons, so that each successive variant adds one forecasting capability while leaving the earlier components unchanged as far as possible.

The staged progression begins with Traditional Analogue (SIC-only), which uses global SIC-only analogue retrieval, and Enhanced Analogue (SIC+BG+Hist), which keeps the same global structure but adds background-climate and recent-history inputs. Regional Retrieval (No Reuse) then introduces the regional retrieval design while keeping the same SIC+BG+Hist inputs and still omitting reuse. On top of this shared regional retrieval backbone, CBR–Reuse (global detrend) adds a coarse pan-Arctic target-time correction, whereas CBR–Reuse (CSA-Adapt) replaces that rule with localized climate-shift-aware reuse. CBR–Reuse+Revise adds disagreement-aware reweighting without changing retrieval or adaptation, and IceCBR adds online bounded-memory retain on top of the same retrieve–reuse–revise pipeline.

All CBR variants use a monthly expanding-window backtest over 2016/01–2023/12. In this setting, the expanding-window protocol is a form of rolling refitting: at each issue month, the CBR system is re-estimated using only the historical prefix available at that time. The deep-learning baselines use the same SIC+Climate predictors and are evaluated on the same effective test coverage, but are trained under a different protocol: a single train/validation/test partition without rolling refitting. We therefore treat them as task-aligned external references under matched inputs, forecast horizon, and test targets, rather than as fully protocol-matched comparisons under identical retraining or temporal-adaptation settings. Accordingly, the DL comparison is intended to show performance under aligned forecasting targets and input design, not to claim strict equivalence of training dynamics, update frequency, or adaptation opportunity across model families. Table 1 lists the shared CBR configuration.

5.2 Metrics

We report mean absolute error (MAE), root mean squared error (RMSE), anomaly correlation coefficient (ACC), and integrated ice-edge error (IIEE). Unless otherwise stated, all metrics are computed over ocean grid points only and are aggregated across lead-time and target-month bins.

MAE and RMSE. For a forecast field $\hat{Y}$ and observed SIC field Y over N ocean grid cells,

$$\mathrm{MAE} = \frac{1}{N} \sum_{i=1}^{N} \left| \hat{Y}^{(i)} - Y^{(i)} \right|, \tag{12}$$

$$\text{RMSE} = \sqrt{\frac{1}{N}\sum_{i=1}^{N}\left(\hat{Y}^{(i)} - Y^{(i)}\right)^2}. \tag{13}$$

ACC. ACC measures how well the forecast captures the temporal variability of SIC anomalies relative to the observations. It is computed as the temporal anomaly correlation at each ocean grid cell and then spatially averaged:

$$\text{ACC} = \frac{\sum_t \left(\hat{Y}(t) - \overline{\hat{Y}}\right)\left(Y(t) - \overline{Y}\right)}{\sqrt{\sum_t \left(\hat{Y}(t) - \overline{\hat{Y}}\right)^2}\sqrt{\sum_t \left(Y(t) - \overline{Y}\right)^2}}, \tag{14}$$

where $\overline{\hat{Y}}$ and $\overline{Y}$ are temporal means at that grid point.

IIEE. To measure ice-edge displacement, SIC is thresholded at SIC > 0.15 to obtain forecasted and observed ice-covered sets SIE_f and SIE_o. We then compute

$$\text{IIEE} = |SIE_f \cup SIE_o| - |SIE_f \cap SIE_o|, \tag{15}$$

reported in million km^2.

5.3 Main Results

Table 2 reports the main comparison at the 6-month horizon over the shared effective target coverage of 2016/01–2023/12. The table is best read as a staged ladder. After the statistical and deep-learning references, the seven analogue-to-CBR variants isolate the effects of input enrichment, retrieval design, reuse, revise, and retain. This organization matters because the gains are not attributable to a single component alone, but accumulate across multiple stages.

The first two transitions isolate the retrieval side. Moving from Traditional Analogue (SIC-only) to Enhanced Analogue (SIC+BG+Hist) improves all four metrics, showing that background climate and recent-history inputs already strengthen analogue forecasting before any adaptation is introduced. Moving from Enhanced Analogue to Regional Retrieval (No Reuse) yields a further improvement while keeping the SIC+BG+Hist inputs fixed, so this step isolates the benefit of changing retrieval from a global analogue rule to the regional retrieval design.

The next four transitions isolate the downstream CBR stages. Relative to Regional Retrieval (No Reuse), CBR–Reuse (global detrend) adds a coarse pan-Arctic target-time correction on top of the same retrieval and improves RMSE from 0.1079 to 0.1044, IIEE from 1.9898 to 1.8576 million km^2, and ACC from 0.6023 to 0.6100. Replacing that coarse reuse rule with CBR–Reuse (CSA-Adapt) yields a much larger gain, lowering RMSE to 0.0928 and IIEE to 1.4753 while raising ACC to 0.6576. Within the downstream CBR stages, replacing CBR–Reuse (global detrend) with CBR–Reuse (CSA-Adapt) gives the largest gain,

Table 2. Main comparison at the 6-month horizon over the shared effective target coverage 2016/01–2023/12. Arrows indicate the preferred direction; IIEE is reported in million km^2.

Method	MAE ↓	RMSE ↓	IIEE ↓	ACC ↑
Climatology	0.0339	0.1086	1.9533	0.6667
Damped persistence	0.0358	0.1072	1.7517	0.6161
SICNet	0.0321	0.1130	1.3578	0.5252
IceDiff	0.0327	0.1087	1.3974	0.5497
IceMamba	0.0249	0.0950	1.1033	0.6396
Traditional Analogue (SIC-only)	0.0562	0.1500	2.6856	0.4225
Enhanced Analogue (SIC+BG+Hist)	0.0489	0.1325	2.3579	0.5175
Regional Retrieval (No Reuse)	0.0374	0.1079	1.9898	0.6023
CBR–Reuse (global detrend)	0.0359	0.1044	1.8576	0.6100
CBR–Reuse (CSA-Adapt)	0.0320	0.0928	1.4753	0.6576
CBR–Reuse+Revise	0.0299	0.0930	1.3393	0.6552
IceCBR	0.0292	0.0905	1.3096	0.6689

indicating that localized climate-shift-aware reuse is more effective than a single global detrending rule under the present evaluation setting. Adding Revise then changes neither retrieval nor reuse, but reweights adapted cases according to internal disagreement; this mainly improves MAE and IIEE while leaving RMSE nearly unchanged and slightly reducing ACC. Finally, IceCBR adds Retain on top of the same retrieval–reuse–revise pipeline and yields a further consistent improvement, reducing MAE to 0.0292, RMSE to 0.0905, and IIEE to 1.3096 while increasing ACC to 0.6689.

Against recent deep-learning baselines, IceCBR exhibits a metric-dependent trade-off rather than uniform dominance. It achieves the best RMSE overall and the highest ACC, including a higher ACC than IceMamba, while IceMamba remains strongest on MAE and IIEE. We therefore position IceCBR as a competitive and interpretable alternative under aligned target coverage and climate-input design, rather than as universally superior across all metrics.

5.4 Ablations and Qualitative Analysis

The main results show that performance improves steadily along the staged progression, but they do not by themselves explain whether the larger downstream gain is better explained by retrieval or by reuse. This subsection therefore focuses on that question by comparing CBR–Reuse (CSA-Adapt) directly against CBR–Reuse (global detrend) under the same regional retrieval design.

Figure 2 traces one forecast episode at the case level. Rather than only comparing forecast maps, the figure exposes the retrieved precedents, their final aggregation weights, and the effect of target-time adaptation. The most infor-

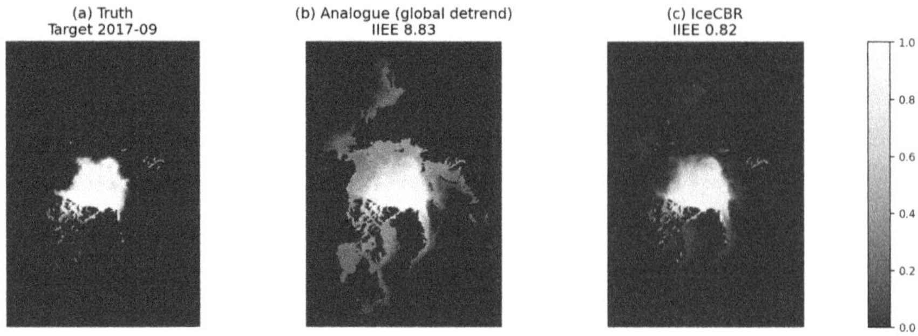

(d) Case trace: retrieved precedents, final weights, and adaptation effect

Retrieved case	Similarity	Final weight	Adaptation Δ extent	Dominant region
2016-05→2016-09	0.562	0.159	-0.004	Central Arctic
2015-05→2015-09	0.558	0.158	-0.043	Central Arctic
2006-10→2007-02	0.498	0.140	-5.245	East Siberian Sea

The 2006-10→2007-02 precedent receives the largest target-time correction, supporting reuse-stage adaptation as the main source of improvement.

Fig. 2. Case-level analysis of an illustrative forecast episode. Panels (a)–(c) compare the verifying observation, CBR–Reuse (global detrend), and IceCBR. Panel (d) traces the top retrieved precedents, their final aggregation weights, and their target-time adaptation effects. An older historical precedent receives the largest correction.

mative pattern is that an older historical precedent receives the largest correction while still retaining substantial weight in the final forecast. This is consistent with the intended role of localized climate-shift-aware reuse: the improvement comes from making historically useful but target-time-misaligned solutions usable again, not from changing the retrieval set itself.

Table 3 shows that this pattern is not confined to a single example. The top-improvement cases span multiple lead times, and all six improve simultaneously on both IIEE and RMSE relative to CBR–Reuse (global detrend). In several cases, the dominant adapted precedent comes from materially earlier years, including 2006/10→2007/02 for the 2017/05→2017/09 query and 2010/07→2010/09 for the 2023/07→2023/09 query. This visible temporal offset supports the same interpretation as the case study: target-time adaptation can recover informative historical futures even when they are subject to target-time climate-shift mismatch. The qualitative example in Fig. 2 should therefore be read as illustrative of a broader reuse pattern rather than as an isolated episode.

The retrieval-side ablations reinforce this interpretation. A recency-decayed retrieval variant performs substantially worse, suggesting that useful precedents cannot be restricted to the most recent years under ongoing climate drift. A climate-state-gated retrieval variant remains closer to the proposed method, but still does not surpass it. Taken together, these results indicate that richer retrieval context is helpful, but retrieval refinements alone do not explain the main gain. Within the downstream CBR stages, the larger improvement is associated with localized target-time reuse, with Revise and Retain providing smaller downstream refinements. This analysis also clarifies the source of IceCBR's interpretability. Forecasts can be inspected through explicit retrieved precedents, adaptation magnitudes, and final aggregation weights, so the mechanism behind an individual prediction remains visible at the case level even when the full pipeline includes reuse, revise, and online retain.

Table 3. Top six cases with the largest improvements under the transition from CBR–Reuse (global detrend) to CBR–Reuse (CSA-Adapt). Positive values indicate gains relative to CBR–Reuse (global detrend). Query and dominant-precedent entries are shown as issue→target month pairs to preserve temporal offsets and seasonal structure.

Query	Lead	ΔIIEE	ΔRMSE	Dominant precedent	Adaptation Δ extent
2017-05→2017-09	4	6.15	0.0438	2006-10→2007-02	-5.245
2017-05→2017-08	3	5.43	0.0318	2006-10→2007-01	-4.868
2017-04→2017-09	5	4.80	0.0227	2007-04→2007-09	-0.158
2017-04→2017-08	4	4.73	0.0251	2007-04→2007-08	-0.279
2023-07→2023-09	2	4.29	0.0242	2010-07→2010-09	-0.258
2022-04→2022-09	5	3.80	0.0331	2021-02→2021-07	-0.904

5.5 CBR Progression Across Lead Time and Target Month

Table 2 reports overall averages, but those means do not show whether the staged gains are uniform across forecast lead time and seasonal target month. Figure 3 addresses this by decomposing the same comparison along both axes.

The retrieval-side progression is relatively broad. Moving from Traditional Analogue (SIC-only) to Enhanced Analogue (SIC+BG+Hist), and then to Regional Retrieval (No Reuse), yields the clearest RMSE and IIEE gains at short-to-mid leads, with weaker but still generally positive improvements at the longest lead. Across target months, these gains remain visible across much of the seasonal cycle rather than being confined to a narrow window. This suggests that richer inputs and regional retrieval mainly strengthen the overall forecasting backbone.

The downstream CBR stages are more differentiated. Adding CBR–Reuse (global detrend) to Regional Retrieval (No Reuse) yields only small and uneven improvements, whereas replacing it with CBR–Reuse (CSA-Adapt) produces the first broadly visible downstream gain. The effect is clearest for RMSE at leads 3–5 and for IIEE at leads 4–5, with stronger month-wise improvements in October–February than in March–May. CBR–Reuse+Revise mainly stabilizes IIEE rather than further reducing RMSE, consistent with its role as a reliability-weighting step, while IceCBR adds a final but smaller refinement through Retain. Figure 3 therefore complements Table 2 by showing that the gains are not only cumulative, but also unevenly distributed across lead time and target month.

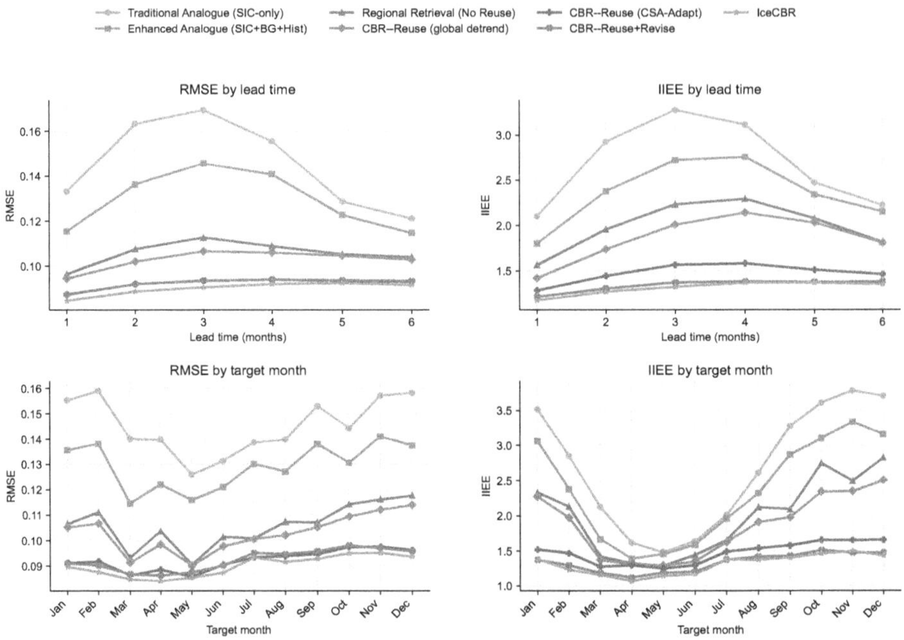

Fig. 3. Staged comparison across forecast lead time and target month for RMSE and IIEE. The figure shows where gains from retrieval, reuse, revise, and retain emerge beyond the overall averages reported in Table 2.

6 Discussion and Conclusion

Arctic sea-ice forecasting is inherently non-stationary: historical analogues remain informative, but their realized futures are not directly reusable under persistent climate drift [20,24]. This makes the problem well suited to a full case-based reasoning formulation rather than retrieval-only analogue forecasting. In this work, we instantiate all four CBR stages for monthly SIC prediction, combining climate-state-aware retrieval, climate-shift-aware reuse through CSA-Adapt, case-specific revision, and bounded-memory retention. Empirically, this staged design improves progressively over statistical and analogue baselines and remains competitive with recent deep-learning models at the 6-month horizon on RMSE and ACC, while preserving transparent case-level diagnostics and interpretable failure modes [2,31].

At the same time, the present study has clear scope limits. Our system is restricted to monthly SIC forecasting, uses deliberately simple adaptation and retention mechanisms, and compares CBR and deep-learning baselines under aligned tasks and inputs rather than fully identical training protocols. In particular, the current reuse rule is region-level: each region receives a single scalar target-time offset, so finer intra-region drift heterogeneity is not modeled explicitly. The deep-learning comparison should therefore be interpreted as task-aligned rather than protocol-matched: IceCBR is competitive on RMSE and ACC in the current setting, but still trails IceMamba on MAE and IIEE. In addition, although the staged gains are consistent in the main aggregate comparisons, we do not claim exhaustive paired statistical superiority across every metric, lead time, and target-month subset in the present page budget. Future work can extend the framework with richer multivariate predictors, more flexible similarity and adaptation functions, stronger significance analysis, and tighter neural–CBR hybrids. Overall, the results suggest that analogue forecasting under climate drift can be strengthened by moving beyond static retrieval toward a full CBR pipeline with adaptation, revision, and case-base maintenance.

Acknowledgements. This research was supported by Shanghai's Key Technology Development Program, under the project 'Intelligent Integrated Arctic Ice-Snow-Atmosphere Observation Platform and Short-to Medium-Term High-Precision Sea Ice Forecasting' (Grant No. 25DZ3102600).

GenAI Statement. Generative AI tools were used for limited language refinement and editorial assistance during manuscript preparation. The authors reviewed and verified the final text and remain fully responsible for the scientific content, experimental results, and conclusions.

References

1. Aamodt, A., Plaza, E.: Case-based reasoning: foundational issues, methodological variations, and system approaches. AI Commun. **7**(1), 39–59 (1994)
2. Andersson, T.R., et al.: Seasonal arctic sea ice forecasting with probabilistic deep learning. Nat. Commun. **12**(1), 5124 (2021)
3. Blanchard-Wrigglesworth, E., et al.: Persistence and inherent predictability of arctic sea ice in a GCM ensemble and observations. J. Clim. **24**(1), 231–250 (2011)
4. Bushuk, M., et al.: Skillful regional prediction of arctic sea ice on seasonal timescales. Geophys. Res. Lett. **44**(10), 4953–4964 (2017)
5. Bushuk, M., et al.: A mechanism for the arctic sea ice spring predictability barrier. Geophy. Res. Lett. **47**(13), e2020GL088335 (2020)
6. Bushuk, M., et al.: Predicting September arctic sea ice: a multimodel seasonal skill comparison. Bull. Am. Meteor. Soc. **105**(7), E1170–E1203 (2024)
7. Craw, S., Wiratunga, N., Rowe, R.: Learning adaptation knowledge to improve case-based reasoning. Artif. Intell. **170**(16–17), 1175–1192 (2006)
8. Delaney, E., et al.: Forecasting for sustainable dairy produce. In: Case-Based Reasoning Research and Development. Lecture Notes in Computer Science, vol. 13341, pp. 365–379. Springer (2022)
9. van den Dool, H.M.: Searching for analogues, how long must we wait? Tellus A **46**(3), 314–324 (1994)
10. Goessling, H.F., et al.: Predictability of the arctic sea ice edge. Geophys. Res. Lett. **43**(4), 1642–1650 (2016)
11. Guemas, V., et al.: A review on arctic sea-ice predictability and prediction on seasonal to decadal time-scales. Q. J. R. Meteorol. Soc. **142**(695), 546–561 (2016)
12. He, Z., et al.: Correcting errors in seasonal arctic sea ice prediction of earth system models with machine learning. Cryosphere **19**(8), 3279–3293 (2025)

13. Hersbach, H., et al.: The ERA5 global reanalysis. Q. J. R. Meteorol. Soc. **146**(730), 1999–2049 (2020)
14. Juarez, J.M., et al.: Maintenance of case bases: current algorithms after fifty years. In: IJCAI, pp. 5457–5468 (2018)
15. Kolodner, J.L.: Case-Based Reasoning. Morgan Kaufmann, San Mateo, CA (1993)
16. Lin, Y., et al.: Optimization of the k-nearest-neighbors model for summer arctic sea ice prediction. Front. Mar. Sci. **10**, 1260047 (2023)
17. Lorenz, E.N.: Atmospheric predictability as revealed by naturally occurring analogues. J. Atmos. Sci. **26**(4), 636–646 (1969)
18. Meier, W.N., Stewart, J.S.: Arctic and Antarctic Regional Masks for Sea Ice and Related Data Products (2023). nSIDC-0780, v1
19. Meier, W.N., et al.: NOAA/NSIDC Climate Data Record of Passive Microwave Sea Ice Concentration, Version 4 (2021)
20. Notz, D., Stroeve, J.: Observed arctic sea-ice loss directly follows anthropogenic CO2 emission. Science **354**(6313), 747–750 (2016)
21. Ren, Y., et al.: SICNet_season v1.0 for seasonal arctic sea ice prediction. Geosci. Model Develop. **18**(9), 2665–2688 (2025)
22. Richter, M.M., Weber, R.: Case-Based Reasoning: A Textbook. Springer, Berlin, Heidelberg (2013)
23. Roach, L.A., Meier, W.N.: Sea ice in 2024. Nat. Rev. Earth Environment **6**(4), 252–254 (2025)
24. Serreze, M.C., Stroeve, J.: Arctic sea ice trends, variability and implications for seasonal ice forecasting. Phil. Trans. R. Soc. A **373**(2045), 20140159 (2015)
25. Smyth, B., Keane, M.T.: Remembering to forget: a competence-preserving case deletion policy. In: IJCAI, pp. 377–383 (1995)
26. Smyth, B., Keane, M.T.: Adaptation-guided retrieval: questioning the similarity assumption in reasoning. Artif. Intell. **102**(2), 249–293 (1998)
27. Smyth, B., McKenna, E.: Competence models and the maintenance problem. Comput. Intell. **17**(2), 235–249 (2001)
28. Sørmo, F., et al.: Explanation in case-based reasoning - perspectives and goals. Artif. Intell. Rev. **24**(2), 109–143 (2005)
29. Stroeve, J., et al.: Predicting September sea ice: ensemble skill of the SEARCH sea ice outlook 2008–2013. Geophys. Res. Lett. **41**(7), 2411–2418 (2014)
30. Stroeve, J.C., et al.: The arctic's rapidly shrinking sea ice cover: a research synthesis. Clim. Change **110**(3–4), 1005–1027 (2012)
31. Wang, W., et al.: Seasonal forecasting of pan-arctic sea ice with state space model. NPJ Climate Atmospheric Sci. **8**(1), 172 (2025)
32. Wei, L., Freris, N.M.: Arctic sea ice prediction based on multi-scale graph modeling with conservation laws. J. Geophy. Res. Atmospheres **130**, e2024JD042136 (2025)
33. Wilke, W., Vollrath, I., Bergmann, R.: A framework for learning adaptation knowledge based on knowledge light approaches. In: European Workshop on Advances in Case-Based Reasoning. Lecture Notes in Computer Science, vol. 1488, pp. 235–249. Springer (1998)
34. Xu, J., et al.: Icediff: High resolution and high-quality arctic sea ice forecasting with generative diffusion prior. In: CVPR, pp. 10567–10576 (2025)
35. Zuo, H., et al.: The ECMWF operational ensemble reanalysis-analysis system for ocean and sea ice: A description of the system and assessment. Ocean Sci. **15**(3), 779–808 (2019)

A Large-Small Model Coordination Framework Based on Tactical Case-Based Reasoning Reward Machine for Adversarial Game Scenarios

Wei Dong[1], Sirui Huang[2], Chong Wang[2(✉)], Guohua Zhang[3], and Yindong Ji[2]

[1] Beijing National Research Center for Information Science and Technology, Tsinghua University, Beijing 100084, China
weidong@tsinghua.edu.cn

[2] Department of Automation Tsinghua University, Beijing 100084, China
huang-sr24@mails.tsinghua.edu.cn, {wangchong,jyd}@tsinghua.edu.cn

[3] Intelligent Science and Technology Academy of CASIC, Beijing 100041, China

Abstract. In complex adversarial game scenarios, multi-agent reinforcement learning methods usually have low training efficiency due to sparse final rewards and lack of macro-tactics guidance. To solve this problem, this paper proposes a large-small model collaboration framework for adversarial games based on a tactical case-based reasoning reward machine. In the framework, a Large Language Model (LLM) is offline responsible for the maintenance of tactical cases and drives the generation of offline training data with dense reward. The small model (i.e., the reinforcement learning model trained on the generated training data) is used for online decision-making. Specifically, first, an LLM combined with Retrieval-Augmented Generation (RAG) technology is used to construct a structured tactical case library and maintain it continuously, so as to enable persistent storage and cross-situation reuse of tactical experience. Second, based on the tactical case library, a reward machine is constructed to model the execution progress and transfer logic between tactical sub-goals. Third, by training the tactical execution utility function on the augmented state space, the sparse final reward is decomposed into dense process reward. Finally, based on the dense reward dataset, the multi-agent reinforcement learning model is trained for online decision-making. Throughout this process, the tactical effects after use and verification are fed back to the tactical case library to promote its continuous optimization. The proposed framework is evaluated on the Google Research Football (GRF) simulation environment to verify its effectiveness in learning efficiency and strategy quality. The experimental results show that in the 11-vs-11 scenario, our method achieves approximately 14% points higher winning rate than the sparse reward baseline under the same number of training steps, and in the 3-vs-1 scenario, reduces the training steps required to reach a 50% winning rate by 55%–63% compared with other dense reward baselines.

L. Malburg and K. Bach (Eds.): ICCBR 2026, LNAI 16780, pp. 455–471, 2027.
https://doi.org/10.1007/978-3-032-33865-5_28

Keywords: Multi-agent Reinforcement Learning · Case-based Reasoning · Large-small Model Collaboration · Adversarial Game · Reward Machine

1 Introduction

Adversarial game scenarios, such as football, are characterized by fine-grained decision-making actions, high real-time requirements, long-term decision-making requiring macro tactical guidance, and sparse final rewards. Multi-agent reinforcement learning can effectively deal with real-time decision-making problems in a fine-grained action space. In recent years, it has been widely studied and applied in adversarial game tasks.

Taking Google Research Football (GRF) as an example, Kurach et al. [1] proposed a benchmark environment. Subsequent works, such as TiKick of Huang et al. [2], TiZero of Lin et al. [3], ACE of Li et al. [4], FoX of Jo et al. [5], and DOTO of Wang et al. [6], have improved performance from the perspectives of demonstration learning, self-play, joint value modeling, and offline-to-online migration. However, these methods mainly rely on the exploration of the reinforcement learning agent itself to discover effective strategies, lacking explicit modeling and guidance of tactical phase structures. Moreover, the agent can only receive feedback when scoring or conceding a goal. This leads to several challenges in long-term adversarial tasks, including low exploration efficiency, difficulty in credit assignment, and limited ability to reuse experience across different situations.

To address the problem of reward sparsity and credit assignment, large language models (LLMs) have provided new ideas for high-level decision-making and reward shaping in adversarial game scenarios, leveraging their rich world knowledge and semantic reasoning ability. The review by Zhang et al. [7] pointed out the potential of LLMs in strategic reasoning. Stride by Li et al. [8] enhanced the interactive decision-making ability of LLMs through tools and memory module. StrategicAI by Alkayyal et al. [9] demonstrated the value of using retrieval to enhance LLMs in complex strategic decision decomposition. In reinforcement learning, Chen et al. [10]'s URI, Pang et al. [11]'s KALM and Liu et al. [12]'s OCaL-RL attempt to use LLMs to generate knowledge, trajectories or cases to assist strategy learning. LaRe by Qu et al. [13] further used LLMs to generate multi-dimensional potential rewards, which provided a new paradigm for time credit allocation in the scenario of sparse reward. However, existing methods still have obvious deficiencies: some rely on LLM online reasoning, leading to large computational overhead and poor real-time performance; others use LLM only as a one-time policy prompter or reward generator, making the output difficult to accumulate, correct, and reuse across situations.

To address the problem of the lack of explicit modeling of tactical knowledge, Case-Based Reasoning (CBR) provides a more appropriate knowledge organization and reuse mechanism. Football tactics naturally have a case structure of "situation-intention-execution-result". Ontanón et al. [14] early demonstrated the feasibility of case-based planning and execution in real-time strategy games, where behavioral knowledge extracted from expert demonstrations in the form of cases can be effectively reused to handle the vast search spaces of adversarial game scenarios. OCaL-RL by Liu et al. [12], DCBRL of Wibowo et al. [15], and Guo et al. [16] show that CBR is helpful for experience reuse, rapid adaptation, and improving the quality of case reuse in reinforcement learning. However, the existing CBR + RL methods mainly focus on case retrieval and policy migration. It is difficult to generalize to unseen situations due to limitations in case matching quality, and it has not yet solved the problem of how to stably map the high-level tactical intentions in the case to time-step learning rewards.

On the other hand, existing reward shaping methods, such as potential-based reward shaping discussed by Müller and Kudenko [17], HPRS by Berducci et al. [18], and VBRS by Hou et al. [19], can alleviate credit assignment difficulties under sparse rewards, but their design relies on human experience, heuristic rules, or general value priors, and lacks structural constraints aligned with the stage progression of football tactics. The Reward Machine proposed by Icarte et al. [20,21] can explicitly describe the task phase and transition logic. Subsequent works by Corazza et al. [22], Alsadat et al. [23], and Ardon et al. [24] have further extended reward machines in stochasticity, automatic generation, and expressive power. However, in existing research, the state space and transition conditions of reward machines are usually statically predefined, lacking the adaptability to couple dynamically with specific tactical situations, and the reward machine alone still struggles to eliminate the reward sparsity within the sub-goals.

To bridge this gap, this paper introduces a tactical case organization mechanism based on CBR, and combines the idea of reward machine and reward redistribution, so as to provide reusable, traceable and adaptable tactical guidance for the reinforcement learning model. Accordingly, this paper proposes a large-small model collaborative framework based on tactical case-based reasoning reward machine for game confrontation scenarios. The core of the framework is the Return Decomposition Based on Tactic-Case Reward Machine (RD-TCRM). In this framework, LLM is offline responsible for the maintenance of tactical cases and dominates the generation of offline datasets with dense rewards. The reinforcement learning small model uses the datasets to learn and make online decisions.

The main contributions of this paper are summarized as follows:

(1) An LLM tactical knowledge structuring method based on case-based reasoning is proposed. The existing LLM-assisted reinforcement learning methods usually use the LLM as a one-time reward function generator or strategy prompter, making it difficult to accumulate, iterate and reuse tactical knowledge across situations. This paper uses the retrieve, reuse, revise, retain cycle of CBR to structure the tactical knowledge generated by the LLM, thus overcoming the limitations of one-time generation mode, i.e., tactical knowledge cannot be accumulated, reused and iterated.
(2) A two-layer decomposition mechanism from tactical cases to dense rewards is designed. The existing reward shaping methods lack the systematic trans-

formation path from high-level tactical semantics to low-level reward signals. This paper constructs a two-layer decomposition mechanism from reward machine to utility function difference. The abstract tactical semantics are refined into step-by-step numerical signals, which effectively alleviates the difficulty of credit allocation caused by sparse final rewards.

(3) A training and deployment framework for large-small model collaboration is constructed. To address the issue that the existing methods cannot meet the real-time requirements of adversarial game scenarios because they still need LLM real-time participation in the reasoning stage, this paper limits the participation of LLM to the generation process of offline datasets with dense rewards, and only requires lightweight small models to make independent decisions during online deployment, thus taking into account the real-time performance of online decision-making and the full use of LLM reasoning ability.

Systematic experimental verification was carried out in the GRF environment. By comparing with benchmark methods, the effectiveness of the proposed method in learning efficiency and strategy quality is verified.

The rest of this paper is organized as follows: Sect. 2 provides the formal definition of problem modeling and key concepts; Sect. 3 describes the overall framework and module design of the RD-TCRM method. Section 4 comprehensively evaluates the method through main experiment, ablation experiment and qualitative analysis. Section 5 summarizes the paper and the future research direction.

2 Problem Modeling

2.1 Problem Background and Markov Decision Process

As shown in Fig. 1, the overall framework of this paper is to use the proposed RD-TCRM algorithm to realize the reward shaping based on case-based reasoning, that is, through the generation, retrieval, execution tracking, and value evaluation of tactical cases, the reinforcement learning offline dataset with dense reward signals is obtained, and it is used to train the reinforcement learning small model, and finally the reinforcement learning small model makes decisions.

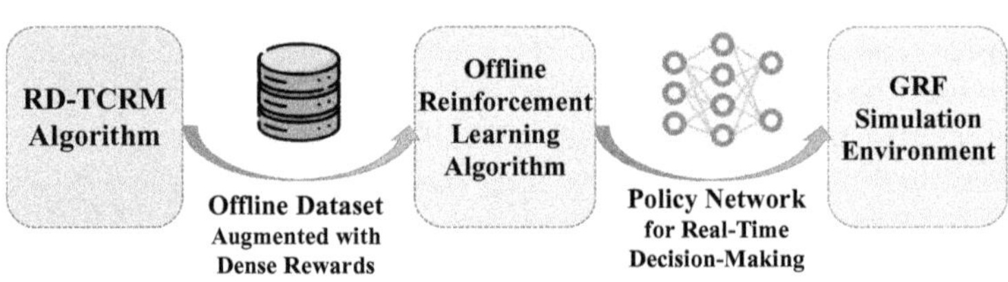

Fig. 1. Application of RD-TCRM Algorithm in GRF Decision System

In this paper, a single football match is modeled as a multi-agent Markov game:

$$\mathcal{G} = \langle \mathcal{N}, \mathcal{S}, \{\mathcal{O}_i\}_{i\in\mathcal{N}}, \{\mathcal{A}_i\}_{i\in\mathcal{N}}, P, r, \gamma \rangle \tag{1}$$

where each symbol is defined as follows:

$\mathcal{N} = \{1, 2, \ldots, n\}$ denotes the set of controlled agents, i.e., the teammates on the controlled side.

$\mathcal{S}$ denotes the global state space, which encodes the positions, velocities, ball possession status, and other match-related information of all players.

$\mathcal{O}_i$ denotes the local observation space of agent i. At each time step, every agent receives a 115-dimensional feature vector $o_i \in \mathbb{R}^{115}$ provided by the GRF environment, which contains information such as player coordinates, velocities, and ball ownership flags from the perspective of that agent.

$\mathcal{A}_i$ denotes the action space of agent i, comprising 19 discrete actions including moving, passing, and shooting. At each time step, every agent independently selects its own action $a_i \in \mathcal{A}_i$, forming the joint action $a = (a_1, a_2, \ldots, a_n)$.

$P : \mathcal{S} \times \mathcal{A}_1 \times \cdots \times \mathcal{A}_n \times \mathcal{S} \to [0, 1]$ denotes the state transition probability, which depends on the global state and the joint action of all agents.

$r : \mathcal{S} \times \mathcal{A}_1 \times \cdots \times \mathcal{A}_n \to \mathbb{R}$ denotes the team-shared reward function, meaning that all controlled agents receive the same scalar reward at each time step.

$\gamma \in (0, 1)$ denotes the discount factor.

2.2 Game Segment Cutting Based on Ball Control State and Tactical Case Definition

Football matches can be naturally decomposed into possession-based segments, each driven by a distinct tactical intention. To segment a match, we define the ball possession state $b_t \in \{\text{own}, \text{opponent}, \text{neutral}\}$ at time step t. A possession switch ($b_t \neq b_{t-1}$) marks the boundary between consecutive segments, yielding $N + 1$ segments for a match with N possession switches. Each segment is represented as a fine-grained state-action transition sequence $(s_t, a_t, s_{t+1}, a_{t+1}, \ldots)$.

Building on this segmentation, we introduce the concept of *tactical case* to encapsulate the high-level semantic abstraction of each segment. This possession-based segmentation aligns with the inherent logic of football: an attacking team must maintain possession to execute offensive tactics and create scoring opportunities, while losing possession signals the interruption of the current tactical intention and necessitates re-planning.

In this paper, tactical cases are defined as:

$$c_i = (x_i, \omega_i, \Pi_i, \mathcal{R}_i, y_i) \tag{2}$$

where x_i denotes the description of the case problem, ω_i denotes tactical intentions, Π_i denotes structured tactical programs, including sub-goal sequences, phase constraints, and predicate templates, $\mathcal{R}_i$ denotes the reward machine compiled by a tactical program, y_i denotes the expected result of the tactical case. A complete match thus comprises multiple tactical cases, each internally progressing through a sequence of sub-goal stages formalized by its reward machine $\mathcal{R}_i$ corresponding to the tactical case.

2.3 Formalization of Tactical Case Intention Based on Reward Machine

In order to make the tactical case intention be used by reinforcement learning, this paper models the tactical intention in each tactical case as a reward machine. A reward machine is a finite state automaton that can track the progress of a task according to changes in the state of the environment and provide a reward signal when specific conditions are met [20,21].

A reward machine is defined as a six-tuple

$$\mathcal{R} = (\mathcal{U}, u_0, \mathcal{F}, \Sigma, \delta, \sigma) \tag{3}$$

where $\mathcal{U}$ denotes the set of reward machine states, with each state $u \in \mathcal{U}$ corresponding to a particular phase of task execution; $u_0 \in \mathcal{U}$ denotes the initial state; $\mathcal{F} \subseteq \mathcal{U}$ denotes the set of terminal states; $\Sigma = 2^{\mathcal{P}}$ denotes the set of propositional symbols generated by the predicate set $\mathcal{P}$, where each predicate $p \in \mathcal{P}$ is a Boolean function defined over the state space, i.e., $p : \mathcal{S} \to \{$ true, false $\}$; $\delta : \mathcal{U} \times \Sigma \to \mathcal{U}$ denotes the state transition function; and $\sigma : \mathcal{U} \times \Sigma \times \mathcal{U} \to \mathbb{R}$ denotes the reward output function.

In the framework of this paper, the reward machine state u represents the stage index of the current tactical execution. Starting from $u = 0$, it passes through each stage in turn until it reaches the termination state $u = K$ (indicating tactical completion), or resets due to timeouts, loss of possession, and other reasons. The predicate p is used to determine whether a specific sub-goal is achieved.

2.4 Tactical Execution Utility Function and Case Reward Shaping

In order to integrate tactical case information in the reinforcement learning framework, this paper extends the original state space to an augmented state space. The augmented state $(s, u, w) \in \mathcal{S} \times \mathcal{U} \times \mathcal{W}$ is defined, where s represents the state of the environment, u represents the state of the current reward machine, that is, the progress of the current case execution, and w represents the fixed coding of the currently activated tactical case.

Inspired by the design idea of potential function, in order to realize the quantitative evaluation of case execution effect, this paper defines the Tactical Execution Utility Function (TEUF) $\Phi_\psi : \mathcal{S} \times \mathcal{U} \times \mathcal{W} \to \mathbb{R}$ on the augmented state space, which is used to estimate the expected cumulative return from the current augmented state. The learning goal of the tactical execution utility function is:

$$\Phi_\psi(s, u, w) \approx \mathbb{E}\left[\sum_{k=0}^{\infty} \gamma^k r_{t+k}^{\text{env}} \mid s_t = s, u_t = u, w_t = w\right] \tag{4}$$

We use a similar potential function shaping method to transform the tactical execution utility function into a dense reward signal. Combining the theory of potential function shaping, the shaping reward is defined as:

$$r_t^{\text{shape}} = \begin{cases} \gamma \Phi_\psi\left(s_{t+1}, u_{t+1}, w_{t+1}\right) - \Phi_\psi\left(s_t, u_t, w_t\right), w_{t+1} = w_t \\ 0, w_{t+1} \neq w_t \end{cases} \tag{5}$$

Finally, the reward signal provided to the reinforcement learning algorithm is a weighted combination of environmental reward and shaping reward:

$$\hat{r}_t = r_t^{\text{env}} + \beta r_t^{\text{shape}} \tag{6}$$

where $\beta > 0$ is the weight coefficient of shaping reward.

3 Algorithm Design

3.1 Overall Framework

The RD-TCRM algorithm proposed in this paper is a tactical case-based reasoning reward design framework for sparse reward multi-agent football tasks. As shown in Fig. 2a, the framework includes:

Tactical case initialization: the tactical case generation module uses the LLM+RAG to develop tactical concepts according to the preset game scene, independently imagine the feasible tactical scheme in different situations, deduce and generate a variety of structured tactical case program drafts, and form the initial tactical case library.

The 4R cycle operates as follows:

Retrieve: At the beginning of each tactical segment, the decision-making LLM retrieves similar tactical cases from the tactical case library according to the current game situation.

Reuse: Based on the retrieved tactical cases, the decision-making LLM combines the current competition situation to adjust the tactics in the case; in the process of tactical execution, the reward machine continuously monitors the achievement of sub-goals; the case execution utility function learning module trains a neural network based on sparse final reward signals to estimate the value of the augmented state, resulting in dense shaping rewards.

Revise: After the execution of the fragment, the case itself is evaluated and modified according to the actual execution trajectory and final effect, and the sub-goal sequence is adjusted, the predicate criterion condition is modified, and the tactical applicability labeling is updated, so that the case can more accurately reflect the effective tactical mode in practice.

Retain: Save the revised case together with its execution track and effect evaluation back to the case library, form a sustainable growth experience memory, and improve the case quality in the case library.

As shown in Fig. 2b, in the inference mode of the RD-TCRM algorithm, the LLM selects the case and its corresponding reward machine from the tactical case library according to the current game situation and makes specific decisions. The single-step dense reward is obtained by tactical execution utility function network reasoning, so as to obtain the offline data set for offline reinforcement learning algorithm training.

In this framework, the role of decision-making LLM is to retrieve the most matched historical case from the tactical case library, reuse its tactical strategy, and modify it according to the current actual situation, and return it to the case

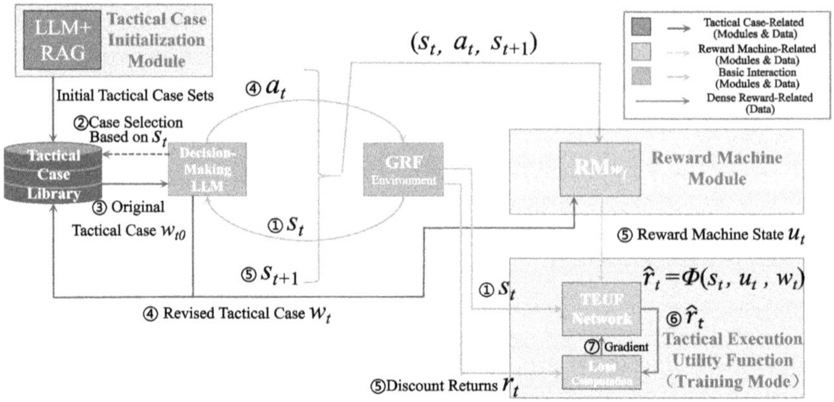

(a) Training Flow Chart of RD-TCRM Algorithm

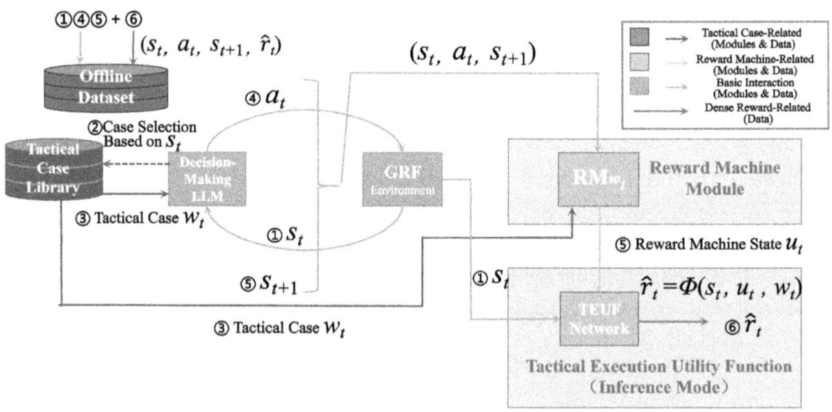

(b) Inference Flow Chart of RD-TCRM Algorithm

Fig. 2. Flow Charts of RD-TCRM Algorithm

library. The reward machine is responsible for tracking the execution progress of case tactics online, and the tactical execution utility function is responsible for deriving dense rewards from the augmented state (incorporating the reward machine's tracking output) for reinforcement learning.

3.2 Initialization and Retrieval of Tactical Case Library

The core task of the tactical case initialization module is to generate a structured tactical case fragment based on a hypothetical initial game situation state, requiring the LLM to output a structured description of the tactical case, including the tactical intention of the case, the sequence of sub-goals, and the observable criterion recommendations corresponding to each sub-goal.

During the Retrieve phase, the LLM is prompted with the current game situation along with a summary list of available cases in the library, and is instructed to select the most situationally similar tactical case by matching the current context against each case's problem description. Figure 3 illustrates a retrieval prompt template.

```
Retrieval Prompt Template
[Role]
You are a football coach. Select the best tactic from the case library based on the current state.
[State]
Ball: <<pos, owner, dir>> | Score: <<score>> | Mode: <<game_mode>>
|Teammates: <<team info list>> | Opponents: <<enemy info list>>
[Case Library]
1: Wing Attack. Desc: Exploit wide flank space via overlapping runs...
2: Counter-Attack. Desc: Fast vertical transition after turnover...
3: Central Penetration. Desc: Through-ball into box via short combinations...
4: ...
[Output]
{"case_id":_, "reason":"..."}
```

Fig. 3. Prompt Template for LLM-Based Tactical Case Retrieval

3.3 Construction and Operation of Reward Machine

The reward machine maintains its state at each time step according to the following logic. Given a state transition (s_t, a_t, s_{t+1}), the module first checks whether a possession switch has occurred. If so, the current tactical case terminates and the reward machine resets to u_0, awaiting re-initialization by the next retrieved case. If possession is retained, the predicate $p_u(s_{t+1})$ associated with the current stage u is evaluated. If satisfied, the reward machine transitions to the next stage via $u \leftarrow u+1$ and the stage timer is reset. Otherwise, the module checks whether the stage has timed out, i.e., $t_{\text{stage}} > T_u^{\max}$, where $T_u^{\max}$ is the maximum allowed duration for stage u. A timeout triggers tactical re-planning, prompting the LLM to retrieve a new matching case. At every time step, the stage timer increments by one, regardless of whether the reward machine advances to the next stage. All predicates are implemented as white-box geometric rules computed directly from the state vector.

3.4 Training of Tactical Execution Utility Function

The goal of tactical execution utility function training is to train a parametric function Φ_ψ to estimate the state value of the augmented state, thereby generating a dense shaping reward signal. We use a neural network as the function approximator for Φ_ψ. The specific architecture is a multi-layer perceptron. The input is a vectorized representation of the augmented state, and the output is a scalar single-step reward value.

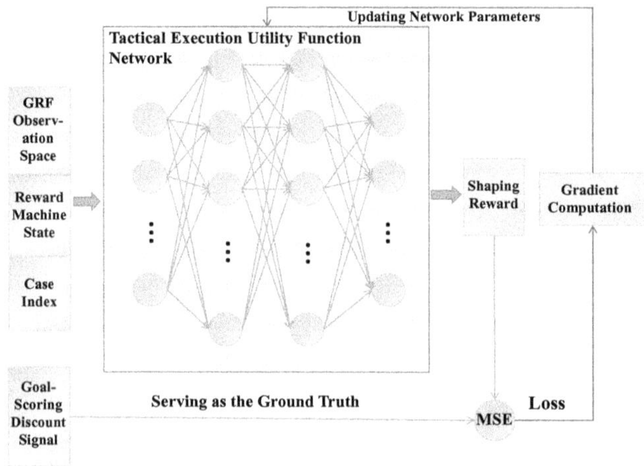

Fig. 4. Training Flow Chart of Tactical Execution Utility Function

As shown in Fig. 4, the vectorized representation of the augmented state is composed of three parts: the environmental state s directly uses the 115-dimensional feature vector provided by GRF; the reward machine state u is encoded by one-hot, and the dimension is $K+1$; the case number w uses a fixed embedded vector to represent the index of the tactical case. After the three parts are spliced, they are normalized and input to the multi-layer perceptron.

The training of tactical execution utility function adopts temporal difference learning method. Assuming that the trajectory data generated by the interaction between the agent and the environment is $\mathcal{D}=\{(s_t,u_t,w_t,r_t^{\text{env}},s_{t+1},u_{t+1})\}$ in a tactical segment, the training loss of the utility function is defined as the mean square timing difference error:

$$\mathcal{L}_{\text{TD}}(\psi)=\mathbb{E}_{(s,u,w,r,s',u')\sim\mathcal{D}}\left[\left(\Phi_\psi(s,u,w)-r-\gamma\Phi_{\bar{\psi}}\left(s',u',w\right)\right)^2\right] \tag{7}$$

where $\Phi_{\bar{\psi}}$ is the target network, and its parameters $\bar{\psi}$ are regularly soft-updated from ψ [17,18]. Since the environmental reward r^{env} is extremely sparse, directly using the above loss function training may cause the function estimation to tend to zero in most states. To alleviate this problem, we introduce auxiliary supervisory signals based on Monte Carlo returns.

For each complete episode, we calculate the cumulative discount return $G_t=\sum_{k=0}^{T-t}\gamma^k r_{t+k}^{\text{env}}$ at each moment and use it as the supervisory target for the utility function estimation. The corresponding Monte Carlo regression loss is defined as:

$$\mathcal{L}_{\text{MC}}(\psi)=\mathbb{E}_{(s_t,u_t,w_t,\text{G}_t)\sim\mathcal{D}}\left[\left(\Phi_\psi\left(s_t,u_t,w_t\right)-G_t\right)^2\right] \tag{8}$$

The final total loss function is the weighted sum of the temporal difference loss and the Monte Carlo loss:

$$\mathcal{L}(\psi)=\mathcal{L}_{\text{TD}}(\psi)+\lambda\mathcal{L}_{\text{MC}}(\psi) \tag{9}$$

where $\lambda > 0$ is the hyperparameter that balances the two losses.

4 Experiment

4.1 Experimental Settings

In this paper, experimental verification is carried out on the GRF environment [1]. We select the following three representative scenarios for experiments: 11v11 complete game scenario[1] (`academy_11_vs_11_stochastic`), which involves the cooperation and confrontation of 22 players in the whole game; 3v1 game scenario (`academy_3_vs_1_with_keeper`), which is a small-scale attack task of three offensive players against one defensive player and one goalkeeper; and RPS game scenario (`academy_run_pass_and_shoot_with_keeper`), where there are two offensive players on one side, and one defensive player and one goalkeeper on the other side.

The observation space uses the GRF default Simple115 feature vector (115 dimensions), and the action space consists of 19 discrete actions.

The tactical execution utility function network uses a three-layer multi-layer perceptron, the hidden layer dimension is 256, the activation function is ReLU, and the input dimension is 115 (state) + 8 (reward machine state one-hot encoding, each tactic up to 8 sub-goal stages) + 16 (tactical intention one-hot encoding embedding, each tactical case library up to 16 tactics) = 139 dimensions. The weighting coefficient λ for combining the temporal difference loss and the Monte Carlo loss is set to 0.5.

In this paper, multi-agent conservative Q learning (MACQL) [25–27] is used for offline reinforcement learning training. The offline dataset is composed of the aforementioned pre-collected policy trajectories. The LLM uses Deepseek-v3 as the initial tactical case generator and tactical case adapter, which is called in the form of API.

4.2 Baseline Methods

We compare RD-TCRM against the following baselines:

Sparse: MACQL trained with only the environment's original sparse reward, serving as the base reference.

Checkpoint Reward: The GRF built-in checkpoint reward [1], a hand-designed dense reward based on ball advancement distance.

LLM-Direct: LLM-generated reward rules [13] that directly provide instant reward feedback to agents without reward machine structures.

Random RM: Replaces the tactical-case-derived reward machine with a randomly generated structure while keeping all other components identical to RD-TCRM, verifying the necessity of the tactical case design.

[1] Names in parentheses are built-in scenario identifiers in the GRF environment.

RD-TCRM (Ours): The complete proposed method, integrating LLM tactical program generation, reward machine runtime tracking, TEUF learning, and shaping reward generation.

We further conduct ablation studies: **RD-TCRM w/o RM** removes the reward machine module and uses only the LLM-output tactical intention index as auxiliary input to the potential function; **RD-TCRM w/o LLM Revise** retains the LLM's ability to retrieve tactical cases from the library but disables runtime adaptation; **RD-TCRM w/o TEUF Shaping** removes the TEUF-based potential shaping reward entirely.

4.3 Evaluation Metrics

We evaluate all methods along five dimensions:

Win Rate: Proportion of wins over 100 evaluation games against the GRF built-in AI, measured at the same number of training episodes across all methods.

Goals Scored: Average goals per game over 100 evaluation games, measured at the same number of training episodes across all methods.

Sample Efficiency: Number of training steps required to reach a 50% win rate threshold.

Tactic Completion Rate: Proportion of tactical segments that successfully reach the reward machine's terminal state, measuring adherence to tactical intentions.

4.4 Main Experimental Results

Table 1 shows the performance comparison of each method on three experimental scenarios.

Table 1. Performance comparison of different methods across three experimental scenarios.

Method	11v11 Win Rate	11v11 Avg. Goals	3v1 Win Rate	RPS Win Rate	Training Steps (to 50% Win Rate)
Sparse	2%	0.05	38%	41%	–
Checkpoint	8%	0.22	61%	57%	7.5×10^6
LLM-Direct	11%	0.28	56%	62%	6.2×10^6
Random RM	4%	0.09	33%	27%	–
RD-TCRM (Ours)	16%	0.41	78%	83%	2.8×10^6

Note: The number of training steps is based on the 3v1 scenario; '–' means that the winning rate failed to reach 50% within 1,000 epochs.

Figure 5 shows the training curves of each method in the 11v11 scenario. The horizontal axis is the number of steps in the training environment, and the vertical axis is the winning rate against the built-in AI.

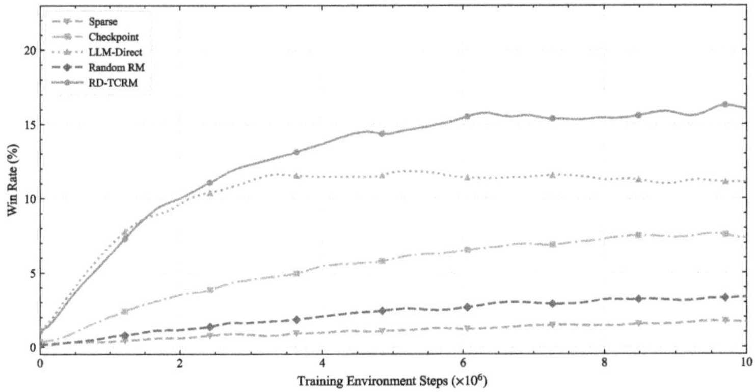

Fig. 5. The Winning Rate Curve in the 11v11 Scenario

Across all three experimental scenarios, the proposed RD-TCRM method achieves the best final performance. Compared with the Sparse baseline, RD-TCRM improves the winning rate by approximately 14 percentage points in the 11v11 scenario under the same number of training epochs, confirming that the shaping rewards effectively alleviate the learning difficulties caused by sparse rewards. RD-TCRM also outperforms Checkpoint, indicating that LLM-generated tactical structures provide more informative learning signals than the built-in distance-based reward shaping in GRF.

Notably, although the LLM-Direct method exhibits faster early-stage learning, its final performance is significantly lower than that of RD-TCRM, with performance degradation observed in some scenarios due to reward hacking. Agents learn to frequently trigger intermediate rewards (e.g., frequent passes) rather than pursue the ultimate goal of winning. This validates the design rationale of RD-TCRM: shaping via potential functions avoids reward hacking. Furthermore, the significantly inferior performance of Random RM compared to RD-TCRM confirms that the LLM-generated tactical structures contain meaningful domain knowledge rather than benefiting from arbitrary structural decomposition.

4.5 Ablation Experimental Results

Table 2 shows the results of ablation experiments.

Ablation results confirm that each component contributes meaningfully. Removing TEUF shaping (w/o TEUF Shaping) causes the largest drop (-9%): although the reward machine state is still available as part of the input, the absence of potential-based shaping leaves agents reliant on sparse environment rewards for credit assignment. Removing the reward machine (w/o RM) leads to a 7-point decline, indicating that explicit stage-wise progress tracking is essential for the TEUF to distinguish tactical phases that share similar environmental states. Restricting the LLM to retrieval without adaptation (w/o LLM Revise)

Table 2. Ablation study results on the 11v11 scenario.

Ablation Configuration	11v11 Win Rate	Relative Change
RD-TCRM (Ours)	16%	–
w/o RM	9%	−7%
w/o LLM Revise	11%	−5%
w/o TEUF Shaping	7%	−9%

results in a 5-point decrease, showing that runtime tactical revision provides tangible gains over static case matching.

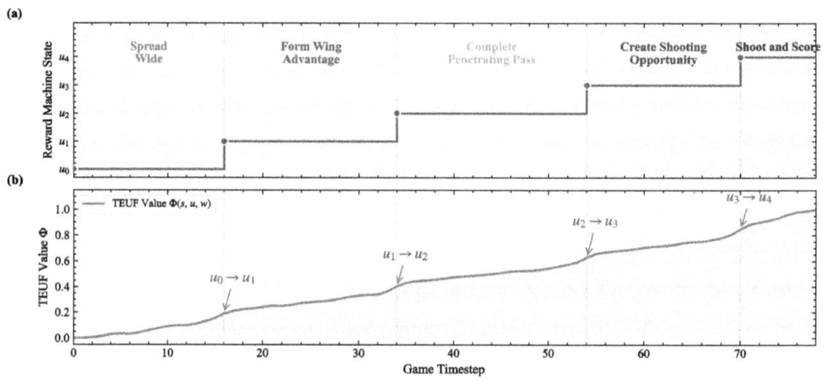

Fig. 6. The Evolution Process of the Reward Machine State and TEUF in the Side Attack Tactics

4.6 Tactical Execution Analysis

In order to deeply understand the behavioral characteristics of the RD-TCRM method, we qualitatively analyze the tactical execution of the agent after training. Figure 6 shows the evolution of the reward machine state in a typical attack clip in a 3v1 scenario. In this example, LLM adopts the side attack tactic according to the initial state, including four sub-goals: widening the width, forming the side advantage, completing the penetrating pass, and creating the shooting opportunity. It shows that the advancement of the reward machine state and the increasing value of TEUF indicate the gradual completion of the sub-goals.

Table 3 shows the execution success rate of some tactical types in 500 3v1 scene games.

Table 3. Execution statistics of different tactical types in the 3v1 scenario.

Tactic Type	Triggers	Completions	Completion Rate	Avg. Execution Steps
Wing Attack	152	51	33.55%	78
Counter-Attack	94	38	40.43%	53
Ball Progression	187	85	45.45%	98
High Press	73	21	28.76%	41

5 Conclusion and Discussion

5.1 Main Conclusions

Experimental results validate the effectiveness of the proposed RD-TCRM method. Ablation studies show that removing the reward machine, TEUF shaping, or LLM revision capability leads to significant performance degradation of 5–9 percentage points in winning rate, confirming the necessity of each component. Compared with baselines such as LLM-Direct and Checkpoint, RD-TCRM achieves higher winning rates in both 3v1 and 11v11 scenarios while requiring substantially fewer training steps (e.g., reaching 50% winning rate at 2.8×10^6 steps versus 7.5×10^6 for Checkpoint), demonstrating superior sample efficiency.

5.2 Future Research Direction

Based on the research in this paper, the following directions are worth further exploration: First, the small model training feedback could be introduced into the CBR correction and retention link to further enhance the adaptive evolution ability of the tactical case library. Second, the dynamic adjustment mechanism within the tactical segment could be studied, allowing dynamic correction of local sub-goals when the reward machine stagnates or the opponent's formation changes, and improving the flexibility in game confrontation. Third, the abstraction and domain adaptation method of transferring the tactical case library to other staged game confrontation tasks could be explored.

Acknowledgments. This work was supported by the BNRist project under Grant No. BNR2024TD03003.

Disclosure of Interests. The authors have no competing interests to declare that are relevant to the content of this article.

Declaration on Generative AI. The authors declare that no generative AI or AI-assisted tools were used in the preparation of this manuscript.

References

1. Kurach, K., Raichuk, A., Stańczyk, P., et al.: Google research football: a novel reinforcement learning environment. In: Proceedings of the AAAI Conference on Artificial Intelligence, vol. 34, pp. 4501–4510 (2020)

2. Huang, S., et al.: Tikick: towards playing multi-agent football full games from single-agent demonstrations. arXiv preprint arXiv:2110.04507 (2021)
3. Lin, F., et al.: Tizero: mastering multi-agent football with curriculum learning and self-play. arXiv preprint arXiv:2302.07515 (2023)
4. Li, C., et al.: ACE: cooperative multi-agent Q-learning with bidirectional action-dependency. In: Proceedings of the AAAI Conference on Artificial Intelligence, vol. 37 (2023)
5. Jo, Y., et al.: Fox: formation-aware exploration in multi-agent reinforcement learning. In: Proceedings of the AAAI Conference on Artificial Intelligence, vol. 38 (2024)
6. Wang, S., Pu, Z., Hu, T., et al.: Diversity-driven offline-to-online multi-player policy learning for football matches. In: 2025 International Joint Conference on Neural Networks (IJCNN), pp. 1–8. IEEE (2025)
7. Zhang, Y., Mao, S., Ge, T., et al.: LLM as a mastermind: a survey of strategic reasoning with large language models. arXiv preprint arXiv:2404.01230 (2024)
8. Li, C., et al.: Stride: a tool-assisted LLM agent framework for strategic and interactive decision-making. arXiv preprint arXiv:2405.16376 (2024)
9. Alkayyal, M., Malberg, S., Groh, G.: An LLM-based decision support system for strategic decision-making. In: Joint European Conference on Machine Learning and Knowledge Discovery in Databases. Springer (2025)
10. Chen, X.-H., et al.: Policy learning from tutorial books via understanding, rehearsing and introspecting. In: Advances in Neural Information Processing Systems, vol. 37, pp. 18940–18987 (2024)
11. Pang, J.-C., et al.: Kalm: knowledgeable agents by offline reinforcement learning from large language model rollouts. In: Advances in Neural Information Processing Systems, vol. 37, pp. 126620–126652 (2024)
12. Liu, H., Liu, Q., Wu, L., et al.: Offline-to-online: case-based knowledge distillation with large language models for reinforcement learning. In: International Conference on Case-Based Reasoning, pp. 142–156. Springer (2025)
13. Qu, Y., et al.: Latent reward: LLM-empowered credit assignment in episodic reinforcement learning. In: Proceedings of the AAAI Conference on Artificial Intelligence, vol. 39 (2025)
14. Ontanón, S., Mishra, K., Sugandh, N., Ram, A.: Case-based planning and execution for real-time strategy games. In: International Conference on Case-Based Reasoning, pp. 164–178. Springer, Heidelberg (2007)
15. Wibowo, A., et al.: Enhancing autonomous space exploration with distributed case-based reasoning and learning (DCBRL) in multi-agent systems. In: International Symposium on Artificial Intelligence, Robotics and Automation in Space (i-SAIRAS) (2024)
16. Guo, S., et al.: Optimizing case-based reasoning system for functional test script generation with large language models. In: Proceedings of the 31st ACM SIGKDD Conference on Knowledge Discovery and Data Mining (2025)
17. Müller, H., Kudenko, D.: Improving the effectiveness of potential-based reward shaping in reinforcement learning. arXiv preprint arXiv:2502.01307 (2025)
18. Berducci, L., et al.: HPRS: hierarchical potential-based reward shaping from task specifications. Front. Robot. AI **11**, 1444188 (2025)
19. Hou, B., Pan, G., Chen, Y.: Enhancing adversarial policy learning via value-based reward shaping. Electronics **15**(2), 463 (2026)
20. Icarte, R.T., et al.: Using reward machines for high-level task specification and decomposition in reinforcement learning. In: International Conference on Machine Learning. PMLR (2018)

21. Icarte, R.T., et al.: Reward machines: exploiting reward function structure in reinforcement learning. J. Artif. Intell. Res. **73**, 173–208 (2022)
22. Corazza, J., Gavran, I., Neider, D.: Reinforcement learning with stochastic reward machines. In: Proceedings of the AAAI Conference on Artificial Intelligence, vol. 36 (2022)
23. Alsadat, S.M., et al.: Using large language models to automate and expedite reinforcement learning with reward machine. In: 2025 American Control Conference (ACC). IEEE (2025)
24. Ardon, L., et al.: Form: learning expressive and transferable first-order logic reward machines. arXiv preprint arXiv:2501.00364 (2024)
25. Kumar, A., et al.: Conservative q-learning for offline reinforcement learning. In: Advances in Neural Information Processing Systems, vol. 33, pp. 1179–1191 (2020)
26. Shao, J., et al.: Counterfactual conservative q learning for offline multi-agent reinforcement learning. In: Advances in Neural Information Processing Systems, vol. 36, pp. 77290–77312 (2023)
27. Zhong, H., Wang, X., Li, Z., et al.: Offline-to-online multi-agent reinforcement learning with offline value function memory and sequential exploration. arXiv preprint arXiv:2410.19450 (2024)

Case-Based Causal Reasoning for Elite Basketball Decision Support: A Human-in-the-Loop Approach to Clutch-Time Strategy Recommendation

Dandan Cui[1(✉)], Yuqiao Qian[2], Mulin Yang[1], and Wenchao Yang[1]

[1] China Institute of Sport Science, Beijing, China
ditto9@gmail.com
[2] Neusoft Institute Guangdong, Foshan, China

Abstract. Elite basketball games are often decided in clutch time—the final minutes when scores are close and every tactical decision matters. However, existing basketball analytics systems focus predominantly on outcome prediction rather than prescriptive strategy recommendation, leaving coaches without actionable strategy recommendations during these critical moments. We propose a novel Case-Based Causal Reasoning (CBCR) framework that integrates data-driven causal inference throughout the entire case-based reasoning cycle to deliver robust, interpretable tactical recommendations. Our human-in-the-loop approach incorporates expert feedback to continuously refine causal models of decision-outcome relationships. We construct a comprehensive dataset of 515 clutch-time possessions from the 2025 FIBA Women's EuroBasket, AmeriCup, and Asia Cup tournaments, encompassing play-by-play actions and contextual game states. Experimental results demonstrate that our CBCR-based system achieves 73.0% score-prediction accuracy (predicted $\geq$ actual), substantially outperforming conventional similarity-based CBR (60.8%), which offers a credible pathway for addressing the unique challenges of data scarcity, risk sensitivity, and high personalization in decision-making for elite sports.

Keywords: Case-Based Reasoning · Causal Inference · Sports Analytics · Decision Support Systems · Basketball · Clutch Performance

1 Introduction

In elite basketball, the final minutes of close games—commonly referred to as "clutch time"—are decisive moments where a single tactical decision can determine the outcome of an entire season. Recent high-stakes competitions have vividly demonstrated this phenomenon. At the 2023 FIBA Women's Asia Cup

L. Malburg and K. Bach (Eds.): ICCBR 2026, LNAI 16780, pp. 472–488, 2027.
https://doi.org/10.1007/978-3-032-33865-5_29

Final, China narrowly defeated Japan 73–71, with the outcome hinging on critical decisions made in the last 30 s. Similarly, at the 2024 Paris Olympics Women's Basketball Final, the USA secured gold against France with a slim 67–66 margin, where strategic choices in the final two minutes proved determinant. These scenarios underscore a fundamental challenge in sports analytics: how to provide coaches with intelligent, real-time decision support during clutch moments when traditional statistical approaches often fall short.

Despite the growing body of research on basketball analytics, decision-making in clutch scenarios remains poorly understood and inadequately supported by existing intelligent systems. Sarlis et al. [26] define clutch time as the final minutes of games where the score differential is five points or less, emphasizing that performance in these critical periods requires distinct analytical frameworks. Vázquez-Estévez et al. [30] analyzed 509 offensive actions from the final two minutes of EuroBasket 2022 and 2021, revealing that trailing teams exhibit higher offensive efficiency and that fast-break strategies completed within 17 s are significantly more effective. However, existing research predominantly focuses on *prediction* of game outcomes [2,6,20] rather than *prescriptive decision support*, leaving coaches without actionable tactical recommendations during these high-pressure moments.

Three fundamental challenges impede effective clutch-time decision support. First, **data scarcity**: clutch scenarios are inherently rare, rendering data-hungry deep learning unreliable. Second, **risk sensitivity**: tactical choices carry asymmetric consequences when trailing versus leading, requiring explicit risk-reward modeling. Third, **personalization**: optimal strategies vary by team strengths, opponent characteristics, and contextual factors (foul counts, timeouts). Generic recommendations ignore these nuances and are unlikely to be adopted by professional coaches.

Traditional machine learning methods excel at identifying correlations (*what happened*) but struggle to explain causation (*why it happened*) [23]. In risk-sensitive domains like elite competitive sports, the path to success must be clearly understood and mechanistically justified. Strategies based on spurious correlations can be not only ineffective but potentially harmful to decision-making outcomes. For instance, while graph convolutional networks have been applied to predict basketball game results [31], such black-box deep learning models are often "red-carded" in elite sports decision-making practice due to their lack of interpretability and vulnerability to spurious patterns [5].

Interestingly, many successful coaches demonstrate a remarkable ability to grasp causal clues from limited historical cases and make sound decisions under pressure. This suggests that human expertise in clutch-time decision-making relies on implicit causal reasoning rather than pure pattern recognition. By explicitly modeling causal relationships between tactical decisions and outcomes, our approach enables the system to (1) distinguish genuine strategic effects from spurious correlations, ensuring that recommended tactics are mechanistically sound rather than artifacts of dataset-specific patterns; (2) generalize robustly from limited clutch-time data by leveraging causal structure to transfer knowledge across contexts with different confounding factors; and (3) provide interpretable explanations that align with coaches' mental models, facilitating trust and adoption in high-stakes decision scenarios.

To address these challenges, we propose a novel **Case-Based Causal Reasoning (CBCR)** framework that synergistically integrates case-based reasoning (CBR) with data-driven causal inference. In this paper, we extend our previous work on case-based causal reasoning for elite sprint training [9,10]. Unlike conventional CBR that relies on surface-level similarity, our framework integrates causality across all five CBR stages—reconstruction, retrieval, reuse, revision, and retention—enhancing reliable inference in high-stakes, personalized, small-data scenarios [13]. We apply this framework to basketball clutch-time decision support, with three key contributions: (1) a causally-augmented CBR architecture that improves reasoning reliability in risk-sensitive domains; (2) multi-stage human-in-the-loop collaboration mechanisms for effective coach-system interaction in complex game contexts; and (3) a working prototype built upon a real-world dataset of 515 annotated clutch-time possessions from 2025 FIBA Women's continental championships, enabling domain-specific evaluation methodologies and empirical validation for basketball clutch-time strategy inference.

2 Related Work

2.1 Clutch-Time Analysis in Basketball

The concept of clutch time in basketball has been rigorously defined by recent research. According to the NBA's official definition [22], clutch time refers to the final five minutes of the fourth quarter or overtime periods when the score differential is five points or less. Sarlis et al. [26] analyzed 20 seasons of NBA data and introduced the Estimation of Clutch Competency (EoCC) metric to evaluate individual player performance under pressure, finding that clutch performance requires specialized competencies distinct from overall game performance.

Vázquez-Estévez et al. [30] employed observational methodology to analyze 509 offensive actions from the final two minutes of EuroBasket 2022 and 2021 finals. Using T-pattern detection, they identified that trailing teams complete more offensive possessions with higher efficiency during clutch moments, and that fast-break plays finishing within 17 s via inside scoring yield significantly better outcomes. However, their analysis remains descriptive—identifying *what works* without explaining *why* these patterns emerge or *how* to prescribe strategies for novel contexts. Current research on clutch time focuses primarily on retrospective pattern mining and factor identification [14,21], but does not provide actionable mechanisms for coaches to select optimal tactics in real-time.

2.2 AI Decision Support in Basketball

The application of artificial intelligence to basketball analytics has predominantly concentrated on outcome prediction rather than tactical decision-making.

Recent systematic reviews [20] report that multilayer perceptron neural networks achieve up to 98.90% prediction accuracy for game outcomes, while hybrid models combining extreme learning machines and XGBoost attain 93.81% accuracy [6]. Comparative studies of machine learning algorithms on NBA and WNBA data report 65–67% accuracy for game-level predictions [2], with European tournament prediction accuracies ranging from 69% to 78% [19].

While impressive, these prediction-oriented approaches suffer from two fundamental shortcomings for clutch-time support: they optimize for probability estimation rather than decision recommendation, and they lack interpretability. As highlighted by Bullock et al. [5], black-box prediction methods in sports medicine deserve a "red card for reckless practice," as strategies based on spurious correlations can be ineffective or even harmful to decision-making outcomes.

Case-based reasoning (CBR) offers a compelling alternative paradigm for sports decision support due to its inherent interpretability and ability to leverage domain expertise [1]. Feely et al. [13] demonstrated the effectiveness of CBR for personalized pacing strategy recommendations in marathon running, where the system retrieves similar past races and adapts their pacing profiles to the target runner's characteristics. Their approach has been extended to marathon performance prediction and training plan recommendations [11], as well as injury risk assessment in running [12]. The human-in-the-loop methodology employed in these studies, which incorporates athlete feedback to refine similarity metrics, provides a valuable template for interactive sports analytics systems. However, directly applying traditional CBR to clutch-time basketball faces challenges: surface-level similarity matching may retrieve cases with fundamentally different causal structures, leading to ineffective recommendations.

2.3 Causal Inference Methods

Causal inference aims to estimate causal relationships from data. As shown in Fig. 1, the field has evolved along two parallel traditions [18,23]. The **social science approach** treats randomized controlled trials (RCTs) as the gold standard and develops statistical methods (instrumental variables, SEM, propensity score matching) to emulate them using observational data [3,16,25]. Rubin's potential outcomes framework [18] provides the foundation for counterfactual estimation.

In contrast, Pearl's **AI approach** [23,24] uses directed acyclic graphs (DAGs) and structural causal models (SCMs) to represent causal mechanisms directly from raw data, without requiring prior causal knowledge. It systematically addresses three core tasks—causal discovery, causal effect identification, and counterfactual reasoning—making it highly suitable for complex scenarios in elite sports. As shown in Fig. 1, the AI approach encompasses three core causal tasks. Causal discovery extracts pathways from observational data [7,27,28]; causal effect identification quantifies interventions via the back-door criterion and *do*-calculus [23]; counterfactual reasoning computes potential outcomes for individual-level decision-making [4,18,24]. Granger causality [17,29] accommodates temporal dynamics.

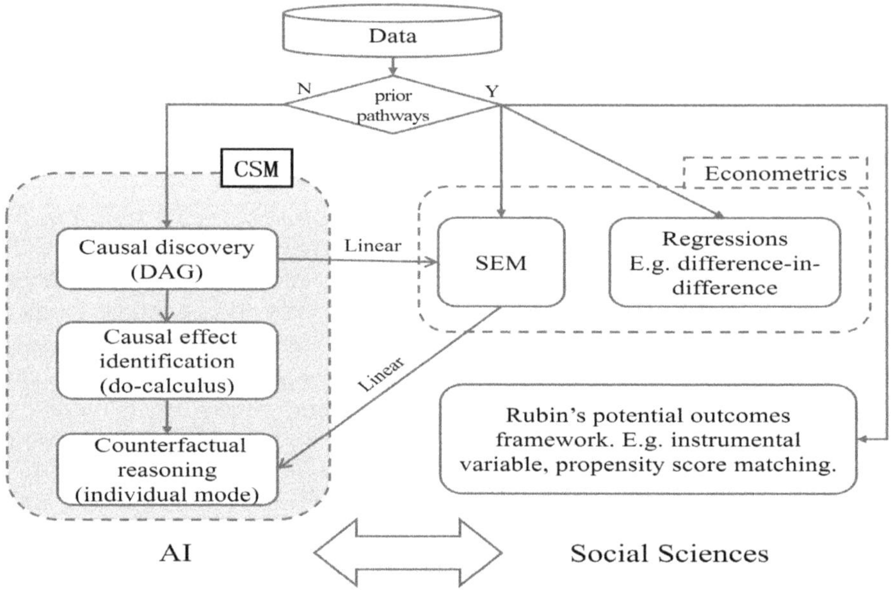

Fig. 1. Framework of causal inference methods. The social science approach (right) focuses on emulating randomized controlled trials using statistical methods, while the AI approach (left, highlighted) employs graphical models to systematically address three core causal tasks: causal discovery, causal effect identification, and counterfactual reasoning. Our CBCR framework adopts the AI approach to construct causal models from clutch-time basketball data.

In basketball research, Gibbs et al. [15] applied Rubin's counterfactual framework to quantify the causal effect of timeouts on stopping opponent scoring runs in the NBA, demonstrating that timeouts exhibit statistically significant effects in specific game contexts. As of March 2026, a search of Google Scholar reveals that, aside from Gibbs et al. [15], no research has applied causal inference to basketball, let alone clutch-time decision recommendation. Our team has pioneered the integration of causal inference into CBR for elite sports. In [9], we initially combined causal inference with CBR by introducing counterfactual diagnosis for personalized 100 m sprint training, though a complete framework had not yet been established. Subsequently, [10] presented the full CBCR framework encompassing all five causal reasoning steps and demonstrated deeper applications in elite sprinting. To the best of our knowledge, this work represents the first application of case-based causal reasoning to clutch-time basketball strategy recommendation.

3 Methodology

3.1 Case Representation

Following the standard CBR paradigm [1], each case in our system represents a single **offensive possession**—the fundamental unit of basketball gameplay. As defined by [30], a possession is "the time that the team has the ball and is attacking," ending when the defense gains possession. We adopt this rigorous definition to ensure consistency with FIBA's official play-by-play data standards.

Our case representation is structured as $C = \langle X, T, Y \rangle$, where X: **description variables** (initial state), T: **offensive strategy variables** (actions taken), and Y: **outcome variable** (possession result).

Variable Selection and Extraction. Variable selection followed a rigorous two-stage process. First, we identified all attributes available in FIBA's publicly accessible play-by-play data. Second, we consulted with professional basketball coaches to select the subset most critical for clutch-time decision-making. This collaborative approach ensures our case representation captures both data-driven insights and domain expertise.

Description Variables X capture the game state at possession start:

- t_s (start_time_sec): Seconds remaining in the quarter
- Δ_s (start_diff): Score differential (offensive team perspective)
- F_d (defensive_team_foul_count): Defensive team fouls accumulated
- F_o (offensive_team_foul_count): Offensive team fouls accumulated

Offensive Strategy Variables T characterize tactical execution:

- n_{shot} (shot_attempted_count): Field goal attempts during possession
- n_{oreb} (offensive_rebound_count): Offensive rebounds secured
- n_{foul} (offensive_foul_drawn_count): Shooting fouls drawn

Outcome Variable Y: p (points_scored) at the end of the possession.

These variables serve as *strategy execution indicators* quantifying tactical outcomes (e.g., shot volume, rebounding effort) rather than complete play diagrams. Coaches retain full authority to translate these indicators into detailed tactical deployments (e.g., pick-and-roll, off-ball screens) based on game context and video analysis. This representation enables causal reasoning about how contextual factors (X) and strategic choices (T) jointly influence scoring outcomes (Y) in clutch scenarios.

3.2 Human-in-the-Loop Case-Based Causal Reasoning

Given the complexity and risk-sensitivity of clutch-time basketball decisions, we extend the automated CBCR framework with a human-in-the-loop paradigm. Our approach integrates causal knowledge and causal reasoning throughout the entire CBR cycle while maintaining close collaboration with coaches.

Framework Overview. Figure 2 illustrates our five-stage framework. Unlike traditional CBR's four R's (Retrieve, Reuse, Revise, Retain), our CBCR framework incorporates an initial *Reconstruction* stage and transforms each subsequent stage with causal reasoning and expert feedback.

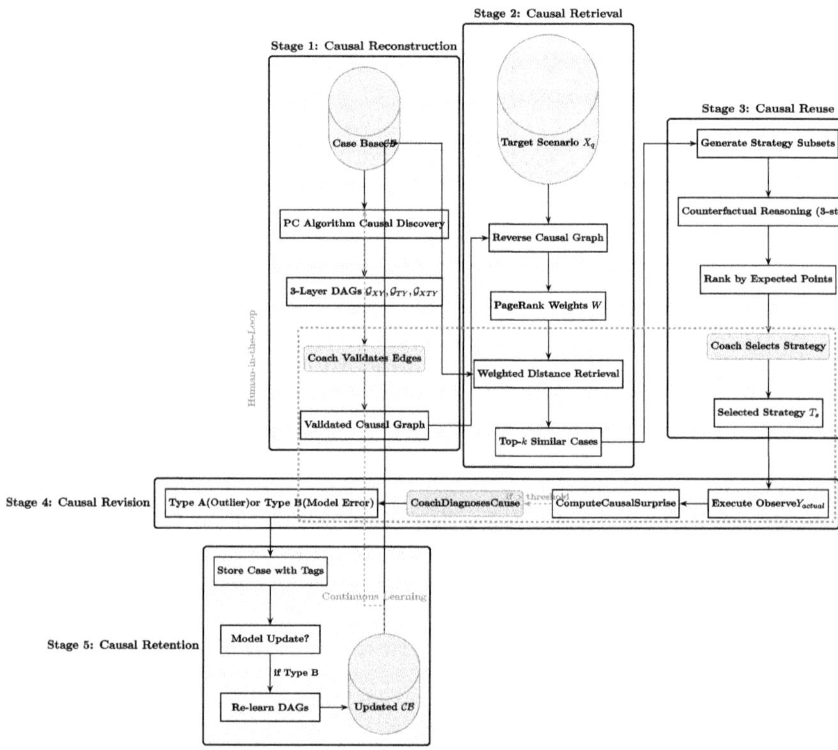

Fig. 2. Human-in-the-Loop CBCR Framework. The system integrates causal knowledge extraction, expert validation, and adaptive learning across five stages: (1) Causal Reconstruction builds three-layer causal graphs with expert validation; (2) Causal Retrieval uses PageRank-weighted similarity; (3) Causal Reuse generates multiple counterfactual strategy options; (4) Causal Revision collects coach feedback and identifies model misalignments; (5) Causal Retention selectively updates causal knowledge based on significant discrepancies.

Stage 1: Causal Reconstruction with Expert Validation. From the case base $\mathcal{CB} = \{(X_i, T_i, Y_i)\}_{i=1}^N$, we construct three causal DAGs: (1) $\mathcal{G}_{XY}$: Context-Outcome graph; (2) $\mathcal{G}_{TY}$: Strategy-Outcome graph; (3) $\mathcal{G}_{XTY}$: Full graph revealing confounding and mediation effects. We apply the PC algorithm for causal discovery, then present the learned graphs to coaches for validation. Coaches can confirm, reject, or suggest missing edges based on domain knowledge. This expert validation is crucial for small datasets, where algorithmic discovery may identify spurious relationships.

Stage 2: Causal Retrieval with PageRank Weighting. Traditional CBR methods measure similarity by independently weighting features. Our approach derives weights from the DAG structure using a PageRank-based method:

1. Construct the reverse causal graph $\mathcal{G}_{XY}^R$ by inverting edges in $\mathcal{G}_{XY}$
2. Apply PageRank on $\mathcal{G}_{XY}^R$ to compute importance scores, where d is the damping factor (typically 0.85), $In(x_i)$ denotes in-neighbors, $Out(x_j)$ denotes out-neighbors, and V is the variable set:

$$w_i^{(k+1)} = \frac{1-d}{|V|} + d \sum_{x_j \in \mathrm{In}(x_i, \mathcal{G}_{XY}^R)} \frac{w_j^{(k)}}{\mathrm{Out}(x_j, \mathcal{G}_{XY}^R)} \tag{1}$$

3. Use converged PageRank scores as retrieval weights:

$$d_{\text{causal}}(X_{\text{query}}, X_i) = \sqrt{\sum_{j=1}^{4} w_j^2 (x_j^{\text{query}} - x_j^i)^2} \tag{2}$$

Root causes (variables influencing outcomes through multiple pathways) receive higher weights. Coaches specify k (number of cases to retrieve), with default $k = 5$.

Stage 3: Causal Reuse via Granular Counterfactual Reasoning. Given a target scenario X_{query} and k retrieved cases $\{(X_i, T_i, Y_i)\}_{i=1}^k$, we generate multiple candidate strategies through granular counterfactual reasoning:

Step 1: Identify Strategy Differences. In post-game analysis where T_{query} and Y_{query} are known, for each case i, compute $\Delta T_i = \{t_j \mid t_j^{\text{query}} \neq t_j^i\}$.

Step 2: Generate Intervention Subsets. Compute the power set $\mathcal{P}(\Delta T_i) \setminus \{\emptyset\}$, representing all partial strategy adaptations.

Step 3: Three-Step Counterfactual Reasoning. For each intervention subset $S \in \mathcal{P}(\Delta T_i)$:

1. *Abduction*: Infer latent characteristics U_{query} from observed ($X_{\text{query}}, T_{\text{query}}, Y_{\text{query}}$) using structural equations from $\mathcal{G}_{TY}$
2. *Action*: Apply intervention $\mathrm{do}(T_S)$ where T_S modifies only variables in S to match case i
3. *Prediction*: Compute counterfactual outcome Y'_{query} under modified strategy

In pre-game and in-game decision-making where T_{query} and Y_{query} are unknown, conversely, perform counterfactual reasoning for each retrieved case i based on $\mathcal{G}_{XTY}$ using the steps described above.

Step 4: Rank and Present Options. Aggregate counterfactual predictions, rank by expected points, and present the top-3 strategy options with causal explanations. Each option represents a causal effect estimate for a given execution pattern (e.g., high shot volume with offensive rebounding), not a complete play diagram. Coaches select the final strategy and translate it into detailed tactical deployments (e.g., specific player movements, screen setups) based on factors not captured in X.

Stage 4: Causal Revision Through Feedback-Driven Diagnosis. After executing the selected strategy T_{selected} and observing actual outcome Y_{actual}, the system evaluates prediction accuracy. If the outcome is significantly worse than expected, we initiate collaborative causal diagnosis by quantifying the discrepancy using causal weights from $\mathcal{G}^R_{XTY}$:

$$\text{Surprise} = \sqrt{\sum_{y_j \in Y} w_{y_j} \cdot (y'_{\text{query},j} - y_{\text{actual},j})^2} \tag{3}$$

If Surprise $> \theta$, the system prompts coaches to diagnose the cause as either (A) temporary contextual factors not captured in X (stored as outlier), or (B) systematic model errors requiring causal graph modification.

Stage 5: Causal Retention with Selective Model Update. New cases are stored in $\mathcal{CB}$ with diagnostic annotations. When accumulated Type B feedback signals consistent model deficiency, the system triggers targeted causal re-learning: (1) re-run causal discovery on updated $\mathcal{CB}$ with coach-suggested constraints; (2) highlight changed edges; (3) request expert validation for modified edges; (4) archive previous model version.

4 Experiments and Evaluation

4.1 Dataset

To evaluate the effectiveness of our CBCR framework for basketball clutch moment decision-making, we collected official play-by-play data from 116 games across four major FIBA women's continental championships in 2025: the FIBA Women's AfroBasket, FIBA Women's AmeriCup, FIBA Women's EuroBasket, and FIBA Women's Asia Cup Division A. These tournaments represent the highest level of competition in their respective regions, featuring national teams with diverse tactical styles and player abilities.

Following the methodology described in Sect. 3, we extracted clutch offensive possessions using three progressively stricter time-based criteria: (1) the last

5 min with the score within 5 points (5min5pts), (2) the last 2 min under the same score conditions (2min5pts), and (3) the last 30 s (30sec5pts). The text content of "plays" is retained to provide coaches with explanatory details. The distribution of clutch possessions across tournaments and time criteria is summarized in Table 1.

Table 1. Distribution of clutch offensive possessions across tournaments and time criteria.

Tournament	5min5pts	2min5pts	30sec5pts
FIBA Women's EuroBasket 2025 (36games)	196	90	20
FIBA Women's AfroBasket 2025 (28games)	152	58	17
FIBA Women's Asia Cup Division A 2025 (20games)	86	36	9
FIBA Women's AmeriCup 2025 (32games)	81	43	13
Total	**515**	**227**	**59**

The dataset comprises 515 clutch offensive possessions under the 5min5pts criterion, 227 possessions under the 2min5pts criterion, and 59 possessions under the 30sec5pts criterion. While causal structures were learned from all three datasets (Fig. 3), systematic evaluation of Stages 2–3 was conducted on 5min5pts ($n = 515$) due to statistical reliability; the smaller datasets were reserved for causal discovery validation but deemed insufficient for robust cross-validation of retrieval and reuse performance. EuroBasket contributed the largest share (38.1% under 5min5pts), reflecting the higher frequency of close games in European competition. The decreasing number of possessions across stricter time criteria demonstrates the natural filtering effect of high-pressure endgame situations.

4.2 Evaluation Methods

Comparison Approaches. We evaluate our proposed human-in-the-loop Case-Based Causal Reasoning (CBCR-HITL) framework against two representative approaches:

1. **CBR-Sim.** The similarity-based CBR method by Feely et al. [13] represents traditional CBR without causal inference, using weighted Euclidean distance (initially uniform weights) for retrieval:

$$d(X_{\text{query}}, X_i) = \sqrt{\sum_{j=1}^{4} w_j (x_j^{\text{query}} - x_j^i)^2} \tag{4}$$

2. **CBCR-Auto.** Our second comparison method is the automated CBCR framework from our previous work [10], which integrates causal inference

into all CBR stages but operates without expert feedback. The system learns causal DAGs using the PC algorithm [28], computes causal weights for retrieval, and performs counterfactual reasoning for strategy adaptation.

Evaluation of Stage 1: Causal Reconstruction. The first stage constructs three causal DAGs ($\mathcal{G}_{XY}$, $\mathcal{G}_{TY}$, $\mathcal{G}_{XTY}$) using the PC algorithm. Evaluating causal discovery results is challenging due to the absence of ground truth causal structures in basketball tactics. Following our previous work on causal knowledge discovery in elite race-walking [8], we focus on the *trustworthiness* of discovered causal relationships through expert validation.

We perform causal reconstruction on all three case bases (Table 1). A basketball scientist (10+ years coaching experience) evaluates the learned DAGs for:

- *Structural validity*: Whether edges align with basketball tactical knowledge (e.g., score differential affects shot attempt patterns);
- *Confounding identification*: Whether known confounders (e.g., time remaining) are correctly identified;
- *Actionability*: Whether causal paths suggest interpretable tactical adjustments.

The expert validates, rejects, or suggests modifications to edges, producing validated causal graphs for subsequent stages. This human-in-the-loop validation ensures causal models are trustworthy before deployment.

Evaluation of Stage 2: Causal Retrieval. Stage 2 retrieves similar cases using different similarity metrics across the three methods. Evaluation was conducted on the 5min5pts dataset ($n = 515$), which provides sufficient sample size for reliable cross-validation; the 2min5pts ($n = 227$) and 30sec5pts ($n = 59$) datasets were used for causal discovery (Fig. 3) but excluded from systematic Stage 2–3 evaluation due to limited statistical power. A fundamental challenge is that similarity scores from different methods are not directly comparable—CBR-Sim uses Euclidean distance, while CBCR-based methods use PageRank-weighted causal distances. Therefore, we evaluate *consistency* of retrieval outcomes rather than score magnitudes.

Using 5-fold cross-validation on the 5min5pts dataset (515 possessions), we compare the top-1 case retrieved by each method for every test query. We report:

- Pairwise consistency: Percentage of queries where two methods retrieve identical top-1, top-3 and top-5 cases;
- Triple consistency: Percentage where all three methods agree.

Evaluation of Stage 3: Causal Reuse. Stage 3 generates strategy recommendations through counterfactual reasoning. Since observed solutions may be suboptimal (coaches under pressure), we cannot use simple accuracy against observed outcomes.

Instead, we evaluate *efficiency* by categorizing test cases into *scoring possessions* (points > 0) and *non-scoring possessions* (points = 0), applying different success criteria:

- **Scoring cases**: Success if the recommended strategy $T_{recommended}$ matches the test case's strategy T_{test} (assuming the test case's successful strategy is worth replicating);
- **Non-scoring cases**: Success if $T_{recommended} \neq T_{test}$ (suggesting a different approach might improve outcome).

Using 5-fold cross-validation on the 5min5pts dataset, we report success rates for each category and overall accuracy. This efficiency metric reflects whether the system provides actionable recommendations that align with successful precedents or diverge from unsuccessful ones.

Stages 4 (Causal Revision) and 5 (Causal Retention) require real-world deployment with continuous expert feedback to evaluate feedback-driven diagnosis and are await full deployment evaluation in the future.

4.3 Results

Results of Causal Reconstruction. We applied the PC algorithm [28] with $\alpha = 0.05$ to learn causal DAGs from the three datasets, incorporating two critical domain knowledge constraints confirmed by the expert: **(1) Exogeneity of time:** `start_time_sec` is purely exogenous—the game clock decreases monotonically regardless of in-game events. **(2) Temporal ordering between variable types:** Context variables X cannot be caused by strategy variables T or outcome variable Y within the same possession as context is determined before possession begins, while strategies and outcomes unfold during possession.

Figure 3 presents the learned causal DAGs for the two larger datasets (5min5pts and 2min5pts); the 30sec5pts dataset ($n = 59$) yielded unstable structures due to insufficient sample size. **Key findings:** (1) The 5min5pts and 2min5pts datasets yield nearly identical causal structures, suggesting stable causal mechanisms in clutch-time basketball. (2) Due to the marginal correlation between `offensive_rebound_count` and `points_scored` ($p = 0.18$), this edge is absent in $\mathcal{G}_{TY}$. However, when conditioning on other strategy variables in $\mathcal{G}_{XTY}$, the partial correlation becomes highly significant ($p < 0.001$). This illustrates the importance of analyzing the full graph $\mathcal{G}_{XTY}$ to capture indirect causal pathways, and the necessity of treating descriptions, strategies, and outcomes as a unified whole in case-based reasoning. Based on the results in Fig. 3, in the case of this paper, we used $\mathcal{G}_{XTY}$ for inference in all subsequent stages.

Results of Causal Retrieval. Table 2 presents the retrieval consistency across the three methods on the 5min5pts dataset using 5-fold cross-validation.

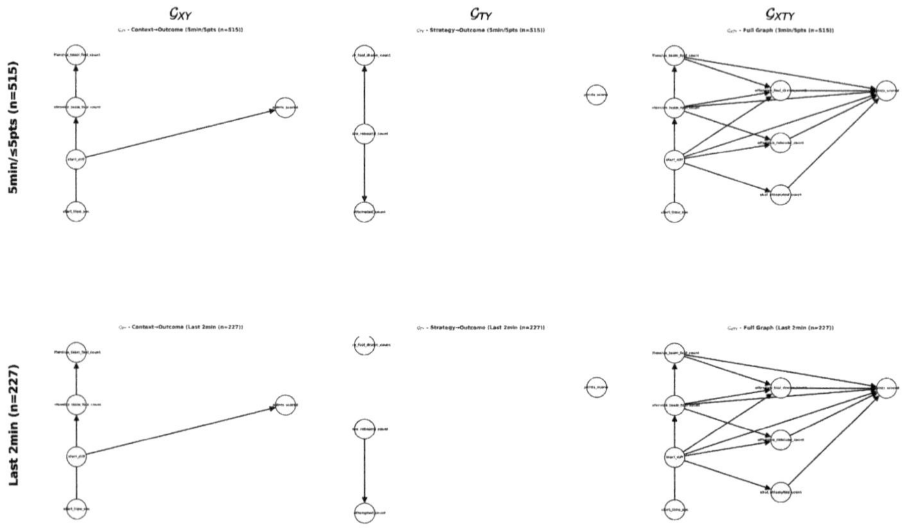

Fig. 3. Learned causal DAGs using PC algorithm on 5min5pts and 2min5pts datasets. Rows represent causal graph types: $\mathcal{G}_{XY}$ (Context→Outcome), $\mathcal{G}_{TY}$ (Strategy→Outcome), and $\mathcal{G}_{XTY}$ (full graph). Columns show results for 5min5pts ($n = 515$) and 2min5pts ($n = 227$). Node colors: blue (context X), orange (strategy T), green (outcome Y).

The near-identical retrieval outcomes between CBCR-Auto and CBCR-HITL (96.7%–97.8%) indicate that causal graph structure drives retrieval results, not precise effect values. In contrast, CBR-Sim shows only 56–61% consistency with CBCR methods, confirming that PageRank-weighted causal similarity fundamentally diverges from Euclidean distance.

Notably, consistency slightly increases with retrieval depth (top-1 to top-5), suggesting that while methods disagree on the single most similar case, they converge on the broader pool of relevant cases with compatible causal mechanisms.

Table 2. Retrieval consistency across methods on 5min5pts dataset (5-fold CV, 515 possessions). Values represent percentage of queries where methods retrieve identical cases.

Method Pair	Top-1 (%)	Top-3 (%)	Top-5 (%)
CBR-Sim vs. CBCR-Auto	58.1	60.3	61.2
CBR-Sim vs. CBCR-HITL	56.1	58.9	60.1
CBCR-Auto vs. CBCR-HITL	96.7	97.3	97.8
Triple Consistency (All three)	**56.1**	**58.9**	**58.3**

Results of Causal Reuse. Due to the high retrieval consistency between CBCR-Auto and CBCR-HITL (Table 2), we compare only CBR-Sim and CBCR-HITL in Stage 3. Figure 4 presents results using two evaluation criteria on the 5min5pts dataset via 5-fold cross-validation. **(a) Strategy consistency-based:** CBCR-HITL outperforms CBR-Sim on non-scoring possessions by 17.1% points (81.5% vs. 64.4%), but shows lower consistency with test case solutions on scoring possessions (25.7% vs. 38.0%).

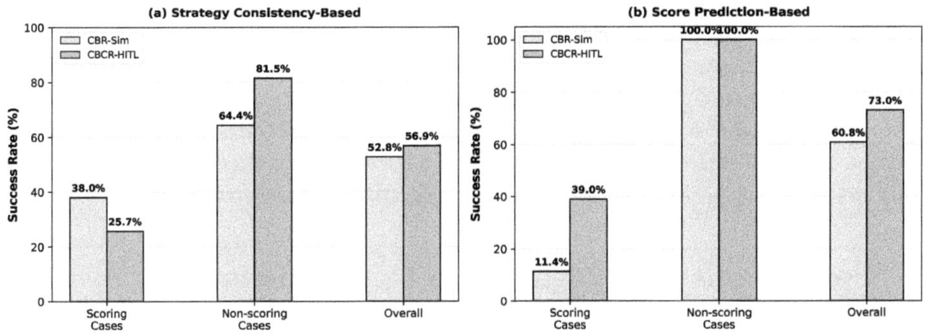

Fig. 4. Stage 3 causal reuse results comparing CBR-Sim and CBCR-HITL. (a) Strategy consistency-based evaluation. (b) Score prediction-based evaluation (predicted $\geq$ actual). Non-scoring cases are 100% by definition since predicted $\geq$ actual $= 0$; the meaningful comparison is on scoring cases. HITL's value lies in Stage 1 (expert-validated causal edges) and Stages 4–5 (feedback-driven diagnosis), requiring real-world deployment for full evaluation.

However, as noted in our evaluation methodology, test solutions are not ground truth—consistency does not equal optimality, as coaches may have made suboptimal decisions under pressure. **(b) Score prediction-based:** Using the criterion *predicted score* $\geq$ *actual score*, CBCR-HITL's counterfactual predictions substantially outperform CBR-Sim (73.0% vs. 60.8%, +12.2 percentage points), with particularly strong improvements on scoring cases (39.0% vs. 11.4%). This superior predictive performance increases our anticipation for real-world deployment evaluations.

5 Discussion and Limitations

This study demonstrates that integrating causal knowledge throughout the CBR cycle—particularly the full causal structure among description, solution, and outcome variables—is essential for clutch-time decision support. The incorporation of causal inference significantly enhances reasoning reliability under data scarcity. By leveraging causal structure rather than pure statistical patterns, CBCR-HITL achieves robust generalization from limited clutch-time observations (515 possessions in 5min5pts, 227 in 2min5pts). Furthermore, the human-in-the-loop design augments interpretability—coaches validate causal edges, diagnose prediction failures, and select strategies based on causal explanations rather than black-box recommendations. This transparency is crucial for adoption in high-stakes competitive environments.

However, several limitations remain. First, data scarcity constrains causal discovery: the 30sec dataset (59 possessions) yields unstable DAGs, preventing reliable inference in the most critical endgame moments. Second, current strategy variables (shot count, rebound count) remain coarse execution indicators; future work will incorporate finer-grained tactical elements such as possession start location, shot type (2pt/3pt), and play diagrams (e.g., pick-and-roll, off-ball screens) to align more closely with coaches' actual whiteboarding practice. Third, current counterfactual reasoning operates at the population level; individual athlete causal models are underdeveloped, limiting personalization in pre-game and in-game scenarios. Fourth, Stages 4 and 5 (feedback-driven revision and selective retention) lack empirical evaluation—their effectiveness in continuous deployment and potential risks of model drift await validation.

6 Conclusions and Pathway to Deployment

This work presents a novel CBCR framework for clutch-time basketball strategy recommendation, addressing the unique challenges of data scarcity, risk sensitivity, and high personalization in elite sports. By integrating causal inference across all CBR stages, we provide a trustworthy, interpretable alternative to black-box prediction models. Beyond basketball, this architecture offers a credible pathway for combining CBR with RAG and large language models, where causal validation can mitigate hallucination risks. Future deployment priorities include: (1) expanding data volume for ultra-clutch scenarios; (2) developing individual-level causal models; and (3) conducting field trials with national teams to evaluate Stage 4–5 performance.

Acknowledgments. Supported by the Fundamental Research Funds for the China Institute of Sport Science (Grant No. 25-03).

Generative AI Statement. The authors used large language models (LLMs), including Kimi (Moonshot AI) and Claude Code (Anthropic), to assist with language polishing, plot drawing and LaTeX formatting during the paper-writing process. The authors assume full responsibility for all content. All research ideas, methodological designs, experimental analyses, and scientific conclusions were conceived and validated by the authors.

References

1. Aamodt, A., Plaza, E.: Case-based reasoning: foundational issues, methodological variations, and system approaches **7**(1), 39–59 (1994)
2. Alves, J.A.M., Barbosa, R.S.: Machine learning for basketball game outcomes: NBA and WNBA leagues **13**(10), 230 (2025)

3. Angrist, J.D., Pischke, J.S.: Mostly Harmless Econometrics: An Empiricist's Companion. Princeton University Press (2009)
4. Bareinboim, E., Correa, J.D., Ibeling, D., Icard, T.: On Pearl's hierarchy and the foundations of causal inference. In: Probabilistic and Causal Inference: The Works of Judea Pearl, pp. 507–556. ACM (2020)
5. Bullock, G.S., Hughes, T., Arundale, A.H., Ward, P., Waterman, B.R., Hanlon, C.: Black box prediction methods in sports medicine deserve a red card for reckless practice: a change of tactics is needed to advance athlete care **52**(8), 1729–1735 (2022)
6. Chen, W.J., Jhou, M.J., Lee, T.S., Lu, C.J.: Hybrid basketball game outcome prediction model by integrating data mining methods for the national basketball association **23**(4), 477 (2021)
7. Colombo, D., Maathuis, M.H., Kalisch, M., Richardson, T.S.: Learning high-dimensional directed acyclic graphs with latent and selection variables **40**(1), 294–321 (2012)
8. Cui, D., Jiang, Z., Zhang, X., Yang, W., He, Z.: A multi-domain collaborative framework for practical application of causal knowledge discovery from public data in elite sports. Appl. Syst. Innov. **9**(2), 43 (2026)
9. Cui, D., Guo, J., Liu, P., Zhang, X.: Using case-based causal reasoning to provide explainable counterfactual diagnosis in personalized sprint training. In: Case-Based Reasoning Research and Development - 32nd International Conference, ICCBR 2024, Proceedings, pp. 418–429. Springer (2024)
10. Cui, D., Guo, J., Liu, P., Zhang, X., Liu, W.: Case-based causal reasoning for elite sport training. In: Case-Based Reasoning Research and Development - 33rd International Conference, ICCBR 2025, Proceedings, pp. 378–391. Springer (2025)
11. Feely, C., Caulfield, B., Lawlor, A., Smyth, B.: Using case-based reasoning to predict marathon performance and recommend tailored training plans. In: Watson, I., Weber, R. (eds.) ICCBR 2020. LNCS (LNAI), vol. 12311, pp. 67–81. Springer, Cham (2020). https://doi.org/10.1007/978-3-030-58342-2_5
12. Feely, C., Caulfield, B., Lawlor, A., Smyth, B.: A case-based reasoning approach to predicting and explaining running related injuries. In: Sánchez-Ruiz, A.A., Floyd, M.W. (eds.) ICCBR 2021. LNCS (LNAI), vol. 12877, pp. 79–93. Springer, Cham (2021). https://doi.org/10.1007/978-3-030-86957-1_6
13. Feely, C., Caulfield, B., Lawlor, A., Smyth, B.: A case-based approach to data-driven pacing strategy recommendations for marathon runners during training. In: Case-Based Reasoning Research and Development - 32nd International Conference, ICCBR 2024, Proceedings, pp. 351–366. Springer (2024)
14. García-Manso, J.M., Martín-González, J.M., Guerra, Y.D.S., Vaamonde, D.: Last minute in NBA games **24**(3), 31–35 (2015)
15. Gibbs, C.P., Elmore, R., Fosdick, B.K.: The causal effect of a timeout at stopping an opposing run in the NBA **16**(3), 1359–1379 (2022)
16. Goldberger, A.S.: Structural equation methods in the social sciences **40**(6), 979–1001 (1972)
17. Granger, C.W.J.: Investigating causal relations by econometric models and cross-spectral methods **37**(3), 424–438 (1969)
18. Imbens, G.W., Rubin, D.B.: Causal Inference for Statistics, Social, and Biomedical Sciences: An Introduction. Cambridge University Press (2015)
19. Lampis, T., Ioannis, N., Vasilios, V., Stavrianna, D.: Predictions of European basketball match results with machine learning algorithms **9**(2), 171–190 (2023)

20. Li, C., Zhang, H., Zhang, Y., Shen, J., An, R.: The application of artificial intelligence techniques in predicting game outcomes of professional basketball league: a systematic review **20**(6), e0326326 (2025)
21. Martins, J.A., Mesquita, I., Mendes, A., Santos, L., Afonso, J.: Current understanding of critical game scenarios in team sports: systematic review **23**(2), 1–11 (2022)
22. National Basketball Association: NBA advanced stats: Clutch traditional statistics (2026). https://www.nba.com/stats/teams/clutch-traditional. Accessed 26 Mar 2026
23. Pearl, J.: Causality: Models, Reasoning, and Inference, 2 edn. Cambridge University Press (2009)
24. Pearl, J., Glymour, M., Jewell, N.P.: Causal Inference in Statistics: A Primer. Wiley (2016)
25. Rosenbaum, P.R., Rubin, D.B.: The central role of the propensity score in observational studies for causal effects **70**(1), 41–55 (1983)
26. Sarlis, V., Gerakas, D., Tjortjis, C.: A data science and sports analytics approach to decode clutch dynamics in the last minutes of NBA games **6**(3), 2074–2095 (2024)
27. Shimizu, S., Hoyer, P.O., Hyvärinen, A., Kerminen, A.: A linear non-Gaussian acyclic model for causal discovery **7**, 2003–2030 (2006)
28. Spirtes, P., Glymour, C.: An algorithm for fast recovery of sparse causal graphs **9**(1), 62–72 (1991)
29. Tank, A., Covert, I., Foti, N., Shojaie, A., Fox, E.B.: Neural Granger causality **44**(4), 4267–4279 (2021)
30. Vázquez-Estévez, C., et al.: Analysis of successful offensive patterns in critical moments in men's EuroBasket 2022 and women's 2021 **14**(23), 10883 (2024)
31. Zhao, J., et al.: Learning graph convolutional networks for multi-behavior recommendation in heterogeneous networks **35**(5), 4684–4696 (2023)

A Case-Based Reasoning System for Meteorological Event Analysis Integrating Multi-source Observational Data

Chenxi Wang, Yan Li, Xinjin Ge, Hanwen Zhang, and Chunli Lv(✉)

China Agricultural University, Beijing 100084, China
{wangchenxi2019,liyantongxue,2022308250211,zhw19,lvcl}@cau.edu.cn

Abstract. Meteorological event analysis typically relies on experience-driven analogical reasoning or data-driven approaches; however, it still faces challenges such as strong heterogeneity in multi-source observational data, difficulties in unified modeling, and a lack of traceable reasoning mechanisms and interpretability. To address this issue, this paper proposes a Case-Based Reasoning (CBR) system for meteorological event analysis that integrates multi-source observational data. The proposed system constructs a unified feature representation by fusing surface meteorological variables and remote sensing cloud images. A multi-dimensional similarity measurement strategy, incorporating dynamic time warping (DTW), is designed to evaluate historical weather processes comprehensively. Furthermore, the system employs Facebook AI similarity search (FAISS) for efficient case retrieval and a Transformer-based evolution analysis module to infer the developmental trends of current weather systems based on similar historical cases. Quantitative experiments demonstrate that the proposed method achieves competitive performance in both historical case retrieval (with a Recall@5 of 0.876) and trend analysis (with a mean absolute error (MAE) of 2.31) compared to mainstream sequence-modeling methods. Moreover, domain expert evaluation indicates that 82.00% of the system's inferred evolution trends can directly serve as operational references.

Keywords: Case-Based Reasoning · Meteorological Event Analysis · Multi-Source Data Fusion · Interpretable Machine Learning · Time Series Modeling

1 Introduction

The analysis and prediction of meteorological events are directly related to agricultural production, disaster prevention and mitigation, and public safety decision-making [21]. In practical operations, meteorological analysts are typically required to determine which historical weather processes are similar to the current atmospheric structure and to infer their subsequent evolution paths accordingly [5]. This experience-based analogical analysis constitutes one of

L. Malburg and K. Bach (Eds.): ICCBR 2026, LNAI 16780, pp. 489–504, 2027.
https://doi.org/10.1007/978-3-032-33865-5_30

the core approaches in meteorological forecasting practice [20]. Taking Wuyuan County in Bayannur City, Inner Mongolia Autonomous Region, China as an example, this region is characterized by a typical temperate continental climate, where spring dust storms, localized convective precipitation in summer, and cold waves in winter are the primary meteorological hazards. A large number of historical weather event records have been accumulated by the Wuyuan County Meteorological Bureau through long-term operational practice, including ground meteorological observations such as temperature, humidity, atmospheric pressure, and wind speed, as well as satellite-based remote sensing cloud imagery from the FY-2/FY-4 series [26]. When analyzing a suspected cold wave process, the current pressure field and temperature variation trends are typically examined, similar historical cases are retrieved from experience, and their evolution processes are referenced to support decision-making [6].

However, this experience-driven analysis approach exhibits several limitations [24]. First, human memory is insufficient to comprehensively retrieve large-scale historical cases accumulated over long richter2013caseperiods [17]. Second, multi-source meteorological data (e.g., remote sensing and ground observations) present structural heterogeneity, which increases the difficulty of integrated analysis [21]. Third, expert experience is difficult to standardize and share, making it challenging for newly recruited analysts to rapidly acquire the reasoning capabilities developed by experienced forecasters. In recent years, deep learning methods have achieved significant progress in meteorological analysis [14]. For example, the ConvLSTM model proposed by Shi et al. introduces convolutional operations into the long short term memory (LSTM) framework to enable spatiotemporal sequence prediction [15], while the Pangu-Weather model developed by Bi et al. leverages a Transformer-based architecture to improve medium-range weather forecasting accuracy [3]. However, such methods are essentially function approximation models that provide predictions without explicit reasoning mechanisms, making it difficult for analysts to interpret the origin and reliability of the results [2]. Case-Based Reasoning (CBR) provides a computational framework that is highly consistent with the workflow of meteorological analysis [4]. By retrieving similar historical cases and reusing their solutions, CBR enables experience-driven reasoning with explicit traceability, thereby improving interpretability and trustworthiness [13]. This paradigm has demonstrated effectiveness in domains such as clinical decision support [11] and explainable recommendation systems [8]. However, applications of CBR in meteorology remain limited and are primarily focused on single data sources, lacking the capability to integrate multi-source meteorological data [17].

To address these issues, a case-based reasoning meteorological event analysis system integrating remote sensing and ground observation data is constructed. Specifically, multi-source meteorological data are first unified through deep visual models and statistical processing methods, enabling remote sensing cloud features and ground meteorological variables to be represented within a common feature space. Subsequently, considering the multimodal and temporal characteristics of meteorological data, a composite similarity measurement method is developed by integrating Euclidean distance, cosine similarity, and dynamic time warping, thereby achieving more accurate case matching. On this basis, an efficient vector retrieval mechanism is employed to improve retrieval efficiency in large-scale case bases. Furthermore, a Transformer-based temporal modeling approach is introduced to analyze the evolution processes of historical meteorological events, providing references for the development trends of current weather systems. Finally, the effectiveness and practical applicability of the system are validated through real-world meteorological observation data and expert evaluation.

2 Related Work

2.1 Meteorological Data Analysis

In recent years, a large number of studies have applied machine learning methods to meteorological data analysis. In the direction of deep neural network-based weather prediction, the ConvLSTM model proposed by Shi et al. [18] introduces convolutional operations into the gating mechanism of LSTM, enabling effective modeling of spatiotemporal sequence data and achieving superior performance compared with traditional optical flow methods in precipitation nowcasting. The Pangu-Weather model developed by Bi et al. [3] employs a 3D Transformer architecture for global medium-range weather forecasting, achieving accuracy comparable to that of the numerical models of the European Centre for Medium-Range Weather Forecasts (ECMWF). The GraphCast model proposed by Lam et al. [12] further utilizes graph neural networks to predict meteorological variables on a global grid. In the fields of time-series meteorological modeling and remote sensing data fusion, recurrent neural networks have been widely used for temperature and wind speed prediction, while deep learning methods have been applied to cloud classification, precipitation estimation, and meteorological object detection [10,27]. Although these approaches have demonstrated strong performance in their respective tasks, they primarily focus on predictive modeling and lack the capability of experience-based reasoning using historical cases. When a prediction is generated, its underlying rationale remains difficult to interpret, and in county-level meteorological scenarios with limited data, model performance is often constrained. This limitation becomes particularly critical in operational contexts where decision justification is required [2].

2.2 Applications of Case-Based Reasoning in Environmental and Meteorological Domains

CBR assists problem solving by retrieving similar historical cases, and its workflow has been summarized as a four-stage cycle consisting of Retrieve, Reuse, Revise, and Retain [1,9,25]. In meteorology-related studies, Ráduly et al. [16] estimated pollutant concentrations by retrieving similar meteorological conditions, and Flash-CBR [7] was applied CBR to early flood warning by leveraging historical flood cases. These studies demonstrate the effectiveness of CBR in environmental event analysis. A key advantage of CBR lies in its inherent interpretability [19]. For instance, Kuhn et al. [11] validated the transparency of CBR in decision-making, while González-Monge et al. [8] further enhanced interpretability by integrating CBR with knowledge graphs to visualize reasoning paths. However, existing CBR studies in meteorology predominantly rely on single-source ground observations and lack the integration of remote sensing data [22,23]. In addition, limitations remain in case representation capability and retrieval efficiency for large-scale case bases. To address these issues, a CBR system integrating multi-source meteorological data is constructed, combined with vector retrieval techniques and Transformer-based modeling to enhance the representation and reasoning performance for meteorological event analysis.

3 Methodology

3.1 Use Case

In practical grassroots meteorological forecasting operations, the CBR-based meteorological event analysis system proposed in this study is primarily designed to assist forecasters in the early identification and trend assessment of complex weather processes. When abnormal fluctuations in meteorological variables or characteristic cloud system changes are detected by the observation network, the current ground observation sequences together with corresponding satellite cloud images can be input into the system. Through unified feature representation and similarity measurement methods such as dynamic time warping (DTW), the system retrieves historical weather processes that are most similar in terms of initial conditions, spatial structures, and recent evolution patterns. Subsequently, the evolution patterns of the retrieved cases are modeled using a Transformer module to infer the development trends of the current weather system, while the actual evolution outcomes and explanatory information of historical cases are presented.

3.2 Case Base

A meteorological case base was constructed based on real-world meteorological observation data. The primary data sources include ground observation data from the Wuyuan County Meteorological Bureau in Bayannur City, Inner Mongolia Autonomous Region, China, satellite-based remote sensing meteorological observations, and historical weather event records.

First, with respect to ground meteorological observations, the data were obtained from the automatic meteorological station network operated by the Wuyuan County Meteorological Bureau. This station network provides continuous hourly observations covering a seven-year period from 2018 to 2024. The observed meteorological variables mainly include air temperature, relative humidity, atmospheric pressure, wind speed, wind direction, and precipitation. Temperature is recorded in degrees Celsius (°C), humidity is expressed as a percentage, atmospheric pressure is measured in hectopascals (hPa), wind speed is measured in meters per second (m/s), and precipitation is recorded in millimeters (mm). The original temporal resolution of the observations is 1 hour. After data cleaning and anomaly filtering procedures, 61,000 valid meteorological observation records were obtained. Second, with respect to remote sensing meteorological observations, satellite cloud imagery corresponding to the timestamps of ground observations was collected. The remote sensing data mainly include visible-spectrum cloud images (9,200 samples) and infrared cloud images (8,800 samples) provided by geostationary meteorological satellites. Each remote sensing image was uniformly cropped and spatially aligned to extract atmospheric cloud structure information covering Wuyuan County and its surrounding regions. The spatial resolution of the satellite observations is approximately 1–2 km, while the temporal resolution ranges from 30 minutes to 1 hour. During the data preprocessing and screening procedure, 18,000 valid satellite cloud image samples were retained.

Temporal information includes observation timestamps (61,000 records), weather process duration records (4,200 records), and weather system evolution stage indicators (4,200 records). The development stages of weather processes were categorized according to the lifecycle of meteorological events, including the formation stage (1,050 cases), development stage (1,150 cases), mature stage (1,050 cases), and dissipation stage (950 cases). Meteorological event outcomes mainly include precipitation conditions (4,200 records), heavy precipitation events (850 records), and extreme weather events (320 records). According to meteorological bureau classification standards, precipitation events are categorized into five levels: no precipitation (1,800 cases), light rain (1,100 cases), moderate rain (750 cases), heavy rain (400 cases), and rainstorm (150 cases). In addition, several types of extreme weather phenomena were documented, including severe convective weather (120 cases), short-duration heavy precipitation (140 cases), and strong wind processes (60 cases). Through the integration and alignment of historical weather records with observation data, 4,200 meteorological event cases were constructed. Each case contains a complete description of meteorological conditions and the corresponding weather event outcome. Finally, all collected data were organized using a unified data structure. Each meteorological case consists of four components: meteorological variable features, remote sensing observation features, temporal information, and meteorological event outcomes. This case base provides the real-world observational data foundation required for the construction of the case-based reasoning system.

3.3 Meteorological Event CBR Reasoning System

Based on the aforementioned multi-source meteorological data processing and modeling methods, a meteorological event analysis system integrating case-based reasoning mechanisms and multimodal learning approaches is constructed. As shown in Fig. 1, the system follows the classical case-based reasoning cycle (Retrieve–Reuse–Revise–Retain), and is implemented as a closed-loop process of unified representation–similarity matching–case retrieval–evolution inference–result revision. Let the current meteorological event to be analyzed be denoted as the query case q, and the historical case base be denoted as $\mathcal{C} = \{c_1, c_2, \ldots, c_N\}$. The overall reasoning process of the system can be formulated as

$$\{q, \mathcal{C}\} \xrightarrow{\phi} \{\mathbf{z}_q, \mathbf{z}_1, \ldots, \mathbf{z}_N\} \xrightarrow{\mathcal{S}} \{\mathcal{S}(q, c_i)\}_{i=1}^{N} \xrightarrow{\mathcal{R}} \mathcal{N}_k(q) \xrightarrow{\mathcal{E}} \hat{y}_q, \tag{1}$$

where $\phi(\cdot)$ denotes the multi-source case representation function, $\mathbf{z}_i \in \mathbb{R}^d$ denotes the case vector in the unified feature space, $\mathcal{S}(\cdot)$ denotes the composite similarity computation, $\mathcal{R}(\cdot)$ denotes the case retrieval process, $\mathcal{E}(\cdot)$ denotes the evolution inference based on historical cases, and $\hat{y}_q$ denotes the final trend analysis and risk assessment result.

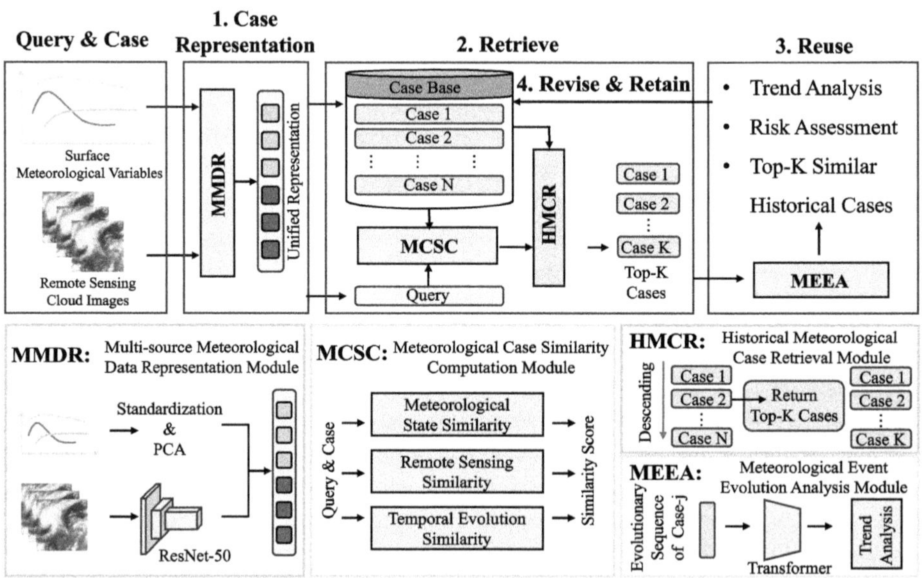

Fig. 1. The overall architecture of the proposed case-based reasoning system, illustrating the workflow of case representation, retrieval, reuse, and revision, along with the detailed structure of its core modules.

Case Representation. In the case representation stage, each meteorological case is modeled as a structured unit consisting of a state description and an evolution outcome, where the state description characterizes the multi-source observational features of the weather system at the current time and within its historical window, and the evolution outcome describes its subsequent development process. For any case c, the raw observations include the ground meteorological variable sequence $\mathbf{X} \in \mathbb{R}^{T \times p}$, remote sensing cloud imagery $\mathbf{I}$, and temporal evolution information. To achieve unified modeling of heterogeneous data, the ground meteorological variables are first normalized to eliminate scale differences, and principal component analysis (PCA) is applied to extract dominant variation patterns, yielding a low-dimensional meteorological state representation $\mathbf{m} \in \mathbb{R}^{d_m}$. Meanwhile, a pre-trained ResNet-50 is utilized to extract high-level semantic features from remote sensing cloud images, resulting in the representation $\mathbf{r} \in \mathbb{R}^{d_r}$. The two types of features are then concatenated to obtain the unified case representation

$$\mathbf{z} = \phi(c) = [\mathbf{m}; \mathbf{r}] \in \mathbb{R}^d, \quad d = d_m + d_r. \tag{2}$$

Through this mapping, the query case q and historical cases c_i are projected into the same feature space, enabling multimodal information to be compared and matched within a unified semantic space.

Similarity Measurement and Case Retrieval. In the retrieval stage, the similarity between the query case and historical cases is computed based on the unified representation. Considering that meteorological events exhibit numerical state characteristics, spatial structural features, and temporal evolution properties simultaneously, a multi-dimensional similarity function is constructed:

$$S(q, c_i) = \alpha S_{\text{met}}(q, c_i) + \beta S_{\text{rs}}(q, c_i) + \gamma S_{\text{ts}}(q, c_i), \tag{3}$$

where S_{met} denotes the Euclidean distance-based similarity on meteorological variables $\mathbf{m}$, S_{rs} denotes the cosine similarity on remote sensing features $\mathbf{r}$, and S_{ts} denotes the DTW-based similarity on raw temporal sequences, with $\alpha, \beta, \gamma \geq 0$ and $\alpha + \beta + \gamma = 1$. After computing the composite similarity, historical cases are ranked according to $S(q, c_i)$, and the Top-k most similar cases are retrieved:

$$\mathcal{N}_k(q) = \text{TopK}_{c_i \in \mathcal{C}}\ S(q, c_i). \tag{4}$$

When the case base is small, exact nearest neighbor search can be applied; in large-scale scenarios, high-dimensional indexing is constructed based on unified feature vectors to enable efficient approximate retrieval. This stage establishes the mapping from multimodal observations to historical experience cases, serving as a critical bridge between the data space and the experience space.

Case Reuse and Evolution Inference. In the reuse stage, the evolution information of the retrieved similar case set $\mathcal{N}_k(q) = \{c_{(1)}, \ldots, c_{(k)}\}$ is utilized to infer the development trend of the current weather process. Let the evolution sequence of the j-th similar case be

$$\mathbf{U}^{(j)} = \{\mathbf{u}_t^{(j)}\}_{t=1}^{L}, \tag{5}$$

where L denotes the evolution window length. To reduce the influence of short-term noise, a moving average is first applied to smooth the sequence:

$$\bar{\mathbf{u}}_t^{(j)} = \frac{1}{w} \sum_{\tau=t-w+1}^{t} \mathbf{u}_\tau^{(j)}, \tag{6}$$

where w denotes the window length. Subsequently, a Transformer model is introduced to model the evolution sequences of multiple cases, capturing long-range temporal dependencies of the weather system. Considering the matching degree between each case and the query case, a similarity-based weighted fusion mechanism is introduced. Let the similarity score of the j-th case be $s_{(j)}$, and its normalized weight is defined as

$$\omega_j = \frac{s_{(j)}}{\sum_{\ell=1}^{k} s_{(\ell)}}. \tag{7}$$

Finally, the trend analysis result of the current meteorological event is expressed as

$$\hat{y}_q = \sum_{j=1}^{k} \omega_j \, g\left(\bar{\mathbf{U}}^{(j)}\right), \tag{8}$$

where $g(\cdot)$ denotes the mapping function from historical evolution patterns to trend estimation or risk scoring. This process realizes the knowledge transfer from similar historical cases to current trend prediction.

Case Revision and Retention. Due to the inherent nonlinearity and regional variability of meteorological systems, even globally similar historical cases may exhibit local discrepancies, necessitating an adaptive, residual-based adjustment of the reused results. In this stage, the system performs a comparative analysis of state deviations between the query case and retrieved historical analogs across key physical indicators, including temperature gradients, moisture transport flux, and dynamic lifting structures. These deviations are utilized as dynamic correction signals to refine the initial predictions; specifically, when the current system demonstrates higher levels of energy accumulation or more intense moisture convergence compared to the retrieved cases, the risk estimation for severe convection or intensified precipitation is proportionally increased. Conversely, if the current observational signals are weaker than the historical baseline, the predicted outcome intensity is adjusted downward to ensure the accuracy of the reference. This mechanism enables the transition from simple analogical mapping to context-adaptive reasoning, significantly improving the system's robustness in complex and shifting meteorological scenarios.

To ensure the continuous evolution of the expertise within the system, a case retention process is implemented to complete the Case-Based Reasoning closed-loop. Once the actual weather process concludes and the ground truth is recorded by the automatic meteorological station network, the new event—comprising its multi-source observational features and verified evolution path—is encoded through the MMDR module into a unified feature vector z. This new case is then integrated into the case base $\mathcal{C}$ to serve as a novel reference. Simultaneously, the FAISS-based high-dimensional index is incrementally updated to incorporate this latest experience, allowing the system to function as a self-learning knowledge repository that progressively adapts to regional climate characteristics and long-term variations.

3.4 Evaluation Concept

To validate the effectiveness of the proposed case-based reasoning system for meteorological events, experimental evaluation is conducted from three perspectives, namely, historical case retrieval, weather evolution trend analysis, and computational efficiency. The former evaluates whether relevant historical cases can be accurately retrieved, while the latter assesses whether reliable future trends can be inferred based on retrieved cases. For the retrieval task, Recall@5, Precision@5, F1@5, MRR, and NDCG@5 are adopted to measure retrieval accuracy, ranking quality, and overall balance. For the trend analysis task, mean absolute error (MAE) and root mean square error (RMSE) are used to evaluate prediction deviation and sensitivity to large errors. To assess the computational overhead, the average inference time per query is introduced as an efficiency metric. These metrics enable a comprehensive assessment of case-matching quality, trend-analysis performance, and system deployment feasibility.

To verify the performance advantages of the proposed method, multiple baseline methods are selected, including ConvLSTM, GraphCast, Pangu-Weather, KNN-Met, KNN-Fusion, FAISS-Fusion, and Transformer-Seq. All experiments are conducted in a consistent training environment with identical hardware and software configurations to ensure fair comparisons. The meteorological case base is partitioned into training, validation, and testing sets with a ratio of 7:1:2. For the multi-dimensional similarity computation, the hyperparameters are empirically set to $\alpha = 0.4$, $\beta = 0.3$, and $\gamma = 0.3$ to balance the contributions of surface meteorological variables, remote sensing features, and temporal evolution sequences. To further analyze the contribution of each module, ablation experiments are conducted based on the full model. For the representation module, w/o Remote Sensing, w/o PCA, and w/o Meteorological Features are introduced. For the similarity computation module, w/o DTW, w/o Remote Sensing Similarity, and w/o Temporal Evolution Similarity are evaluated. For the evolution analysis stage, w/o Transformer is considered, where only similarity-weighted aggregation is retained. These settings allow the roles of multi-source representation, similarity modeling, and temporal evolution analysis to be systematically examined. Furthermore, the relevant code is publicly available at https://github.com/Aurelius-04/cbr4meteorology.git.

In addition, domain expert evaluation is introduced to assess practical applicability and interpretability. During evaluation, randomly sampled cases and their initial observations, including meteorological variables and cloud images, are presented to experts, who provide blinded scoring on three aspects: evolution trend analysis, Top-5 retrieved cases, and generated explanations. For trend rationality, scores of $+1$, 0, and -1 are assigned for accurate, partially correct, and incorrect predictions, respectively. For case similarity, scores of 2, 1, and 0 are assigned based on the consistency between retrieved and current cases. For explanation quality, scores of 2, 1, and 0 reflect the clarity and correctness of reasoning. The mean score for each case is computed, and the proportion of cases with positive trend scores is recorded. This evaluation framework provides qualitative and quantitative support for system effectiveness in terms of usability, reliability, and interpretability.

3.5 Technical Evaluation

This section quantitatively validates the performance of the proposed case-based reasoning system for meteorological events in terms of retrieval capability and evolution analysis accuracy. To evaluate overall performance, the proposed method is compared with multiple baseline models. Subsequently, ablation experiments are discussed to analyze the contributions of multi-source feature fusion and similarity modeling.

Table 1. Performance comparison results between the proposed method and mainstream meteorological forecasting and retrieval models.

Model	Recall@5	Precision@5	F1@5	MRR	NDCG@5	MAE	RMSE	Avg. Time (s)
ConvLSTM	-[a]	-[a]	-[a]	-[a]	-[a]	3.12 ± 0.18	4.45 ± 0.22	1.25 ± 0.15
GraphCast	-[a]	-[a]	-[a]	-[a]	-[a]	2.85 ± 0.15	3.98 ± 0.19	2.10 ± 0.25
Pangu-Weather	-[a]	-[a]	-[a]	-[a]	-[a]	2.58 ± 0.12	3.32 ± 0.14	1.85 ± 0.20
Transformer-Seq	-[a]	-[a]	-[a]	-[a]	-[a]	2.45 ± 0.10	3.15 ± 0.12	0.85 ± 0.10
KNN-Met	0.684 ± 0.021	0.584 ± 0.018	0.630 ± 0.019	0.662 ± 0.020	0.648 ± 0.017	3.28 ± 0.20	4.67 ± 0.25	0.45 ± 0.05
KNN-Fusion	0.811 ± 0.015	0.742 ± 0.014	0.775 ± 0.015	0.795 ± 0.016	0.772 ± 0.014	2.85 ± 0.16	3.98 ± 0.21	0.65 ± 0.08
FAISS-Fusion	0.804 ± 0.016	0.735 ± 0.015	0.768 ± 0.016	0.791 ± 0.015	0.768 ± 0.015	2.88 ± 0.15	4.02 ± 0.20	0.15 ± 0.02
Proposed System	0.876 ± 0.012	0.804 ± 0.010	0.838 ± 0.011	0.852 ± 0.013	0.831 ± 0.012	2.31 ± 0.08	3.18 ± 0.10	0.95 ± 0.12

[a] "-" indicates not applicable. ConvLSTM, GraphCast, Pangu-Weather, and Transformer-Seq are pure predictive models that do not perform case retrieval or ranking.

Table 1 presents the overall performance of different methods on case retrieval and trend analysis tasks. Mainstream deep learning-based predictive models, such as ConvLSTM, GraphCast, and Pangu-Weather, demonstrate competitive accuracy in trend prediction (MAE/RMSE) but lack the inherent interpretability provided by historical evidence retrieval. Compared to nearest-neighbor-based methods, multi-source fusion approaches (KNN-Fusion, FAISS-Fusion) significantly outperform KNN-Met, highlighting the necessity of integrating remote sensing data with ground observations. The proposed method achieves the best performance across all retrieval metrics, indicating that the unified representation and comprehensive similarity design—incorporating dynamic time warping—can more accurately capture the intrinsic similarity between weather events. In trend analysis, while Pangu-Weather and Transformer-Seq achieve high predictive precision, the proposed system attains the best MAE (2.31), demonstrating that strong predictive accuracy is maintained alongside superior retrieval capability. Overall, the hybrid framework of case retrieval and evolution modeling exhibits clear advantages in operational meteorological analysis where both accuracy and decision justification are required.

From the perspective of multi-source representation, as shown in Fig. 2, removing either remote sensing features or meteorological variables leads to significant performance degradation, with the removal of meteorological features

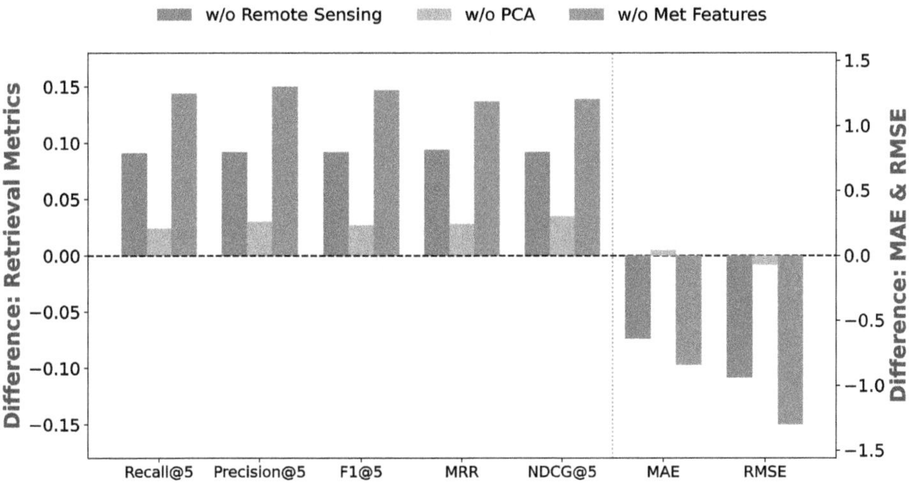

Fig. 2. Ablation results of the multi-source meteorological representation module.

causing the most severe decline, indicating that they serve as the core information source, while remote sensing provides important complementary spatial information. Removing PCA results in relatively minor changes, suggesting that its primary role is to stabilize feature representation. From the similarity computation perspective, as shown in Fig. 3, removing temporal evolution similarity causes the most substantial performance drop, indicating that temporal information is critical for case matching, while DTW and remote sensing similarity also provide independent contributions. Finally, as shown in Fig. 4, removing the Transformer leads to a clear increase in trend prediction errors, demonstrating that deep temporal modeling plays a key role in evolution inference. Overall, the optimal performance is achieved through the synergistic effect of all modules.

3.6 Expert Evaluation Results

To evaluate the practical usability and interpretability of the system, a domain expert evaluation experiment is conducted. A total of 100 representative test cases are randomly selected, and three meteorological experts are invited to perform blinded evaluations on the system outputs, including trend analysis, retrieved cases, and explanations. The results are summarized in Table 2. The experimental results indicate that the system performs well under expert evaluation. A total of 82.00% of cases achieve directly applicable trend analysis results, with an average score of 0.76, demonstrating strong practical usability. In terms of case similarity, 68.00% of retrieved cases are considered highly consistent, confirming the reliability of the retrieval mechanism. For explanation quality, 70.00% of outputs are evaluated as logically clear, indicating strong interpretability. Overall, the system is recognized by experts in terms of predictive capability, evidence reliability, and transparency.

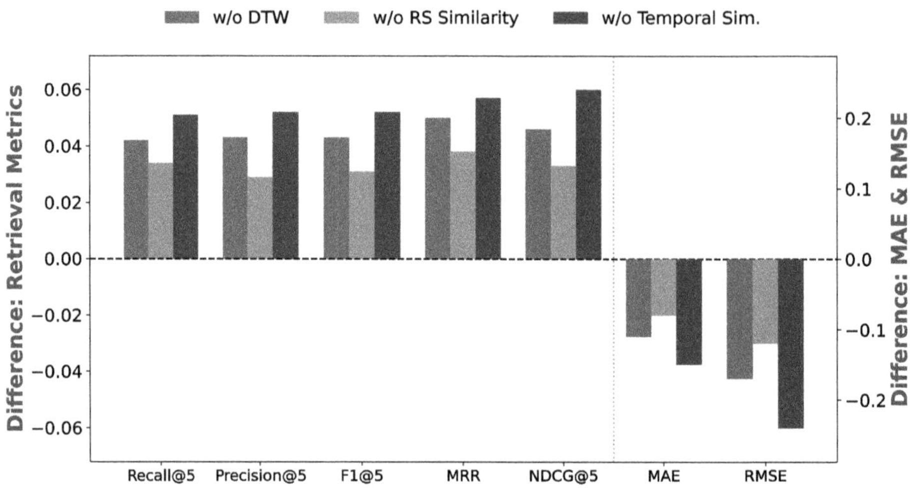

Fig. 3. Ablation results of the case similarity computation module.

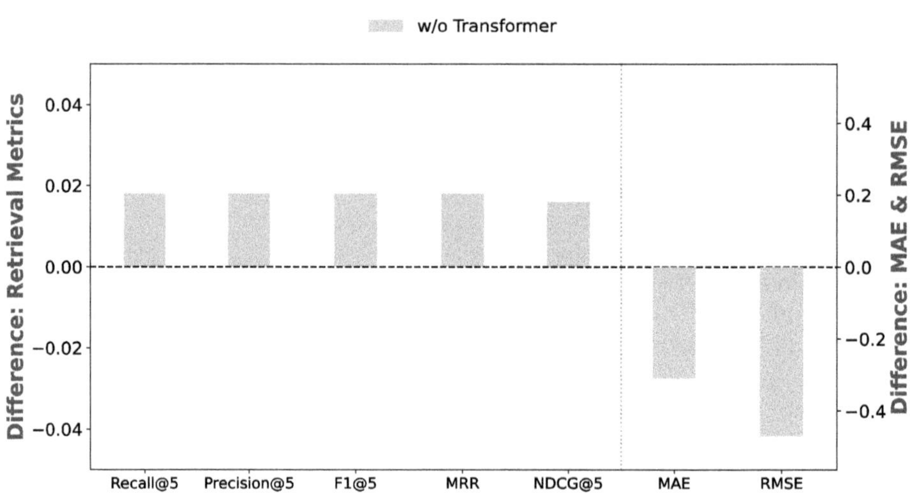

Fig. 4. Ablation results of the weather event evolution analysis module.

Table 2. Statistical results of expert evaluation for the meteorological system.

Evaluation Dimension	Evaluation Level	Score	Count	Proportion (%)
Recommendation Rationality (Avg. Score: 0.76)	Directly applicable	+1	82	82.00
	Basically correct, needs minor adjustment	0	12	12.00
	Contradicts physical laws (Unusable)	−1	6	6.00
Historical Case Similarity (Avg. Score: 1.61)	Highly consistent	2	68	68.00
	Partially similar	1	25	25.00
	No substantial association	0	7	7.00
Decision Explanation Quality (Avg. Score: 1.62)	Clear and logically sound	2	70	70.00
	Basically reasonable, but lacking details	1	22	22.00
	Logical errors or hallucinations	0	8	8.00

4 Discussion

This study proposes a multi-source CBR system for meteorological event analysis, alleviating the reliance on manual experience and improving the interpretability of deep learning models. Achieving performance comparable to cutting-edge time-series models and an 82.00% positive operational feedback rate, the system effectively transforms historical weather processes into reusable references. Specifically, historical cases are transferred to current trend predictions through a similarity-weighted aggregation mechanism; the temporal evolution sequences of retrieved analogous cases are processed by a Transformer module, mapping past development patterns to estimate the current system's trajectory.

The scale of 4,200 historical cases adequately covers primary weather patterns in the target mid-temperate region, demonstrating the feasibility of CBR reasoning under small-sample conditions typical of county-level operations. However, data preprocessing techniques such as standardization, PCA, and rescaling inevitably introduce certain errors. While essential for unified dimensional representation and noise reduction, PCA discards minor variance components that might contain subtle meteorological signals, and rescaling can suppress extreme outlier values. These information losses slightly constrain the representation of highly anomalous states.

Consequently, handling unseen or extreme meteorological events remains a challenge within this small-sample context. To address unprecedented weather patterns, the system utilizes the multi-dimensional similarity score as an out-of-distribution indicator. If the retrieval scores of the Top-K cases fall below a predefined confidence threshold, the event is flagged as an anomaly to alert forecasters. Concurrently, the revision module adapts the closest available partial matches by dynamically adjusting outcome intensity estimations based on physical state deviations.

Furthermore, the system has regional and data source limitations. The current case base relies on mid-temperate continental climate data, necessitating cross-regional sample expansion for broader applicability. Additionally, the multi-source fusion lacks Doppler weather radar data, which is crucial for meso- and micro-scale convective systems. Future work will integrate radar echo sequences and natural language processing into the CBR framework to further enhance the capability to analyze and explain sudden and extreme meteorological events.

5 Conclusion

This study constructs a CBR system for meteorological event analysis integrating multi-source observational data, aiming to provide a decision-support tool that combines accuracy and interpretability for meteorological evolution analysis. By designing a unified multi-source feature representation method and a multi-dimensional similarity measurement strategy combined with DTW, the system can effectively map heterogeneous surface meteorological variables and remote sensing cloud image features into the same space for comprehensive comparison. Building upon this, by integrating vector retrieval techniques with a Transformer-based evolution modeling module, the method retrieves relevant historical weather processes while achieving a reasonable inference of the developmental trends of the current meteorological system. Quantitative experiments and expert evaluation results indicate that the proposed system performs comparably to mainstream time-series deep learning models in both retrieval performance (e.g., reaching a Recall@5 of 0.876) and trend analysis accuracy (with MAE reduced to 2.31). Furthermore, expert blind evaluation shows that 82.00% of the system's evolution inference results can be directly used as operational references, validating its effectiveness in providing specific and intuitive historical evidence for forecasting results. This relatively transparent analysis mechanism provides a feasible path to alleviate the issues of weather forecasting overly relying on individual subjective experience and deep learning models lacking logical interpretability. Overall, this study validates the potential value of the case-based reasoning paradigm in complex meteorological data analysis and operational applications, providing a reference technical framework for the digital accumulation of meteorological domain knowledge and the construction of trustworthy decision-support systems.

Declaration on Generative AI. During the preparation of this work, the author(s) used ChatGPT, Grammarly in order to: Grammar and spelling check, Paraphrase and reword. After using this tool/service, the author(s) reviewed and edited the content as needed and take(s) full responsibility for the publication's content.

References

1. Aamodt, A., Plaza, E.: Case-based reasoning: foundational issues, methodological variations, and system approaches. AI Commun. **7**(1), 39–59 (1994)
2. Arrieta, A.B., Díaz-Rodríguez, N., Del Ser, J., et al.: Explainable artificial intelligence (XAI): concepts, taxonomies, opportunities and challenges toward responsible AI. Inf. Fusion **58**, 82–115 (2020)
3. Bi, K., Xie, L., Zhang, H., Chen, X., Gu, X., Tian, Q.: Accurate medium-range global weather forecasting with 3D neural networks. Nature **619**, 533–538 (2023)
4. Dash, B.K., Caezza, J.A., Malandra, F.: Experimental analysis of the impact of weather on signal strength in the CBRS frequency spectrum. In: 2025 IEEE International Conference on Communications Workshops (ICC Workshops), pp. 1664–1669. IEEE (2025)
5. Doutreloup, S., et al.: Historical and future weather data for dynamic building simulations in Belgium using the regional climate model mar: typical and extreme meteorological year and heatwaves. Earth Syst. Sci. Data **14**(7), 3039–3051 (2022)
6. Du, K., Huang, J., Wang, W., Zeng, Y., Li, X., Zhao, F.: Monitoring low-temperature stress in winter wheat using tropomi solar-induced chlorophyll fluorescence. IEEE Trans. Geosci. Remote Sens. **62**, 1–11 (2024)
7. Fernandez, E., Villar, J.R., Navarro, A., Sedano, J.: Early detection of flash floods using case-based reasoning. Eng. Proc. **18**(1), 19 (2022)
8. González-Monge, M., Díaz-Agudo, B., Recio-Garcia, J.A.: Explaining translational embedding models in recommender systems using knowledge graphs and language models. In: ICCBR 2025. LNCS (LNAI), vol. 15662, pp. 81–95. Springer (2025)
9. Jimenez-Diaz, G., Díaz-Agudo, B.: Visualization of similarity models for CBR comprehension and maintenance. In: International Conference on Case-Based Reasoning, pp. 67–80. Springer (2024)
10. Jin, Y.Q., Lu, N., Lin, M.: Advancement of Chinese meteorological Feng-Yun (FY) and oceanic Hai-Yang (HY) satellite remote sensing. Proc. IEEE **98**(5), 844–861 (2010)
11. Kuhn, M., et al.: Clinical decision support for skin tumor treatment: a case-based reasoning approach. In: ICCBR 2025. LNCS (LNAI), vol. 15662, pp. 407–422. Springer (2025)
12. Lam, R., Sanchez-Gonzalez, A., Willson, M., et al.: Learning skillful medium-range global weather forecasting. Science **382**(6677), 1416–1421 (2023)
13. Li, J., Guo, X., Zhang, K., Zhao, W.: A knowledge-enabled approach for user experience-driven product improvement at the conceptual design stage. AI Edam **37**, e22 (2023)
14. Liu, M., Zhang, W., Lou, Y., Dong, X., Zhang, Z., Zhang, X.: A deep learning-based precipitation nowcasting model fusing GNSS-PWV and radar echo observations. IEEE Trans. Geosci. Remote Sens. (2025)
15. Malashin, I., Tynchenko, V., Gantimurov, A., Nelyub, V., Borodulin, A.: Applications of long short-term memory (LSTM) networks in polymeric sciences: a review. Polymers **16**(18), 2607 (2024)
16. Ráduly, B., Gernaey, K.V., Capodaglio, A.G., Mikkelsen, P.S., Henze, M.: Artificial neural networks for rapid WWTP performance evaluation. Environ. Model. Softw. **22**(8), 1208–1216 (2007)
17. Schultheis, A., Zeyen, C., Bergmann, R.: An overview and comparison of case-based reasoning frameworks. In: International Conference on Case-Based Reasoning, pp. 327–343. Springer (2023)

18. Shi, X., Chen, Z., Wang, H., Yeung, D.Y., Wong, W.K., Woo, W.C.: Convolutional LSTM network: a machine learning approach for precipitation nowcasting. In: Advances in Neural Information Processing Systems, vol. 28 (2015)
19. Sørmo, F., Cassens, J., Aamodt, A.: Explanation in case-based reasoning–perspectives and goals. Artif. Intell. Rev. **24**(2), 109–143 (2005)
20. Stuart, N.A., Schultz, D.M., Klein, G.: Maintaining the role of humans in the forecast process: analyzing the psyche of expert forecasters. Bull. Am. Meteor. Soc. **88**(12), 1893–1898 (2007)
21. Su, M., et al.: Improving rice leaf area index monitoring accuracy via robot-integrated multi-sensors and meteorological data fusion with explainable machine learning. Comput. Electron. Agric. **245**, 111581 (2026)
22. Valdez-Ávila, M.F., Pérez-Pérez, G.A., Sarabia-Osorio, H., Bermejo-Sabbagh, C., Orozco-del Castillo, M.G.: A case-based explanation method for weather forecasting. In: ICCBR Workshops, pp. 153–164 (2022)
23. Wiratunga, N., et al.: CBR-RAG: case-based reasoning for retrieval augmented generation in LLMs for legal question answering. In: International Conference on Case-Based Reasoning, pp. 445–460. Springer (2024)
24. Wu, B., et al.: Hysteresis in flag leaf temperature based on meteorological factors during the reproductive growth stage of wheat and the design of a predictive model. Comput. Electron. Agric. **232**, 110113 (2025)
25. Yan, A., Cheng, Z.: A review of the development and future challenges of case-based reasoning. Appl. Sci. **14**(16), 7130 (2024)
26. Yang, J., Zhang, Z., Wei, C., Lu, F., Guo, Q.: Introducing the new generation of Chinese geostationary weather satellites, Fengyun-4. Bull. Am. Meteor. Soc. **98**(8), 1637–1658 (2017)
27. Yousaf, R., Rehman, H.Z.U., Khan, K., et al.: Satellite imagery-based cloud classification using deep learning. Remote Sens. **15**(23), 5597 (2023)

Case-Based Identification of Anti-coagulation Therapy for Pregnant Women Using Approximation and Interpolation of Sequences

Erwan Diebold[1], Jean Lieber[1(✉)], Nabila Merah[1,2], and Aurélie Bannay[1,2]

[1] LORIA, Université de Lorraine, CNRS, Inria, 54000 Nancy, France
{erwan.diebold,jean.lieber,nabila.merah,aurelie.bannay}@loria.fr
[2] CHRU-Nancy, Medical Information Department, Université de Lorraine, LORIA, Nancy, France
{nabila.merah,aurelie.bannay}@univ-lorraine.fr

Abstract. In a current medical study about anti-coagulation therapy for pregnant women, an issue of missing data has been raised. This issue is modeled as a problem-solving task where a problem is a description of the known data of a patient and the solution is her missing data. A case-based approach is used for inferring missing data, where a case is a complete data. The approaches of approximation (using a similarity relation) and interpolation (using a fuzzy betweenness relation) are considered for implementing such a CBR system. A technical difficulty is that the problems in this application are represented using temporal sequences, and the issue of implementing similarity and betweenness on such sequences had to be addressed. The proposed approach is based on similarity paths, i.e., paths in the problem space. The evaluation had to be made on generated data but has shown the efficiency of these approaches.

Keywords: case-based reasoning · approximation · interpolation · missing data · anti-coagulation therapy for pregnant women

1 Introduction

Case-based reasoning (CBR [20]) is classically based on the binary notion of similarity according to the principle "If those problems are similar then it is plausible that their solutions are similar.", which is called in this paper the *approximation pattern*. Other relations can also be exploited, such as the ternary relation of betweenness: "If a problem is between two other problems, then it is plausible that its solution is between the solutions of these problems.": this is called the *interpolation pattern* [16]. These simple patterns have proven useful for building an efficient CBR system in which problems and solutions are represented by tuples of real numbers [2].

Now, do these approaches apply to more complex representations, such as sequences? This is what this paper deals with for a medical application in which case-based inference aims at inferring missing data.

This medical application is described in Sect. 2. Section 3 presents some preliminaries, in particular on CBR, approximation, and interpolation. The representation of cases

L. Malburg and K. Bach (Eds.): ICCBR 2026, LNAI 16780, pp. 505–520, 2027.
https://doi.org/10.1007/978-3-032-33865-5_31

in this application is detailed in Sect. 4. Sections 6 and 7 present the approximation and interpolation approaches applied to this application, and their evaluation is presented in Sect. 8. Section 9 provides a discussion of this work, concludes the paper, and outlines directions for future work. Many technicalities due to the complexity of the application domain are not presented here but can be found in [7].

2 Application Context: Anti-coagulation Therapy for Pregnant Women

Anticoagulants are recommended medications for the treatment and prevention of different pathologies, including thromboembolic events which are common during pregnancy and can lead to maternal death [4]. They occur when a blood clot forms in a vein. Three pharmacological classes are used: heparin injections, vitamin K antagonists (VKAs), and direct oral anticoagulants (DOACs) [3]. DOACs are more manageable because they are administered orally, unlike heparins, and do not need monitoring, unlike VKAs [6]. Their prescription relies on national recommendations and clinical guidelines. The posology and duration of treatment differ according to the underlying treated disease, and the drug prescribed. The three pharmacological classes share common indications such as the prevention and treatment of deep venous thrombosis (VTE) and pulmonary embolism, and thromboembolic events following knee and hip surgery. However, specific indications exist for each class: certain DOACs are recommended for the prevention of stroke in patients with heart arrhythmia, VKAs are used for the prevention of heart disease complications and heparins are indicated for patients enduring a prolonged bed rest [13]. However, even though they are the more manageable, DOACs are not recommended during pregnancy. Currently, heparin injections are the only recommended anticoagulants in this population. VKAs expose to the risk of foetal loss or malformation syndromes while DOACs are contraindicated as a precautionary measure due to the lack of studies on their safety during pregnancy [4]. This underlines the need for more evidence. To address this issue, pregnancy outcomes were compared among pregnant women accidentally exposed to DOACs with those exposed to VKAs and heparins, in France, between 2012 and 2018, using data from the French National Health Data System (Système National des Données de Santé - SNDS). This database collects individual real-world data, covering all health insurance beneficiaries in France. It provides information on outpatient care (physician visits, medical procedures, and reimbursed drugs). It also records hospitalisation data such as diagnoses, and procedures performed during the stay [21]. By targeting pregnant women reimbursed for anticoagulants during their pregnancies, it is possible to track their health trajectories, up to the end of pregnancy.

However, estimating the association between DOACs and pregnancy outcomes requires distinguishing the effect of the drug from that of the underlying disease that led to its prescription, since the pathology itself can lead to an unfavorable pregnancy outcome. Unfortunately such information is not available in this database [21]. Using CBR to infer this missing data could allow approximating the likely indication for treatment by anticoagulant, by comparing the observed treatment sequences with national recommendations.

Table 1. Example of recommendation rules for venous and pulmonary thromboembolic events.

Rule	Step 1			Step 2		
	Anticoagulant	Daily dose	Duration	Anticoagulant	Daily dose	Duration
R1	Rivaroxaban	30 mg	21 d	Rivaroxaban	20 mg	500 d
R2	Enoxaparin	8 000 - 20 000 UI aXa	10 d	Sintrom	4 mg	500 d
R3	Enoxaparin	8 000 - 20 000 UI aXa	10 d	Rivaroxaban	20 mg	500 d

Anticoagulant Prescription Recommendations. Anticoagulant prescription recommendations serve as a reference to guide sequence comparison and transformation. These recommendations are structured as follows. For each group of indications, recommendations are formalized as a set of prescription rules. Each rule is composed of one to three successive steps, representing successive phases of treatment. A step specifies the prescription of an anticoagulant, the recommended daily dose, and the duration of treatment.

Table 1 illustrates examples of recommendations for venous and pulmonary thromboembolic events. Each row represents a therapeutic pattern, with an initiation phase followed by a maintenance phase. These rules capture the main therapeutic patterns recommended for the indications considered and serve as theoretical reference sequences in the proposed similarity framework.

3 Preliminaries

This section recalls some classical and less classical notions on which this paper is based. After a section introducing classical mathematic notions (Sect. 3.1), CBR is introduced in general (Sect. 3.2). Then, the notion of betweenness relations is presented in Sect. 3.3; it is used afterwards for one of the approaches to CBR presented in Sect. 3.4.

3.1 Mathematical Notions and Notations

$\mathbb{R}$ denotes the set of real numbers. $\mathbb{R}_+$ is the set of nonnegative real numbers. For $a, b \in \mathbb{R}$ such that $a \leq b$, $[a, b]$ denotes the set of $x \in \mathbb{R}$ such that $a \leq x$ and $x \leq b$.

A distance function on a set $\mathcal{U}$ is a mapping $\mathtt{dist} : \mathcal{U} \times \mathcal{U} \longrightarrow \mathbb{R}_+$ such that, for all $a, b, c \in \mathcal{U}$:

$$\mathtt{dist}(a, b) = 0 \quad \text{iff} \quad a = b$$

$$\mathtt{dist}(b, a) = \mathtt{dist}(a, b) \qquad \text{(symmetry of dist)}$$

$$\mathtt{dist}(b, c) \leq \mathtt{dist}(b, a) + \mathtt{dist}(a, c) \qquad \text{(triangular inequality of dist)}$$

3.2 CBR: Notions and Notations

This section presents some notions and notation related to case-based reasoning, with some choices consistent with the approach presented in this paper.

(a) Situation where $[b\text{-}a\text{-}c]_{\texttt{dist}}$ holds (with the canonical Euclidian distance): $\texttt{dist}(b, a) + \texttt{dist}(a, c) = \texttt{dist}(b, c)$.

(b) Situation where $[b\text{-}a\text{-}c]_{\texttt{dist}}$ does not hold though $\mathcal{FB}_{\texttt{dist}}(b, a, c)$ is closed to 1: $\texttt{dist}(b, a) + \texttt{dist}(a, c) - \texttt{dist}(b, c)$ is relatively small.

Fig. 1. Illustration of (a) exact betweenness relation and (b) fuzzy betweenness relation.

In particular, in this paper, a *case* is given by an ordered pair $(\mathtt{x}, \mathtt{y})$ where $\mathtt{x}$ is a *problem* and $\mathtt{y}$ is a *solution*, these notions of problem and solution being dependent on the application domain. Moreover, a binary relation $\leadsto$ relating problems and solutions is assumed to exist, such as $\mathtt{x} \leadsto \mathtt{y}$ is read "x has for solution y", although this relation is not completely known to the CBR system.

However, some cases $(\mathtt{x}^{\mathtt{s}}, \mathtt{y}^{\mathtt{s}})$ such that $\mathtt{x}^{\mathtt{s}} \leadsto \mathtt{y}^{\mathtt{s}}$ are supposed to exist; they are called the *source cases* and constitute the *case base* $\mathtt{CB}$.

Case-based reasoning consists of using a case base (and other sources of knowledge) to solve a problem called the *target problem* and is denoted by $\mathtt{x}^{\mathtt{tgt}}$. The inference part of CBR usually consists of 2 steps. (1) Retrieval aims to select the source cases k that are relevant for solving $\mathtt{x}^{\mathtt{tgt}}$. (2) The adaptation aims to use these cases retrieved from k to propose a solution $\mathtt{y}^{\mathtt{tgt}}$ such that the relation $\mathtt{x}^{\mathtt{tgt}} \leadsto \mathtt{y}^{\mathtt{tgt}}$ is plausible. Further steps of CBR (validation and storage of the newly formed case) are not considered here.

3.3 Betweenness Relations

A betweenness relation on a set $\mathcal{U}$ is a ternary relation noted (in this paper) $[b\text{-}a\text{-}c]$ for $a, b, c \in \mathcal{U}$ which models the relation "a is between b and c." Such relations have been studied in [1], within the framework of the conceptual spaces introduced by Peter Gärdenfors [10]. In particular, the following postulate is assumed;

$$\text{for } a, b, c \in \mathcal{U}, \text{ if } b = c \text{ and } [b\text{-}a\text{-}c] \text{ then } a = b \tag{1}$$

One way to define such a betweenness relation is by using a distance function $\texttt{dist}$ on $\mathcal{U}$:

$$[b\text{-}a\text{-}c]_{\texttt{dist}} \quad \text{is defined by} \quad \texttt{dist}(b, a) + \texttt{dist}(a, c) = \texttt{dist}(b, c)$$

for $a, b, c \in \mathcal{U}$. Thus, $[b\text{-}a\text{-}c]_{\texttt{dist}}$ corresponds to the situation of equality in the triangular inequality, as illustrated by Fig. 1(a).

A fuzzy version of this relation is given by a function of "fuzzy betweenness" $\mathcal{FB}_{\texttt{dist}} : (b, a, c) \in \mathcal{U}^3 \longrightarrow [0, 1]$ such that, for $(b, a, c) \in \mathcal{U}^3$, $\mathcal{FB}_{\texttt{dist}}(b, a, c) = 1$ iff $[b\text{-}a\text{-}c]$ holds. In particular, $\mathcal{FB}_{\texttt{dist}}$ can be defined as the fuzzification of the $[\cdot\text{-}\cdot\text{-}\cdot]_{\texttt{dist}}$ ternary relation as follows. Figure 1(b) illustrates this idea: a is not exactly between b and c, but it is not far from a h which is between b and c. The idea is then to consider the value $\texttt{dist}(b, a) + \texttt{dist}(a, c) - \texttt{dist}(b, c)$, which is nonnegative according to the triangular equality: for fixed values b and c, the lower this value is, the more a is between b and c, and the closest to 1 is $\mathcal{FB}_{\texttt{dist}}(b, a, c)$. Now, assuming that $b \neq c$, the difference given above can be normalized by $\texttt{dist}(b, c)$, which leads to the proposed definition of $\mathcal{FB}_{\texttt{dist}}$ (where $\alpha > 0$ is a parameter):

$$\mathcal{FB}_{\texttt{dist}}(b, a, c) = \left[1 - \alpha \frac{\texttt{dist}(b, a) + \texttt{dist}(a, c) - \texttt{dist}(b, c)}{\texttt{dist}(b, c)}\right]_+ \qquad \text{(for all } a, b, c \in \mathcal{U} \text{ such that } b \neq c\text{)}$$

$$\text{with } [u]_+ = \begin{cases} u & \text{if } u \geq 0 \\ 0 & \text{else} \end{cases} \qquad \text{(for } u \in \mathbb{R}\text{)}$$

3.4 CBR by Approximation, Interpolation and Extrapolation

Various approaches to CBR exist. In [16], three approaches are described, corresponding to $k = 1$, $k = 2$ and $k = 3$ retrieved cases.

***k* = 1.** The approach for $k = 1$ is quite classical in CBR, and called *approximation* in the following. For $(\mathrm{x}^{\mathrm{s}}, \mathrm{y}^{\mathrm{s}}) \in \texttt{CB}$, it states that if x^{s} is similar to $\mathrm{x}^{\texttt{tgt}}$ then the searched solution $\mathrm{y}^{\texttt{tgt}}$ is such that y^{s} is similar to $\mathrm{y}^{\texttt{tgt}}$, thus this can be summarized by applying the following plausible inference rule

$$\frac{\mathrm{x}^a \simeq \mathrm{x}^b}{\mathrm{y}^a \simeq \mathrm{y}^b}\text{approximation}$$

with $(\mathrm{x}^a, \mathrm{y}^a) = (\mathrm{x}^{\mathrm{s}}, \mathrm{y}^{\mathrm{s}})$ and $(\mathrm{x}^b, \mathrm{y}^b) = (\mathrm{x}^{\texttt{tgt}}, \mathrm{y}^{\texttt{tgt}})$. This idea has been studied in depth in particular in the work about credible CBR [12]. In the work presented in this paper, approximation is used in a simple but effective way by stating that $\mathrm{y}^{\texttt{tgt}} = \mathrm{y}^{\mathrm{s}}$([1]) and the similarity between problems is represented thanks to a distance function. The assumption here (which is typical of CBR) is that the lowest is the distance between x^a and x^b, the more plausible is the above inference rule. The extreme case $\texttt{dist}(\mathrm{x}^{\mathrm{s}}, \mathrm{x}^{\texttt{tgt}}) = 0$ entails $\mathrm{x}^{\mathrm{s}} = \mathrm{x}^{\texttt{tgt}}$ so, if $(\mathrm{x}^{\mathrm{s}}, \mathrm{y}^{\mathrm{s}}) \in \texttt{CB}$ and $\mathrm{y}^{\texttt{tgt}} = \mathrm{y}^{\mathrm{s}}$, then $\mathrm{x}^{\texttt{tgt}} \rightsquigarrow \mathrm{y}^{\texttt{tgt}}$.

***k* = 2.** The approach for $k = 2$ is called *interpolation*. It is based on the notion of *betweenness* between problems and between solutions. The principle is as follows. If $(\mathrm{x}^b, \mathrm{y}^b), (\mathrm{x}^c, \mathrm{y}^c) \in \texttt{CB}$ and $\mathrm{x}^{\texttt{tgt}}$ is between x^b and x^c then it is plausible that $\mathrm{y}^{\texttt{tgt}}$ is between y^b and y^c. This consists in applying the following plausible inference rule:

$$\frac{[\mathrm{x}^b\text{-}\mathrm{x}^a\text{-}\mathrm{x}^c]}{[\mathrm{y}^b\text{-}\mathrm{y}^a\text{-}\mathrm{y}^c]}\text{interpolation}$$

with $(\mathrm{x}^a, \mathrm{y}^a) = (\mathrm{x}^{\texttt{tgt}}, \mathrm{y}^{\texttt{tgt}})$. Now, given $\mathrm{x}^{\texttt{tgt}}$, the situation $[\mathrm{x}^b\text{-}\mathrm{x}^{\texttt{tgt}}\text{-}\mathrm{x}^c]$, with x^b and x^c, the problem parts of source cases, is rare in many problem spaces, hence the idea of

[1] This is justified in the application by the fact that the set of solutions is finite: the application problem can be seen as a classification problem.

using the fuzzy version of the betweenness relation. So, with a distance function dist between problems, retrieval aims to select $(\mathtt{x}^b, \mathtt{y}^b)$ and $(\mathtt{x}^c, \mathtt{y}^c)$ in CB that maximize $\mathcal{FB}_{\mathtt{dist}}(\mathtt{x}^b, \mathtt{x}^{\mathtt{tgt}}, \mathtt{x}^c)$. Then, it is plausibly inferred that $\mathtt{y}^{\mathtt{tgt}}$ is between $\mathtt{y}^b$ and $\mathtt{y}^c$.

In this paper, because the solution space is finite and rather small, to make this simpler, this principle is applied to retrieved cases with the same solutions: $\mathtt{y}^b = \mathtt{y}^c$, which involves that $\mathtt{y}^{\mathtt{tgt}} = \mathtt{y}^b$ according to (1). Therefore, the way the interpolation principle is applied in this paper is the following:

- Select the pair $\{(\mathtt{x}^b, \mathtt{y}^b), (\mathtt{x}^c, \mathtt{y}^c)\}$ of source cases such that $\mathtt{y}^b = \mathtt{y}^c$ maximizes $\mathcal{FB}_{\mathtt{dist}}(\mathtt{x}^b, \mathtt{x}^{\mathtt{tgt}}, \mathtt{x}^c)$;
- The proposed solution $\mathtt{y}^{\mathtt{tgt}}$ is set to $\mathtt{y}^b$.

***k* = 3.** *Extrapolation* is presented here briefly, since it has not yet been applied to our application problem: it constitutes a future line of work. An analogical proportion on a set $\mathcal{U}$ is a quaternary relation denoted by $a : b :: c : d$ and read "a is to b as c is to d", for $a, b, c, d \in \mathcal{U}$. Extrapolation is based on two analogical proportions: one in the problem space, the other one in the solution space. The principle is (1) to select $k = 3$ source cases $(\mathtt{x}^a, \mathtt{y}^a)$, $(\mathtt{x}^b, \mathtt{y}^b)$ and $(\mathtt{x}^c, \mathtt{y}^c)$ such that $\mathtt{x}^a : \mathtt{x}^b :: \mathtt{x}^c : \mathtt{x}^{\mathtt{tgt}}$ holds. (2) in assuming that the corresponding relation $\mathtt{y}^a : \mathtt{y}^b :: \mathtt{y}^c : \mathtt{y}^{\mathtt{tgt}}$ holds in the solution space, this relation being an "analogical equation" with unknown $\mathtt{y}^{\mathtt{tgt}}$, whose solving plausibly gives a solution to the target problem.

These approaches have been successfully applied to a problem of cleaning old images of text [2]. In the application domain of this previous work, both problems and solutions were represented by tuples of numbers. In the application described below, the main technical difficulty was that the representation was more complex: one problem attribute takes sequences as values and each solution is a class of a taxonomy.

4 Case Representation

This section explains the chosen representation of cases and introduces a few source cases and a target problem that are used as illustrations in the next sections. A problem describes a patient and her anticoagulant treatment, while a solution corresponds to a group of medical indications that contains the one that motivates this treatment.

Consider a 26-year-old patient who gave birth on November 23rd 2016. She previously experienced a thromboembolic episode before her pregnancy, which was treated from October 24th 2015 to January 28th 2016. During her pregnancy, she received preventive treatment from August 14th to November 15th in order to avoid a recurrence. In the SNDS data, the sequence refers to drug deliveries (represented by the attribute `deliveries`). Each delivery corresponds to a medication package collected at a pharmacy and is represented by an object d defined by the following attributes: `deliveryDate` is the date when patients pick up their drugs at the pharmacy (format: YYYY/MM/DD), `class` is the type of anticoagulant (DOAC, Heparin, or VKA), `dose` is the dose per medication unit in the box, `deliveredQuantity` is the number of medication units in the box, `inn` is the international nonproprietary name (INN) of the active

Table 2. A patient's anticoagulant delivery history.

`deliveryDate`	`class`	`dose`	`inn`	`deliveredQuantity`
2015/10/24	Heparin	4000 UI aXa	Enoxaparin	6
2015/10/24	Heparin	4000 UI aXa	Enoxaparin	2
2015/11/01	Heparin	4000 UI aXa	Enoxaparin	6
2015/11/14	DOAC	15 mg	Rivaroxaban	28
2015/12/03	DOAC	20 mg	Rivaroxaban	28
2015/12/31	DOAC	20 mg	Rivaroxaban	28
2016/01/28	DOAC	20 mg	Rivaroxaban	28
2016/08/14	Heparin	4000 UI aXa	Enoxaparin	6
2016/09/11	Heparin	4000 UI aXa	Enoxaparin	2
2016/09/11	Heparin	4000 UI aXa	Enoxaparin	6
2016/10/13	Heparin	4000 UI aXa	Enoxaparin	6
2016/11/15	Heparin	4000 UI aXa	Enoxaparin	6

substance. Table 2 presents the complete delivery sequence of the patient described previously. A delivery sequence is then defined as $\mathtt{Seq} = (d_0, \ldots, d_{n-1})$, where each d_i is a delivery ordered chronologically by `deliveryDate`.

In the proposed system, the solution part of a case corresponds to a set of medical indications associated with that treatment. These indications are encoded using ICD-10 [11] (International Classification of Diseases) or CCAM (French procedure codes). For example, venous thromboembolism is encoded as "I26" when the thrombosis occurs in the pulmonary artery, and "I80", "I81" or "I82" when there is deep vein thrombosis. These events share the same recommendations. The solution associated with our running example is therefore $\{\mathtt{I26}, \mathtt{I80}, \mathtt{I81}, \mathtt{I82}\}$, which includes the code of the patient's indication.

A patient and her treatment are represented by a problem x defined by the following attributes:

- `age`: age of the patient at the beginning of the treatment,
- `D`: temporal landmark object relative to the estimated date of conception.
  In our example, the conception date is estimated to be February 16, 2017. All temporal values are expressed as numbers of days.
  - $\mathtt{D} \cdot \mathtt{get30}()$[2] is the number of days between the date 30 days before conception (January 17, 2016) and the first anticoagulant delivery. For example, if the delivery of anticoagulants was on October 24, 2015 $\mathtt{D} \cdot \mathtt{get30}() = -93$, that is, the prescription occurred 93 days before this reference date.
  - $\mathtt{D} \cdot \mathtt{get365}()$ is defined in the same way using the date 365 days before conception (February 17, 2015).

[2] In this article, the value of an attribute a for an object o is denoted by $\mathtt{o} \cdot \mathtt{a}$.

Table 3. Sequences of prescriptions obtained by inferring treatment duration and daily dosage, and by aggregating consecutive deliveries sharing the same INN.

$\mathtt{Seq}^1 =$

beginningDate	class	dailyDose	inn	duration
2015/10/24	Heparin	1530.6 UI aXa	Enoxaparin	21
2015/11/14	DOAC	21 mg	Rivaroxaban	100

$\mathtt{Seq}^2 =$

deliveryDate	class	dailyDose	inn	duration
2016/08/14	Heparin	866.7 UI aXa	Enoxaparin	120

Table 4. Sequence of prescriptions of the target problem.

$\mathtt{Seq}^{\mathtt{tgt}} =$

beginningDate	class	dailyDose	inn	duration
2017/07/05	Heparin	9653 UI aXa	Enoxaparin	7
2017/07/12	VKA	3.7 mg	Sintrom	15
2017/07/25	Heparin	6312 UI aXa	Enoxaparin	253

  - $\mathtt{D} \cdot \mathtt{pregnancyOutcome}$ is the number of days between the first delivery and the date of pregnancy outcome. For example, if the delivery date is November 23th 2016, $\mathtt{D} \cdot \mathtt{pregnancyOutcome} = 380$.
- `prescs`: sequence of prescriptions, each of which being an object defined below.

In this context, a prescription denotes a period during which a patient receives anticoagulant therapy based on the same active substance, reconstructed from successive deliveries. A prescription object `presc` is represented by the set of attributes $\mathtt{presc} = \{\mathtt{beginningDate}, \mathtt{duration}, \mathtt{class}, \mathtt{inn}, \mathtt{dailyDose}\}$ where `beginningDate` is the start date of the treatment, `duration` is the treatment duration (in days), `class` is the type of anticoagulant (DOAC, Heparin, VKA), `inn` is the international nonproprietary name (INN) of the active substance, `dailyDose` is the estimated daily dose of the active substance.

Observing the sequence of delivery in Table 2, a gap of several months (from January 28 to August 14) can be observed between two consecutive deliveries. Since this gap is greater than 90 days, it is considered a treatment interruption. This gap separates the patient's history into two distinct treatment episodes, producing two cases $(\mathtt{x}^1, \mathtt{y}^1)$ and $(\mathtt{x}^2, \mathtt{y}^2)$.

The corresponding prescription sequences are shown in Table 3.

These correspond respectively to two distinct cases $(\mathtt{x}^1, \mathtt{y}^1)$ and $(\mathtt{x}^2, \mathtt{y}^2)$, where: $\mathtt{x}^1 \cdot \mathtt{age} = \mathtt{x}^2 \cdot \mathtt{age} = 26$, $\mathtt{x}^1 \cdot \mathtt{D} \cdot \mathtt{get30}() = -93$, $\mathtt{x}^2 \cdot \mathtt{D} \cdot \mathtt{get30}() = -333$, $\mathtt{x}^1 \cdot \mathtt{D} \cdot \mathtt{get365}() = 240$, $\mathtt{x}^2 \cdot \mathtt{D} \cdot \mathtt{get365}() = -213$, $\mathtt{x}^1 \cdot \mathtt{D} \cdot \mathtt{pregnancyOutcome} = 380$, $\mathtt{x}^2 \cdot \mathtt{D} \cdot \mathtt{pregnancyOutcome} = 92$, $\mathtt{x}^1 \cdot \mathtt{prescs} = \mathtt{P}^1$, $\mathtt{x}^2 \cdot \mathtt{prescs} = \mathtt{P}^2$ and $\mathtt{y}^1 = \mathtt{y}^2 = \{\mathtt{I80}, \mathtt{I81}, \mathtt{I82}, \mathtt{I26}\}$.

Let $\mathtt{x}^{\mathtt{tgt}}$ be a new problem for which the solution is unknown. It corresponds to a patient who gave birth on April 3rd, 2018 and whose reconstructed prescription sequence is shown in Table 4.

$\mathtt{x}^{\mathtt{tgt}} \cdot \mathtt{age} = 26$, $\mathtt{x}^{\mathtt{tgt}} \cdot \mathtt{D} \cdot \mathtt{get30}() = -27$, $\mathtt{x}^{\mathtt{tgt}} \cdot \mathtt{D} \cdot \mathtt{get365}() = -362$, $\mathtt{x}^{\mathtt{tgt}} \cdot \mathtt{D} \cdot \mathtt{pregnancyOutcome} = 272$, $\mathtt{x}^{\mathtt{tgt}} \cdot \mathtt{prescs} = \mathtt{Seq}^{\mathtt{tgt}}$.

Throughout this report, our objective is to determine the set of medical indications (the solution) associated with this target problem.

5 Distance Functions on Cases

As presented in Sect. 3.4, the approximation and interpolation approaches in CBR rely on the relations of similarity and betweenness in problems, which can be defined thanks to distance functions. In this section, the distance between problems is defined as a weighted sum of attribute distances.

$$\mathtt{dist}(\mathtt{x}^1, \mathtt{x}^2) = \sum_{\mathtt{a:attribute}} \mathtt{dist}_{\mathtt{a}}(\mathtt{x}^1 \cdot \mathtt{a}, \mathtt{x}^2 \cdot \mathtt{a})$$

The following sections detail the distance functions associated with numerical attributes (Sect. 5.1) and for sequences of prescriptions (Sect. 5.2), as well as the distance defined on solutions (Sect. 5.3). All proposed distance functions rely on attribute weights. A learning method is described to automatically estimate these weights (Sect. 5.4). A more detailed version of this section can be found in [7].

5.1 Distance on Numerical Attributes

Numerical attributes refer to age or pregnancy-related dates. For bounded attributes such as age, a normalized distance is used:

$$\mathtt{dist}_{\mathtt{age}}(\mathtt{x}^{\mathtt{s}} \cdot \mathtt{age}, \mathtt{x}^{\mathtt{tgt}} \cdot \mathtt{age}) = |\mathtt{x}^{\mathtt{tgt}} \cdot \mathtt{age} - \mathtt{x}^{\mathtt{s}} \cdot \mathtt{age}| / B_{\mathtt{age}},$$

where $B_{\mathtt{age}}$ denotes the maximal possible difference. In our dataset, patient age ranges from 13 to 55, so $B_{\mathtt{age}} = 42$.

Pregnancy-related dates ($\mathtt{D} \cdot \mathtt{get30}()$, $\mathtt{D} \cdot \mathtt{get365}()$, $\mathtt{D} \cdot \mathtt{pregnancyOutcome}$) are represented as day offsets relative to the first delivery of anticoagulants. Since these values are unbounded, a decreasing bounded function, namely a sigmoid, is used to normalize the distance function:

$$\mathtt{dist}_a(\mathtt{x}^{\mathtt{s}} \cdot a, \mathtt{x}^{\mathtt{tgt}} \cdot a) = \sigma\big(|\mathtt{x}^{\mathtt{tgt}} \cdot a - \mathtt{x}^{\mathtt{s}} \cdot a| \;, \lambda, -\alpha, \beta\big) \text{ with}$$
$$\sigma(x; \lambda, \alpha, \beta) = 1/(1 + e^{-\lambda(\alpha x + \beta)}).$$

This ensures that the distance approaches 0 for close dates and gradually increases to 1 as the temporal difference grows. The parameters α, β and λ are solution-dependent parameters since the number of possible solutions is small, these parameters can be estimated for each solution (the solution $\mathtt{y}^{\mathtt{s}}$ of the source problem $\mathtt{x}^{\mathtt{s}}$ being known). More precisely, α controls how much the distance increases when the difference grows, β shifts the curve and determines when two values start to be considered different, and λ controls how fast the transition is between similar and dissimilar values.

5.2 Distance Between Sequences of Prescriptions

Given the sequence $\texttt{Seq}^{\texttt{s}}$ and $\texttt{Seq}^{\texttt{tgt}}$, their distance is the aggregation of 3 values. The first value estimates the normalized distance between the total durations of the sequences. The total duration of treatment of a prescription sequence is computed as the sum of the durations of its individual prescriptions. For example, the duration of the target sequence $\texttt{Seq}^{\texttt{tgt}}$, presented in Sect. 4, is equal to $7 + 15 + 253 = 275$ days.

The second value measures the theoretical incompatibility with the source solution $\texttt{y}^{\texttt{s}}$ of the first class of anticoagulants in the sequence $\texttt{Seq}^{\texttt{tgt}}$. This choice is motivated by the fact that the initial class of anticoagulants is a strong indicator of the underlying medical indication. Indeed, according to clinical recommendations, only a limited number of indications allow the use of DOACs or VKAs as first-line treatments, whereas most treatments typically start with heparins. For the target sequence $\texttt{Seq}^{\texttt{tgt}}$ of our example, the initial prescription is *Enoxaparin*, which belongs to the heparin class. According to the recommendation rules associated with the indication group $\texttt{I80}, \texttt{I81}, \texttt{I82}, \texttt{I26}$ (Table 1), heparin is an acceptable option for the initial treatment phase. As a result, when comparing $\texttt{x}^{\texttt{tgt}}$ with either case $\texttt{x}^1$ or $\texttt{x}^2$, the initial treatment is considered theoretically compatible, and the corresponding incompatibility score is set to 0.

The third step aims to evaluate the coherence between $\texttt{Seq}^{\texttt{tgt}}$ and $\texttt{Seq}^{\texttt{s}}$ through a *similarity path* [17] based on a series of allowed transformations. This step computes the transformation cost between a source sequence $\texttt{Seq}^{\texttt{s}}$ and a target sequence $\texttt{Seq}^{\texttt{tgt}}$. The idea is to progressively transform both sequences into a common intermediate sequence $\widehat{\texttt{Seq}}$ through a series of operations, each associated with an elementary cost. The weighted sum of these costs defines the final distance between the two sequences:

$$\texttt{transCost}(\texttt{x}^1 \cdot \texttt{prescs}, \texttt{x}^2 \cdot \texttt{prescs}) = \sum_i \texttt{w}_i \cdot \texttt{cost}_i,$$

where $\texttt{cost}_i$ denotes the cost of each elementary operation and $\texttt{w}_i$ represents solution-dependent weights.

$$\texttt{Seq}^{\texttt{tgt}} \xrightarrow[\texttt{cost}_1]{} \texttt{Seq}^1 \dashrightarrow \cdots \rightarrow \widehat{\texttt{Seq}} \leftarrow \cdots \dashleftarrow \texttt{Seq}^{n-1} \xleftarrow[\texttt{cost}_{n-1}]{} \texttt{Seq}^{\texttt{s}}$$

Transformation of $\texttt{Seq}^{\texttt{tgt}}$ and $\texttt{Seq}^{\texttt{s}}$ into the intermediate sequence $\widehat{\texttt{Seq}}$ is performed in four successive steps, each contributing to an elementary cost $\texttt{cost}_i$. First, the source sequence $\texttt{Seq}^{\texttt{s}}$ is replaced by a theoretical reference sequence $\texttt{Seq}^{\texttt{th}}$ using the operator "selection of the theoretical sequence". Second, if the two sequences have different lengths, the shorter one is adjusted to obtain sequences of equal size using the operator "sequence length adjustment". Third, the operator "INN substitution" is used to align prescriptions so that the corresponding elements use the same active substance to guaranty a valid position-wise comparison. Finally, the remaining quantitative differences in daily dose and duration of treatment are evaluated using the operator "dose–duration alignment". Each step produces an associated cost $\texttt{cost}_i$, and the weighted aggregation of these costs defines the total transformation cost between $\texttt{Seq}^{\texttt{s}}$ and $\texttt{Seq}^{\texttt{tgt}}$.

Selection of the Theoretical Sequence. A theoretical sequence $\mathtt{Seq}^{\mathtt{th}}$ is selected among the recommendations associated with the source solution $\mathtt{y}^{\mathtt{s}}$ by maximizing the overlap of active substances (the attribute `inn`) with the target sequence $\mathtt{Seq}^{\mathtt{tgt}}$. This overlap is measured using a Jaccard similarity between the sets of INNs. If there is no overlap, the search is extended to recommendations of solutions close to $\mathtt{y}^{\mathtt{s}}$, with an additional penalty cost.

In the running example, $\mathtt{Seq}^{\mathtt{tgt}}$ (Table 4) contains *Enoxaparin* and *Sintrom*. Among the three theoretical sequences candidate associated with the source solution $\mathtt{y}^{\mathtt{s}}$ (Table 1), R2 is selected because it achieves the highest overlap score.

Sequence Length Adjustment. Prescription sequences must be of the same length to be compared. When their lengths differ, the shorter sequence is expanded by splitting some prescriptions while preserving their order. This transformation is formulated as a search in a state space, where states represent partial alignments between the two sequences, and transitions correspond to editing operations on the shorter sequence.

In the running example, the selected theoretical sequence contains fewer prescriptions than $\mathtt{Seq}^{\mathtt{tgt}}$. The *Sintrom* prescription is therefore split into two consecutive segments to match the structure of $\mathtt{Seq}^{\mathtt{tgt}}$, resulting in sequences of equal length.

INN Substitution Operation. Prescription-level comparisons require aligned active substances at each position. When this is not the case, the target sequence is modified by substituting incompatible INNs with compatible theoretical prescriptions derived from the recommendations associated with $\mathtt{y}^{\mathtt{s}}$. For each position where INNs differ, a consistent theoretical prescription is selected according to the treatment phase, while preserving the original duration. If the theoretical prescription is derived from a different indication than the source solution, this substitution is accounted for using a substitution cost.

In the example, the third prescription of $\mathtt{Seq}^{\mathtt{tgt}}$ uses *Enoxaparin* while the aligned theoretical prescription is *Sintrom*. The *Enoxaparin* prescription is therefore replaced by *Sintrom* from rule R2, keeping the original duration.

Dose–Duration Alignment. Once the prescriptions are aligned by active substance, this operator quantifies their mismatch in terms of daily dose and treatment duration. At each position, the normalized deviations between theoretical and practical doses and durations are computed and aggregated using anticoagulant-specific weights. This yields a single alignment cost that reflects the overall quantitative difference between the two sequences.

In the example, dose and duration differences are evaluated position-wise (e.g., a 3-day duration gap for *Enoxaparin*), and combined into a weighted cost.

5.3 Distance Between Solutions

As presented in Sect. 2, each solution is associated with a set of theoretical recommendations represented as a set of theoretical prescription sequences derived from clinical guidelines. The distance between two solutions is computed by comparing these sets.

Theoretical sequences are first aligned by solving an assignment problem [5] that minimizes the total distance between the matched sequences, allowing comparison of solutions associated with different numbers of recommendations. The distance between two sequences is computed by aligning their prescriptions in order, aggregating prescription-level distances, and penalizing differences in sequence length. Finally, the distance between two theoretical prescriptions is defined only when they share the same INNs and is based on normalized differences in daily dose and duration of treatment; prescriptions with different INN are considered to be maximally distant. The distance between solutions is used in Sect. 5.2 to support operations "selection of theoretical sequence" and "INN substitution", which requires retrieving a solution y^* that is as close as possible to the solution y^s.

5.4 Weight Learning

Several parameters are used in the weights used in the weighted distances. Parameter learning relies on triplets $((\mathtt{x}, \mathtt{y}), (\mathtt{x}, \mathtt{y})^+, (\mathtt{x}, \mathtt{y})^-)$, where $(\mathtt{x}, \mathtt{y})^+$ shares the same solution as $(\mathtt{x}, \mathtt{y})$, and $(\mathtt{x}, \mathtt{y})^-$ does not. For distance-related weights, learning aims to minimize distance between $(\mathtt{x}, \mathtt{y})$ and $(\mathtt{x}, \mathtt{y})^+$ while maximizing distance with $(\mathtt{x}, \mathtt{y})^-$. For transformation-related weights, the objective is to penalize transformations toward $(\mathtt{x}, \mathtt{y})^-$ and to favor transformations toward $(\mathtt{x}, \mathtt{y})^+$.

6 Approximation

Given a target problem $\mathtt{x}^{\mathtt{tgt}}$, the approximation approach corresponds to retrieving $k = 1$ source case $(\mathtt{x}^{\mathtt{s}}, \mathtt{y}^{\mathtt{s}})$ [16]. It relies on a distance function between cases, based on the assumption that if $\mathtt{x}^{\mathtt{s}}$ is close to $\mathtt{x}^{\mathtt{tgt}}$, then $\mathtt{y}^{\mathtt{s}}$ is likely to be close to the requested solution $\mathtt{y}^{\mathtt{tgt}}$.

The approximation approach returns a solution profile rather than a single solution. Each candidate solution $\mathtt{y}$ is assigned a plausibility score in $[0, 1]$, defined as the maximum similarity between $\mathtt{x}^{\mathtt{tgt}}$ and any source problem associated with $\mathtt{y}$:

$$\mathtt{score}(\mathtt{y} \mid \mathtt{x}^{\mathtt{tgt}}) = \max\{1 - \mathtt{dist}(\mathtt{x}^{\mathtt{s}}, \mathtt{x}^{\mathtt{tgt}}) \mid (\mathtt{x}^{\mathtt{s}}, \mathtt{y}^{\mathtt{s}}) \in \mathrm{CB} \text{ and } \mathtt{y}^{\mathtt{s}} = \mathtt{y}\}.$$

The solution $\mathtt{y}$ with the highest score can be interpreted as the solution predicted by the system, as it is the most plausible candidate for the target problem $\mathtt{x}^{\mathtt{tgt}}$.

7 Interpolation

Interpolation is performed using a CBR approach relying on a fuzzy betweenness relation (Sect. 3.4). Given a target problem $\mathtt{x}^{\mathtt{tgt}}$, the method retrieves $k = 2$ source cases $(\mathtt{x}^b, \mathtt{y}^b)$ and $(\mathtt{x}^c, \mathtt{y}^c)$ sharing the same solution $\mathtt{y}^b = \mathtt{y}^c$. The underlying assumption is that if $\mathtt{x}^{\mathtt{tgt}}$ is between $\mathtt{x}^b$ and $\mathtt{x}^c$ in the problem space, then it is plausible that it shares the same solution.

To ensure a consistent context for distance comparison, the betweenness relation for solutions is restricted to equality: for $y^a, y^b, y^c \in \mathcal{S}$, $[y^b \text{-} y^a \text{-} y^c]$ holds iff $y^b = y^a = y^c$. This ensures that interpolation is performed within the same therapeutic reference.

The interpolation process also returns a solution profile. For a candidate solution y, its plausibility score is defined as the maximum fuzzy betweenness degree between the target problem and any pair of source problems $(\mathtt{x}^b, \mathtt{x}^c)$ such that $\mathtt{y}^b = \mathtt{y}^c = y$:

$$\mathtt{score}(\mathtt{y} \mid \mathtt{x}^{\mathtt{tgt}}) = \max\{\mathcal{FB}_{\mathtt{dist}}(\mathtt{x}^b, \mathtt{x}^{\mathtt{tgt}}, \mathtt{x}^c) \mid (\mathtt{x}^b, \mathtt{y}), (\mathtt{x}^c, \mathtt{y}) \in \mathtt{CB}\}$$

Therefore, a solution is considered plausible for $\mathtt{x}^{\mathtt{tgt}}$ if the target problem lies between two similar source problems associated with the same solution.

8 Evaluation

The approaches presented in Sects. 6 and 7 have been evaluated on generated data (Sect. 8.1), results are presented in Sect. 8.2.

8.1 Generated Data

Real-world data were not available on time due to legal and ethical constraints related to sensitive healthcare information. Synthetic data were generated to preserve key statistical properties of the real dataset. A preliminary statistical analysis identified the main distributions of clinical indications, prescribed active substances, and transitions between successive substances, including deviations from official guidelines. These statistics guided the generation process.

Patient ages and pregnancy-related dates were sampled to match the observed distributions. Prescription sequences were generated from theoretical recommendation patterns associated with the selected indication while allowing controlled variations in active substance, dose, and duration to reflect real prescribing behavior. The resulting synthetic data closely follow the real-world distributions. A total of 100 000 cases were generated. The dataset was split into 80 000 cases for parameter learning, 512 cases for the case base, and 19 488 cases for testing. This ensures that, for each solution, multiple cases are available in each subset.

8.2 Results

Let $\mathtt{n}_{\mathtt{tgt}}$ be the size of the test set, i.e., the number of target problems, $\mathtt{n}_{\mathtt{a}}$ the number of answers produced by the system and $\mathtt{n}_{\mathtt{ra}}$ the number of right answers. Let $\mathtt{S}_{\mathtt{sim}}$ denote the sum of similarities between the predicted solution (i.e., the solution having the highest score in the returned solution profile) and the expected solution. The system is evaluated using exact-match metrics, precision $\mathtt{prc} = \mathtt{n}_{\mathtt{ra}}/\mathtt{n}_{\mathtt{a}}$, recall $\mathtt{recall} = \mathtt{n}_{\mathtt{ra}}/\mathtt{n}_{\mathtt{tgt}}$, similarity-based metrics, average similarity $\mathtt{meanSim} = \mathtt{S}_{\mathtt{sim}}/\mathtt{n}_{\mathtt{a}}$, and average quality $\mathtt{meanQlt} = \mathtt{S}_{\mathtt{sim}}/\mathtt{n}_{\mathtt{tgt}}$. The coverage $\mathtt{coverage} = \mathtt{n}_{\mathtt{a}}/\mathtt{n}_{\mathtt{tgt}}$ is also reported, which measures the proportion of target problems for which the system produces an answer.

Table 5 reports the global performance of the system for different case-base sizes $|\mathtt{CB}|$ and for $k \in \{1, 2\}$, corresponding to approximation ($k = 1$) and interpolation ($k = 2$). For approximation, coverage is always 1.0 showing that a nearest case is always retrieved. Recall increases with the size of the case base and stabilizes around

Table 5. `prc`, `recall`, `meanSim`, `meanQlt` and `coverage` for $k = 1$ (approximation) and $k = 2$ (interpolation) for different sizes of the case base $|\texttt{CB}|$.

	$\|\texttt{CB}\| = 16$		$\|\texttt{CB}\| = 32$		$\|\texttt{CB}\| = 64$		$\|\texttt{CB}\| = 128$		$\|\texttt{CB}\| = 256$		$\|\texttt{CB}\| = 512$	
k	1	2	1	2	1	2	1	2	1	2	1	2
`prc`	0.68	1.00	0.70	1.00	0.75	0.93	0.79	0.59	0.79	0.68	0.78	0.69
`recall`	0.68	0.20	0.70	0.32	0.75	0.41	0.79	0.52	0.79	0.64	0.78	0.69
`meanSim`	0.94	1.00	0.94	1.00	0.93	0.95	0.93	0.76	0.93	0.80	0.93	0.78
`meanQlt`	0.94	0.20	0.94	0.32	0.93	0.42	0.93	0.67	0.93	0.75	0.93	0.78
`coverage`	1.00	0.20	1.00	0.32	1.00	0.44	1.00	0.88	1.00	0.94	1.00	1.00

0.79. The average similarity remains high (around 0.94), showing that the incorrect predictions are similar to the expected solution. For interpolation, coverage is low on small case bases but increases with $|\texttt{CB}|$, reaching 1.0 for $|\texttt{CB}| = 512$. When coverage is low, precision is close to 1.0, indicating a behavior that is both highly selective and accurate. As coverage increases, precision decreases, showing the loss of selectivity. While recall increases with coverage, it stabilizes at a level lower than that of approximation. In general, approximation ensures stable performance, while interpolation is very accurate on small case base, but becomes less precise as it answers more frequently. This suggests future work based on a smart combination of these approaches.

9 Discussion, Conclusion and Future Work

This paper has presented an application of the approximation and interpolation approaches of CBR to the domain of the completion of missing data, more specifically to the domain of inferring the medical indication of anticoagulant prescription, given this treatment. In previous studies, interpolation was studied with simple structures, such as Boolean tuples [16] or real number tuples [2], whereas in this work, it was necessary to take into account sequence structures of elements associated to knowledge in domain ontologies. Another possibility to address this task would have been to embed sequences in a vector space, as it was done in [8] and in [22]. It was chosen not to follow this path, because of the domain-specific information attached to the elements of the sequences. However, a potential future work would consist in using this embedding approach in order to speed up retrieval, under a MAC/FAC principle [9].

The proposed approach can be further improved. First, since two approaches are used, the question raised is how to efficiently combine approximation and interpolation. One idea would be find a mean to make a choice between the result proposed by these approaches (when they disagree), using the scores associated with them, i.e. the similarity for approximation and the fuzzy betweenness for interpolation. Both approaches can also be individually improved. In particular, approximation is a very simple way to apply the "Similar problems have similar solutions" hypothesis, but there are more sophisticated and more efficient ones, such as the approach of credible CBR proposed by Eyke Hüllermeier [12].

A future work aims at applying also the approach of extrapolation, which involves being able to define analogical proportions between sequences. In [14, 15, 18, 19] are described approaches for analogical proportions between sequences of characters (i.e., words, sentences, etc.) and should be inspiring for this future work. A difference here is that the element of the sequences are associated with knowledge and are not just mere characters, so, the question here is how to take into account pieces of knowledge in these analogical proportions.

Acknowledgments. The authors wish to thank the anonymous reviewers for their work.

Declaration on Generative AI. During the preparation of this work, the authors used the tools ChatGPT and Writefull. Writefull was used for grammar and spelling checking. ChatGPT was used to suggest paraphrasing and improvements to writing style in some passages where the authors had doubts about formulation. The suggestions were reviewed, selectively adopted, and adapted by the authors. The author carefully reviewed and edited the final text and takes full responsibility for the content of the publication.

References

1. Aisbett, J., Gibbon, G.: A general formulation of conceptual spaces as a meso level representation. Artif. Intell. **133**(1–2), 189–232 (2001)
2. Astier, É., Iopeti, H., Lieber, J., Mathieu Steinbach, H., Yvoz, L.: Case-based cleaning of text images. In: Massie, S., Chakraborti, S. (eds.) Case-Based Reasoning Research and Development, Proceedings of the 31st International Conference on Case-Based Reasoning, vol. 14141, pp. 344–358. Springer, Cham (2023). https://doi.org/10.1007/978-3-031-40177-0_22, https://hal.science/hal-04393829
3. Bates, S.M., et al.: American society of hematology 2018 guidelines for management of venous thromboembolism: venous thromboembolism in the context of pregnancy. Blood Adv. **2**(22), 3317–3359 (2018). https://doi.org/10.1182/bloodadvances.2018024802
4. Bukhari, S., Fatima, S., Barakat, A.F., Fogerty, A.E., Weinberg, I., Elgendy, I.Y.: Venous thromboembolism during pregnancy and postpartum period. Eur. J. Intern. Med. **97**, 8–17 (2022)
5. Crouse, D.F.: On implementing 2D rectangular assignment algorithms. IEEE Trans. Aerosp. Electron. Syst. **52**(4), 1679–1696 (2016). https://doi.org/10.1109/TAES.2016.140952
6. DeWald, T.A., Washam, J.B., Becker, R.C.: Anticoagulants: pharmacokinetics, mechanisms of action, and indications. Neurosurg. Clin. N. Am. **29**(4), 503–515 (2018). https://doi.org/10.1016/j.nec.2018.06.003
7. Diebold, E., Lieber, J., Merah, N., Bannay, A.: Case-based identification of anti-coagulation therapy for pregnant women using approximation and interpolation of sequences (extended version). Tech. rep., LORIA (Université de Lorraine, CNRS, INRIA) (2026). https://hal.science/hal-05557015
8. Dolphin, R., Smyth, B., Dong, R.: Industry classification using a novel financial time-series case representation. arXiv:2305.00245 (2023)
9. Forbus, K.D., Gentner, D., Law, K.: MAC/FAC: a model of similarity-based retrieval. Cogn. Sci. **19**, 141–205 (1995)
10. Gardenfors, P.: Conceptual Spaces: The Geometry of Thought. MIT Press (2004)
11. Hirsch, J., et al.: ICD-10: history and context. Am. J. Neuroradiol. **37** (2016). https://doi.org/10.3174/ajnr.A4696

12. Hüllermeier, E.: Credible case-based inference using similarity profiles. IEEE Trans. Knowl. Data Eng. **19**(6), 847–858 (2007). https://doi.org/10.1109/TKDE.2007.1017
13. Jourdi, G., et al.: Anticoagulation therapy in France: state-of-the-art in 2020. Ann. Blood **5** (2020). https://aob.amegroups.org/article/view/5396
14. Lepage, Y., Denoual, É.: Purest ever example-based machine translation: detailed presentation and assessment. Mach. Transl. **19**, 251–282 (2005)
15. Lepage, Y., Lieber, J.: Case-based translation: first steps from a knowledge-light approach based on analogy to a knowledge-intensive one. In: ICCBR 2018 - 26th International Conference on Case-Based Reasoning. Stockholm, Sweden (2018)
16. Lieber, J., Nauer, E., Prade, H., Richard, G.: Making the best of cases by approximation, interpolation and extrapolation. In: Cox, M.T., Funk, P., Begum, S. (eds.) ICCBR 2018. LNCS (LNAI), vol. 11156, pp. 580–596. Springer, Cham (2018). https://doi.org/10.1007/978-3-030-01081-2_38
17. Lieber, J., Napoli, A.: Using classification in case-based planning. In: Wahlster, W. (ed.) 12th European Conference on Artificial Intelligence, Budapest, Hungary, August 11–16, 1996, Proceedings, pp. 132–136. John Wiley and Sons, Chichester (1996)
18. Marquer, E., Alsaidi, S., Decker, A., Murena, P.A., Couceiro, M.: A deep learning approach to solving morphological analogies. In: Keane, M.T., Wiratunga, N. (eds.) Case-Based Reasoning Research and Development, pp. 159–174. Springer International Publishing, Cham (2022). https://doi.org/10.1007/978-3-031-14923-8_11
19. Murena, P.A., Al-Ghossein, M., Dessalles, J.L., Cornuéjols, A.: Solving analogies on words based on minimal complexity transformation. In: International Joint Conference on Artificial Intelligence, pp. 1848–1854. IJCAI (2020)
20. Riesbeck, C.K., Schank, R.C.: Inside Case-Based Reasoning. Lawrence Erlbaum Associates Inc. (1989). available on line
21. Tuppin, P., et al.: Value of a national administrative database to guide public decisions: from the système national d'information interrégimes de l'Assurance Maladie (SNIIRAM) to the système national des données de santé (SNDS) in France. Rev. Epidemiol. Sante Publique **65**, S149–S167 (2017). https://doi.org/10.1016/j.respe.2017.05.004, https://www.sciencedirect.com/science/article/pii/S0398762017304315, réseau REDSIAM
22. Weich, J., Schultheis, A., Hoffmann, M., Bergmann, R.: Integration of time series embedding for efficient retrieval in case-based reasoning. In: Bichindaritz, I., López, B. (eds.) Case-Based Reasoning Research and Development, pp. 328–344. Springer, Cham (2025).https://doi.org/10.1007/978-3-031-96559-3_22

Knowledge-Guided Generative Adaptation in Case-Based Reasoning for Automatic Art Exhibition Generation

Jorge López-Varela, Javier Vega Domínguez, Belen Diaz-Agudo, Juan A. Recio-Garcia(✉), and Antonio A. Sánchez-Ruiz

Facultad de Informática, Universidad Complutense de Madrid, Madrid, Spain
jareciog@ucm.es

Abstract. Museums increasingly publish open collections as knowledge graphs and Linked Open Data, yet assembling coherent exhibitions from these sources remains an open challenge. In this paper we present a hybrid system that generates virtual painting exhibitions from open cultural data stored in an RDF knowledge graph. A Case-Based Reasoning (CBR) engine retrieves past exhibitions and adapts them to new curatorial requests through a *knowledge-guided generative adaptation* strategy. When a retrieved case contains a room whose movement conflicts with the new query, the adaptation module searches the knowledge graph for compatible replacements and regenerates the affected rooms. The knowledge graph integrates multiple sources into over 40,000 RDF triples with explicit provenance. We describe the ontology design, two similarity functions for movement and painting queries, and the adaptation mechanism, illustrating the approach with a worked example that shows how the SKOS concept hierarchy drives explainable case reuse.

Keywords: CBR · Knowledge Graphs · Adaptation · Cultural Heritage · Art Exhibitions · Semantic Similarity · Linked Open Data

1 Introduction

The digitisation of museum collections has produced a large volume of open cultural data. Platforms such as Wikidata, Europeana, and museum APIs now expose millions of artworks as Linked Open Data [2], described through vocabularies such as the Getty Art & Architecture Thesaurus (AAT) [9] and ontologies such as CIDOC CRM [4] and the Europeana Data Model (EDM) [6]. Europeana alone aggregates over 50 million cultural heritage objects from thousands of European institutions[1], yet this integration does not by itself turn raw data into coherent exhibitions. A visitor does not want a list of paintings; they want a *curated experience*: rooms that flow from one theme to the next, contextual movements that illuminate the anchor style, and a selection principle that is transparent and reproducible.

[1] https://www.europeana.eu/en/about-us.

L. Malburg and K. Bach (Eds.): ICCBR 2026, LNAI 16780, pp. 521–536, 2027.
https://doi.org/10.1007/978-3-032-33865-5_32

The intended users of the system are not visitors but curators and museum staff, particularly in institutions where the ratio between available curatorial personnel and collection size makes the manual design of exhibitions impractical. The system does not produce a deployment-ready exhibition: it delivers a conceptual structure (a set of thematically coherent rooms with their constituent works), not the curatorial narrative, interpretive texts, visitor-facing presentation, or mapping to a specific floor plan that a finished exhibition requires. The output is venue-agnostic, in the sense that the rooms are logical groupings rather than physical assignments; whether the resulting exhibition is then realised online, in a physical gallery, or as a hybrid is a downstream decision that depends on the institution's medium and constraints. It assists the preselection stage that precedes those decisions by proposing groupings of movements and works that a curator can then refine. This preselection task scales poorly with collection size and is precisely where understaffed teams struggle most: navigating a catalogue of thousands of items and identifying meaningful thematic axes is time-consuming even for specialists.

This paper addresses the problem of automatically generating *virtual painting exhibitions* from open cultural data. Given a user query, either an anchor artistic movement (e.g., *Impressionism*) or a specific painting, the system must produce a structured exhibition comprising ten thematic rooms, each presenting up to ten artworks with full metadata. The challenge is threefold. First, the data are heterogeneous: movements, artists, and paintings are spread across multiple sources with different schemas and identifier spaces. Second, the notion of a *good* exhibition is inherently subjective, making fully automatic evaluation hard. Third, when the system reuses a previously generated exhibition for a similar but distinct query, it must adapt the case in a principled way rather than blindly copying it.

A purely generative module always produces the same exhibition for the same query and never learns from past results. CBR addresses this by treating every user-validated exhibition as reusable curatorial knowledge: subsequent similar queries reuse the room combinations a curator already found coherent, modifying only what the new anchor demands. The case base thus accumulates curatorial memory: the knowledge graph provides vocabulary and data; the cases capture how that data has been successfully organised before.

We propose a hybrid system that combines an RDF knowledge graph with a Case-Based Reasoning (CBR) engine. The knowledge graph serves a dual role: it supplies the instance data (paintings, artists, institutions) and, via the SKOS hierarchy inherited from Getty AAT, it provides the structural knowledge that guides adaptation. Concretely, our main contributions are:

1. An integrated multi-source RDF pipeline that combines Getty AAT, Wikidata, the Metropolitan Museum of Art (MET) API, the Art Institute of Chicago (ArtIC) API, and the Museo del Prado via Europeana into a single coherent knowledge graph with explicit provenance.
2. Two complementary similarity functions, one for movement-anchored queries and one for painting-anchored queries, based on structural path similarity

over the SKOS hierarchy and Jaccard overlap over instance sets, following the approach in [11].
3. A knowledge-guided generative adaptation mechanism that exploits the SKOS concept hierarchy to detect and resolve semantic conflicts in retrieved cases, regenerating affected rooms with semantically compatible content.
4. A cold-start mitigation strategy in which the generative module acts as an on-demand case factory, eliminating the need for a hand-crafted initial case base.

The rest of the paper is organised as follows. Section 2 reviews related work. Section 3 describes the CBR system in detail, including the knowledge graph, case representation, similarity functions, and the adaptation mechanism. Section 4 presents evaluation results. Section 5 concludes and outlines future work.

2 Related Work

CBR has been applied to creative and open-ended domains since the early 1990s. Systems such as CHEF [10] and JULIA [12] demonstrated that adaptation guided by domain knowledge is essential when cases from the case base do not perfectly match new problems. In cultural heritage, CBR has been used for museum tour recommendation [15], content-based artwork retrieval [5], and personalised itinerary planning [17]. However, these systems typically treat artworks as atomic items to be retrieved or recommended, without constructing *structured exhibitions* or thematic groupings. Our work differs in that cases represent entire curated exhibitions, that is, multi-room structures with semantic coherence constraints, and adaptation must preserve that structure.

The publication of cultural heritage data as Linked Open Data has fostered a rich and increasingly interoperable ecosystem of knowledge sources. Authoritative vocabularies such as the Getty Art & Architecture Thesaurus (AAT) and the Union List of Artist Names (ULAN) provide controlled terminologies that support semantic consistency across museum collections [9]. Wikidata functions as a central alignment hub, aggregating persistent identifiers from hundreds of cultural catalogues and facilitating cross-source integration without extensive manual mapping [18]. At the modelling level, the Linked Art initiative promotes CIDOC CRM as a shared interchange framework, while Europeana's Data Model (EDM) harmonises metadata from thousands of European institutions [6].

These resources have enabled a range of cultural heritage applications, including unifying heterogeneous collections into knowledge graphs and supporting reasoning over structured cultural data [1,13]. MuseKG provides a knowledge graph over museum collections that allows querying across semantic relations [13]. CHAD-KG represents both descriptive metadata and digitisation paradata using RDF and CIDOC-CRM, preserving provenance through a reproducible pipeline [1]. Our work builds on these approaches by integrating multiple sources via a reproducible pipeline with explicit provenance using the

W3C PROV ontology [19], and by using the resulting knowledge graph not only for retrieval but as a structured substrate for CBR adaptation. Ontology-based semantic similarity has a long history [16,21]. Path-based measures, such as the Wu-Palmer metric [21], compute similarity as a function of the shortest path between concepts in a hierarchy and the depth of their least common subsumer. Embedding-based alternatives (e.g., node2vec, TransE) capture richer relational patterns but sacrifice explainability [20].

Automatic generation of structured cultural content from knowledge graphs has also attracted growing interest [8]. In [7] authors generated textual descriptions of artworks from ontological features. [14] used semantic web technologies to support museum storytelling. Closest to our work, [3] proposed a planning-based framework for virtual exhibition layout, but did not address multi-source data integration or case reuse. Our system is, to the best of our knowledge, the first to combine a multi-source cultural knowledge graph with a CBR engine whose adaptation phase is explicitly guided by the hierarchical structure of a controlled vocabulary.

3 The CBR System for Exhibition Generation

A data integration pipeline constructs an RDF knowledge graph by combining four external sources plus the Getty AAT vocabulary. The CBR engine then operates over this graph, implementing the classical cycle. User interaction is mediated through a web interface that exposes the generation and revision controls.

The system supports two generation modes. In *movement mode*, the user selects an anchor artistic movement (e.g., Impressionism) and a grouping criterion for the rooms (author, medium, genre, decade, institution, sub-movement, or movement). In *painting mode*, the user selects a specific anchor painting, and the system identifies the most similar artworks and organises them according to the chosen criterion. In both modes, five rooms are dedicated to the anchor concept and five contextual rooms present semantically related movements selected from the SKOS hierarchy.

3.1 Knowledge Graph Construction

The construction of the knowledge graph begins with the extraction of a sub-tree from the Getty Art & Architecture Thesaurus that covers artistic movements and styles. Starting from a root node representing the general domain of painting styles, a breadth-first traversal downloads each concept in Turtle format, preserving the full SKOS structure (`skos:broader`/`skos:narrower`, `skos:prefLabel`, multilingual labels). This ensures that the hierarchical relationships used later for similarity computation and adaptation are stable, controlled, and reproducible without relying on string matching. A representative fragment of the resulting graph is shown in Fig. 1, illustrating how the external vocabularies and artwork records are integrated into a single RDF structure.

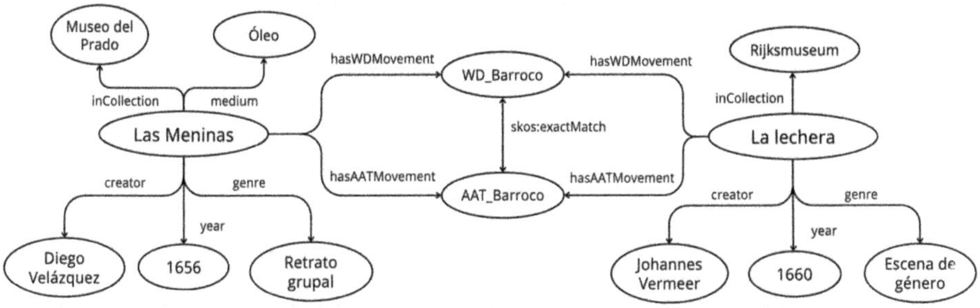

Fig. 1. Fragment of the RDF knowledge graph, showing the connections between AAT movements, Wikidata entities, paintings, and descriptive metadata.

Many artistic movement entities in Wikidata carry the property `P1014` (Getty AAT identifier), enabling automatic, identifier-based alignment between the two sources. This alignment is computed in batches over the Wikidata SPARQL endpoint and materialised in the graph as bidirectional `skos:exactMatch` links. The result is a direct, unambiguous projection: if a painting is associated with a movement in Wikidata via `P135`, it can immediately be anchored to the corresponding Getty AAT concept without any manual mapping.

The initial AAT sub-tree contains many concepts unrelated to painting (e.g., architectural and sculptural movements). To reduce this noise, a first filter retains only those AAT concepts with a corresponding Wikidata match, together with all ancestors up to the root so that the hierarchy remains connected. A second, stricter filter then removes movements for which no painting with a retrievable image exists in Wikidata, again preserving the necessary ancestors. This double filtering substantially reduces semantic noise and produces a hierarchy that accurately reflects the coverage of the available instance data. The process is illustrated in Fig. 2 using the Impressionism branch as an example: the input AAT concept is first aligned with its Wikidata counterpart, then the relevant ancestors are recovered to preserve the tree structure, and finally the filtered movement is connected only to paintings that satisfy the availability constraints.

For each movement retained after filtering, a SPARQL query retrieves up to thirty paintings with metadata: author (`P170`), creation date (`P571`), image (`P18`), holding institution (`P195`), artistic genre (`P136`), and depicted subject (`P180`). Queries are issued via HTTP POST with exponential back-off to handle rate limits. Results are cached locally to ensure reproducibility.

Wikidata often contains identifiers pointing to specialised museum catalogues. The system activates enrichment only when a reliable identifier is present: if a painting has a MET object ID (`P3634`), the MET Open Access API is consulted to add medium, dimensions, credit line, curatorial department, and the official museum URL; if it has an ArtIC ID (`P4610`), the Art Institute of Chicago API provides medium, dimensions, a textual description, and the official artwork URL. For paintings held by the Museo del Prado (`P195`) with a known inventory number (`P217`), Europeana's dataset (downloaded in XML and indexed

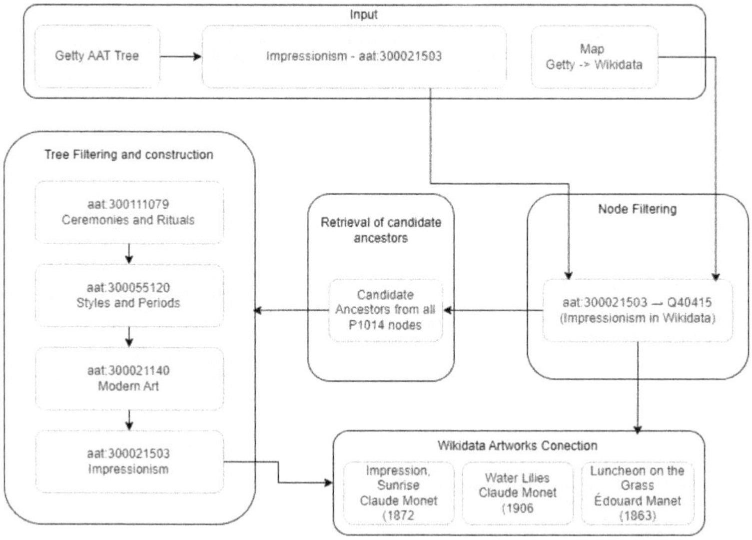

Fig. 2. Two-stage filtering process applied to the Impressionism branch.

locally) is used, adding medium, dimensions, textual description, and date. The linking criterion is the inventory number, which is the most stable identifier across sources. Every enrichment triple carries a `prov:wasDerivedFrom` assertion recording the source, ensuring full traceability. For the final ontology alignment, a local ontology defines five classes, `Painting`, `Artist`, `Museum`, `Exhibition`, and `Room`, aligned to established standards via `owl:equivalentClass` and `owl:equivalentProperty`:

$$\texttt{local:Painting} \equiv \texttt{schema:VisualArtwork}$$
$$\equiv \texttt{crm:E22\_Man-Made\_Object} \equiv \texttt{edm:ProvidedCHO}$$

$$\texttt{local:creator} \equiv \texttt{dcterms:creator} \equiv \texttt{schema:creator}$$
$$\equiv \texttt{wdt:P170} \equiv \texttt{crm:P14\_carried\_out\_by}$$

These equivalences are declared directly in the graph, making interoperability explicit without depending on external inference. The final knowledge graph contains **40,126 RDF triples**, **5 OWL classes**, **8 object properties**, and **3023 instances**.

Given the seed AAT concepts that define the domain scope, the entire pipeline runs end-to-end without manual curation: hierarchy traversal, Wikidata alignment, double filtering, and source-conditional enrichment are all driven by the SKOS structure and the presence of stable identifiers, with no hand-mapping between sources. Adding a new museum source within the same domain only requires registering its identifier property and enrichment endpoint; extending to a different AAT sub-tree is equally automated once the new seed concepts are specified.

3.2 Case Representation

Each case in the CBR base represents a previously generated (and user-validated) virtual exhibition. Cases have four components:

Description. The query parameters that generated the exhibition: *mode* (`movement` or `painting`), *anchor URI* (the Getty AAT or Wikidata URI of the anchor concept or painting), *grouping criterion* (one of: author, medium, genre, decade, institution, sub-movement, movement), *min_works* (minimum number of paintings a neighbouring movement must have to be eligible as a contextual room; movement mode only), and *top_n_similar* (number of similar paintings to pre-compute before grouping; painting mode only).

Solution. The exhibition title and a list of ten rooms. Each room has a thematic label and a list of up to ten painting URIs together with cached metadata (author, date, medium, institution, image URL, external link).

Justification Metadata. Timestamp, save status, and the similarity score at which the case was retained.

Cold-start handling. When no stored case exceeds the similarity threshold for a new query, the generative module produces a fresh exhibition on the fly (see Sect. 3.4) and offers it to the user for revision. Once approved, it is stored as a new case. This dynamic seeding eliminates the need for a hand-crafted initial case base and makes the system immediately usable with zero cases.

3.3 Similarity Assessment (Retrieve Phase)

The retrieval phase computes a weighted similarity between an incoming query and every case in the base, returning the top-2 cases that exceed a user-configurable threshold τ. Two distinct similarity functions are used depending on the generation mode.

Movement Mode Similarity. Two attributes drive the comparison: the structural similarity between the anchor movements, and the proximity of the *min_works* parameter.

$$\mathrm{sim}_{\mathrm{mov}}(q, c) = 0.70 \cdot \mathrm{path\_sim}(q.\mathrm{anchor}, c.\mathrm{anchor}) + 0.30 \cdot e^{-\lambda |q.\mathrm{min\_works} - c.\mathrm{min\_works}|} \tag{1}$$

where path_sim is a Wu-Palmer-style path similarity computed over the SKOS hierarchy: it rewards concepts that share a deep common ancestor and penalises those connected only through the root. The mode and grouping criterion act as hard constraints: cases with a different mode or grouping are excluded from the candidate set, as mixing these would produce structurally incompatible adaptations.

Painting Mode Similarity. For painting-anchored queries, similarity is computed in two stages. First, a painting-level similarity aggregates multiple facets of the anchor painting:

$$\begin{aligned}\text{sim}_{\text{paint}}(q, c) = {} & 0.35 \cdot \text{path\_sim}(\text{AAT mvt}) + 0.15 \cdot J(\text{creator}) + 0.15 \cdot J(\text{genre}) \\ & + 0.20 \cdot J(\text{depicts}) + 0.10 \cdot J(\text{institution}) + 0.05 \cdot e^{-\lambda|\Delta\text{year}|}\end{aligned} \quad (2)$$

where $J(\cdot)$ denotes Jaccard similarity over the corresponding URI sets. This painting-level similarity is then combined with the proximity of the *top_n_similar* parameter:

$$\text{sim}_{\text{final}}(q, c) = 0.70 \cdot \text{sim}_{\text{paint}}(q, c) + 0.30 \cdot e^{-\lambda|q.\text{top\_n} - c.\text{top\_n}|} \quad (3)$$

The weights in Eqs. 1–3 were set by domain reasoning: the structural movement similarity is the dominant signal because the thematic coherence of an exhibition is primarily determined by the anchor movement, while depicted subjects receive higher weight than institution or year because they are more directly predictive of the room content.

3.4 Knowledge-Guided Generative Adaptation (Reuse Phase)

The adaptation phase is the core contribution of this paper. When the user selects a retrieved case for reuse, the system must transform the stored exhibition, built for a different (though similar) anchor, into a coherent exhibition for the new query. The central challenge is that the five contextual rooms (rooms 6–10) were populated with movements that are semantically appropriate neighbours of the *original* anchor but may be inappropriate for the *new* anchor. Specifically, if one of those contextual rooms uses a movement that is an ancestor, descendant, or the anchor itself, presenting it as a neighbour would be misleading or redundant.

Conflict Detection. For each contextual room r_i, the system flags its thematic movement m_i for replacement if any of the following holds:

1. $m_i = a$ (identity conflict),
2. m_i is an ancestor of a in the SKOS hierarchy (`skos:broader*`),
3. m_i is a descendant of a in the SKOS hierarchy (`skos:narrower*`).

Replacement Strategy. The replacement search exploits the SKOS hierarchy in a three-step cascade (Fig. 3):

1. **Narrower concepts.** Retrieve all `skos:narrower` children of a not already used in the exhibition and with at least *min_works* paintings with images. Select the child with the highest path_sim to the conflicting movement m_i.
2. **Sibling concepts.** If step 1 yields no candidate, retrieve all concepts sharing the same `skos:broader` parent as a (excluding a itself and concepts already used) that meet the *min_works* threshold. Select the sibling with the highest path_sim to m_i.

3. **Broader expansion.** If step 2 also fails, move one level up the hierarchy and repeat from step 1 with a's parent as the new pivot.

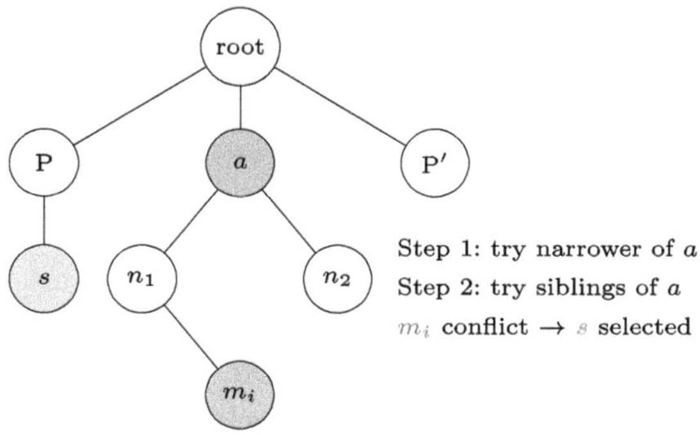

Fig. 3. Knowledge-guided replacement. The conflicting movement m_i (red) is a descendant of a (blue), triggering replacement. Step 1 finds no suitable narrower concept of a with enough paintings; Step 2 selects the sibling s (green) based on path similarity. (Color figure online)

Room Regeneration. Once a replacement movement m' is selected, the system queries the knowledge graph for paintings associated with m', filters to those with an image URL, and selects up to ten, preferring works that are already in the graph's enriched subset (MET/ArtIC/Prado) for richer metadata display. The contextual room is then rebuilt with this new set of paintings and the label of m'. Rooms that passed conflict detection without a conflict (i.e., movements that are genuine semantic neighbours of a) are retained unchanged from the retrieved case, preserving as much of the original solution as possible.

Generative Fallback (cold Start). When no stored case clears the threshold τ, the generative module constructs an exhibition from scratch using the same SKOS hierarchy. In movement mode, it queries the graph for all paintings of the anchor movement, groups them by the chosen criterion, selects the five groups with the most paintings (the *anchor rooms*), and then computes path_sim for all movements in the hierarchy to find the five most similar movements with at least *min_works* paintings (the *contextual rooms*). In painting mode, it first retrieves the *top_n* most similar paintings by the painting-level similarity (Eq. 2) and then organises them into ten rooms according to the grouping criterion. This generative fallback produces a valid exhibition immediately, which the user can then revise and optionally retain as a seed case, progressively building the case base without any bootstrapping effort.

To illustrate the adaptation mechanism end to end, Table 1 traces the transformation of a Post-Impressionism case, manually seeded into the case base for expository purposes, into an exhibition for the new anchor Impressionism. The trace is intended as a worked example of the conflict-detection and replacement cascade described above, not as quantitative evidence; the empirical evaluation of the structural component is reported in Sect. 4.

Table 1. Adaptation example: Post-Impressionism case adapted to Impressionism. Room 6 of the retrieved case uses Post-Impressionism itself as contextual movement, which is a descendant of Impressionism and therefore a conflict, so it is replaced.

Room	Retrieved case (anchor: Post-Impr.)	Adapted (anchor: Impressionism)	Change
1–5	Anchor rooms (Post-Impressionism)	Anchor rooms (Impressionism)	Replaced
6	Post-Impressionism (contextual)	Realism (sim = 0.60, 45 ptgs.)	Replaced
7	Symbolism	Symbolism	Kept
8	Neo-Impressionism	Neo-Impressionism	Kept
9	Fauvism	Fauvism	Kept
10	Romanticism	Romanticism	Kept

Rooms 7–10 pass the conflict check (none is an ancestor or descendant of Impressionism in AAT) and are preserved. Room 6 contains Post-Impressionism, a descendant of Impressionism, and is flagged. Step 1 finds no eligible narrower concept; Step 2 searches the siblings of Impressionism (Realism, 45 paintings, path_sim = 0.60; Romanticism, 38, already used; Naturalism, 12), selects Realism as the best available, and regenerates room 6.

3.5 Revision and Retention

Revise. After adaptation, the system presents the exhibition to the user through the Gradio interface. The user may deselect individual paintings from any room or add paintings from a suggestion panel. Suggestions are generated by querying the knowledge graph for works associated with the room's thematic movement that are not yet in the exhibition, ranked by the presence of enriched metadata (images, descriptions). This constrained suggestion mechanism preserves the semantic coherence of each room while providing genuine curatorial agency, without requiring the user to have deep art-historical expertise.

Retain. Retention is manual: once satisfied with the exhibition, the user explicitly saves it to the case base. The saved case records the adapted problem parameters, the final room structure (including any manual modifications), the timestamp, and the similarity score at which the base case was retrieved. Manual retention is justified by the subjective nature of curatorial quality: automatic retention would accumulate low-quality cases that degrade future retrieval.

4 Evaluation

The evaluation in this section targets the structural component of the system, namely the integration of the knowledge graph with the generative module that produces exhibitions from scratch when no validated cases are available (Sect. 3.4). The complete CBR cycle, in which retrieve and reuse operate over a case base of curator-validated exhibitions, is not evaluated here: its central value, the accumulation of curatorial memory over time, is intrinsically subjective and requires a longitudinal study with domain experts that lies beyond the scope of this paper. The mechanism of knowledge-guided adaptation is illustrated separately in Sect. 3.4 (Table 1) on a manually seeded case base. We therefore designed an automated pipeline to measure what can be measured objectively in the structural component: its robustness against data sparsity, its curatorial diversity, and its structural semantic coherence when generating exhibitions in cold-start mode.

4.1 Baseline

To evaluate our semantic adaptation, we compare against a strict relational baseline, denoted *NaiveBaseline*. This baseline simulates a traditional exact-match retrieval system.

When the query is an artistic movement, *NaiveBaseline* simply retrieves artworks tagged with that exact movement ID. When the query is anchored by a specific artwork, it extracts the primary movement of that artwork and uses it as the search key. We chose the artwork's movement as the relational anchor rather than other attributes (such as author or decade) to establish a fair comparison: using the author would be overly restrictive and artificially penalise the baseline due to data scarcity, while grouping by decade would be excessively broad, retrieving semantically disconnected artworks. Matching by movement provides the most balanced strict-relational scenario.

Crucially, *NaiveBaseline* lacks semantic expansion: if the repository does not contain enough exact matches to fill the exhibition, the retrieval process terminates prematurely, resulting in an incomplete exhibition.

4.2 Metrics

Completion Rate and Volume. The primary metric for robustness against data sparsity is the system's ability to produce a full exhibition. We measure the *Average Rooms* generated per query and the *Completion Rate* (the percentage of queries that yield the target number of rooms).

Curatorial Diversity (Entropy). To measure the variety of a generated exhibition based on the selected grouping mode, we use *Shannon Entropy*, defined in Eq. 4. We calculate both the distinct number of curatorial categories ($N_{categories}$) and the overall entropy:

$$H(X) = - \sum_{i=1}^{N_{categories}} p_i \log_2(p_i) \tag{4}$$

where p_i is the proportion of artworks belonging to category i over the total number of artworks in the exhibition. To contextualise this value, we bound it by the theoretical maximum for equiprobable categories, $H_{max} = \log_2(N_{categories})$.

Normalised Semantic Coherence (C_{norm}). To fairly evaluate both exact-match retrieval and semantic expansion when the query is anchored by a movement, we partition the exhibition rooms into two subsets: Anchor Rooms (R_{anchor}), containing paintings from the queried movement, and Related Rooms (R_{rel}), containing paintings from semantically neighbouring movements.

For a set of rooms R, let P_R be the set of all paintings in those rooms and $M(p)$ the set of movements associated with a painting p. The coherence of a room set is:

$$C(R) = \frac{1}{|P_R|} \sum_{p \in P_R} \max_{m \in M(p)} SKOS_{sim}(m_a, m) \tag{5}$$

We define $C_{anchor} = C(R_{anchor})$ and $C_{rel} = C(R_{rel})$. To penalise failure in both fidelity and expansion equally, we combine them with equal weight: $C_{norm} = 0.5 \cdot C_{anchor} + 0.5 \cdot C_{rel}$

Anchor Artwork Centrality (C_{art}). When the query is anchored by a specific artwork rather than a movement, we measure the structural cohesion of the exhibition by computing the average similarity between the anchor artwork a and all other paintings. The anchor itself is excluded from the averaging pool to avoid artificial inflation:

$$C_{art} = \frac{1}{|P \setminus \{a\}|} \sum_{p \in P \setminus \{a\}} sim_{paint}(a, p) \tag{6}$$

where P is the set of all paintings in the exhibition and sim_{paint} is the painting-level similarity defined in Eq. 2. A higher centrality score indicates that the retrieved artworks remain tightly aligned with the anchor piece.

4.3 Experimental Setup

The evaluation was conducted over the knowledge graph described in Sect. 3.1. We executed 1,000 randomised curatorial queries (500 anchored by specific artworks and 500 by artistic movements). The minimum threshold for a valid room was set to $min\_works = 8$. For painting-mode queries, the retrieval parameter was $top\_n = 50$. For movement-mode queries, the system used a 5/5 split (anchor vs. contextual rooms), selecting contextual movements via $path\_sim$ over the SKOS hierarchy. A fixed random seed (42) was used across all iterations to guarantee reproducibility.

4.4 Results

The comparison between *NaiveBaseline* and the proposed *Knowledge-Guided* strategy reveals a clear performance gap, particularly in robustness and curatorial richness. Table 2 summarises the results across 1,000 queries.

Table 2. Cold-start exhibition generation: NaiveBaseline vs. Knowledge-Guided Generative Module.

Metric	NaiveBaseline	KG Generative Module
Avg. Rooms Generated (out of 10)	3.98	8.99
Full Exhibition Completion Rate	19.2%	82.1%
Avg. Distinct Categories	3.85	12.30
Mean Entropy (H)	1.171 (58.6%)	2.710 (75.6%)
Artwork Centrality (C_{art})	0.470	0.290
Anchor Coherence (C_{anchor})	1.000	0.775
Related Coherence (C_{rel})	0.000	0.266
Normalised Coherence (C_{norm})	0.500	0.520

Robustness and Diversity. One of the contributions of our approach is the mitigation of data sparsity. NaiveBaseline fails to produce complete exhibitions in over 80% of cases, while the Knowledge-Guided module completes most of them. Curatorial diversity rises substantially in both distinct categories and entropy, indicating that semantic traversal not only finds more artworks but produces a more varied selection.

The Semantic Coherence Trade-Off. The results validate C_{norm} as a fair aggregate metric. *NaiveBaseline* achieves a perfect C_{anchor} of 1.000 because it only retrieves exact matches, but its inability to expand yields $C_{rel} = 0.000$ and a global C_{norm} of 0.500.

In contrast, the Knowledge-Guided module accepts a controlled decrease in anchor fidelity ($C_{anchor} = 0.775$) to enable meaningful semantic expansion ($C_{rel} = 0.266$), resulting in a higher normalised coherence (0.520 vs 0.500).

Although artwork centrality is higher in the baseline (0.470 vs 0.290), this is a direct consequence of the baseline's failure to expand beyond the immediate neighbourhood. The Knowledge-Guided centrality of 0.290 shows that, even when populating 10 rooms under sparse conditions, the retrieved items maintain a meaningful bond with the anchor.

5 Discussion and Conclusions

We have presented a hybrid CBR system that generates virtual art exhibitions from open cultural data. It brings together Getty AAT, Wikidata, and three museum sources into a single RDF knowledge graph with over 40,000 triples, which serves both as instance repository and as structural guide for adaptation.

The main contribution is a knowledge-guided adaptation mechanism that uses the SKOS concept hierarchy to detect semantic conflicts in retrieved cases and resolve them through a hierarchical replacement search. Because every replacement traces back to a path in the AAT thesaurus, adaptation remains transparent and explainable. A generative fallback tackles the cold-start problem: when no suitable case exists, the system produces a valid exhibition on demand and seeds the case base as users validate results.

The quantitative results confirm that this approach mitigates data sparsity effectively. By relying on the structural hierarchy, the system maintains thematic coherence regardless of the query region, which is especially useful when no prior cases are available.

However, the evaluation revealed a tension between thematic focus and semantic expansion. The fixed 5/5 split (anchor vs. related rooms) ensures diversity but can produce abrupt transitions for certain curatorial goals. The system is designed to complement, not replace, human curatorial judgement.

The evaluation in Sect. 4 characterises the structural component of the system in cold-start mode; it does not assess the CBR cycle itself, whose value depends on the accumulation of curator-validated cases over time and requires the longitudinal study outlined below.

A clear vulnerability is the reliance on knowledge graph completeness: gaps in the triples or unpopulated nodes lead directly to empty rooms. For real deployments we propose a validation threshold that reports an error when the traversal cannot find enough artworks to meet a minimum coherence score, rather than generating a fragmentary exhibition.

We see four directions for future work: (i) extending coverage to institutions such as LinkedArt/Rijksmuseum once SPARQL access to movement metadata becomes stable; (ii) formalising exhibition quality metrics, including diversity indices for author, technique, and period; (iii) conducting a longitudinal study with curators to evaluate the CBR cycle in its own right, measuring how curatorial memory accumulated over multiple sessions affects retrieval quality and the perceived coherence of adapted exhibitions; (iv) broadening multilingual label normalisation to support non-English queries.

The applicability of this approach beyond visual art is not unrestricted: as stated in Sect. 1, any candidate domain must provide a controlled vocabulary with a SKOS-style hierarchy and a meaningful structural distance over it. Where that prerequisite holds, the adaptation mechanism transfers directly; where it does not, the contribution is methodological rather than directly reusable.

Acknowledgements. This work was developed within the Knowledge-Based Reasoning course of the Master in Artificial Intelligence at Universidad Complutense de Madrid. Supported by the UCM (Research Group 921330). Supported by Grant PID2023-150566OB-I00 (AUDITIA-X) funded by MCIN/AEI /10.13039/501100011033 and by ERDF/EU (https://gaia.fdi.ucm.es/research/auditia-x/).

Generative AI Statement. Claude Sonnet 4.5 was used for proofreading and improving the English language of the manuscript. The authors take full responsibility for the content of the publication.

References

1. Barzaghi, S., Moretti, A., Heibi, I., Peroni, S.: CHAD-KG: a knowledge graph for representing cultural heritage objects and digitisation paradata. arXiv preprint arXiv:2505.13276 (2025)
2. Bizer, C., Heath, T., Berners-Lee, T.: Linked data - the story so far. Int. J. Semant. Web Inf. Syst. **5**(3), 1–22 (2009)
3. Chakraborti, T.: Planning-based virtual exhibition layout. In: Proceedings of the AAAI Workshop on Planning in Cultural Heritage (2020)
4. CIDOC CRM Special Interest Group: Cidoc conceptual reference model (2023). https://cidoc-crm.org/. Accessed 2024
5. Colombo, C., Del Bimbo, A., Pala, P.: Semantics in visual information retrieval. IEEE Multimedia **6**(3), 38–53 (1999)
6. Europeana: Europeana data model documentation (2023). https://pro.europeana.eu/page/edm-documentation. Accessed 2024
7. Falomir, Z.: Describing paintings from features and semantics. In: Proceedings of the ECAI Workshop on Artificial Intelligence for Cultural Heritage (2018)
8. Gatt, A., Krahmer, E.: Survey of the state of the art in natural language generation: core tasks, applications and evaluation. J. Artif. Intell. Res. **61**, 65–170 (2018)
9. Getty Research Institute: Art & architecture thesaurus (2024). https://www.getty.edu/research/tools/vocabularies/aat/. Accessed 2024
10. Hammond, K.J.: CHEF: a model of case-based planning. In: Proceedings of the AAAI Conference on Artificial Intelligence, pp. 267–271 (1986)
11. Jiménez-Díaz, G., et al.: Interpretable clusters for representing citizens' sense of belonging through interaction with cultural heritage. ACM J. Comput. Cult. Heritage **17**(4), 74:1–74:22 (2024). https://doi.org/10.1145/3665142
12. Kolodner, J.L., Riesbeck, C.K.: Experience, Memory, and Reasoning. Lawrence Erlbaum Associates (1989)
13. Li, J., Qi, J., Han, S.C., Holden, E.J.: MUSEKG: a knowledge graph over museum collections. arXiv preprint arXiv:2511.16014 (2025)
14. Mulholland, P., Collins, T., Zdrahal, Z.: Exhibit: using narrative to develop museum web-site stories. In: Proceedings of Museums and the Web (2012)
15. Pérez-Marín, D., et al.: Case-based museum tour recommendation. In: Proceedings of the European Conference on Case-Based Reasoning (ECCBR). Lecture Notes in Computer Science, vol. 3155, pp. 441–455 (2004)
16. Resnik, P.: Using information content to evaluate semantic similarity in a taxonomy. In: Proceedings of the International Joint Conference on Artificial Intelligence (IJCAI), pp. 448–453 (1995)
17. Ricci, F., Mirzadeh, N., Venturini, A.: ITREC: an interactive travel recommender system. In: Proceedings of Information and Communication Technologies in Tourism (2002)
18. Vrandečić, D., Krötzsch, M.: Wikidata: a free collaborative knowledge base. Commun. ACM **57**(10), 78–85 (2014)
19. W3C: PROV-O: The PROV ontology (2013). https://www.w3.org/TR/prov-o/. Accessed 2024

20. Wang, Q., et al.: Knowledge graph embedding: a survey of approaches and applications. IEEE Trans. Knowl. Data Eng. **29**(12), 2724–2743 (2017)
21. Wu, Z., Palmer, M.: Verbs semantics and lexical selection. In: Proceedings of the Annual Meeting of the Association for Computational Linguistics (ACL), pp. 133–138 (1994)

Security, Workflows, and CBR Development

CBR-PAR: LLM-Augmented Case-Based Reasoning for Provenance-Based Alert Reduction

Canhua Chen[1,2], Yaqin Cao[1,2], Xinyu Liu[1], Baihang Liu[1,2], Yongjun Wang[1,2], Xiaoyu Wang[1(✉)], and Qixu Liu[1,2]

[1] Institute of Information Engineering, Chinese Academy of Sciences, Beijing, China
{chencanhua,caoyaqin,liuxinyu,liubaihang,wangyongjun,wangxiaoyu, liuqixu}@iie.ac.cn

[2] School of Cyber Security, University of Chinese Academy of Sciences, Beijing, China

Abstract. Provenance-based intrusion detection systems achieve near-perfect recall for Advanced Persistent Threats but generate tens of thousands of alerts within hours, overwhelming security analysts. We observe that case-based reasoning (CBR) offers a promising approach to reducing massive false alarms. Unlike static whitelists or fixed rules, CBR maintains a dynamically evolving case base, enabling the system to automatically retrieve and reduce false alarms. We present **CBR-PAR**, the first framework to formalize provenance alert reduction as a complete CBR cycle. CBR-PAR models an alerted process as a graph-text case representation through rarity-guided subgraph extraction and enhanced evidence completion, then follows the complete CBR cycle for alarm elimination and intrusion detection. It retrieves benign source cases from the case base by jointly analyzing structural and behavioral similarity. LLM reuses the retrieval results as benign baseline to assess the threat of given case. Security analysts dynamically revise and selectively retain new cases that exhibit significant deviation from existing ones. Evaluation on three DARPA benchmarks shows that CBR-PAR reduces raw alerts by 700× to 3,800× while preserving 86.7% to 100% of true threats. Removing the case base increases false positives by up to 10×, confirming that grounding judgments in retrieved experience is the primary driver of noise elimination. The local-online split further cuts cloud API costs by 50×. Beyond quantitative gains, CBR-PAR's case-based comparative reasoning uncovers ground-truth labeling errors and discovers previously unlabeled attack components—demonstrating that decisions anchored in concrete past cases are both more transparent and more robust than opaque anomaly scores.

Keywords: Case-Based Reasoning · Provenance Graph · Intrusion Detection · Large Language Model · Alert Reduction

L. Malburg and K. Bach (Eds.): ICCBR 2026, LNAI 16780, pp. 539–559, 2027.
https://doi.org/10.1007/978-3-032-33865-5_33

1 Introduction

Cyber attacks are occurring at an unprecedented scale and frequency, posing serious threats to critical infrastructure, financial systems, and national security worldwide. Advanced Persistent Threats (APTs) are an increasing threat to government and industrial organizations, causing severe societal and economic damage. As adversaries continuously innovate to evade detection and persist within compromised systems, defenders have turned to Intrusion Detection Systems (IDS) as a frontline response tools that continuously monitor system activity and raise alerts when suspicious behavior is observed. Among the most powerful class of IDS are Provenance-based Intrusion Detection Systems (PIDS), which have attracted growing attention from both academia and industry for their ability to reason over causal dependencies between system events. Rather than examining individual log entries in isolation, PIDS construct a provenance graph—a directed graph in which nodes represent system entities (processes, files, network sockets) and edges represent causal interactions such as file reads and writes, process creation, and network communication. By reasoning over this causal structure, PIDS can trace an attacker's actions across process and host boundaries, linking seemingly unrelated events into a coherent picture of an intrusion. State-of-the-art systems achieve recall rates exceeding 99% on standard benchmarks [5,12,19,23].

However, alert fatigue problem remains the central unsolved challenge in provenance-based intrusion detection. To ensure no malicious activity is missed, PIDS flag not only core attack events but also the large volume of benign system activity causally connected to those events within the provenance graph. On standard benchmarks, state-of-the-art detectors generate between 12,000 and 94,000 alerts within just a few hours of system activity—a volume no human analyst can sustainably review. Each alert requires manual examination of its provenance context: command-line arguments, file accesses, network connections, and causal dependencies. This phenomenon, known as alert fatigue, is the central obstacle to deploying PIDS in practice, as analysts cannot manually verify thousands of flagged entities within practical time constraints.

Traditional false alarm reduction relies on maintained whitelists or static rules, which often fail in the context of provenance graphs because false positives typically manifest as complete, semantically normal process dependency chains rather than isolated nodes [10]. We observe that experienced analysts reason from experience, not formal rules. When handling a new alert, they recall similar past patterns, compare the current activity, and judge whether it reflects a known legitimate variant or an actual threat. A process reading /etc./resolv.conf and contacting a DNS server is recognized as routine due to the familiar pattern. The same process reaching out to an undocumented external IP raises concern precisely because no prior experience matches. This process aligns with the core principle of CBR that a case base stores historically confirmed false alarm graph structures. Upon a new alert, CBR performs structural and semantic similarity retrieval against the case base. If the alert's subgraph is sufficiently similar to the retrieved cases, the system directly flags it as a false alarm, bypassing the more expensive LLM invocation and manual analysis queue.

In this paper, we propose **CBR-PAR** (**C**ase-**B**ased **R**easoning for **P**rovenance-based **A**lert **R**eduction), a framework that implements the full CBR cycle with alert analysis mechanisms and LLM augmentation. In CBR-PAR, each alert is represented as a case constructed using dual-modal graph–text representation by the rarity-guided subgraph extraction algorithm to compress million-node provenance graphs into compact behavioral sketches, and the local Small Language Model (SLM) to complete missing causal evidence via tool-augmented graph traversal. And then, we propose a "Local-Profile, Online-Judge" architecture that confines sensitive raw provenance data to the local environment while reserving cloud LLM calls exclusively for lightweight comparative judgment over sanitized behavioral summaries.

In summary, this paper makes the following contributions:

- **A CBR Formulation for Provenance Alert Reduction.** We align the alert triage workflow with case-based reasoning paradigm. By establishing alert reduction as a case classification problem, we present CBR-PAR, the first framework to apply the full CBR cycle to provenance-based alert reduction.
- **Domain-Adapted Case Representation and Retrieval for Provenance Graphs.** We design a dual-modal graph–text case representation that captures both the causal structure of provenance subgraphs and a natural language behavioral summary, enabling effective similarity-based retrieval over a benign case base built from operational history.
- **Empirical Validation on Real-World APT Benchmarks.** Evaluation on CADETS, THEIA, and TRACE shows alert reductions of 700× to 3,800× while preserving attack coverage. Ablation confirms the value of the CBR retrieval–reuse cycle: removing case retrieval increases false positives by up to 10×, demonstrating that grounding judgments in retrieved precedents is essential.

The remainder of this paper is organized as follows. Section 2 surveys related work and provides background on provenance graphs and CBR. Section 3 formalizes the alert reduction task within the CBR framework. Section 4 details the design of CBR-PAR. Section 5 presents our experimental evaluation, and Sect. 6 concludes the paper.

2 Background and Related Work

2.1 Provenance-Based Intrusion Detection and Alert Management

System-level provenance data record causal dependencies between kernel objects as directed graphs [3,13,18]. A provenance graph is a directed multigraph $G = (V, E)$, where nodes V represent system entities (processes, files, network sockets), and edges E represent causal dependencies, including system calls such as `Read`, `Write`, `Execute`, `Fork`, `Sendto`, and `Receivefrom`. Each node carries type-specific attributes such as command lines, pathnames, IP addresses, and each edge is annotated with an event type and timestamp.

PIDS analyzes provenance graphs to identify malicious activities, employing signature matching [16,17] or anomaly detection based on graph embeddings [5, 9,12,19,23]. Although near-perfect recall has been achieved, the alert volumes remain overwhelming.

Existing alert management falls into two categories. *Alert correlation* methods group causally related alerts: RapSheet [10] aggregates alerts matching ATT&CK tactics, while SteinerLog [4] extracts cohesive subgraphs. *Priority ranking* methods score alerts by anomaly: NoDoze [11] assigns rarity-based scores, and RAPID [15] optimizes investigation priorities.

These methods share a critical limitation from a CBR perspective: they reorder alerts without eliminating them, and none maintains an explicit case base of benign behaviors to determine whether an alert represents a genuinely novel threat or a known benign pattern. CBR-PAR addresses this gap by introducing a case-based filtering layer that proactively eliminates false positives through retrieval and comparison against benign source cases.

2.2 Case-Based Reasoning and LLM Integration

CBR solves new problems by retrieving and adapting solutions from previously encountered situations [1,20]. The classical 4R cycle, Retrieve, Reuse, Revise, and Retain, provides a principled framework for experience-based problem solving. A distinctive strength of CBR is its inherent explainability: each decision is linked to past cases, making the reasoning trace interpretable and auditable [8]. CBR has been applied to security tasks including network intrusion detection [7], fault diagnosis [14] and malware classification [22], demonstrating its suitability for anomaly-based classification problems.

However, classical CBR struggles with high-dimensional, structured inputs such as provenance graphs, where defining compact and informative case representations remains a fundamental challenge. Recent work has explored the combination of CBR with LLMs to address this limitation [2,24,25]. LLMs bring two capabilities that complement CBR: the ability to synthesize structured summaries from complex heterogeneous data, enabling case authoring at scale; and the capacity for nuanced comparative judgment between a target problem and retrieved source cases, enabling flexible reuse beyond exact matching. Critically, the CBR framework reciprocally constrains the LLM: grounding every judgment in concrete retrieved cases mitigates hallucination and ensures verdicts are explainable through specific precedents. Despite this natural synergy, LLM-enhanced CBR has not been applied to provenance-based alert reduction. CBR-PAR fills this gap.

3 CBR Formalization of Alert Reduction

This section formalizes provenance alert reduction as a case-based reasoning task, defining the case representation, the case base, and the reasoning task that the subsequent design sections instantiate. We follow the classical CBR framework of Aamodt and Plaza [1].

Case Representation. A case $c = (\mathbf{d}, \mathbf{s})$ consists of a *problem description* $\mathbf{d}$ and a *solution* $\mathbf{s}$. In our domain, the problem description captures a process's behavioral context within the provenance graph, while the solution records the triage result. Formally:

$$c = (\underbrace{(G_{sub},\ t)}_{\text{problem description } \mathbf{d}},\ \underbrace{(l,\ r)}_{\text{solution } \mathbf{s}}) \tag{1}$$

where:

- $G_{sub} = (V_{sub}, E_{sub})$ is a compact provenance subgraph centered on the focal process, capturing its causal neighborhood. Each node $v \in V_{sub}$ carries a type label $\tau(v) \in \{\text{PROCESS}, \text{FILE}, \text{SOCKET}\}$ and a semantic descriptor $\sigma(v)$ (e.g., command line, file path, IP address). Each edge $e \in E_{sub}$ carries an event type $\lambda(e) \in \{\texttt{Read}, \texttt{Write}, \texttt{Execute}, \texttt{Fork}, \texttt{Sendto}, \texttt{Recvfrom}\}$ and a timestamp.
- t is a structured textual behavioral summary generated by a language model, describing observed actions without attributing intent.
- $l \in \{\textit{malicious}, \textit{benign}\}$ is the classification label.
- r is a reasoning chain explaining the classification decision, generated by the Judger during the Reuse phase. For stored cases in the benign case base, r may be empty or a default annotation.

The case representation is deliberately *dual-modal*: G_{sub} preserves the precise causal topology needed for structural comparison and local evidence completion, while t compresses behavioral content into a natural-language narrative suitable for efficient semantic comparison and privacy-preserving transmission across the local-to-cloud boundary.

Case Base. The *benign case base* $\mathcal{CB} = \{c_1, \ldots, c_n\}$ is a collection of stored cases constructed from known-clean system operation, each with $l = \textit{benign}$. This case base serves as an experiential model of normal system behavior, against which new alerts are compared. A *new case* $q = (\mathbf{d}_q, ?)$ represents a newly alerted process whose problem description is constructed through the same procedure, but whose solution is unknown.

Task. The alert reduction task is: given a new case $q = (\mathbf{d}_q, ?)$, determine its solution $\mathbf{s}_q$ by executing the classical CBR cycle [1]—Retrieve, Reuse, Revise, Retain—over the benign case base $\mathcal{CB}$. A prerequisite is that stored cases and new cases share a common representation space; we ensure this by applying the same case construction procedure to both (Sect. 4.1).

4 Design of CBR-PAR

Designing an LLM-enhanced CBR system for provenance-based alert triage presents three domain-specific challenges. **(C1)** Large-scale case construction. A provenance subgraph extracted from an alert may contain millions of nodes and edges, far exceeding the capacity for direct use as a case representation. **(C2)** Case completeness. Heuristic extraction from large graphs often misses critical causal dependencies, such as parent processes, network connections, or file relationships, leading to inaccurate similarity judgments during retrieval. **(C3)** Privacy-aware case reasoning. Provenance data often contains sensitive operational information, yet high-quality case comparison requires the sophisticated reasoning capabilities of frontier LLMs, which are typically accessed via cloud APIs.

Figure 1 provides an overview of CBR-PAR, which addresses these challenges through four stages: case construction, retrieval, reuse, as well as revision and retention.

Case construction (Sect. 4.1) addresses C1 and C2 by extracting compact behavioral subgraphs from million-scale provenance graphs and augmenting missing causal evidence using a tool-enhanced local SLM (reasoner). This process yields comparable representations shared across both the benign case base and new alerts.

Retrieval (Sect. 4.2) combines provenance-aware graph kernels with sentence embedding similarity to accurately locate the most relevant benign precedents.

Reuse (Sect. 4.3) adopts an architecture of local profiling with online judgment, where each alert is compared against retrieved precedents via a cloud-hosted LLM to produce a verdict.

Revision and retention (Sect. 4.4) incorporate analyst feedback to correct errors and continuously update the case base.

4.1 Case Construction

The first challenge in applying CBR to provenance data is constructing a meaningful case description from a graph that may contain millions of nodes. We address this through a *behavioral profiling* procedure that maps any focal process into the unified dual-modal case representation defined in Eq. 1: a compact provenance subgraph G_{sub} capturing causal structure, and a textual behavioral summary t capturing semantic intent. The procedure involves two stages: *subgraph extraction* produces a compact behavioral sketch G_{sub}, and *evidence completion* enriches it with missing causal links and finally generates the textual summary t.

Applying this same procedure to both populations ensures that stored cases and new cases inhabit a common representation space, a prerequisite for meaningful similarity computation in CBR [1]. When populating the benign case base, the procedure is applied to processes sampled from known-clean provenance logs; during alert processing, it is applied identically to each alerted process P_{alert}.

Rarity-Guided Subgraph Extraction. Not all edges in the provenance graph are equally informative for characterizing a process's behavior. The standard k-hop expansion is too coarse: small k misses critical causal context, while large k floods the case with irrelevant benign activity that degrades retrieval quality. To extract a compact yet discriminative subgraph G_{sub}, we perform N biased random walks of length L from the focal process p (Algorithm 1), where each transition is guided by two complementary scores computed from benign training data.

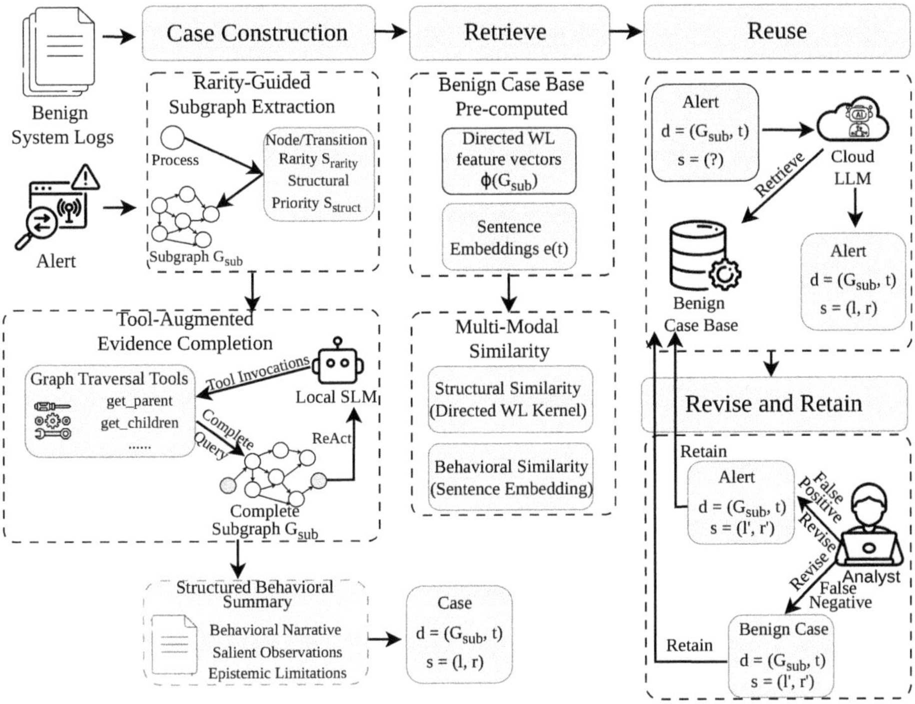

Fig. 1. Overall Architecture of CBR-PAR.

The first score captures *statistical rarity.* We quantify edge rarity at two levels: *node name rarity* $R_{node}(n) = -\log P(n)$, measuring how unusual an entity name is in benign data, and *conditional transition rarity* $R_{cond}(u, v, e) = -\log P(n_v \mid n_u, a)$, measuring how unusual a specific interaction pattern is given the source entity and event type. Their sum $R(e) = R_{node}(v) + R_{cond}(u, v, e)$ is normalized via a sigmoid centered on the benign mean μ_R:

$$S_{rarity}(e) = \frac{1}{1 + \exp(-(R(e) - \mu_R))} \tag{2}$$

yielding values in $(0, 1)$ where common edges score below 0.5 and rare edges above.

The second score encodes *structural priority.* A function S_{struct} assigns differentiated weights ω to transition types based on their relevance to typical attack chains, subject to the ordering $\omega_{fwd} > \omega_{r2p} > \omega_{p2r} > \omega_{def} > \omega_{bwd}$. Forward process lineage (ω_{fwd}) and sibling data flows receive the highest priority, as APT attacks typically propagate through process creation chains. Resource-to-process (ω_{r2p}) and process-to-resource (ω_{p2r}) transitions receive intermediate priority, while backward lineage (ω_{bwd}) receives the lowest, since excessive backtracking leads away from the attack's downstream impact. The specific weight values are reported in Sect. 5.1.

Algorithm 1: Rarity-Guided Subgraph Extraction

Input: Provenance graph $G = (V, E)$, Focal process p, Walks N, Length L, Rarity bias β, Base exploration γ
Output: Behavioral subgraph G_{sub}

$V_{visited} \leftarrow \{p\}$; $Excl_{hop1} \leftarrow \emptyset$
for $i \leftarrow 1$ **to** N **do**
  if $|Excl_{hop1}| \geq |\mathcal{N}(p)|$ **then** $Excl_{hop1} \leftarrow \emptyset$
  $Path \leftarrow [p]$; $u \leftarrow p$; $v_{prev} \leftarrow$ null
  for $j \leftarrow 1$ **to** $L - 1$ **do**
    $Cand \leftarrow []$; $Wts \leftarrow []$
    foreach *neighbor* v *of* u *via edge* e **do**
      if $v = v_{prev}$ ***or*** $v \in Path$ **then**
        continue
      if $j = 1$ ***and*** $v \in Excl_{hop1}$ **then**
        continue
      $w \leftarrow S_{\text{struct}}(v_{prev}, u, v) \cdot (\gamma + \beta \cdot S_{rarity}(e))$
      Append v to $Cand$; Append w to Wts
    if $Cand = \emptyset$ **then**
      if $v_{prev} = null$ **then break**
      $u \leftarrow v_{prev}$; $v_{prev} \leftarrow$ null; **continue**
    $v_{next} \leftarrow \text{Sample}(Cand, Wts/\text{sum}(Wts))$
    Append v_{next} to $Path$
    $v_{prev} \leftarrow u$; $u \leftarrow v_{next}$
  $V_{visited} \leftarrow V_{visited} \cup Path$
  if $|Path| > 1$ **then** $Excl_{hop1} \leftarrow Excl_{hop1} \cup \{Path[1]\}$
return $G.subgraph(V_{visited})$

At each step, the transition weight to a candidate neighbor combines both scores:

$$W = S_{struct} \cdot (\gamma + \beta \cdot S_{rarity}) \tag{3}$$

where β controls rarity bias and γ ensures common edges retain non-negligible sampling probability. The algorithm enforces path diversity through first-hop exclusion, cycle avoidance, and dead-end backtracking. The resulting G_{sub} typically contains only a few dozen nodes—three orders of magnitude smaller than k-hop alternatives—while preserving the security-relevant causal context.

This extraction is equally appropriate for benign and suspicious processes. For benign processes entering the case base, the walk captures the *distinctive tail* of the behavioral distribution—precisely the rare-but-legitimate patterns that drive false positives—while γ ensures common behaviors are still sampled for context. For alerted processes, the same rarity bias naturally gravitates toward the most anomalous aspects of behavior, producing subgraphs that highlight potential attack indicators.

Algorithm 2: Tool-Augmented Evidence Completion

Input: Provenance graph G, Subgraph G_{sub}, Focal process p, Iteration limit R_{max}, Tool budget T_{max}

Output: Structured behavioral summary t

$\mathcal{M} \leftarrow \text{InitializeContext}(G_{sub}, p)$; $\mathcal{C} \leftarrow \emptyset$; $n_{tools} \leftarrow 0$
for $r \leftarrow 1$ **to** R_{max} **do**
    $response \leftarrow \text{SLM}(\mathcal{M})$
    $(reasoning, action, params) \leftarrow \text{Parse}(response)$
    $\mathcal{M} \leftarrow \mathcal{M} \cup \{response\}$
    if $action = Terminate$ **then return** *ExtractSummary*$(response)$
    $key \leftarrow (action, params)$
    if $key \in \mathcal{C}$ **then**
        $evidence \leftarrow \mathcal{C}[key]$
    else
        if $n_{tools} \geq T_{max}$ **then return** *PartialSummary*$(\mathcal{M})$
        $evidence \leftarrow \text{ExecuteTool}(action, params, G)$
        $\mathcal{C}[key] \leftarrow evidence$; $n_{tools} \leftarrow n_{tools} + 1$
    $\mathcal{M} \leftarrow \mathcal{M} \cup \{\text{FormatEvidence}(evidence)\}$
return *PartialSummary*$(\mathcal{M})$

Tool-Augmented Evidence Completion. The extracted subgraph G_{sub} is compact but potentially incomplete: stochastic walks may miss critical causal links, producing a case description that lacks features essential for accurate retrieval. Evidence completion requires iterative graph queries that generate large token volumes, making cloud delegation both costly and privacy-violating. We therefore deploy a local SLM as the Reasoner, a tool-augmented agent that iteratively identifies evidential gaps and retrieves missing context from the full provenance graph G.

The agent employs the ReAct paradigm, interleaving chain-of-thought reasoning with invocations of specialized graph traversal tools (Algorithm 2). These tools are organized into three groups: *process lineage tools* (`get_parent`, `get_children`, `get_lineage`) for exploring creation chains, *resource access tools* (`list_file_accesses`, `list_network_flows`) for querying file and network interactions, and *multi-hop expansion tools* (`expand_neighbors`) for discovering indirect causal paths. Critically, all tools query the *complete* provenance graph G, not merely G_{sub}, enabling evidence retrieval beyond the extraction boundary. The loop runs for at most R_{max} iterations with tool budget T_{max}, and memorization eliminates redundant queries.

Structured Behavioral Summary. Upon completing evidence gathering, the agent synthesizes its findings into a structured behavioral summary t following a tripartite structure: a *Behavioral Narrative* (temporally-ordered account of observed actions, framed factually without attributing intent), *Salient Observations* (noteworthy findings anchored to specific evidence), and *Epistemic Limitations* (unresolved questions or missing causal links). This summary is explicitly *descriptive rather than judgmental*, since the same procedure is applied to both benign and suspicious processes. It also serves as a privacy-preserving abstraction layer, transforming fine-grained provenance data into sanitized natural-language descriptions that can safely cross the local-to-cloud boundary. Together with the behavioral subgraph G_{sub}, this summary completes the dual-modal problem description $\mathbf{d} = (G_{sub}, t)$ of each case.

4.2 Retrieve

Given a new case q, the Retrieve phase identifies the k most similar stored cases from $\mathcal{CB}$. Since each case description $\mathbf{d} = (G_{sub}, t)$ contains both a provenance subgraph and a textual behavioral summary, our similarity measure operates on both modalities: a *graph kernel* captures causal-structural correspondence between subgraphs, while a *sentence embedding* captures behavioral-semantic correspondence between summaries.

Structural Similarity via Directed WL Kernel. We measure structural correspondence through a directed Weisfeiler-Leman (WL) graph kernel [21]. The standard WL kernel is designed for undirected homogeneous graphs and is therefore unsuitable for provenance graphs, where edge direction encodes causal flow and node types carry semantic meaning. We make two domain-specific adaptations.

First, we initialize each node's label by jointly encoding its type and semantic descriptor: $\ell^{(0)}(v) = \text{hash}(\tau(v), \sigma(v))$, where $\tau(v)$ is the node type and $\sigma(v)$ encodes attributes such as process command line, file pathname, or IP address. This ensures the kernel is sensitive to entity identity, not just graph topology.

Second, we preserve causal directionality by aggregating in-neighbors and out-neighbors separately, with edge types included:

$$\ell^{(i)}(v) = \text{hash}\Big(\ell^{(i-1)}(v),\ \mathcal{M}_{in}^{(i-1)}(v),\ \mathcal{M}_{out}^{(i-1)}(v)\Big) \tag{4}$$

where $\mathcal{M}_{in}^{(i-1)}(v) = \{\!\{(\lambda(e), \ell^{(i-1)}(u)) : (u,v) \in E_{sub}\}\!\}$ is the sorted multiset of (edge-type, label) pairs from in-neighbors, and $\mathcal{M}_{out}^{(i-1)}(v)$ is defined symmetrically. This adaptation ensures that the kernel distinguishes, e.g., a process that `Reads` a file from one that `Executes` it.

After h iterations, the graph-level feature vector concatenates histograms of node labels across all iterations:

$$\phi(G_{sub}) = \bigoplus_{i=0}^{h} \text{hist}(\{\ell^{(i)}(v) : v \in V_{sub}\}) \tag{5}$$

The structural similarity between two cases is then the cosine similarity of their feature vectors:

$$\text{Sim}_{graph}(q, c_i) = \frac{\phi(G_{sub}^{(q)}) \cdot \phi(G_{sub}^{(i)})}{\|\phi(G_{sub}^{(q)})\| \cdot \|\phi(G_{sub}^{(i)})\|} \tag{6}$$

This computation is $O(h \cdot |E_{sub}|)$ per graph and reduces to a sparse dot product for comparison, making it efficient for our compact subgraphs.

Behavioral Similarity via Sentence Embedding. The graph kernel captures causal topology but cannot capture the higher-level behavioral abstractions produced during evidence completion. For instance, the SLM might summarize a process's behavior as "performed network reconnaissance after privilege escalation"—a semantic characterization that has no direct counterpart in the graph's node labels or edge types. To capture such correspondences, we compute the cosine similarity between sentence embeddings of the behavioral summaries:

$$\mathrm{Sim}_{text}(q, c_i) = \cos\big(\mathbf{e}(t_q),\ \mathbf{e}(t_i)\big) \tag{7}$$

where $\mathbf{e}(\cdot)$ denotes a pre-trained sentence encoder. This component is complementary to the graph kernel: two processes may access different files through different causal paths yet perform functionally equivalent operations that the SLM describes in similar terms.

Combined Retrieval. The overall case similarity combines both modalities:

$$\mathrm{Sim}(q, c_i) = \alpha \cdot \mathrm{Sim}_{graph}(q, c_i) + (1 - \alpha) \cdot \mathrm{Sim}_{text}(q, c_i) \tag{8}$$

where $\alpha \in [0, 1]$ controls the relative weight. For each case in the case base, $\phi(G_{sub}^{(i)})$ and $\mathbf{e}(t_i)$ are pre-computed and indexed offline. At retrieval time, we compute the combined similarity against all stored cases and return the top-k as the retrieved set $\mathcal{R}(q)$, whose behavioral summaries serve as reference baselines for the Reuse phase.

4.3 Reuse

The Reuse phase leverages the retrieved benign cases as analytical context to assess whether a new case represents a genuine threat or a benign behavioral variant. Since system behaviors are inherently dynamic, retrieved cases serve not as exact templates for matching, but as reference examples that ground the LLM's reasoning on whether observed deviations are security-relevant. We delegate this judgment to a cloud-based LLM (the Judger) that analyzes the target case in light of retrieved benign precedents.

Comparative Analysis. The Judger receives a structured prompt containing three components. First, a *role definition* assigns the LLM the role of a security analyst specializing in provenance-based intrusion detection. The task is framed as contextual analysis: assess whether the new process's behavior can be explained as a normal variant of known benign patterns, or whether it exhibits security-relevant deviations that the benign precedents cannot account for. Second, the *evidence* presents the new case's behavioral summary t_q alongside the behavioral summaries $\{t_{(1)}, \ldots, t_{(k)}\}$ of the retrieved stored cases, together with the retrieval similarity scores to indicate the degree of correspondence. Third, the *judgment guidelines* instruct the LLM to reason about *whether and why* observed behavioral differences matter from a security perspective, rather than requiring exact behavioral alignment. The LLM produces:

$$\mathbf{s}_q = (l_q,\ r_q), \quad l_q \in \{benign,\ malicious\} \tag{9}$$

where r_q is a reasoning chain documenting which retrieved cases were consulted, which behavioral aspects are consistent with benign precedents, and which raise security concerns. A process that accesses different files or connects to different ports than the retrieved cases may still be judged benign if the LLM determines these differences reflect normal operational variation; conversely, subtle deviations such as unexpected payload staging or anomalous process lineage may trigger a malicious verdict even when the overall behavioral profile appears superficially similar to a benign case.

This design addresses a key limitation of anomaly-based detection: without benign context, any rare behavior appears suspicious, leading to massive false positives. By providing the LLM with concrete benign precedents, we shift the task from "is this behavior abnormal?" to the more tractable question "can this behavior be explained by known benign patterns?" The retrieved cases ground the LLM's reasoning in documented operational experience rather than relying on its parametric knowledge alone, reducing hallucination and enabling verdicts that are both informed and auditable.

Privacy and Explainability. A critical design constraint is that only the sanitized behavioral summaries t cross the local-to-cloud boundary, never the raw provenance subgraphs, log entries, or tool invocation results. The entire case construction process (extraction, completion, summarization) runs locally on the SLM, with the cloud LLM receiving only high-level behavioral descriptions. This "Local-Profile, Online-Judge" architecture ensures that sensitive operational data (usernames, file paths, IP addresses, command lines) remains confined to the trusted local environment, while reserving the expensive cloud API calls exclusively for the lightweight final verdict.

Every verdict is *explainable through specific retrieved cases*: the reasoning chain r_q documents which stored cases were compared, which behavioral aspects were consistent or divergent, and the rationale behind the verdict. An analyst can inspect both the target's profile and the retrieved benign precedents to verify the decision independently, a distinctive advantage over black-box anomaly scores.

4.4 Revise and Retain

An analyst's expertise grows with every case they handle: misdiagnoses are corrected, and newly encountered behavioral patterns become part of their mental baseline. CBR-PAR replicates this learning through revision and retention mechanisms that enable the case base to evolve with operational experience.

Revision via Analyst Feedback. Analyst feedback serves as the primary revision mechanism, targeting two types of errors. *False negatives* occur when a genuine threat is dismissed because its behavioral profile superficially matches a benign stored case, indicating that the matching case lacks sufficient discriminating features or that evidence completion failed to retrieve attack-indicative context. The analyst's corrected verdict is logged with the reasoning behind the correction, and the matching stored case is annotated to prevent future over-generalization. *False positives* occur when a benign process is flagged because no sufficiently similar stored case exists. This signals a coverage gap in the case base, directly motivating the retention of the corrected case.

Selective Retention Policy. Confirmed benign processes are retained in the case base, particularly those representing rare-but-legitimate activities that initially triggered alerts—these directly reduce future false positives for behaviorally similar alerts. Confirmed malicious processes are excluded from the benign case base to prevent them from incorrectly covering future attacks during retrieval. To avoid redundancy, near-duplicate cases (similarity above threshold θ_{dup}) are not retained.

Table 1. Alert Reduction Results. Stage 1: raw PIDS output (nodes). Stage 2: process aggregation. Stage 3: CBR-PAR output. TP/FP shown in parentheses. GT = ground-truth malicious processes.

Dataset	Upstream PIDS	Stage 1 (Nodes)	Stage 2 (Processes)	Stage 3 (CBR-PAR)	Total Reduction
CADETS (15 GT)	Threatrace	14,209	142	**18** (**13**/5)	**789**×
	Flash	13,571	235	**15** (**13**/2)	**905**×
	Magic	13,575	133	**17** (**13**/4)	**799**×
THEIA (23 GT)	Threatrace	29,062	267	**35** (**23**/12)	**830**×
	Flash	27,193	130	**29** (**23**/6)	**938**×
	Magic	25,774	184	**33** (**23**/10)	**781**×
TRACE (8 GT)	Threatrace	94,156	2,208	**28** (**5**/23)	**3,363**×
	Flash	71,187	2,881	**31** (**5**/26)	**2,296**×
	Magic	68,641	515	**18** (**5**/13)	**3,813**×

5 Evaluation

We evaluate CBR-PAR to validate the effectiveness and characteristics of our case-based approach. Our experiments address five research questions:

- **RQ1 (Alert Reduction Effectiveness):** Does CBR-PAR successfully reduce alert volume while preserving genuine threats?

- **RQ2 (Value of the Case Base):** How critical is the benign case base to system performance?
- **RQ3 (Case-Based Insight):** Can comparative reasoning against retrieved cases provide interpretable insights beyond anomaly scores?
- **RQ4 (Case Construction Quality):** How does rarity-guided extraction compare to alternative case construction strategies?
- **RQ5 (Model Sensitivity and Operational Cost):** How sensitive is CBR-PAR to model selection, and what are its operational costs?

5.1 Experimental Setup

Datasets and Baselines. We evaluated CBR-PAR on three datasets from the DARPA TC program [6]: CADETS, THEIA, and TRACE, which capture whole-system provenance during simulated APT attacks mixed with benign activity. CBR-PAR operates as a refinement layer atop existing detectors; we use three representative upstream systems—Threatrace [23], Flash [19], and Magic [12]—whose alerts serve as input.

Ground Truth and Metrics. We adopt ground truth labels from prior work [23], filtered to process-type nodes to reflect operational reality. We report the *Alert Reduction Factor* (ARF $= |A_{initial}|/|A_{final}|$) and absolute True Positive (TP) and False Positive (FP) counts.

Configuration. Experiments use Llama-4-Maverick as the local Reasoner and Claude-3.7-Sonnet as the online Judger. The behavioral profiling process involves several hyperparameters whose values were determined through preliminary experiments on a held-out validation set from the CADETS benign period. For subgraph extraction (Algorithm 1), we use $N = 5$ walks of length $L = 10$, rarity bias $\beta = 1.0$, base exploration $\gamma = 0.5$, and Laplace smoothing $\alpha_s = 1$. The structural priority weights are set to $\omega_{\text{fwd}} = 1.0$, $\omega_{\text{r2p}} = 0.5$, $\omega_{\text{p2r}} = 0.4$, $\omega_{\text{def}} = 0.3$, and $\omega_{\text{bwd}} = 0.2$, reflecting a descending priority from forward attack propagation to backward lineage traversal. For profile completion (Algorithm 2), we set the iteration limit $R_{max} = 6$ and tool budget $T_{max} = 6$. For retrieval, we use $k = 3$ nearest stored cases and similarity weight $\alpha = 0.4$ (Eq. 8).

5.2 Alert Reduction Effectiveness(RQ1)

Table 1 summarizes the alert reduction across all datasets and upstream detectors. CBR-PAR reduces raw node-level alerts by **781**$\times$ **to 3,813**$\times$ while retaining 86.7–100% of ground-truth malicious processes. On CADETS, 13,000–14,000 initial alerts become 15–18 actionable alerts; on THEIA, all 23 threats are preserved from 25,000–29,000 initial alerts; on TRACE, 68,000–94,000 alerts are distilled to 18–31.

These results validate that the case-based approach effectively distinguishes genuine threats from rare-but-legitimate activities that dominate raw PIDS output. The subsequent research questions examine *why* this approach succeeds.

5.3 Value of the Case Base (RQ2)

The central claim of our CBR approach is that grounding judgments in retrieved benign cases is essential for effective alert reduction. We test this claim through an ablation study on CADETS, comparing the full system against a variant where the Judger renders verdicts *without* retrieving cases from the benign case base.

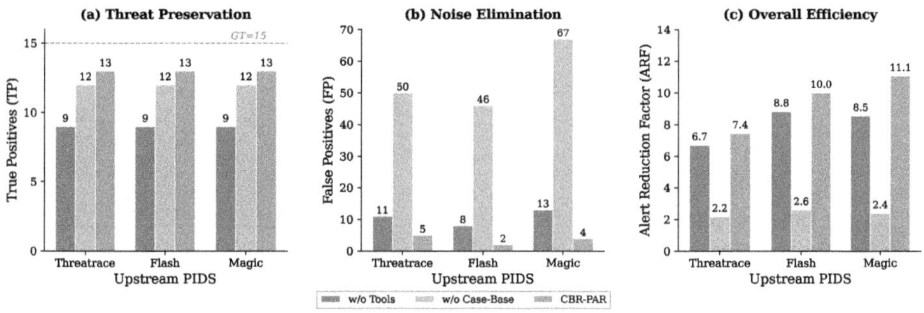

Fig. 2. Ablation Study on CADETS. (a) True positives preserved best by Full CBR-PAR system. (b) Removing the case base increases FP by up to 10×, confirming that grounding judgments by retrieved cases is essential. (c) Full CBR-PAR system achieves the highest ARF.

Figure 2 presents the results. Removing the case base causes false positives to increase substantially: from 5 to 50 with Threatrace (**10**× increase), from 2 to 46 with Flash (**23**×), and from 4 to 67 with Magic (**16.8**×). Meanwhile, true positive counts remain stable, indicating that the case base primarily affects noise filtering rather than threat detection.

This finding directly validates the CBR paradigm. Without retrieved benign precedents, the LLM Judger operates in a "zero-shot" mode where any rare behavior appears suspicious, systematically over-flagging legitimate activities. The case base provides the normative context that transforms the intractable question "is this behavior abnormal?" into the answerable question "can this behavior be explained by known benign patterns?" The 10× false positive increase when this context is removed demonstrates that retrieval-based comparison is the primary driver of effective noise elimination.

We additionally ablate the evidence completion stage. Removing tool-augmented graph traversal reduces true positives from 13 to 9 (30.7% degradation) because incomplete profiles may incorrectly match benign cases. This confirms that both components contribute complementary capabilities: complete profiles enable accurate case matching, while the case base provides the reference context for judgment.

5.4 Case-Based Insight (RQ3)

A distinctive strength of CBR is that decisions are anchored in specific retrieved cases, enabling verification and insight generation unavailable with opaque anomaly scores. We demonstrate this through two qualitative findings.

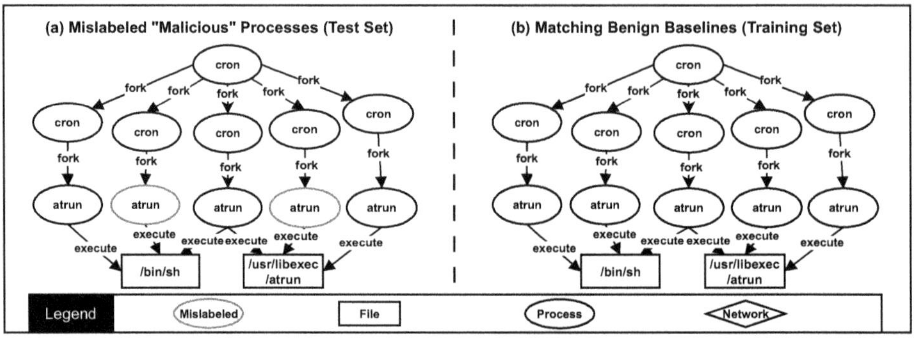

Fig. 3. Ground Truth Error Detection via Case Comparison. (a) Two `atrun` processes labeled "malicious" in the benchmark. (b) Structurally identical benign cases retrieved from the case base. The match demonstrates these are mislabeled scheduled tasks.

Finding 1: Identifying Labeling Errors. Two `atrun` processes labeled as malicious in the benchmark were correctly classified as benign by CBR-PAR. Figure 3 shows the evidence: panel (a) displays their behavioral profiles (characteristic `cron`→`atrun` fork chains), while panel (b) shows structurally identical cases retrieved from the benign case base. The strong structural correspondence provides transparent evidence that these are legitimate scheduled tasks. An analyst can inspect both profiles, verify the similarity, and understand precisely why the system reached its verdict. Manual cross-referencing with DARPA's official attack documentation confirms these processes are absent from the reported attack scenarios, indicating that prior evaluations may have included mislabeled benign processes in their ground truth.

Finding 2: Discovering Unlabeled Attacks. Conversely, processes including `nginx`, `sendmail`, and `main` on CADETS were flagged by CBR-PAR despite being absent from benchmark annotations. These processes were flagged because their completed profiles had *no matching cases* in the benign case base.

Figure 4 illustrates how evidence completion enables this discovery. Starting from the alerted `uname` process (red borders), the tool-augmented Reasoner retrieves missing causal evidence (blue borders), reconstructing the complete attack chain: compromised `nginx` → C2 communication with `76.56.184.25` → payload staging in `/tmp` → reconnaissance via `uname`. Without completion, this chain would remain fragmented, and the profile would incorrectly match a benign case. Cross-referencing with DARPA's official reports confirms these were genuine attack components omitted from the ground truth.

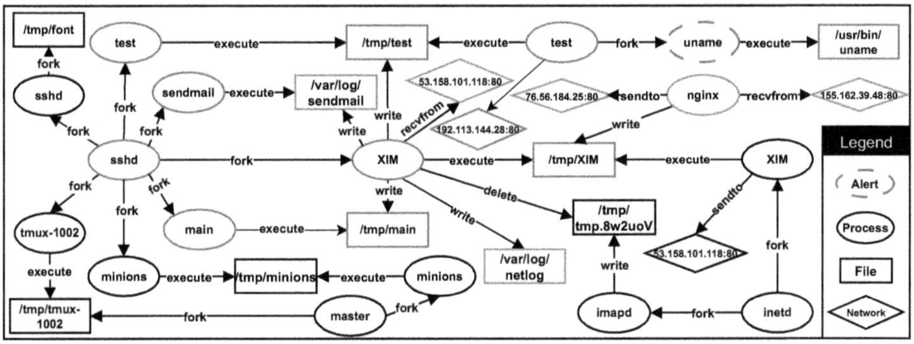

Fig. 4. Attack Chain Reconstruction via Profile Completion. Red borders: initial extraction centered on the alerted `uname` process. Blue borders: evidence discovered through tool-augmented completion, revealing the full attack chain from compromised `nginx` through C2 communication to reconnaissance.

These findings illustrate that case-based decisions are both more *transparent* (analysts can inspect retrieved cases) and more *robust* (the system identifies mislabeled benign activity and unlabeled attacks) than black-box anomaly scores.

5.5 Case Construction Quality (RQ4)

Effective CBR requires case construction that is both compact enough for efficient retrieval and specific enough for accurate case matching. We compare our rarity-guided extraction with the standard k-hop neighborhood expansion on CADETS.

Table 2. Subgraph Extraction Strategies on CADETS.

Strategy	Avg. Size (Nodes)	Alerts (TP/FP)	ARF
1-Hop Expansion	9	23 (3/20)	618×
2-Hop Expansion	4,979	34 (6/28)	418×
3-Hop Expansion	26,427	45 (3/42)	316×
Rarity-Guided	**33**	**18** (**13**/5)	**789**×

Table 2 shows the results. The fixed k-hop expansion faces a fundamental trade-off: 1-hop produces minimal profiles (9 nodes) that capture only 3 of 15 threats, while 3-hop generates 26,427-node profiles that overwhelm the comparison process with irrelevant context (42 false positives). Our rarity-guided algorithm achieves compact profiles (33 nodes on average) while capturing 13 of 15 threats with only 5 false positives, achieving the best performance across all metrics.

By biasing random walks toward statistically rare and structurally significant edges, the algorithm selectively captures the behavioral features most relevant to distinguish malicious from benign activity. This produces case representations that are three orders of magnitude smaller than 3-hop alternatives while being substantially more discriminative for retrieval.

5.6 Model Sensitivity and Operational Cost (RQ5)

We examine two practical properties of CBR-PAR: whether performance is sensitive to model selection for each architectural role, and whether the Local-Profile, Online-Judge design yields meaningful cost reductions relative to a fully cloud-based alternative.

Table 3. Model sensitivity analysis on CADETS. Group A varies the Reasoner while fixing the Judger; Group B varies the Judger while fixing the Reasoner.

Reasoner	Judger	Alerts (TP/FP)
Group A: Reasoner Variation (Judger = Claude-3.7-Sonnet)		
Qwen3-30B-A3B	Claude-3.7-Sonnet	19 (11/8)
Llama-4-Scout	Claude-3.7-Sonnet	21 (13/8)
Llama-4-Maverick	Claude-3.7-Sonnet	**18 (13/5)**
Group B: Judger Variation (Reasoner = Llama-4-Maverick)		
Llama-4-Maverick	**Claude-3.7-Sonnet**	**18 (13/5)**
Llama-4-Maverick	GPT-5.1	22 (13/9)
Llama-4-Maverick	GPT-OSS-120B	33 (13/20)

Model Sensitivity. We test sensitivity on CADETS with two groups: Group A fixes the Judger (Claude-3.7-Sonnet) and varies the Reasoner; Group B fixes the Reasoner (Llama-4-Maverick) and varies the Judger. Table 3 reveals asymmetric sensitivity. The Reasoner exhibits low sensitivity: all models achieve TP $\in$ [11, 13] and FP $\in$ [5, 8], since evidence completion is a structured retrieval task constrained by tool invocations. The Judger shows markedly higher sensitivity: replacing Claude-3.7-Sonnet with GPT-OSS-120B increases false positives from 5 to 20 (4$\times$), indicating that comparative judgment demands frontier-level reasoning. This asymmetry validates the architectural split: evidence completion can be delegated to efficient local models, while comparative judgment benefits from frontier LLM capabilities.

Operational Cost. We compare CBR-PAR against a *Pure Online* baseline where both evidence completion and comparative verdict are executed by the cloud LLM on CADETS. As shown in Fig. 5, CBR-PAR reduces per-alert API cost by **51.9**$\times$ (from \$0.14 to \$0.0027) and processing latency by **3.5**$\times$ (from 1.18 s to 0.34 s). The Pure Online baseline incurs high cost because iterative evidence completion generates approximately 474K tokens per alert through multi-round tool invocations, whereas CBR-PAR delegates this phase locally and invokes the cloud API only for the final comparative verdict (average 9K tokens). Sub-second latency enables near-real-time triage, and the reduced costs make LLM-augmented detection economically viable for production deployment.

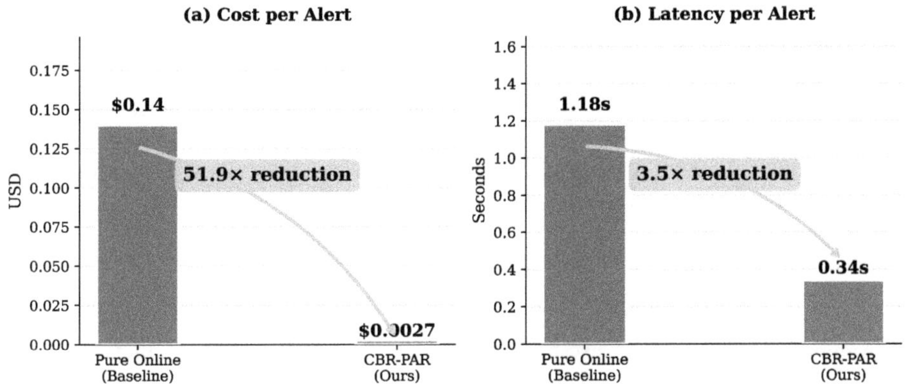

Fig. 5. Operational Efficiency Comparison. (a) Per-alert API cost comparison between CBR-PAR and the Pure Online baseline. (b) Per-alert processing latency comparison. Error bars indicate standard deviation across alert instances.

6 Conclusion

Provenance-based Intrusion Detection Systems achieve high recall for APT detection but generate overwhelming alert volumes. This paper addressed this challenge by reformulating provenance alert reduction as a case-based reasoning problem, introducing CBR-PAR, a framework implementing the full CBR cycle with provenance-specific mechanisms and LLM augmentation.

The core insight is that most false-positive alerts correspond to rare-but-legitimate behaviors with benign precedents. CBR-PAR addresses this through three contributions: a rarity-guided extraction algorithm that constructs compact case representations from million-node provenance graphs; a tool-augmented SLM agent that dynamically completes cases by retrieving missing causal evidence; and a cloud-based LLM that implements the Reuse phase through comparative judgment against retrieved benign stored cases, grounding every verdict in concrete past experience.

Evaluation demonstrates 700× to 3,800× alert reduction while preserving 86.7%–100% of threats. Ablation confirms the value of both evidence completion (removing it degrades threat preservation by 30.7%) and the case base (removing it increases false positives by 10×). The hybrid architecture cuts API costs by 51.9×. Qualitative analysis further shows that comparative reasoning identifies labeling errors and discovers unlabeled attacks, demonstrating that experience-grounded decisions are more transparent and robust than opaque anomaly scoring.

Acknowledgements. This work is supported by National Natural Science Foundation of China (Grant No.92467201) and the Youth Innovation Promotion Association CAS (Grant No.Y2023047), the Key Laboratory of Network Assessment Technology at Chinese Academy of Sciences and Beijing Key Laboratory of Network Security and Protection Technology.

Declaration on Generative AI. During the preparation of this work, the authors used ChatGPT and Claude to assist with grammar checking and language polishing. All AI-assisted content was carefully reviewed and edited by the authors. The authors take full responsibility for the content of this publication.

References

1. Aamodt, A., Plaza, E.: Case-based reasoning: foundational issues, methodological variations, and system approaches. AI Commun. **7**(1), 39–59 (1994)
2. Bach, K., et al.: Case-based reasoning meets large language models: a research manifesto for open challenges and research directions (2025)
3. Bates, A., Tian, D.J., Butler, K.R., Moyer, T.: Trustworthy {Whole-System} provenance for the Linux kernel. In: 24th USENIX Security Symposium (USENIX Security 15), pp. 319–334 (2015)
4. Bhattarai, B., Huang, H.: SteinerLog: prize collecting the audit logs for threat hunting on enterprise network. In: Proceedings of the 2022 ACM on Asia Conference on Computer and Communications Security, pp. 97–108 (2022)
5. Cheng, Z., et al.: Kairos: Practical intrusion detection and investigation using whole-system provenance. In: 2024 IEEE Symposium on Security and Privacy (SP), pp. 3533–3551. IEEE (2024)
6. DARPA Information Innovation Office (I2O): Transparent computing (TC) engagement 3 datasets. https://github.com/darpa-i2o/Transparent-Computing (2018). Accessed 26 Oct 2025
7. Esmaili, M., Balachandran, B., Safavi-Naini, R., Pieprzyk, J.: Case-based reasoning for intrusion detection. In: Proceedings 12th Annual Computer Security Applications Conference, pp. 214–223. IEEE (1996)
8. Gates, L., Leake, D., Wilkerson, K.: Cases are king: a user study of case presentation to explain CBR decisions. In: International Conference on Case-Based Reasoning, pp. 153–168. Springer (2023)
9. Han, X., Pasquier, T., Bates, A., Mickens, J., Seltzer, M.: UniCorn: runtime provenance-based detector for advanced persistent threats (2020). arXiv:2001.01525 arXiv preprint
10. Hassan, W.U., Bates, A., Marino, D.: Tactical provenance analysis for endpoint detection and response systems. In: 2020 IEEE Symposium on Security and Privacy (SP), pp. 1172–1189. IEEE (2020)
11. Hassan, W.U., et al.: NoDoze: combatting threat alert fatigue with automated provenance triage. In: Network and Distributed Systems Security Symposium (2019)

12. Jia, Z., Xiong, Y., Nan, Y., Zhang, Y., Zhao, J., Wen, M.: {MAGIC}: Detecting advanced persistent threats via masked graph representation learning. In: 33rd USENIX Security Symposium (USENIX Security 24), pp. 5197–5214 (2024)
13. King, S.T., Chen, P.M.: Backtracking intrusions. In: Proceedings of the Nineteenth ACM Symposium on Operating Systems Principles, pp. 223–236 (2003)
14. Liu, F., et al.: MicroCBR: case-based reasoning on spatio-temporal fault knowledge graph for microservices troubleshooting. In: International Conference on Case-based Reasoning, pp. 224–239. Springer (2022)
15. Liu, Y., Shu, X., Sun, Y., Jang, J., Mittal, P.: Rapid: real-time alert investigation with context-aware prioritization for efficient threat discovery. In: Proceedings of the 38th Annual Computer Security Applications Conference, pp. 827–840. (2022)
16. Milajerdi, S.M., Eshete, B., Gjomemo, R., Venkatakrishnan, V.: POIROT: aligning attack behavior with kernel audit records for cyber threat hunting. In: Proceedings of the 2019 ACM SIGSAC Conference on Computer and Communications Security, pp. 1795–1812 (2019)
17. Milajerdi, S.M., Gjomemo, R., Eshete, B., Sekar, R., Venkatakrishnan, V.: Holmes: real-time APT detection through correlation of suspicious information flows. In: 2019 IEEE symposium on security and privacy (SP), pp. 1137–1152. IEEE (2019)
18. Pasquier, T., et al.: Practical whole-system provenance capture. In: Proceedings of the 2017 Symposium on Cloud Computing, pp. 405–418 (2017)
19. Rehman, M.U., Ahmadi, H., Hassan, W.U.: Flash: a comprehensive approach to intrusion detection via provenance graph representation learning. In: 2024 IEEE Symposium on Security and Privacy (SP), pp. 3552–3570. IEEE (2024)
20. Richter, M.M., Michael, M.: Knowledge containers. Readings in case-based reasoning, Morgan Kaufmann Publishers (2003)
21. Shervashidze, N., Schweitzer, P., Van Leeuwen, E.J., Mehlhorn, K., Borgwardt, K.M.: Weisfeiler-Lehman graph kernels. J. Mach. Learn. Res. **12**(9) (2011)
22. Wang, H., Hardy, J., Kandah, F.: Case-based reasoning with diffusion model for ransomware detection. In: International Conference on Case-Based Reasoning, pp. 469–483. Springer (2025)
23. Wang, S., et al.: ThreatRace: detecting and tracing host-based threats in node level through provenance graph learning. IEEE Trans. Inf. Forensics Secur. **17**, 3972–3987 (2022)
24. Watson, I.: A case-based persistent memory for a large language model (2023). arXiv:2310.08842 arXiv preprint
25. Wilkerson, K., Leake, D.: On implementing case-based reasoning with large language models. In: International Conference on Case-Based Reasoning, pp. 404–417. Springer (2024)

Vision-Based Retrieval of Semantic Workflows in Process-Oriented Case-Based Reasoning

Maxim Hotz[1,2], Lukas Malburg[1,2], Kokulan Thanabalan[1,2], and Ralph Bergmann[1,2(✉)]

[1] Artificial Intelligence and Intelligent Information Systems, Trier University, Trier, Germany
{s4mahotz,lukas.malburg,thanabalan,bergmann}@uni-trier.de
[2] German Research Center for Artificial Intelligence (DFKI), Trier, Germany
https://www.wi2.uni-trier.de

Abstract. *Process-Oriented Case-Based Reasoning (POCBR)* relies on retrieving similar semantic workflow graphs, but accurate retrieval typically requires computationally expensive graph matching. To improve scalability, existing systems often employ two-stage retrieval strategies such as *MAC/FAC*, where a fast but less accurate prefilter reduces the search space before detailed matching. Recent approaches use *Graph Neural Networks (GNNs)* for this prefiltering step, but they still involve trade-offs between approximation quality, efficiency, and interpretability. This paper investigates whether semantic workflows can instead be retrieved by visual comparison. To this end, we analyze existing graph visualization strategies regarding their suitability for vision-based retrieval and propose a multi-step pipeline that transforms semantic workflows into deterministic visual representations. These representations are then used in combination with modern vision models for similarity-based retrieval. Experiments in two *POCBR* domains indicate that the proposed approach yields substantial speedups while producing retrieval quality that is generally below but still competitive with established methods. The results demonstrate that vision-based retrieval is a promising alternative for use as a *MAC-stage* filter in *POCBR*.

Keywords: Vision-Based Retrieval · Vision Transformer · Semantic Workflows · Similarity Assessment · Process-Oriented Case-Based Reasoning

1 Introduction

The methodology of *Case-Based Reasoning (CBR)* [1] is based on the principle that similar problems have similar solutions [34]. Thus, a suitable and efficient similarity assessment is crucial in modern *CBR* applications [12]. However, the use of complex case representations, such as in *POCBR* [7], where cases represent procedural experiential knowledge as semantic workflow graphs, introduces

L. Malburg and K. Bach (Eds.): ICCBR 2026, LNAI 16780, pp. 560–576, 2027.
https://doi.org/10.1007/978-3-032-33865-5_34

new challenges for similarity-based retrieval. Unlike traditional attribute-value case representations used in *CBR*, semantic workflow graphs require similarity measures that account for both structural topologies and semantic descriptions of workflows [7]. This increased complexity results in a graph matching/mapping problem that must be solved to accurately assess similarity. This process is significantly more challenging than the simple comparison of attribute values in classical *CBR*. For several years, we have been investigating this issue by proposing novel approaches for similarity-based retrieval in *POCBR* (e. g., [7,20,21,25,29,42]). These approaches range from heuristic algorithms like A* [7,42] to compute node and edge mappings between workflow graphs to GPU-accelerated graph matching [21,29] and graph embedding approaches [20,25] that are used as a prefiltering step in a MAC/FAC retrieval [15]. Nonetheless, some of the proposed approaches lack scalability, which poses challenges for large case bases or complex workflows. This scalability barrier is particularly problematic in settings where fast retrieval is essential, not only for overall system performance but also for user satisfaction and the acceptance of a *CBR* application.

In recent years, a potential alternative is the use of methods based on *Large Language Models (LLMs)*, which have also gained increasing attention in the *CBR* community (e. g., [2,6,27,31,39,40]). Hereby, approaches can be used to assess similarity that mimic how human experts assess similarity between objects: by comparison of visual cues such as patterns, shapes, or colors, such as product designers do in product development with technical drawings [26]. Unlike many existing approaches (e. g., [20,25]), which often operate as black boxes and offer limited explainability of retrieval results, a visual representation is a first step toward making the similarity assessment process transparent for users by visually exposing individual graph elements (i. e., nodes).

In addition, modern vision-based machine learning models, such as *Convolutional Neural Networks (CNNs)* [33] or Vision Transformers (ViTs) [14], help to remedy the scalability issues. Once trained, these models provide constant inference time during retrieval, regardless of workflow complexity. Furthermore, because they could learn to extract domain-agnostic visual features rather than relying on domain-specific data, these models have the potential to generalize to entirely unseen domains. However, existing applications focus on domains with standardized visual encodings (e. g., finance [37]) and lack the ability to integrate workflow semantics. Hence, the question remains of how both the structure and semantics of workflow graphs in *POCBR* can be jointly encoded. The contribution of this paper is twofold: 1) we discuss requirements for vision-based retrieval in *POCBR* and compare current state-of-the-art approaches based on these requirements, and 2) we propose two visual encoding methods that are combined with generated node embeddings for vision-based retrieval in *POCBR*. The vision-based retrieval approach is evaluated on two datasets containing different kinds of semantic workflow graphs.

The paper is structured as follows: Sect. 2 introduces relevant foundations and provides an overview of related work. The set of requirements is presented in Sect. 3, followed by the proposed vision-based retrieval approach. Section 4 discusses the experimental evaluation of the proposed approach, and Sect. 5 concludes the paper and outlines future work.

2 Foundations and Related Work

The foundations for this paper comprise the *NEST* graph representation for semantic workflow graphs in *POCBR* and the associated similarity assessment by Bergmann and Gil [7]. Furthermore, the general properties of Vision Transformers (ViTs) are fundamental to this work. Hence, they are introduced in the following along with related approaches for visualizing graph-structured data.

2.1 Similarity Assessment in POCBR

Cases in *POCBR* consist of procedural experiential knowledge [7] in the form of semantic workflow graphs. In this work, we use the *NEST* graph formalism [7] to encode these graphs. A NEST graph represents a workflow as a semantic workflow graph, which is a directed, typed, and semantically enriched graph. A semantic workflow graph W is hereby defined by the quadruple $W = (N, E, S, T)$ where N denotes a set of nodes and $E \subseteq N \times N$ is the set of edges between N. In addition, every node and every edge is strictly typed with $T : N \cup E \longrightarrow \Omega$ and also assigned a semantic description $S : N \cup E \longrightarrow \mathcal{E}$ out of a metadata language. Figure 1 depicts an exemplary NEST graph representing a sandwich recipe from the cooking domain.

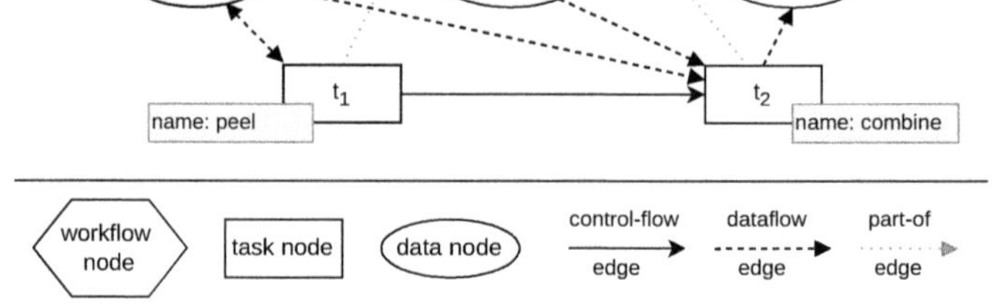

Fig. 1. Exemplary NEST Graph Representing a Cooking Recipe.

To determine similarity between NEST graphs, the knowledge-intensive similarity measure for semantic workflow graphs [7] is used in this context. This measure evaluates graph similarity by constructing a best-possible mapping between the nodes and edges of two graphs under the condition that only nodes and edges of the same type can be mapped. For every mapped pair, some local similarity measure (e. g., taxonomic similarity or Levenshtein distance [5,7]) is applied to the semantic descriptions of the mapped graph items. These local similarity scores are finally aggregated into an overall similarity value following the local-global principle [7].

2.2 Vision Transformers

For many years, deep learning in computer vision was dominated by *CNNs* [27]. More recently, attention-based architectures have become increasingly important, with *ViTs* emerging as a prominent alternative to *CNNs*-based models. *ViTs* transfer the transformer architecture, originally developed for natural language processing, to image analysis. Instead of processing an image with convolution operations, a *ViT* divides the image into fixed-size patches. These patches are transformed into embedding vectors and enriched with positional embeddings to preserve spatial information. The resulting sequence is then processed by transformer encoder layers based on self-attention [14]. In contrast to *CNNs* that mainly focus on local spatial neighborhoods [27], *ViTs* can model relationships between distant image regions directly through self-attention. This makes them well suited for learning global contextual information in images [14].

2.3 Related Work

Related approaches in the field of graph visualization form a taxonomy [4] that can be broadly categorized into explicit, implicit/abstract, and hybrid visualizations. Explicit methods, such as node-link diagrams and adjacency matrices, directly depict graph topology. In this context, Goh et al. [16] demonstrate with *Chemception* that *CNNs* can learn chemical properties directly from 2D molecular drawings that resemble node-link drawings. Lyu et al. [28] present matrix-based *Graph-Preserving Grid Layouts* that project graph nodes onto a 2D grid while integrating node features. Hybrid approaches like *NodeTrix* [18] or *MatLink* [19] combine matrices and node-link diagrams by rendering dense subgraphs as matrices and connecting them with edges while prioritizing readability for humans. Conversely, implicit and abstract approaches apply algorithmic transformations to represent graphs. In this context, Bartz et al. [3] propose a space-filling representation for argument graphs in *CBR*. Tixier et al. [38] represent graphs as 2D density histograms of node embeddings for *CNN* classification. Similarly, Sharma et al. [36] introduce *DeepInsight* to convert non-image data into *CNN*-compatible structured images, and Cakmak et al. [10] present *dg2pix* that stacks embedding vectors as pixel rows to visualize temporal graph changes.

While these approaches demonstrate the general compatibility of visual graph representations and vision models, a significant research gap remains regarding the complex semantic workflows applied in *POCBR*. Classic explicit methods (node-link, matrices) represent structure well and remain intuitive for humans, yet they cannot incorporate multi-type semantic annotations without clutter or simplification. Spatialization and projection-based approaches capture semantic similarity effectively but typically fail to preserve explicit graph structure and are often stochastic (e. g., t-SNE, UMAP), which is problematic for reproducible vision-based ML pipelines. Hierarchical and space-filling methods usually require true hierarchies and therefore do not fit sequential NEST graphs with branches and loops, while creating artificial hierarchies risks breaking directed flow and losing information. Finally, many methods cannot produce compact, fixed-size outputs, and embedding-based visualizations often either ignore semantics or aggregate information too strongly, making them potentially too lossy for similarity regression. Consequently, there is currently no unified representation for semantic graphs that would allow the complete encoding of structure and semantics required for vision-based similarity regression.

3 Vision-Based Retrieval Approach

In this section, we present our novel vision-based retrieval approach. The approach is based on the idea of transforming semantic workflow graphs into visual representations that can be processed by state-of-the-art vision-based machine learning models. For this reason, we present in the following a set of requirements that the visual representation must fulfill to be suitable for encoding workflow graphs for similarity-based retrieval. Afterwards, we present a conceptual overview of the components of our approach and describe the individual steps in more detail.

3.1 Requirements Analysis

To guide the development and evaluation of a novel visual representation for semantic graphs, we derive the following functional (FR) and non-functional (NFR) requirements based on a literature review and the inherent properties of NEST graphs.

FR 1 – Representation of Graph Structure: The representation must encode the directed topology of a NEST graph. This includes nodes, edges, and control-flow patterns (sequences, parallel branches, loops), which serve as a structural foundation.

FR 2 – Integration of Semantic Annotations: The encoding mechanism must allow the integration of semantic descriptions of workflow nodes into the structural representation. The integration of semantic descriptions for nodes is essential, as current A*-based approaches rely on the local-global principle, where the overall similarity is typically aggregated from node-level semantic similarities [7]. Encoding edge semantics is optional, as they contribute less to overall similarity and are often mapped implicitly.

FR 3 – Preservation of Node and Edge Types: The representation must visually distinguish between different node and edge types (e. g., via shape, color, or texture). This is necessary to accommodate the strict type-preserving mapping constraints of A* [7].

FR 4 – Multi-Type Attribute Encoding: The visual representation must be capable of encoding different data types found in composite semantic descriptions (e. g., numerical, ordinal, nominal). It should also be flexible enough to represent semantic information at different levels of abstraction, supporting both the direct encoding of individual attributes and the encoding of aggregated node-level similarity scores.

FR 5 – Compatibility with Input Requirements of Vision Models: The output must adhere to the constraints of vision models, such as producing fixed-resolution tensors for *CNNs*. For *ViTs*, it should ideally preserve semantically connected components when the image is divided into patch sequences [14].

FR 6 – Flexible Parametrization: The encoding mechanism must be configurable for diverse application domains. This ideally also includes toggling between structure-only and semantics-inclusive encodings, as well as adjusting the granularity of the semantic representation.

NFR 1 – Deterministic Encoding: The encoding mechanism must produce deterministic and reproducible visual representations, such that encoding the same NEST graph multiple times yields identical visual outputs.

NFR 2 – Generalizability Across Domains and Case Representations: The visual encoding approach should generalize across different workflow domains (e. g., cooking recipes [32], cyber-physical systems [30]) and thereby also accommodate for the different case representations linked to the respective domains (e. g., flat cases in classical *CBR* or time series in *Temporal Case-Based Reasoning (TCBR)*).

Table 1. Comparison of Visualization Approaches Against the Requirements.

Req.	Explicit		Hybrid	Implicit / Abstract		
	Node-Link *Std. Layout*	Matrix-Based *Adj. Matrix*	NodeTrix / MatLink	Space-Filling / Hierarchical	Spatialization *t-SNE Layout*	Embedding-Based
FR1	✓	✓	✓	✗	✓	✓
FR2	(✓)	(✓)	(✓)	✓	(✓)	✓
FR3	✓	(✓)	✓	✓	✓	✓
FR4	✗	✗	✗	✓	✗	✓
FR5	✗	(✓)	✗	✓	✗	✓
FR6	✓	✓	✓	(✓)	(✓)	✓
NFR1	✗	(✓)	✗	✓	✗	✓
NFR2	(✓)	(✓)	(✓)	(✓)	(✓)	(✓)

✓= *fulfilled*, (✓) = *partially fulfilled*, ✗= *not fulfilled.*

Table 1 summarizes the assessment of current approaches and the categories presented in related work regarding the derived requirements. The results reveal a critical trade-off that is consistent across most investigated approaches: While explicit layouts attempt to preserve the human-readable topology of a graph, they struggle to comply with the strict input requirements of modern vision models and also lack the ability to encode complex semantic descriptions adequately. Conversely, abstract and implicit approaches generally yield better semantic-encoding capabilities, but their abstract properties diminish interpretability. Ultimately, we identify embedding-based visualizations as the best candidate for this work, as they are the only approach that allows the simultaneous encoding of complex semantic descriptions and graph topology while adhering to the strict input requirements of modern vision models.

3.2 Architectural Overview

Based on the presented requirements, we develop a novel approach for vision-based retrieval of semantic workflow graphs. Figure 2 illustrates the components of our architecture.

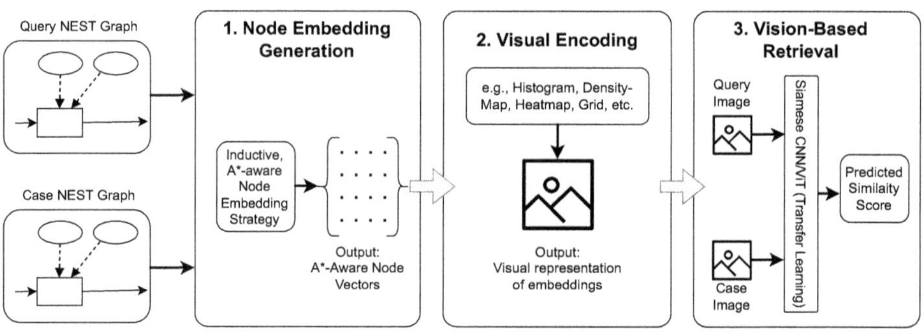

Fig. 2. Architectural Overview for Vision-Based Retrieval.

The first stage addresses the challenge of converting both query and case NEST graphs (input phase 1) into a set of embedding vectors (output phase 1) while fulfilling the requirements stated above. It is the goal to employ a specialized, inductive embedding technique that ideally considers node-level A* ground truth labels from the case base during training the embedding function. Based on the resulting vector representation (input phase 2), the second stage consists of an algorithmic process that transforms the high-dimensional vectors from the first stage into a 2D visualization (output phase 2). Finally, the third stage addresses the challenge of learning to approximate graph-level A* similarity scores by employing a Siamese [9] similarity regression architecture. At this stage, the network is trained on the visual representations of graphs (input phase 3) contained in the case base with the ultimate goal of performing online retrieval on unseen graph visualizations. Together, these steps represent the full conceptual pipeline for the vision-based retrieval process.

3.3 Node Embedding Generation

Semantic bag-of-feature approaches like *StarSpace* [25,41] are transductive and suffer from context pollution when attempting to integrate structural information, while structural embedding approaches such as *Node2Vec* [17] are oblivious of semantics. Therefore, a hybrid, inductive, embedding strategy is used that can handle the composite nature of A* similarities. *Graph Neural Networks (GNNs)* are capable of generating node embeddings by iteratively combining a node's own features with aggregated features from its neighbors [35]. Figure 3 depicts the *GNN* architecture used in our approach.

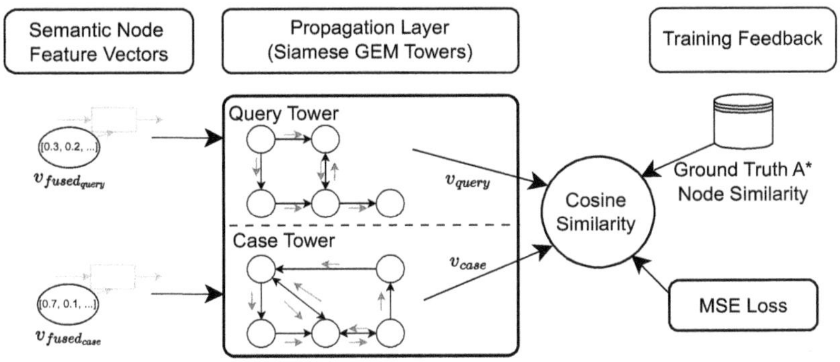

Fig. 3. Siamese Graph Embedding Model Architecture. (Source: Based on [23])

3.4 Visual Encoding

The second component of the proposed architecture addresses the transformation of the high-dimensional node embeddings into a fixed-size image representation. Approaches such as *dg2pix* [10] demonstrate that embedding vectors can be encoded as "pixel-bars" that are essentially sequences of pixels where the color intensity represents the value of a vector dimension. This concept is adopted in our approach and extended by proposing two different layout strategies: a *Grid* layout and a *Linear* layout (see Fig. 4), which each complement different properties of state-of-the-art vision models.

Based on the task and data nodes in the graph, the created node embeddings are transformed into grayscale patterns while the padded zones are rendered as black tiles (0). In addition to this, we transform the *NEST* graphs directly into node-link diagrams, rendering nodes as geometric shapes and edges as directed connecting lines. We use these diagrams as a structure-focused baseline to evaluate whether vision models can directly parse explicit human-readable graph topologies. To improve their machine-readability, the node-link drawings are optimized in terms of layout and color palette before being used as input for vision-based retrieval. In detail, this is achieved through a compacting layout

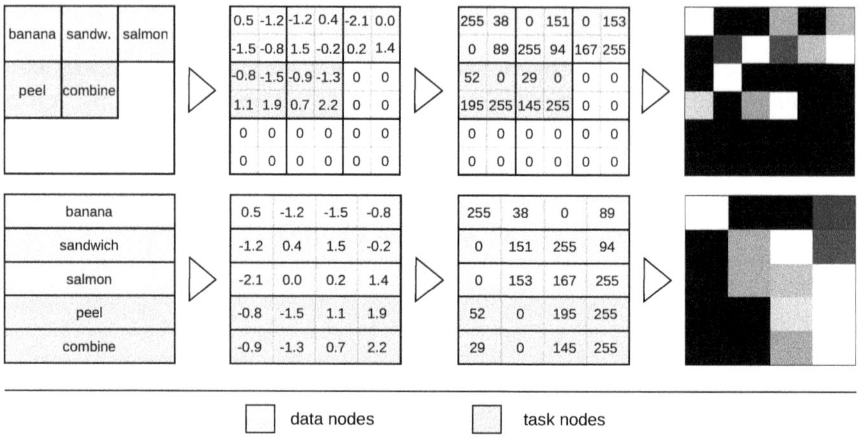

Fig. 4. Grid and Linear Layout of the Exemplary Cooking Recipe.

algorithm that minimizes white space and edge crossings and by employing a high-contrast color scheme to differentiate between item types.

3.5 Vision-Based Retrieval

Based on the generated node embeddings and their visual encoding into the proposed *Grid* or the *Linear* layout, a Siamese neural network is used to process the images for a query and the cases from the case base. Figure 5 depicts this process where both images in a grid or linear layout or as node-link diagrams are input to a Siamese 2D *CNN*/*Vit*. The neural network transforms the input into vectors with which the similarity is assessed based on cosine similarity. The Siamese model is trained based on the ground truth A* graph similarities and optimized based on an *Mean Squared Error (MSE)* loss.

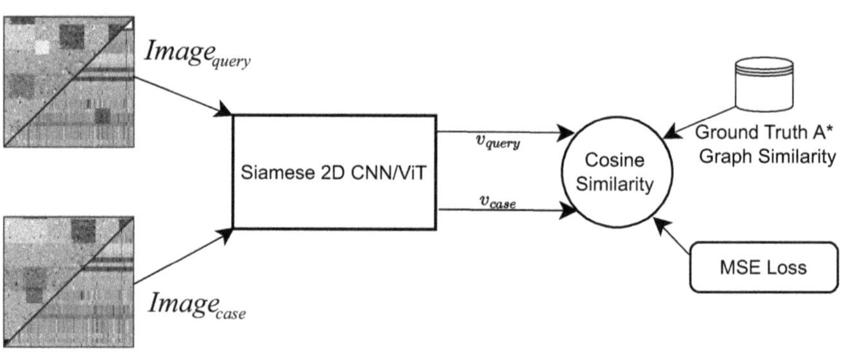

Fig. 5. Siamese Retrieval Architecture.

4 Experimental Evaluation

Based on the vision-based retrieval approach presented in the previous section, this section presents the experimental evaluation of the proposed approach compared to other available approaches such as the A* similarity assessment. In the evaluation, we assess the suitability of the proposed visual encoding based on the grid and linear layouts, as well as the appropriateness of the use of node-link diagrams as an alternative visualization strategy.

In the evaluation, we investigate the following four hypotheses that are structured according to the components of the architecture: Initially, the design choice regarding the visual encoding is validated in a first experiment to assess (H1 and H2), followed by an assessment of the pipeline's qualitative performance (H3). In a second experiment, the robustness of the approach regarding incomplete queries (H4) is investigated.

H1 The embedding-based visualizations allow a better approximation of the A* similarity by vision models than the direct node-link visualizations.
H2 The space-filling properties of the linear layout result in a better A* similarity approximation than the grid layout.
H3 The vision-based retrieval approach achieves a retrieval quality that is comparable to current state-of-the-art *GNN* approaches.
H4 The vision-based retrieval pipeline maintains a high retrieval quality even when queries are incomplete.

4.1 Experimental Setup

For the experimental evaluation, we use two domains from our *ProCAKE* [5] system. The *Cooking Domain* [32] is taken from the graph embedding benchmark [20] and consists of a total of 800 workflows, split into a training set of 660 cases, a validation set of 60 cases, and a test set of 80 cases. As the cooking domain is quite small and consists of a relatively simple workflow case representation, the second domain is selected to be more complex and larger in scale. The *Cyber-Physical Systems (CPS)* domain [30] is taken from a process augmentation study [22] that has been conducted in the same research context with the goal of investigating the impact of process augmentation techniques on deep learning techniques, including the graph embedding approach. The data set used in this context contains a total of 3350 workflows. Since the original study [22] evaluated performance on the original, non-augmented test set, a dedicated augmented test set is manually created. This is achieved by splitting the augmented validation set of 350 cases in half. This results in a final partitioning of 3000 training cases, 175 validation cases, and 175 test cases.

Similar to the evaluation by Hoffmann et al. [20,22], a *Hold-Out* retrieval evaluation scenario is applied in the experiment, i. e., every case in the unseen test set acts as the query. The approach is then tasked to assess the similarity between this query and all cases in the train set, effectively taking the role of the case base. Applied to the specific datasets, this results in the full computation of the $N_{test} \times N_{train}$ similarity matrix, meaning 80×660 for the cooking domain and 175×3000 for *CPS* respectively. To compare the results and to assess the quality of the similarity computations, we calculate the *Mean Absolute Error (MAE)* to the A* similarity that is the baseline for our approach. In addition, we calculate the global *Correctness* $\in [-1, 1]$ [11] to rate the resulting ranking quality, the *Hits* rate and the *k-NN Quality* $\in [0, 1]$ [25] for the first $k = 25$ most similar cases of the resulting ranking. It is important to note that the A* similarity baseline achieves the best possible MAE of 0, the best possible *Correctness* of 1, the highest possible *Hits* of 25 with $k = 25$, and the best possible *k-NN Quality* of 1. The training of the models is performed on a GPU cluster consisting of eight *Nvidia Tesla V100 (32GB VRAM)* GPUs, dual *Intel Xeon Gold 6138* CPUs (40 cores), and 768GB of RAM. The evaluation is performed on a consumer-grade *Windows 11* machine with a single *Nvidia GeForce GTX 1660 (6GB VRAM)*, an *AMD Ryzen 5 3600* CPU (6 cores), and 32GB of RAM. All experiments are conducted using the same hyperparameters[1].

In the first experiment, three different configurations are applied. In the first and second configurations, the vision model is fine-tuned on the proposed grid and linear layouts, respectively. In the third configuration, the model is trained on the alternative node-link visualization, which does not rely on the upstream pipeline components. In the second experiment, incomplete user queries are simulated by systematically manipulating and reducing the existing query graphs. For this purpose, nodes are randomly omitted from the graphs of the respective test sets of both domains,such that four different instances of the test set corresponding to reduction levels of 10 %, 25 %, 50 %, and 75 % are produced for each domain.

4.2 Experimental Results

As an additional non-neural baseline, the *Feature-Based Retriever (FBR)* [8] with explicitly constructed features for the case representation in the *MAC* phase is included in the comparison. The first experiment investigates hypotheses H1-H3 and analyzes the retrieval performance of the proposed visual encoding. The results of this experiment for the cooking domain (CB-I) and *CPS* domain (CB-II) are shown in Table 2. Bold numbers indicate the best-performing visualization strategy for each domain and metric, while underlined numbers indicate the second-best-performing strategy.

In the cooking domain, the node-link visualization significantly outperforms both embedding-based visualizations in all recorded metrics. Especially in terms of *Hits* and global *Correctness*, this discrepancy becomes evident. In the more complex *CPS* domain, both embedding-based layouts achieve a significantly better performance, not only in comparison to the node-link visualization but also compared to their performance in the cooking domain. Furthermore, it appears

[1] See https://github.com/wi2trier/Vision-Based-Retrieval-ICCBR-2026 for more details.

Table 2. Evaluation Results of the A* Approximation Experiment.

	Recipes (CB-I)				CPS (CB-II)			
Retriever	MAE ↓	Corr. ↑	Hits ↑	Quality ↑	MAE ↓	Corr. ↑	Hits ↑	Quality ↑
Grid	0.102	0.111	1.090	0.496	<u>0.101</u>	<u>0.312</u>	<u>13.140</u>	<u>0.568</u>
Linear	<u>0.096</u>	0.127	0.930	0.493	**0.101***	**0.313**	**13.510**	**0.582**
Node-Link	**0.086***	<u>0.280</u>	<u>2.438</u>	<u>0.528</u>	0.108	0.210	2.931	0.185
FBR	0.200	**0.601**	**10.160**	**0.694**	-	-	-	-

* indicates that the superiority of this visualization is statistically significant ($p < 0.001$) in terms of MAE compared to the other visual layouts using the Wilcoxon signed-rank test [13].

that the performance of the node-link visualization deteriorates in the complex *CPS* domain, which becomes evident by considering the *k-NN Quality*, which constitutes the lowest score recorded across all configurations. These findings align with the preliminary assumptions that the drawbacks of node-link diagrams (e. g., sparsity or visual clutter) are aggravated in complex domains with large graphs. Since these results indicate that embedding-based visualizations are necessary to maintain retrieval quality in complex domains while being outperformed by the node-link visualization in simpler domains, Hypothesis H1 is partially accepted.

While it has been assumed that the space-filling properties of the linear layout outperform the grid layout (H2), the results only indicate a marginal improvement over the grid layout. In the cooking domain, the performance is almost identical. While the linear layout achieves slightly better MAE and global *Correctness*, the grid layout exhibits better *Hits* and *k-NN Quality* metrics. However, in the *CPS* domain, the linear layout surpasses the grid layout in almost every metric except for the MAE. This advantage can likely be attributed to the composition of the workflows in *CPS*: the discrepancy between the largest graph in the domain and the average graph size, which puts the grid layout at a natural disadvantage due to the introduction of void space (i. e., zero padding). Although the advantage is only marginal, the overall better performance of the linear layout leads us to accept Hypothesis H2.

Since the recent learning-to-rank variation of the *GNN* baseline [24] does not report an MAE metric, the vision-based pipeline is compared against earlier *GNN* architectures [23] in terms of MAE. Both studies [23, 24] employ the exact same data split for cooking recipes as used in this work, which makes a combined assessment feasible. For the remaining metrics, [24] is used for comparison. The results for the cooking domain indicate that the proposed visualization, especially the node-link variation, can compete with the *GNN* baselines. Regarding the similarity regression capabilities, the node-link visualization achieves a MAE of 0.086, which even outperforms the best equivalent Graph Embedding Model (GEM) retriever with 0.158 [23]. The best pointwise GEM retriever achieves a global *Correctness* of 0.055 in the cooking domain, while the node-link visualization obtains a value of 0.280. Furthermore, the best GEM retriever achieves a *Hits* rate of 0.225 and a *k-NN Quality* of 0.471, while the node-link visualization exceeds these values with a *Hits* rate of 2.438 and a *k-NN Quality* of 0.528. It is important to note that both grid and linear layouts also surpass the point-wise GEM retrievers in all metrics in the cooking domain. For the *CPS* domain, all proposed visualization approaches exhibit a significantly better MAE (0.101, 0.101, 0.108) than the 0.1729 for the GEM retriever [22]. Regarding the ranking metrics, the best pointwise GEM retriever achieves a global *Correctness* of 0.389, a *Hits* rate of 11.778, and a *k-NN Quality* of 0.600. In contrast, the best-performing visualization strategy (i. e., the linear layout) achieves slightly inferior global *Correctness* (0.313) and *k-NN Quality* (0.582) metrics. Only the *Hits* rate of 13.510 exceeds the baseline. Despite these results, it is important to note that the more complex *Graph Matching Network (GMN)* architectures [22] achieve significantly better results across both domains than the proposed approaches. Nevertheless, when comparing the novel approaches against the equivalent GEM architectures, it becomes evident that they can compete with the baseline performance. Consequently, Hypothesis H3 is accepted.

In the second experiment, Hypothesis H4 is investigated by analyzing the robustness of the vision-based approach. The experimental results are displayed in Fig. 6 that visualizes the relative decline of the retrieval quality for both domains across all reduction levels.

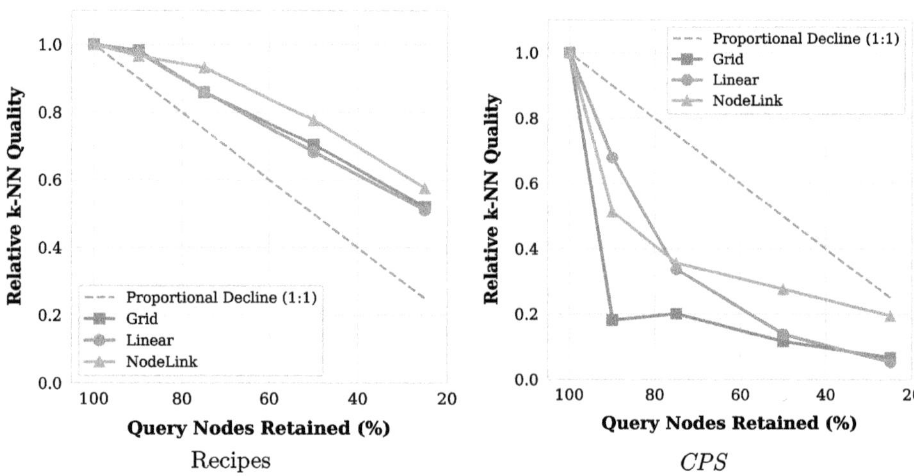

Fig. 6. Retrieval Performance Degradations.

For this purpose, we choose the *k-NN Quality* metric as it constitutes the most sophisticated of the reported measures since it not only considers the overlap of the retrieval result list but also integrates the weighted similarity quality. In addition, the relative *k-NN Quality* is normalized against the 100 % baseline ($Q_{rel} = Q_r/Q_{100\%}$) such that the decline rates can be directly compared to a proportional decline, which is indicated by the diagonal dashed line. As illustrated, the performance declines vary largely depending on the domain. In the cooking domain, all three visualizations exhibit a better than proportional decline. For instance, when 50 % of query nodes are removed, all three variations can retain roughly 70 %80 % of their original retrieval quality. This constitutes a promising result regarding the real-world applicability, as it provides evidence for the robustness of the vision-based retrieval approach in simple application domains. On the contrary, in the *CPS* domain, all three visualizations show a performance collapse at the 90 % level, which stabilizes throughout the higher deletion levels. Here, the grid layout suffers the most, as a 10 % removal leads to an 80 % loss of retrieval quality. As previously discussed, this behavior can likely be attributed to the varying graph sizes in the *CPS* domain, rendering the grid layout a bad choice. Due to the placing mechanism of tiles, the deletion of nodes causes the remaining node tiles to shift in two dimensions, i. e., horizontally and potentially also vertically. In contrast, the removal of nodes in the linear layout only causes a shift in the vertical dimension, potentially explaining the superior performance of this layout variation further. Furthermore, the grid layout requires pre-calculated dimensions, meaning it cannot process queries that exceed the size of the largest workflow in the case base. Combined with the aforementioned node shifting, this constitutes a major limitation in this context. Considering the results of the second experiment, Hypothesis H4 is partially accepted. While the vision-based pipeline shows a graceful degradation across all visualizations in the cooking domain, the collapse in the more complex *CPS* domain hinders a full acceptance of the hypothesis[2].

5 Conclusion and Future Work

In this paper, we present a novel vision-based retrieval approach for complex *POCBR* domains. For this purpose, a set of requirements toward a visualization approach for semantic graphs is derived and used to score existing visualization approaches w. r. t. their suitability for this task. Based on this analysis, two embedding-based visualization layouts have been introduced and evaluated by practical experiments. These experiments indicate that embedding-based visualizations, especially the linear layout, provide promising retrieval performance as candidates for a *MAC* retriever in complex application domains such as *CPS*. In addition, the evaluation results indicate that the direct use of node-link renderings in combination with modern *ViT* architectures can already yield sufficient A* approximation performance in simpler domains such as cooking. Overall, the evaluation demonstrates that the proposed vision-based retrieval approach can compete with current state-of-the-art *GNN* baselines w. r. t. similarity regression while also pointing toward broader decision-support applications. In particular, the results promise that vision-based retrieval can also support product design processes in which similar technical drawings must be retrieved efficiently from

[2] A table with the experimental results for all quality metrics and all levels can be found in the GitHub repository.

large repositories. In such settings, the approach could serve as a scalable preselection mechanism that identifies visually and structurally related prior solutions before more detailed engineering analysis is applied. In conclusion, although the proposed architecture is tailored to semantically enriched workflow graphs, its transferability mainly depends on whether arbitrary case representations can be converted into graph-like structures or suitable visual encodings.

In future work, the impact of alternative optimization objectives during training should be explored. Recent work in this context [24] moves toward a learning-to-rank paradigm in which models are optimized for ranking case lists rather than for similarity regression. In addition, the proposed implementation currently translates semantic descriptions of graph elements into a key-value-based representation. While this proved effective in preliminary experiments, it should be investigated to what extent the quality of the semantic embeddings produced by the *LLM* can be improved by replacing this input format with a representation that is closer to natural language, which may better exploit the language processing capabilities of the *LLM*. Another important direction for future research is hyperparameter tuning, as well as the evaluation of the proposed retrieval concept on design-oriented representations such as technical drawings.

Acknowledgments. Funded by the Deutsche Forschungsgemeinschaft (DFG, German Research Foundation) – 543073350.

Declaration on Generative AI. During the preparation of this work, the author(s) used ChatGPT, Gemini, and LanguageTool in order to: Generate images, Paraphrase and reword, improve writing style, Grammar and spelling check, Citation management, and Formatting assistance. After using this tool/service, the author(s) reviewed and edited the content as needed and take(s) full responsibility for the publication's content.

References

1. Aamodt, A., Plaza, E.: Case-based reasoning: foundational issues, methodological variations, and system approaches. AI Commun. **7**(1), 39–59 (1994)
2. Bach, K., et al.: Case-based reasoning meets large language models: a research manifesto for open challenges and research directions **hal-05006761** (2025)
3. Bartz, K., et al.: Retrieving argument graphs using vision transformers. In: ArgMining 2025, pp. 32–45. ACL (2025)
4. Beck, F., et al.: A taxonomy and survey of dynamic graph visualization. Comput. Graph. Forum **36**(1), 133–159 (2017)
5. Bergmann, R., et al.: ProCAKE: a process-oriented case-based reasoning framework. In: ICCBR Workshops, pp. 156–161. (2019)
6. Bergmann, R., et al.: EXAR: a unified experience-grounded agentic reasoning architecture. In: ICCBR 2025, pp. 3–17. Springer (2025)
7. Bergmann, R., Gil, Y.: Similarity assessment and efficient retrieval of semantic workflows. Inf. Syst. **40**, 115–127 (2014)
8. Bergmann, R., Stromer, A.: MAC/FAC Retrieval of Semantic Workflows. In: FLAIRS 2013, AAAI Press (2013)

9. Bromley, J., et al.: Signature Verification Using a "Siamese" Time Delay Neural Network. In: NIPS 1993. pp. 737–744 (1993)
10. Cakmak, E., et al.: dg2pix: Pixel-Based Visual Analysis of Dynamic Graphs. CoRR **abs/2009.07322** (2020)
11. Cheng, W., et al.: Predicting partial orders: ranking with abstention. In: ECML PKDD 2010, pp. 215–230. Springer (2010)
12. Dalal, S., et al.: Case Retrieval Optimization of Case-Based Reasoning Through Knowledge-Intensive Similarity Measures. Int. J. Comput. Appl. **34**(3), 12–18 (2011)
13. Demšar, J.: Statistical Comparisons of Classifiers over Multiple Data Sets. J. Mach. Learn. Res. **7**, 1–30 (2006)
14. Dosovitskiy, A., et al.: An image is worth 16x16 words: transformers for image recognition at scale. In: ICLR 2021 (2021)
15. Forbus, K.D., et al.: MAC/FAC: a model of similarity-based retrieval. Cogn. Sci. **19**(2), 141–205 (1995)
16. Goh, G.B., et al.: Chemception: a deep neural network with minimal chemistry knowledge matches the performance of expert-developed QSAR/QSPR models. CoRR **abs/1706.06689** (2017)
17. Grover, A., Leskovec, J.: node2vec: scalable feature learning for networks, pp. 855–864 (2016). KDD 2016
18. Henry, N., et al.: NodeTrix: a hybrid visualization of social networks. IEEE Trans. Vis. Comput. Graph. **13**(6), 1302–1309 (2007)
19. Henry, N., Fekete, J.D.: MatLink: Enhanced matrix visualization for analyzing social networks. In: INTERACT 2007, pp. 288–302. Springer (2007)
20. Hoffmann, M., et al.: Using Siamese graph neural networks for similarity-based retrieval in process-oriented case-based reasoning. In: ICCBR 2020, pp. 229–244. Springer (2020)
21. Hoffmann, M., et al.: GPU-based graph matching for accelerating similarity assessment in process-oriented case-based reasoning. In: ICCBR 2022, pp. 240–255. Springer (2022)
22. Hoffmann, M., et al.: Augmentation of semantic processes for deep learning applications. Appl. Artif. Intell. **39**(1), 2506788 (2025)
23. Hoffmann, M., Bergmann, R.: Using graph embedding techniques in process-oriented case-based reasoning. Algorithms **15**(2), 27 (2022)
24. Hoffmann, M., Bergmann, R.: Ranking-based case retrieval with graph neural networks in process-oriented case-based reasoning. In: FLAIRS 2023 (2023)
25. Klein, P., et al.: Learning workflow embeddings to improve the performance of similarity-based retrieval for process-oriented case-based reasoning. In: ICCBR 2019, pp. 188–203. Springer (2019)
26. Kunz, L., et al.: XDP-Opt: experience-based design process optimization for industrial manufacturing. In: Workshop SIG Knowledge Management (FG WM). CEUR-WS.org (2025)
27. Lenz, M., et al.: LLsiM: large language models for similarity assessment in case-based reasoning. In: ICCBR 2025, pp. 126–141. Springer (2025)
28. Lyu, Y., et al.: Graph-preserving grid layout: a simple graph drawing method for graph classification using CNNs. CoRR **abs/1909.12383** (2019)
29. Malburg, L., et al.: Improving similarity-based retrieval efficiency by using graphic processing units in case-based reasoning. In: FLAIRS 2021 (2021)
30. Malburg, L., et al.: Adaptive management of cyber-physical workflows by means of case-based reasoning and automated planning. In: EDOC Workshops 2022, pp. 79–95. Springer (2022)

31. Minor, M., Kaucher, E.: Retrieval augmented generation with LLMs for explaining business process models. In: ICCBR 2024, pp. 175–190. Springer (2024)
32. Müller, G., Bergmann, R.: CookingCAKE: a framework for the adaptation of cooking recipes represented as workflows. In: ICCBR Workshops, pp. 221–232 (2015)
33. O'Shea, K., Nash, R.: An Introduction to Convolutional Neural Networks. CoRR **abs/1511.08458** (2015)
34. Richter, M.M., Weber, R.O.: Case-Based Reasoning - A Textbook, Springer (2013)
35. Scarselli, F., et al.: The graph neural network model. IEEE Trans. Neural Netw. **20**(1), 61–80 (2009)
36. Sharma, A., et al.: DeepInsight: a methodology to transform a non-image data to an image for convolution neural network architecture. Sci. Rep. **9**(1), 11399 (2019)
37. Sood, S., et al.: Visual time series forecasting: an image-driven approach. In: ICAIF 2021, pp. 1–9 (2021)
38. Tixier, A.J.P., et al.: Classifying graphs as images with convolutional neural networks. CoRR **abs/1708.02218** (2017)
39. Wilkerson, K., Leake, D.: On implementing case-based reasoning with large language models. In: ICCBR 2024, pp. 404–417. Springer (2024)
40. Wiratunga, N., et al.: CBR-RAG: case-based reasoning for retrieval augmented generation in LLMs for legal question answering. In: ICCBR 2024, pp. 445–460. Springer (2024)
41. Wu, L.Y.: StarSpace: embed all the things! In: AAAI 2018, pp. 5569–5577. AAAI Press (2018)
42. Zeyen, C., Bergmann, R.: A*-based similarity assessment of semantic graphs. In: ICCBR 2020, pp. 17–32. Springer (2020)

Neuro-Symbolic Temporal Reasoning: A Hybrid Case-Based Approach for Robust Expiration Date Recognition

Hao Peng(✉), Juan Bayon, Joaquin Recas, and Maria Guijarro

Universidad Complutense de Madrid, Avda. de Séneca, 2 Ciudad Universitaria, 28040 Madrid, Spain
penghao@ucm.es

Abstract. Accessing expiration dates is a critical safety requirement for individuals with visual impairments, yet automated recognition is hindered by text orientation and semantic ambiguity. We propose a hybrid neuro-symbolic system combining RepViT-based computer vision with a **Case-Based Temporal Disambiguator (CBTD)**. The CBTD resolves ambiguities via a format-voting memory bank that dynamically adapts to localized structural layouts. Experimental results on real-world datasets demonstrate an end-to-end accuracy of 91.64%, while the CBTD reasoning engine achieves 100% logic accuracy. This approach confirms that grounding perceptual deep learning in a case-based reasoning framework provides a robust and explainable solution for assistive technology.

Keywords: Case-Based Reasoning · Visual impairment assistive technology · Computer vision · Temporal Disambiguation

1 Introduction

Access to expiration dates is a critical component of personal health and safety; yet, it remains a significant barrier to independence for individuals with visual impairments. These indicators are often printed in small, low-contrast fonts and placed inconsistently on packaging, making them nearly impossible to locate. Real-time recognition technology is vital in this context, as it allows users to scan products freely without needing to precisely align the camera. By instantly detecting dates regardless of their orientation or position, such systems empower visually impaired users to independently manage their nutrition and medication, thereby mitigating the health risks associated with consuming expired goods.

Recent advances in deep learning have enabled computer vision-based target detection, particularly using Convolutional Neural Networks (CNNs), to achieve promising results in practical, real-world applications. Seker et al. [11] presents a generalized end-to-end framework that detects and semantically understands expiration dates on product packages by identifying the day, month, and year components rather than only recognizing digits. It demonstrates robustness to

L. Malburg and K. Bach (Eds.): ICCBR 2026, LNAI 16780, pp. 577–589, 2027.
https://doi.org/10.1007/978-3-032-33865-5_35

real-world challenges—dot-matrix fonts, blur, reflections, skew, multiple dates per image, and varied backgrounds—and releases a new dataset (ExpDate) to support training and evaluation. Takeuchi et al. [13] present an expiration date recognition system designed for visually impaired users. The approach first detects the date region on a product package and then uses multiple Spatial Transformer Networks (STNs) to localize and rectify each digit before recognizing them with a CNN, thereby improving robustness to skew, misalignment, and partial occlusion. Peng et al. [9] present a lightweight, mobile-oriented OCR pipeline for recognizing and parsing expiration dates on product packages, with a focus on accessibility for visually impaired users. The system combines an FCOS-based date detector, a CRNN recognizer, and a date-time parser that supports 17 date formats, and it emphasizes model quantization and Android deployment for edge devices.

The methods above, though, achieve strong performance in detection and recognition; however, their ability to detect rotated images is limited. Consequently, research in arbitrary shape text detection is emerging. Liao et al. [8] introduce a real-time scene text detection method that combines Differentiable Binarization (DB) with an Adaptive Scale Fusion (ASF) module to improve detection accuracy and speed on natural images. The approach frames binarization as a learnable, differentiable operation inside a segmentation network, enabling end-to-end training and sharper text region boundaries for irregular text shapes. Zhu et al. [17] propose Fourier Contour Embedding (FCE) and an associated detector, FCENet, to represent and detect arbitrarily shaped scene text by modeling text contours in the Fourier domain rather than the image spatial domain. The method encodes each text contour as a compact Fourier signature vector and reconstructs contours via inverse Fourier transform, enabling accurate fitting of highly curved and irregular text shapes. Zhang et al. [16] introduce TESTR (Text Spotting Transformers), an end-to-end transformer-based framework that unifies detection and recognition for arbitrarily shaped scene text by using a single encoder and dual decoders: one for predicting control-point coordinates (polygons or Bezier curves) and one for predicting character sequences, thereby eliminating RoI operations and many heuristic postprocessing steps.

However, the aforementioned models are not lightweight, making edge deployment difficult. Furthermore, while these computer vision methods achieve strong performance in the perceptual extraction of characters, they operate completely divorced from semantic temporal reasoning. Once raw text is extracted, expiration dates present severe structural ambiguity (e.g., deciding whether "08 06 21" represents August 6th, June 8th, or the year 2021). Traditional static rule-based parsers fail to adapt to regional format variations, causing dangerous temporal hallucinations.

To bridge the gap between noisy visual perception and complex semantic reasoning, Case-Based Reasoning (CBR) offers a highly adaptable solution. Recent literature highlights the efficacy of CBR in handling noisy, real-world logic tasks. For instance, Li et al. [6] introduced a two-stage CBR framework that improves

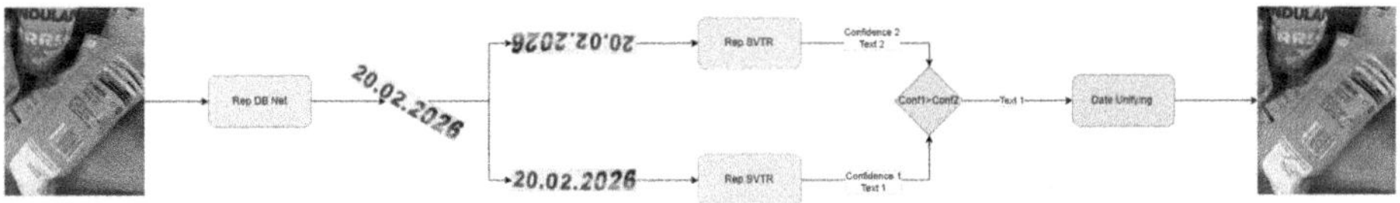

Fig. 1. General workflow of expiration date recognition.

financial distress prediction by mitigating the impact of label noise. Similarly, Guillotel et al. [3] demonstrated that case-based similarity approaches effectively identify eligible patients from noisy, real-world EHR data. Furthermore, Sun et al. [12] proposed a unified framework integrating CBR to automate complex end-to-end design logic.

Inspired by these reasoning architectures, this study proposes a hybrid neuro-symbolic pipeline. For the perception layer, we chose DBNet [7] equipped with a lightweight RepViT backbone to achieve fast, multi-oriented text detection. For character recognition, we utilize RepSVTR, an improved, lightweight variant of the SVTRv2 [2] model. Finally, the noisy textual output from this perception pipeline is passed into our novel Case-Based Temporal Disambiguator (CBTD), an experience-guided reasoning module designed to logically resolve the semantic ambiguity of the extracted date components.

The main contributions of this work are as follows:

1. We introduce the **Case-Based Temporal Disambiguator (CBTD)**, a hybrid reasoning engine that resolves ambiguous expiration dates. By combining symbolic regex generation with a format-voting CBR memory, it dynamically adapts to regional structures, overcoming the brittleness of static parsers.
2. We propose a specialized perception layer utilizing RepViT [14] as the backbone for DBNet and as the encoder for the SVTRv2 [2] recognition pipeline.
3. We demonstrate that this RepViT-driven architecture outperforms standard heavy and light baselines (ResNet [4] / MobileNetv4 [10]) in the Accuracy vs. Efficiency trade-off, enabling robust edge deployment.

2 Methodology

As illustrated in Fig. 1, the proposed workflow begins by localizing the expiration date on the food packaging. Using the detected four corner points, a perspective transformation is applied to rectify the region of interest (ROI) into a horizontal alignment. To address potential orientation ambiguity (i.e., if the text is inverted), the system generates a 180-degree rotated copy of the rectified image. Both the original and rotated candidates are fed into the recognition model simultaneously. The system then selects the output text associated with the higher confidence score. Finally, the raw text is passed to the Case-Based Temporal Disambiguator (CBTD) to logically interpret and standardize the semantically ambiguous date components.

2.1 Detection Network

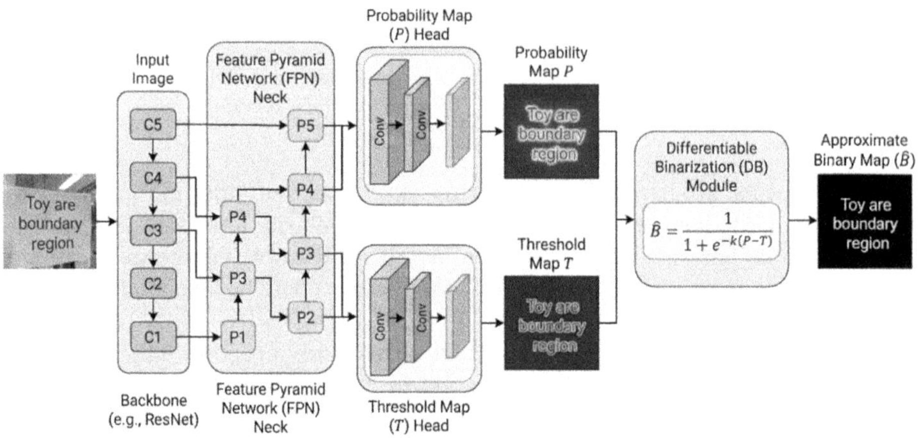

Fig. 2. Architecture of expiration date detection model.

Figure 2 shows that the proposed architecture adopts the DBNet framework [7], which consists of three primary components: a feature extraction backbone, a fusion neck, and a dual-head prediction mechanism. Usually, a ResNet-50 backbone [4] is employed to extract visual representations; the backbone is replaced with the RepViT [14] module in this work, which is subsequently enhanced by a Feature Pyramid Network (FPN) neck to ensure robustness across varying text scales.

The processed features are fed into two parallel convolutional branches: (1) the probability head, which predicts the segmentation map of text regions, and (2) the threshold head, which generates an adaptive threshold map. These two outputs are fused via a Differentiable Binarization (DB) function. This differentiable mechanism allows the network to dynamically optimize the binarization thresholds for each pixel during training, resulting in sharper boundaries and improved separation of closely spaced text instances.

The basic structure of Repvit is shown in Fig. 3. RepViT [14] is a lightweight convolutional neural network architecture designed to optimize the trade-off between inference latency and accuracy on mobile edge devices. It systematically integrates the topological efficiency of Structural Re-parameterization with the architectural design principles of Vision Transformers (ViTs) [1].

Unlike standard ViTs, which suffer from high memory access costs due to self-attention mechanisms, RepViT employs a pure convolutional structure that mimics the MetaFormer [15] token-mixing paradigm. The core innovation lies in the decoupling of training-time and inference-time architectures:

1. Training Phase (Multi-branch Topology): The network utilizes complex, multi-branch blocks (e.g., parallel convolution branches and identity shortcuts) to improve gradient flow and feature capture capabilities.

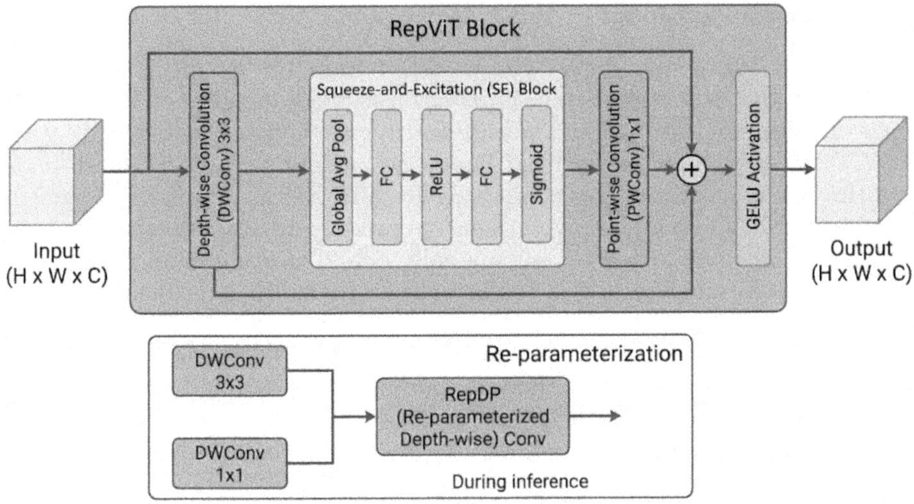

Fig. 3. RepViT module.

2. Inference Phase (Single-Branch Topology): Through structural reparameterization, these parallel branches are mathematically merged into single 3×3 convolutional kernels. This results in a streamlined, linear topology that significantly reduces memory access costs (MAC) and computational overhead without sacrificing the learned representational power.

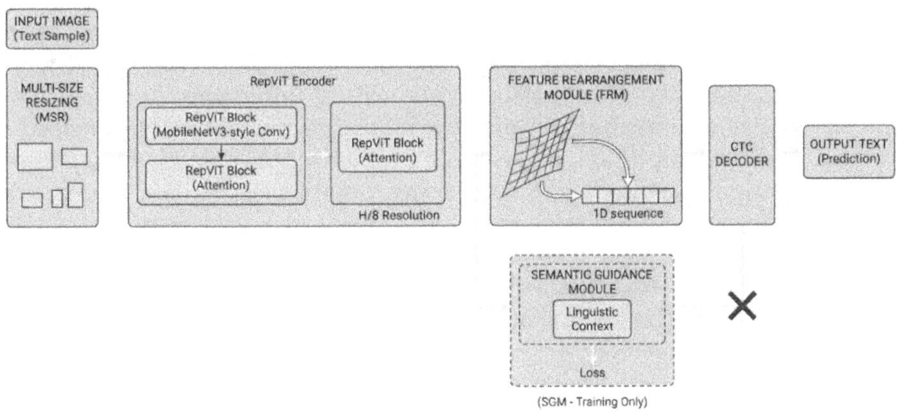

Fig. 4. The structure of RepSVTR model.

2.2 Recognition Model

As shown in Fig. 4, the RepSVTR, modified from the SVTRv2 [2], has an architecture that is a streamlined, pure-vision network designed to process text images in four efficient stages: The core feature extraction is performed by the RepViT Encoder. This hierarchical backbone processes the normalized visual data through sequential stages comprising RepViT Blocks, which hybridize efficient MobileNetV3-style [5] convolutional operations with attention mechanisms. The encoder outputs high-level, semantically rich 2D feature maps with spatial dimensions downsampled to H/8 resolution relative to the input height.

To facilitate sequence transcription, these 2D spatial features are forwarded to the Feature Rearrangement Module (FRM). The FRM transforms the spatially arranged features—potentially accounting for irregular text geometry—into a flattened, temporal 1D sequence. This sequence serves as the input to the CTC Decoder (Connectionist Temporal Classification), which performs parallel decoding to generate the final Output Text prediction.

Complementing the primary inference path is an auxiliary branch designated as the Semantic Guidance Module (SGM). Utilized exclusively during the training phase, the SGM accepts features from the encoder to model explicit linguistic context, generating an auxiliary loss signal for enhanced supervision. As indicated by the 'X' marker, this semantic branch is architecturally decoupled and inactive during the inference phase, maximizing speed.

2.3 Case-Based Temporal Disambiguator (CBTD)

While the perception layer extracts raw text (T_{raw}) from product packaging, expiration dates frequently suffer from severe structural ambiguity (e.g., "05.06" as May 6th or June 5th). To map perceptual text to semantic understanding, we introduce the Case-Based Temporal Disambiguator (CBTD), a hybrid neuro-symbolic engine governed by the traditional Case-Based Reasoning (CBR) cycle.

Retrieve (Candidate Generation): The CBTD normalizes T_{raw} to remove OCR artifacts and evaluates it against symbolic regex constraints. Instead of forcing a single interpretation, it generates a robust set of competing hypotheses. Each candidate is a tuple (d_i, t_i), comprising a mathematical date d_i restricted to a logical physical domain (e.g., years 2015–2035) and a structural format tag t_i (e.g., `YEAR_FIRST`).

Reuse (Ambiguity Resolution): When multiple unique dates D are generated, the CBTD relies on historical experience to resolve the ambiguity. It utilizes a dynamic case base memory M, which tracks the historical success rate of each structural tag t. The engine calculates a confidence score $S(d)$ for each candidate date:

$$S(d) = \sum_{t \in T_d} M(t)$$

The system outputs the candidate date d^* that maximizes this historical structural popularity, dynamically adapting to regional format preferences without rigid geographical logic.

Revise (Temporal Fallback): In scenarios where M is uninitialized or structural scores tie, the CBTD revises its decision using a temporal proximity heuristic. It selects the tie-breaking candidate by minimizing the absolute temporal distance to the current system date $d_{current}$:

$$d^* = \arg\min_{d \in D} |d - d_{current}|$$

Retain (Continuous Learning): Finally, the system retains the successful extraction to improve future disambiguation. The memory is updated by incrementing the weights of the winning tags: $M(t) \leftarrow M(t)+1$. To prevent permanent entrenchment in early biases—a standard practice in Case-Based Maintenance—a global exponential decay factor λ (e.g., 0.995) is applied to M before each parse. This allows the system to seamlessly unlearn older biases if the dataset transitions to new geographical distributions.

3 Datasets and Implementation Details

To systematically evaluate the performance of our proposed pipeline, we utilize the benchmarks established by Seker et al. [11]. These benchmarks are bifurcated into two distinct datasets, **Products** and **Date**, designed to assess the detection and recognition modules, respectively.

The **Products** dataset is used for the main task of detecting expiration date regions. To mitigate the limited availability of annotated bounding boxes in real-world settings, it leverages a *Sim-to-Real* transfer approach. The training split includes 12,000 synthetic images, enabling the model to acquire knowledge of varied spatial configurations from generated samples. In contrast, an additional collection consists of 1,102 real images for training and 510 real images for testing, providing a stringent evaluation of the model's robustness and generalization in noisy, real-world conditions.

For sequence recognition, we utilize the **Date** dataset. Unlike the detection benchmark, this dataset focuses on transcribing specific characters from localized regions and relies entirely on real-world data to capture genuine image degradations, such as blurriness and dot-matrix artifacts. It contains 1,102 real-world images for training and 510 real-world images for testing. Crucially, these 510 real-world test samples also serve as the validation set for the Case-Based Temporal Disambiguator (CBTD). By evaluating the CBTD on the text strings extracted from this unseen test set, we accurately measure its ability to logically resolve semantic ambiguity and dynamically adapt to local format layouts without prior data leakage.

3.1 Model Training Details

the models are trained using the pytorch framework in an environment with a single NVIDIA GeForce RTX 3090 with 24 GB of VRAM. the model configurations are described in Tab. 1

Table 1. Hyperparameter and Architecture Configuration for Detection and Recognition Models.

Category	Parameter	Detection	Recognition
Architecture	Backbone	RepViT	RepSVTREncoder
	Neck/Head	RSEFPN / DBHead ($k = 50$)	CTCDecoder (Dim: 256, Depth: 2)
Input and Data	Train Input Size	800×800 (Crop)	48×320 (Padding)
	Eval. Input Size	960×960 (Padding)	48×320 (Padding)
	Batch Size/GPU	24	256
	Augmentation	Flip, Rotate ($\pm 180°$), Resize	Shear, Rotate ($\pm 30°$), Trans.
	Dataset	Products	Date
Optimization	Epochs	100	100
	Optimizer	Adam	Adam
	Learning Rate	0.001	0.0001
	Weight Decay	5.0×10^{-5}	3.0×10^{-5}
	Scheduler	Cosine (2 ep. warmup)	Cosine (5 ep. warmup)
Loss	Type	DBLoss (Dice + BCE)	CTCLoss
	Precision	Mixed Precision (AMP)	Mixed Precision (AMP)
Post-Process	Method	DBPostProcess	CTCLabelDecode
	Thresholds	Binary: 0.6, Box: 0.7	Max Length: 25
	Output	Polygons (Unclip: 1.5)	Text String (Char dict v1)

4 Results

4.1 Detection Results

To evaluate the localization performance of the Detection Model, we utilize the standard DetMetric protocol, with H-mean serving as the primary indicator. This metric provides a balanced assessment of the model's ability to accurately and completely localize text regions.

The evaluation relies on three key components:

1. Precision (P): The proportion of predicted text regions that correctly match ground-truth polygons. It measures the model's ability to avoid false positives (detecting background as text).
2. Recall (R): The proportion of actual ground-truth text regions that are successfully detected by the model. It measures the model's ability to avoid false negatives (missing actual text).
3. H-mean (F-measure): The harmonic mean of Precision and Recall, offering a single score that penalizes the model if either accuracy or completeness is lacking. It is calculated as:

$$\text{H-mean} = 2 \times \frac{P \times R}{P + R}$$

From Table 2, the experimental results highlight a distinct trade-off between robustness and efficiency across the evaluated backbones. ResNet50 prioritizes recall and overall accuracy (H-mean 85.75%) but incurs a heavy computational penalty (81.5 GFLOPs). Conversely, MobileNetV4 [10] achieves the highest inference speed (80.83 FPS) and the smallest footprint; however, it suffers a substantial drop in robustness (H-mean 70.49%). RepViT effectively bridges this gap, delivering the highest precision (78.45%) and retaining competitive accuracy (H-mean 82.53%) while reducing model size by nearly 5× compared to ResNet50, identifying it as the optimal architecture for balanced performance.

Table 2. Comparative Analysis of Backbone Architectures for DBNet

Backbone	Precision	Recall	H-mean (F1)	Params M	Model Size (Pytorch)	FLOPs (GFLOPs)	FPS (CUDA)
RepViT	0.7845	0.8706	0.8253	4.932	19.25 MB	18.872	43.48
MobileNetV4	0.6338	0.7939	0.7049	**0.546**	**2.24 MB**	**4.391**	**80.83**
ResNet50	**0.7842**	**0.9458**	**0.8575**	24.026	91.98 MB	81.507	54.88

4.2 Recognition Results

To improve date interpretation, we have added all character types to the character dictionary, including symbols and spaces, for use in the recognition model.

Sequence Accuracy measures the percentage of samples for which the predicted text string matches the ground truth label exactly, character for character.

$$\text{Accuracy} = \frac{N_{\text{correct}}}{N_{\text{total}}} \times 100\%$$

Normalized Edit Distance measures how close the prediction is to the ground truth by quantifying the number of character-level errors (insertions, deletions, or substitutions) relative to the string length.

$$\text{Norm Edit} = 1 - \frac{D(S_{pred}, S_{gt})}{\max(\text{len}(S_{pred}), \text{len}(S_{gt}))}$$

where a higher value is preferable.

The recognition results of three different recognition models, as shown in Tab. 3, reveal a significant trade-off between transcription fidelity and computational throughput. SVTRv2 clearly delivers the highest accuracy, whereas CRNN offers the fastest inference speed on GPU. Thanks to CUDA acceleration, SVTRv2 attains higher FPS than RepSVTR, even though it uses more parameters and FLOPs.

Table 3. Comparative Analysis of Text Recognition Architectures

Model	Acc (%)	Norm Edit Dist	Params (M)	FLOPs (G)	FPS (CUDA)	FPS
RepSVTR	91.76	0.9865	**6.28**	1.25	17.10	
CRNN	84.12	0.9896	8.36	**0.91**	**2847.81**	
SVTRv2	**96.86**	**0.9954**	20.98	6.69	32.65	

Table 4. Baseline vs. Proposed CBTD Performance

Model	Overall Acc.	Ambiguity Acc.
Static Heuristic Baseline	90.20%	83.08%
Proposed CBTD (Voting)	**99.61%**	**100.00%**

4.3 Evaluation of the Case-Based Temporal Disambiguator (CBTD)

We conducted an ablation study comparing our format-voting CBTD against a static Baseline Parser (greedy regex and `dateutil` fallback). Accuracy was measured across **Overall** and **Ambiguity** (e.g., "05.06") metrics.

As shown in Table 4, the CBTD's experience-guided memory significantly outperforms the baseline, which drops to 83.08% on ambiguous formats. Qualitatively, the baseline suffers from "numerical condensation" (e.g., parsing "AUG 11 2021" as November 20th by stripping letters) and "temporal hallucinations," where standard libraries inject the system clock's current day into partial dates (e.g., "NOV 2021"). The CBTD mitigates these risks by isolating text-based structures and resolving partial dates via its case base rather than the system clock.

Despite achieving 100% accuracy on standard ambiguities, two "double-valid" symmetrical errors remained (e.g., "30|10|21" parsed as 2030 instead of 2021). In these cases, the CBR memory's aggressive adaptation to regional formats overrides imported anomalies. Furthermore, a "temporal fallback" error occurred on "21-02-28" due to insufficient memory initialization, resulting in a selection based on proximity to the current year. Resolving such symmetrical overlaps remains a future multimodal challenge.

4.4 End-to-End System Performance

The end-to-end performance of the proposed hybrid pipeline is evaluated on the test set established by Seker et al. [11]. For a prediction to be considered successful, the system must not only extract raw characters with high fidelity but also logically resolve them into a standardized semantic date format (e.g., transforming the extracted string "01/12/2025" into the unified ISO-style "2025-12-01"). Any failure in temporal reasoning or structural misinterpretation by the Case-Based Temporal Disambiguator (CBTD) is strictly penalized as false recognition.

Table 5. Comparative Analysis: Proposed Hybrid Pipeline vs. State-of-the-Art (SOTA)

Method	Orientation	Det. (%)	Rec. (%)	Throughput (img/s)
Seker et al. [11]	Horizontal Only	98.31	97.74	1.03
Ours (Hybrid)	**Full Angle**	82.53	91.76	0.75

Table 5 contextualizes our results against the current state-of-the-art. While Seker et al. report a higher end-to-end accuracy (97.74%), our pipeline operates under significantly more rigorous operational constraints. Specifically, our system evaluates images across a **360-degree rotation spectrum**, whereas the baseline is restricted to near-horizontal orientations. Furthermore, our perception-reasoning pipeline processes complex, noisy strings containing arbitrary symbols and varying separator logic, while the baseline is optimized for digit-only recognition.

Despite these challenges, the system achieves a robust end-to-end accuracy of 91.64%. Notably, the final semantic accuracy (91.64%) exceeds the initial detection H-mean (82.53%). This is attributed to our strategy of expanding detected bounding boxes by 5 pixels; while this expansion introduces additional background noise and "cropped" character artifacts, the CBTD reasoning engine effectively filters these inconsistencies by mapping extracted candidates to a dynamic memory of valid temporal structures.

Finally, Fig. 5 demonstrates the framework's visual robustness in assistive scenarios. The system successfully localizes and interprets expiration data under extreme physical conditions, including large tilts (Fig. 5a), complete upside-down inversions (Fig. 5b), and standard alignments (Fig. 5c).

(a) (b) (c)

Fig. 5. Visual comparison of detection results. The system robustly handles (a) large tilt, (b) upside-down orientation, and (c) near-horizontal alignment.

5 Conclusion

This work introduced a hybrid neuro-symbolic system for expiration-date recognition, specifically designed to assist individuals with visual impairments. By integrating a lightweight RepViT-driven perception layer with a novel **Case-Based Temporal Disambiguator (CBTD)**, we achieved a 91.64% end-to-end success rate across diverse layouts and unconstrained viewing angles. Our results demonstrate that while deep learning effectively extracts raw visual features, the inclusion of a case-based reasoning framework is essential for resolving the inherent semantic and structural ambiguities of temporal data. The CBTD's ability to achieve 100% logic accuracy on ambiguous candidates proves that an experience-guided memory bank can overcome the brittleness of static, rule-based parsers. This system provides a practical, robust, and explainable foundation for real-world assistive technology.

6 Future Work

Future research will focus on enhancing the Case-Based Reasoning module by incorporating multimodal cues, such as manufacturer logos or regional packaging styles, to resolve "double-valid" symmetrical date ambiguities. We also intend to expand the system's linguistic reach through multilingual support and cross-format generalization. Finally, we aim to implement a user-centered feedback loop where the CBR memory can be personalized to a specific user's common household products, further improving recognition speed and reliability in real-time edge deployment scenarios.

Acknowledgments. This work was partially supported by the Ministry of Science and Innovation (Grant no. PID2021-125596OB-I00 and PID2024-158638OB-I00) and the UCM-ONCE-Tiflotechnology Chair.

Code Availability. https://github.com/AnanasPizzaMigliore/Repvit-recognition

Declaration on Generative AI. During the preparation of this work, the author(s) used ChatGPT and Writefull in order to: Paraphrase and reword, improve writing style, and Grammar and spelling check. After using this tool/service, the author(s) reviewed and edited the content as needed and take(s) full responsibility for the publication's content.

References

1. Dosovitskiy, A.: An image is worth 16×16 words: transformers for image recognition at scale (2020). arXiv:2010.11929 arXiv preprint
2. Du, Y., Chen, Z., Xie, H., Jia, C., Jiang, Y.G.: SVTRV2: CTC beats encoder-decoder models in scene text recognition. In: Proceedings of the IEEE/CVF International Conference on Computer Vision, pp. 20147–20156 (2025)

3. Guillotel, L.A., Lesimple, T., Zekri, O., Cuggia, M., Campillo-Gimenez, B.: Case-based reasoning for clinical trial recruitment tools in oncology: when you need patients to find patients. Int. J. Med. Info., 106301 (2026)
4. He, K., Zhang, X., Ren, S., Sun, J.: Deep residual learning for image recognition. In: Proceedings of the IEEE Conference on Computer Vision and Pattern Recognition, pp. 770–778 (2016)
5. Koonce, B.: MobileNetV3. In: Convolutional Neural Networks with Swift for TensorFlow: Image Recognition and Dataset Categorization, pp. 125–144. Springer (2021)
6. Li, M., Yu, L., Liu, C.: A case-based reasoning-driven clustering imputation and noise-resistant classification learning paradigm for financial distress prediction with missing and noisy data. Eng. Appl. Artif. Intell. **167**, 113955 (2026)
7. Liao, M., Wan, Z., Yao, C., Chen, K., Bai, X.: Real-time scene text detection with differentiable binarization. In: Proceedings of the AAAI Conference on Artificial Intelligence, vol. 34, pp. 11474–11481 (2020)
8. Liao, M., Zou, Z., Wan, Z., Yao, C., Bai, X.: Real-time scene text detection with differentiable binarization and adaptive scale fusion. IEEE Trans. Pattern Anal. Mach. Intell. **45**(1), 919–931 (2022)
9. Peng, H., Bayon, J., Recas, J., Guijarro, M.: Efficient expiration date recognition in food packages for mobile applications. Algorithms **18**(5), 286 (2025)
10. Qin, D., et al.: MobileNetV4: universal models for the mobile ecosystem. In: European Conference on Computer Vision, pp. 78–96. Springer (2024)
11. Seker, A.C., Ahn, S.C.: A generalized framework for recognition of expiration dates on product packages using fully convolutional networks. Expert Syst. Appl. **203**, 117310 (2022)
12. Sun, T., Wang, B., Huo, X.: Knowledge-driven automated design of industrial robots: a unified graph-based framework with multi-engine reasoning. Adv. Eng. Inform. **69**, 103995 (2026)
13. Takeuchi, Y., Suzuki, K.: Expiration date recognition system using spatial transformer network for visually impaired. In: International Conference on Computers Helping People with Special Needs, pp. 517–524. Springer (2024)
14. Wang, A., Chen, H., Lin, Z., Han, J., Ding, G.: RepViT: revisiting mobile CNN from vit perspective. In: Proceedings of the IEEE/CVF Conference on Computer Vision and Pattern Recognition, pp. 15909–15920 (2024)
15. Yu, W., et al.: Metaformer is actually what you need for vision. In: Proceedings of the IEEE/CVF Conference on Computer Vision and Pattern Recognition, pp. 10819–10829 (2022)
16. Zhang, X., Su, Y., Tripathi, S., Tu, Z.: Text spotting transformers. In: Proceedings of the IEEE/CVF Conference on Computer Vision and Pattern Recognition, pp. 9519–9528 (2022)
17. Zhu, Y., Chen, J., Liang, L., Kuang, Z., Jin, L., Zhang, W.: Fourier contour embedding for arbitrary-shaped text detection. In: Proceedings of the IEEE/CVF Conference on Computer Vision and Pattern Recognition, pp. 3123–3131 (2021)

Challenges and Support Potentials in the Development of Case-Based Reasoning Applications

Lisa Grewenig[1], Christian Zeyen[1(✉)], Alexander Schultheis[1,2], Lukas Malburg[1,2], and Ralph Bergmann[1,2]

[1] German Research Center for Artificial Intelligence (DFKI), Branch Trier, Behringstraße 21, 54296 Trier, Germany
{Lisa.Grewenig,Christian.Zeyen,Alexander.Schultheis, Lukas.Malburg,Ralph.Bergmann}@dfki.de

[2] Artificial Intelligence and Intelligent Information Systems, Trier University, 54296 Trier, Germany
https://www.wi2.uni-trier.de

Abstract. Developing *Case-Based Reasoning* (CBR) applications is a knowledge-intensive task that consists of numerous demanding and time-consuming development steps. Major challenges are posed by knowledge engineering since CBR systems depend on capturing, validating, and maintaining domain knowledge in an explicit, machine-interpretable form. This usually can be done only in a close interdisciplinary collaboration between CBR and domain experts. To support development, previous works put forth a broad spectrum of support functions but mostly have not yet addressed the synergies of support functions or the potentials for involving domain experts, particularly those without knowledge-engineering experience. To further improve the accessibility of CBR frameworks and to reduce the effort of development, this paper consolidates development challenges along with corresponding support methods. In addition, we address the potentials for involving domain experts in the development with the help of support functions. We derived development challenges and support potentials from literature and conducted an explorative survey in the CBR research community.

Keywords: Case-Based Reasoning · CBR Applications · Knowledge Engineering · Domain Experts · Development Support

1 Introduction

Developing CBR applications requires both knowledge engineering and specific CBR-related development steps. Regarding knowledge engineering, one has to elaborate, populate, validate, and maintain the so-called knowledge containers [31], i.e., vocabulary, case base, similarity model, and adaptation knowledge. CBR-related development steps comprise application- and domain-dependent

L. Malburg and K. Bach (Eds.): ICCBR 2026, LNAI 16780, pp. 590–607, 2027.
https://doi.org/10.1007/978-3-032-33865-5_36

design decisions and their implementation to ensure effective and efficient knowledge acquisition, user interfaces, retrieval, adaptation, maintenance, and deployment. Domain experts play a key role in the development process but are usually inexperienced in knowledge engineering. Ideally, they can express their knowledge like knowledge engineers in terms of formal attributes, categories, and relationships rather than narrative descriptions or holistic judgments. With the rapid development of *Generative AI* (GenAI) methods and, particularly *Large Language Models* (LLMs), new support potentials for various aspects such as knowledge acquisition, maintainability, and explainability are opening up [6]. The CBR research community regularly presents new approaches to support the development of CBR applications. These efforts are also reflected in the ongoing development of CBR frameworks [36]. However, related works have not yet addressed the synergies of support functions and potentials for involving domain experts.

The objective of this paper is to form a basis to further improve the accessibility of CBR frameworks or specific applications and to reduce the effort and, consequently, the costs for development in future work. To this end, we investigate the challenges of typically required development steps along with the potentials for support methods.

The contribution of this work is (1) a literature-based synthesis of existing support for development steps in CBR, (2) a survey-based assessment of CBR experts on involvement and support of domain experts regarding the identified development steps, and (3) a synthesis of challenges in each development step along with potentials for support methods.

In the remainder of this paper, related work on existing support for developing CBR applications is presented in Sect. 2. Section 3 presents the results of an explorative survey conducted in the CBR research community with a focus on involving domain experts. Section 4 describes the derived challenges and support potentials for each identified development step. Finally, Sect. 5 summarizes the main findings, limitations, and proposes future work.

2 Existing Support for Developing CBR Applications

This section investigates related work along the development steps that we derived from CBR literature. Figure 1 illustrates how the development steps can be mapped to the traditional CBR model, i.e., knowledge containers [31] and CBR cycle [1].

Please note that the steps are organized in an ideal-typical sequence. In practice, it can happen that steps are skipped or that there are iterations. In complement to this work, the INRECA methodology [9] has been proposed to provide practical guidelines from collected CBR development experiences, represented as software process models. In [36], we provided an overview[1] of the features of existing CBR frameworks.

[1] Please refer to https://git.opendfki.de/easy/overview-and-comparison-of-cbr-frameworks/-/raw/main/Overview-Table.pdf for an overview table (from 2023).

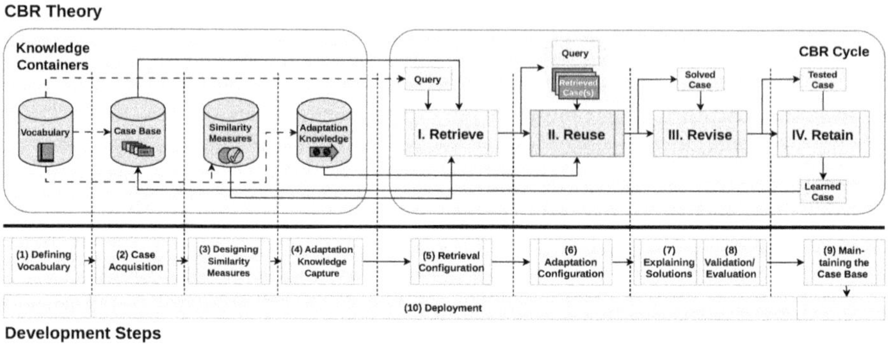

Fig. 1. Mapping of Elements of the CBR Model to Development Steps.

Defining Vocabulary is supported in the myCBR framework through interactive knowledge modeling. It also provides extensions such as integrating linked open data for taxonomy construction [4,36,40]. The ProCAKE framework provides a GUI-based object editor for system and custom data classes and automatic derivation of data models from input data [10,36].

Case Acquisition is supported by ProCAKE through visual case editing for structural and process-oriented cases and automated imports from CSV and JSON [10,36]. myCBR also supports importing content from unstructured documents into an existing vocabulary [4]. The proposed competence modeling method makes coverage and competence regions visible to guide case acquisition and support maintainers in targeting under-covered regions [39].

Designing Similarity Measures is frequently addressed by related work with a focus on the design, tuning, and explanation of similarity measures. myCBR supports interactive similarity modeling and testing through a workbench with integrated execution support and immediate feedback [36,40]. Bach and Mork [3] provide visualizations of global similarity and local contributions. Marín-Veites and Bach [24] add ranking summaries and per-case-pair views with global similarity, local similarities, and weighted contributions. For process-oriented CBR, visualization-based similarity explanations provide mapping-oriented graph views and heatmaps [37]. Building on this, point-mapping methods are investigated as visualization techniques for similarities in temporal CBR [34]. The tool SimViz provides coordinated views for case comparison and similarity distributions, including taxonomy-based inspection for semantic similarities, and supports identifying modeling errors and data quality issues [17,18]. A combination of SimViz with the CBR framework CBRkit [21] supports iterative similarity design with immediate feedback, partial interactive reconfiguration, and recomputation-based inspection, and explicitly targets CBR designers rather than end users [19].

Adaptation Knowledge Capture is less supported by existing CBR frameworks [36]. Frameworks mainly provide implementations of adaptation mechanisms. myCBR 3 supports rule-based completion and adaptation through integration with a rule engine [2]. Several approaches for learning adaptation knowledge exist in research (e.g., [12,13]), but no concrete support function for accessibility of such approaches is provided. ProCAKE includes an integrated rule engine that enhances the representation, maintainability, and runtime behavior of adaptation rules [23].

Retrieval Configuration is supported by workflow-oriented tooling regarding retrieval strategy configuration and evaluation through guided steps and visual inspection, including scatter plots and clustering [15].

Adaptation Configuration is also less supported by existing CBR frameworks [36]. To optimize adaptation chains, Hotz et al. [16] investigate search algorithms for determining optimal sequences in rule-based adaptation.

Explaining Solutions is an important aspect of *Explainable CBR* (XCBR) where dedicated tools support transparency and communication [35]. The similarity visualizations described above can also be used for user explanation. The myCBR tool provides explanation support for understanding retrieval outcomes during development, and myCBR reports provenance information in concept explanations [2,7]. For end-user-facing explanation in the medical domain, Lamy et al. propose a visual CBR interface combining a polar multidimensional scaling scatter plot with rainbow boxes [20].

Validation and Evaluation is supported by the eXiT*CBR framework through an executable environment with a GUI for navigating experiments and comparing alternative configurations through visual analytics such as receiver operating characteristic curves and cost curves [22]. It also supports experiment replication by managing and backing up experiment artifacts. Workflow-oriented tooling further supports retrieval strategy configuration and evaluation through guided steps and visual inspection [15].

Maintaining Knowledge is supported by eXiT*CBR through human approval workflows for adding cases and instance selection techniques for pruning [22]. The framework CloodCBR supports retain-side functions such as forgetting cases and recomputing similarities [36]. The tool SimViz supports maintenance-oriented inspection [17,18]. Competence modeling makes coverage and competence regions visible to guide case acquisition and maintenance decisions [39]. Interactive visualization supports redundancy and outlier detection and makes case base evolution transparent [25].

Deployment is supported by the CloodCBR framework, which exposes CBR functionality through a microservice-oriented REST architecture [26,36]. myCBR provides a REST interface for modeling and runtime functionality [5]. ProCAKE exposes its functionality via REST and provides a Docker-based setup, facilitating its use as a service in external applications. CBRkit supports embedding and deployment through a REST interface, a command-line interface, and a Docker image [21].

General Support Functions span multiple development steps. Frameworks typically provide support by dedicated GUI, API, and deployment-oriented infrastructure [36]. jColibri provides guided configuration and generation, including interactive testing of partially configured systems and generation of deployable applications such as standalone CBR systems and web interfaces [14,36]. Within the COLIBRI ecosystem, system design itself is treated as a CBR problem by retrieving and recommending templates based on project requirements [27]. Semantic templates add a graphical template editor, multi-level template libraries, and semantic annotations to compute template similarity and guide adaptation under dependency constraints [28]. COLIBRI Studio stores architectures as templates, tries them as executable implementations, and adapts them through component selection [30,33]. The COLIBRI Open Platform adds publishing support and a central repository for data, executable systems, and experimental protocols, thereby strengthening reuse and reproducibility of complete designs [29]. myCBR further supports rapid prototyping and provides practical modeling guidance and documented workflows in accompanying documentation rather than tool functionality [4,40]. CloodCBR adds dashboard-based inspection and transparency, including parallel plots for reviewing outcomes and supporting revision through interactive analysis [26].

3 Explorative Survey in the CBR Research Community

To ensure that important development steps and support methods are not missed and to gather practical insights from the CBR research community regarding the involvement of domain experts, we conducted an explorative survey [42].

Setup - In three internal workshops of the authors, the goal and purpose of the survey have been determined, and we iteratively refined the set of questions, items, and measurement scales. The survey consists of seven questions, which are divided into four categories: (1) Background of the participant, (2) rating of the difficulty of development steps for domain experts, (3) rating of the utility of support functions for domain experts, and (4) the experience of the participant in developing CBR applications in collaboration with domain experts. The development steps and support functions have been derived from the literature, complemented with our experience in developing CBR applications. We used the mailing list of the *International Conference on Case-Based Reasoning* (ICCBR) to invite all subscribers to participate in our survey. The survey ran for two weeks in Q1 2026 and we received 22 responses. In the following, we summarize the results.

(1) Background of the Participants - Figure 2 depicts the profile of survey participants. The survey mainly reflects the viewpoints of academic researchers (16 out of 22). Most responses came from people with more than three years of experience with CBR (16 out of 22) and most people have practical experience in developing CBR applications together with domain experts in the past (15 out of 22).

(2) Rating of the Difficulty of Development Steps for Domain Experts - In this category, we asked participants to rate the difficulty of development steps for domain experts without knowledge engineering experience on a 5-point Likert scale (1 – not difficult to 5 – extremely difficult). Participants also had

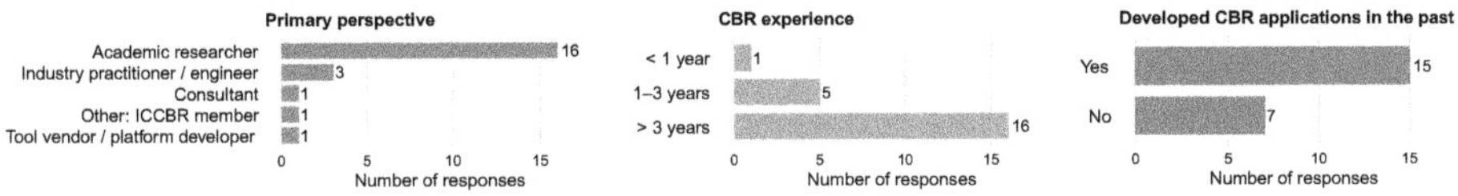

Fig. 2. Profile of Survey Participants.

the option to name one additional development step along with a rating. The phrasing of the question and development steps, along with the participants ratings, are depicted in Fig. 3.

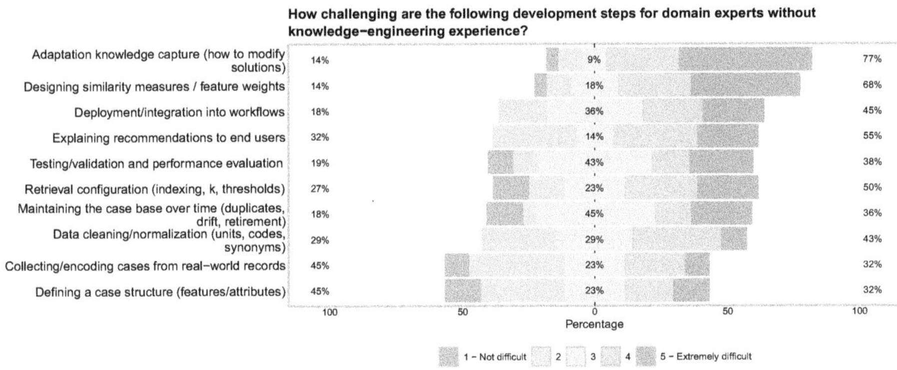

Fig. 3. Difficulty Rating of Development Steps.

The diagram shows aggregated percentages for positive, neutral, and negative assessments. The items are sorted by the average Likert scores in descending order. The steps *capturing adaptation knowledge* and *designing similarity measures* stand out with an assessment of mostly being extremely difficult. Regarding the other end of the scale, the picture is not so clear. There is a tendency that *defining case structures* and *collecting cases* are rather rated as less or not difficult. There is not a single task that was not rated as extremely difficult by at least one participant. Other development steps along with a difficulty rating (in parentheses if available) specified by the participants are *fixing incompatibilities in the knowledge base* (4), *unit testing* (3), *training domain experts* (-), *deployment and support in an industrial context* (4), *licensing* (5), and *building a deep learning CBR* (5).

(3) Rating of the Utility of Support Functions for Domain Experts - In this category, we asked participants to rate the utility of support functions for domain experts on a 5-point Likert scale (1 - not useful to 5 - extremely useful). Participants also had the option to name one additional support function along with a rating. The phrasing of the question and support functions, along with the participants ratings, are depicted in Fig. 4 analogous to the previous diagram.

One can see that there is a tendency for participants to rate all features towards (extremely) useful.

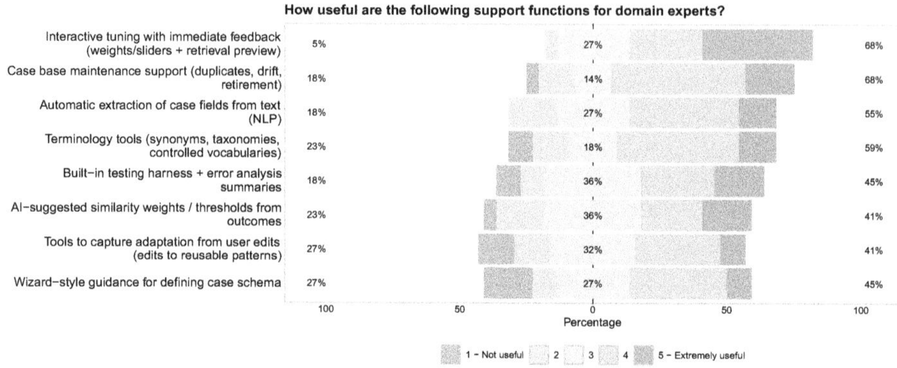

Fig. 4. Utility Rating of Support Functions.

The support by *interactive tuning with immediate feedback* stands out as being considered the most useful. Other support functions along with a utility rating specified by the participants are *automatic vocabulary extraction* (3) and *AI-based generation of an initial complete CBR application based on a data set and a given objective in natural language* (5).

(4) Experience of the Participants in Developing CBR Applications in Collaboration with Domain Experts - In this category, 15 out of 22 participants stated that they have such development experience. In this case, we asked follow-up questions concerning the used CBR tools, role of the domain experts, and the most challenging aspects of the collaboration. Participants stated that they used open-source CBR frameworks (six different frameworks in total), proprietary implementations, and their implementations. The most commonly mentioned roles of domain experts are *providing data and knowledge* (11 mentions), *modeling knowledge* (3 mentions), and *testing and evaluation* (5 mentions). The most challenging aspects of working with domain experts with at least two mentions are *finding a common vocabulary* (6 mentions) and *explaining the CBR paradigm and similarity* (3 mentions). It is noticeable that although the survey participants rated defining a case structure and collecting/encoding cases as least difficult for domain experts, it is mentioned as most challenging to find a common vocabulary when collaborating. The participants rated similarity modeling as the second most difficult challenge for domain experts, which is in line with the mentioned aspect that they need to understand the notion of similarity.

4 Development Challenges and Support Potentials

After analyzing the existing support functions proposed by related work and the practical insights gained through the survey results, we refined the development challenges and conceptualized corresponding support potentials. In the following section, we describe them for each development step.

4.1 Defining Vocabulary

A central challenge in the development of a CBR system is defining an appropriate case structure and vocabulary to describe cases [31]. This task requires experts to translate often tacit and experience-based domain knowledge into an explicit, structured representation that can be processed by a CBR system. In practice, this involves determining which attributes are relevant for describing a case, deciding on appropriate levels of abstraction, defining data types and value ranges, and ensuring that the resulting structure captures the aspects of a problem that are important for similarity assessment and retrieval. This step requires a combination of domain expertise and knowledge engineering skills. Consequently, this step typically requires interdisciplinary collaboration.

Schema Definition can be supported by analyzing existing data sources (e.g., CSV, JSON, Excel, databases, or unstructured text) representing past problem–solution situations and suggesting candidate attributes together with inferred data types, value ranges, units, and default values. E.g., automatic vocabulary extraction can help identifying relevant terms and relationships as a basis for further processing with terminology tools. Complementary acquisition interfaces, such as structured input forms, data import tools, or guided interview prompts (e.g., chatbots), can help transform real-world examples into well-formed cases while simultaneously refining the underlying case schema.

Terminology Management can support consistent use of domain terms when defining attributes and values, e.g., with visual editors. Such tools may provide mechanisms for managing synonyms, aliases, taxonomies, and controlled vocabularies [2], while automatic normalization harmonizes heterogeneous value representations (e.g., units or codes).

Consistency Checking - To reduce modeling errors, maintaining vocabulary and case structure as a single source of truth can ensure consistency across the case base and related knowledge artifacts. Changes made to the case schema should therefore be propagated automatically to other knowledge containers. This can be supported with visual editors that show the relationships between knowledge artifacts.

4.2 Case Acquisition

Case acquisition relies on past problem–solution situations that are typically contained in historical data sources or exist as implicit experiential knowledge. However, such experiences are rarely available as ready-to-use cases and must instead be constructed from recorded information. Consequently, relevant information about problems, decisions, and outcomes is often embedded in narrative descriptions or distributed across multiple records. Identifying suitable cases therefore requires collecting and interpreting these records and transforming them according to the defined case structure into explicit cases.

Semi-Automatic Case Extraction can assist in identifying candidate cases within existing data. By detecting recurring problem–solution patterns or suggesting potential cases from historical data, these tools can reduce manual effort while keeping domain experts involved in validating and refining the extracted cases. Natural language processing (NLP) techniques can further support this process by automatically extracting relevant case fields from unstructured text and mapping them to elements of the case representation.

Interactive Case Acquisition – Adaptive input forms or conversational interfaces (e.g., chatbots) can support users in capturing problem situations and solutions while dynamically adapting inputs based on the case schema and previously entered information. Such environments can ensure that newly created cases conform to the defined structure [10] and can reveal gaps or inconsistencies in the schema or vocabulary, linking acquisition with data analysis in 4.1. In addition, elements of case base maintenance (see Sect. 4.9) can already be incorporated during acquisition by enforcing quality constraints, for example, by preventing the inclusion of incomplete or inconsistent cases.

Case Base Exploration – Visualization and analysis techniques can support case acquisition by enabling users to explore and interpret existing cases while assessing the coverage of the problem space. Adaptive visualizations based on the case schema can support clustering or filtering of cases according to user-defined criteria, helping users identify patterns and relationships. Complementary analysis methods, such as competence- or coverage-based approaches, can reveal underrepresented regions and boundary areas where additional cases are needed [39]. Based on these insights, systems can guide domain experts to contribute counterexamples or boundary cases that capture rare but critical scenarios, which is particularly important in safety-critical domains.

Support for case base maintenance may already be integrated into the acquisition process to ensure that newly created cases satisfy basic quality criteria and do not introduce avoidable inconsistencies or redundancies.

4.3 Designing Similarity Measures

Similarity assessment is central to CBR, as retrieval relies on identifying cases that are most similar to a given problem [1]. However, defining similarity is often non-trivial because the relative importance of different attributes may vary across domains and contexts [31]. Domain experts typically possess intuitive knowledge about which aspects of a case are more relevant for comparison, but translating this knowledge into formal similarity functions and numerical weights requires knowledge engineering expertise. Furthermore, different attribute types may require different similarity models, such as numerical distance functions, symbolic comparisons, or taxonomy-based similarities [8]. Poorly designed similarity measures or inappropriate feature weights can significantly affect retrieval results and reduce the usefulness of the CBR system [39].

Configuration Recommendation can assist in configuring similarity models by suggesting both appropriate similarity functions and parameter settings, such as feature weights or thresholds. Based on attribute types (e.g., numeric, symbolic, hierarchical), such assistants can guide domain experts in selecting suitable similarity functions while also proposing reasonable default configurations. Machine learning or optimization techniques can further refine these suggestions by analyzing historical cases and retrieval outcomes to improve retrieval performance. In addition, such tools can highlight potential modeling issues and provide transparent explanations to help users understand and validate the proposed similarity model.

Interactive Similarity Tuning – Graphical editors can enable users to adjust feature weights and select similarity functions for individual attributes through sliders or parameter controls. Immediate previews of retrieval results allow users to observe how configuration changes affect case ranking. Such interactive feedback supports what-if analyses by showing how retrieval outcomes change when feature values or weights are modified, allowing experts to explore the sensitivity of the similarity model and identify attributes that dominate or have little influence on retrieval results (see Sect. 2).

Efficiency and Scalability Analysis – As similarity computations directly influence retrieval performance, tools can support domain experts in assessing the computational efficiency of similarity models. This may include estimating computational costs, identifying expensive similarity functions, or recommending optimized configurations that balance retrieval quality and runtime performance.

4.4 Adaptation Knowledge Capture

Adaptation knowledge denotes the knowledge required to transform the solution of a retrieved case into one that fits a new problem [1,31]. Although CBR frameworks may provide technical adaptation mechanisms [2,36], the underlying adaptation knowledge is usually not available explicitly. Instead, it has to be elicited from domain experts, formalized, and configured for use in the system. As a result, the acquisition and validation of adaptation knowledge typically require substantial effort.

Adaptation Capture – One promising support potential is the capture of adaptation knowledge from user edits. In such a setting, domain experts can modify proposed solutions directly, while the system records these changes and generalizes recurring edits into reusable adaptation patterns or candidate rules. Similarly, adaptation knowledge may be learned from pairs of original and adapted cases, reducing the effort of making such knowledge explicit. Machine learning methods can further support this process by identifying regularities across repeated corrections [13].

Visual Editing - Visual adaptation knowledge interfaces can lower the barrier for specifying rules, operators, or constraints by providing intuitive authoring environments instead of purely symbolic representations. Such environments may also support the structured validation and refinement of adaptation knowledge in an interdisciplinary and collaborative fashion.

4.5 Retrieval Configuration

Retrieval determines which cases are considered relevant for a given problem specification and therefore directly influences the quality of the proposed solutions [1]. It may be challenging for users to translate a current problem into a formal query according to the defined case structure. Thus, it is important to provide suitable query interfaces. Designing an effective retrieval configuration involves selecting appropriate retrieval strategies, defining indexing structures, and tuning parameters such as the number of retrieved k-nearest neighbors, similarity thresholds, or ranking mechanisms. These decisions depend on domain-specific similarity notions, case base characteristics, and task-specific retrieval requirements. Poorly configured retrieval mechanisms may lead to irrelevant cases being retrieved or useful cases being overlooked.

Visual Retrieval Pipeline Configuration – Dedicated configuration tools can support designers in defining the retrieval workflow as a sequence of retrieval and filtering steps [21]. A graphical retrieval pipeline creator can allow users to compose and configure stages such as candidate selection, similarity-based ranking, and post-filtering. Such tools help make the retrieval process explicit and easier to adjust, especially in systems with multi-stage retrieval strategies. Furthermore, such a pipeline should also include a feature for editing the query—based on the methods of *Interactive Case Acquisition*—which also allows for configurations related to retrieval.

Indexing Support – As case bases grow, efficient indexing becomes increasingly important for maintaining acceptable retrieval performance. Tools can automatically suggest suitable indexing strategies or partitions based on key attributes or data distributions. Such assistance can help balance retrieval accuracy and efficiency without requiring deep expertise in indexing techniques.

Parameter Recommendation can assist in selecting appropriate retrieval parameters, such as the number of retrieved cases (k) or similarity thresholds. By providing default values, parameter suggestions, or feedback based on retrieval behavior, such mechanisms can help iteratively refine the retrieval configuration.

4.6 Adaptation Configuration

The Reuse step focuses on applying adaptation knowledge to tailor solutions. The configuration can be challenging, for example, when multiple adaptation steps need to be chained together and a (runtime) optimized sequence is required.

Visual Adaptation Pipeline Configuration – Support can also be provided during the practical application of adaptation knowledge. Interactive adaptation environments may suggest similar adaptation steps, potentially in a case-based manner, from which users can select, revise, or refine appropriate actions. Such environments may also support chained adaptations by suggesting and managing sequences of dependent adaptation steps. In addition, LLMs may support the formulation, proposal, or explanation of adaptation steps.

4.7 Explaining Solutions

Explaining solutions is relevant within the Revise phase, where users need to assess, understand, and potentially modify the proposed solution. The difficulty lies both in explaining why a particular case is considered similar to the query case and in explaining how the final proposed solution emerged from the retrieved case and its adaptation [3,24,37].

Retrieval Explanation describes why a particular case is considered similar to the query. Support functions include visualizations of global similarity, local attribute contributions, and ranking behavior, which make the influence of individual features and weights more transparent [3,17,24,37]. In addition, interactive exploration with side-by-side comparisons of past retrieval results can further support understanding.

Adaptation Explanation complements similarity explanation and describes how the final solution emerged from the retrieved case. Adaptation trace explanations and side-by-side comparisons of the query, retrieved case, and adapted solution can help users understand which parts were reused, modified, or newly introduced. Natural-language explanations, potentially supported by LLMs, may further help communicate adaptation decisions in a more understandable way.

4.8 Validation and Evaluation

This step is part of the Revise phase, where the proposed and, if applicable, adapted solution has to be assessed regarding its usefulness for the target problem. Depending on the application, this may require real-world testing, expert assessment, user feedback, or simulation-based evaluation. The challenge is highly domain-dependent, since suitable evaluation criteria vary with the task and the extent to which outcomes can be observed directly. It is also often difficult to distinguish between weaknesses in retrieval and weaknesses in adaptation.

Evaluation Environments enable testing of proposed or adapted solutions under controlled conditions before being applied in practice. This may include simulation sandboxes, replay settings, or other domain-specific test environments.

Feedback Capture supports a structured feedback process. Interactive interfaces can guide domain experts in assessing the usefulness of proposed solutions based on ratings, qualitative feedback, and domain-specific criteria.

Evaluation Analysis supports a systematic interpretation of evaluation results. This may include performance metrics, comparisons of alternative configurations, and error analyses that distinguish between weaknesses in retrieval and weaknesses in adaptation. This may also include (technical) malfunctions, which are subject to testing.

4.9 Maintaining Knowledge

This step can be performed in the Retain phase to ensure the long-term efficiency and effectiveness of the case base. In practice, maintenance has to address duplicates, near-duplicates, obsolete or invalid cases, and domain drift, i.e., changes in the application context that make previously useful cases less representative over time [11,41]. At the same time, reducing the case base should not lead to a loss of competence. In addition to the case base, all knowledge containers are subject to maintenance activities and their close interdependencies have to be considered and coordinated [32].

Continuous Case Base Inspection supports identifying problematic or maintenance relevant cases. This includes the detection of duplicates, near-duplicates, outliers, obsolete cases, and possible signs of domain drift [18,25]. Such support can help domain experts review the current state of the case base more systematically and identify cases that may require further attention.

Remembering to Forget Analysis goes beyond general inspection and supports deciding which cases should be removed, merged, or retained without unnecessarily reducing the competence of the case base. Such support can build on competence-oriented analyses, e.g., by considering coverage or the contribution of individual cases to future problem solving, and can provide recommendations for competence-preserving deletion or consolidation decisions [8,38].

Maintenance Dashboards complementarily support the accessibility of inspection results and maintenance recommendations. Such dashboards can highlight likely deletion, merge, or retention candidates with explanations and thereby support informed maintenance decisions. In addition, they can visualize dependencies between knowledge containers, helping users identify required updates in related components and avoid inconsistencies across the overall knowledge base.

4.10 Deployment

The difficulty of this step does not only lie in making a CBR system technically available but also in integrating it into the software context. This may require integrating CBR functionality with existing process steps, user roles, data flows, and surrounding software systems, as well as onboarding and supporting users.

Interface Generation - To provide easy access to the functions of the CBR system, interfaces and reusable connectors can be provided, e.g., based on REST or MCP, as well as support for common data exchange formats [5,21,26].

Onboarding and Runtime Support supports the introduction and practical use of a CBR system in its target context. This includes onboarding materials such as documentation, tutorials, or explanatory videos that help users understand the workflow of the application and the principles of CBR. Conversational support, potentially based on LLMs, may complement such functionality by providing application-specific assistance across the broader software environment. During runtime, it may further assist users by explaining system functions, clarifying process steps, and guiding them through typical usage situations.

4.11 General Support Functions

Beyond support functions tailored to individual development steps, our analysis revealed several mechanisms that provide benefits across all challenges.

Implementation Recommendation provides guidance for selecting a suitable technological basis for a given application scenario. This includes choosing appropriate frameworks [36] and considering aspects such as extensibility, deployment options, integration requirements, and licensing constraints.

Guided Modeling Support in the form of wizard-style guidance can provide step-by-step assistance across multiple stages of the CBR development process, addressing all previously introduced challenges. Such guidance can be realized through intuitive, low-code graphical interfaces that reduce technical complexity (see e.g., jColibri [14], myCBR [40], eXiT [22], CloodCBR [26]) and enable domain experts to actively participate in system development. Error-tolerant interaction design, including validation and immediate feedback, can help prevent modeling errors and support incremental refinement. Interactive or conversational components, such as chatbot-like interfaces, can further facilitate knowledge elicitation and user engagement.

Template-Based System Design can support the development of CBR systems by enabling the reuse of previously defined system designs across multiple stages of the development process. Instead of constructing models from scratch, designers can retrieve and adapt existing templates that capture case structures, similarity models, or retrieval strategies [15], effectively treating system design itself as a case-based reasoning task. The COLIBRI ecosystem exemplifies this approach by providing reusable and adaptable CBR system templates that can be selected and refined based on project requirements [27,28,30,33]. This idea can be further extended by intelligent assistants that generate initial CBR system configurations from data and high-level user objectives, for example expressed in natural language, as proposed in our survey by a participant.

5 Conclusion, Limitations, and Future Work

In this paper, we investigated the development challenges for CBR applications with corresponding support potentials. We explored the current landscape of support functions and elicited practical insights from the literature and the CBR community on involving domain experts in the development. To summarize, there is a wide range of support functions already available but mostly considered for specific tasks. There is a potential to leverage synergies by integrating different support functions to provide support across different development steps. This work could be a first step in this direction. There might also be a potential to increase involvement of domain experts for various steps, such as defining a case structure or collecting cases. But support is needed, particularly for explaining the CBR paradigm to novices and for supporting the interdisciplinary collaboration to efficiently find a common, shared vocabulary.

Our study has some limitations that should be considered. In the literature review, we investigated related works with a strong focus on CBR that typically do not focus on domain experts and rarely distinguish between different stakeholders. The survey has been conducted with a limited number of participants who are mainly academic researchers and experienced in the development of CBR applications. Furthermore, the survey posed rather high-level questions with a selection of items derived from literature. To reduce effort for participants, we did not distinguish between types of CBR applications or domains, although CBR covers a broad application field with varying complexity. Consequently, the results should be considered as a first indication of the potential of domain expert involvement and support. Moreover, a prioritization for future framework development heavily depends on various factors such as CBR tasks, domain, and user knowledge.

In future work, a more extensive survey is needed that includes perspectives beyond academia and, in particular, more direct input from domain experts. Based on the identified challenges and support potentials, future research should prioritize relevant support functions for a selected CBR framework, implement them in a user-friendly environment, and evaluate their usefulness for involving domain experts. Existing support functions should be reused and connected through suitable interfaces where possible. In addition, the identified challenges and support potentials could be investigated in a more domain- and application-specific manner to address specific requirements.

Furthermore, recent advances in LLMs and agent-based approaches offer additional opportunities for supporting CBR development, in particular, assisting in generating an initial CBR system configuration and coordinating continuous evolutions over time across all knowledge containers. While current limitations, such as the limited availability of CBR-specific training data, may restrict their immediate applicability, leveraging generative and agent-based AI represents a promising direction for future research.

Acknowledgments. We would like to thank all people from the CBR research community who participated in our survey. This work is partly funded by Rhineland-Palatinate and the EU as part of the IMPACT project under grant no. 86003522 and by Trier University and DFKI as part of the development of the ProCAKE framework.

Declaration on Generative AI. During the preparation of this work, the authors used ChatGPT and LanguageTool to: paraphrase and reword, improve writing style, Grammar and spelling check, peer review simulation, and content enhancement. After using this tool/service, the authors reviewed and edited the content as needed and take full responsibility for the publication's content.

References

1. Aamodt, A., Plaza, E.: Case-based reasoning: foundational issues, methodological variations, and system approaches. AI Commun. **7**(1), 39–59 (1994)
2. Bach, K., Althoff, K.: Developing case-based reasoning applications using myCBR 3. In: 20th ICCBR Proceedings. LNCS, vol. 7466, pp. 17–31. Springer (2012). https://doi.org/10.1007/978-3-642-32986-9_4
3. Bach, K., Mork, P.J.: On the explanation of similarity for developing and deploying CBR systems. In: 33rd FLAIRS, pp. 413–416. FloridaOJ (2020)
4. Bach, K., Sauer, C., Althoff, K.D., Roth-Berghofer, T.: Knowledge modeling with the open source tool myCBR. In: 10th KESE Workshop. CEUR Workshop, vol. 1289. CEUR-WS.org (2014)
5. Bach, K., et al.: Demonstrating the myCBR Rest API. In: 27th ICCBR Workshops Proceedings. CEUR Workshop Proceedings, vol. 2567, pp. 144–155. CEUR-WS.org (2019)

6. Bach, K.: Case-based reasoning meets large language models: a research manifesto for open challenges and research directions (2025). https://hal.science/hal-05006761
7. Bahls, D., Roth-Berghofer, T.: Explanation support for the case-based reasoning tool myCBR. In: 22nd AAAI Proceedings, pp. 1844–1845. AAAI Press (2007)
8. Bergmann, R.: Experience Management: Foundations, Development Methodology, and Internet-Based Applications. LNCS, vol. 2432, Springer (2003)
9. Bergmann, R., et al.: Developing industrial case-based reasoning applications: The INRECA Methodology, LNCS. Springer (2003). https://doi.org/10.1007/B94998
10. Bergmann, R., Grumbach, L., Malburg, L., Zeyen, C.: ProCAKE: a process-oriented CBR framework. In: 27th ICCBR Workshop Proc., vol. 2567, pp. 156–161. CEUR-WS.org (2019)
11. Chebel-Morello, B., Haouchine, M.K., Zerhouni, N.: Case-based maintenance: Structuring and incrementing the case base. Knowl. Based Syst. **88**, 165–183 (2015). https://doi.org/10.1016/j.knosys.2015.07.034
12. Cordier, A.: Engineering and learning of adaptation knowledge in case-based reasoning. In: 15th EKAW Proc., LNCS, vol. 4248, pp. 303–317. Springer (2006). https://doi.org/10.1007/11891451_27
13. Craw, S., Wiratunga, N., Rowe, R.C.: Learning adaptation knowledge to improve case-based reasoning. Artif. Intell. **170**(16–17), 1175–1192 (2006). https://doi.org/10.1016/J.ARTINT.2006.09.001
14. Díaz-Agudo, B., González-Calero, P.A., Recio-García, J.A., Sánchez-Ruiz-Granados, A.A.: Building CBR systems with jColibri. Sci. Comput. Program. **69**(1–3), 68–75 (2007). https://doi.org/10.1016/J.SCICO.2007.02.004
15. Fornells, A., Recio-García, J. A., Díaz-Agudo, B., Golobardes, E., Fornells, E.: Integration of a methodology for cluster-based retrieval in jColibri. In: 8th ICCBR Proceedings. LNCS, vol. 5650, pp. 418–433. Springer (2009). https://doi.org/10.1007/978-3-642-02998-1_30
16. Hotz, M., et al.: Advanced search techniques for determining optimal sequences of adaptation rules in process-oriented case-based reasoning. In: 33rd ICCBR Proc., LNCS, vol. 15662, pp. 236–251. Springer (2025). https://doi.org/10.1007/978-3-031-96559-3_16
17. Jiménez-Díaz, G., Díaz-Agudo, B.: Visualization of similarity models for CBR comprehension and maintenance. In: 32nd ICCBR Proceedings. LNCS, vol. 14775, pp. 67–80. Springer (2024). https://doi.org/10.1007/978-3-031-63646-2_5
18. Jiménez-Díaz, G., Díaz-Agudo, B.: SimViz: interactive visualizations to analyze similarity measures. SoftwareX **32**, 102454 (2025). https://doi.org/10.1016/J.SOFTX.2025.102454
19. Jimenez-Diaz, G., Lenz, M., Malburg, L., Díaz-Agudo, B., Bergmann, R.: A framework for supporting the iterative design of CBR applications. In: 33rd ICCBR Proceedings. LNCS, vol. 15662, pp. 252–266. Springer (2025). https://doi.org/10.1007/978-3-031-96559-3_17
20. Lamy, J. B., Sekar, B., Guezennec, G., Bouaud, J., Séroussi, B.: Explainable artificial intelligence for breast cancer: a visual case-based reasoning approach. Artif. Intell. Med. **94**, 42–53 (2019). https://doi.org/10.1016/J.ARTMED.2019.01.001
21. Lenz, M., Malburg, L., Bergmann, R.: CBRKit: an intuitive case-based reasoning toolkit for Python. In: 32nd ICCBR Proceedings. LNCS, vol. 14775, pp. 289–304. Springer (2024). https://doi.org/10.1007/978-3-031-63646-2_19
22. López, B., Pous, C., Gay, P., Pla, A., Sanz, J., Brunet, J.: eXiT*CBR: a framework for case-based medical diagnosis development and experimentation. Artif. Intell. Med. **51**(2), 81–91 (2011). https://doi.org/10.1016/J.ARTMED.2010.09.002

23. Malburg, L., et al.: Improving complex adaptations in process-oriented case-based reasoning by applying rule-based adaptation. In: 32nd ICCBR Proc., LNCS, vol. 14775, pp. 50–66. Springer (2024). https://doi.org/10.1007/978-3-031-63646-2_4
24. Marín-Veites, P., Bach, K.: Explaining CBR Systems Through Retrieval and Similarity Measure Visualizations: A Case Study. In: 30th ICCBR. LNCS, vol. 13405, pp. 111–124. Springer (2022). https://doi.org/10.1007/978-3-031-14923-8_8
25. McKenna, E., Smyth, B.: An interactive visualization tool for case-based reasoners. Appl. Intell. **14**(1), 95–114 (2001)
26. Nkisi-Orji, I., Wiratunga, N., Palihawadana, C., Recio-García, J.A., Corsar, D.: Clood CBR: Towards Microservices Oriented Case-Based Reasoning. In: 28th ICCBR Proc. LNCS, pp. 129–143. Springer, Cham (2020). https://doi.org/10.1007/978-3-030-58342-2_9
27. Recio-García, J.A., Bridge, D., Díaz-Agudo, B., González-Calero, P.A.: CBR for CBR: a case-based template recommender system for building case-based systems. In: 9th ECCBR Proceedings. LNCS, vol. 5239, pp. 459–473. Springer (2008). https://doi.org/10.1007/978-3-540-85502-6_31
28. Recio-García, J.A., Díaz-Agudo, B., González-Calero, P. A.: Semantic templates for case-based reasoning systems. Knowl. Eng. Rev. **24**(3), 245–264 (2009). https://doi.org/10.1017/S0269888909990051
29. Recio-García, J.A., Díaz-Agudo, B., González-Calero, P.A.: The COLIBRI open platform for the reproducibility of CBR applications. In: 21st ICCBR Proceedings. LNCS, vol. 7969, pp. 255–269. Springer (2013). https://doi.org/10.1007/978-3-642-39056-2_19
30. Recio-García, J.A., González-Calero, P.A., Díaz-Agudo, B.: Template-based design in COLIBRI studio. Inf. Syst. **40**, 168–178 (2014). https://doi.org/10.1016/J.IS.2012.11.003
31. Richter, M.M.: Knowledge containers. In: Readings in Case-Based Reasoning, Morgan Kaufmann Publishers (2003)
32. Roth-Berghofer, T.: Knowledge maintenance of case-based reasoning systems - the SIAM methodology, Kaiserslautern University of Technology, Ph.D. thesis (2003). https://d-nb.info/967388635
33. Roth-Berghofer, T., Sauer, C., Garcia, R.A.J., Bach, K., Althoff, K.D., Agudo, B.D.: Building case-based reasoning applications with myCBR and COLIBRI studio. Expert Update **13**(1) (2013)
34. Schander, R., Schultheis, A., Bergmann, R.: Explanation of similarities in temporal case-based reasoning by visualization. In: 34th ICCBR Proc. LNCS, vol. 16780, pp. 169–185. Springer (2027). https://doi.org/10.1007/978-3-032-33865-5_11
35. Schoenborn, J. M., Weber, R.O., Aha, D.W., Cassens, J., Althoff, K.D.: Explainable case-based reasoning: a survey. In: AAAI-21 Workshop Proc. (2021)
36. Schultheis, A., Zeyen, C., Bergmann, R.: An overview and comparison of case-based reasoning frameworks. In: 31st Proc. LNCS, vol. 14141, pp. 327–343. Springer (2023). https://doi.org/10.1007/978-3-031-40177-0_21
37. Schultheis, A., Hoffmann, M., Malburg, L., Bergmann, R.: Explanation of similarities in process-oriented cbr by visualization. In: 31st ICCBR. Proc. LNCS, vol. 14141, pp. 53–68. Springer (2023). https://doi.org/10.1007/978-3-031-40177-0_4
38. Smyth, B., Keane, M.T.: Remembering to forget: a competence-preserving case deletion policy for case-based reasoning systems. In: 14th IJCAI Proc., pp. 377–383. Morgan Kaufmann (1995)
39. Smyth, B., McKenna, E.: Modelling the competence of case-bases. In: 4th EWCBR Proceedings. LNCS, vol. 1488, pp. 208–220. Springer (1998). https://doi.org/10.1007/BFB0056334

40. Stahl, A., Roth-Berghofer, T.: Rapid prototyping of CBR applications with the open source tool myCBR. In: 9th ECCBR Proceedings. LNCS, vol. 5239, pp. 615–629. Springer (2008). https://doi.org/10.1007/978-3-540-85502-6_42
41. Wilson, D.C., Leake, D.B.: Maintaining case-based reasoners: dimensions and directions. Comput. Intell. **17**(2), 196–213 (2001)
42. Wohlin, C., Runeson, P., Höst, M., Ohlsson, M.C., Regnell, B., Wesslén, A.: Experimentation in Software Engineering, 2nd edn., Springer (2024). https://doi.org/10.1007/978-3-662-69306-3

Author Index

L. Malburg and K. Bach (Eds.): ICCBR 2026, LNAI 16780, pp. 609–610, 2027.
https://doi.org/10.1007/978-3-032-33865-5

www.ingramcontent.com/pod-product-compliance
Ingram Content Group UK Ltd.
Pitfield, Milton Keynes, MK11 3LW, UK
UKHW021642180926
475650UK00002B/81